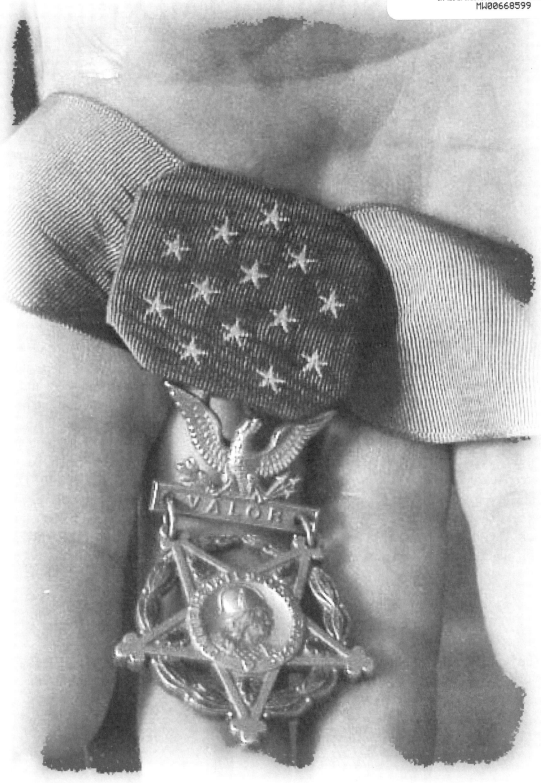

*Dedicated to those who served their country, and to those who
lost their lives on the line of duty in Vietnam.*

ACKNOWLEDGEMENTS

Vietnam Experience: Stories of a Troubled Past would not be possible without the support of the Wisconsin Humanities Council, Community Foundation of North Central Wisconsin, Weyerhaeuser, Rotographics, D.P.I./CESA 9 Service Learning Grant. Nystrom provided us with several maps for the book. The efforts of many people have made this project possible. We greatly appreciate Melvin Laird's contributions to this project -- allowing students to interview him and writing the forward for the book. His time and energy are greatly appreciated. We also greatly appreciate Diane Carlson-Evans contributions. We used numerous pictures from her book *Celebration of Patriotism and Courage*. We would like to acknowledge the professors that helped critique student essays and were project consultants. This includes William Skelton (Professor of History at UWSP), Paul Mertz (Professor of History at UWSP), and Michael Stevens (Wisconsin Historical Society) and the author of *Voices from Vietnam*. Dennis Uhlig, an English teacher from Milwaukee Hamilton High School spent numerous hours critiquing the students essays. D.C. Everest English teachers Brenda Grosskreutz and Len Fike, along with Mr. Uhlig read student essays and chose which ones would be included in the book. We appreciate the technical assistance provided by Derek Casta and his initial design for the book. We are greatly indebted to Cindy Zuleger at Roto-Graphic Printing, Inc., who assisted by training students to use QuarkXpress™ designing unit pages and providing technical assistance. We would also like to thank the D.C. Everest Yearbook Staff for their donation of the student graduation pictures, and the D.C. Everest Marketing Class for developing creative ways to market this book. Several foundations have supported previous oral history projects upon which the foundation for this project has been built: Gannett Foundation, D.C. Everest Area Education Foundation, Judd S. Alexander Foundation, Verizon Foundation, and the Hagge Foundation.

Special Note

The oral histories have been conducted in a manner that adheres to the guidelines set forth by the Oral Histories Association. The recordings have been transcribed to the best of our abilities.

STUDENT PROJECT LEADERS

The Vietnam Oral History Project, *The Vietnam Experience: Stories of a Troubled Past,* was truly a student-led project. Students completed all aspects of the project - interviewing, transcribing, editing, desktop publishing, and layout. The following students were project leaders.

Senior Managing Editor
Meghan Casta, senior at D.C. Everest

Director of Layout
Megan Meverden, senior at D.C. Everest

Staff Manager
Jacalyn Schultz, senior at D.C. Everest

Editor in Chief
Jenna Hazaert, junior at D.C. Everest

Chief Formatting Editor
Jessica Dabler, junior at D.C. Everest

Chief Photographer
Kesa Jenks, senior at D.C. Everest

Asst. Managing Editor
Karen Ho, senior at D.C. Everest

Interviewing Specialist
Jenni Marcell, junior at D.C. Everest

Asst. Director of Layout
Katie Anderson, senior at D.C. Everest

Editor of Photography
Vicki Karcher, senior at D.C. Everest

Web Page Designer
Ryan Plisch, senior at D.C. Everest

Assistant Transcriber
Andrew Miller, senior at D.C. Everest

Asst. Editor of Photography
Ashley Geisendorfer, senior at D.C. Everest

Head of Transcription
Kristy Isberner, senior at D.C. Everest

STAFF INVOLVEMENT

The D.C. Everest Vietnam Oral History project *The Vietnam Experience: Stories of a Troubled Past* has been prepared by D.C. Everest students and staff. The staff listed below helped to facilitate this student-directed oral history project. The project also included collaboration with staff from the Wisconsin State Historical Society and the University of Wisconsin – Stevens Point.

Project Coordinator
Paul Aleckson, *D.C. Everest Social Studies Coordinator*

Project Manager
Nancy Gajewski, *Social Studies Teacher*

Editorial Managers
Julie Fondell, *D.C. Everest Language Arts Coordinator*
Jim Kegel, *Social Studies Teacher*
Anne Jagodzinski, *English Teacher*

Technical Manager
Sandi Jaipuri, *Mathematics Teacher*

Staff
Greg Peterson, *Social Studies Teacher*
Trish Masanz, *Learning Disabilities Teacher*
Beth Schultz, *Administrative Assistant*
Brenda Grosskreutz, *English Teacher*
Len Fike, *English Teacher*
Patty Mayo, *English Teacher*
Lori Bychinski, *English Teacher*
Polly Hirn, *5th Grade Teacher,* Wausau School District

Community Collaboration
Michael Stevens, *State Historian*, Wisconsin State Historical Society
Paul Mertz, *Professor of History,* University of Wisconsin – Stevens Point
William Skelton, *Professor of History,* University of Wisconsin – Stevens Point
Dennis Uhlig, *English Teacher,* Milwaukee Hamilton High School

PROJECT SUPPORT

The D.C. Everest Oral History Project *The Vietnam Experience: Stories of a Troubled Decade* was made possible by the generous support of the following foundations and organizations.

Wisconsin Humanities Council

Community Foundation of North Central Wisconsin

D.P.I. CESA #9 Service Learning Grants

Weyerhaeuser

Roto-Graphic Printing, Inc.

D.C. Everest Area School District

SUCCESS
is taking root.

Working together gets things done. That's nothing new to us at Weyerhaeuser. We've been teaming up with schools, businesses, churches and civic groups for almost 100 years. It's the best way to make our communities better places to work and live. This is our home and we're proud to be here.

 Weyerhaeuser

HELPING OUR COMMUNITY GROW.

TABLE OF CONTENTS

Appendices

FORWARD
Melvin Laird
Secretary of Defense
1969-1973

Those U.S. Army soldiers and Marines serving in Vietnam, and the Air Force and Navy personnel supporting them in close proximity to Southeast Asia, are all **HEROES** to me. These young men and women have never truly been recognized for their sacrifices, patriotism, and valor in a very unpopular war.

Representing Wisconsin's Seventh Congressional District in the United States House of Representatives (encompassing D.C. Everest Area School District) at the time President Kennedy changed the 8,000 man Vietnam mission from the role of military advisors to combat participants, one did not fully realize the magnitude of this 1962 decision. We had recently experienced the Cuban Missile Crisis and were at the height of the Cold War with the Soviet Union. The French had pulled back their support of South Vietnam and the Russians were increasing their support for North Vietnam. During the next six years, under the leadership of President Johnson, the Vietnam War was Americanized. By the end of 1968, our combat forces totaled 540,000 in country on the ground, and an additional 1,200,000 men and women were assigned in direct support of the war. These 1,200,000 military personnel consisted of a vast naval force with its carriers, battleships, destroyers, and support ships; multiple Air Force bases out of country, but in striking distance; and a vast military logistic group.

After nine terms representing our area in the U.S. Congress, it fell upon me in 1969 as the new Secretary of Defense to change the terms of America's involvement in the Vietnam War. U.S. public opinion was no longer supporting our massive involvement. The plan was set in motion to de-Americanize the war — prepare and train the South Vietnamese to handle their own military and economic problems, fight their own war, and ready themselves for negotiations with North Vietnam. The American military, while training the South Vietnam forces, would withdraw in an honorable and orderly fashion, while still giving the South reasonable military and economic aid comparable to the Russian support for North Vietnam.

This was the beginning of *Vietnamization*. Every month during my tenure as Secretary of Defense our manpower commitment was decreased. By the end of 1972, we had no ground combat forces involved in Vietnam. On January 30, 1973, the Vietnam Peace Treaty was signed in Paris. The U.S. pledged to give South Vietnam ammunition, military equipment replacements and spare parts. The Russians indicated their agreement to follow the same course in the North. In 1975, however, the U.S. Congress, after considerable debate, withdrew our country's support of the South. As a result, South Vietnam collapsed soon thereafter. The incentive for any negotiated settlement between the North and South became a moot issue as the Russians continued their support of the North.

This is now old Cold War history. The men and women who answered the call of their country must never be forgotten. The time spent with them on many occasions in Vietnam was very special and personal to me. The POWs, MIAs, and their families were always my utmost concern. To all those brave men and women who served in Vietnam and never returned home, my prayers are with them and their families. To those surviving this Southeast Asian conflict, our country's continued salute of special appreciation and extra support is deserved. They are all our **HEROES**.

Melvin R. Laird
U.S. Secretary of Defense 1969-73
Nine-Term U.S. Congressman from Wisconsin
World War II Purple Heart recipient
and veteran of the Pacific
www.lairdcenter.org

PREFACE

When I entered high school in 1968, the Vietnam War had reached its peak with over 500,000 American soldiers stationed in Vietnam. Between 1968 and 1972 I became more and more aware of the possibility of being drafted. By 1970 college deferments were a thing of the past, replaced by a new lottery system that hoped to provide equity to the draft. As a high school student however, I was more interested in playing basketball and doing just enough studying to get good grades. I received my selective service card with the lottery number 41 in January of 1973, just as the peace treaty was being signed. By 1972, my senior year, Vietnam had begun to fade with only 70,000 American troops there. Few Americans were drafted out of the class of 1971. Even the anti-war movement had settled down after 1971. I guess everyone knew the war was about to end for the U.S. Most talk was about getting the POW's back and of course the government succeeded at that.

Vietnam, however, remained of interest to me. What had our men experienced? Was it worth it? Why were we in Vietnam? As a history major at the University of Wisconsin, I began my study of Americas' longest war. I studied all facets, even learning a great deal about the anti-war movement from my brother Jon who was working on the documentary the *War at Home*, a case study of Madison, WI, and the Vietnam War.

As a history teacher at D. C. Everest I had a burning desire to teach more than just the customary 2-3 days on the Vietnam War, so in the late 1980's, I began teaching a six-week unit on the war in my American History Seminar course. At that time it was difficult to find Vietnam veterans who were willing to share their stories. The few that did come into my class were brief and to the point. They just had not had enough time to open up. It was at this time that President Reagan alerted the country to the sacrifices that our Vietnam vets had made for our country. It always bothered me that these men were blamed for our failure in Vietnam and not the politicians. It just did not make sense that these men and women who served their country were not being honored properly. I wanted my students to understand the history behind the Vietnam War and why we should not have been in that war. But I also wanted the students to understand that our soldiers had no choice but to fight in an unpopular war and should be honored just like our vets from WWII.

By the early 90's with group therapy and a better understanding of PTSD (post traumatic stress disorder), the vets that I brought into my class began to open up. You could tell they were feeling better about themselves. Then in 2000 I decided that my students needed to go beyond just listening to a speaker. They needed to go out and personally interview a veteran. At that time we had just finished the WWII oral histories project and we were about to publish *The Hmong and their stories*. After discussing my idea with Nancy Gajewski, project manager for World War II: Stories from our Veterans I decided to coordinate an oral histories project titled The Vietnam Experience. I wanted a balanced book, one with both combat veterans and support veterans. I also wanted the anti-war side told. I wanted this book to be completely done by D.C. Everest students. Teachers had done a lot of work on transcribing and editing on the previous books, and I wanted this to be a total student effort. The project caught on like wildfire. Students in all four sections of American History Seminar became responsible for creating questions, interviewing, transcribing and editing. Then we bought QuarkXPress™ software so that the students could do the layout for the book. All aspects of the project are student driven, including the marketing and sale of the final product.

I would like to share some of the major themes of the war that I had learned throughout the study of the Vietnam War from teachers and books that I now can confirm from the works of our veterans:

• Vietnam was a winnable war if the politicians had not tied the hands of the soldiers. Most vets indicated they couldn't fire at the enemy due to no fire zones. They also couldn't go into Cambodia, Laos or North Vietnam.

• The Viet Cong and the North Vietnamese Army had the advantage at first, due to the element of surprise. They did most of the ambushing. But once we called in the firepower, artillery, helicopters, and jets, it was all over for them.

• Friendships were hard to make because of so much death. Some vets kept in touch after the war, but most did not. Many vets tell stories of buddies being killed when they should have taken the bullet or stepped on the booby traps. Survival guilt was common.

• Most vets felt bad that the public did not receive them as war heroes. The antiwar movement has always been difficult for Vietnam veterans to understand. Why takeout the frustration of an unpopular war on the soldiers rather than the politicians?

• The veterans were very young. Most were 18-20, physically fit, and looking for excitement, but instead lived through lots of periods of boredom. Many vets describe their Vietnam experience as long periods of boredom interspersed with short bursts of adrenalin rush (combat).

• Clearly there were little or no racism or relationship problems between minorities and whites in combat areas. Only in the rear did the minorities congregate together with secret handshakes and black power salutes. Problems were worse later in the war (after 1968).

• Most veterans attest to seeing drug use, but did not partake themselves. Clearly the drug use problem got worse late in the war.

• Most vets alluded to the problem of not knowing who the enemy was. Most couldn't trust the villagers, even children, for fear of a mine or booby trap.

• Most vets expressed little or no understanding of the reasons for the war other than to stop communism. Most came out of the experience wondering why we were there.

• The Vietnam veteran espoused lots of courage, incredible acts of bravery, yet little bragging. They were just "doing their job."

• Medevac helicopters and medical technology kept a lot of wounded alive.

• Most vets blame the politicians for bad decisions and tying their hands. The military fought well.

• There appeared to be some deterioration in military discipline after 1970. This could have been due to more draftees fighting the war. You start to hear "search and avoid" rather than "search and destroy."

• Most vets seemed to enjoy themselves when they stood down for periods of three to four days back at the base camp before returning to the boonies to search and find the enemy.

• It seems that everyone in helicopters and armor has a great respect for the grunt or infantryman who didn't have it so good.

• Some vets spoke of post traumatic shock disorder (PTSD). Clearly combat veterans and nurses suffered the most. To some degree, the war haunts them all.

You will read some incredible stories from nurses, helicopter pilots, grunts, and support soldiers. The stories are real and as vivid as if they were told in the late 60's during the war. You will also read essays, journals and poems from high school sophomores who interviewed the veterans and spent a good portion of the semester reading and learning about the Vietnam experience. I think you will find the interviews and stories to be interesting, shocking, emotional, and informative.

Paul Aleckson
Vietnam Experience Project Coordinator
D.C. Everest Social Studies Coordinator
paleckson@dce.k12.wi.us

U.S. INVOLVEMENT GROWS
1957–1964

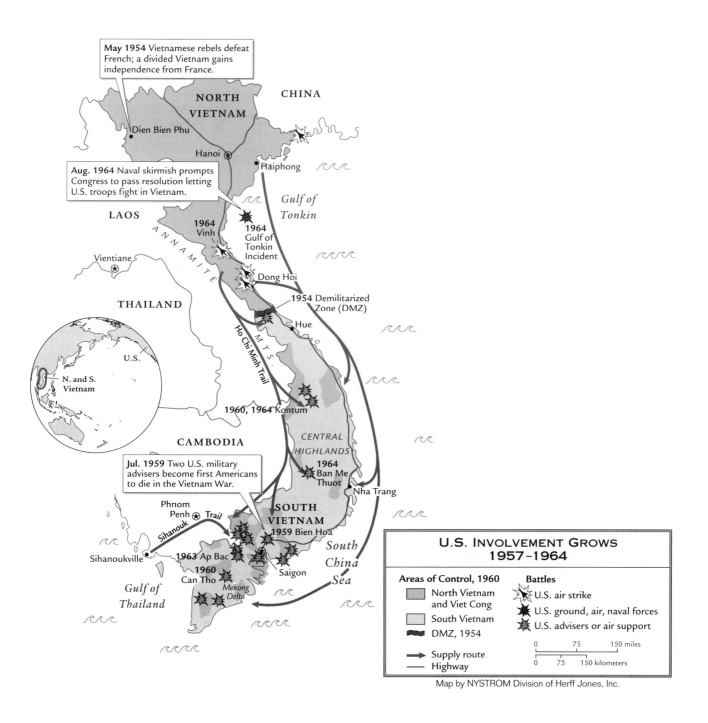

May 1954 Vietnamese rebels defeat French; a divided Vietnam gains independence from France.

CHINA

NORTH VIETNAM

Dien Bien Phu

Hanoi

Haiphong

Aug. 1964 Naval skirmish prompts Congress to pass resolution letting U.S. troops fight in Vietnam.

Gulf of Tonkin

LAOS

1964 Vinh

1964 Gulf of Tonkin Incident

Vientiane

Dong Hoi

1954 Demilitarized Zone (DMZ)

THAILAND

Hue

Ho Chi Minh Trail

U.S.

N. and S. Vietnam

1960, 1964 Kontum

CENTRAL HIGHLANDS

CAMBODIA

1964 Ban Me Thuot

Jul. 1959 Two U.S. military advisers become first Americans to die in the Vietnam War.

Nha Trang

Phnom Penh Trail

SOUTH VIETNAM

1959 Bien Hoa

Sihanouk

South China Sea

Sihanoukville

1963 Ap Bac

1960 Can Tho

Saigon

Gulf of Thailand

Mekong Delta

U.S. INVOLVEMENT GROWS
1957–1964

Areas of Control, 1960

North Vietnam and Viet Cong

South Vietnam

DMZ, 1954

→ Supply route

— Highway

Battles

✶ U.S. air strike

✸ U.S. ground, air, naval forces

✹ U.S. advisers or air support

0   75   150 miles

0   75   150 kilometers

Map by NYSTROM Division of Herff Jones, Inc.

AAH_09_108_M2_vietnam57-64

U.S. TROOPS CARRY THE LOAD
1965-1968

CHINA

NORTH VIETNAM

U.S. TROOPS CARRY THE LOAD
1965-1968

Areas of Control, 1966
- North Vietnam and Viet Cong
- South Vietnam
- DMZ, 1954
- → Supply route
- — Highway
- U.S. 7th fleet

Battles
- U.S. air strike
- U.S. ground, air, naval forces
- No U.S. involvement

0   75   150 miles
0   75   150 kilometers

Map by NYSTROM Division of Herff Jones, Inc.

1965–68 Hanoi

1965–68 Haiphong

LAOS

Gulf of Tonkin

Vientiane

1965–68 Vinh

1965–68 Mu Gia Pass

Mar. 1965 First U.S. combat troops arrive in Vietnam.

1966–68 Khe Sanh DMZ

1968 Hue

Da Nang

THAILAND

My Lai

1966–67 Dak To

1968 Kontum

Pleiku

1965 Ia Drang Valley

CAMBODIA

CENTRAL HIGHLANDS

Jan. 1968 Tet Offensive by the North fails militarily, but erodes U.S. public support for the war.

1968 Ban Me Thuot

Phnom Penh

Sihanouk Trail

SOUTH VIETNAM

Cam Ranh Bay

Sihanoukville

1968 Can Tho

South China Sea

1968 Saigon

Gulf of Thailand

Mekong Delta

ANNAMITE

Ho Chi Minh Trail

M T S.

AAH_09_109_M1_vietnam65-68

U.S. TROOPS WITHDRAW, THE WAR ENDS
1969-1975

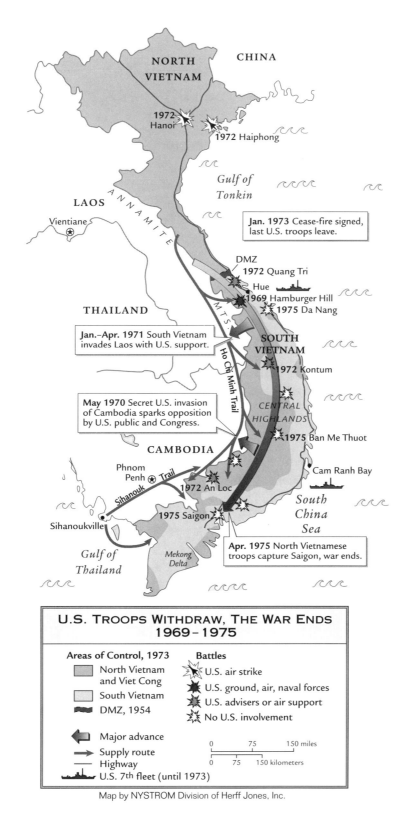

CHINA

NORTH VIETNAM

1972 Hanoi

1972 Haiphong

Gulf of Tonkin

LAOS

Vientiane

Jan. 1973 Cease-fire signed, last U.S. troops leave.

DMZ
1972 Quang Tri

Hue
1969 Hamburger Hill
1975 Da Nang

THAILAND

Jan.–Apr. 1971 South Vietnam invades Laos with U.S. support.

SOUTH VIETNAM

1972 Kontum

CENTRAL HIGHLANDS

May 1970 Secret U.S. invasion of Cambodia sparks opposition by U.S. public and Congress.

1975 Ban Me Thuot

Cam Ranh Bay

CAMBODIA

Phnom Penh

Trail

Sihanouk Trail

1972 An Loc

1975 Saigon

South China Sea

Apr. 1975 North Vietnamese troops capture Saigon, war ends.

Sihanoukville

Gulf of Thailand

Mekong Delta

Ho Chi Minh Trail

ANNAMITE MTS.

U.S. TROOPS WITHDRAW, THE WAR ENDS
1969 – 1975

Areas of Control, 1973
- North Vietnam and Viet Cong
- South Vietnam
- DMZ, 1954

- Major advance
- Supply route
- Highway
- U.S. 7th fleet (until 1973)

Battles
- U.S. air strike
- U.S. ground, air, naval forces
- U.S. advisers or air support
- No U.S. involvement

| 0 | 75 | 150 miles |
| 0 | 75 | 150 kilometers |

Map by NYSTROM Division of Herff Jones, Inc.

POLITICAL

Political Scene

Eisenhower was president when the French were struggling in IndoChina. This conflict was not seen as a nationalistic movement but as communist aggression. The leaders of the free world had seen the Soviet Union absorb smaller countries in their quest for world domination, and the events in southeast Asia seemed to be part of the overall conquest. The French, who asked for and received American financial aid, fought the Viet Minh and were defeated in 1954. Near the end of the struggle, the French asked Eisenhower to intervene militarily, and he declined. The Geneva Accords divided Vietnam into two parts, North and South. Once the government of South Vietnam took the reins of authority, they became a part of SEATO and asked the US to aid them militarily. The US sent military advisors to train the South Vietnamese military and other civilian officials to promote the startup of the organization of civic programs in the country. The US changed leadership during that time.

Kennedy, a cold war warrior, was intrigued by guerilla warfare and the means to fight it. He recognized that the Soviets and their allies were using this type of warfare. He was a fan and a supporter of the US Special Forces and was instrumental in allowing the soldiers to wear the green beret as their symbol. Kennedy viewed the Special Forces as one answer to the guerilla warfare that was taking place in Vietnam. American involvement increased, and more and more advisors were sent to the country to assist the army of South Vietnam. During the early 60's, helicopter units were dispatched and began flying in the country. By the time of Kennedy's assassination, approximately 16,000 military personnel were stationed in South Vietnam. When Lyndon Johnson came to the White House, he recognized that the survival of South Vietnam demanded a strong US presence, and he increased the troop deployment in that country. This time also saw the Gulf of Tonkin Resolution and the intense bombing of North Vietnam that would follow. It was during Johnson's administration that the war effort reached its greatest numbers and also its greatest casualties. Broken by the war, Lyndon Johnson decided not to run in 1968 and was replaced in the fall election by Richard Nixon who promised an end to the war with honor. Nixon, through his Secretary of State Henry Kissinger, negotiated a settlement to the war after several years of talks. Mounting pressure at home and a reluctant Congress pressed for a solution, and one was found. The US removed itself in 1973, and the North Vietnamese defeated the South in April of 1975.

Melvin Laird

He became Secretary of Defense during the Nixon Administration from 1969-1973. Laird was quoted as the "architect of Vietnamization," a plan to bring our soldiers home.

I would like to say that I am delighted to have the opportunity to be with you today. I will be glad to answer any of your questions. My interest in Vietnam operations goes back many years before becoming Secretary of Defense. As you probably know, I was very critical of the Johnson administration. You may have read some articles where I felt they had not prepared themselves for the long haul in Vietnam. They kept committing more and more and more. During the Eisenhower administration, there were 371 American troops. Kennedy increased that to 18,000. When I became Secretary of Defense at the end of the Johnson administration, there were 540,000 troops on the ground and another 1,200,000 in the Navy and Air Force in Thailand. There were around 2,000,000 men and women committed to that war when I took over as Secretary of Defense. They had "Americanized" the war. They had taken it over and said: "No, you Vietnamese stay away; this is going to be our operation." I was very critical of that and critical of Secretary McNamara. As the ranking member of the Defense Appropriations Committee, I did not think that war should have been "Americanized."

After becoming Secretary of Defense, I started a new program – "Vietnamization" – turning over more of the responsibility to the Vietnamese every month, with the idea in mind that when I finished my term, there would not be a single American combat troop in Vietnam. We prepared the Vietnamese to take over and to handle their war. At that particular time, we were in the midst of the cold war. The Russians were supplying more than $2.5 billion in arms and ammunition either by railroad or by ship into the north of Vietnam. They were the main suppliers. That is why President Johnson felt he had to challenge the Russians. He did it the wrong way by "Americanizing" the operation completely and not depending more on the Vietnamese to carry out their responsibilities. We immediately began to prepare the Vietnamese to do that.

In the Paris Peace Accord of January 1973, you will recall that there was an agreement made that we would not supply anything but replacement arms and ammunition, replacement equipment, and replacement spare parts. The Russians acquiesced to the same thing. The only problem was that the Russians kept up their flow of arms and ammunition. The Congress in 1975, however, turned down a request for $350 million dollars for spare parts and ammunition for the South Vietnamese forces. That broke the back of the South Vietnamese because there was nobody else who would supply arms and ammunition. In 1975, we did not have Americans on the ground fighting, but the South Vietnamese needed the pledge that Kissinger made in January 1973 that they would get the replacement arms and ammunition. This action by the Congress broke the back of the South Vietnamese, and there was no will to fight when they found out the Russians were continuing at the rate of about $2 billion a year and the United States was not willing to carry out its pledge of the Paris Agreement. The Vietnamization program failed that day; the vote was held in the Congress of the United States. I have been critical of Secretary Kissinger, and I have been critical of President Jerry Ford from time to time for not doing more to get a majority vote in the Congress of the United States at that time, because Kissinger had made that commitment in Paris. We let South Vietnam go down the drain.

Now, I will be glad to answer any of your questions, but I wanted to give you a little background. When I became Secretary of Defense, there were three things I wanted to do. I wanted to get Americans out of Vietnam, I wanted to turn over the responsibility to South Vietnam, and I wanted to end the draft and establish an All-Volunteer Force. The draft had been used by the United States military since 1939. Any time the Defense Department needed additional people, they could just put out a draft call. That would put pressure on young people to join the Marines, Navy, and the Air Force, and they would fill Army requirements. The draft was very unfair, and President Johnson used it instead of the Guard and Reserve because he thought it would create too much of a political disturbance if we called up various units from around the United States. It was not fair to the people who served because people could get college deferments and everything else. I have the greatest respect and admiration for those individuals called to serve. I

cannot adequately express my affection and appreciation for those who served in Vietnam during that very difficult period. It was not an easy war and many people received deferments. I stopped college deferments when I became Secretary of Defense. I set up a lottery system so it would be fair. I did away with the draft and set up the volunteer service, which is serving this country well. I think you will find that every Secretary of Defense since then has supported my position.

What were you critical of in prior administrations?
First, I felt that they were misleading the people on what the war cost. One of the speeches I made while in Congress and serving on the Defense Appropriations Committee outlines my thoughts. By the way, Hillary Clinton helped my staff write that speech. She was interning in my Congressional office. This was before she met Bill Clinton. It was a speech on how we were robbing from NATO, taking things from all over the world – from our military forces, and diverting it to Vietnam. Preparedness in NATO was going down the drain. We had taken $10 billion of material to hide $10 billion in costs, as far as the war was concerned. I thought the American people should be advised and told what the war was costing, not only in human lives and in casualties, but that was certainly the big loss. However, there was also a hidden cost. They did not come to the Congress for approval. Hillary helped on that speech and she is very proud of it.

Did you agree with General Westmoreland's strategy?
Well, I had great respect for General Westmoreland, but we did have some disagreements. General Westmoreland was not a great believer in Vietnamization. I called it "Vietnamization"; he was for giv-

ing more and more responsibility to the American forces during that period. In fact, when President Johnson left office, there was still a request on the desk of the President and on Secretary Clark Clifford's desk, for 200,000 more ground combat forces. That was not the way to go. The American people were fed up with that war and you have to have public support if you are going to pursue any kind of a war successfully. Public support had gone down the drain at that particular time. President Nixon beat Hubert Humphrey in the election of 1968 because he promised he would do something about Vietnam. If Hubert Humphrey had broken with Lyndon Johnson and even given some indication of turning over more responsibility to the South Vietnamese, he would have been elected President of the United States. That was a very close election and Nixon would never have been elected President if Humphrey had shown some inclination to change the direction of the war. It was like the campaign when Ike first ran against Stevenson. You probably do not remember this, but you read about it, I'm sure, and he said, "I will go to Korea – we are going to end the war in Korea." That statement elected Ike by a tremendous majority. Nixon, in 1952, said he had a plan, the Republican platform, in which I wrote, "We will de-Americanize that war."

What was it like working for President Nixon?

I had known him for a long time. I was in Congress with him, as you know, and I traveled with him in his campaigns just as I had traveled with Eisenhower in the 1956 campaign. Nixon was running for Vice President at that time. During my travels with President Nixon, I pointed out various members of the Congress and Senate. My Seventh Congressional District was good to me. They let me take some time off during those campaigns to work with the presidential campaign. I traveled with Nixon during the 1968 campaign on a part-time basis, alternating weekly with Bryce Harlow. Nixon was a very bright and intelligent person. He would have been a great president if he had not lied about the cover-up of Watergate. He did not know about the break-in, but he lied about the cover-up. When I found that out, it was a great disappointment, because he also lied to me. I put that question to him before I went back over to the White House as his Domestic Counsellor. The office of the President of the United States is very important and cannot allow untruths told in order to protect friends. One should not lie – it only becomes deeper and deeper. Nixon lied about the cover-up. He knew about the cover-up and the tapes finally proved it. I remember when I first learned about it. Fred Buzhardt, whom I had recommended to

Secretary Laird consulting President Nixon

the White House as my general counsel at Defense, came to me at the end of May or early June, and told me that Nixon had lied. The tapes show that he was involved in the cover-up. That was a great mistake and one of my greatest disappointments in politics. I could not forgive him for that.

Regarding Vietnam, did you and Nixon agree or disagree on American policy?

We had disagreements. We had disagreements regarding a faster withdrawal at times. I was for the Cambodian bombing, but I did not want it secret. Nixon, the Secretary of State, and Kissinger, insisted on keeping it secret. I thought it would be a terrible thing to do because full disclosure is always the best policy. I had twelve thousand men who knew about the bombing of Cambodia. I was all for taking out the North Vietnam sanctuaries. They were coming over and hitting our U.S.

troops. Those sanctuaries in Cambodia were occupied territory of the North Vietnamese. I had no prob-
lem hitting them, not a bit, but I had a problem about keeping it secret. The secrecy blew in *The New York Times*. It was a catastrophe as far as public opinion was concerned. Yes, I did have disagreements but you know, I had my chance to make my case. The day the bombing was authorized, I told those in the White House that I had 12,000 people who knew about it or would know about it. The operation was largely run from Guam and Thailand. It is impossible to keep a secret when 12,000 people are involved.

Would you have done things differently?

Well, I felt that full disclosure was the best way to go. The Pentagon papers caused Kissinger to go "straight up the wall," and Rogers and President Nixon did not like the Papers being released. I did not release them. They accused me of releasing them, but I did not. The Papers had to do with what had been happening during the seven previous years. The responsibility of running the Department of Defense at that time, included 3,000,000 men and women in the military and 2,000,000 civilian employees. It was, and is now, a big job. I had to get the funds and support from the Congress. It was not just Vietnam. Vietnam was the most important problem, but there were other areas of the world that were also important. We had just gone through the 1967 war in the Middle East, we had men in Egypt, we had our NATO commitment at the time, we had 200,000 men in NATO at the time, we had 60,000 in Japan, and we had 52,000 in Korea. There were many other places deserving the attention of the Secretary of Defense.

Do you think Vietnam was a winnable war?

A painting done by a veteran and given to Laird.

I think that it would have been a winnable war if it had been properly approached in 1962-63. However, it was not a winnable war unless the South Vietnamese were given the kind of support they needed. You cannot expect Americans to support that sort of an operation for that many years. They had not prepared the Vietnamese at all. We had started preparing the Vietnamese, but then Congress pulled the plug on them in 1975. When the plug was pulled, we did not have any more American combat forces involved.

In 1969, you went to Vietnam. Can you describe the event?

I think that February or March is when I drew up the Vietnamization program with Abrams. I went to all four corps areas to visit the troops, and I went from the north down to the Riverine forces. Admiral Zumwalt commanded the Riverine forces at that time in IV Corps, and I spent a day or two with each corps commander.

How was morale at that time?

The morale was always much better than expected. You cannot fault the troops. I disagreed so much with McNamara's book. In his book, he does not have one good thing to say about a single soldier fighting in Vietnam. There are people who performed a dedicated service, and they kept their morale up better than imagined. It was not a pleasant place to be. I agreed with President Eisenhower when he disciplined Vice President Nixon. Nixon said we should be sending combat troops in there, and Ike said never, never get involved in a land war in Southeast Asia. Ike was so right. He was so right, and Nixon had the rug cut out from under him because Nixon thought we should come in and support the French. Ike said that it was not the place to be.

Can you explain more about your trip?

I spent time trying to seek out young military men, women, and nurses in Saigon, to spend time individually with them. I tried to get a better understanding of the drug problem and the morale problem. I was interested in our people. One of the speeches I gave was about people, not hardware, being the most important thing in the Department of Defense. You can have all the airplanes, all the tanks, all the weapons of war you want, but the people are the important component. Those individuals behind the guns, running the tanks, those in front of the aircraft – all our military personnel supporting our aircraft and ships – for them, morale is so important.

Was there any certain person that you had a chance to meet who stands out in your mind?

I met over 500 of them. I could tell you all sorts of stories. The pictures on the wall tell the story. For example, the one that is hand-painted – an enlisted man painted this picture knowing I was coming to visit the troops. Up in I-Corps they presented me with a Russian sub-machine gun and a Russian rifle.

They were so proud. You cannot imagine how touching that is. It is tough when you are Secretary of Defense and you see those casualties coming in every day. I wanted to cut the casualties back as fast as I could.

On base conversing with troops in Vietnam.

Was the purpose of your trip to Vietnam to set up a program?

I went to Vietnam to establish a program that we would follow for the next four years. As you know, Abrams was my Commander. Creighton Abrams was one of the greatest Commanders of our Army. He was a tank commander with Patton during World War II. Do you know Abrams' history? He always found a way to do something. Westmoreland was in Washington at that time as Chief of Staff of the Army and was always saying, "You cannot do it." Abrams was always saying, "You can do it." That was the difference -- Abrams was a "can do" general.

Did Abrams die three years after the war?

Abrams died of complications with cancer. There were many great people over there. I remember a year and half later, after the trip, I was sitting there having dinner with Abrams and the commanders of each of the four corps areas. I was getting fed up with what was happening in Laos. The State Department was running that operation along with the CIA. We were putting in many arms, and ammunition to those forces up there, but there was no accountability for their actions. I looked down at the end of the table, and there was Jack Vessey. At that time, Vessey's rank was Major General, and I said we needed a military man in Laos because this thing is getting out of hand. I asked Abrams if we could spare Vessey if we sent him to Laos. That night we sent Vessey to Laos, and he was there for two and a half years. He came back and later became Chairman of the Joint Chiefs. Vessey and I traveled all over Russia when I went there for a national intelligence mission for President Reagan. We were having problems with our US Embassy in Russia, and President Reagan asked me to go and clear it up. Once again, I asked Vessey to help me on an important mission.

How did Johnson's administration deal with the Tet offensive?

The situation regarding Tet was badly handled by Westmoreland and the military command. That was not a defeat for the American forces; they performed very well. It was not handled well from a public perception. I feel badly that the American troops did not get the credit and recognition they deserved for a job well done. The only thing I fault was that the Vietnamese depended almost exclusively on the US forces. That was my criticism all the time: the South Vietnamese forces were not being used properly. There were not many North Vietnamese in the country. I think that public affairs in Tet were handled badly, providing even more reason why we needed to have a new program and get the South Vietnamese training in high gear. Although I was still in Congress at the time, Tet was not a defeat for our forces.

What are your thoughts about the Hmong and the Secret War?

My concern for the Hmong is one reason for my sending Jack Vessey to handle things in Laos. The Hmong forces were very good fighters, and they performed very well when they were given the proper arms and ammunition, but you can't expect the Hmong forces to be responsible for closing off the Ho Chi Minh trail. They were not in that league, but they performed well, and I have nothing but the greatest respect for the Hmong forces. I meet with them from time to time. My honest opinion is the Lao situation was not handled very well. They left Vessey's predecessor up there for many years, and events finally were turned around when Vessey arrived in 1970.

Can you explain why Cambodia and Laos were off limits?

The State Department felt both were independent countries, and because of their independence, they could not be invaded or have their borders crossed. They had not declared neutrality, although they were supposed to be neutral. I think it was right to hit the sanctuaries, which were controlled by the North Vietnamese forces and the Viet Cong. I had a disagreement with the State Department over that because they were killing Americans by in-and-out raids. In March when I was there, I authorized Abrams to carry on and pursue the enemy. I called it "protective reaction," and it drove the State

Laird with Kahn in Vietnam

Department up the wall, but I did not think it was right for our forces to chase the enemy and then stop after the enemy crossed the border. Those sanctuaries were responsible for many American casualties. I did not support the secret bombing, but I supported the bombing and the incursions into Laos. There is a difference.

How long did your meeting with Abrams take to establish "Vietnamization?"

I convinced Abrams that we had to change our planning with respect to public opinion in the United States. We had to show progress in turning the responsibility to the South Vietnamese. We Americans could not be there forever. Arrangements had to be made to get my Vietnamization program going. At first, Abrams was not gung ho on doing this. I began our conversation and explained to him what was going to take place. He listened, and from then on, he was completely cooperative all the way. I did not have all team players in the Pentagon, but I had a team player in Abrams. They would send back channels to him, and Abrams always shared those back channels with me.

I also had back channels through a different source. As Secretary of Defense, the National Security Agency reported to me. I put my man in there immediately – Admiral Gayler. Never before had anybody been promoted to four stars who held that job. I told him if he did a good job, he would be leaving this place wearing four stars. However, at the same time, I also told him that if did a bad job, he would be out of there pretty darn fast. He did a great job, and I was kept well informed on all channels. I never had a problem with any military or civilian person not keeping me informed with what they were doing. They might disagree with you, as General Westmoreland disagreed with me on the All-Volunteer Force. Tom Moorer, my Chairman did not like it. However, he publicly came along and supported the program.

I never got Westmoreland to support it 100% but I got General Chapman and four other Chiefs on the Joint Staff to agree with me. It took a while to convince them that the All-Volunteer Force was the way to go. The military thought it was a lot cheaper to use the draft, but I felt the young men and women should be paid on a comparable basis with everyone else in our society. Unfortunately, our service personnel were not sufficiently compensated, and we are still trying to get the pay scale up to the level of firemen and policemen. One of the first things my friend Les Aspin did as Secretary of Defense for a period of nine months, was try to do away with the retirement program for the military. He broke the contract and I told Les that I went to the Congress, although no longer in office, and fought this through. We finally changed it back. The military has a far more dangerous job day in and day out. Deployed military cannot spend much time with their family.

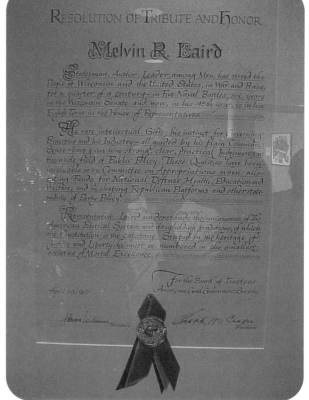

Resolution of Tribute and Honor

Not long ago, I met with pilots from Northwest, and most of them came from the military. I asked why they had left the military – was it a question of pay? They said it was not just pay, but they had been deployed on carriers in Europe and around the world and did not see their families for ten months at a time. At Northwest, they are home twenty-two nights a month. Not only are they being paid more, but also they are home! The wives have an influence on this, and you have to consider that. If you use the draft to solve all your military manpower requirements, it is not fair and it is like a reverse taxation.

WISCONSIN ALUMNI ASSOCIATION
DISTINGUISHED SERVICE AWARD
presented to
MELVIN R. LAIRD, JR.
In recognition of outstanding professional achievement
a record of alumni citizenship that has brought credit
to the University of Wisconsin, and
for loyalty and service to Wisconsin.

May 14, 1966

In Vietnam, did you notice any problems with whites and Afro-Americans?

From time to time, there have been racial issues; there is no question about that. I did everything I could to have a better understanding of those problems. I cannot say I did not run into racial issues because I did from time to time. People living in close quarters with one another can create friction, but they get along much better than other sections of our society. I am proud of the way the Navy, Army, Air Force, and Marines handled the situation.

I traveled much with a great fighter pilot, Chappie James. He was one of my public affairs people. He ran our base in Libya, and when I became Secretary of Defense, I only had sixty days to close that base because Johnson had made that agreement. I called up Chappie and told him I wanted everything out of Libya. He told me he could not do that because the agreement said everything had to stay. I told him to fly at night and get everything out of there. Chappie was a large, towering African American. At the time, he had the rank of colonel. I promoted him to general. He was something. He was a fighter pilot from Tuskegee and when he got back from Libya, I told him he was going to work for me in my office in public affairs. He complained to me that he was a fighter pilot and no public affairs officer. I told him he had been a fighter pilot. From then on, we were all right. Once while delivering a speech before the Council of Churches in Chicago, a demonstration erupted. I turned up the microphone because the crowd was chanting. I told them that we would now hear from General James, whom I had just promoted, and he would lead us in hymns. Chappie stepped up to the microphone and began to sing a beautiful spiritual hymn. He quieted down the crowd at the Stevens Hotel in the first few bars of that hymn. I will never forget it.

Tell us your thoughts about the anti-war movement.

I had a son in the anti-war movement. He was a student at Eau Claire. He led a parade in protest of the war. We talked almost every day. Once, he appeared on the front page of *The New York Times* and I told him he had a perfect right to be against the war. I told him I understood completely but I had to do everything I could to terminate our involvement there. I told him I admired him for taking a position. The New York Times had a great editorial about how I handled my son. He married a young lady from Chetek in the summer of 1969. The whole family gathered in Chetek for the wedding and they thought there would be demonstrations. It turned out to be a lovely, very peaceful event.

Did the anti-war demonstrations bother you?

Oh sure they bothered me. Nixon and some other members of the Administration did not understand the feelings of these young people. I remember my niece and her friend Jim Doyle coming into my office. They were in Washington to demonstrate, but I heard they were in town so I invited them to come to my

Pentagon office. It was good to hear their opinion. I sent the Secretary of the Navy and others to listen to the demonstrators because it was good to hear them out, let them know we were interested in their viewpoint. That was all we could do. They are going to demonstrate anyway, and our responsibilities were quite different from theirs. By the way, my niece and Jim married, and Jim is now Attorney General for the state of Wisconsin.

How did you get American troops out of Vietnam?

Our first step was to set up a training program for the South Vietnamese forces. We established this as our primary mission – to train one platoon at a time. Next, we had to equip them. Our plan was to train and draw down U.S. forces. We probably could have drawn down a little faster but not much faster. The first withdrawal I recommended was 50,000. That was at Midway. President Thieu was there, and he was against any withdrawals. Kissinger was against any withdrawals. Rodgers was against any withdrawals. I was fighting for 50,000. They all said you cannot do that, and I said we have to do it. We have to show movement. The President did not give me as much as I wanted -- 25,000. That was the first withdrawal announced at Midway. The next withdrawal was announced at 90,000. We had to stage it as the South Vietnamese took over. They had not had full responsibility. They did not have the best leadership, and we had to quietly get good people in responsible jobs in their military.

Do you think the South Vietnamese could have defeated the North?

I do not think the South Vietnamese could have defeated the North Vietnamese, but the South would not have had to capitulate. There would have been a negotiated settlement between the South and the North, I am sure of that. There was no chance of negotiations, with the North when they knew there would be no more support for the South Vietnamese forces. Therefore, in 1975 I understand what happened. Many South Vietnamese who had really been gung ho wanted to come to the United States as fast as they could. They wanted to get out of there when they found out there was no military or economic support for them from the United States.

One of four pens used to sign the peace treaty.

Discuss the Christmas bombing in 1972.

Henry Kissinger came back from Paris and briefed us that everything was at a standstill. There was no chance of negotiations and we had to do something rather dramatic. On that recommendation, we carried out the bombing. They came back to the peace table in early January. I have the pen on my desk that was used to sign the peace treaty.

Tell us about the peace treaty.

One of the most important things for me was assurance on the POWs. I spent regular time with all POW and MIA wives. They had free access to my office. I took the wives and kids to the Thanksgiving Redskins football game against the Dallas Cowboys. I had them brought in from all over the country. I wanted the POWs to get publicity because the Johnson administration wanted the POW matter kept secret. Harriman, who was negotiating in Paris, even came to see me in January when I announced I was going public on the POW matter. He said going public was a mistake. He felt the enemy would want too much for the POWs for their return. That was not my concern. I did not think they were being treated properly from information coming through mail through the Red Cross. We had certain ways of reading the letters from the Air Force. They were well trained. That is why we had the Son Tay raid, which I authorized. The prisoners had been moved. The Son Tay raid was a beautiful operation. We did not lose a single person, but the prisoners had been moved. The letters we were getting had been delayed several months. The letters were through the International Red Cross. Photo recon was not much help as they kept things covered up. The prisoners were only let out at night. I wanted the return of all prisoners as part of the peace accord. The accord was negotiated and the bombing stopped. The South Vietnamese and North Vietnamese were to be responsible for future negotiations. The United States and the Russians indicated they would supply only equipment, replacement parts, and ammunition. All this was agreed to in Paris on January 31. I was still Secretary of Defense at that time and had not left Defense. There were problems getting Elliot Richardson confirmed.

The confirmation process took a couple of months. As soon as he was confirmed, my responsibilities were over, but only after all POWs were returned.

What was your reason for leaving?

I do not think people should serve more than four years in that position. I had been critical of McNamara and remember telling him that after he had been there six years. I told him one day that he needed a good vacation or a rest because the stories are always the same when you return from Vietnam. I told him no Secretary should serve more than four years. I had made that statement and felt I should honor it.

Did you see any of the propaganda coming out of North Vietnam?

We saw all the propaganda and we got everything.

What was in it?

We listened to the broadcasts. We taped all the propaganda coming out of Hanoi involving our people. They used their names on a regular basis. We had good coverage.

A drawing on display in Laird's office

What kind of things did it say? I read John McCain's book.

We got their letters, which we decoded. We knew the POWs were being treated very harshly. John McCain, in his book, points out that as soon as I went public about their condition, things improved. Things got better after the Hanoi raid. The Son Tay raid was a great morale booster for those POWs because they knew we cared about them. John McCain is an interesting person, as you know. I served with John McCain's grandfather in the Pacific and his grandfather was the first naval officer I ever saw in my life when he came to Marshfield. I appointed John's father Commander in Chief of the Pacific and then John came to the House of Representatives. His father was a lobbyist for the Navy and was the legislative representative for the Navy when he was a young commander while I was on the Defense Appropriations Committee. I regularly walked over to the committee with Rickover on Tuesdays and with McCain on Wednesdays. They would fill me up with questions. I was in the Longworth building, and we would walk through the tunnel – bending my ear all the way. I knew his old man very well and knew his mother and his aunt. McCain's mother and her sister were identical twins. While staying with the McCain's in Hawaii, I asked the Admiral how he could tell the twins apart. His comment was, "that's their problem, not mine." I told this story to his son, and he put it in his book.

How did McCain's father handle his imprisonment?

Very well. He handled it very well; they were threatening to do things to his son. We were getting that from our intelligence sources. McCain, in his book, points out that he did not get any special treatment because of who his father was. Many people do not realize the Marshfield connection with the McCain family. I saw his grandfather on an island in the Pacific. We did not drink on the ship, but when we hit the island, we were allowed four cans of beer. He remembered Marshfield and said he remembered the young kid that followed him around town.

Can you comment on Agent Orange?

I stopped Agent Orange. The thing that influenced me most was Admiral Zumwalt who became Chief of Naval Operations. I knew him before he reached that position. I passed over a large number of other admirals to appoint him to that post. Many people thought I had made a bad mistake. When I was in four corps in Vietnam, they were using Agent Orange. Zumwalt was using it on the Ho Chi Minh trail, and I became concerned. Agent Orange is a variant of the chemical used along our highways. You have to be very careful with this stuff. You have to be careful even when using Roundup. Caution must always be exercised when using any type of chemical. I did not think Agent Orange was doing too much good on the Ho Chi Minh trail, and we stopped using it.

How about the side effects?

We did not see the side effects until years later. There have been some health problems. Admiral Zumwalt's book is a confession of the person who used the chemical. He lost his son. You should read his book about his use of Agent Orange. McNamara authorized that. I am blamed for many things, but I think we have to take care of those troops. We need to recognize that this country owes them. I have no problem with that. You heard the big deal about nerve gas. I never put nerve gas in that area. When I became Secretary of Defense, I found that some very lethal gas had been shipped to Okinawa, and I immediately got it out of Okinawa and had it sent to a remote island. Nobody used it, but I did not think it should be there.

Collage displayed in the Melvin Laird Center in Marshfield.

Can you describe the Phoenix program?

Bill Colby was running this program to neutralize certain Viet Cong leaders. It was designed to take them out of action. It is like the program being discussed now in Iraq. The Democratic leaders of both the House and Senate in recent interviews came out in favor by saying that all means possible should be used to take out the leader of Iraq. That is assassination. The Phoenix program did have that as one of its underlying goals. That was approved before I got involved, and we pulled back from that. I did not think it was accomplishing very much.

What is your background?

I had a great mother and father. My dad was a Presbyterian minister and also was elected Chairman of the Wood County Board and a Wisconsin State Senator. My mother, a long-time member of the Board of Regents of the University of Wisconsin, also served as head of Mortar Board as a student at the University, and she was very active. My grandmother was one of the first graduates of the University of Wisconsin. My grandfather had been head of the Republican Party when Bob LaFollette was first elected Governor, and then in 1908, Bob LaFollette went to the United States Senate. My grandfather was chairman of the party and Lt. Governor when LaFollette was elected by the legislature to the U.S. Senate. That was the time when my grandfather was very active in getting Bob elected Governor. I have lived around politics all my life. When my father ran for the state senate, I was still in high school, and I made more speeches on his behalf than he did. It was a family interest, and I went to a small school up in Northfield, Minnesota, Carleton College. I attended law school at the University of Wisconsin while in the State Senate. I still work for Reader's Digest. I became good friends with the founders. The Digest operates in forty-four countries and publishes in eighteen languages. We are the biggest magazine in Russia, Germany, and Great Britain, and market a lot of magazines, books, and tapes. The owner passed away in 1994 and willed everything they owned to charity, as they had no children. I then became involved in setting up charitable trusts, as we had to unload 50% of the stock by the year 2000. Charitable trusts cannot be used to retain control of a corporation. The trusts were established with $5.5 billion dollars. Getting back to my family, I lost my two older brothers and my youngest brother is formerly head of the English department at UCLA. He received his Ph.D. in English at the University of Wisconsin, went to Oberlin, and taught there. He lived in Los Angeles, California for thirty years, but is now retired, living here in Marshfield.

It is wonderful to have these five lovely women here today for this interview, along with your teacher. You know, there was never a female general or admiral in the history of the Department of Defense until I became Secretary of Defense. They presented me with that picture displayed on the wall at my last luncheon in the Pentagon. Those are the seven women I raised to flag rank. The picture given to me that day was mounted on a different sort of background. I considered it too racy so I never used it that way. We cut the top matting off because the women had all signed it at the bottom, but along the top it read, "The Women Mel Laird made at the Pentagon." Not very appropriate!

Laird speaking with former President, Gerald Ford in Laird's new office.

Do you have a message for young people about the war?
There is no better place to serve your country than in the military. A few years in the military is very good training, and there are great opportunities for young people. I really do feel that way. I have encouraged many people to get involved in the military.

My first campaign chairman was D.C. Everest, for whom your school is named. His grandson, John Weaver, was appointed to Annapolis. I used to go down and see him play football at Annapolis and tried to get as many good people as possible appointed there. At one time, I had as many as fifteen appointments at Annapolis. D.C. Everest called me when Reed Murray passed away in 1952 and said I must run for Congress. I was very happy as Chairman of the Legislative Council, a very important role for a state senator in Madison. I thought I would stay in the state legislature and possibly run for governor, but the old man said no. He told me it was important to go to Congress and asked whom I wanted for campaign treasurer. I told him about a young man in Stevens Point, Robert

Froehlke, who had just graduated law school. I mentioned that Froehlke did not have enough time in his position to be released to do that kind of job. D.C. picked up the phone and called Carl Jacobs, who was CEO of the company in Stevens Point, where Froehlke was employed. Everest asked Jacobs how long it would take him to come to Rothschild. Shortly, both the CEO and this young man were in Rothschild. Everest gave Froehlke a check for $10,000 that day, making the first contribution to my election campaign. D.C. said it was not his money, he was going to raise it from other people, but the check was a start to the campaign. From that day forward, Froehlke served as Treasurer to all nine campaigns and never accepted a dollar from outside the district.

I represented the Seventh Congressional District for nine terms until I resigned to become Secretary of Defense. When I got out of the Navy, I was twenty-three and not eligible for the House. Therefore, I ran

Katie Anderson and Meghan Casta with Laird at the interview table.

for the state Senate, still in Naval uniform. My father had passed away, and I was elected to fill his seat. I had a very pleasant time in the State Senate and served as secretary to Gov. Kohler for a time, performing both jobs. In Congress, I was ranking member on Defense and also on Health, Education and Welfare.

I visited with Jim Bradley (author of "Flags of Our Fathers") the other day in a restaurant in Pleasantville, New York, near the Digest headquarters. Jim was visiting Pleasantville to speak before the Westchester Marine Corps reunion. The waitress told Jim I was on the second floor of the restaurant, and he came charging up there and asked me to come back downstairs with him. We visited for some time. I knew his old man in Antigo pretty well. He was kind of a recluse there at the end, but I would go up there occasionally and enjoyed spending time with him.

As you know, we are writing a book. Most of our vets are all local guys, and there are many combat veterans. We also have a large number of nurses; some were located in Pleiku and one nurse served on a ship.

Those nurses have tough duty. When we saw those nurses in World War II, we all thought it was a big deal. The nurses would come over on the islands occasionally on liberty outings. We had not seen a woman in a long, long, time. I remember when I was hit by a kamikaze; they transferred me to the battleship *Wisconsin*. Very attractive nurses served on this ship, and I was sorry to have to return to my destroyer.

I am proud of the Laird Center building. Bob Froehlke raised all the money for this building. We did not want to use federal construction money, although some federal money funds research. Bob raised $18 million dollars in a very short time. Almost all of it from close friends and associates who worked with me in business and government. Bob visited with Dave Packard, who served as my Deputy in Defense. As a little background, before coming to Defense, Dave served as Chairman of the Board at Stanford and had been on a small advisory board on medical research. I was promoting medical research in Congress. Soon I convinced Dave to come to Washington, and we established the Laird-Packard Team at Defense. We had a great association together. Dave was a fine person to have on board. Anyway, Bob met with Dave in California to gain his interest in contributing to the Laird Building. Dave asked how much Bob wanted. Bob says, "How about a million dollars." Dave wrote a check immediately. The next day Dave called me and said that Bob was the worst fundraiser he had ever seen. Dave said he would have given him five million! All joking aside, Froehlke is a good fundraiser. For the University of Wisconsin, Bob was very successful in securing private, outside funding -- $850 million. He and Donna Shalala were traveling all over the country raising that money. We have a Clinic Board meeting this Thursday and Friday. You may wish to look at the Laird Day Dedication brochure. I think you will get a kick out of some of those articles. Hillary was interviewed the day before the story broke on Monica. You will read she thought about working for me as an intern in the Congress. I do not think she would have given the interview had it been one day later.

Thank you for visiting the Laird Center at the Marshfield Clinic campus. Now I would like to take you on a tour of this splendid facility.

Melvin Laird served as a member of the House of Representatives for 9 terms from 1950 -1968. He has received several different honorary degrees and has been accredited for a multitude of medical research through the Marshfield Clinic. The Melvin R. Laird Center was erected in honor of Laird in 1998.

Interviewed by Meghan Casta, Katie Anderson and Jenni Marcell
Pictures taken by Jacalyn Schultz and Kesa Jenks.

COMBAT INFANTRYMEN

Infantry in Vietnam

Vietnam was a country of differing climates and terrain. The fighting for men in the delta was different from that in the central highlands, yet there were common threads of experience for all these men.

The majority of fighting units in Vietnam were infantry units that formed the many divisions fielded by the United States. Whether it was Army units in the field or Marine units, the common denominator for the infantry was the individual soldier.

When the United States changed its role in Vietnam in the earl 60's and introduced units to the countryside, it soon became apparent that they would be responsible for their own security. The South Vietnamese could not provide the coverage and protection that was needed. This became evident after the attacks made by sappers to the American airfield outside Da Nang. In 1965 Marines landed to provide security for that airfield, and eventually the protectors began to demand patrols to protect themselves. This escalation demanded the increase of military strength, and the rest is well known.

Infantry units have the responsibility to meet and destroy the enemy after they have been located. Recon forces were responsible for the location, and the infantry units were transported by the helicopter units available. Once the fight was over, these units were removed and allowed to recover before the next confrontation. It is in this sequence of events that makes up the history of the Vietnam War.

Dennis Francl

Dennis Francl enlisted in the Marines and volunteered to go to Vietnam. He was injured within his first two weeks of combat. He was in Vietnam for 16 months.

Do you want to tell us your story, when you got over there to when you got out and coming home?
When I first got there I went to De Nang and right into combat within 72 hours of arrival. I started getting shelled right away. We received a lot of incoming artillery fire at this base. I saw my first marine get killed from there, just patrols looking for the enemy. I was wounded for the first time within two weeks upon arrival. I spent some time in the hospital, was released and went back to the field. I got real lucky for the next year and wasn't hit again until the end of my tour. Coming home, after I was released from the hospital, I spent a few days in Okinawa and from there I went to San Francisco then to New Orleans and saw my family. That's about 16 months of my life in a minute or two.

How did you become involved in the Vietnam War?
I enlisted in the Marines core as a 17 year- old. I went to boot camp after graduation from high school, and a year and a half later, I volunteered to go to Vietnam.

Can you explain the training you went though before you went to Vietnam?
The basic training, or boot camp, was 10 weeks long was an introduction to military life, mystery tactics. Upon graduation from boot camp into infantry training, helicopter training, tactics, and training on various weapons and then to Vietnam.

What did you think when you first arrived in Vietnam?
I thought it was awful hot. We landed in De Nang, which was a huge military air base, from De Nang to various places. One of them being the DMZ, after being at the DMZ we traveled to various fire bases and to the surrounding jungle. It was pretty hot.

What were the base camps like?
I spent very little time in any base camps but they were mostly for support for the people in the field

Did you fight against the Vietcong or the NVA regular units?
NVA regular units.

Can you describe the enemy?
Very determined, well trained, well equipped, fierce.

Can you describe what an average day was like during the war?
An average day would consist mostly of a big cat and mouse game. We would look for them and they would look for us and it would go from extreme boredom to extreme terror in an instant.

Were you involved in any fire fights?
Yes. I don't know how many. I was actually in the jungle or the bush from one side of the DMZ to the other. That area was considered a northern eye core area, which was all up and down the DMZ, east and west.

"WE WOULD LOOK FOR THEM AND THEY WOULD LOOK FOR US AND IT WOULD GO FROM EXTREME BOREDOM TO EXTREME TERROR IN AN INSTANT."

Vietnam was considered a guerrilla war. What was meant by guerrilla warfare?
A lot of small unit combat and quick strikes, quick in and quick out, as opposed to large troop movements.

Did you ever do an ambush?
Yes, ambushes were primarily conducted at night where we would set up an area that we knew the enemy was moving through and usually along a suspected trail that we had found evidence that they had been there. Primarily consisted of very strong unit of about eight or ten people and they were placed strategically and if the ambush was sprung, we would just fire with everything we have and leave the area before their support troops came.

Can you tell us what is meant by search and destroy or search and destroy?
Search and destroy was consisted of usually us being transported from one area to another by helicopter. A short notice given, trying to really spring the surprise on the enemy. We would sweep through and area looking for people, weapon patches, anything that they could utilize and if it was found it was destroyed.

Could you explain any experience you had with body counts or kill ratios?
My unit, which was forth Marine regiment, was never asked to give body counts. I'm sure somebody counted but I never counted any personally. I was not aware of my unit placing an emphasis on that. I had heard other units in the U. S. Army placed more emphasis on that than we did. Usually there wasn't a whole lot left to find.

Did you use helicopters to get around?
Yes, helicopters were considered troop transport I think we had common DH 46's. They probably held 30 people with equipment and weapons. Those were primarily used for transport and there were other smaller helicopters used for medical evacuation and quicker movement.

Were you in Vietnam during the time of the TET offensive? Can you describe it?
Yes, we were near an area called Khe Sahn, which was a major fire base and experienced several human wave assaults in different areas. It didn't really seem like much difference than what we had already experienced.

Were drugs a problem for the soldiers?
No, there were a few guys that smoked, some smoked pot. Usually where we were, which was way out there, we had very little to no contact with any type of a drug source, so it really wasn't much of a problem. People that did smoke were really looked down upon because we were in really hot areas so we need everyone to be focused on what they were doing and not drugged out.

How was the relationship between the whites and blacks in you unit?
It was very strong, we didn't see any color difference. They were our brothers.

Did you have any opinions regarding the anti-war movement back in the States while in Vietnam?
We were not aware of how strong the anti-war movement was, because we were simply not informed. What we did find in a lot of our operations was medical supplies that had been donated by a number of United States universities and that shocked us and made us angry. It caused more confusion than anything. For the most part we were not aware of how strong the movement was.

> *"EVEN TO THIS DAY WHEN I NEAR A HELICOPTER I FLASHBACK AND THEN AT THAT POINT A LOT OF DIFFERENT IMAGES GO THROUGH MY MIND."*

What was the hardest part of being in the war?
Probably being away from the world, the United States. Also being separated from our friends and family, most of us were fairly young, right out of high school then into military training and then into war. That was somewhat of an adjustment.

Was there a lot of emotional or physical stress that you had to endure?
Yes both. From an emotional standpoint, maintaining discipline under very prying circumstances. From a physical standpoint, constant movement through the jungle, horrible living conditions, very little water, very few hot meals, and horrible sleeping conditions.

Is there one particular experience that stands out in your mind?
No I don't think I could pinpoint any particular one. I remember many of them. Even to this day when I hear a helicopter I flashback and then at that point a lot of different images go through my mind.

Do you think the U.S could have won the war? Why?
Yes, I think that we had superior firepower, that should have done it for us, and I think our strategies that we were employed were not effective. There were major decisions made on troop movements from Washington. They were 10,000 miles removed from what was actually happening. I think that one thing that was a got us was the tour itself. Most people knew that if they lived they were only there for a certain period of time and our enemy, the NVA, they were committed and they had a sense of purpose, a sense of direction and for the most part we did not. Our main thing was to survive.

Did you make any lasting friendships during the war?
Yes and do I still keep in touch with people? No, that faded away after I was here for a number of years. For as far as friendships are concerned when one Vietnam veteran meets another one there is almost an instant friendship whether you knew the guy or not because you knew what each other had been through, there is a bond there.

What kind of reception did you get when you came back to the United States?
From strangers very poor, from my family a good one. From strangers, I was actually spit upon at the airport in San Francisco.

What did serving your country mean to you during your active duty and now as a Veteran?
There was a lot of pride in the Marine corps. I don't think that we felt we were really defending our country, we were doing a job that our country had asked us to do. Now as I look back upon it I think that the country as a whole has learned a great deal on the way a lot of the veterans were treated upon the return, and I have a sense of pride and knowing what I did.

Did you have difficulties dealing with the memories when you were back home?
Yes, I think that if anything I had some survivors' guilt for a while. It was difficult for me to make any close or lasting relationships for a number of years and it took several years for that to slide.

Did you have nightmares?
Yes, they are fewer and farther between thankfully.

What did you personally do in the Vietnam War?
I was a Marine corps squad leader for an infantry unit.

Is there anything else you would like to share with us?
Just that not all of the experiences were negative and horrible. The overall experience taught me a lot about myself and it taught me a lot about other people. I know what my limits are and a lot of discipline that I learned then I still use today. There's a certain sense of satisfaction knowing that I had done what I did and I came though it pretty much in one piece and I'm proud of what I did and what others around me did.

Mr. Francl is now working with the American Fidelity Assurance Company as the National Director for brokerage development.

Interviewered by Amber Esch and Jackie Gierczak
Transcribed by Amber Esch

Lee Gebert

Lee Gebert served from 1970-71 with the 1st Battalion, 11th Infantry.

Were you drafted?

Yes. I went into the army on March 17th, 1970. I did my basic training at Fort Bragg in North Carolina. I was in the 1st/11th Infantry – 5th Mech. We were attached to armored but I wasn't armored. I was a ground pounder, a grunt. I flew into Bien Hoa and was processed there and then went to Quang Tri to Camp Roberts. That was thirty some years ago. It's hard to remember it all.

What did you do when you first arrived?

The first week we went out on a search and destroy mission. We spend seven to ten days out, and then we'd be back for two to three days. When things would hit the crap you'd have to jump on a chopper and go out even if you were back in the rear. The land there was highlands before you came to the triple canopy jungle. It was hilly in the west. It was really pretty country, and it was a shame that it had to be used for that purpose.

When you went on that first search and destroy mission, what was it like?

You were scared shitless. Everyone who was a new kid on the block was so scared. The other guys were cool because they'd been there. But when you were new you didn't know what to expect. It's hard. Other P's I talk to say the same thing. It's a weird feeling because you don't know from one day to the next if it's going to be your number. That's the worst part – never knowing if you're going to catch the big one. You're closer than family with those people. I mean you have your friends, but these people were much more than friends. You're protecting each other's ass. When I left I promised Grandma I'd personally come back and hug her, so I had to come back. In the search and destroy missions we were sent out by platoon. We'd be out walking around looking to try and make contact, clearing the area. But these people [North Vietnamese] – it was their country, and they knew it like the back of their hand. But some big generals would say, go out here, go there and clear it out. When you were on a search and destroy mission you usually couldn't see the enemy until you made contact. During one search and destroy mission Cully Jasper (from Tennessee) stepped on a pressure detonated anti-personnel device. Both of his legs were blown off. He was going to get out in two weeks. He should have been in the back. Everyone scrambled like crazy to open up a hole in the triple canopy so the medevac chopper can lower a stretcher to winch him up and get him out. I found out later that he "made it." Yeah, he made it but at what price? He shouldn't have even been in the bush as he was "real short." The point man thought he had seen someone run off the hill before we got to the top. The dog should have been released to check out the area before anyone else was allowed up there. Just a dammed waste!

In January of 1971 we reopened Khe Sanh. It was very scary. We were the first unit to land on the tarmac. It had been years since there had been anyone in Khe Sanh, and they had got their asses kicked. We had to reopen it in January of '71. There hadn't been any troops there since 1968. It was scary as hell because there were NVA out there and we were in numerous firefights. In March my friend Jerry Danay from Illinois caught it. I had been flown back to the rear and went on R & R. They made contact with the NVA and he caught an R.P.G. As I said, I was on R & R at the time, and when I got back I found out. It was really depressing. We were really a tight unit. That contributed to most of us making it back OK. Everyone was tight. We looked out for each other.

All of the firefights were really scary. There were bullets flying everywhere, mortars coming in and everything is blowing up all around you. You are trying to make some sense of what's going on. It was chaotic but it was a controlled chaos. You're trained to react to a certain situation, but it's not like in the movies. It's very surrealistic – having to try and kill a human being, which is not the way we were brought up. Everyone's firing. I prayed to God I didn't kill anyone. I aimed at people and shot. You just can't understand what it's like unless you were there. One of the worst firefights was at Khe Sanh. We were lucky that there were trees in front of us. There were bullets flying everywhere. Everything just broke loose all over.

Dear Mom and Dad and Lyle,
It sure is nice to have only seven-day operations again. The guys don't get so uptight and they don't suffer from being out in the bush so damm long like at Khe Sanh. Everyone's nerves are back to normal again. Have you been to Milwaukee lately? I'd give a million to be back there again. I wonder how all my buddies are doing down there. I can just imagine all the fun they're having. Have you done any fishing lately? I have, but the only thing I've been catching is bottle bass. Saturday I really caught my limit. That was the first good one I hung on to since I've been in this hole. I guess it really isn't all that bad but sometimes it really puts a guy down.

Love, Lee

How did you feel about the NVA?

I hated them, but I also knew they were just doing their job like us. One firefight we came upon a small group of NVA on a trail. They lost two guys. It's hard to deal with when you look in their packs and see pictures of their wives and kids, and they were just doing their job and so were we. Oh man…it's not something you ever want to do, but if you have to do this for your country you'd do it. We would take their weapons and anything that pertained to troop movements. It would be taken back to the rear and given to people in charge of intelligence.

Did you help the ARVN forces?

One mission was Lamson 719. [The name Lam Son 719 came from a victory the Vietnamese people scored over the Chinese six centuries ago, with 719 standing for the current year and the tactical highway number.] We cleared it out for the ARVN so they could make the push toward Laos to where all the NVA were. We pushed to wipe out resistance on the western border. I remember sleeping on the ground at night and the B-52's would be bombing the Ho Chi Minh Trail. The ground would actually be shaking. That was 5-10 miles away. It was a white light show at night.

> *"WE WERE SO AFRAID OF BOOBY TRAPS. YOU WERE ON EDGE EVERY MINUTE OF THE 365 DAYS YOU WERE OVER THERE BECAUSE YOU NEVER KNEW IF IT WAS YOUR TURN."*

What was one of the hardest things about being in Vietnam?

Out in the bush you didn't know who the goddamm enemy was. They were your friends during the day and your enemy at night. So I was only close to the guys in my unit. You couldn't get close to anyone else. Someone would be on guard duty at night, and they would see the enemy, and it would be someone who was on the base during the day. That was the bad part -- you couldn't trust anyone but the people in your unit. Another difficult thing was that there were booby traps all over the place. You never knew where they were. I'd rather be dead than have half my body blown off. We were so afraid of booby traps. You were on edge every minute of the 365 days you were over there because you never knew if it was your turn. One minute a guy's right there next to you, and the next minute he's gone. You'd be thinking, "Is this a bad dream?" You've heard the saying, "When I die I'm going to go to heaven because I've already spent my time in 'Nam."

What was the countryside like?

In the part we were in it was open country, then rolling hills, and then next was the triple canopy jungle. It was beautiful country. The villages where I was at were mostly secured, so we really never went into the villages. They were secure in 1970.

Where did you go on R & R?
I went to Bankok. It was great there. It really did help to get away for awhile.

Dear Mom and Dad and Lyle,
I'm really sorry I haven't written sooner but ever since I went on R & R, things have been pretty hectic around here. By this I mean I've been goofing around down here in Danang going to the beach and generally having a good time. Bangkok was absolutely outa sight. It seemed like time went so fast when I was there. It was really great to see how the people there lived. So many things reminded me of back home. I caught myself feeling homesick a few times but I got over it. While I was there I saw old custom dances, some really beautiful temples and a miniaturized version of Thailand called "Timland." We saw elephants working, cockfights, (a national sport), Thai boxing and some of the biggest snakes I ever saw in my life. One guy walked out of a building with a twenty- foot python around his neck and you should have seen the people run. We took a day and a half and spent it at the ocean. I thought I'd get sick when we went on the boat ride but after about five minutes it didn't even bother me. The beer there is 18%! Could only drink a couple of bottles but it sure is better than American brew. That salt water seems to clear up your skin. It makes you feel a lot better after a few days there. Really had fun catching waves and "body surfing."

Love, Lee

Since you went over in 1970, you knew about the protesting going on at home. Did you hear about it over there?
Yes, I knew about the protesting. I was very unsure of what I wanted to do about Vietnam. I had a friend in Milwaukee who worked at Briggs who could have helped me get to Canada. But look where I was raised – here in Stetsonville, Wisconsin. Was I one to run? You do what you have to. I knew that Ma and Pa had gone through a lot in their lives, too. While I was over there I had a friend, Rick, from West Virginia who went home on leave. He came back and told us they were marching on the streets and a lot of stuff was going down. They were protesting in Madison. He was like a walking encyclopedia of information. He said, "Man, you wouldn't believe what's going on…there's talk that the war will be over." Nixon decided to pull everyone out. The ARVN's were supposed to take over, but they really didn't want to fight. Right now I'm remembering a time on a hilltop overlooking Laos.

"THERE AIN'T NO WINNING OR LOSING IN WAR. EVERYONE TALKS ABOUT WINNING AND LOSING. THE ONLY THING YOU LOSE IS LIVES. IT CHANGES YOU FOREVER."

Those chicken shits [ARVN] threw down their guns and ran. It was March of 1971 on a hill overlooking Highway 9 east of the Laotian border. The ARVN troops were running back to Dong Ha. We were supposed to be supporting them, and they didn't really want to fight. It was weird. We gave them all kinds of support – aerial, artillery. They didn't really want to be there. What was it all about? It was a civil war. They probably had relatives fighting for the other side. We shouldn't have been there. The French couldn't beat them. Way back in history the Chinese couldn't beat them. How are you going to beat a people who are fighting for their country. But when we were there, we did what we had to. There ain't no winning or losing in war. Everyone talks about winning and losing. The only thing you lose is lives. It changes you forever. You can't understand unless you've been there. This was the first media covered war and it really opened people's eyes to the horror of war – the waste it really was. I had a lot of hate and distrust for the government when I got back. It wasn't about fighting communism. It was about American interest. They had a puppet government. We set up the leader and then he got assassinated.

Was it difficult toward the end when you were in Vietnam – the last few weeks?

You were back in the rear then, but it was hard. You were marking days off on a "short calendar." At that time things were winding down and they were getting ready to pull American units out. We didn't give a damm what they did in Vietnam once we got out of there. We had a high survival rate in my unit because the leaders were good. They were good people. We were really green weenies when first got there. All the training you do back home, training for fighting in the jungles and dealing with the Vietnamese – when you get over there they tell you to forget all that stuff you learned back home. We have our own rules over here. You quickly adjust. It's not like what you read about or see in the movies. The best captain we had was from Illinois. He was an excellent captain. He was there the first half of my tour, and then he went home. He was excellent. He had his shit in order. He looked out for his men. If we needed something, he'd get on the horn and say I need it now.

How did you deal with memories after the war?

In 1990 I was assessed for PTSD. Shit was coming up in my life that I didn't know how to deal with. They got me to tell them about when the guy got his legs blown off. It was horrible. The dog was acting weird and everyone was freaking out trying to get the medevac. I knew I had something inside of me for years after the war. I always felt anxious. After I got out of the war, everything was different; your viewpoint on life changes. A lot of vets, myself included, had the feeling "it don't mean nothing." Have you heard that before? Many things in life over here seem so trivial. People get stressed out over things that don't matter – "it don't mean nothing" – it's not important enough to worry about. The war made me a stronger person in some ways. It really affected me. There isn't a day that doesn't go by that I don't think about it still. It affects me still.

What was it like when you came home?

We were filtered back into society. It wasn't so bad around here regarding how they treated the soldiers coming back. People around here supported their sons and daughters. I read reports about soldiers getting spit on. That didn't happen to me. You were just supposed to come back and resume your life. With 'Nam you went by yourself and came back by yourself. It was like I went away and did a job for a year. I used to have a lot of flashbacks and I always woke up at 3:00 a.m. in the morning no matter what time I went to bed. We must have had something bad that happened at that time when I was in Vietnam. I had a lot of flashbacks to Vietnam. Vets try to put it in the back of their heads and not think about it, and then when they get with other vets and start talking about it, it comes back. Other vets are the only ones who truly understand. A buddy of mine, John from Pennsylvania, was the leader of a platoon. He gave a command to take a certain position. They got pinned down. Only three people made it out alive. To this day when he thinks of it he breaks down because he thinks, "What could I have done differently to prevent those deaths?" The highlight of my Vietnam tour was when I jumped on that big bird at Cam Ranh Bay and got the hell out of there. When I got out of the plane when I got back, I kissed the earth. I would have liked to have had my life go a different way, but that's how it is. I try to be a productive person. If you study the history of Vietnam vets, you'll see they have higher percentages of divorce and drug and alcohol use. I was at the original dedication for the High Ground at Neilsville. At first they just had the American flag and the POW flag. There were lots of tears. It felt a little better after being there. You walked away and felt just a little bit better than before. The guys I was with in 'Nam – people who actually served there - were some of the finest people you'll ever meet. We were like a family. We had to rely on each other.

Lee Gebert works at Hurds Millwork in Medford, Wisconsin.

Interviewed by Nancy Gajewski

©2002 D.C. Everest Area Schools Publications

Randall Gorski

Attached to Company C, 1st Battalion, 2nd Infantry, Gorski was wounded on patrol in Tay Ninh province in November, 1968. He was transferred to Japan and then sent back to the United States to finish his enlistment.

Could you please introduce yourself and tell us about your experiences in Vietnam?

Hi, this is Randy Gorski, and I'll give you a brief history of my time spent in the military service. My induction date was 9 April '68. I was inducted out of Wausau, Wisconsin, and I was discharged on 8 April '70. My basic training, which were completed at Fort Campbell, Kentucky, was about a 2-month ordeal. And I took AIT training at Fort Ord, California. The time spent in Vietnam and dates of service in Republic of Vietnam was 12 Sept '68 through 5 Dec '68. At that time I was attached to C Company 1st battalion 2nd infantry 1st infantry division. During my time in Vietnam, I had duty in Saigon, Cam Ranh Bay, Bien Hoa, Loc Ninh, Da Nang, and the Mekong Delta. I was wounded at Tay Ninh Province November 4, 1968. At that time I spent a few weeks in Vietnam, and was sent to Camp Drake, Japan. December 22, I arrived at Fitzsimmons General Hospital in Denver, Colorado. After spending a few days there, I was given convalescent leave and went home for a month at Wausau, WI. February 8th, 1969, I arrived at Fort Riley, Kansas. I was fortunate enough to be attached to the 24th Admin. Company. My job description at that time was that I had the opportunity to process all incoming troops according to their MOS. I assigned them job duty at that time. Decorations and medals I received during the Vietnam conflict were the Campaign Ribbon, National Defense medal, Vietnam Service medal, and the Vietnam Campaign medal. The high point of the war was 1963. President Diem was killed and sadly President Kennedy was assassinated. In 1965, the Marines landed in South Vietnam to defend the air base at Da Nang. At that time we had 75,000 men, which increased to 125,000 troops on active duty in Vietnam. In 1966, the number escalated to 385,000 ground troops. In 1967, President Johnson increased the troop forces to 525,000, on the advice of Gen. Wm. Westmoreland, because apparently the enemy and their efforts at that time were escalating. Another high point was 1968 when President Johnson decided not to run for re-election. In 1969, President Nixon won the presidency and announced at that time that he would start the troop withdrawl.

Can you talk more about how you got involved? Were you drafted? Were you in high school at the time?

I graduated from the North Central Technical Institute. I spent two and a half years there. I was 23 years old at the time of my induction.

How did you feel when you were drafted? Did you even want to go into the war?

At that time I thought it was a very just cause and that it was an honor for me to be called upon my country to serve. I still consider it an honor to be able to serve my country.

Were most of your friends drafted?
A percentage of them were, although a large percent went on to different colleges throughout the country. Some continued seeking a higher level of education.

Did you fight against the Viet Cong or NVA?
We fought mainly against the Viet Cong and some N.V.A.

What were they like?
I never had really an opportunity to meet a live one. But at that time it was difficult to determine if you were fighting the NVA or the Viet Cong. During the day, on the troop maneuvers going through some of these communities and searching amongst the peasants, it was really hard to determine who'd be a Viet Cong or who your real enemy was.

What was an "average" day like for you in Vietnam?
Well, on an average day you'd be concerned with your military duties and you went out on missions to search out and destroy the enemy. We did a lot of helicopter runs where we were dropped in a certain area like the Mekong Delta and were on search and destroy missions.

What did you do when you were on search and destroy?
My primary duty was point man with the radio. They would give me the readings, and I would basically stay in communication with the commanding officer. I was probably the first one out in front of the rest of my company.

Were you scared to do that?
Well, at that time, you were young, and I'm sure in situations, yes, you were quite frightened. Especially when you came in contact, or when we came under fire, or had the misfortunes to see one of our comrades killed or wounded in action.

Did any of your close friends ever die?
Yes, they did.

Is there one particular experience that stands out in your mind?
Well, I think the one experience that really stands out in my mind is when I was wounded November 4, 1968, in Tay Ninh Providence.

> *"WE DID A LOT OF HELICOPTER RUNS WHERE WE WERE DROPPED IN A CERTAIN AREA LIKE THE MEKONG DELTA AND WERE ON SEARCH AND DESTROY MISSIONS."*

That time really stands out sadly because Steven W. Burnam, who served with me in Vietnam, and Billy W. Wilkinson, who was a 19-year veteran, were killed at that time. We were subjected to a lot of enemy fire, and I am sure others were probably wounded or killed during that conflict. It seemed like an eternity to get the chopper in to evacuate us. Once on the chopper, I don't really remember a lot until I arrived at the military hospital. I think that was in Bien Hoa.

Where were you hit?
I was hit in the left, upper chest area, and it went through the left lung and they took out a couple, or three ribs, and they did a rib resection. Sometimes I feel very blessed and fortunate to have survived the war.

How were you injured? What were you doing?

I was on patrol, setting course for the others in the country. I can remember looking at the radio after being hit, and I tried to get up at that time, and I forget what I attempted to do, but one of my comrades pulled me down. I remember looking at the radio, and it had quite a hole in it. I think I was round with AK-47 at that time, which was sniper fire. I believe I was the first one to get hit. And Steve Burnam, whom was from Wichita, Kansas, at that time, was the medic. He was hit shortly after I was, and he expired right next to me.

Was there a lot of emotional or physical stress that you had to endure?

I'm sure there was. I've always been an emotionally strong person. I came from a strong family background, and I was able to persevere, and I was a survivor and I felt blessed for that. After being released from Fitzsimons Hospital, I was fortunate to get assigned to 24th Admin Company in Fort Riley, Kansas. And my MOS was changed from 11b 10 which is infantry to 24b 10. I had a clerical position assigning incoming troops duty according to their MOS. It was a change; I enjoyed it. I met a lot of interesting people that were assigned to Fort Riley.

How long were you in the hospital for?

I was in Ben Hoi for about three weeks. I was wounded November 4, '68 and I was discharged from Fitzsimons, Denver, Colorado, on February the 8th of '69. I arrived at Fort Riley, Kansas, on February 8th or 9th. I had convelesant leave for probably about a month over the Christmas holidays. I spent time with my family and arrived back at Fort Riley on February 8th, 1969.

Were you happy to be home and injured rather than back in Vietnam still fighting?

It's hard to say what ran through my mind. I guess I was just happy to be alive; I didn't give it much thought, whether I was back in Vietnam or back in the U.S. I guess I felt very happy to be a survivor. There were some difficult times after being injured, with surgery, and prior to that I was in excellent physical shape. It took a long time to recover and build up to a point where I could do the type of work I was accustomed to after that injury took place. But I certainly felt fortunate. I think of my army buddies, especially the ones that perished and died over there, many times. I feel very happy to be a survivor.

Were you in involved in any firefights?

Right we were.

Can you describe some of those?

That's been so long ago that it's really hard to give an accurate description or an account of really what happened.

Did you ever do an ambush?

Probably not, no. I don't care to get into that aspect of it.

What was the hardest part of being in the war?

Probably the hardest part was not having a thorough understanding or idea at that time why we were fighting it. You were just basically sent out on these patrols, on search and destroy missions. You never really had an accurate account of how many we were going up against or what these locations were. I'm sure if I'd been in the country longer it would have been (harder). It was a very short period of time I served in Vietnam.

When you were back in the U.S. did you see a lot of the anti-war movements?
We did.

Where you involved in any of them?
I was never involved in any. I was on discharge the 8th of April and back working the 14th, two weeks later. I followed the protestors and totally disagreed with them. But my feelings were that during the war a lot of soldiers, sailors, airman, and marines fought with valor and determination under a lot of extreme conditions, and when they came back a lot of them were typecast as baby killers, druggies, which I certainly didn't agree with. These individuals gave their lives for the cause of freedom, and they really were not given any good recognition at that time until President Reagan initiated the Vietnam Veterans Memorial. Prior to that, we just kind of had to adjust back into society and get on with our lives. They had stories about Lt. Calley and how they'd go into these villages and kill innocent people, but those are the harsh facts of war. Occasionally innocent people will be victims. And as to what degree that happened, I can't accurately state.

How long was your basic training for?
That was about two months.

So were you mostly in the hospital when you were in the war?
No, I was actually released from Fitzsimmons probably about December 22nd, 1968. Then I went home for convalescent leave for about a month. Then I came back and saw the surgeon and was discharged from the hospital, and then I was

> *"BUT MY FEELINGS WERE THAT DURING THE WAR A LOT OF SOLDIERS, SAILORS, AIRMEN, AND MARINES FOUGHT WITH VALOR AND DETERMINATION UNDER A LOT OF EXTREME CONDITIONS."*

attached to Fort Riley. I received my orders for Fort Riley, Kansas, under the 11b-10 mos, 1st Inf. Division. But with my education that I was coming through the lines I was fortunate to be picked out. I was attached to the 24th Admin. Company. I would give all the incoming troops speeches, discussions, or orientation, and then assign them a duty.

What were the hospitals like?
At that time, the care I received, I thought they were adequately equipped. They had good surgeons and gave the veteran or the injured individual the best care that they possibly could. I'm sure medical advancement over years would have improved. I was satisfied. I had no complaints.

What did serving your country or "patriotism" mean to you during active duty?
I just felt that I was fighting a just cause and serving my country. I guess I was proud to be part of the cause over there. I just felt that looking back now, things could've been done more differently, and it's a shame that we lost 58 thousand American boys and 300 thousand wounded, and there's something like 25-26 hundred unaccounted for MIAs. That certainly doesn't please me and the fact that South Vietnam fell to North Vietnam in the end. But there are no guarantees.

Did you lose any friends in the war?
Well they are always there, the friends that you lost. It's been thirty some years, and I think of Doc Burnam and Billie Wilkinson, and some of the other individuals, and they've been gone for that period of time. It's something you never forget. And it does enter your mind on occasion. You could be doing anything, and it will surface.

You mentioned before that things could have been done differently. What do you think should have been done?
I think we should have bombed more aggressively, like the Ho Chi Minh trail and North Vietnam.

Are there any other particular experiences that you could share with us?
Not really. That's pretty much it.

Is there a message that you have for young people today about the war?
As to the Vietnam Conflict? I think it's great that in the schoolroom they go through the horrific events of World War I, World War II, and Korean Conflict, and I'm sure the Vietnam Conflict is discussed, too. I think it's great for the young people to find out and realize what patriotism and being an American is. It's freedom, and the lifestyle we are able to enjoy as a result of the freedom that we do have. Of course, I need not mention the horrific events that took place at the World Trade Centers. I think now the world has changed for all of us, and it's a different world that we now live in. We're fighting a different enemy.

Randall Gorski studied and became an optician following the Vietnam War. He practiced opticianiary in Wausau from 1970 - 1983. Currently, Mr. Gorski farms ginseng and is involved in real estate.

Interviewed and transcribed by
Jenna Tomcek and Katie Klein

Ken Hansen

Hansen was trained as an infantryman and served in the Chu Lai area conducting patrols. He later was stationed near Da Nang. He served there from October 1970 to October 1971.

I was in the 196th infantry brigade. I was there from Oct.1970 to Oct.1971. We worked in Chu Lai. and stayed there for 6 months; then I was in Da Nang for the last six months.

How did you become involved in the Vietnam War?

I was drafted. I had a nice low lottery number, and I was selected for the draft. When I got the paperwork, it told me I had to go to the state of Washington for my basic training. There were several other young men in the community that were also going. We had to go from the city I lived in to a train station that took us to Chicago. When we got to Chicago, we had a physical. We all passed, and they put us on an airplane for Seattle, Washington. We did our basic training at Fort Lewis. Basic training consisted of laws in the military such as discipline, following orders, marching, exercising, and how to build up your body. Then there was some training on different things you would be asked to do in the army like weapons, military procedures, and different things like that. After I finished the eight weeks of basic training, we were shipped to different places in the country. However, my advanced technical training was at Fort Lewis, so I moved to the other side of the fort and started my training for Vietnam. I was going to be in the infantry in Vietnam, so we were trained on different weapons like the M16 and the M60 machine guns. There was another weapon called a 79 grenade launcher and a 203 weapon that was also new. It was an M16 with a grenade launcher mounted to it. We were taught how to throw hand grenades, too. You were taught how to detect booby traps, set booby traps, and how to disassemble booby traps.

How did you go about doing that?

Well, you had to be very patient. When you found one you had to look very closely at it. Some of them were little holes dug in a trail; the hole would be about a foot square. They would take little twigs, branches and leaves and lay them over the hole so you couldn't see it. Some of these trails were very narrow with very thick brush on the sides, so it was very hard to see a booby trap. They would take a C-ration can and mount or wire it into the side of a tree and stick a grenade in the C-ration can. They would run a wire across the hole and tie it to the other side. Then when your foot stepped on the hole, it would get caught on the wire, which was attached to the hand grenade. That is how many men lost their legs and their lives.

Did you personally find any of these booby traps?
Yes, I found several of them, and I was able to disassemble them, so thankfully no one was injured.

Did you fight against any enemy in Vietnam?
Yes I did. At that time, it would have been north of the city of Da Nang. This was thirty years ago, and I don't remember the city or provinces where we were at, but it was north of the city of Da Nang where we had the most of our conflicts. The contact in Chu-Lai, wasn't as much as we had in the Da Nang area.

Were you involved in any fire fights?
Yes.

What were they like?
We were pinned down, and you had bullets flying over

> *"I WALKED POINT, AND THAT IS WHERE I FOUND A LOT OF THOSE BOOBY TRAPS."*

your head. You could hear them flying through the air and hitting along side of you. The closest bullet was in a tree eight inches above my head. I carried a M60 machine gun for six months. You had a lot of firepower with that. That is where the enemy would concentrate on, the firepower. So after I carried it for 6 months, I was able to get rid of that, and I became a point man. I walked point, and that is where I found a lot of those booby traps. Sometimes if the point man missed one, it would be the second guy that would step on it. Luckily, when I was walking point, we didn't have any of those problems; we were able to find them all.

What does guerilla warfare mean to you?
You did not know who the enemy was. It could be a young boy walking in the village. He could have a hand grenade strapped to his back. Or it could be a young girl carrying a satchel bag that had explosives in it. It could be a woman; it could be anyone. All the people dressed alike. It was hard to distinguish who was who. Everyone wore black; they looked like black silk pajamas. If you came into a village and they were running from you, most of the time that was the enemy.

Did you meet a lot of people in the field?
Yes. We would go through villages and come across their little homes called hootches. Most of the time they were friendly. We came across a hooch one time, and it had a small baby crying in it. Evidently, they were the VC, and they had left and didn't take the baby because they were afraid that it would give away their position, so we called in a helicopter and sent the baby to an orphanage.

Did you set up a lot of ambushes?
Well, you would sit out there in the rain and hide so they couldn't see you. You could tell who was who, because if they had weapons, you could eliminate them. Search and destroy is when you did a patrol and if you would come across an enemy you would eliminate them or capture them. I caught a Vietcong doctor one time. We found a trail leading up to this hooch. It was a booby trap. The doctor had captured one of our M16 weapons and had tripwired it across the trail. When I got there, I found it and disassembled it. Then, quietly, we went into the hooch and we captured the Vietcong doctor. We then called in a helicopter and we sent him to the rear for interrogation. That happened a lot, and that was just one that I found. I used many helicopters to get around. I had flown so many times in one that they sent me an air medal. The first time was really an experience. We had been taught how to jump out of helicopters and rappel. When your helicopter would come in and hover over a rice paddy, then you would jump out. The

helicopter had a pilot, a co-pilot and two gunners with machine guns on each side. A helicopter would hold approximately six more people. There would be two people sitting on the floor with their feet hanging out on each side, and 2 sitting in the middle. The helicopter would hover over the area you were going to patrol. Each man weighed at least 100 lbs., plus a backpack that weighed another 100 lbs., so every time a man would jump out, that was another 200 lbs. less weight in the helicopter the helicopter would rise a couple more inches so when all of these people jumped out, the last guy out had the farthest way to go. So, on my first trip out, I was the last one. I didn't know any better; I had never jumped in a rice paddy before. When I jumped out, I got stuck in the rice paddy because the helicopter was so high in the air. I took my backpack off and I held my weapon so it didn't get full of mud from the rice paddy, and tried to get out. Everyone else was off in the bush and out of sight, undercover. Everyone's saying, "c'mon, c'mon, get over here!" I was stuck. I couldn't go anywhere. It took me a few minutes to get out of there. Everywhere we went, we flew by helicopter. If there was a place they could hover over land and get out without

Hanson with a M-16 machine gun and ammo

being in a rice paddy, they would do that. But sometimes there was no place to go but a rice paddy because they were everywhere

What kind of training did you have for this?

They taught us how to bring in a helicopter and how to guide them. We had smoke grenades, and we would pop smoke, and then the helicopter would be able to see us. You would tell him the color of your smoke so he knew it was a friendly smoke, not the enemy, because sometimes the enemy would try to confuse him by having a radio and same color smoke as you so they could bring him in and shoot at him.

What happened?

There was a massive attack in that area; they were overrunning a lot of American firebases. The company I was put into in 1970 had just been eliminated; we were all new except for four or five others. They had just been in a big fight, and most of the company had just been eliminated.

Were drugs a problem?

Yes, they were a problem, but I was in the field and we didn't allow any. It wasn't a big problem for me. Most of it was occurring in the rear areas. There were cooks. and supply people that could get the drugs. I think they were just bored and didn't have much to do. I think that is where most of the problems were. When we were out in the field, you couldn't tolerate that. You had to depend on your buddy and everybody looked out for each other in the field.

> *"WHEN I JUMPED OUT, I GOT STUCK IN THE RICE PADDY BECAUSE THE HELICOPTER WAS SO HIGH IN THE AIR."*

Have you kept in contact with the men from your company?

I haven't kept in contact with them. I visited them ten years after we were out of Vietnam, but after that, no.

Were there racial issues?

We had two blacks in our company. They were really nice guys and got along good with everybody. They were there six months, and then their time was up and they left to go home. I didn't have a lot of contact with other blacks at that time.

Can you describe an average day?

Well you would pull guard duty every night for four hours. There were usually twenty of us in one area at a time. We would all be hidden in fox holes, and we set up three guard posts. Three of us would be pulling guard duty during the night. Most of the time it was raining, and so you had a poncho that you sat out with. You had to keep on oiling your weapon so it wouldn't rust. Then you would get up in the morning and have some breakfast. You would heat up some C-rations, have a cup of instant coffee, the water was usually from a stream. I carried about four quarts of water with me at a time. If you couldn't find good water, iodine tablets were the way to go. Then we would go out on patrols. You usually took your lunch with you. You would have the platoon lieutenant stay at a base camp. We called it night loggers. You set up camp for the night, get something to eat, and caught a few hours of sleep, then pulled some more guard duty. Every 3-4 days the helicopter would come back out and re-supply you with your C-rations. Sometimes they would bring you a can of Coke or Pepsi. I would get mail, too. My fiancée at that time would write me every day. They only came once a week, so every time it came, I had a bunch of letters. One time, she had sent me a package when I was in training. I was in the

Viet Cong hootch where an abandoned Viet Cong baby was found.

states, and it never got there. She had sent it in September; I went into Vietnam in October. One day the helicopter came. It was Christmas, and Santa Claus was on the helicopter. Santa gave me a package that she had sent in September, and it had finally caught up to me, and it was some homemade chocolate chip cookies. They were moldy, but we ate them anyway. There was some Kool-Aid that we could put into the water along with the iodine tablets to help the taste a little bit. Everyday she would send me a letter for the whole year, and I got the newspaper from the city once in awhile. But anywhere we went, we had to burn our garbage, so it was hard to carry around that kind of stuff.

Did you hear from your family?

Yes, every week they would send notes and stuff. I would write them back too.

How heavy was your back pack?

It got to be quite a load with four quarts of water, C-rations for four days, ammunition, bed roll.... that got to be quite a load! I have a bad back today because of it.

Did you find any snakes or reptiles?

Have you ever hear of the viper snake? We called it the step-and-a-half. It was bright green (well, everything was green in Vietnam, even our uniforms) and a foot long. After it bit you, you only went a step and a half and you were dead. I did find one of those and was able to kill it before it got to me. That is

why we called it "the step and a half" I also found a tarantula. We tried to make new paths since the main ones were usually booby-trapped. So I was cutting the trail, and this big tarantula fell on my arm. Using my natural instinct, I took the machete and removed him from my arm. I now have a scar from the machete.

Young villager posed for picture for a package of cigarettes.

What other problems did you encounter with the environment?

We were on an ambush and along came two of the snakes crawling by, but we kept still. The mosquitoes were bad. We had mosquito nets we put over our heads at night. Malaria was a big thing since it rained all the time. We took pills for that. The leeches look like nightcrawlers in the water. We had blousing rubbers that we had on our legs to keep them from crawling up your leg. We had bug juice that we kept in our hat all the time. When you squirted them with that, they would fall right off. Ticks were another big thing. They were all over, falling out of trees and bushes. There were some wild boars and chickens, but there were not a lot of bigger animals. There were also a lot of water buffalo though.

What were some of the emotional and physical stresses?

No one likes to get shot at. When you get shot at, there is a lot of emotional stress there. You get depressed since you are in the rain all the time. You count your days on your hard hat, and when 360 days were up, you would soon be going home. That was a big deal. The hardest part of being in the war was killing people; I didn't like to do that. I thought there was other things I was better qualified for than being in the infantry, but they thought different, so that is where I ended up. We had good morale in our company. One guy was from Guam; he was a good friend of mine. We would run out of food sometimes since the helicopters couldn't come in due to rain. The worst thing I would have to say about Vietnam was being shot at. Some people couldn't handle stress, which was hard on many.

> *"ONE TIME WE SAW HUNDREDS MARCHING THROUGH THE HO-CHI-MINH TRAIL LATE IN THE NIGHT. IT'S PRETTY SCAARY WHEN THERE ARE ONLY THREE OF YOU!"*

Could the US have won the war?

Yes, we definitely could have. We had the firepower, but we couldn't cross certain borders. If the enemy ran over there, we couldn't follow. I think we could have won, but the restrictions held us back. The Vietcong liked to use the element of surprise. They were small and were able to move, they didn't carry much and moved very well throughout the bushes. We had starlight scopes that we could see the enemy move really well. One time we saw hundreds marching through the Ho-Chi-Minh trail late at night. It's pretty scary when there are only three of you!

How was your reception when you got back?

I was glad to be home; my family was glad to see me. When I got back to the city, everyone was glad to have me back and were very happy and nice. If they would start a draft, anyone in that age bracket should be willing to go serve. If the country calls on you to help, I think you should go. Without the draft now, the military seems to have enough people, and that is good. After men get out of the service, the government helps them get an education, and that is nice. I have relatives that have done this. I didn't have a lot of difficulty with memories. When you are in the country for a year, you have all the guns going off, you get a little gun shy. I was visiting my fiancé, and the cement plant across the street was doing some blasting in the quarry. I ducked down under the car; I thought someone was shooting at us. To this day, when someone shoots I am always ducking down to get out of the way. My reactions were quick, but slowing down now. That was thirty years ago. I don't recall any nightmares or anything, but my sister tells me I did have some.

Is there a message you have today for young people about Vietnam?

I learned a lot. I was glad I went and had a chance to serve my country. If the opportunity ever arises, I hope the younger generation would feel the same way and protect their country. It helped me in my life. I learned a lot of discipline, and I think it made me a better person. I was 21 years old when I was there, so it was a good learning experience, but I still don't go hunting today. I don't own a weapon.

It was nice that our city had a veteran's parade and built a big monument in our town for recognition of all the Vietnam Veterans. The government is helping out the veterans that have trouble.

Overall, you get to meet a lot of men from all over the country. That was neat. People from Kansas, Massachusetts, Oklahoma, and California. It was nice to learn about their families and what they were going to do when they got home.

Ken Hansen has had a number of occupations following the war. He had a drain-cleaning business, was a shift foreman at a cement plant, and was an assistant street department superintendent.

Interviewed by Jacalyn Schultz

Ken Hanson carrying M-16 machine gun and backpack.

Dan Hazaert

Hazaert enlisted in the Marines and served in Vietnam in the 26th regiment of the 9th Marine Amphibious Brigade in 1969. Participating in a number of major Marine operations, Hazaert was seriously wounded.

This interview is intended for the exclusive use of *Vietnam Experience*, © 2002, D. C. Everest Area School District, Weston, WI 54476. As a part of the class project, my daughter, Jenna Hazaert ,and a classmate, Nicole Berry, conducted an interview with me. Without exception, I have agreed to the interview and its publication with the understanding the reader(s) will not approach me to elaborate or talk about the interview or my Vietnam experiences. In advance, thank you for honoring my request and privacy. This experience has provided me a perfect opportunity to talk with my daughter and family about my painful experiences, most of which I have kept to myself for years. I only hope the interview helps my family and others understand the silent pain of family members.

How did you become involved in the Vietnam War?
I enlisted.

What years did you serve in Vietnam?
I served in Vietnam from January until May of 1969.

What branch of the service were you in?
I am a retired U.S. Marine.

What operations did you participate in?
Actually, as a U. S. Marine, I was assigned to Indian ("I") Company, 3rd Battalion, of the 26th Regiment. "I" Company was part of the 9th Marine Amphibious Brigade in 1969 and 1970, referred to as "I" Company 3/26th Marines, 9th MAB.
The operations I participated in included:
- Operation Bold Marnier, January 13 – February 9, 1969
- Operation Russell Beach, January 13 – February 9, 1969
- Operation Defiant Measure, February 10 – March 8, 1969
- Operation Taylor Common, February 10 – March 8, 1969
- Operation (Unnamed) on Hill 55, March 8 – March 23, 1969
- Operation Oklahoma Hills, March 31 – April 8, 1969

Can you describe what the Amphibious Brigade was?
The 26th Marine Regiment is a part of the 5th Marine Division, which raised the flag on Iwo Jima during World War II. In 1966, the 26th Marines were reactivated under the command of the 9th Marine

Amphibious Brigade, a special landing force. Deactivation of the 26th Marine Regiment occurred in 1970, and the Colors were again retired.

As a part of "I" Company, 3/26th Marines, 9th Marine Amphibious Brigade, in January 1969 I was assigned to the U.S.S. Tripoli, which was on its second tour of duty. The Tripoli participated in amphibious operations during my assignment. The first of these was Operation Bold Mariner, which was hailed as the largest such in the world since the allied force entered World War II. It was aimed at the Batangan Peninsula of Quang Ngai province, where the entire population was considered hostile. The operation sought to cordon off the peninsula and trap the 300 or so guerillas operating there. Both landing forces Alpha and Bravo joined the South Vietnamese troops and soldiers of the American Division in forming the cordon. Following a feint near Mo Duc, the amphibious force headed for the real landing area. Navy guns softened the objective beaches and the troops went ashore on January 13th, all by helicopter. While the operation continued, the Tripoli remained offshore providing Marines with their ever-needed logistical support and medical facilities. By February 6th, the troops ashore had thoroughly combed the peninsula for Viet Cong troops, so the 3/26 turned the mop-up operation over to the American and South Vietnamese soldiers and returned to the ship. Actually, I joined the U.S.S Tripoli about January 15, 1969, for Operation Bold Mariner. The Tripoli operated off the coast of South Vietnam; helicopters airlifted Marines inland to "hot spots" of combat action.

U.S.S. Tripoli

Operation Russell Beach, was on the China Sea. What I remember most about this operation was hundreds of Marines all went skinny dipping and relaxed in the ocean. We were in the water for about two hours. It was kind of fun. It was a time to relax for a few hours, with the realities of war all around us.

Operation Taylor Common, February 9, 1969, the U.S.S. Tripoli launched their last amphibious operation of the deployment. The expected enemy Tet Offensive required South Vietnamese troops to be withdrawn from Operation Taylor Common, then in progress near An Hoa in Quang Nam province. Bravo "B" Company was to replace those troops in Operation Defiant Measure. In the middle of the day it was very hot, about 110 degrees Fahrenheit. The ships were shooting artillery rounds all around the area for several hours. The humidity in the air was so thick that a few artillery rounds actually blew up in the air (an air burst).

During this operation on February 20, 1969, an air burst from a U.S. artillery round "hit" me with a large piece of shrapnel. I was sent to the Battalion Aide Station for medical care. The initial assessment of my injury was, I had approximately a ten–inch in diameter shrapnel wound on my left shoulder and back which included 2nd-degree burns. As a result of the x-ray exam, I was treated for malaria. The medical staff put me in a bed with an electrical cooling blanket, because of the diagnosis of malaria. I was with about twenty-five guys, all of whom had malaria. I remained at the aide station from February 20 until March 2, 1969. As it turned out, I really had a large lung contusion and abrasion to the left shoulder and back with 2nd-degree burns. I was sent to light duty for an additional five days. I spent the five days at base camp. I remember meeting "Cage" (Kenneth Blackwell) at base camp. He was also recovering from an injury. We became good friends quickly.

One day when I went to the "head" (bathroom)… I walked past the area of camp where the garbage was burned. I saw a pile of paper. I looked closer and I saw that the paper was actually hundreds of records of Marines. I also saw hundreds of pieces of unopened U.S. mail being burned. I picked up some of the mail. Some of it was from the Marines being sent to the states. Other pieces of mail were from individuals in the states to the Marines. I asked myself why are the records and mail being burned? This made me angry! As I looked closely I saw a small package and picked it up. It belonged to "Cage," so I brought

Dan at the Battalion Aide Station

it back to him. He began to cry and got very angry. The package was his Bronze Star Medal, which he was sending to his parents for safekeeping. I reported the situation to the sergeant. However, I do not think anything was done to stop the burning. I left the area within a few days. I then went to Operation (Unnamed) Hill 55. The memories of this operation are vivid. We changed ship or server from the amphibious brigade to the U.S.S. Valley Forge. I actually never went onto the Valley Forge. "I" Company just stayed inland on operations and stored our gear on the ship. Operation (Unnamed) Hill 55 was a very intense operation because we had several people who were killed in the operation. The Viet Cong had dug into this hill and were in little holes. When the Viet Cong fled the area, commanding officers called in artillery rounds and napalm on the hill. After three days of hitting the hill, Ray Fassio and

I had to go get the body of a dead Marine, who was on the hill. We had to search for the parts of his body after it had been lying in the hot sun for three days. We had to carry the pieces down in our ponchos. The smell and experience is unforgettable, beyond words…

The 58 days from January 13th through March 28th, the 26th Marines officially had 90 killed in action, a minimum of 313 wounded in action. Twenty-one of the Marines were killed in alphabetical order. Yes, that's right, in alphabetical order. (www.geocities.com/Pentagon/Bunder/8600/)

Operation Oklahoma Hills seemed to come up quickly. The choppers picked us up quickly and dropped us off in another area. I was really upset; I had no idea of where we were. Later I learned we were on the western end of Happy Valley. We were rushed into action. We climbed a path going up a mountain and there were very thick trees, two and three canopies thick. It took us two days to get up the mountain. It was very difficult to walk through the thick jungle. The climate was now different; it was cold and rained most of the time. On April 4, 1969, around 10:30 AM the machine gun fire started at the point (the head of the company line). Most men fell to the ground right away. I was standing behind a huge rock, I felt protected by the rock so I stood there. The guys started to yell at me to get down. I had 100 pounds of firepower on my back and felt safe where I was, so I remained standing.

The radioman called in 4.2 mortar rounds. These are the largest of the mortar rounds. They are 22 inches long and weigh 25.5 pounds. The radioman called in the wrong ordinances from the map. He called in the rounds, right on us! The first of three rounds landed ten feet from me. I was thrown approximately 30 feet from the blast. I

"THE RADIOMAN CALLED IN THE WRONG COORDINATES FROM THE MAP. HE CALLED IN THE ROUNDS, RIGHT ON US!"

remember the body parts of other men around me and the piles of blood and body abdomens. I remember a numbing pain all over my body. I could not move. I was later told I was the only man in the immediate area to live. Because I was standing, I was hit mostly in the legs and abdomen. I was covered with a thick heavy mud from the crater caused by the blast. I was told the mud was so thick it reduced my bleeding. Three to six men were blown into pieces. They were hit in the head and chest, two to three men on each side of me. Cage was on point and was shot through his liver. I remember him sleeping next to me that night. I was later told he died that night. He bled to death.

I remember some things from going down the mountain trail in a poncho. We did not have stretchers. I was unconscious for most of the three days it took to carry and drag 32 dead and wounded Marines down the mountain. I remember falling out of my poncho two or three times; it was numbingly painful. I remember waking up to throw-up and getting shots of morphine. I knew I would not be going back to action. I really do not know how I made it down…alive!

"BEING ON A WARD WITH MEN WHO HAVE NEW AMPUTATIONS IS ONE OF THOSE UNFORGETTABLE EXPERIENCES."

Operation Oklahoma Hills officially ended on May 29, 1969. In all, 44 Marines were killed in action, 439 were wounded in action, and 456 were injured with broken bones sprains or lacerations (caused by falls in the rugged, slippery jungle terrain). (http://www.mikeco.31.com/Stories/operationoklahomahills.html)

I spent several weeks in a hospital in Vietnam. I was hit with a minimum of 40 shrapnel wounds from my face to my feet. The most life threatening injuries were to my abdomen, groin, and right leg. I was unconscious most of the time I was in the hospital. My wounds were cleaned and the bandages were changed several times each day. The concern for infection was high. I remained in Vietnam until they could close my abdomen. I could not fly in an airplane until my abdomen was closed.

I was brought to Guam Naval Hospital. There I saw my legs for the first time. My legs were severely injured; I had huge wounds to the bone on both of my legs. The medical staff continued to frequently change my bandages and clean out my wounds. They gave me anesthesia, and I slept for a few days. I was told I might lose my right leg and never walk again. A large muscle mass was removed from my right thigh. Infection continued to be a concern, and the circulation in the leg was not good. I was repeatedly told I would probably never be able to have children. I still could not move. I could see a hole in my right hip about the size of a half-dollar; I could actually see my hipbone. I was in an open ward with about 40 other men, most of whom had some type of amputation. Being on a ward with men who have new amputations is one of those unforgettable experiences. The screams of pain, fear, desperation, crying, feeling of loss, and depression is beyond words! The middle of the night was the worst … a lasting memory… Lives were changed forever!

When I was in Guam, my friend, Phil Stover was also there and came to visit me. He had been shot between his helmet and his helmet liner. He suffered seizures from this wound. Phil was with me when I was "hit" both times. He actually helped carry me down the mountain. The doctors found I had a broken wrist, hand,

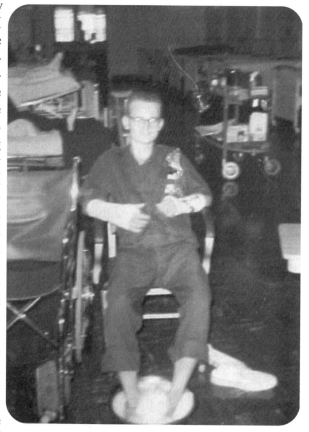

Dan at the Guam Naval Hospital

and right leg. Shrapnel shot through my right hand. I had casts on both of my wrists. My leg did not require a cast because I could not walk for months.

I was eventually transported to the Great Lakes Naval Hospital in Illinois. I was there from May 8 to September 3, 1969. I was glad to be able to see my family. My older brother and his girlfriend brought

me home on weekends until my mobility improved. I received physical therapy on my hands and right leg. I had to learn how to walk again…slowly. After a while I was able to take the train home for weekend visits. At that time, I weighed 110 pounds, fully dressed. I remember getting a new physician, right out of medical school. He wanted me to be sent back to active duty! He told me if I went to school I would be discharged. So that weekend, I went home (for the weekend) and enrolled in the technical school, on a Saturday. I went back to the hospital with my notice of acceptance to the technical school. I was discharged in September of 1969.

I went to school for part of a semester. In November, 1969 I was admitted to Veterans Administrations Hospital, Wood, Wisconsin. I had abdominal surgery and was discharged from the hospital on Christmas Eve of 1969. I remember they had the first lottery for military service when I was in the hospital. My num-

Dan at Guam Naval Hospital preparing to return to the United States

ber was 340+. Sure!

In the late 1960's if you were coming out of high school there was a high likelihood of your being drafted into the service. That was one of the reasons I enlisted: because I wanted to go in and get it over with. Several of my friends tried to get out of going to service by going to school or getting married and having kids. However, most of them ended up in the armed services anyway.

What was it like to come home?

One of the strange things about coming back home was the military did nothing to help Vietnam Veterans with readjustment. No one helped them to mentally prepare for coming home. It was not uncommon for twenty-year old men to be in combat action in Vietnam and in their family's living room within 48 hours. A few vets from high school ended up killing themselves. A lot of guys ended up drinking a lot and taking drugs for a lot of reasons. Many did not have a supportive family. Many had major readjustment problems. Life had a completely different meaning from a few years ago. Many did not have anything to structure their time and did not structure goals for themselves.

When I returned from Vietnam, I was a 20

"SURVIVAL GUILT, PHYSICAL PAIN, HOPELESSNESS, A SENSE OF LOSS, LOSS OF FELLOW MARINES, AND CONTINUAL ABSENCE OF A CLEAR ACCEPTANCE OR 'WELCOME HOME' ALL CONTRIBUTED TO A DEEP SENSE OF SHAME."

year old, which was a legal minor. The general public was very inconsistent in their response to veterans. I tried to forget and hide the fact I was a veteran as much as I could. I did not want to debate the issues. I felt a deep sense of shame, like I had done something wrong. The discussions were and remain too painful! Survival guilt, physical pain, hopelessness, a sense of loss, loss of fellow marines, and continual absence of a clear acceptance or "welcome home" all contributed to a deep sense of shame. I have been very fortunate to have supportive parents, three brothers, a sister, other family members, and Ray and

Phil, all of whom have helped me with my readjustment. Setting career goals and working toward them helped me tremendously in easing the pain. My family has made life meaningful. Against all medical odds, my wife (Jennifer) and I are extremely fortunate to have two wonderful daughters, Jonica and Jenna. They give life true meaning!

Do you have anything else you think is important?
In sharing this interview with my daughter and her classmate, I am hopeful it gives a perspective of how difficult life can be at times. Many people experience a tragedy sometime in their life, in one form or another. As you live, you will find, life will be what you make it. My experience is, there is support in the world...find it! Make a life for yourself...set goals for yourself and follow through with them. Most importantly, share your life with others you care about. Make the world a better place because you were here! What will your positive contributions be? Keep your faith! Believe in yourself! The challenges are yours! The next generation is in your hands. Be all you can be! You are our future.

Dan Hazaert is an assistant superintendant for the D.C. Everest Area School District.

Interviewed and Transcribed by Jenna Hazaert and Nicole Berry

Ron Jones

Drafted in 1967, Jones served in the 1st Air Cavalry Division in the central highlands. He was outside Hue when the Tet offensive occurred and later served near the DMZ.

How did you become involved in the Vietnam War? Were you drafted?
I was drafted in 1967.

Do you remember what the base camps were like?
Over in Vietnam you mean?

Yes.
A base camp, which I saw when we first went into the country, was a big firebase, a lot of barbwire, guard towers, sand bags, and that type of thing.

Did you fight against the Viet Cong or the N.V.A. regular units?
Both.

Could you describe them for us?
I was in the First Air Cavalry Division, and we were in the Central Highlands, and there we fought against the Viet Cong mainly, although we had quite a few North Vietnamese regulars at the same time. When we went up on the Demilitarized Zone in Tet of '68, we fought almost exclusively North Vietnamese.

Were they in bunches of groups or were they mixed in with Viet Cong?
It would be both. We would run into North Vietnamese regulars and other times we would run into a lot of Viet Cong in black pajamas and that type of thing, that type of clothing.

Could you describe what an average day was like during the war?
Okay. Our average day, we'll start in the morning. We get up in the morning and eat breakfast, pack up, kand the helicopters would come in and sling our gear out, and we would be prepared then. Soon after that we would do what we call "saddle up," get our gear on and get ready to go. Helicopters would come in, we'd hop on them six to a helicopter, and we'd go make a combat assault. We'd come in, sometimes they were hot, so we'd come in and we'd take fire some times; most of the time not, thank goodness. We'd go, we'd sweep through a village perhaps, or just go on patrols, and then on a particular day, we'd

walk through the jungle most of the day. Then at night, stop, make camp, dig foxholes. They'd bring in supper. If you got so stay in your perimeter, you would have to be on guard duty. On two hours, off two hours, on two hours, off two hours. If you weren't able to stay in the perimeter, sometimes you would have to go on a listening post with two or three of you. After dark you would put a radio on, grab a machine gun and our other weapons, and go out three or 400 meters and sit quiet and listen for the enemy to go by. You would try not to engage them, because you would probably be vastly outnumbered. Usually about every ninth night, five or six of us would go out on a night ambush and do the same thing. You would find what you think is a suspected trail, set up on that trail and kill anything that would go by. That would be a typical day; we would do that 27 days out of 30.

> *"AFTER DARK YOU WOULD PUT A RADIO ON, GRAB A MACHINE GUN, AND OUR OTHER WEAPONS AND GO OUT THREE OR 400 METERS AND SIT QUIET AND LISTEN FOR THE ENEMY TO GO BY."*

Could you describe what one of these ambushes would be like?
Scare the daylights out of you. You are going out after dark and sitting on the trail just praying to God nothing comes by. If anything did, you engaged them to try to kill them.

That was in the Tet Offensive?
This was all the time.

Could you describe the Viet Cong and how they used guerrilla warfare?
The Viet Cong, and for that matter the North Vietnamese Regulars, too, would only want to engage us when they thought they had an advantage. They would almost exclusively hit us at night.

Did you ever experience firsthand how the Viet Cong used their tunnels, and did you chase them?
Yes, very much so. We had to send guys down into the tunnels with a flashlight and a .45. I've been into some of the tunnels, not too often thank goodness. It's scarier than a night ambush.

What was meant by the search and destroy missions?
Search and destroy. When I first got to Vietnam in 1967 we would make an assault into what we called unfriendly territory. We'd make a sweep, like I said before on a typical day. We'd go into a village, and if it were an unfriendly village, we'd sweep it and then destroy it. Later, as the political climate changed in the United States, they changed it from search and destroy to search and clear. We'd make the sweep through, and just leave it. It got worse than that later on; we were able to fight less and less because of the rules that were placed on us.

So then you just went through the village, and then when you found the Vietcong you would take them or engage them if you could. Could you explain the experience you had with body counts or kills?
The officers, they would go through the casualties. For example the day I was wounded, we lost eight of us, killed, and 29 wounded but we killed 84 in the engagement that we were in. Yeah, they would line them up and count the bodies. Pretty gruesome.

Did you use helicopters?
Everyday.

Could you describe what it was like to be in the helicopters?
The unit that I was in was the First Air Cavalry, the first unit ever in history to use helicopters in warfare. We would typically go in and there would be six helicopters carrying troops of 36 men; a platoon was about 36 men. We also got gunships, so when we would be going in a combat assault, the gunships would be strafing to clear the jungle around you. They'd come in and we'd jump off. The helicopter could be ten feet in the air or it might just be close enough off the ground.

> *"IN 1967 AND '68 WHEN WE GOT BACK TO THE FIREBASE, SOME OF THE GUYS WOULD SMOKE MARIJUANA, THERE'S NO QUESTION ABOUT IT. BUT OUT IN THE FIELD THERE WAS JUST AN UNWRITTEN RULE; IT WAS NOT ALLOWED."*

Was there a drug problem?
I was in an infantry unit, a line unit, so we were out in the bush, as I said before, 27 days out of 30. Three days a month we would get to come back in and guard a firebase. In 1967 and '68 when we got back to the firebase, some of the guys would smoke marijuana, there's no question about it. But out in the field there was just an unwritten rule; it was not allowed. Everybody had to cover each other's back, and the last thing you needed was the guy next to you being high on drugs. And it just didn't happen, or not very much.

Could you describe the Tet Offensive?
We were just outside of Hue City, and there was a pretty famous battle that took place there, at Hue City. It was very heavy, very intense fighting around the Tet Offensive. I didn't get into Hue City; some of the 1st Cavalry did along with the Marines. We were on a company size ambush, and we did have a lot of contact in the Tet Offensive. Yes, that would be quite a bit of contact. We were still up in the DMZ.

How was the relationship between blacks and whites?
Again, describing myself in a line unit, it just wasn't a problem. The riots were happening in Los Angeles when I was there. Everyone had to help everyone else-- color didn't matter

So, when you're on the field it's pretty much just survive, and there were no problems with drugs and stuff like that?
There were no drugs, and that's not to say there weren't any racial issues there. But I really can't put my finger on any. Not enough that it really sticks out in my mind.

Do you have any opinion regarding the anti-war movement back in the United States?
You don't want me to go there, (laugh). Very much so. I think they killed a lot of GI's. I think it just encouraged the North Vietnamese to hang on longer. If these protests wouldn't have happened, if Jane

> *"IF THESE PROTEST WOULDN'T HAVE HAPPENED, IF JANE FONDA HAD NOT GONE WHERE SHE DID...I REALLY THINK THAT AMERICANS WERE KILLED BECAUSE OF THAT."*

Fonda had not gone where she did...I really think that Americans were killed because of that.

Do you think the U.S. could have won the war?
No question about it!

Why?
Back to your question about the search and destroy and search and clear. The minute they stopped the bombing they started coming out. You know if they would just let us fight that war the way it was supposed to be fought, I think we could have won the war. The politicians lost it.

What was the hardest part of being in the war?
I think that changes. When you first get there and you were so afraid of getting killed, you know, being in an infantry unit and getting contact, 'cus you don't know what you're doing, you're afraid of getting yourself, or even worse, getting your buddy killed. Boredom- it was tough, you know. You would go hours and hours with nothing. All of a sudden it just hits the fan. I think being afraid of getting killed or being maimed or wounded by shrapnel, was probably some of the hardest things. The humping was hard, you know. Living like an animal for 27 days at a time wasn't easy.

> *"BOREDOM-- IT WAS TOUGH, YOU KNOW, YOU WOULD GO HOURS AND HOURS WITH NOTHING. ALL OF A SUDDEN IT JUST HITS THE FAN."*

Did you experience a lot of booby traps?
Oh, absolutely, every day, every day. [I have] Lost friends to booby traps; friends lost their legs and arms.

Was there a lot of emotional stress or physical stress?
Oh yeah, definitely. Definitely a lot of emotional stress. Physical stress, you know, just the longer you're there the better condition you're in. You know that stress kind of went away. Yeah, a lot of emotional stress, although you took the attitude that, "if today's my day, that's it." So that's kind of how you evolved and survived.

Did you have any difficulties dealing with the memories?
When I first got back, I can remember my mother saying, when I was in bed and I was going to college, she said when she walked by I would just jump. I was just so on edge yet because you just hear anything and you're up. Post-traumatic stress or any of that, not really. I think about it every day; it never goes away.

You did a lot of waiting and stuff didn't you?
A lot of what?

Just waiting. What did you do to pass time when you were not doing anything?
In the field there's not much waiting. We'd make a combat assault, we'd sweep a village, we'd get up, and we'd maybe have to hump maybe a mile, a mile and a half and set up camp. That took up pretty much the whole day. So when you were out in the field you were busy all the time. You came back in the rear,

and there were three or four days when you had to guard a firebase and you'd get a break. Yeah, the waiting during the day. You could go to the little village, drink a lot of beer. You know, what a typical 21 year-old kid would do. Goof off as much as you can. When we were lonesome we'd get to guard the bridge and we'd get to swim in the river; you know those kinds of things. Write letters home, I read a lot of books. It was really neat to get mail. Wait for guard duty just after we ate supper. We played a lot of cards. A couple of friends and I played a lot of three-handed bridge. There were only three of us who knew how to play. So a lot of that type of thing. Good question.

Could you describe the conditions in Vietnam?

Yes, leeches were just awful. Mosquitoes, to this day I'm paranoid about mosquitoes, because malaria was such a problem. So today we'll sit outside, and when mosquitoes start, I'm in the house; to this day can't handle it. So, yeah a lot of bugs, a lot of bugs. Snakes, a lot of snakes. We'd get back and we'd be in the bunkers. Rats were a problem. One guy got bit by a rat, and every day he would have to go by helicopter in the morning and get his rabies shot and come back out; so that was an issue. Snakes we had. We

Ron holding SKS Rifle he captured on DMZ- 1968

had a pet mongoose, so we'd always send that mongoose into bunkers, and they're littered with snakes. So yeah, snakes were a problem. Especially, Mr. Two-steps, which was a bamboo viper. Because you'd go out at night and chop bamboo to make your hooch, and you always had to worry about that old Mr. Two-steps, because the rumor was that if he bites you, you get two-steps and you're down, so it was a very poisonous snake. So we had a lot of that stuff.

Did you ever see anybody get bit by a Two-step?

No, it could've been a wives tale, I don't know. Kept us careful. Getting back to your question, probably the toughest thing that happened to me over there was when I was on point. Do you know what I mean when you're on point? We went through a village and this was right before Tet. The South Vietnamese army was supposed to take over the bridge that we were guarding, so we walked out, and they didn't show up so we had to turn around and come back. Coming back, I missed seeing the ambush, and a close friend was killed. I've never gotten over that one.

Following his return, Ron Jones went back and graduated from college and became a realtor.

Picture getting ready to go on combat assault in Central Highlands- 1967

Interviewed by Matt Moore and Chad Meinel

Allan Juedes

Juedes was a Marine stationed in Da Nang. He was part of the perimeter defenses at Red Beach conducting patrols and guarding against infiltration. He served in Vietnam in 1968.

Where were you stationed and what did you do?

I was in the Marine Corp for three years. I went through my jungle training at Okinawa by going oversees, and I was over there for eleven months. I also had two brothers over there at the same time. I had one in the Air Force and one in the Army. And the whole time I was there, we were all trying to get each other out of there because you can only have one brother in country at the same time, so that's how I got out of there two months early. One of my brothers finally got through, and he stayed his full tour. He was a gunner on a helicopter gunship. Other than that, it was an experience. I was stationed in Da Nang. When I first got over there it was a real experience... something not everybody should go through.

What did you do? Were you on the ground fighting?

I started out, believe it or not, as a clerk typist. I was there for one week, and then I started doing the supplies, the logistics part of it and one month is when I got my first purple heart. I just asked to be on patrol and then from there on out pretty much I was on patrol, just on the perimeter of Red Beach, wherever I needed to go or where they needed somebody. Our main job was to find these eight foot rockets that were being shot into the bases and find out where they were coming from and to either destroy them before they were fired or do the best we could to stop them from getting there.

Can you describe an average day during the war? What did you do everyday?

When I was stationed at Red Beach, you were up early and you went to bed really late. In fact, a lot of times you slept in your bunker because you had no idea when you were going to be attacked or anything. A typical army day... up early and to bed late. Most of the time I was out on patrol, and that was my job.

What did you do on patrol?

Well, most of the time we were out looking for infiltrators trying to get onto the base, trying to keep them from getting onto the base, and most of the time we were looking for these rocket launchers. Most of the time all they were using was the crotch of a tree. And all they would do was lean them into this tree, light them, and it was like a huge eight-foot firecracker. I have some pictures on what happened to some of our stuff from these rockets. They would make holes big enough to hide a tank. The bunkers at Red Beach... everything was dug with cranes. They were at least eight feet deep, and this is where we lived, down in these bunkers. This would be the perimeter of Red Beach, and the infiltrators would try coming in through the fence. Our job was to be outside and get them before they even came that close. The first rocket attack that I ever went through, they just destroyed everything that was there. The Air Force guys lived fairly decent. They had barracks where they slept. We chose to sleep under ground. The only thing was the spiders and the snakes and the things that crawled in the night. We would call in for supplies and then choppers would bring in stuff that they couldn't land, and they would usually draw a lot of gunfire. That is the way we got all of our stuff. C130s, they just came over and dropped whatever we needed... food, ammunition. And hopefully it dropped in our perimeter because otherwise they would get our stuff. It was a different experience.

What did you get to eat from the packages?
C-rations. It was cans of everything you could name. You could even get good stuff like meatballs. Some of it was horrible like scrambled eggs because they always turned green. For some reason whenever you opened them up, they would turn green. That's why I always laughed at Green Eggs and Ham. It always turned out that way. We got to see one USO show when we were over there, and I don't even remember who they were because they weren't like Bob Hope or any of those people. They were just a small group that came through. You got a very nice tan.

Was it really hot over there?
It was very hot, 120 degrees. That was nothing. But once you got over there, it wasn't bad at all. You got used to it just like we get used to winter here.

So you were married and had a one-year-old child when you left?
Yes, I was married with just a little son when I left. If you ask her[my wife], she thought it was pretty bad when I was leaving, but I was trained to do something and that's what I did.

How long were you there?
Eleven months, from right after New Year's, '68 to just before Christmas of '69.

Were you drafted?
No, I joined the Marine Corp.

Were there drug problems for the soldiers in Vietnam?
I guess so. I tried marijuana when I was over there, but it didn't do anything for me. A Camel cigarette was better. I mean, they had no filter and they were just as strong. Before I left, the hard stuff was bad, and I think a lot of guys lost their lives because of it. They figured they could do more then they really could do; they just weren't in their right head.

Did you use helicopters to get around? How did you get around when you were stationed in different places?

Usually helicopters. Once they opened up the roads to some of the bases, then we would convoy in at night, no lights, go as fast as you can. If you were lucky they didn't mine the road or anything so you could get through, get your supplies as fast as you could get them, and have the truck get out of there because they were just sitting ducks, those guys. Mostly by helicopter and by feet, lots by feet. We walked and walked and walked. But it was a lot safer, and that is why I wanted to go on patrol and in the jungle because it was safer there because I felt like it was one-on-one in there and back on the base, you couldn't fight the rockets that were coming in. I felt I was safer out there.

Did you ever come across any booby traps or anything like that?
Yes. There were lots of them on the trail. I saw a lot of GIs; a lot of my friends got killed with all kinds of rigs. They had a genius way of hurting people. Especially their punji sticks that were saturated with human wastes and stuff like that. They did that a lot. You would put your foot in and the sticks would come out. As soon as you tried to pull your foot back out... See, there were some in the bottom of the pit and as soon as you hit those your reaction was to pull your foot back out. Well they also had the sticks that came out from the sides so when you pulled your leg out, those came out from the side. A lot of them lost their legs because of that. Even to leave C-ration can lying somewhere or anything, they would booby-trap them with a grenade and all kinds of stuff. They knew how to mess you up.

What were the base camps like?
The base camps weren't bad, except when they were getting rocketed or mortared. A lot of the times you might get a warm beer or something special, especially a warm meal, something different than C-rations or whatever you could scrape out of the village. Some of the villagers were very friendly, but raw rice and fish heads isn't very good. That is what they would offer you. But to them it was good. But the base camps were decent. The only thing was, they were very unsafe.

> *"THEY HAD A GENIUS WAY OF HURTING PEOPLE. ESPECIALLY THERE PUNI STICK THAT WERE ATURATED WITH HUMAN WASTE..."*

What did you do when they were getting rocketed?
First thing for me as soon as they started rocketing, I had to go cover my squad and then I would go cover the helicopter path. If there were any dignitaries or anything there, they were getting off of that base, and the choppers was their only way to get out because after the rocket attacks or mortars, you would always have the infiltrators. They would try sneaking through the wires and stuff like that, and once they got on

the base then they would throw grenades and whatever they wanted to do. Everybody on that base when we were getting hit had a place to go, either in the bunker or some place on the perimeter usually just to make sure that they weren't coming at you.

How was the relationship between whites and blacks in your unit?
From what I can remember, and this is a long time ago, there really weren't any racial problems that I can remember where I was stationed. Going over before we ever got to Vietnam you always have, and I don't care if they were white or black, some good ones and you always have some bad ones. And I remember in Okinawa we had some trouble, but once we got over there you were all just like brothers because one had to try to keep the other guy in line and that in turn he kept you in line. I saw very little that ever happened over there. Now between officers that was different. Didn't matter if they were black or white if they were not a good officer then they always ended up leaving one way or another.

What would happen with the officers if there were a fight between them and the enlisted?
A handful of them would fight. I don't know if it was bred into them in their cadet school or what, they

think were better, so they should be treated better. Well you were all there to do a job and to get back home. Some of the young officers, the second Lieutenants were just coming out of OCS, Officer Candidate School, or wherever, right out of college. I would say most of them ended up dead because they wouldn't do what the ones who really knew what was going on said; they wouldn't listen to them. They would think that they knew better, and they just didn't last.

Do you think that the U.S was a political war?
Yes it was. We had the war won; we actually did ,and they pulled us back, and that's when we first realized that it was a big political war. That is what really hurt our troops. I still think today that a lot of people still know that is exactly what it was.

Do you think that we could have won if there would have been more troops down there instead of withdrawing them?
Well we could have won if it wouldn't have been a political war. We had it won when they started with the political stuff. Then everything started to fall apart. It was a long time ago and I don't remember all the ins and outs, but when we found out in our own minds that it was a political war; it hurt.

What do you think the U.S. could have done differently?
I think they could have let us go and just keep going instead of leaving us go to a certain point and then pulling us back. Then the Viet Cong would come back in and take the same area that we had just taken, and it would just go back and forth, back and forth. If they would just let us keep going right now, Vietnam would be won and Thailand and all those would be, I wouldn't say Democratic, but I think their

government would be a lot better.

What about the Ho Chi Mihn Trail? Do you think we could have cut off supply?

Oh yes, that was their main supply route. We knew it; we could have stopped them anytime, I think. Nothing seemed to work for us; we were losing more people and not getting it done. We could have taken it, I think, and we could have held it. Who knows, hard to say?

What encounters did you have with the Vietnamese people and the Viet Cong?

The Vietnamese people as a whole while we were out on patrol, it was very hard to tell who was your friend and who was your enemy. You could go to a village and think they were your friends, but as soon as you would turn your back they would... For some reason the Viet Cong would know exactly where we were going and what we were doing because the people in the village would send somebody out to warn them that we were coming, or which way we were going, or what we were doing. Not always, and not all of the Vietnamese people were Viet Cong, but you didn't know who was or who wasn't. One sure way was them shooting at you; you knew then that they weren't very friendly, so you would shoot back.

Did you ever try and avoid fighting?

Oh yes. We were usually patrols with anywhere from ten GIs to sometimes a company size, but most the time it was between ten and 14/15. Anytime you got in a position where there were ten or fifteen guys coming up against a company size element, we didn't fight; we hid, if we could hide. If you couldn't hide, you just fought as hard as you could, called for evacuation helicopters, and got out of there, because you didn't have a chance.

"MOST OF THE TIME YOU DIDN'T WANT TO WALK ON THE TRAILS ANYWAY BECAUSE THEY WERE BOOBY-TRAPPED..."

Where did you hide if you did?

Over there, it was like this centerpiece. It was so thick that a lot of times, you couldn't even see the trails that they were using. Most of the time you didn't want to walk on the trails anyway because they were booby-trapped, so you always went through the jungle or wherever you could get. It was so thick that a lot of times you couldn't even see the guy ahead of you.

Can you describe the Tet Offensive in 1968?

Yes. Most of the time, you never even saw the inside of the base because you were always out on the perimeter because they were trying to get in. In fact, I was at Red Beach when Tet was going on, and we stayed on the perimeter day and night because they would try getting through the wire. And once they did, they really created a lot of hell inside the base. Our job was to keep them out. The ones that they did overrun were a mess. Those were really times that you would like to forget; it kind of gets to you.

Was there a lot of physical and emotional stress while you were there?

Yes, in just about every guy that came back. When I left Vietnam, I left right out of the field, and so did the whole company that I was with. They flew us out on commercial jets, charter jets that would come in, because they could get off the ground a lot faster than our C130s. They were being fired at as we were taking off. When I got home, yes, I had some problems. I didn't sleep very well, and I had very bad nightmares. I was on some drug just to relax me. And just about every guy that came back with me had at least that problem. A few of them couldn't take it and actually committed suicide. The biggest thing, was as soon as we got off the plane in the states, people were there calling us baby killers, throwing things at us, and it wasn't our fault. We did what we were trained to do for the United States, and that's what we had done. A lot of them that came back and a lot of them that are still living today have a lot of problems. Luckily, I don't.

How did you feel when the Vietnam Wall was built?
I joined the Guard after the war, and I was on active duty working for the guard. I won an award and went to Washington D.C., and the Wall was one place I could not go. I don't know if I ever will be able to because to me that is one of the most sacred things, and I just couldn't go there. One of our tours was there, and I just couldn't do it. Someday, I'll grow up and go there.

How did you feel about going into war when you knew that you were going to have to leave?
I was young. I was only 19, but I was trained. The Marine Corps. trained me the way that I think everybody should be trained, and when I went, I was ready. The thing was that I didn't go over there to get killed, but I went over there to fight for my country. If I would have gotten killed, to me that's just part of the job.

What do you think was the hardest part of going to war?
I think the hardest part was coming home finding that people weren't behind us and that they felt the way they did. They called us baby killers and everything else. I know that was only a handful of people, a minority of them, but I think that was the worst thing.

Did you make any friendships when you were in Vietnam?
We tried not to because as soon as you did, you never knew if they would be here tomorrow. You always had your friends, you just didn't get real friendly. You didn't even know if you would be here tomorrow.

Is there one particular experience that stands out in your mind?
I think joining the Marine Corp was the best thing I ever did. I was fairly wild and they straightened me out. I was glad to get back home. That was the best experience. We came back in to L.A. and that's where we discharged out of. It was good to get back to Wisconsin, even with the snow. I hadn't seen snow in almost a year.

Do you have a message for young people today about war, especially seeing the events of September 11th?
I think my message is that right now everybody has to back the President. Terrorists cannot keep getting away. Talk doesn't work with these people. There would be more of the same terrorism if all we did was talk. Look what we have now. We don't know if you can open your own letters anymore. These people have to be stopped. We have to stick together. We have to be united and just stay behind our president because this is not going to be a couple months. This could be years like in Vietnam. One way or another we will defeat them.

Do you have any last stories?

I do have one story that I like. One time I was on one of the bases. On this base, the officers had an officers' club. The enlisted guys very seldom had a place they could go. So during one of the rocket attacks, myself and three other guys broke into the officers' club and stole all their liquor and cases of beer when the rockets were coming in. We made it through. We were sick afterwards, though. We always ran from the rockets but this time we didn't.

Following his return, Allan Juedes joined the National Guard and was on active duty with that organization.

Interviewed and Transcribed by Lindsey Walstrom and Ashley Zollpriester

Bruce Kleist

1945-1981

Bruce Kleist served in Vietnam in 1969. He was part of the army field artillery.

Vietnam Memories - The following was written by Evelyn Kleist about her son's Vietnam War Experience.

1969…man walked on the moon. What a marvelous and unbelievable event to watch. To my son, Bruce, it didn't mean much.

Boys and girls of D.C. Everest, I pray you will never have to experience such a senseless war. According to the World Almanac1995, the following statistics were given: War…Aug. 4, 1964-Jan. 27, 1973.

No. Serving	8,744,000
Battle Deaths	47,369
Other Deaths	10, 799
Wounded	153,303
Total	211, 471

This was just for the army and did not include other forces.

Bruce was a graduate of D.C. Everest, former teacher of art at D.C. Everest. He enjoyed life, like you do. He was an eagle scout, enjoyed playing in the band, and swimming. He was a lifeguard. He attended college and then was drafted. He was sent to Vietnam without much training in field artillery. Conditions in Vietnam were horrible. He could not wear contacts (a minor thing) as it was too dusty, so he had to wear glasses. He was extremely nearsighted. He sent home for a warm jacket as the nights in the tower were cold. He was told not to fire unless you could see the whites of their eyes. Soldiers coming in from the jungles had shoes rotted off their feet and were not welcome in the PX. Sometimes they had no ammunition. My nephew was a helicopter pilot and earned many medals. Bruce did not earn any medals. Bruce came home, married his childhood sweetheart, graduated from college with a degree in art, taught, as I mentioned, at D.C. Everest, and before he died in 1981, he was the first educational curator at the Leigh Yawkey Woodson Museum.

Kleist was a teacher at D.C. Everest. He had a degree in art and was the educational curator at the Leigh Yawkey Woodson Museum.

Submitted by "Toots" Kleist, Bruce's mother

Wayne Kroening

Kroening served with the 1st of the 26th Infantry which was part of the 1st Division. He served west of Saigon near the Cambodian border. He was drafted in 1968.

What was your rank in Vietnam and what was your job there?
I got there as a private and three months later I became a sergeant, mostly because other guys either went home or got wounded, and my job was just to go where they told us to go and keep the guys alive.

Where exactly were you in Vietnam?
I was in a couple different places. I was in Quan Loi for about three months and then we went to Lai Kai. That was about 60 miles from Saigon, right on the Cambodia border.

Were you mad that you had to go to the war?
No, at the time it was just something that most of us kids had to do. They had the draft, and everybody I knew got drafted, so it was just part of it. And after you got out of high school you got a job and then got drafted. That was part of life at the time.

How old were you when you went into the war?
I was 20 years old when I got drafted and went into basic training in January in 1968.

How many years were you there?
I was in Vietnam for one full year and in the service for two.

How long were you supposed to be there?
Usually everybody did a tour in Vietnam, which was for one year, unless you reenlised or volunteered to stay there longer. Most of them didn't reenlist or volunteer to stay longer.

How were you treated when you came home?
I wasn't treated that bad at all. I heard different stories of young guys coming home from the war, and they were picked on or whatever, but not here, not in Wausau, Wisconsin. They were pretty decent.

Did you know exactly what you were fighting for in the war?
No, no we really didn't find out until we got back that it was more politics then anything, but we were over there just to do what we were told. That was about it. We really didn't know much what was going

on back here. They weren't going to tell us that there were demonstrations. It would have hurt the morale.

Did you feel like the South Vietnamese were doing their part in the war?
We really didn't mingle with them a lot, because we were mostly out in the jungle. The guys that did serve with us were mostly Cambodian. The Vietnamese, they didn't fight as much.

Did you have any friends that died in the war?
Yeah, several of the guys that I actually served with and the guys I got to know from different platoons and stuff like that. They got killed or wounded during the course of serving in the war.

"It's just that the bad times were bad and he good times were better."

Did you ever come close to dying in the war?
I came as close as I wanted to be. There was a few low flying blows and stuff that'd make you dig deep holes if you could.

Do you have any stories to tell or anything?
No, some of the stories are.... I could tell you I was in 17 firefights while I was there, so that's not a lot if you look at 365 in the country and you only got in 17 firefights. A lot of the stories I guess that I could tell you are a lot more. We had some good times in Vietnam. It wasn't all just bad, because the times you weren't fighting, we went back to get new troops or just to rest or whatever. That was the best times and you would do like you did any place else. We played some football games. We went out and kind of enjoyed the small towns. It wasn't all bad. It's just that the bad times were bad and the good times were better. You made a lot of good friends, and I've seen some through the years, that came into town to look me up. I got phone calls from some of them and called a few just to stay in touch.

What was your infantry called exactly?
I was in the 1st of the 26th. The first infantry battalion in the 26th infantry. That was, I guess they called the "Big Red One." That was the patch that we had. It was part of what they called the "Blue Spaders." It was a group of us guys that pulled a lot of day and night time ambushes and day time recons and that kind of stuff.

Wayne Kroening now works at Hammerblow Corporation in Wausau, Wisconsin. He and his wife Marla have three children.

Interviewed and Transcribed: Shannon McCulloch and Adam Michalik

Dennis Kruger

Arriving in Vietnam in March of 1968, Kruger was assigned to a Marine artillery outfit in Phu Bai as a radio operator. Later he became a forward observer.

I joined the Marine Corps when I was in high school - my senior year, along with a friend of mine; we went in together. We went to boot camp the end of August of 1967 in San Diego, CA, and six months later we were in Vietnam. After I came home from boot camp, we had a leave of ten days. I returned and was assigned to radio school where you're taught how to correctly operate a radio - different procedures and things like that, along with the different types of radios you could use. I was on the February draft to go to Vietnam, and on March 9, I arrived in Da Nang, South Vietnam. It's the largest base in the northern part of the country. I was attached to, or supposed to go with, the 11th Marines, so we took a smaller airplane up to Phu Bai where they were located. I was then assigned to Alpha 1/11, which is a field artillery battery.

Khe Sanh was a large base located right south of the DMZ and on the Laotian border. There had been a 77-day siege where the North Vietnamese surrounded the place, and there were two battalions of Marines defending. For 77 days they couldn't get anything in or out. I mean, they could drop their supplies by helicopter, parachute… The big thing was, it was kind of a political battle because when the Vietnamese fought the French in the 50s, they surrounded a place called Dienbienphu up in North Vietnam, and this was supposed to be the Dienbienphu of the South. The NVA were going to overrun the Marines and capture the base. Well, they never did.

Anyway, I was there for about a month, and my job was as a radio operator. The infantry would work out in the fields, and when they would run into a problem or meet the enemy or need artillery, they would call back into Khe Sanh. My job was to take the message, and other Marines would plot it on a map, so the artillery could shoot out in support of the infantry. I did that for about a month, and then I volunteered to go out into the field as a forward observer, which is: you go with the infantry and when you engage the enemy and you want artillery fired, say, on that hillside because that's where the enemy is, your job is to figure out on a map where it is, call the coordinates back to the battery, and then adjust the fire onto your target. We were on the hills around Khe Sanh. I was on hill 558; we stayed there for about a week, and then we went up on another hill, 861. These were some of the bigger hills they had battles on during the siege and prior. You always see them nowadays where they talk about [spending] weeks trying to fight for the top of this hill, win it, and then fly away a week later, and all these casualties for what?

The end of June, June 29, we were overrun one night, and I was wounded that night. There were three forward observers attached to Delta Company, First Marines, and all three forward observers were wounded that night along with three other grunts, infantrymen. Things got pretty bad after that; we lost about two-thirds of the company. I was wounded again on July 7, and on July 8 I left the hill, because when you have two Purple Hearts - when you've been wounded twice - they take you out of the front lines and put you in the rear, because if you get wounded a third time they have to take you out of the country. So they try to hide you somewhere where you won't get hit again.

From there I went to a field hospital in Dong Ha, which was a small village near the coast. Then I was sent back to Da Nang and put with the 11th Marine Regiment. It was the headquarters where all the higher officers and records are kept. They controlled all the 11th Marines, which were all the artillery units in northern Vietnam. I spent my last six months in country there. It was real easy; I'd stand a radio watch for four to five hours a day and had hot roast beef for supper every night.

You were in Vietnam from when to when?
March 9, '68 to the end of March '69. In the Marine Corps you had to spend - what did they say, the tour was thirteen months. So it was like, 12 months and 22 days I was there.

Did you ever kill anyone?
Not directly that I know of. I directed artillery, you know. There were bodies from the artillery barrages, but to say, did I take a rifle and shoot at anyone, no. That wasn't my job. Everyone had his or her job, and if I picked up a rifle and tried to shoot at someone, there would be no one there to call in the artillery. When I first went out into the field there were four of us on this - what you would call an FO team; we were artillery forward observers. My job was, if we were on patrol or on top of a hill, and if all of a sudden we started to get enemy fire or the enemy started to attack from one side, my job was to figure out where that was on the map, call it into the rear, and then direct the artillery onto whatever was trying to get through. If we'd chase them off the hill, and if you see them moving away or something like that, my job was to shoot artillery onto them.

"I WAS WOUNDED AGAIN ON JULY 7, AND ON JULY 8, I LEFT THE HILL, BECAUSE WHEN YOU HAVE TWO PURPLE HEARTS - WHEN YOU'VE BEEN WOUNDED TWICE - THEY TAKE YOU OUT OF THE FRONT LINES AND PUT YOU IN THE REAR BECAUSE IF YOU GET WOUNDED A THIRD TIME, THEY HAVE TO TAKE YOU OUT OF THE COUNTRY."

When I first went out with this company it was Delta Company, First Battalion, First Marines there were four of us, and the first night when we got hit, when I got wounded, like I mentioned prior, all three of the FO's, except the lieutenant, he didn't get hit that night, but all three of us did. One of them, it was his second heart, so that left three of us there. On about the 4th of July, the lieutenant was wounded. He was in a bunker that was struck by a mortar round with a delayed fuse. Instead of hitting and blowing up right away, this penetrates into something, so it doesn't matter how big your roof is, and it goes down in, and then it explodes. He was wounded, and then he was taken out onto a hospital ship.

Anyway, so the lieutenant was gone; there was just myself and this other private first class. On July 7, he was killed, and I received my second heart, so I left by helicopter the next day. Then, three other companies came over to support the hill and what was left of Delta Company, and they stayed there until, like July 12. When they left there, that was the last hill - Khe Sanh had been abandoned. When they pulled out of there, they left all the hills at the time. That was the end of the battles up in that area.

Was everyone there always aware of what they were really fighting for?
You really didn't know much about what was happening back in the United States. One thing that surprised me was you'd see these pictures of Nixon doing this all the time (victory sign) but you know you didn't you're 17 or 19 years old -- you didn't pay too much attention to that stuff. So you know all the protests there were supposedly in '68; there was a lot of protesting going on. When I left here in '67,

Antigo was kind of a small town in northern Wisconsin, you know that. And you really didn't know, or pay that much attention to, what was going on in the cities and all this stuff. Sometimes someone would have a radio or get letters from home, and you'd hear things about what was going on.

I think everyone had a different reason why we were there. Everyone was there because we were sent there, but why they went into the service - lots of different reasons at the time. I went in just because I wanted to join the Marine Corps. I knew there was a war and I'd probably end up over there. But knowing what was going on back in the States at the time, not that much. A little bit, but you really didn't care. It wasn't something you were worried about.

What was your base camp like during your average day?

Well, I had, like, two tours in Vietnam. I always felt sorry for the guys that did their time in Vietnam down south because they had booby traps and they had the Viet Cong, which were civilians that, during the day, they might be working in your area or out working in the field. But at night they'd come find their rifles and they're out setting mines for you to step on the next day. Up north there was nothing like that. It was like there was a North Vietnamese army and the Marines. And it was almost like a fair fight. There were no booby traps really to speak of. There were mines that we'd each put out, but they were in regular mine fields. It wasn't put down the middle of a road where you'd step on it or civilians and stuff like that. During the rest of the day, you might have work parties where you had to clean up the area, regular stuff, you know. So you'd have jobs, cleaning up the area, just different work parties, things to keep people busy and jobs that had to be done.

They'd always send a patrol out, every day, and one of the four FO's would go out, and there'd be maybe 30 other Marines would go out on this patrol. You'd go down off the side of your hill and just move around the edges of it. Just to kind of keep an eye on your area to make sure they weren't building something or digging trenches up towards the top to get closer to you. So you'd do this patrol and you might do that once a week, twice a week, and then that would take all day. There wasn't much foliage around Khe Sanh and the hill because B-52 bombers and perhaps Agent Orange had bombed everything off. When a bomb would hit, it would probably make a hole about the size of this living room {12' by 13' by 8'} and twice as deep. But it would blow all the trees and everything around it from like here to the middle of the road would all get blown down.

So you could sit on top of 689, you could sit there and you could look straight south, and without turning your head, you could look out of your side of your eye and you could see Laos and it's just as green and pretty as can be, and just look out the other side and you could see the ocean. That's how narrow it was up there, but everything in that area was brown. As soon as you crossed the river into Laos, it was all the green jungles again, and it was pretty.

Otherwise, the rest of the day you might set up artillery fires, so the night before you might add some little traps where they try to come up and mess with you, try and get through the wire, or just throw a few hand grenades at us, something like that. Well, you'd go over and maybe set up some defensive fires where you program it in and if needed to call on a fire mission, it's all set up. The rounds will start landing on this ridge right here. This finger that comes up your hill, so you don't have to sit there in the middle of the night with a flashlight and try to get this artillery fire directed. You'd do it during the daytime. You'd have these plotted on your map, so if all of a sudden something was happening here, you could look at your map and say, OK, I got this fire mission right here and it will hit where these guys are coming from right now. You call it in right away. Back in Khe Sanh the gunman would set the directions and elevations to put on so everything went real quick. So you'd do that during the day.

You spent a lot of time writing letters. It's as boring as it can be, a war. You sit up on these hills or you'd sit in Khe Sanh, and it would be so boring. There would be nothing going on, nothing to do, and then all a sudden something would happen, and it's like instant, I'd say terror, but instantly you're going, oh man I wish it would go back to the way it used to be. It's like all the excitement is squeezed into about ten minutes of all the ten days that nothing has happened.

Were there problem with blacks and whites in the army together?

I keep hating to split this thing up… up north, no, because everyone relied on each other. It really didn't matter up there. When you got down south, there would be black and white divisions and all that. In Vietnam, maybe after the early '70s or so - early '69, maybe into the '70s and that - they got worse. I always heard it did, but I never saw it. The unit I was in down south - I don't think there was that many black Marines in there. Up north there were. It didn't matter. You sleep in the same hole, the same trench line.

Did you lose a lot of friends that you were close to?

Ah, this one other FO. His name was Mike Singer, and I joined up with him when I went out in the field. We were together for about three months. It was his job to teach me how to direct fire from the artillery batteries. There was this other Mike I met after boot camp. His name was Mike Enochs. Him and I went through radio school together and did some training together, and staging battalion - which is where you get ready to go to Vietnam. We went to Okinawa together and then we went to 11th Marines [regiment] in Da Nang. There were probably about ten of us, and they said, "OK, we want you three guys to go here and you two guys to go here." It was him, me, and about five other guys . We were sent up to alpha battery. He was still with me. You know you didn't get to say, "I want to stay with him." They told you where you were going and

> *"I ALWAYS FELT SORRY FOR THE GUYS THAT DID THEIR TIME IN VIETNAM DOWN SOUTH BECAUSE THEY HAD BOOBY TRAPS, AND THEY HAD THE VIET CONG, WHICH WERE CIVILIANS THAT, DURING THE DAY, THEY MIGHT BE WORKING IN YOUR AREA, OR OUT WORKING IN THE FIELD."*

all this. Well, it got down to him and me were the final two left. We stayed together. We went to Khe Sanh together.

When we both volunteered to go up the field, I went with Delta Company, and he went with this other company, and then after we had been out and Delta Company had so many problems on the hill, you know most of them got killed or wounded, then they brought the other three companies over. Well, he came over then too that night. So I was able to talk to him. He was probably the closest friend I had there. I was on one side of the hill, and he was on the other with his unit. Mike Singer, the other FO I'd lived with, and myself were the only FO's left in Delta Company. He took one side of the hill, and I took the other. And this Mike Enochs, the old friend, was somewhere else. The next morning, I been wounded that night, the next morning this lieutenant came by and I said, "Where is Mike?" He said, "Mike got killed last night." I was talking about the Mike Enochs and he was talking about Mike Singer that I had lived with the last three months. The guy that I lived with for three months got killed, but the real close friend didn't. So, you made friends that last a lifetime. But there were different guys that got killed that were good friends. You didn't try and make real strong friendships, you would know people and get along with them, but you didn't really make… you knew better because something could happen to them. So, I made friends and I lost some.

You said you got two wounds. Where were those wounds? What happened to you?

The first night when we got overran when I said the three FO's got hit, and then that was… I was sleeping in the bomb crater down on the side, and all the sudden you can hear all this shooting. One FO come down that got wounded and woke up this other guy Singer, that got killed later, and says they got through the wire. We need to get an FO on top the hill to help out in case they need artillery. Well, he said, "I got to go on patrol tomorrow; send Kruger." This is my first action. I am all thrilled and ready to go. I grab my radio and rifle and see these people run on top the hill, and I'm charging up there, and all of a sudden they all started talking Chinese, it sounded like to me, and I realize those are the bad guys. So then I jumped in this big bomb crater, which was probably about the size of the living room here {12' x 13' x 8'} looking out towards the top of the hill. There was shooting up there. It was with Marine we called Chief. Well, someone else came and said we have to get someone the backside of this hole in case they come up that way. Because we were facing up towards the top of the hill. Well, if you move over and you lay on the other end of this hole, your whole body is exposed. Well, I was there for maybe an hour, and someone threw a hand grenade. A piece of it went through underneath the bottom of my arm and out the other side. I remember it was raining and cold and I could feel this warm blood. It didn't hurt that bad, so I kind of felt good to feel something warm. I knew I wasn't hurt that bad. Um, the second one was later on just before I left. I was in a trench line and a mortar went off. That is where they shoot it up and it comes straight back down, where guns usually shoot a straight line. Well a mortar goes up that way and it can go down into the trenches. That is why they use mortars. I had my arm back and I got hit in the wrist by a piece of shrapnel. So, my purple hearts weren't too bad.

What was the hardest part of being in the war? The hardest thing you had to do?
The only thing that sticks is the boredom. It's, like I said, it's days and weeks on end with nothing happening. You just get so bored. It was awful hot a lot of the times. You would go out on these patrols and there would be these bomb crates, and they would be full of water from all the rain. You'd be so hot you'd wade through these. When you got back you had to go pick all these leeches and bloodsuckers that would be all over you. I guess the biggest thing was the boredom then. It was bad.

With all that extra time did you get really homesick?
Oh sure. You'd write letters, and I kept all my letters. My wife, she was my girlfriend back then. And we got married a couple months after I got back. From the time I got there until July, April, May, June, July, say five months; I had every letter she wrote me. I probably kept some from my parents and cousins too. You'd sit there and you'd read them. You would go back and start from the beginning and read them over again. I had all these letters and some red licorice, she would send me red licorice, and Chesterfield cigarettes because you couldn't get them, and I had all this in my bunker, a hole in the ground. And one day I went out on one of these patrols where you went around, and when I came back, they had buried all the trenches because they were supposedly leaving. That is when they buried all my cigarettes and letters. They're still over there somewhere.

What was your most memorable event from the war, that you remember the most?
I guess it would be when I talked about before, when I asked that one lieutenant where Mike was, and I was looking for the friend of mine from Detroit and he told me that Mike got killed, but we were talking about two different people. I think that always stuck with me because I felt kind of, when I found out it wasn't Mike Enochs, the

"WELL, WHEN WE GOT TO OKINAWA ON THE WAY BACK, OUT OF TWELVE OR FIFTEEN OF US, EVERYONE MADE IT. THAT WAS KIND OF RARE BECAUSE THEY ALWAYS SAID ONE OUT OF FOUR USUALLY, IF YOU ARE IN AN INFANTRY TYPE UNIT, GETS KILLED. BUT EVERY ONE OF US GOT BACK."

friend from Detroit, instead it was Mike Singer, the guy I had lived with for about three months, when I found out it was him, I had always felt bad that one of the Mikes got killed, but I felt good that it wasn't the one from Detroit. That has always bothered me, that I felt that way about one of them.

Were you glad when you got to leave or were you sad that you were going to miss people?
Well, you are always glad when you leave there. You know. I know when I first got there, when you get

off the plane. There are people waiting to get on the plane you came on. You know. And they are all yelling, "There's my replacement!" It was a different war. World War II or Korean War, you went as a unit. To Vietnam you went as an individual. If you went there, you were going to be there twelve months and twenty-two days in my case, or thirteen months. Where if you went during the Korean War or WW2, your whole unit went. You left when it left. If it was going to be there six months, you were there six months. If it was going to be there for four years, you were there the whole four years. It kind of depends, so you were glad to go because you knew you were coming back home. In my position, when we went through radio school and staging battalion to prepare you for Vietnam, there was twelve or fifteen of us who all hung out together. We would go to town at night and we all went to radio school together. We got to Vietnam; we all got split up except me and Mike Enochs from Detroit. Our plan was that when we came back, we all had to stop on Okinawa on the way back to get your clothes, to get cleaned up, and make sure your uniforms fit again because you were pretty thin again, and then you would fly back to the United States. Well, when we got to Okinawa on the way back, out of twelve or fifteen of us, everyone made it. That was kind of rare because they always said one out of four usually, if you are in an infantry type unit, gets killed. But, every one of us got back.

What did serving your country or patriotism mean to you during the war and now?
Oh, now I guess I am a lot more proud of it. It is getting to be a lot easier now to be a Vietnam veteran. I knew when I first got back I was on recruiting duty. I stayed in the Marine Corps another four years after I came back. The war in Vietnam was over in 1973. So two years after I came back, the Marine Corps side of the war was over. The war went on until 1975, but the Marine Corps combat troops didn't go over. There were a lot of bad feelings about the war and the people who were in it. So I just put it behind me. I didn't talk about it and if I didn't talk about it, they wouldn't know that I was in the war.

Now, I think that the general public has realized what the veterans and the Marines or anyone that was in the Vietnam War went through, and they are a lot more appreciative, and in the last two years I have gotten in touch with a lot of friends that I was in Vietnam with.

Did you have any difficulties dealing with memories you had from the war?
Not really. There are things you think of. I guess you feel bad about it, but you realize that is the way it is. One of the things they always talk about is the survivor's guilt.

"I GRAB MY RADIO AND RIFLE AND SEE THESE PEOPLE RUN ON TOP THE HILL, AND I'M CHARGING UP THERE, AND ALL OF A SUDDEN, THEY ALL STARTED TALKING CHINESE, IT SOUNDED LIKE TO ME, AND I REALIZE THOSE ARE THE BAD GUYS."

Sometimes you think about all the guys that got killed or wounded real badly, and you figure, and you feel bad that it happened to someone else. At the time there was always a saying, "Better him than me." Someone got killed, he might be a friend, but he is still a fellow Marine. He is lying there and you're not. It is better him than me. It is still someone else. You have this survivor's guilt, and you still have that now where you look back and say why did that happen to someone else. And then you feel like maybe I didn't do enough, didn't do enough that, not that it happened to him or I got him killed or anything, why did it happen to him and not me? There is always that guilt there of just something. We had this one night, me and this other guy were in a fighting hole, and this is when we were on this hill up north, we were goofing off. We were painting our faces black, we were going to sneak down and steal some food because we were only getting one meal. There wasn't much food up there at the time. This bomb went off, it was a rifle-propelled grenade, and it is where they shoot a grenade off a gun. Well, it went off right in front of us. It knocked me down and the two guys behind us. But this guy who was standing directly next to me, we were leaning against each other, he got hit in the throat and everything.

He ended up, they had to do a tracheotomy on him to keep him breathing. I met him last spring. I went back and saw him. I finally found him through the Internet. He is from Saginaw, Michigan. I went to see him. He is pretty bad off. One side is kind of paralyzed. Little parts of it went into his spine, which went into his nervous system. So he is pretty messed up. He is, you know, about my age, a little older, but he lives alone and he walks really badly, and it is hard to understand him. Here is a guy that, if I had just been standing on the other side of him, it would have been different. That still bothers me.

Following his return, Dennis Kruger became a deputy sheriff.

Interviewed and transcribed by Ashley Harder, Stephanie Barnard, and Shanna Hanson

Don Masterson

Masterson served in Vietnam from February 1968 to February 1969 with the 1st of the 5th Cavalry in the 1st Air Cav. Division. He was a medic serving in the central highlands.

Could you please say your name and where you were stationed?

My name is Don Masterson; I was in Vietnam in February of 1968 to February 1969. I was with Company D 1/5th 1st Air Cavalry division, airmobile.

How did you become involved in Vietnam?

I enlisted in the United States Army, I thought it was something that I had to do at that time. I knew the draft was available; I went to the University of Stevens Point, Wisconsin for a year after I graduated from high school and that just did not keep me occupied, so to speak. My interest was in Vietnam, so I enlisted in the United States Army.

Can you explain to us what the base camps were like?

Base Camps: My base camp was An Khe. When I entered and left the country were the only times I was there. The rest of the time I was stationed at firebases consisting usually of an artillary battery surrounded by razor wire, barbed wire, trip flares, claymore mines, and bunkers or fighting positions.

Did you fight against the Viet Cong or NVA regularly?

I fought against both of them.

What was the enemy like?

That's hard to explain. The Viet Cong, in my opinion, were not well armed or trained, but the NVA (North Vietnamees Army), on the other hand, were well trained and they had some better armaments than the V.C. did. The Viet Cong had a lot of Chinese made, or leftovers from some other wars, German Mausers, bolt action. They had grenades, which looked like a piece of metal on a stick, but they weren't very effective, and their weapons were not very effective. However, the NVA were armed with 30 caliber machine guns and AK-47s, and they had rockets. They had some artillery, and they had some tanks in the area and were a formidable force, for what they had.

Was it hard having to deal with their tunnels?

Well, that I never really got involved in. I was sniped at from a tunnel a couple of times, but there was a group called tunnel rats, and they would actually go down into these tunnels. My unit with the First Cav. was about 120 men strong. I was assigned there as a medic; there was supposed to be one medic per platoon. There was also supposed to be a senior-aid man that was attached to the company commander so you were supposed to have five medics, but most of the time we had three. I think, during the time I was there, there were over 500 thousand troops. I think it was very fortunate that I got the first cavalry because they were a force in that country, but because they were a force, we had air power, and we worked with the Navy, with their big guns plus our choppers. Basically, if we asked for support, we got it. It was a very mountainous country. Where I was located was called the Central Highlands. We would go out in a strength of about 120 people for approximately 30 days at a time. Our protection at night consisted of trip flares, claymore mines, four M-60 machine guns, M-16 rifles, small arms, and our radios. We had a forward observer when we moved he moved with us, and he actually had artillery pointing toward us from any point in that country, and all he did was get on the radio and call in fire. The first Cav. Division was there, and it really made a statement. There were probably other units that wished they had some of our support. If I had a man injured or somebody wounded, I could call in a " Dust-Off" or a helicopter and supposedly, within eight minutes they could reach hospital ships or division aid stations, whatever was there.

> *"THE V.C. LOVED TO PLANT MINES AND SUCH IN THE ROAD, SO WE WOULD HAVE TO DO SWEEPS AND CLEAR SECTIONS OF ROADS, FROM ONE FIREBASE TO ANOTHER."*

Can you describe what an average day was like during the war?

Well if I put them all together, I would say you were always a little bit on edge. At no place in that country were you really safe, like we're sitting here right now. And maybe after the September 11th attacks, maybe you guys don't feel as safe anymore. Well that feeling was kind of the feeling in Vietnam. There was no what you call "front lines." In Korea and WWII and past wars you had a "line drawn in the sand" so to speak, and you try to gain ground, and you didn't want to give anything up, and you had objectives and goals. Well, the thing in Vietnam was that we were 120 men in a unit, and that's the ground we held. There was a DMZ or "de-militarized zone" that split Vietnam into North Vietnam and South Vietnam. You had your North Vietnamese Capital, Hanoi, and you had your South Vietnamese capital, Saigon, and that's about as far as it went. There was no place that you could actually feel safe. There was a lot of boredom. Some days we'd maybe cover a "click." Now a click is about 1000 yards. And sometimes we'd go one direction and come right back the next day or even the same day. As average soldiers, you didn't see the whole picture. We were always prepared to go before dawn; this is something that the enemy always thought we were a little lacking in. We kept a vigilance all night long. You were always hungry and tired. What we ate were called C-ration; it's a canned food. They had over 12-15 different meals. It came in a little 6x8 cardboard box, and inside of it were your meals. When we went to the fields, we took our meals and put them in our socks. We used a metal-framed backpack, kind of like what students use to go to school with now, and we filled them up with our belongings. My very first job in the morning was to make sure that the guys got salt tablets, and malaria pills. When we were at our firebases, our basic jobs there were security at night, absolutes at night and road clearing in the morning. The V.C. loved to plant mines and such in the road, so we would have to do sweeps, and clear sections of roads, from one fire-base to another. We did this so the roads would be safe to travel on.

So, basically, you were ready and alert the whole time?

Yeah, at night you posted two hours at a time. And none of those guys fell asleep, no matter how tired we were. Sometimes we got one or two hours of sleep. Out of all the time I was there, we were hit two, maybe three times at night. It was just small, little attacks. Mainly to see if we were awake or not, type of attacks. These attacks involved hand-grenades, and we would throw a few back. The one thing you didn't want to do is give away your position by opening fire, with rifles or machine guns. We were never threatened a lot at night. I did see LZ Evans go up. I was at LZ Jane, which was around two miles away, on another mountaintop. The First Cav. was in charge of making this base Evans, and when they were about half done, the V.C. got the best of it. There were flares and fighting all night, and you could see it from a distance. The next two days we went in there and bombed the crap out of them, letting them know they didn't really prove anything. I still don't understand why they did this; there was no ground to be gained. When I first got there, I was all full of piss and vinegar. I thought oh boy, we are going to kick these guys' asses, but it just didn't work that way. I think our military was prepared to make the right decisions at the time. I don't know if our presidential leaders were prepared. I do know that we had enough manpower in that country to just make it happen. What I really hated were the "no-fire zones," where if we get near a village, or what was called a friendly area, if we actually got fired on, we couldn't return fire. In early '68 we used to go on what was called search and destroy missions, and actually, if the village was hostile, we would just burn it down. There wasn't too much to burn down though; it was all just dried bamboo. Politics changed in the time I was there, and we just couldn't do the things we could prior to mid '68.

"I SAW A LITLE CUBBYHOLE, AND CRAWLED IN. THERE WAS A V.C. HIDING THERE IN BLACK PAJAMAS. THIS WAS ONLY MY THIRD OR FOURTH DAY IN THE BUSH, SO I STUCK MY M-16 IN HIS EAR, AND THE GUY JUMPED UP! I THOUGHT I WAS DEAD."

What were the search and destroy missions like?

We would try to find where there was a stock of weapons and body counts. We would try to find V.C. in these villages. About the only good way we had to find a V.C. was to rip his shirt off and check his shoulder for strap marks. If we got hit going into a village, we wouldn't hesitate at all. We would just burn it down. After awhile I just didn't feel sorry for those people. One of the first things I ever did over there was capture a V.C. We had 120 guys, plus about 30 ARVN's with us (which was someone I had no respect for). ARVN's were the Army of The Republic of Vietnam. We were in this sandy area, with a heavy over-growth, and we got shot at by four or five V.C. So we attack them. When we got into the heavy under-brush, there was this great big path probably thirty feet wide. I saw a little cubbyhole, and crawled in. There was a V.C. hiding there in black pajamas. This was only my third or fourth day in the bush, so I stuck my M-16 in his ear, and the guy jumped up! I thought he was dead. I still say to this day that if that guy would have had a knife, I would have gotten killed, because I wasn't expecting him alive. He was just a-blabbering, scared as all hell. His eyeballs had to be as big as half dollars. He thought I was going to shoot him, and I probably should have. Anyways, to make a long story short, I got him back to the

Unit, and they were all saying, "Oh look, the new doc got a prisoner. Shoot him!" I gave him to the ARVN's, and they tied his hands behind his back, blind-folded him, took a BAR, (Browning Automatic Rifle), which is as tall as a Vietnamese, and he cracked the V.C. right on the skull. He went down to one knee, but he never passed out. That was amazing to me.

Later that year on search mission, we got into a battalion firefight, near the arms. We called in the jets, the Navy, and our helicopters. For two days, we chased these guys around, and we killed so many at one time, that they just couldn't take the bodies away. One thing I remember, one of the bodies, was a Chinese advisor. Everyone was looking at him because he was Chinese, and they were concerned that the North was attempting to get Chinese forces to get into this thing. That guy brought a lot of attention. We killed lots of new troops that had just come from North Vietnam, and they didn't have a clue about what they got into.

Masterson currently works at the Department of Work Force Development in the Job Center. He helps Veterans find jobs. He has been married for 30 years and has one son and two grandchildren.

Interviewed by Chris Rupel and Ahmed Chadi

Gary Meyer

Volunteering for the service, Meyer served in the infantry in Vietnam, being wounded in action by grenade fragments.

How did you become involved in the Vietnam War?
A friend of mine and I volunteered to go in for two years in the army.

When did you go in?
I graduated from high school and worked for one year at Greenheck, and then I went over to Vietnam.

Can you describe what an average day was like during the war?
We did a lot of walking, building different bunkers because we were setting up different CPs, all over and we were the support brigade, so we would go where different units wanted us. We would helicopter in to these different areas.

Were you in combat?
Yes, we engaged the enemy. They would be hiding and shooting rockets on you, and we would run ambushes at night, and we would see a few but not many. They played hide and seek with us. If we found them we would engage.

What was a battle like?
One time we went for twenty-four hours. We heard some digging one night when we were on ambush, so we set up to listen, and then in the morning when it got light we could see these guys laying in a hammock, and they had underground bunkers and stuff like that. It was a big swampy area and flying overhead you couldn't see them and our captain called in some air strikes during the daytime with napalm to try to get as many out as you could, and then we went in to see what we got. The majority left a lot of information which the captain kept and took back, and they dragged off a lot of bodies, but there were a few that were in the bunkers. We went and checked to see what was left in there. We lost a few guys but we cleared out what was in there, and it was a long, long day. There were a few scary moments. One time we were coming down by these dikes and the Captain called in this air support from some helicopters and the helicopters must have got the coordinates screwed up and they were coming right down to the area where we were laying behind these dikes and the Captain called in that we were "friendly" and that they would be firing on us if they didn't pull back. So they pulled back, and the napalm bombs kind of shook the ground.

Did you ever receive any battle wounds?

A grenade wounded me when we were out on ambush with some Vietnamese troops that threw some grenades on us. Three of us that were in the platoon were over in the hospital in Cam Ranh Bay. I was in there for fifty-four days. Nothing serious, but they hit my wrist, and I couldn't use my hand. It was fractured.

What was an average day like in the war?

Over there we did a lot of patrolling. A lot of patrols looking for the enemy, but we could never run across them because they were a hit and miss person because they liked to hit you at night. You set up your CPs or if you are in a village, or the ARVN compound, they would stand on top of roofs and shoot rockets and mortars on you and if you are in the field, they would set up grenades with trip wires and stuff like that to slow you down. Basically your day consisted of resting or moving around. You eat, sleep, and go on ambushes. It wasn't that often that you ran into the enemy. I think I was in three different fights over there.

Were drugs a problem for some of the soldiers?

When I was in the mortar platoon, in charge of that, I had one person that used to go into the ARVN compound where we were stationed at, and he was taking some drugs. I got wind of that, and that was the only incident with somebody taking drugs. I gave him the choice of staying with the company or another option.

Was there a good relationship between blacks and whites?

The majority of blacks got along pretty well. The only problem we ran into was if you get too many blacks in a group, you could have a problem. They seemed more aggressive; I don't know what caused them to do that. When we were in basic training, we ran into the same problem. Alone they were OK, but if they got in a group of ten or so, you had to watch out because they would over power you. One night we were walking down a sidewalk near the headquarters. A group of blacks were coming down and there were only three of us and all of a sudden they were coming down the sidewalk and they separated on the right and left hand side of us. They tried to jump us, and we starting swinging. One guy got a knife wound in the leg, and the MPs came, and they all took off. Over in Vietnam there wasn't too much of a problem. They knew they had to watch themselves over there. An accident can happen.

So there was racism?

I think there was some.

Did you make any lasting friendships over there?

I made a few good friends over there. I don't know where they live anymore, but I had some friends over there, and I lost a few good friends over there.

Have you ever attempted a reunion?

No, we have never had a reunion. I have thought about writing to the Army and maybe try to locate some of these men. I think one is in North Carolina and a few are up in Michigan. We always got along pretty good.

What was the hardest part for you about being a Marine?
Probably seeing my friends die.

When one of them died in battle, what was your reaction?
Basically if we ran into a group like that, the firefight would only last so long. If somebody got killed you wouldn't know right away until things got cleaned up and then you would know. We had a long line and we were spread out and then someone would come and tell us who got killed. That was about the only time you found out.

Were there any battles you were in where there were major losses?
Not really, the most people we lost in a day were about three. There weren't too many firefights that you ran into. Most of the time they were hiding. I think people ran into a lot more before I arrived in Vietnam. Things were winding down when I got over to Vietnam.

Did you encounter trip wires?
I tripped on a trip wire one time, and they didn't set it up properly so it didn't pull the pin out of the grenade. Otherwise I saw friends that ran into those traps and had a foot blown off.

So you were in the lead?
Sometimes I was in the lead and sometimes I was in the back. A lot of times we rotated.

Was the wire hard to see?
Oh yes, they are hard to see. When I tripped it, somebody hollered "hit it" and luckily it didn't go off.

Can you go into detail about your experience with battle?
The battles are hard to describe because they are "hit and miss." Once when I was in the mortar platoon that one night I was in charge of them. We got a couple of army platoons come into this compound that we had made for our mortars and everything that went with that, and they were just going to stay overnight, and some Vietnamese got on top of some house roofs and stuff like that to fire these rockets over the fences in the hope of blowing up our mortars. We always kept our charges away from the mortars so they weren't easy to blow up. Some guys from the platoons were hit, and I think we lost five guys that night. Hit and miss, they would sneak up on you, get on the roofs, and shoot something at you and then disappear. They had a lot of tunnels and bunkers built under the ground, and some were hard to find. The other fight I got into was the one where we were on ambush that night and heard the digging so we staked out that area that night and that's when the Captain called in the air strikes and napalm. They would take their dead with them, and there were some that were alive. We had to kill them before we could secure the area. I lost three of my friends in that.

Is there one particular experience that stands out in your mind?
The biggest experience is the one where I lost my friends in that firefight. One time we were in this platoon headquarters where we had set up. I was in the mortars for four months, I was in the hospital for two months and when I got back, I went into the ground troops for my second MOS. We were set up one night in this compound with a different company, and they sent a rocket in, and we all headed for our bunkers and there was a medic tent set up and that rocket hit right on top of that medic tent and took care of the tent and the medic. It was a pretty good sized rocket.

Was the helicopter your primary transportation?
Yes, about half-and-half. Sometimes we would go on our daily walks and sometimes we were in the field for weeks setting up ambushes and patrolling. We would move around during the day and set up the ambushes at night. One night we were close to a company of NVA that was settled near a swamp. They knew that we were around them, and they tried to sneak out at night. So our Captain called in helicopter support, and he set us up with strobe lights in a diamond shape, and he called in the helicopters and told them to shoot on all sides of the diamond shape. That way none of the enemy could get at us. We wounded quite a few that night, and we were able to take some to headquarters. The rest scattered all over. That night we didn't know how many would be coming out. Once in a while, a firefight would last a day or two, but most were fast. We were patrolling looking for caches of weapons that they might have buried in the ground.

Did you ever burn a village?
No, we never got into a situation where we had to burn villages.

Was there a lot of emotional and physical stress that you had to endure?
I would say that the emotional part was when my friends were killed but nothing else.

What was your reception like when you returned?
When I got back to the states, I went to Colorado and spent the last six months of my service there. That was at Ft. Carson, and that was basically an Army reserve station, so anybody that came back from Vietnam just stayed in the barracks. In the morning, some guys wouldn't come out, and they left us alone. Our reception consisted of family that were glad to see that you made it.

Was it hard to readjust?
Somewhat, not real bad. If I had been there earlier when more stuff was going on in Vietnam, it may have been harder. If the fighting had been more fierce, it would have made it tougher. My brother was also in Vietnam, and he made it home. He was in one bad fight, but basically he had it pretty good. By the time I got there, they were cleaning up.

Anything you would like to add?
One time we were up in the mountains of the north, and they chopper people in and out because of the

terrain. We were living on a pile of rocks in the hills. Living conditions weren't the best, at least we had food and water. Sometimes we would take water from the river or from pools made by bomb craters. We would put iodine tablets in the water and drink it that way because sometimes you couldn't get things flown in right away. Basically you would stay occupied during the daytime because at night you would be ready to go out on ambush.

Did you stay in the basecamps or in the field?
We were out in the field a lot, and sometimes we would come back to the basecamp. If we were out in the field for two or three weeks, we would be in the basecamp for a week.

Was it harder in the field?
Yes, I would say so because of mosquitoes and rain. Monsoon season was not fun. When we got back to the base-camp you got dry socks. People had problems with their feet. You would be loaded down with food in your pack and little else. One time we were patrolling on a river, patrolling an area. One time we were supposed to go, and they changed it to 3rd platoon instead of 1st platoon. They went out on two or three boats, and the Vietnamese had set up ambushes, and only two people survived. We found the boats, and they were riddled with machine gun fire.

Did you have problems with bugs?
Not really but snakes were a concern. One night we encountered a cobra, and some guys killed it with a shovel. We saw a snake about ten to fifteen feet long. A bamboo viper crawled over my stomach, and I jumped, and there was a separation of about twenty feet. Rats set up in wooden boxes, and one guy was bit reaching into a wooden box. He had to go back and get his shots. You always had to look out for yourself.

Did you serve in any free fire zones?
About half-and-half. Sometimes we set up curfews and people had to be off of their fields by seven that night. Otherwise, if we saw people, we considered them the enemy. We would shoot over their heads to see what they would do.

Capture any prisoners?
Only one which we turned over.

Meyer has worked as a custodian in the D.C. Everest School District for 32 years. He has a wife, Donna, and one son, Travis.

Interviewed by Carmen Erdman

Floyd Moore

Moore joined the Navy and was trained as a corpsman. Sent to Vietnam in 1966, Moore was assigned to a Marine combat unit and was in action right away. He did serve in a recon unit and was wounded in action. He served two tours in Vietnam.

Were you drafted or did you enlist?
I graduated from high school in 1966, and I was drafted ten days later. Then I got out of the draft by joining the Navy.

Where did you go for basic training?
I went to Great Lakes Training Center right by Waukegan, Illinois. Boot camp was sixteen weeks, and then I came home for a week or two, and then I went back to corps school at Great Lakes, and then I went to Camp Lejeune in South Carolina for combat corpsman training for doing stuff under fire after corps school. Then I came home, and after that I went to Vietnam.

What made you decide to go into that type of training?
To be a corpsman? They needed them and I filled the billet. The tests you take, how I ranked, I am not really sure, but I was real high in clerical, administrative stuff like that, and I was real low in mechanical stuff. So I went and talked to a counselor in the Navy and they lined me up after taking all these aptitude tests, so they tell you what you are most qualified for. Back then, the Vietnam War was going on and getting at its peak, so in '66 they needed corpsmen, so they song and danced me around asking me if I would like to be a corpsman, would I like to work in a hospital, and I said yes. We were supposed to go there with the idea of choosing or having four or five job schools to sign up for out of corps school, to the different naval bases in the United States for different training and I think putting down corpsman was my eleventh or twelfth choice, and that's what they picked for me. All the other guys that became corpsmen were needed, so that is how I went to corps school.

> *"THERE WAS NO TRAINING OR ORIENTATION. YOU LANDED AND YOU WENT OUT. I WAS WOUNDED ON MY FOURTH DAY IN COUNTRY."*

What was the training and orientation like when you got to Vietnam?

There was no training or orientation. You landed and you went out. I was wounded on my fourth day in country.

Where did they send you?

I flew into Da Nang and went to Hill 452 where we checked in, and then we stayed somewhere overnight and then I went off with Charlie Company, First Marine Division, Charlie Company. And then the fourth day I went out on patrol and we were ambushed. I was wounded on the first patrol. I was with the 1st Recon Battalion. We would go out with a six man team and they would take us by helicopter and drop us off. They would get information from the area Vietnamese that there was enemy movement around the area, so then when we hear about it they'd send us out to look for it. They would drop us off maybe a couple hundred yards or half a mile from where they had sightings, and then we would go and look for them and try and sneak up on them and count them and see what they were carrying, if they have ammunition, or which way they were going or what they were doing, and that's all we did.

They ambushed you instead?

They put us down too close to where they were, so we got ambushed. I think we lost one or two guys and there were six of us and two of the other Marines were wounded plus

> *"YOU GO FROM BEING AFRAID, TO BEING MAD, TO ANGRY, TO GETTING EVEN."*

myself. I was hit by a Chi-com grenade that hit the tree in front of me and knocked me out. I was out for ten or fifteen minutes and lost some hearing, which now after all these years I have hairline cracks or fractures on my skull which give me reoccurring headaches all the time, so that's what they have finally diagnosed after all these years.

Did you ever come face to face with the Viet Cong?

No. I saw them.

What was an average day like?

An average day was taking care of wounded Marines. I think I made something like thirty-eight patrols. I think that twenty-five or twenty six of them were ambushed and we were medevaced. I did a couple of LPs. That is where you go and sit on top of a hill and watch valleys and low range areas and watch for movement, and you stay up there for two weeks or so. We got overrun on one of them, but I took care of the wounded and it just set you up, if you read my poem. You can tell there are different stages of how emotions take control and how you become over there. You go from being afraid to being mad, to angry, to getting even.

Did you know the men you treated?

Some you do. You get to be good friends with them, and after one or two get wounded and you lose them, you stop making friends, and after about a month over there (I started out being the new guy on the block, I think in my company there were twelve or thirteen corpsmen) and after five weeks, I was the senior corpsman. The rest were wounded, gone, or had died. I think somebody said the life expectancy of a corpsman over there was three minutes, so it's a rude awakening when you get over there.

How many tours did you serve?

I did two; I was over from November 1968 to July 1970.

Were you there for the Tet offensive?
I just missed the first Tet offensive, but I was there for the Tet offensive of 1969.

Were you a corpsman both times?
Yes.

Did you use helicopters to get around?
All of our patrols used helicopters. We were picked up at the LZ, the landing zone, and taken out to the bush. Then we were dropped off, and then we stayed in constant radio communication with our main company, and then when our patrol was up and our time was up, they would come and pick us up.

Did you do body counts or kill ratios?
A body count is when you count bodies, either the enemy or ours. Most of the numbers were fabricated anyway. A lot was made up.

Were there blacks in your unit?
Yes, maybe fifty-fifty. Probably one-third white, one-third hispanic, and one-third black. Everyday was fighting; nobody got along with anybody. You had to make all the patrols with two from each ethnic group: two blacks, two hispanics, and three whites on our team all the time, and it rotated all the time, and I got along with most of them. You had to over there.

Were there drug problems?
Everybody was doing drugs when I first got there. I didn't do any for quite a while, and then after a while I did it.

What did you do?
I smoked marijuana. I didn't get into any hard stuff till after I got home; then I flirted with that for a while. I used that to escape reality, to relax and forget about what was going on.

What percentage of soldiers were using drugs?
Probably ninety percent of the people over there did drugs, that is people from my unit and the companies I was with. I don't know about some of the other ones. I would assume we were close to that.

Did that affect your unit's performance?
Nobody did any of that when we were out in the field that I know of. Somebody would have taken care of them if they had done that. When we were back in the rear area and done with our patrol, that's when people did drugs. On all my patrols, something always happened to somebody, and if we didn't get drunk, we would smoke marijuana.

What was the hardest part of being in the war?
Emotionally it is hard. You get over there, and you are afraid, and then you start seeing everybody get-

> *"YOU HAD TO MAKE ALL THE PATROLS WITH TWO FROM EACH ETHNIC GROUP: TWO BLACKS, TWO HISPANICS, AND THREE WHITES ON OUR TEAM ALL THE TIME, AND IT ROTATED ALL THE TIME, AND I GOT ALONG WITH MOST OF THEM."*

ting wounded and losing your friends, and all of a sudden the next thing you know is you are afraid it's going to happen to you, and then it keeps happening to everybody else, and you keep losing everybody. I was wounded several times. I got hit with shrapnel but not seriously enough to get shipped home. You go through mental stages. For me at first I was just afraid, and then you make friends with people. The people that are there the longest don't want to make friends with you, and they let you know that. Nobody wants to talk to you so the guy that has a week or two longer then you will make friends with you. Somebody is always the new guy on the block. Nobody wants to make friends with the first guy, so it takes a while before you become friends with somebody, and then half the time you lose that friend. Then you turn into the guy that has been there a year, and you don't want to make friends with anybody because you are going to lose them. It's a constant; you meet somebody and you lose them, you meet them and you lose them. It might be two days after you meet them or it might be six months after you meet them. So you just alienate yourself from everybody else, or you pick up on somebody that is the same way you are, and that's who you chum around with.

Then after you are there for awhile, the more I was resenting the new people because they did a lot of dumb things, and somebody else was at risk then; if they didn't react quick enough or handle their job in a combat situation, you didn't want them around. You were told right away, like when I first got to Vietnam, the sergeant walked up to me, and I had only been with the company, Charlie Company, and I was taken to the company area and I was told what platoon I was going into, and I went to that hooch, which is a wooden tent like deal. The sergeant came out and shook my hand and just looked at me, and he asked me if I knew what they did to bad corpsmen. I didn't know what to say or do, and he just walked away from me. That's after thirty-six hours there. It doesn't take long and people have no use for people who can't pull their weight.

"For me, taking care of the wounded immediately all the time, they told me in corps school that I would be the father, mother, brother, whatever and that is exactly how it ended up being."

So then you struggle with all of that, and then at night, the first night I am in Vietnam, my emotions are running absolutely crazy, and off in the distance you can hear the explosions from the bombing they were doing at night, called "Arc Light," with B-52s. They just dropped a whole bunch of bombs over a whole area, and you could see that off in the distance and hear it. You could see all that red flame at night, so my first night was sleeping through all that which was true of anybody that went over there. From then on, it was just one big stepping stone after another. You go from all these different emotions. You try to act like it doesn't bother you because you are hard and tough, but inside you are just shaking. It can unravel the toughest man in a couple seconds just hearing that stuff, and smelling the stuff and seeing it.

For me, taking care of the wounded immediately all the time, they told me in corps school that I would be the father, mother, brother, whatever, and that is exactly how it ended up being. I wasn't prepared for that. I never got to tell anybody how I felt over there because they all came to me, and I was perhaps six months to a year older than the guys in my squad and in my platoon. They all came to me with all their problems, problems with breaking up with girlfriends, family problems, being lonely and everything, and I had to always sit and rationalize with all these people and smooth everything over, and I never got to tell anybody that I was scared. My girlfriend wasn't writing to me or something, and all of my feelings got shoved off to the side. Now I am making friends and I am treating them. So after a while, a month of being there, I just stopped making friends, being around them, started drinking a lot more to get away from the reality of what has been going on.

Then all that happens is you get up and go on patrol in the morning, you get ambushed, you get into a firefight, you get medevaced. The whole time it's taking care of the wounded, and you lose somebody else, another person comes back into the team. I always used the analogy that if you are on the volleyball team, there are six people, so when the ball comes over the net and one of your friends hits it, it explodes and they are gone. The wounded are dead, and you replace them. It's the same as rotating your people off the bench. All of a sudden someone comes in who can't handle it, and they replace your best friend, and they are gone. That keeps happening for a month or two months. All of a sudden you don't want anything to do with anybody new or anybody that can't handle something. It keeps going through your mind and stuff, and it just hardens you; it makes you angry.

I went from being afraid when I got wounded and I came to, I didn't know how to react to the first Marine I took care of. I sat up and I couldn't hear nothing, and every time I sat up I fell back down into the dirt, and all the serum that is around your brain in your skull had run out of my ears and my nose so I had this unbelievable headache and I couldn't really see. All I can remember is that I could smell, and I could not

> *"EMOTIONALLY I HAD ALREADY BEEN SCARRED AND I FELT IT WOULD BE BETTER IF I STAYED THERE AND I KNEW WHAT TO DO AND I KNEW WHAT TO EXPECT AND I WANTED TO GET EVEN BECAUSE I HAD LOST A LOT OF FRIENDS AND THERE WERE OTHER MARINES WHO FELT THE SAME WAY AND I WENT BACK TO MEET THEM."*

hear a word. It was really a goofy feeling, and everytime I got up to my knees, I fell forward. I would fall into the dirt, and everything would stick to my face, the leaves and stuff, because that serum was running out. It was really weird. I could tell the Marine I was laying next to was wounded. He kept grabbing me and I could see he was mouthing "corpsman, corpsman," pointing to where the patrol was. So by the time I got up there, it took forever to get that twenty, thirty feet, and I got my first wounded Marine.

This has been my training for all this, and my dreams and nightmares have revolved around this. Here he is with a piece of shrapnel that had hit his ankle and his boot was full of blood, and I knew I wanted to get that boot off to see how bad it was and put a bandage on it. In all of my excitement, with the headache and everything going wrong with me, I had zero senses. All I could use was my smell and my taste, I pulled out my knife to cut the strings of the boot and I jammed the knife right into his ankle. I went in a good inch to an inch and a half, and he screamed and he punched me right in the face. He just hit me, and then he grabbed me and he said, "Doc, calm down and relax," and after that I was fine.

Never had a problem after that. It was just that I was caught off guard and scared; I was unbelievably scared. You have to act like it's just a football game or a baseball game and the ball got hit to you, and it's so loud and vicious, and it's a nightmare. It happens in a split second. When that firefight started, it took about one second, not even one second, and there were guys screaming. I remember diving behind a tree and bringing up my gun to look around to see what was happening, to see if I should return fire or whatever. I can remember all this yelling, and next thing, I heard a sound of metal hitting a tree and then I was out.

Did those injuries bother you in Vietnam?

Yes, I have been suffering from headaches and now there is some vision problems. I make my trips to the VA all the time. After my first tour when I came home and I was on leave for thirty days and then when I went back, that's when I really had a lot of emotional problems. That's when everything caught up to me, everything that had happened to me. You're a man and you are not supposed to cry and you got to be tough and hard, and then when I went back, a lot of my friends were gone. But the time I got back after the thirty days leave and I was starting all over, that was emotionally hard.

"I WANTED TO WALK POINT AND I STARTED KIND OF RUNNING THE TEAM A LITTLE MORE INSTEAD OF WHEN I WAS JUST A CORPSMAN."

What made you go back?

Revenge. I honestly felt that I was lucky and I would make it and I knew what to do. Emotionally I had already been scarred, and I felt it would be better if I stayed there, and I knew what to do, and I knew what to expect, and I wanted to get even because I had lost a lot of friends. There were other Marines who felt the same way, and I went back to meet them.

How were you going to get even?

I would take care of other corpsmen, saving Marines and going out there, and I started losing my perspective on what my duties were. I started becoming more of a Marine instead of a corpsman. I wanted to walk point, and I started kind of running the team a little more instead of when I was just a corpsman. When I was a corpsman, I would follow along waiting for a wounded guy. I started reading a map and planning out our patrols and all this other stuff. My role as a corpsman became a squad leader, and after you start losing everybody, that's what started happening to me. I wanted to do more than save people, and that role changed after a while when I had to go treat somebody. I felt they should know better. I was getting mad about that because there were other things I wanted to do. I wanted to lead the team and not worry about the wounded. Emotionally, I went through all these different roles, and it was hard when I came home. One day I am in the jungle with my gun and my backpack and stuff and with these guys, and twenty-four hours later I am sitting in my living room in my house, no gun and no debriefing. That probably was the worse thing. Everybody that left Vietnam should have been taken somewhere for a month to talk about the things that happened to them and get it off their chests. Tell somebody what was driving you or what wasn't driving you.

How did you emotionally adjust?

I didn't. I tried to act like nothing was wrong. I started drinking a lot when I came home. I was already doing drugs when I came home, but the drugs and the alcohol doubled and tripled. When I came home, I got a job right away working for six years at Wausau Homes, but I got fired because of drugs and alcohol abuse and stuff. After that I did odd jobs and stuff for fifteen years or so, and then I went to Tomah hospital and they looked at my drug and alcohol issues and stuff and I went through a PTSD (Post Tramatic Stress Disorder) clinic. People are becoming more familiar with that term. Then I was diagnosed with that, being a corpsman. They are ranked the highest for that as far as PTSD goes. They had a program set up for the corpsmen, and I went through that twice, and I went through the drug and alcohol thing twice. I was there for almost a year.

Did you feel that the programs worked?
Yes, I faced a lot of my fears and nightmares and all my reoccurring nightmares that I have.

What kind of reoccurring nightmares did you have?
Just things that happened to me while I was over there. Every week I have one or two. It is just an ongoing thing. Now they are just not as fearful. I wake up, but I can go back to sleep, and I don't run to get a drink. I can rest better now, and I don't have this fear of someone coming into my house and adjusting to the war. I always sit in a corner in a restaurant so I can see everything and know where all the exits and who is all in the area. You never lose that feeling. I don't like being in crowded areas. I have lived alone ever since coming home from Vietnam.

Has talking to the classes helped?
Yes, I enjoy doing that. For me, I get excited, and it is hard to talk because I am choking because there are so many emotions and they are running wild. I can't have a decent train of thought for awhile because they are such a pattern of the first day to a year and a half; that so many things happened on each of those days to form how I was mentally the last day I was there. The escalation of emotion that changes you. You are young and you see too much too fast, too vicious, too vulgar, too disgusting. You know you are in a climate that is one hundred degrees every day and it's humid and it's backwards. No electricity, the constant violence of people hitting booby traps, snipers constantly. Every day was something, everyday somebody else was wounded or hurt, and you never got to rest, and you were always alert

"THEN I WAS DIAGNOSED WITH THAT, BEING A CORPSMAN. THEY ARE RANKED THE HIGHEST FOR THAT AS FAR AS PTSD GOES."

every minute of every hour, of every day. Any noise, any distraction, any smells would just make all your senses come alive and make you get ready to do something. You always had to react, and its an everyday, every minute thing.

I think I read somewhere that of all the wars, Vietnam was the most....World War I and World War II and the Korean War, the guys would be in an area fighting for a period of time, and then they would go back to the rear. You would be there for awhile, and then you would be shipped out. In Vietnam, you went for a year and for a year you were in the front lines or whatever your duties were. I was a corpsman, so I had to spend six months in the bush and six months in the rear. Some corpsmen go to the rear for the first month working in a battalion aid station or a hospital, and then they go out into the bush. I don't think I could have handled that, taking care of wounded people for six months in a hospital and then have to go out into the field. I would have been a basket case. But when my six months were up, they sent me back to the rear for about a month, but then I transferred back into my old company. I couldn't handle being in the rear; I couldn't be around the non-combatants. We would take a hill and the next morning pack up and leave it. We would walk over somewhere else, and two weeks later, if your company didn't retake it, somebody else would. You would lose the same amount of men again. It was ridiculous. Go take it, leave it, take it, leave it. It was like that all the time. Go on patrol and then leave.

There were all kinds of booby traps, and you had to learn not to touch or kick things. They were masters at booby trapping things. You couldn't trust the kids because they would blow themselves up while talking to Marines. You had a fear of the Vietnamese because any of them could take your life. When we went through the villages, we never let them get close to us. You have to learn that lesson first. You might get wounded but you learned.

What feelings did you have regarding serving your country?

We didn't hear much about the rioting going on. We got newspapers. McDonalds sponsored the newspaper for me from Schofield. It was always about two weeks late and I would read that, but when I read those things I threw it away. The thing that hurt me the most was when I got discharged in July 1970. We flew from Vietnam to Okinawa, and there we changed into military uniforms from our jungle stuff and then we flew to California, and when we landed we went down the steps of the airplane into a bus and they took us into a hanger. They took all our military clothes away from us and made us put on civilian clothes, and then we got on a bus right inside the hanger, and when they drove us out, there were hundreds of people throwing eggs, tomatoes, and holding signs and all kinds of stuff. I wasn't in the US for two hours, and I am being egged. It was the same thing when I came home. People called me "baby killer" and stuff like this.

One or two guys went to Canada from here that were friends of mine, and I have seen one since then. Everybody had to do what they had to do. When I look at how that war played mentally on me versus these guys that went to Canada, they are just as stressed as the vets, and when the President gave them amnesty, I thought that was a bad deal, but I don't think they deserved that at all.

Do you have a message for young people today?

My message would be to get as good an education as you possibly can. I floated through school looking out the window waiting to go hunting or fishing and not applying myself, and when I was in boot camp, it was a brutal awakening not being able to answer all the questions and write and read because I didn't apply myself. I should have gotten a much better education in high school to prepare me for what was going to happen to me. When I started corps school, I was probably at the bottom of the class, and when I graduated from corps school, I was in the top twenty people out of 126 people. I had to study every night, all night long. I didn't get to go have fun like the other guys did because if you flunk out of this I might have had to become a cook. I don't know what would have happened to me if I would have flunked out of corps school. Then the pressure that every day reminds me I am going to Vietnam and I have to get my act together.

If I could go back thirty-five years to the first day in high school, I think I would have been a bookworm. For that three or four years of high school, to get a good

A Corpsman

I am a corpsman, true and true,
Fixing the wounded, is what I do.
I've got to do it, as fast as I can,
As for myself, I can't give a damn.

The men I've seen fallen, were the best
To fix 'em and keep 'em alive, would be the test.
I've gotta go now, can't take a break
I've gotta bring 'em back, for God's sake.

The pain and suffering, that I let slide,
Now eats away, at my insides.
The blood, the guts, the pieces I find,
Are forever deeply embedded in my mind.

His screaming and crying, for a mother's hand,
Are not heard, in a distant and far away land,
The voices at night, are so hauntingly real,
The begging of God, to make a deal.

I came with morals and ideals to save,
And the killing and brutality, to now I'm a slave.
To save and to heal, was the hand I would lend,
Thou shall not kill, was the rule I would bend.

I feel angry and guilty, withdrawn and depressed,
I'm terrified and doomed, and I pray for some rest.
With nightmares and flashbacks, it's impossible to sleep.
With alcohol and chemicals, I'm in way too damned deep.

All the agony and despair, make my life feel so dim,
And now I must live, with all these feelings with-in.
The war is over, and twenty years have past,
I want peace and tranquility, and the will to last.

To forget Vietnam, is how I'd like to be,
With goals and a future, and a mind that can be free,
To be happy and peaceful, and not to be alone,
To have a family, and a place to call home.

I'm a corpsman, true and true,
Fixing the wounded, is what I do.
I've got to do it, as fast as I can.
As for myself, I can't give a damn.

I'm a corpsman, true and true,
Fixing me, is what I'd want to do.

Floyd "Doe" Moore
"C" Ca. 1st Recon Batt.
1st Marine Div. 1968, 69, 70
June 2, 1988
COPYRIGHT 1988

education is a drop in a bucket when it comes to leaving high school to going to a war or something like this until you are an adult. I am fifty-three now. That three years in school is a blink of the eye. You need to have that education. You really do. You need the best out of that. I would have been much better prepared for everything that happened to me. The day I went to boot camp, with that education, I would have been more mature, and things would not have affected me as severe as they did. The education is very important, and I realized that right away, and I have to serve and work with people who had zero education.

I do not know how they got into the Marine Corps; they were terrible. Most of these guys I was with were felons. They had a choice of serving for two years in the Marines, and they didn't go to jail. Some of these people had been in reform school since they were twelve. Many had police records already. With me being the corpsman, I was with humans that were expendable. The dumb ones were at the front lines, the people who didn't have an education. I was with a college teacher. Corporal Carroll was a teacher at Cornell University, and he wanted to serve his country. We had a guy who was a policeman in our platoon. Another guy had eight years of medical school. Then there were guys that never went to grade school. Some of the Hispanics and some of the Blacks were in jail so they never went to school.

I would probably go again tomorrow so somebody else would not have to serve. I don't regret going there, I don't regret anything that has happened to me. I could have handled things a little differently, and you get into that mode and sometimes it takes a long time to get out of it. You adapt; you will do anything to survive. Some panic, and they are not here. It is all your frame of mind. You do what you have to do.

Following his return, Floyd Moore dealt with a number of medical and psychological problems. He overcame these problems to become a successful electrician.

Interviewed by Natasha Zuidema

David Schilling

Drafted into the Army, Schilling arrived in Vietnam in 1970. Initially assigned as an infantryman in the 196th Light Infantry Brigade, he later transferred to the Green Berets. He worked in the Chu Lai area with a six-man killer team.

Mr. Schilling, how did you first enter the Vietnam War? Were you drafted or did you enlist?
I was drafted. Then they just give you numbers, if you went to Germany, if you went elsewhere, and most of us went to Vietnam. You didn't have a choice.

Where were you trained?
I was trained at Fort Campbell for basic training and advanced infantry was at Fort Polk, Louisiana.

What branch of the service were you?
I was in the U.S. Army.

What year were you drafted? What years were you in Vietnam?
I was drafted in 1969, but I was in Vietnam all of 1970.

When you got there, what was the first base camp like that you got to? What were the base camps like?
The first base we got to was like where they're going to split you up and send you to the various outfits. So we actually retrained for two weeks and learned jungle warfare because everything we learned in the U.S. they told us to forget. And then they sent me, it was in Cam Ranh Bay close to Saigon, north to Chu Lai.

In the base camps was there some segregation among the blacks and say Latinos and then the white people?
You had a black power movement back then, and if the blacks were in the rear they'd have constant hitting of the hands or they show black power and they'd always cried to get all the rear jobs.

What kind of unit were you put in? Were you in a combat situation?
Yes, I was always in combat. I was put in an infantry unit to start, and you never knew when you were going to hit combat. You could go seven days and not see anybody, and then you could run into a whole day of constant firing. After that then they put me in the Green Berets, and I was assigned to a six man killer team with a dog, and there you used your equipment and helicopter (loaches) and searched for the enemy. You did it through urine smell or gun shell smell the dogs would pick up of the enemy.

So you were drafted at first, right? That's what you said?
Right.

And exactly how did you end up in the Green Berets?
You take a test. In order for us, anyway, to advance in rank or even if you wanted to be an E-3 or PFC or sergeant you had to go back to the rear base camp and take a test. Part of it was written and part of it was verbal, just like school. And that's basically how it all was set up.

In what part of Vietnam did you fight in mostly?
By the Central Highlands and a little bit of the Lowlands around Chu Lai was the main part. All I remember is mostly rice paddies and the hills. The fire supported bases were all on little knobby hills like on Rib Mountain, or something like that, so you could see.

The civilians that you encountered in South Vietnam, what were they like? Would they come right up to you and try to talk to you or try to talk you into buying something?
Yes. They would sell you your American soda for a dollar a can back in 1970 for military payment certificate (MPC) - paper money. You didn't have U.S. currency; you had military payment certificates. But the civilians would come up. Viet Cong were the black pajammie people, and those you would see at night, and they mostly tried not to be seen. The girls were beautiful. A lot of them were French Vietnamese, and they wore all bright colored silks like we do now. And I always got along good with the civilians.

Were you ever suspicious of the civilians?
Yes, you are because our hooch maids that actually helped us clean our bunks and stuff were from the civilians and you never knew if they were Viet Cong or if they were civilians.

What was your enemy like? Was it the NVA or the Viet Cong mostly, or both?
We very seldom saw the NVA. They were smart; they were tactical. I liked them sometimes more than us. And they'd plan their attacks. The Viet Cong would be scattered and they'd mostly harass. They'd shoot mortars in just when you're perfectly comfortable in a guarded perimeter area; they'd shoot a mortar in the middle just to upset you. If the night was peaceful they'd just throw a grenade or something out there just to get your attention. But they were constantly harassing. They didn't let up.

What kind of weapons did you carry with you? What kind of weapons did you use?
I mostly used the M-16, which was the rifle. It was fairly decent, lightweight plastic. But I also at times carried the M-79 grenade launcher to shoot a small grenade through a barrel. And then we were all required to carry M-60 rounds for the machine gunner because no way could he carry more than five hundred rounds. We always carried grenades.

You'd shoot the M-60s too?
If I needed to, I'd help, yeah. I never liked them; they weren't accurate anyway. Actually the ones we like the best were the captured AK-47s from the North Vietnamese. That was a better rifle than our M-16, so we tried to keep them.

Can you describe the M-79 you said?
Yes.

How big was it about?
It's about the size of a shotgun, and a breech would brake in the middle, and it would be one shot. You just put one grenade in and fired, and you'd do it all over again.

"THE M-60 COULD JAM BECAUSE THE BARREL WOULD GET HOT AND BEND, AND THAT'S WHEN I GOT SCARED AND DIDN'T WANT TO FIRE THEM BECAUSE YOU DON'T KNOW WHERE THAT BULLET'S GOING. IT MIGHT BE IN YOUR LAP."

Did you ever have any problems with the weapons jamming? Like the M-16?
No, we kept them pretty clean. We'd clean ours probably every two to three days because you'd get bored and you'd take them down and clean them. A certain amount of people would keep theirs in case the enemy would show up, but if they ever did, we could have put it back together rather quickly. The M-60 could jam because the barrel would get hot and bend, and that's when I got scared and didn't want to fire them because you don't know where that bullet's going. It might be in your lap. (Lost part of a finger in barrel.)

Describe your average day when you were there. What time did it start? And I know that a lot of infantry units stayed up all night?
Yes, well you'd shift. I think we all got fairly enough sleep unless you were leery the enemy was around; then you didn't sleep. But we'd take shifts; there always be some up, some sleeping. After awhile, it was just like a job; you got used to it. They got a firefight over there about a click away, let them fight, and we're going to sleep. Just like a railroad train going past your house; after awhile, you get used to it. The days were quite mundane or boring because it would be the same thing. You did a lot of walking. That's why I liked it when I got assigned to the helicopter teams, but the walking was quite tiring. The food was the same old boring stuff, the C-rations. But you start probably about seven in the morning, and about five, six at night we're already starting to make camp.

"THEY (SAPPERS) KNEW HOW TO WIGGLE THEIR WAY RIGHT THROUGH, AND THEY NEVER GOT CAUGHT. AND THEN THEY'D THROW C-4 OR SATCHEL CHARGES AND MESS EVERY-THING UP."

Could you estimate how many firefights you took part in?
I never kept track. I'd say about thirty, forty, but I never kept track. Just like killer counts, I never kept track.

How often did they occur?
Well you never knew. You could have two a day, and then you could go a week without one. A lot of times when you thought it was a safe, secure area, like in a fire support base which was on a hill, the sappers would come because they could get through concertina wire quicker than we could get through a Gym Cyclone fence. They knew how to wiggle their way right through, and they never got caught. And then they'd throw C-4 or satchel charges and mess everything up.

Describe the firefights? How long were they?

They just never quit. I mean some were short, and the enemy would retreat. It depends upon whether we called in bombs through the navy, through the marines, through the air force. That was a neat thing. When I became sergeant, I could call on the bombers, call in a lot of the other stuff, your artillery, helicopter squadrons with their rockets because a helicopter could carry thirty-six rockets. We'd start working those around us. The enemy knew enough to either get into their bunkers or leave.

Did you ride helicopters frequently?

Yes, that was the mode to get to anywhere. The only other way was walking. A bike would have been nice, a motorbike.

If you were put into a place with a lot of Viet Cong or if you were under fire, would the helicopter touch the ground?

No, you'd jump out, and a lot of people wrenched ankles and legs that way because you were in full gear. That's much more weight going down, and the terrain was never even, and you never knew what was under that elephant grass. It could be rocks. It could be anything.

Were drugs a large problem when you were there? Were there a lot of people in the army that were using drugs?

Not in my outfit. They stayed pretty straight. The big drug of choice was alcohol because we got a beer ration of about thirty cans a month for ten bucks. That was reasonable, and we learned to drink it warm. But no one really wanted to be too much on heroin or anything. I know there were some outfits that had it, but you wanted to stay alert because you wanted somehow to get home.

Was the antiwar movement in the United States, when you were in Vietnam, going yet?

I think it probably was. I didn't notice. I got the hometown paper of Mosinee because I grew up near Halder, and they didn't talk much of it and the *Record Herald* didn't talk a whole bunch. But when I came back, I realized it was going on. I wasn't aware of it; I didn't really care. They didn't do much to convince Tricky Dick to change his mind or LBJ.

Do you think the United States could have won the war under different circumstances?

I don't know. I've thought of that a lot, but I don't think so. There were too many unpredictable things you weren't trained for, and then politics was different over there than over here. And the understanding of the war, the legislatures and that, I don't think they ever did or will understand it. So I don't know how it could have been won.

Did you make any lasting friendships while you were in Vietnam?

No, we tried to stay away from that. I did anyway. You'd be acquaintances, but you didn't want to get too close because that buddy might be killed tomorrow.

How were you received when you returned to the United States?

I don't know. When I came to the Mosinee airport the only ones who greeted me were my folks and my fiancée. That was it. But I don't know if I cared to have anybody else greet me either. When I was in the hospital for eighteen months in Denver, an army hospital, the media twisted everything we said to their benefit. I guess they do that a little bit yet.

When you look back on the war today, do you think it was a worthwhile cause?
Yes I do. I'd do it again. I might think a little harder next time, but it'd probably be the same thing, your not knowing what you're getting into.

Talking about spider holes, did you encounter any Viet Cong or NVA that used spider holes or the underground tunnels and stuff?
I only went into, I think, two tunnels. One had so many snakes. They got out of there quicker. The other one was a hospital on the side of the mountain and I could have stayed there for about three, four days. I was just fascinated that that hospital was better equipped than any of our base camps.

"THE OTHER ONE (VC TUNNEL) WAS A HOSPITAL ON THE SIDE OF THE MOUNTAIN, AND I COULD HAVE STAYED THERE FOR ABOUT THREE, FOUR DAYS. I WAS JUST FASCINATED THAT THAT HOSPITAL WAS BETTER EQUIPPED THAN ANY OF OUR BASE CAMPS."

Underground?
Yes, totally underground. It had all U.S. equipment. IVs, you name it. And it was totally ready to take endangered people, wounded. But that's the only two I was in. I didn't really care to be a Tunnel Rat, as they called them.

What emotional effect has or did this war have on you today?
It still does. I still get worked up, good and bad. Like this weekend, Memorial Day Weekend, there's a lot of good because I go to the parades and enjoy it. I'm proud to be a member of Veterans' Organizations. I'm proud to be a veteran. But yet at times you get so worked up because it seems like we're going into the same quagmire as what we did then only more high-tech. And we haven't learned so you get frustrated; benefits are slow and coming. Like Tom and I got Agent Orange and we haven't received a thing for it. We got diabetes and now they're trying to say it's hooked but Congress passes a law for some compensation last November but they don't know how to interpret it. And it's that type of frustration that just winds you up.

Tell me a little bit more about being a Green Beret? Any experiences that you had just in battles when you were a Green Beret or whatever?

We mostly stayed in the helicopter and went down in to hot LZs. You searched for hot LZs; you were a team so you had a loach helicopter that flew low. Then you have the Huey slicks, which was ours, and the troop carriers. And then you had your gunships, and if need be, even you had your fan of jets from whatever because we can call other branches. We could call the navy, or whatever, for support, so we always went down hot. And then you tried to end it as quickly as possible and get retrieved and taken out. The Green Beret, that's what they assigned us. It was long ago. I've been trying to find stuff on it, but everything is hidden. But it wasn't that long that they did it that way with killer assault teams. I don't know. They probably got too many people wounded and too many people killed. It was dangerous to do it that way. You're setting yourself up as a decoy to go in and hope you trap them.

I don't know if you feel comfortable, but if you could, tell me how you were wounded?
It was in one of those hot firefights, and the NVA was that particular enemy that time, and they knew enough to funnel us into a minefield, and I hit a Bouncing Betty. The guy in front of me was killed. I was walking, I believe, third because I was sergeant and squad leader, and the ones behind me were all okay. But a Bouncing Betty is a mine that's like a truck's spring, and you stand on it. As long as you stand on it, nothing will happen but what saved me was I was inside the killer range, which is right on top of the mine, which is weird because most times you think it the other way. And the shrapnel seeks out; some comes in but most shoots out, so that's why the guy in front got killed. But I originally only lost my right foot. It's just I took about ten, twelve pounds of shrapnel, and they debriefed me for about two days, and then I went into high fevers, and then they had to keep amputating. I had sixteen amputations. Right now 42 surgeries had come. But it just was one of those days where it seemed like everything was in chaos. It had been known that they don't tell you everything at the start of a mission, or you might not go out; you might go out and get drunk. So when we got there, our other squad was on fire. All the helicopters were down, and then the adrenaline kicks in, and then you want to help them, and then we all got caught. It was a mess.

> *"IT WAS IN ONE OF THOSE HOT FIRE-FIGHTS AND THE NVA WAS THAT PARTICULAR ENEMY THAT TIME AND THEY KNEW ENOUGH TO FUNNEL US INTO A MINE-FIELD AND I HIT A BOUNCING BETTY."*

Can you tell me about the period when you were in the army hospital? How long were you in there and what was it like?
It was probably, about eighteen months. Two and a half weeks in Vietnam and they shipped me to Camp Zama, Japan, which was an army hospital there. I think it was an old WWII hospital because you felt like you were in the catacombs and all the equipment was old. All I remember was nine weeks of a circle bed, wherever they put you. And then after that I went to Fitzsimmons Army Hospital, Denver, which is an army hospital in Denver. I had a choice; they gave me Valley Forge, Pennsylvania, or Denver, and I thought, I heard Denver you heal faster, and I don't know if it's true to this day. But anyway, we went there, and I'd be there for a month and then come home for a month. I'd be a month at my fiancée's and live at her house because my folks didn't want me home. They didn't understand why I got injured. They were real religious there. Since then it's been resolved a little, I guess. I had a total of sixteen surgeries in the eighteen months, so it was constant rehabbing and trying to get your strength back. The only thing I can remember that I loved about it, well there was a few things, you could eat around the clock, 24 hours a day, and I loved fruit, and they had the best fruit bar in Denver, and it was always full. They wanted you to just pack as much as you could in. The other thing was a Playboy Club was open, and they'd take us down there. They'd take us to sporting events; all the nurses were looking for what we called free rides. They knew we were going to get a pension and these nurses would try to latch you in hopes that they could marry you so they got a sure bet going. In fact, most of the people I know that were in hospitals all married nurses. It was just one of those things, and it could be the empathy of the gals, too. But it was boring at times but we tried to make the best of it. We'd have the bingos or whatever, and we'd just be

kids in the hospital and try to make light of everything. It was the only way you could survive.

Back to the emotional part of it, did you ever receive treatment? I know there is a place down in Tomah. Did you visit there?

Yes. I've gone through two programs there. Currently, I just had a real bad accident at Cedar Creek last fall, and it's bringing back some of the stuff because it's a feeling that I couldn't move, and they had to take me by ambulance. But yes, I go to Minneapolis and I have my psychological follow up there. I'm finally getting some of this stuff done locally, but I did for years go to Tomah. Me and a lot of guys really have trouble adjusting to this crazy civilian life. It's different, authority, all kinds of issues -- anger. In fact, we go to a group once a month at Family Practice Center and family counseling in Wausau and all that's there is about 9 to 15 of us Vietnam Vets, and we just jaw about what went wrong this month. Actually none of us talked like this probably for six, seven years. No one cared to talk.

Any other interesting facts that you would just like to share?

I think it's neat that you young people do want to know and that hopefully learn from our mistakes. I always told my son, I wish you wouldn't make the same mistakes I do, and I know sometimes you have to make the mistakes to learn. And once I realized that, we got along better. But still, I'd hate to see us go to war under the same pretenses we went, and I think Desert Storm wasn't perfect but it was better.

> *"THE FLAG TEARS US UP WHEN WE SEE A CEREMONY WITH A FLAG, IT STILL RIPS RIGHT TO MYSELF."*

A lot of Vietnam Veterans went to Desert Storm, but they wouldn't come back and have a victory parade, with the other troops because they still had that stigma of Vietnam. For years, we didn't even care to be recognized. Now there's a bunch of us go to parades and we really don't care what people think. We're just going to try to pass and tell how we feel.

And I think society is maybe making a turn for the better. I'd like to think that. But if we get into another war, we'll see. And China was close last month over that plane. And it's not only the damage to us. It's our kids. I know my son is definitely got authority problems. He's twenty-nine and he still does. And it makes you wonder, does some of this go into dramatics and we can have big arguments there, but could it be that Agent Orange chemicals do strange things. And I know chemicals have definitely altered my body to the effect that I got to take other chemical pills to fight against what they say didn't happen. And my diabetes is the result of injury, stress, and other stuff. And if Uncle Sam would just admit it and give us the validation that we need, that's all we want. I want them to salute the flag as if it was high, wave, and say thanks. That's all you got to do. That would be overwhelming to me if they just do those three little things. But there's people out there who don't even want to respect the flag. I really do. The flag tears us up when we see a ceremony with a flag. It still rips right to myself. I guess that part of it, the army did teach me right and the service because we were taught, drilled, in ceremonies to respect and all that.

But I think it's neat that I give talks at Newman because I know Rick Lohr the history professor from Marathon and what amazes me even more is how less timid the Asian people have got. They will ask questions now. For years, they wouldn't ask a question; they wouldn't approach us; they'd probably thought we'd kill them with a slingshot. She's going to be a doctor in two months in psychology, she's full-blooded Vietnamese. And ten years ago, I wouldn't have had no Vietnamese work on me and so I'm breaking down too with time. I think time heals, but they didn't really give us all the tools to heal with.

One example I'll give you is I was in Japan and we had this doctor, and I have respect for doctors, there's no way I could be a doctor and I'm amazed at some of the things they can do. And this doctor, he was just one of the glorious doctors I've ever seen in my life. He comes in and he says while you were on the table and I had you all cut up and parted and everything else I took 36 pictures. I would like you to send them home to your fiancée. I thought, you asshole, get out of the room, but then I was thinking he might have done that so that I would fight. See, a lot of times they would use reverse psychology so that you would turn around and get so angry that you fight. But it taught us to be angrier. We were already angry. And to this day I'll bring it up with some doctors, and they said that's unethical. That guy should have lost his license. That's just not humane. But strange things happen in service that don't happen in civilian life. And I went to seminary for five years with tight religious values. They had a convent in St. Nasianz that was across the lake from us. Every chance us young dudes had, we were over there trying to talk to the future nuns. That's the way service was; it almost kept you locked in. You didn't know what was going on in the rest of the world. And that's where we think at times lost two, three years of our life that we could have been here with a hot car and hot babe. Instead we were in the old man's army.

David Schilling became an insurance micro-filmer following the war and later was self-employed. He is a free lance writer and land-scape design artist.

Interviewed by Eric Doescher
Transcribed by Vicki Karcher

Ken Schmirler

Drafted into the Army, Schmirler was trained in artillery. Assigned to the 23rd Infantry, he served in the northern part of Vietnam.

How did you become involved? Were you drafted, enlisted?
I was drafted.

How did you feel about that?
It was the least fun I had that particular day. It was like waking up with a bad hair day.

How old were you when you got drafted?
Nineteen.

What kind of training did you go through?
I had eight weeks of basic infantry training. Then after that I had advanced training in artillery.

What was basic training like?
Basic training was mostly physical. More physical training, conditioning than anything else. Then they taught you how to shoot if you didn't know, because everybody needs to know how to shoot just in case you have to shoot somebody.

Did you know how to shoot when you went in?
Yes.

Did you actually see combat?
Yes.

Describe the enemy. What was it like? What did they look like?
They looked like the people that you had working inside the compound, doing tasks like working in the kitchen, cooking meals, doing dishes, filling sand bags. You couldn't tell who was who. There was times when VC or NVA would actually be working for the U.S. government or for the soldiers, cleaning your barracks, polishing your shoes, something. Doing your laundry, but you didn't know it. They all looked the same. You couldn't tell the difference. They weren't in uniforms. They didn't wear uniforms saying yoo-hoo, here I am.

What was an average day like?

I was in fire direction for the artillery unit. I worked eight hours on, eight hours off. You really didn't have time to get bored or anything else because you worked eight hours, and if it happened to be the day shift, you had eight hours on, eight hours off. So after supper, you could maybe catch a movie if they had one; then go back and work until morning, so you were just kept busy enough.

So it was usually sixteen-hour days?

Some days were sixteen, some only eight. With that type of rotation one day would only be eight and the next would be sixteen.

What was it like? Did you go out into the bush?

I didn't. Being in the artillery, we didn't go and do, like shaking up the ground, like ground troops. Like the infantry would've. We shot cannons.

U.S. Tank inside perimeter.

You basically had the camps, and you waited for them to come to you?

If we stayed long enough we had a fence up. A perimeter put up with some guard towers or whatever, for lookouts. Sometimes we didn't stay long enough to get setup like that, but there was always a perimeter set up; and there was usually an infantry unit with us to guard these guns because these guns were the protection for the infantry in the field. If they got in trouble, the first person they called were the artillery. The bad guys are over here. Put some of the big bullets there.

> *"THERE WAS ALWAYS A PERIMETER SET UP; AND THERE WAS USUALLY AN INFANTRY UNIT WITH US TO GUARD THESE GUNS BECAUSE THESE GUNS WERE THE PROTECTION FOR THE INFANTRY IN THE FIELD."*

Did you ever see any guerrilla warfare or guerrilla tactics being used?

No.

Did you ever get ambushed?

Yes, the VC tried to get past the perimeter wire. We caught them in the middle of the night. That's where I had the occasion that I had to shoot at somebody.

What was your specific platoon or regiment with body counts ratios? Do you know off hand what yours was at all?

No, but I know when the forward observers would call in a fire mission where they would want to drop some shells on a particular area, they would call it suspect enemy location. It looked like this was not supposed to be right. They'd drop in a few shells and see what would come running out of the bushes. They'd be in a helicopter, calling in one of these fire missions. Occasionally they would say, well, we got something when they came flying out of the holes in the ground. Then they'd fly over in a helicopter and start gunning them down. As far as a body count, every once in awhile a forward observer would call back, yeah we got some. It paid to shoot.

Did you use helicopters to get around at all?
Almost fell out of some.

Why?
I fell asleep. I was tired.

Were drugs a problem for soldiers at your time?
Yes it was. There were a lot of guys that got messed up big time because they were easy to get. They were there. Real wild. It was just bad.

Do you know of any soldiers that went into battle high or drunk?
Yes.

Did they perform poorly because of it?
No. Not personally. I know it happened, and I seen it happen.

Were more of the soldiers users or not users? What was the majority rate?
Non users. There were more guys that didn't do it.

Can you describe the relationship with blacks in your unit? Was there a definite friction there?
No. Certain guys had a problem with it and certain guys didn't. I myself didn't care what color people were as long as if we get into trouble let's remember we're all on the same side.

"FROM WHAT I REMEMBER, THE LITTLE BIT OF NEWS CLIPS WE'D GET, THE ARMY RADIO STATION OR WHATEVER, ABOUT THE ANTI-WAR MOVEMENT, I WISH I WAS A PART OF IT [THE ANTI WAR MOVEMENT] BECAUSE I STILL TO THIS DAY DON'T REALLY KNOW WHY I WAS THERE."

As a general rule they didn't get treated any different?
Not in my experience.

Did you have any opinions regarding the anti war movement back in the states?
From what I remember, the little bit of news clips we'd get, the army radio station or whatever, about the anti-war movement, I wish I was a part of it because I still to this day don't really know why I was there. I know I accomplished nothing. I know over 80,000 guys were lost for nothing. I wish I had been part of the anti war movement instead of being there, but I got drafted.

What was the hardest part about being in the war?
Being away from home. I was 19 years old. After the first month, then it was two months, and you don't get to see any of your family or friends. You've got new friends that you make in this little "adventure" in the southeast. You get home-sick. That was the worst.

How did you come to be there longer than a year?
I elected to stay there longer so I could get out of the army earlier. There was an option they gave you. If you extended your service in Vietnam for a certain length of time, they'd take you for an 180 day early

out, so rather than going over, spending a year, coming back here and then serving a couple months state-side. I elected to stay there- it was actually two months, and to take me to the 180-day point, and I would have had to stay another 180 days. Then when I came home I was out of the army. I was done. Otherwise I would have had to stay in the army until May of the following year. I was out in December of '71, I was supposed to stay in until May of '72.

Was there a lot of emotional or physical stress that you had to endure?
We had some fun, but we didn't know.

Is there one particular experience that sticks out in your mind?
We had a fun day once. They call the fire mission, and then we got the tubes loaded. There's something about these guns that when you put the shells in, if you don't shoot them and pull them back out, you can't put them back in and reuse them. It was hot. It was really hot. It was the dry season and near a hundred degrees, nasty and we had all these shells that were put in the guns and taken back out, and we couldn't shoot them, so we took them down to the river. Loaded them in a truck and took them down to the river. Got some high explosives and some blasting caps. We hooked them all together in a big bunch,

in the middle of the river, and made a huge pond, a swimming hole and we'd all take turns, and a couple guys standing guard. Got to go swimming that day. I'll never forget that, and the CO, our commanding officer didn't know anything about it. We were just supposed to take them out in the jungle and blow them, because that's what you did, because you couldn't reuse them, and we set them in the river and made a swimming hole. Every platoon took turns sneaking a couple guys out there to take a swim. Something so simple as that made your whole day like a whole month. That was like the activity of the month, that you got to go swimming.

Prepariing to shoot cannons.

Do you think the U.S. could have ever won the war?
Oh, absolutely.

Why?
We had the technology, we had the manpower, the revenue, and we're the most powerful nation in the world. There wouldn't have been any problem at all to end this, to win this. It was a political thing. Somebody needed to make some money. Politicians needed something to do. As far as the United States Government we could've won the war. If they had let us shoot where we wanted to, when we wanted to, we could've leveled the whole country. It's nothing but jungles. We could've stood in a field and seen all the way across. We could've leveled the whole thing.

So what went wrong?
The politicians wouldn't let us. It was a political thing. It wasn't correct. Because it wasn't our war, so

we were supposed to be there in aid to the South Vietnamese in preserving their supposed government democracy. There was no reason for us to say, "Let's win it," because it wasn't our war. We were supposed to be there just helping them, but they didn't want to help themselves. A lot of times it would be a thing where you train them to use the most modern equipment, the best stuff money could buy from all your U.S. tax payers money, buying this stuff, and the government doesn't buy stuff cheap. They would have it for two, three days, and it wouldn't work anymore. It would be junk, because they didn't take care of it. It seemed like it was their war, but they didn't want to fight.

Did you make any lasting friendships during the war?
Of the guys that I was there with, I haven't seen any of them the last thirty years.

Did you have friends, or were they more of just acquaintances?
I had friends. I had real good friends there. We just kind of drifted apart. Nobody contacted me and I never contacted anybody else. There was just a few guys that I knew really well, not many.

"THEY'D SCRUB YOU UP, GET YOU A NEW SET OF CLOTHES, GIVE YOU A STEAK DINNER, PUT YOU ON A PLANE, AND SEND YOU HOME."

What kind of reception did you get when you came back to the U.S.?
From the military standpoint, they were proud of us. I got the best steak dinner I ever had in the army. They ran us through, this "bring you home ceremony." They'd scrub you up, get you a new set of clothes, give you a steak dinner, put you on a plane and send you home. At the airport there weren't protestors. It was just nothing. When I got here, it was like huh, welcome home. I was here. It never went any farther than that. I was home, it was over.

Did you have any difficulties coming back?

U.S. Tank.

No not really.

Any nightmare?
The only active duty I saw was second step back. There were only a couple of circumstances that I saw were the VC or NVA were trying to get into our position and I had to shoot. When they'd be spotted, the flares and sirens would go off and everybody would get up to see what's going on. Other than those couple of instances when I actually saw what was going on, I was pretty much in the back, because with the guns we had, you could shoot 17 miles away and hit a city block.

How did you get out?
I was done. I was drafted, I served my time and then I was done.

Is there a message about the war that you would like to say, or anything else you'd like to say about the war?

I just hope it never happens again. It's sad, but I look at the news, and what's going on in Kosovo. It's scary that it's looking like it's not very far from Vietnam. U.S. troops are already there, supposed to be keeping the peace, just as advisories, or little helpers. I don't know what they're supposed to be. If this would get to be something where politicians want to have some fun and games with American lives, it could blow up out of proportion, and again, be a Vietnam. It's not ours, we don't want to win it, but it's something to do. Why kill people for something to do? That's all that Vietnam was. Just something that somebody wanted to do. It served no purpose, no value. Nothing was accomplished, not a thing. All we did was postpone the communist takeover. It still happened.

You think that something like that could happen today?

Sure it could.

Do you think that because people are more learned, they have a little more education that they would allow something like that, or do you think there would be more draft dodgers?

The thing is there is no draft anymore. For something of this magnitude, you'd have to reinstate the draft, because the volunteer army that we have right now is volunteer. They'd send them all over there, and then we'd need some more people. To reinstate the draft takes an act of congress, so now you're going to have to spend a little time there, because politicians love to talk, and while they're talking they're killing time, so we're saving lives. The people are no more educated now, then they were then. You had your college graduates, and you had your doctors and lawyers, PhD's, and there were scholars in every corner that you looked. The war protesters were probably some of the most intelligent people, because they actually had the insight to say, hey this isn't right. They caught on first to what was really happening, and that it was a waste of time. Waste of time, and a waste of lives.

September 1970.

Following his return, Ken Schmirler worked as a laborer.

Interviewed and transcribed by Kristy Isberner

Carl Sitka

Drafted in 1965, Sitka was a platoon leader in the 196th Light Infantry Brigade which was formed in the U.S. and sent to Vietnam as a unit. They operated around Saigon and were involved with a number of large unit actions. He was the recipient of the Army Commendation Medal, the Purple Heart, and the Vietnam Cross of Gallantry with a Bronze Star.

How you became involved with the Vietnam War? Were you enlisted or drafted

I was drafted in 1965. I went to Fort Devens, Massachusetts and took basic training there. The 196th was a special unit that was formed, completely airmobile. It was an infantry unit and the biggest guns that we had were 106 Howitzers. They pulled them around with jeeps.

Did you get drafted right out of high school?

No, I was out of school for about two years. I worked on the railroad and got drafted. I got one of those letters that say your fellow neighbors have selected you. I went down on a train to Milwaukee and they processed us through. During the war they processed you pretty fast. You got drafted, and you got your papers when you went down for your physical. You passed your physical, and they put you on a train. We had gone to Milwaukee, did the physical, went to Chicago, then to Kentucky to a holding company and stayed there for two weeks. They wouldn't tell us anything about where we were going. We couldn't call home; we couldn't do anything! After two weeks, they put us all on a plane and flew us up to Ford Devins, Massachusetts, about 40 miles out of Boston. That was the first they let us do anything. They issued us clothes and gave us our shots in Kentucky, but they wouldn't tell you anything. Then we formed the 196, a special infantry unit. Everybody did their training together. The normal military did basic training in Kentucky or Fort Diggs, and then you would get transferred to another unit someplace. We did everything together, all of our training. Noncommissioned officers and some of our ranked sergeants were older enlisted people that did all the training; they stayed with us, but other than that it was all completely new people.

Do you believe that they kept you together to help your morale?

Yes. We pretty well prepared each other. Our whole unit, for the first six months that we were in Vietnam, stayed together completely. Everything from the time we did our training until we went over, and when we got over there was together. Then after six months they decided that they couldn't afford to have 3,000 leave at

one time -one unit, so then they started filtering in people after that. But our original unit that stayed together -- about half of us still stayed together and never did split up until we came home except for a few people that reenlisted. Other than that we all did our whole tour together.

Were you involved in one tour?
I was involved in a tour for one year.

Where were you stationed?
The first nine months our main base camp was set up in the middle of a field. We cleared it all out and  set our camp up. It was down in Tay Ninh, which is thirty miles out of Saigon. It's near the Cambodian border. The base camp stayed there. We did all our operations. We would go out anywhere from 30 to 60 days at a time. We would leave base camp, and we wouldn't see base camp again. You come in for two days, and they would ship you back out again on other operations. We would go set up a base camp with just our company near Cambodia's border or Saigon and run the operations we were on. Every night you would go out on ambush patrols. You took a squad, ten guys, and went out and set up in the jungle some place just before dark near an edge or clearing where you could watch. We weren't supposed to engage anybody. We were just supposed to watch how much traffic was going through at night; how the Viet Cong moved everything, the box carts in the middle of the night. Then you would just report that back in. Then the next day you would go back in the morning. You would get up, go back into your base camp, and then probably have breakfast or something. Then you'd go out and do a search operation for activity out at night. You go out and search that area and see what they were doing in the area. During the day we didn't travel too many trails. We stayed in the jungle as much as we could. You're kind of a sitting target out there. You would spread out and go up through the jungle instead of walking on the trail, so you wouldn't get caught. They had little booby traps and mines that they would set up on the trails. If you walked on the trail they would get you! In the jungle there was a patch probably 200-300 feet wide of thick jungle. Then there would probably be some little trail going through. If you walked on the trail, they would get you!

Did you encounter any major problems on your tour?
Yes, in operations, Junction City and Cedar Falls, and we did search and seizure between Saigon and Tay Ninh. There was 25 miles of tunnels where they had a hospital, ammunition, food storages, and warehouses all under ground. They had been fighting for 25 years against the French before we got there, so the jungle was all grown up. Then there would be little holes where they would go in. They were a little bit smaller than we were, so they could fit in a little hole. Usually the smallest guy we had would be our tunnel rat.

You were a bigger one?
Yes. I was the squad leader. I went into a few, but most of them I was too big to get into. There was one guy who loved to go in there, and he went. You never knew what was in there. You would throw a hand grenade down before you would go in there. Sometimes it was like a cubby hole, a little 6 by 6 area, sometimes 12 feet. We never knew how long. Tunnels just kept going

"YOU WOULD SPREAD OUT AND GO UP THROUGH THE JUNGLE INSTEAD OF WALKING ON THE TRAIL, SO YOU WOULDN'T GET CAUGHT."

on for miles all connected. One area just out of Saigon was declared a Viet Cong stronghold. For about 25 miles, they had cleared a 12 mile wide strip and bulldozed it down-everything, completely flat. They bombed it first with B-52's, and then went in there. It was a Vietnamese strong hold. They would go in there, and nobody could get them out because there was no way to fight them. We cleared the area of all the civilians; the villages were small, 8 – 10 huts in a village, and there would be women and kids. Basically we would move them out and ask if there was anybody else. As soon as you got all the women and kids out, and you were walking away with them-get them on choppers or take them out to a field or a rice paddy-then you would get shot at from behind from the village. You go back in there, and they would be in all these little fox hole tunnel complexes. You never knew.

Basically the majority of times you fought were against the Viet Cong?
Yes, the Viet Cong and a couple times we fought against the North Vietnamese regulars, the regular North Vietnamese Army. We encountered a whole North Vietnamese division near the Cambodia border that was underground. A 360 bed hospital underground with tons of food, ammunition, and gas. They used to come down the Ho Chi Minh Trail. They came out of Hanoi through Cambodia right along the border. A unit from the 25th division that actually got sent in, got pinned down. They sent in a platoon and they got pinned down, and the Colonel for some reason or another just kept sending people in. They had the whole brigade in there. They lost everybody. Only seven out of that whole unit survived. Then we got called in, and it took us three days to fight our way in to where they were. This was after we bombed for three days -B-52's trying to push them back and get into where they were. The colonel ended up calling military air strikes right on his own position because they got overrun. The first guys went in there. They got pinned down by a machine gun bunker, so they couldn't do anything. Eventually it took us three days to get them out-to drag out all the people, so it was getting pretty bad towards the end of the third day. We were in there three or four more days clearing the area. It was so thick that you couldn't see in front of you, five or six feet. In the middle of the night the Viet Cong would still come in. We would dig a fox hole and sleep in it. We got ourselves down low, as low as we could get. The whole year I was over there I spent maybe ten days in the main base camp. We did a lot of operations where we would get on a helicopter and were taken out in the middle of someplace and dropped off. We would have to work our way back in. Sometimes the whole company would go, sometimes just a couple squads. During the day we were mine sweeping roads for probably about a month, on the supply route from Saigon to Tay Ninh; They set up mines every night. We would have to take tools and go out and clear the road. We only had so much road to clear each day, and we would use those little hand mine detectors. Two guys sweep back and forth across the road, and when we picked one up, we dug

"WE ENCOUNTERED A WHOLE NORTH VIETNAMESE DIVISION NEAR THE CAMBODIA BORDER THAT WAS UNDERGROUND, 360 BED HOSPITAL UNDERGROUND, TONS OF FOOD, AMMUNITION, AND GAS."

around and found where it was. Weset off the charge, loaded up, and went on to the next one.

You said you were along the border of Cambodia and around Laos too? Was your division ever brought into those two countries?
Cambodia. We operated on the Cambodian border. We were up there probably a good month, working the border. We set up the base camp on the border, and we'd go into Cambodia searching for camps. If we found a camp we would destroy it and go to the next one.

Was it guerilla warfare, and can you describe it?
There wasn't a front line anywhere; it wasn't considered a war. It was a police action. That's what we were told all the time we were there. Our main thing was to keep the North Vietnamese people from com-

ing down to steal the rights from the south. We were supposed to be a police action where we encountered Viet Cong, probably three or four times a week. We would get into a little fire fight someplace. When we weren't on the major operations, we would just go and see if there was any activity in the area.

We would always get sniper fire. The Viet Cong took three guys and set up on the other side of a rice paddy. If we would walk out in the open, they would shoot at us and run. Then they might move down a half a mile; we never knew where they were! We always stayed in the jungle as much as we could, just kept from getting shot at. They would try to entice us into the trail, and they would take off through the jungle. If we ran down the trail chasing them, that's where a lot people got killed, trying to go around and find out where they went. It was different. There was no front line. In Desert Storm they were all lined up in the bunkers and they just overran bunkers; that took care of that whole unit there. It was over in no time because they pushed everybody back. Where we were, you never had any clear areas. Whenever you would have a firefight they'd want to know how many were wounded, how many you captured and brought in alive and how many dead; they kept a running tally.

How were helicopters useful?

Basically, over there that's the one way you can get around in the jungle. We fly out on helicopters, land and set up our perimeter. The rest of the company would move in, and you would go out and do your operation. You might be out there a week, a month, or whatever, but then they would come and pick you up. They would go out and spray an area with machine guns at each side, and you jumped out. Most of the time they were about three or four feet off the ground when we were getting shot at. If you weren't getting out fast enough, the machine gunners would push you out because they were sitting ducks up there. When the choppers were moving fairly fast they're hard to hit, but when they were pushing people out, they have to kind of hover on the grass and are easy targets. They can't get down too low because they get tangled up in elephant grass 10, 12, 14 feet high. The first time I went up in one when they turned corners you were looking straight down and reaching, trying to grab the guy next to you and hang on.

But after the first trip it's just like a ride in the carnival.

> *"FIRST TIME I WENT UP IN ONE (HELICOPTER) WHEN THEY TURNED CORNERS YOU'RE LOOKING STRAIGHT DOWN AND REACHING, TRYING TO GRAB THE GUY NEXT TO YOU AND HANG ON, BUT AFTER THE FIRST TRIP IT'S JUST LIKE A RIDE IN THE CARNIVAL."*

Did you have blacks in your unit, and what was their relationship?

The platoon that I was in had four or five. We never had any problem and most of them as long as they were with us were pretty good. When they got with their buddies they would act different and go to a different tent. We had a couple of black sergeants. I never had a problem with any of them. We had one that was in another platoon. We were running an operation and we were getting some sniper fire. He came back into the base camp one day and said he was getting out of there. Later on in the afternoon he walked down to the other end of the bunker and shot himself in the foot; he was going home, but other than that, we never had any problems.

Were there drug problems with soldiers in Vietnam?

Some units were pretty bad. There were drugs over there if you wanted them. Little kids sold them, just like going down and buying a candy bar. If you had the money you could buy it, and it was cheap over there. I don't think anybody in my platoon had it, but there were other people in our company that were using it. They had some pretty good stuff over there-little stronger than the normal street stuff over here. A couple of them really lost their mind on it. There were people up in headquarters that were using it. They were pretty bad. Some of the rear end people that stayed behind in the base camps had a little more free time to get into it. We didn't have any free time.

What are your opinions regarding the antiwar movement?

I didn't think too highly of it. I figured if they went to Canada or some other country that's where they should have stayed. They should have never been let back into the country. If you want to run up to Canada to get away from having to fight the war and defend the country, then you shouldn't be allowed to live in the country. Clinton, I don't have much use for him; he was a draft dodger. He went over to England or France during the war. The draft dodgers got more of a welcome back to the country than we did. When I came back home there were college riots. Everybody protested the war.

What was the hardest part of the war?

There was never a line-no place, no direction; you were out in the jungle. There wasn't a safe area. No matter where you went, you were never safe. In Saigon you could get shot at just as you could out in a village. There wasn't a definite line any place. In the base camps they would mortar you at night. Our main base camp got hit with mortars almost every night. Square mile base. You never knew where they would hit. They would go in, shoot off three or four mortars and then take off. When they shot the mortars we could almost pinpoint where they were coming from, but it took time to figure out where they were. Once you figured out where they were coming from, you could drop mortars over in that area, but by that time they were gone. It was almost safer out in the jungle than it was in the base camp.

> *"IT WAS ALMOST SAFER OUT IN THE JUNGLE THAN IT WAS IN THE BASE CAMP."*

Emotional and physical stress -- was there more before, or after you came home?

Probably more when you came home. Over there you are under stress all the time, but you were busy all the time; you didn't have time to think about it. Once in a while if you got a couple days back at the base camp, then it kind of got to you, but out in the field you are more worried about trying to stay alive. We had a few people that cracked up over there from stress. A normal day was in the jungle and getting shot at. We didn't have any facilities or anything out there. We found a rice paddy, jumped in, washed up, and washed our clothes during the day. Then we put everything right back on again. You didn't pack any extra clothes because you carried all the ammunition. I'd rather have more shells than an extra shirt. You weren't worried about your fashion over there.

Is there one particular experience that stands out?

We rode in tanks four times the whole time I was over there. Once we hit a land mine, and I got some shrapnel in my arm. We rode in a personnel carrier. It was smaller than a tank with a 50-caliber machine gun on top, 12 feet long x 18 feet wide, stood about 6 feet high, and the back door would open. We were riding in one of those and hit a mine. Instead of being turned up, it was turned down. The charge went down instead of coming up, but it still had enough explosion to blow the tracks off. It was probably a week before I could sit down again. It hit the bottom of the track and blew it up on us so hard, that your ears rang for a week, and your butt was sore for a week. Another time riding in an open one-they can go through water-when riding through the jungle in that, we got hit a couple of times with fire. Every time I was in a tank something happened, so I felt safer walking than I did riding.

What did you think of the South Vietnamese Army?
They had their own small company areas, block square units. They weren't very aggressive. Most of them were afraid of the Viet Cong, and they never went out at night-never did any ambushes. They were supposed to be out protecting the people, but the only thing they protected was their little base camp that they stayed in. Most of the units were pretty bad, didn't have much use for them.

What did you think about the guns that were used?
We had M-16s. They weren't that great of a gun. They were a piece of junk. They jammed all the time and got dirty. The M-14 or M-1's were automatic. You could lay down in the dirt and they would keep on firing. They would even fire blanks, and they never fouled up. If the M-16s laid down in the dirt, the thing would jam, and you had to take it apart and clean it to get it to work again. They were a pain.

Did you hear any stories about fragging? Eliminate the command?
Only once. They had a headquarters company, and we had one guy there, 2nd Lt., who came there from the states. He had the platoon stand out there in formation everyday, and he wanted to have inspection out in the field everyday. He would line up a whole platoon out there and wanted their shoes polished, guns cleaned and everything everyday. They kept getting fired on everyday. About the 3rd day someone eliminated him, but not much became of it. That is the only case of fragging I know about.

Do you believe that if the U.S. committed more of their forces and declared it a war not a conflict, do you believe that we could have won, and why or why not?
Yes, I believe we could have won. If they had committed more forces, went into North Vietnam and Cambodia, and actually had a front line which they could have done, they would have eliminated a lot of the supply coming into the South. Local people were affected a little bit when we did go up north and bombed Hanoi a few times. If they would have had to protect their own country instead of coming down and taking over the South they would have been up north fighting in their own country. There could have been a line someplace, and you could have defeated them, but not the way they went at it.

Did you make any lasting friendships during the war and are still in contact with?
Yes, six of my buddies get together every year since the day we got out. February of every year we party. Parties aren't as big as they used to be. They don't last as long any more. When we first got out we had some pretty good parties-3 day parties.

What does serving your country mean to you? During active duty or now that you are a veteran.
I'm proud that I served. It is hard to explain. More people are more aware today like the wall in D.C. I still feel like we have to defend the country, and I'm proud I did it. I think we need to wake up and realize what we have here compared to other countries. Vietnam had nothing. The people lived in grass huts and ate whatever they could scarf up. We would haul our food out everyday when we got done in the base

"BASICALLY YOU ARE BRAIN-WASHED. THAT'S WHY THEY LIKE YOUNG RECRUITS; THEY CAN SET THE TONE AND KEEP IT POUNDED INTO THEM EVERYDAY, SO WHEN YOU DO GET INTO A FIREFIGHT, YOU PROTECT THE GUY NEXT DOOR TO YOU AND FIGHT SIDE BY SIDE."

camps. We loaded up everything on a dump truck - all the garbage - and these people would be out there scarfing up everything we dumped for food.

Did you have post-traumatic stress disorder – difficulties dealing with memories?
Yes, for the first few years when I got back it was pretty hard. When I first got back thunderstorms and the loud banging made you duck and look for a foxhole. Natural instinct. I had trouble sleeping nights. There were a lot of people that should have had help, but the government never gave any help to people that really needed it. We have a lot of veterans that are in bad shape. If they had been rehabilitated when they came back instead of turned out into the streets - nobody cared. A lot of them ended up with crappy jobs, and the job they had when they left was either eliminated or they just kind of got left behind.

Do you have a message for young people today about the Vietnam War?
The military has changed so much since I was in it. Now there are women in the military looking for rank. You can't touch a new recruit. Back when we did our training, it was pretty rough. Go back to a little more pressure, and build the people up to handle the pressure. I don't think most of them can handle it right now because they haven't been hardened into it. Basically you are brainwashed. That's why they like young recruits; they can set the tone and keep it pounded into them everyday, so when you do get into a firefight, you protect the guy next door to you and fight side by side. The way it is today I think it is everyone for themselves. Maybe with the turn of events in New York, people will start to realize how vulnerable we are and the need the protection.

Following the war, Carl Sitka was an iron worker and truck driver.

Interviewed by David Powers and Scott Schippers

Dwight Stienke

Drafted in 1967, Steinke arrived in Vietnam and was assigned to an infantry unit. He began as an RTO (Radio Telephone Operator) and later became a tunnel rat. He was later promoted to sergeant and led a machine gun squad.

How did you become involved in the Vietnam War?
I was drafted.

When were you involved in Vietnam?
I was there from June of '67 to June of '68.

Do you remember having any attitudes or feelings about being drafted?
No, I didn't.

What was your actual job in Vietnam?
I was in the infantry. I worked in combat, the machine gun squad. Well, at first I carried the radio for the sergeant. As a young guy, when you first come, they give you that job first. Then I went from that to being a tunnel rat, actually going into the holes. Then later on, I was on a machine gun squad. I was a sergeant of a squad.

Do you remember what the base camps were like?
They were pretty nice. It was almost like being on the State side. We didn't get carried back very often. Fights outside, the whole time I was there. Once when I went back from being wounded, there were knifes, they had clubs, and stuff. They had nice showers though.

Do you have any specific experiences when you were at the camps, things that you remember about them?
No, not really. Just rest. A lot more rest. I felt more secure back there at camp, because you could rest easy because somebody else would do it for you.

How often were you actually out in the battlefield?
About six months. We didn't go to base camps very often. We went to artillery camps, where they would have artillery set up, then you'd go back there and do guard duty for them. That was considered a reprieve from being out in the field, but that would happen maybe once or twice a month. Otherwise we were right out in the hot jungle.

Could you describe what an average day was like during the war?
Well, you'd get up in the morning, and they would fly breakfast in for us. I was with the first cav. so we had a lot of helicopters and they flew in twice a day, at breakfast and then at supper. Then the rest of the time you had c-rations. We'd get up, and then they would pick certain areas to go and check out. We did most of our's at night, because that is when the Viet Cong were coming into the villages, at night. They were getting supplies and that. We would circle the village. It was mostly search and destroy.

Did you actually do any fighting?
Oh yeah.

A lot?
Oh yeah.

Were you ever wounded while fighting?
Twice. Two purple hearts. I have two purple hearts, three bronze stars, and a silver star.

Would you mind sharing those experiences of when you were wounded?
Well, the first time was, I don't think I was there a month and we were on a search mission and I was pulling the slang on the plank guard and I snapped a line and the column of the guys and I had guys on the side watch and we got hit by snipers. I fell into the monkey pit. You know those are snakes and rats bit my leg and all. That was the first time. The second time I didn't really get hit, but we were in a fight and there were seven of us that called up into the village and we were supposed to throw small bombs and the helicopters would come and shoot their missiles at anything in front of it, but we ran out of smoke and when they made their last pass they shot at the guys from a distance and I lost my hearing and out of seven men I was the only one to survive.

> *"I HAVE TWO PURPLE HEARTS, THREE BRONZE STARS, AND A SILVER STAR."*

Did you know any of those people personally?
Yes, they were all my guys. Seven of us you know.

Did you ever participate in any ambushes?
Yes, we called them night crawls and every so often you would have to go out on a night crawl and go to your spot. Anybody ever tell you it wasn't hysteria, it's a lie, but you adapt. It's amazing how you adapt to situations.

Were you ever ambushed?
Yeah, we got ambushed. We lost some pretty good guys that way. See that's the way he liked to fight the war. I'm talking about Charlie. We'll call him Charlie. That's the way he liked to fight it. Just bang, bang, hit.

Could you explain any experiences that you had with body counts or kill ratios?
Well, that Christmas, the year of 1967, we went out. We were supposed to go check out a village, they

woke us up, that was one of the times we were back at base camp. They woke me up in the morning and said, "Get the guys going." We had a village to check out that day. They had intercepted a message that there were supposed to be some Viet Cong in this village and high, important ones so they just wanted us to go check it out. Well, we ran into nine oppositions that day. I melted down two machine gun barrels. There was seventeen hours of walking. I lost my . . . that day. Then they had a body count after it was all over. We lost about a hundred and some that day.

What was the war like in your stationed area, compared to some of the other areas of Vietnam?
It was more mountainous, more ravines, where down by Saigon that was more flat lands. It was harder to fight up in the mountains 'cause you had so many tunnels, so many places to go that we didn't know. As soon as you found something, they didn't want us to engage. We'd pull back, and then they'd send in the artillery and machine gun ships.

Are there any actual experiences on the battlefield or in camp that goes through your mind? Did you have any other frightening experiences?
Well, I don't know. Every time you got into a firefight it was scary. One time we went- it was called Hill 724. It was the first division, it was a big hill and they were trying to take the top of it and Charlie was up there. He really was ready for them when they just about wiped the whole company out, and they flew us into the top of the hill to relieve them, I noticed when we jumped out of the helicopters we were jumping into bodies, dead bodies, and there were bodies hanging in the trees, and everything, legs, soldiers with arms and

"I MELTED DOWN TWO MACHINE GUN BARRELS."

legs off. That night we were on guard duty. We were in bunkers doing guard duty. The next day our helicopters come in and they wanted me to go upto the top, and I was going to go, and another guy says, "I'll go." He went up there and Charlie hit him with a rocket launcher, blew everybody up. I had a very good friend that was a Lieutenant, When we left, he got me that leave early. When we left he told a guy that he had never seen a guy more luckier than me. I should have been gone, but nine lives. There was quite a few odds and ends where it was close that's why I went on furlough.

You mentioned different jobs that you performed. Was there one in particular that you preferred over the others?
Not really, I took the tunnel rat job to get away from carrying that radio, I didn't like that. After I caught a couple of guys in the hole, that was close and after that I became a point man for the squad. That has a lot of responsibility. You have to move at night and you have to watch for booby traps, trip grenades and everything. I wasn't the Indian scout that I thought I was. I liked the machine gun squad. You have a lot of firepower there, we had the M-60 machine gun and you had ten guys and the radio man.

Can you describe what the radioman does?
You followed your sergeant around wherever he went and anytime he had to call the other commanders he would talk or if he had to call in airstrikes . That is another job of the squad leader to call in artillery strikes. That radioman has to be there all the time no matter where he goes, you got to go. The radio weighed about eight pounds and you had a pack. Everything you owned you had to carry, food, you carried everything. The supplies came in the evening but not very often.

Did you have any experiences with booby traps?

Well, as far as grenades, we crossed a lot of them and we had to disarm them or blow them, whatever they wanted.

Do you think drugs were a problem for U.S. troops in Vietnam?

There was marijuana that was smoked, but not a whole lot, not that I saw in my groups. There was some that was relaxing, like having a beer. Maybe it was just the start of it back then. Later on it got worse.

Were there any African Americans in your unit?

We had seven black guys and our relationship was good. They were good. We were all kids and every-body was in there to stay alive, to survive. I got along with them good. I got real anxious once. We flew to the top of a hill on a helicopter and then they dropped us off. You had to police everything down the hill and one night we were out there and the guys by the doors used to hang out on the skids when they were coming down. I was sitting out there and Charlie is shooting away at us, taking pot shots. I bailed off and I didn't realize I was as high as I was. I didn't break anything but that was quite a fall with a full pack on and I really twisted my ankle pretty good and about halfway down the hill I couldn't make it down and two blacks guys came up and one took my pack and the other one grabbed me and threw me on his shoulder and carried me down the hill. No white guys offered, not even to take my pack. I haven't forgotten that.

> *"THE QUESTION IS: DID WE REALLY STOP COMMUNISM?"*

Did you use helicopters very often?

Yes, we were with the 1st Air Cav which is a helicopter unit and we could move up a whole division and move it in a week's time. We used a lot. They would take you on a helicopter and drop you off and police the area and come back.

How did you feel about the anti-war movement back in the states?

Tell you the truth, we didn't know what was going on. We didn't get much news over there. We didn't have any idea what was going on. First I heard of it was when we were getting ready to come back home and the 1st Cav always came through San Francisco. They stopped shipping the 1st Cav through there and we came home through Seattle and guys were shot at by people who had lost loved ones. Guy got shot through the shoulder. That was the first we heard about it. I knew that demonstrations were going on when we first left but nothing like what we saw when we came back. We weren't very well liked. We were doing what we were told for our country.

Do you feel as if you were serving your country?

Yes, I thought I was and I felt proud of myself when we came back. I probably don't feel as proud now as I did back then. It was just a political war. The Hmong people felt the same way that we did. My attitude changed and maybe we were wrong. The question is: did we really stop communism? At the time I thought that we were and that we were there for a reason, to help a group of people that were help-ing us. I am not so sure about that.

What was most difficult for you in Vietnam?

Losing friends. That was the most difficult. Also being wounded. I was in the hospital for three weeks with a leg wound.

What was it like in the hospital?

I got a lot of sleep. I never got a lot of sleep because you slept with one eye open always. When you are back in the artillery base, or in a hospital like that, you can sleep. You are still in a war zone but you can sleep.

How did you get out of the war?

Well, you just served your twelve months and the Marines served thirteen months.

"IT WAS A GOOD FEELING TO BE BACK AND PROBABLY THE BEST SINGLE FEELING I HAVE EVER HAD IN MY LIFE, EVEN BETER THAN HAVING KIDS."

What kind of reception did you get when you returned home?

Very good. My family was there. It was a good feeling to be back and probably the best single feeling I have ever had in my life, even better than having kids.

How was your return to civilian life?

There wasn't too much that was special, everybody knew they should leave me alone until I decided I was ready. It wasn't easy for me but it helped later to talk about. There are some things I won't talk about but overall it has helped with the years going by. The people who had trouble with it kept it all inside. I don't think they saw much worse than I did but they keep it inside.

Were awards special to you?

At the time it was important. It was a reward for doing your job. I was proud of it and I thought my kids would be more proud of it but I don't think they are. In World War I and World War II you had all the big heroes. The Silver Star was my highest decoration.

Stienke currently works at Wausau Papers in Brokaw. He is married, has two children and four grandchildren.

Interviewed by Philip Beck
Transcribed by Kristy Isberner

George Theiss

Enlisting in the Marines, Theiss was trained as a mortarman. When he arrived in 1968, he was assigned as a rifleman and spent his time in "I" Corps in the northern part of Vietnam.

I enlisted in the Marine Corps in 1967. In 1968, I was sent to Vietnam. I had been trained as a mortar man. But when I arrived in Vietnam, my unit (G Company, 2nd Battalion, 4th Marines, 9th MAB, 3rd Marine Division) had been hard hit in an ambush. I was told, "We don't need mortar men. We need riflemen. You are now a rifleman." I spent my entire tour in Vietnam as a rifleman. I was "in country" only a few days when my battalion (2/4) was sent to stop the 320th NVA Division from taking Dong Ha. Dong Ha was the Headquarters of the 3rd Marine Division at that time. The Battle for Dong Ha centered in the village complex of Dai Do. It was one of the least known, and yet one of the bloodiest battles of the Vietnam War.

We lost 68 Marines killed and 323 wounded seriously enough to require medical evacuation (TIME Magazine, May 10, 1968, p.32). The number of dead rose to 81 as more died from wounds.

We had another 100 "walking wounded" – those with minor wounds. The 320th NVA Division outnumbered us at least 6 to 1. An NVA division has at least 6,000 soldiers. A Marine battalion, at full strength, has about 900 men (four rifle companies and HQ).

The NVA (North Vietnamese Army) regulars had reliable AK-47s, RPGs (rocket

> *"THE NVA (NORTH VIETNAMESE ARMY) REGULARS HAD RELIABLE AK-47S, RPGS (ROCKET PROPELLED GRENADES) 12.7 MM HEAVY MACHINE GUNS, ANTI-AIRCRAFT GUNS, MORTARS, AND 130 MM ARTILLERY SUPPORT FROM NORTH VIETNAM. WE HAD THE "GUARANTEED-TO-JAM" M-16 RIFLES."*

propelled grenades) 12.7 mm heavy machine guns, anti-aircraft guns, mortars, and 130 mm artillery support from North Vietnam. We had the "guaranteed-to-jam" M-16 rifles. The combat lasted three days (30 April 1968 to 2 May 1968). On May 3, we got to pick up our 68 dead Marines. The NVA had left over 800 of their dead behind (TIME Magazine, May 10, 1968 Issue, p.32). The Marine rifle companies involved were:

E ("Echo") Company, 2/4
F ("Foxtrot") Company, 2/4
G ("Golf") Company, 2/4
H ("Hotel") Company, 2/4
B ("Bravo") Company, 1/3

A Marine rifle company at full strength was about 200 men. But all 5 companies went into Dai Do at less than full strength, due to previous losses in combat. By May 3, not one of the 5 companies could muster more than 40 men.

We were torn to shreds in three days of intense fighting, but we had stopped a vastly superior enemy force from taking Dong Ha, the eastern anchor of our defense facing North Vietnam. Dong Ha is about 8 miles south of the DMZ (demilitarized zone). My Company Commander, Captain Vargas, was wounded three times; winning the Congressional Medal of Honor, in hand to hand combat at Dai Do (The Congressional MEDAL of HONOR Library – Vietnam by Dell Publishing, Inc., © 1984, page 217). He had won a Silver Star and two Purple Hearts before Dai Do. Captain Livingston of Echo Company was also wounded three times winning the Medal of Honor at Dai Do. Several Marines were decorated posthumously for bravery. Our Battalion Commander, Lt. Col. Weise, was wounded winning a Navy Cross. Our Battalion Sgt. Major, "Big John" Malnar, a combat veteran of WWII and Korea, was killed at Dai Do winning a Silver Star. All of this has been documented in a book based on official Marine Corps records and eyewitness accounts: *The Magnificent Bastards*, by Keith Nolan, © 1994 (Hardcover Edition by Presidio; Paperback Edition by Dell). Also, a professional video was put together by the 2nd Battalion, 4th Marines Association: *Memories of Dai Do* by Empire Video, Inc. (Phone: 1 (703) 866-1934).

My company ("G", 2/4) alone was hit by 250 rounds of enemy mortars and artillery shells. This is confirmed by Marine Corp Historical Reference Pamphlet: *A Brief History of the 4th Marines* by James S. Santelli, 1970, page 49. My company (Golf, 2/4) had 75% casualties at Dai Do (see *The Magnificent Bastards* by Keith Nolan, Chapter 15 "God, Get Us Out Of Here"). That's three out of every four men in my rifle company were either killed or seriously wounded at Dai Do. There were three platoons in a rifle company. At full strength a platoon would number over forty men. By the end of three days of combat, not one platoon in Golf Co. could number 10 men.

After Dai Do, I was transferred from Staff Sgt. Wade's 1st Platoon to Lt. Morgan's 2nd Platoon. Why? Because it had only 3 men in it. 1st Platoon still had about 7 men left. Golf Co. was shelled mercilessly on 30 April as we attempted to join our Battalion at Dai Do. We arrived on "mike boats" (LCM-8s) with two tanks. Air strikes were called in and I saw anti-aircraft tracers shooting at our planes. I knew these were not just Viet Cong. My guess was that they were NVA. I later found out they were well trained, well-equipped NVA regulars, fresh from North Vietnam (TIME Magazine, May 10, 1968 Issue, p.32). I prayed, "Lord Jesus, please get me out of here alive." He did. After the air strikes, we had to cross a rice paddy and above ground burial mounds to reach the tree line where the central village, Dai Do, was located. The first wave of Marines ahead of me got down in the tall grass under enemy fire. At first they seemed to be taking cover. But one Marine crawled ahead, then came back and said they were all seriously wounded or dead. To my left, I saw a Marine machine gun crew set up on a burial mound. Then the gunner was shot dead. We had to leapfrog forward in the tall grass, without firing, till we got past the wounded Marines. While behind one burial mound, an NVA soldier charged us. Lance Cpl. Robert Allen shot him in the chest with an M-79 grenade launcher. I shot another NVA. Then Robert asked me if I wanted to help him rescue some wounded Marines under fire. I said "OK". We crawled on our bellies and pulled one Marine (whose intestines were hanging out) to safety. Then we went back for a second one. While crouched over the wounded, an NVA soldier shot at us. A bullet struck my M-16 rifle stock, cracking the hard plastic open and stung my left hand painfully. I picked up a wounded Marine's rifle and returned fire. As the NVA fell over, we heard a thump. Robert was glad and said, "You got him!" We then proceeded to pull the second wounded Marine out and told the third one that we'd be back for him. He didn't want to wait. He rolled over, intestines hanging out, and tried to crawl out. Still approaching the tree line, I passed another burial mound and caught an NVA soldier (in uniform, AK-47 on his lap) sitting behind it. I swung my rifle towards him and he threw his hands up. Another Marine on the other side shot him through the head. Eventually, we reached the tree line. I was ordered to crawl to help evacuate some wounded Marines. Several were already dead when I got there. I laid my rifle down to help drag out another Marine with his intestines hanging. We got maybe 15 yards to a shallow ditch by a hedgerow, under intense enemy fire. A radioman was being shot up right next to us so we quickly pulled him into the ditch with us. I watched the bullets burn in his butt, leg and radio as we pulled him. It looked like the little sparks a cigarette lighter makes when you first light it. It all happened very fast. Three guys got up and ran. Then I noticed some leaves about 10 yards in front of us begin to move. They were leaves on the helmets of NVA soldiers. Three stood up, AK-47s pointing from their hips, but they were looking at other Marines in an adjacent shallow ditch, not at me. I told the Marine with his intestines hanging out what I saw. He said, shoot them. I couldn't get back to my rifle, so I picked up another. It jammed!! The noise by now was deafening. I tried to get one of the wounded Marines to fire at the enemy or give me their rifle, but none would. It was very hot and they were drinking from their canteens. They didn't even see the NVA coming. Then, Anthony Fauer jumped in next to me and asked, "Theiss, what are you doing here?" I told him that they kept me in the States until after I turned 18 years old. I had just arrived in Vietnam. We had gone through Parris Island together. He still remembered me. We were shoulder to shoulder when he was shot in his left shoulder, next to my right shoulder. I saw it go in, but it was a minor "flesh" wound. He said, "That's one Purple Heart." Before he was done speaking, he was hit in the other shoulder. He shouted, "That's two Purple Hearts. I'm out of here." He jumped up and ran. Two Purple Hearts could get a man out of a combat unit. Then I noticed Lt. Morgan, lying on the ground, talking on the radio. He shouted, "Let's get the hell out of here." I found out later that Capt. Vargas had ordered him to pull back. The NVA were advancing from all sides. Once out of the tree line, I was given my third M-16 in a day. Golf Company was now surrounded by NVA. We formed a tight perimeter on the edge of the tree line. I was on a one-man hole watch all that night. My M-16 was off safety, in the fire position, in my hand all night. I half-pulled the pins on all my grenades. I never slept. Friendly artillery slammed close in front of us all night. The enemy still probed our lines. We were low on ammo. We drove through the village again the next day. Some of my memories blur now. I remember the enemy having well-camouflaged, fortified positions.

"HE SAID, THAT'S ONE PURPLE HEART.' BEFORE HE WAS DONE SPEAKING, HE WAS HIT IN THE OTHER SHOULDER. HE SHOUTED, THAT'S TWO PURPLE HEARTS. I'M OUT OF HERE.' HE JUMPED UP AND RAN. TWO PURPLE HEARTS COULD GET A MAN OUT OF A COMBAT UNIT."

We fought hard all day. On May 3, it was mostly over. As a new guy, most guys didn't know me. Nor did I know most of them. I was assigned to help place the dead Marines in body bags. I counted 68 bodies. One was a Cpl. Smith, who befriended me when I first arrived. He had 12 months in country and was almost ready to go home. He was shot through the head at Dai Do. I had to tie a rope to his arm, move away, and roll his body to check for booby traps.

Another Marine I picked up had blond hair, but no face left. I remember a dead black Marine, laying face up, with flies moving in and out of his nostrils. The stench from the dead bodies was so bad, that when I had time to finally eat, I couldn't. We captured many enemy weapons: AK-47s, RPGs, two 12.7 heavy machine guns, SKS sniper rifles, etc. Dead NVA bodies were everywhere. During the Battle, when ammo ran out, or M-16s jammed, some Marines would grab an AK-47 and start firing.

The AK-47 had a different crack (sound) than the M-16 when fired. At least one Marine was accidentally mistaken for NVA and shot by fellow Marines when he fired an AK-47 while partly hid in the brush.

After the Battle, the unit was given three days of rest. Replacements were brought in to fill in our depleted ranks. I was promoted twice in Nam, making Corporal (E-4) when still 18 (1 Nov. 68). I served as a Fire Team Leader and briefly as a Squad Leader.

My Service Record shows a **5.0** performance rating (the highest possible rating) for my time in

Vietnam. I later received a Certificate of Commendation for courage under fire, while in Vietnam. Lt. General H.W. Buse, Jr signed it.

How many were in your company when you started compared to when you left Dai Do?

" THE STENCH FROM THE DEAD BODIES WAS SO BAD, THAT WHEN I HAD TIME TO FINALLY EAT, I COULDN'T.

I don't know the exact number. But I do know that we took 75% casualties at Dai Do (confirmed by MAGNIFICENT BASTARDS by Keith Nolan, Chapter 15).

You were a Fire Team Leader then?
No, not at Dai Do. I was just a Private First Class, a new guy from the States. I was promoted twice after Dai Do, probably because I was one of the few survivors.

How long did you serve in the infantry after that?
I was in Nam as a rifleman ten full months (19 April 68 to 18 February 69). Then my Mom died and they sent me home for the funeral. Enlistment for 17 year olds in 1967 was three years. I received a year early out with Honorable Discharge in July 1969.

As a rifleman, your job was pretty much to go out and get the enemy.
Yes. After Dai Do we did a lot of "Search & Destroy" missions near the DMZ, in the hills near Khe Sanh, and by the Laotian border, under our new CO, Captain Dwyer.

What went through your mind each day as you got up in the morning?
It was a hard job. I wanted to get home safely. Each man carried about 80 lbs. in ammo & food in extreme heat and heavy rains, up hill, down hill. Half of each night was spent on hole watch. You slept with your loaded rifle. You never knew if you'd be hit.

Could you tell us a little about the training you had before you went to Vietnam?
At Parris Island, they told us they would try to break us. "Better break here, than in combat. " They did all they could to break us emotionally and physically. I'd rather go back to combat, than to go through Parris Island again.
After that was Advanced Infantry Training (Camp Lejeune). Then I was stationed with the 28th Marines (Camp Pendleton) until after I turned 18 and was sent to Vietnam. The 28th Marines was mostly combat veterans who helped encourage 17 year olds like me.

Following the war, George Theiss has had a variety of occupations including working for the New York Telephone Co, insurance sales and benefit consultant. He also re-enlisted in the Army for four years.

Interviewers: Amanda Zimmerman and Shannon Whitman

Roy Woytasik

Woytasik served in C Company of the 2nd Battalion, 12th Cavalry as a combat infantryman. He was in Vietnam from October 1966 to October 1967.

I am talking to Roy Woytasik, C Company, 2nd Battalion, 12th Cavalry. He is going to be sharing his views and experiences from the Vietnam War.

What is meant by combat infantry?
Today it's called light infantry I always considered there were two types of soldiers out there in the combat infantry: the rifleman and others. We were not the same. The others fought the war differently. They had time to think about it. They talked the talk; we walked the walk. Statistics. We were told to look left and right; two out of three won't make it for three months...K.I.A...or M.I.A...or W.I.A...Sent home early! I flew over with 208 guys on a cargo ship. We returned, we could only count eight guys that made it. Only four of us were on the plane...one in twenty-nine guys were combat infantry. I had twenty-eight guys getting me K-rations and two cans of beer a month.

How did you become involved in the Vietnam War?
I volunteered for the draft.

What were the base camps like?
They sucked. The big base camp was just like the states. The L-Z or artillary camps that I quarded were the war camps; the front line. When we walked into the big base camps they were afraid of us. They would fence us in like cattle and wouldn't talk with us because we were "grunts." If you got in our way, we were the interview.

What was basic training like?
Basic training destroyed you as a person and rebuilt you to fight.

Did you fight against the Viet Cong or the NVA regulars?
Yes, I hunted the Viet Cong, the NVA, the Chinese, the gooks, and chicken, pigs, and dogs. I drew the line on the water buffalo. The enemy was any one or anything that got in your way.

Can you describe what the average day was like?

That was a twenty-four hour day. We fought twenty-four hours a day. We didn't fight six, eight hours; it was a twenty-four hour day. Probably marched all of daylight till it was dark at night. Nine o'clock, we marched till nine, dig a fox-hole till ten, two hours on, and two hours off, till five o'clock. Too boring for detail...No or little sleep, pushed past your limits, like living ten years in one. If you made a mistake you died.

Describe what is meant by a "guerilla" war.
Fighting a coward, getting shot in the back, getting 1,000 of them to 90 of us. Having little kids come up to you with hand grenades and toss them. Tracking and hunting the enemy. They were out there; you just didn't see them. When you did, you were ambushed. Basically hit and run, that's basically what it was; maybe small groups, ten, fifteen, a hundred, two hundred. The main battles weren't guerilla wars, like the Tet Offensive, ten thousand, twenty thousand, fifty thousand guys.

Did you ever participate in an ambush and please describe it?
Probably about twenty to forty of them. I have been ambushed about twenty to thirty times. Getting ambushed is like getting caught in a mouse trap with a cat waiting to finish you off.

Words You Ask
What is it like to be a soldier
Words that I can say
Words that I can not say
Words I don't mean
Words that you don't know what
They mean: until you get there,
one of the 58,000 names

What Did Patriotism Mean To You
I think of the Past
I think of the Memories
I think of the way it Was
I think of the Lost Memories
I think of all of This
And it lost its Meaning

I Just Happened To Be There
If you were to ask me
What am I doing in this
I just happened to
Be in Vietnam 1967: 68 dgrees Hor.:61 degrees
An American experience to be told
Age 21 years old and no one to tell it to
Objective- Search and Destroy

© Printed with permission from:
Roy Woytasik

Can you explain any experiences you had with body counts or kill ratios?

We killed a hundred a week in our platoon. Our company was about ninety guys. We lost eight hundred and killed five thousand. I always thought we killed a lot more. The ratio was 10-1. Ten to one odds was a fair fight. To get beat the B-52, the jet, the helicopter, and the artillary killed so many you couldn't even count or estimate. I wondered where they got the 5,100 K.I.A. The way we fought for what and how they counted you never knew...since we moved on other units came and counted.

Did you use helicopters to get around?
All the time, probably twenty, thirty helicopters taking whole platoons and companies, and battalions. They gave me some kind of medal for making over twenty or thirty assault landings.
I jumped out of the helicopters, jumped out on mine fields, landed in ambushes, and hot L&Z. Reinforced their companies as they were getting over run, getting shot as you landed and getting shot as you left.

Were drugs a problem for the soldiers in Vietnam?
No, everyone took drugs.

How was the relationship between blacks and whites in your unit.
They all died the same. Color didn't make much difference.

Do you have any opinions regarding the anti-war movement back in the states while you were in Vietnam?
Yes, the American people were basically cowards. They sent us out there to fight and deserted us.

"I NEVER THOUGHT WE LOST THE WAR. WE NEVER LOST ANY BATTLES."

What was the hardest part of being in the war?
Just being there.

Was there a lot of physical and emotional stress that you had to endure?
Probably every day, just routine.

Is there one particular experience that stands out in your mind?
No, probably about a half a dozen.

Do you think the United States could have won the war?
I never thought we lost the war. We never lost any battles. It took twenty years to realize we lost the war. President Nixon explained how we lost the war. I know we lost the war because the "boat" people are here. This is why the Asians are here. If we would have won the war they would not be here.

Did you make any lasting friendships during the war?
Most of them got killed; maybe two or three people that survived. In two or three weeks, they were killed. You make new friends, and in a day or a month they are gone. After awhile you made no friends; you saw too many die; you walked alone.

What kind of reception did you get when you returned to the United States?
None.

What did patriotism mean to you during your active duty and now as a veteran?
You still fight for your country. The words and terminology are different today from then, but they have the same meaning.

Woytasik on search and destroy

Do you have any difficulty dealing with memories?

No, I had no problems there, and I had no problems here. You either live with the memories or die.

Is there a message you have for young people today?

Yes, don't get involved in war. Fighting the battles in Vietnam is no different than walking the halls of school; students, teachers, and workers. When it gets tough just try to survive. I never lost a battle when I was in Vietnam; I just lost the war. Over and over and over when I was in Vietnam, over when I was back. The riots, being called a baby killer...Years later a liar for writing this down and telling these true experiences. Live to tell them; there may be some TRUTH to them, and they have good stories.

What was the hardest part of the war?

The hardest part of being in the war was the anti-war movement back in the states and being called a "baby killer."

What were base camps like?

I saw a base camp three times- once when I got there, actually four times, twice when we were down to thirty guys, third time when I went on R & R in Hong Kong, and the fourth time when I left to go stateside. Basically a base camp was just as secure as stateside with thirty, forty thousand troops.

This is my short version of Vietnam. There has got to be a start but since we are restricted to time, probably I am getting ready to fly to Vietnam sitting there waiting in San Francisco off the plane, and I looked up and there comes two hundred guys. They look like the angel of death, the grim reaper. They had the look of death in their eyes, and then I am on the plane, first class in a cargo plane, kind of like a cattle truck of some type. There were no seats. I remember dropping ten thousand feet and I thought I was dead before I got there. Don't worry; you still have twenty thousand feet.

I get off the plane and it's 110 degrees, 120 if you add in the humidity. It was like walking in the twilight zone. I thought I would see Jesus walking there. We went 1900 years back in time, seeing people farm just like two thousand years ago. They were backward like time never moved. Huts looked like they were two thousand years behind. I would have guessed three out

"I ONLY HAD ONE JOB THERE, TO SURVIVE AND KILL. NOTHING ELSE. NO ETHICS, NO VALUES."

of four were communists, and the one out of the four was a farmer and he didn't care anyway. Generally we were young, and we thought the people were nice. So we thought about the ethics of killing people. I was sitting there looking at the ground, playing soldier for a couple of days, and I was pushing a stick into the ground and kicking over some ants. Look at all the ant soldiers, and I considered myself an ant soldier. What does an ant soldier do? Kills. That is their sole function. That is what I did. As to the hierarchy, I was on the bottom of the scale. I only had one job there, to survive and kill. Nothing else. No ethics, no values.

I don't think I was out there two or three days, fell asleep on guard, got up and this guy wakes me up to go on guard duty and says: " I am dreaming I am in Vietnam. Mom, I don't want to get up." He says, "I'm not your mom, and you are in Vietnam." Wake up kid. No problem, you don't die in your dreams.

I moved on, and in November of 1966 I went to Bong Son. I dug a foxhole ten inches deep so I could lay in that, and I had a radio and I am listening, and I look up the hill and there is ten to fifteen thousand on that hill, and they are bombing it. I am listening, and then a squad is ordered there to see if the enemy is up there. Some poor sucker has to go up there. They ordered the third platoon, and I didn't want to go. They sent thirty guys up with a one way ticket because there are fifteen thousand guys up there. Starting walking up the mountain to see the whites of their eyes, NVA and I never shot, probably hundreds and we didn't shoot back, probably scared. The B-52s just dropped ten planes worth, about 250,000 pounds. We went to the top of the mountain and it was like the twilight zone. The coffee was hot and the clothes were on the line. They weren't dry, and no, there were no soldiers. Nobody was there. They were all gone! I'm making coffee, and there's nobody there. Sitting there wondering where are they? There must have been fifty guys, twenty five for sure, How was that? Count the number of legs and divide by two. The

B-52s just bombed them. If there was fifty guys and there was a crater, thirty feet deep, filled with body parts. We were maybe ten minutes behind them, fifteen thousand guys. Then it started to rain, started coming down the hill, crossed a brook. I don't know how those guys could swim, swimming against the current. We came down, the hill and there were no soldiers down there. We would go up and get killed, like Marines in a video game. I was like one of those little guys you send in. We were a company where all the soldiers had brothers and we were expendable. So they would send us in first all the time.

Were you in any firefights?

I was involved in a hundred, maybe two hundred. We were on "red alert" which means another company had just been overrun in a fight, and I think "B" company with ninety guys had run into twelve hundred to two thousand guys. They come in and drop us right on top of "B" company, and I am coming down in a helicopter and I see the enemy, a couple hundred. I was a machine gunner, so I start shooting at them, and I shot thirty or so before I hit the ground. I was shooting, kind of walking; a thirty round burst coming down in a helicopter, walking it on the ground, and I walked it right to where they were marching. I fired about eight hundred rounds, and I shot thirty of them. I got so involved in shooting them that I forgot to jump, so they kicked me out. They kicked me out in between the enemy and our unit. There was all dead guys around me, so I went to sleep for a couple of hours. They called for me, and someone said I was dead. "No I'm not, I'm just asleep," I said.

"Why don't you come in?"

"You will shoot me for a gook" I said. "Don't shoot."

One captain, got shot in the back. I don't understand why. I came back and crawled in. They pointed to a bank about eighty yards away and I stood up and I walked eighty yards, and I shot thirty to forty guys on that bank. They stood there and froze and I shot them all. I took the machine gun and raked them, and they froze, and I shot. They were sitting there hiding behind bamboo sticks, a guy a foot and a half wide hiding behind an inch and one half stick. As I walked the gunfire and the bullets would bounce in the dirt, and I would walk it on to you. I just started shooting them all. I ran out of ammo and the rest of the guys came up. I guess Rambo wasn't invented yet, but that was a small version of it. At night, in the dark, I dug a foxhole and I jumped in the foxhole. Woke up in the morning about four o'clock with a red alert, pulled guard, and here comes the enemy, marching down the road, and my foxhole is in the middle of the road. They marched right down the road, and the guy on guard fell asleep. Actually, all four of us were asleep. They had a point guy about thirty yards in front, and it's foggy and he couldn't see us, but I could sense him. I got up and grabbed my pistol which is hanging on a tree, and I couldn't get it out, so we grabbed this guy and beat the daylights out of him. This was a company that was coming in, and we gunned them down, and they wondered why we had captured this one guy. Most of the VC were cowards. In daylight, I looked behind me, and there was an enemy soldier with a BAR pointed at me, and I captured him. My machine gun was in front of his machine gun. Can you imagine that?

An eleven man patrol went for a walk. I was smoking a cigar with my sleeves rolled back. As a kid I played soldier like this, and I looked to my right, and there was a camera crew. I should get myself on the TV. That was cool. I was carrying a machine gun, and I had a camera crew following me. So I go out there with an eleven man patrol, and I was the tenth guy. We were walking out maybe three hundred yards, and I stepped on a body, and the guy's alive. I stepped on him, and I was carrying the machine gun, and that's like carrying an ice auger. I am stepping on a guy, and if he moves, kill him. The guy behind me is stuttering. You cannot panic; you have to shoot. You never hesitate. He should have shot him but we captured him, so then they interrogated him and found out where their division headquarters was.

My penalty for taking him alive was to send our platoon to see if the division headquarters was there or not. So they get a guy a helicopter ride and we went out to find out if what he had told us was true. So we went out that night. You put your hand out in front of you, and you couldn't count your fingers. It was dark. The way you moved was to hang onto the belt of the guy in front of you. We were walking down a creek, and if you didn't hang on to the guy, you never saw him. You can't see your fingers in front of you. When we get there, we had specific instructions to follow a road, and we went down that road and came into fifteen thousand troops, right in the

I Walked The Valley of Death
As I was walking
The Valley of Death; I stopped
and time paused for a second or two.

The marines have a saying-
I walk The Valley of the Dead I fear no evil
I know no evil for I am...

I pause again, I think
I say "God"
(I walk The Valley of Death
I know no evil I fear no)

Reality sets in...
I hear the sound of an AK-47
I say "God"
(I would like to take back those words - I fear
Evil, and these are evil people)

I continue marching or walking
to the front to Search and Destroy
I smile I think;
The marines must be tough sons-of
bitches to say that!

© *Printed with the permission of:*
Roy Woytasik

center of the camp. We had a platoon of thirty guys. A platoon is approximately thirty to forty guys. What do we do? Fifteen thousand guys, an army of people. We were in the center of their base camp. We want to retreat, but the line is so long because they are still coming into the base camp. One guy turns to his right, and the next guy turns to his left. A guy shoots to the right and the other shoots to the left. We must have covered three hundred yards over bodies. We stepped over bodies and never touched the ground. They couldn't shoot inside their perimeter because they would be shooting their own guys. They just grabbed you by the leg, and you shot them on the ground. We shot the ground for a couple of hundred yards. Once we were out of the perimeter, they opened up with a heavy machine gun. We called in mortars, artillery, and aircraft. It was like a videogame. The mortars and the artillery wiped out a large number. They hunted us for over a week. Now we were the hunted, and they tracked us with companies. We got out of there at night and looked over cliffs. We never moved because they would find you. So we would sleep. A 155mm round came in one night and landed between me and another guy and didn't explode. We knew we needed to move because the shell was live and didn't explode.

I was listed as dead a number of times. I came back once and my name wasn't on the roster because they said I was dead. I told them who I was, and they said I was dead. OK. Once a sniper hit the hair of my eyes, and I was knocked out for over half an hour. They left me for dead. The firefight continued for over half an hour, and later I woke up and didn't know if I was dead. There was nobody there. I had no map, compass, or radio, and they left me. Now what do you do? I had two thousand rounds, and I was on the high ground, and I opened up and decided to kill as many as I could before I died. I would shoot bursts of ten rounds, and I shot a water buffalo. Finally the guys came back and found me. Why did you come back?

I Cry In My Sorrows

I cry in my sorrows
Not for Me
but for the others: who
Who fought so well and lost.
So Young, Dead and Forgotten
Remembered by just the few
Who were there; not imagine
What it is like to be there (you can not)
You try to forget; It
Goes away when they die
Forgotten
Or you die forgotten Forever

© *Printed in tribute to all people who fought their own battles and lost something, with the permission of:*
Roy Woytasik

We heard the shooting, and we knew it was you. If you have lives, I used up five or six. I was going on R & R to Hong Kong. This one guy says he wants to be just like me. He wanted the machine gun. They listed him as dead, and he could have gone home. All I know is he was from Maine. This guy could have gone home, but he decided to take the machine gun when I went on R & R. I got on the airplane with 160 guys, and I was five hours of flying time away, and the enemy killed one hundred of those guys. The guy that took my place was killed from a bullet in the back. He was hit by a .51 caliber enemy round. Mistakes were made and people died. I was going to Hong Kong to enjoy myself, and when I got back there were thirty-five guys left out of 160 in seven days. A four star general comes up and wants to congratulate us, and we wanted him to leave. I used another life when I was eating. We watched an unarmed guy come up and start throwing hand grenades where there are no people. B company and A company should have lined up, but they didn't. There should have been foxholes there but there were none. Nobody shot at him, and I decided I would give him three hundred yards before I opened up. I ate and watched him tossing the grenades. He never realized that nobody was there because the lines never locked up. He started to run, and I wasn't going to shoot him until he reached three hundred yards. There was a machine gun that opened up on me, but I was not going to be hit. I gave that guy a going away present and turned the machine gun on the other machine gun. I fired about one thousand rounds.

"I WAS LISTED AS DEAD A NUMBER OF TIMES."

When I got back to base camp, I was sitting down and my chin strap about an inch past my ear comes a piece of artillery shell, hits the chin strap and goes in the ground. I go to dig out the piece but it's seven feet deep. Do you know how close that is? It knocked the glasses off. A fragment hit the glasses. No problem. I go out there about one hundred yards and pulled OP. If they come they will overrun me and then the rest of the guys. Those guys forget I am out there, and they open up on me. We had to pull back and retreat. There were ten thousand guys coming at us like on parade ten guys wide. We dropped the first shell, and it hits them and then "fire for effect." The first round was a spotter round, but the next sixteen hit them hard. We moved at night. We basically ran, and they were marching. They were going to wipe us out. That was their mistake. We marked three spots. They came at "A" and we called and they dropped a shell. Later that day we marched and then had another fire-fight. It was just a typical day. We killed more than 10 to 1. That is what they told us. A hundred a week, we killed. I saw our company turn over eight times in one year. Sixty to Seventy guys died a month, and there were only ninety guys in our company.

If you made it three months, you made it. If you didn't get the first three months, you were killed. If you made three months, you would make it. After three months I developed a sixth sense, and I could hunt them like a dog. Actually I was better than a dog. I could sense them over one hundred yards away. I would light a cigar and sit back on guard duty. I was the only guy that did that. It did not bother me at all to light up a cigar at night. I would sit there and talk right in the middle of the jungle. I could see them in the dark and shoot them in the dark. I could shoot them without seeing them. Other guys could see the enemy as well and they would make bets to see if the guy would get me. They didn't shoot one time because they wanted to see if the enemy was going to kill me. The guys that had been watching captured the enemy guy. Another time we were watching an enemy soldier in a bunker. We were high up on a hill and watching down below. I couldn't shoot so I just watched. Here comes a jet and he drops a bomb and the guy comes back out of the bunker and takes his carbine and shoots at the jet. The jet comes back and drops another bomb on the bunker and the guy pulls out his little carbine and shoots again. The guy must have thought he was something, shooting at the jet. The jet called somebody else and they dropped a 500 lb. bomb on the bunker. The bomb left a thirty foot deep crater and damaged the bunker because the guy decided to run. I was watching and he gave me a hand gesture. I took a burst at him from about one thousand yards away and I walked up the rounds. He made a hand gesture and I lined up my sights and I got him. Guys were crossing a river and I walked the rounds up the river and when they looked I wiped them out. All that remained was their hats floating on the

A Letter

I made it!

When I arrived in Vietnam
I wrote 4 letters to people
I loved and liked.

When leaving Vietnam
I picked up the 4 letters
I could not read them.

I had changed.

I knew, I had no home to go to,
the people I once knew
had also changed

They called ME a Baby Killer!
They asked if I liked killing!

Twentry-five years later
they asked what it was like
being there
They call me a liar.
Now they say I wasn't there.
(They have their own ideas what a Hero should be)

I smile-
They are lucky not to fought or be in a war.
They are lucky just to imagine it or
play soldiers.

To the rest-
Be tough.

© Printed with the permission of:
Roy Woytasik

water.

What is it like to be shot?

Like getting hit by Mohammed Ali. You don't have any pain, just the shock. One guy got shot in the heel and died. I saw these guys. One guy got hit nine times in the chest. I am eating my lunch looking at these two body bags and this is the first time I have seen dead people that had been shot. The guy that had been hit in the heel must have died from the shock. The guy that had been hit nine times in the chest lived in the end. Some people were mentally tough.

How long were you in the war?

To me I was in Vietnam for one year and in the army for two years. An expendable soldier...the real soldiers were the RAs...the soldiers that volunteered. They made it their life and died for it. I was not in that class. Amen!

Following the war, Roy Woytosik became an industrial engineer. He followed that with a career in the postal service.

Interviewed by Joel Line

Bob Yuska

Robert Yuska was born on March 27, 1948. He served in the army and went to Vietnam from April 1969-April 1970. In Cu Chi, Bob served with the 25th Division, 1st Battalion, 5th Infantry Unit.

How did you get involved in the service?

I got drafted. What actually happened was some very close friends of mine had gotten their draft notices, and I had a student deferment. I was actually going to school to avoid the draft; however, my daily attendance was poor, so I felt that one day I might become draft eligible. My buddies were to report to the induction center on the 28th of October, and I thought that if I had to go, it would be best to go with them. I had a relative that was on the draft board that I spoke with about dropping my status from 2S (student) to 1A (draft eligible). She was able to speed up the appeal process given to an individual with a change in draft status which I believe was thirty days, and this being the beginning of October, things needed to move quickly. I got my letter to report the 28th of October. (Thanks Auntie!) I got drafted with three other guys that I grew up with, and we went in together. I might add that the lottery came out when I was in the service, and had I not gone and volunteered for the draft, my lottery number would have been way up, and I would have been a civilian for life.

Can you describe what basic training was like?

Actually, it wasn't bad. The fact, I was there with some friends from the neighborhood; made the adjustment easier. We had some fun, but it was still the Army. AIT (Advanced Infantry Training) was more difficult. That's where they work on you mentally and physically to prepare for combat.

What was your daily schedule during training?

I received basic training at Fort Knox, Kentucky, and Advanced Infantry Training at Fort Ord, California. Early to rise was mandatory throughout training. Verbal harassment was also normal for the course along with a lot of PT (physical training) and, of course, marching. In AIT, learning was geared more towards combat skills; learning how to operate different weapons, finding your way with a compass, entering and searching simulated Vietnamese villages, and learning how to work with people. We'd have speed marches on Saturday morning with full gear, romping through the sand hills. Fort Ord was a beautiful place to train; however, I was there in January and February which I believed was their monsoon season. Most of our training took place way up in the hills where it was cold and wet with no place to warm up or dry off. It was miserable. However, on weekends we'd get a pass after our speed march allowing us to visit the City of Carmel by the ocean. I never got to meet Clint Eastwood though.

"WE WERE ON AN AIR-CONDITIONED COMMER-CIAL PLANE, AND WHEN THE DOOR OPENED, IT WAS SO HOT, I THOUGHT I ENTERED HELL."

How did you feel as you prepared to enter Vietnam?

While I was training, Vietnam seemed like a long way off. I believed that perhaps they would send me somewhere else. I thought that perhaps I'd be too tall to become a grunt. For some unexplained reason, perhaps stupidity on my part, I didn't have a fear of Nam till the orders were issued at the end of AIT. That's when reality set in. We were given a 30-day leave to visit home before we had to depart. When my 30-day leave was over and I said goodbye to my parents, that's the only time I believe I saw my father break down and cry.

Can you explain your first impression of Vietnam when you arrived?

I still have the memory of the plane door opening upon arrival. We were on an air-conditioned commercial plane, and when the door opened, it was so hot, I thought I entered hell. As my tour in Nam pro-

gressed, I found out I did. Before I was assigned a unit, I spent four or five days at Ton San Nhut Airbase doing busy work like filling sandbags and other things that I thought were useless. In addition, all newcomers going into the field had to go through a couple of days of jungle school, where they had simulated things that a person would encounter out in the field. They had the areas that were booby-trapped with smoke grenades. During an exercise, I tripped a wire attached to a smoke grenade. Someone ran up and jumped all over me and told me that I had just blown myself up. They also informed those around me in not so polite terms that they also were history for clustering up together. This was a valuable lesson because spacing in Nam was critical.

After going through schooling, I received my orders to report to the 25th Infantry Division, 1st Battalion, 5th Infantry Mechanized. My fear factor was now at a level of 10. I was terrified. I was transported out to a fire support base and assigned a squad. The first night an ambush patrol is to go out, and they needed one more body, I thought, "Oh, no, not me; I just got here." So did this other guy. He had the bad luck of the draw, however, and he went. Someone told me they were having a Mass and asked if I wanted to attend. War makes a person find religion and make many promises. At Mass some guys asked the Chaplain to say a special prayer for someone that just died in combat. That night as I was sleeping, we received some incoming mortar rounds. Then the next morning upon leaving the base camp, a truck hit a land mine. I was not sure I could survive the year out there. This was, after all, my first day in the field.

What was your role during the war?

I was in a mechanized unit, which means we had armored personnel carriers (APC). I usually carried the 60-caliber machine gun.

> *"OUR DRIVERS HAD EXTENSION PEDALS FOR THE ACCELERATOR AND THE STEERING BECAUSE IF WE HIT A MINE OR BOOBY-TRAP, NO ONE WOULD SURVIVE INSIDE THE TRACK."*

Were you in combat?

Yes, I was in infantry for about ten and a half months. Usually when someone got to the end of their tour, they would try to place you in a position that may not be quite as hazardous. I was assigned into the mortar platoon, which means I was still out in the field, but I didn't have to go out on night ambush patrols, be at the point during sweeps, and things like that. Instead of being on the outer edge of the perimeter, I was now located in the middle. My job was to drop the mortar round down the tube when someone said "fire."

When you were in combat, did you come across any booby traps?

The area that I was in was Northwest of Saigon. The village was called Cu Chi. The area was infested with tunnels and booby traps. We had many Vietcong in our area, and it was almost impossible to tell them from the civilians during the day. At night if they moved outside of their homes, they were fair game. Because of the area being heavily mined, everybody in our company had to ride on top of the tracks. Our drivers had extension pedals for the accelerator and the steering because if we hit a mine or booby-trap, no one would survive inside the track. RPG's (rocket-propelled grenades), posed another danger to our APC's (armored personnel carriers.)

Can you describe what an "average" day was like during the war?

We were going constantly. We performed search and destroy missions. At night we were required to go on ambush patrols. We did whatever we could to engage the enemy and kill them. Some days we performed road security or acted as a reactionary force for other units. There were also times we would escort convoys to Cu Chi if they were running late and it was getting dark. A successful day, according to military standards, was getting a body count. A successful day was also if you and your comrades survived.

Could you explain any experience you had with body counts or kill ratios?

The war was defined in terms of body counts. There was no land that we went out and took and said, "This is our land." We went out, and our job was to make contact with the enemy. A successful day was a high body count with low casualties on our side.

Were the animals or insects a problem at all?

It was just a fact of life that you had to deal with. One of the many things we dealt with were little red ants. They would get on your skin and bite into you. They had to be picked off. They hurt. Mosquitoes were in abundance. They were very difficult to deal with. They gave you repellent, but it never seemed to work. The mosquitoes also transmitted malaria. I can not recall anyone taking their pills, the thought being it would have been an admirable way out of the country. The rats there were really big. Returning from an ambush in the morning, you would see young children from the villages gathering up their traps with rats in them. There were snakes, too, but that was just part of the turf. It was just something you adjusted to. I believe that anything that God put on this earth, you came across in Vietnam.

Did you make any lasting friendships during the war?

I had served with a guy named Doug Gardner from Connecticut during most of my tour. He was a driver of the APC I was assigned to, the (2-3) track. I had his name and phone number, but I never had the nerve to call him up. Last Fourth of July, my wife and my daughter had taken a trip, and I was sitting at home by myself, and I finally got the nerve to call him. He knew me right away. My wife and I drove to Connecticut at the end of July and had dinner with him and his family. The next day we drove home. It was great to see him. I also met a Second Lieutenant that I served with that lives in Sheboygan, Wisconsin. His name is Eldon Burgh. It's a small world.

Can you describe the medical treatment that was available to the citizens and soldiers?

We had great medics. If we would go through a village and someone needed medical care, they were treated. If someone was hurt in combat, the medic was always there. They never seemed to be concerned about their own safety.

"I BELIEVE THAT ANYTHING THAT GOD PUT ON THIS EARTH, YOU CAME ACROSS IN VIETNAM."

Were you able to communicate with your family at all?

Yes, through the mail. I never was able to call. I don't remember having access to a telephone. My wife, who I was going out with prior to going in the service, wrote me a lot. My family, of course, wrote to me and sent care packages. They would send things that wouldn't perish. Fruitcakes were a real big thing. I don't know anybody who liked a fruitcake. They were terrible, and they weighed so much.

Is there one particular experience that stands out in your mind?

I've had some good experiences as well as bad. Everyday that goes by I think of something that occurred during my tour of duty there. One story I will share is our mortar platoon had a dog named "Short Round." The dog was killed. They buried the dog and put up a little marker. It said, "Here lies Short

Round. Born in hell. Went through hell. Died and went to Heaven."

"ONE STORY I WILL SHARE IS OUR MORTAR PLATOON HAD A DOG NAMED 'SHORT ROUND'. THE DOG WAS KILLED. THEY BURIED THE DOG AND PUT UP A LITTLE MARKER. IT SAID, 'HERE LIES SHORT ROUND. BORN IN HELL. WENT THROUGH HELL. DIED AND WENT TO HEAVEN.'"

What kind of reception did you get when you came back to the United States?
I came back, and my family didn't expect me. When I arrived home, no one was there. I had to sit on the front porch for an hour waiting for a family member. I've heard that other vets were called "baby killers" and other things. I didn't have that problem. No one called me anything. No one even said, "welcome home" outside of my family and my girlfriend and her family. But then again, I wasn't expecting a parade. I knew this country was in chaos over this war. I am. however,, glad I never met Jane Fonda.

Is there a message you have for young people today?
It's been 32 years since I served. The memories are with me. I'm grateful to those who serve our country and hope that young people realize the sacrifices made. I wish going to war on no one. It's ugly, but sometimes necessary.

Bob Yuska is currently a teacher and a coach at Merrill High School. He has been employed there since 1977. He has been married to his wife, Judy, for 29 years. They have two children, Erik (26 years old) and Melissa (23 years old).

Interviewed by Alex Hollman and Jenessa Ng
Transcribed Alex Hollman

Thomas Zunker

Thomas D. Zunker enlisted in the Marine Corps in 1969. He served from 1969 until 1970 in the Delta 1-7 Infantry unit. He worked as point man and also as a squad leader on Hill 55.

Tom, please share your story with us today. Share any memories you may have. The more you talk the better. We'll ask questions at the end.

I went to Vietnam in 1969. I started out as a point man because all of the new recruits get that position because it is the dirtiest job. We maneuvered through different valleys and stayed in villages with the people that were supposed to be friendly towards us. We went on patrols out of the villages, got shot at, and tried to get friendlier with the people. We tried to get to know them and let them get to know us. We also had the night maneuvers where we went out on night patrols, and a lot of times we were hit by the enemy and had to fight for our lives.

How did you become involved in the Vietnam War? Were you drafted, or enlisted?

I was drafted after I had already enlisted in the Marine Corps.

So, you never tried to dodge the draft or anything like that?

No, I do not believe in it. This is our country, and we should do anything that we have to do to keep it free.

Did you know anyone else who did dodge it? Any of your friends?

No, everybody I knew went.

Could you explain a point man's responsibilities?

I walked point for eight months. I led the troops to day positions and night positions, ambushes and day patrols. I had to watch for land mines, pungi pits, and booby traps. My job was to protect the troops.

What did you do after that?

I became a squad leader.

What are a squad leader's responsibilities?

He is in charge of the squad. He gets the orders from his commander and then goes down to the squads. Then he takes his squad out to do day maneuvers and ambushes. They go into the villages and try talking to the people. They have to find out where the enemy is and help the villages.

How long did you do that?

For five months.

Where were you stationed in Vietnam?
I first was stationed on Hill 55. The base camps are just hills over there. Then I was stationed on L Z Baldy.

Was that in the hills or in the flatlands?
It was in the flatlands, but the highest point in the area. They made base camps there so that you could watch the entire area around you.

Where did most of the fighting take place?
There were territories that we called, for example, Arizona Territory and Death Valley. We were on the base camp hill for four days, and then the rest of the time was spent out in the jungles.

How long did the battles usually last?
Sometimes ten minutes, sometimes an hour, sometime three days.

How long were you in Vietnam?
Thirteen months.

Can you describe what an average day was like during the war?
An average day was hot, very hot. Usually we were in the villages during the day. Then we did patrols. We would have different squads that would take patrols out to find the enemy and do what we had to do with them.

How many men did you work with on a daily basis?
There were about 55 men in my platoon. Usually we worked under a company, and there were probably about 300 men in that.

What kinds of weapons did you use daily?
We all carried grenades. I carried an M16 when I first came into the country. I carried an M79 grenade launcher for a short period, but for most of my tour in Vietnam, I carried an M14.

Did you use helicopters to get around?
Yes, anytime we needed gun support, or if we were being surrounded. We always had helicopters taking out our dead and wounded.

Do you have any experiences from battle that you'd like to share? Any difficult experiences?
I had to fight with a bayonet once. That is one on one. That's where my first confirmed kill was. In addition, finding U.S. servicemen beheaded by the Vietcong. Also, leaving one-night patrols you would be talking to a close friend next to you and the next thing you know he is dead, shot between the eyes. You are thinking that it could have been you. The reason the men were beheaded was because the Vietcong believed that if part of the body was missing that person would not go into the next life.

How many people did you kill?
Twenty-one confirmed kills. I kept grenade pins and hooked them in my bush cover to keep track of how many enemies I killed.

Could you explain any experiences you had with body counts or kill ratios?
I think it was August that we were in a big battle. It is the battle that I was wounded in. We were hit by about 2000 gooks. We actually ran out of ammunition. We had to go at them with bayonets.

How did being wounded have an impact on your role in the war?
Not much. I just had shrapnel in my face and arms. It did not affect me.

Were you ever involved in an ambush? Could you describe it?
Yes I was. It is where you go out in the evening, just before dark, and find a trail where you know the enemy has been moving through, and you set an ambush for them.

Did you ever have any experience working as a tunnel rat?
Yes, I did work as a tunnel rat for a while. I had to crawl in tunnels with a light and a 45 and search out the enemy.

Did you ever have any problems in the tunnels encountering booby traps?
Yes. Booby traps were part of everyday over there. However, combat rather than booby traps killed most men.

While you were there, did you ever take prisoners or was anyone you know taken prisoner?
We took prisoners. We tried to take them all prisoners. We had one corpsman that was taken prisoner ,and we found him two days later, dead, with his eyes burnt out.

What did you do with the prisoners once you took them?
We would question them, and we had Kit Carson scouts, or I think that is what they were called. They were actually North Vietnamese that had turned to our side. We would question them, and then we would call in helicopters to take them to our base camps.

Did they ever help you learn where the enemy was located?
Some information; sometimes we found out where they were located.

Were they reluctant to give you any information?
Yes, extremely reluctant.

Did you ever see any of your friends die?
Yes, we lost a lot of friends. Every man in my unit was a friend. One minute they would be by you, and the next minute they would be dead. You felt as if you were next, or why him, he was one of the best. You feel sick, then you get mad, and then you want to get even.

Did you make any lasting friendships during the war?
I believe so.

Are you still in contact with any of those people today?
The one that I was in contact with has since been killed in a car accident.

"WE HAD ONE CORPSMAN THAT WAS TAKEN PRISONER, AND WE FOUND HIM TWO DAYS LATER, DEAD, WITH HIS EYES BURNT OUT."

While you were in Vietnam, what did serving your country and patriotism mean to you.
My country means a lot to me. I would have done anything I could have to serve well.

Was that the main reason that you went to fight?
Yes, and because we didn't know what Vietnam really was. The way that they fought the war, we could have won Vietnam. We had a few greedy people back here that were making too much money off of Vietnam. That's why we were there so long.

Was Vietnam how you expected it to be when you enlisted?
Not really. I didn't think that it was going to be as pretty as it was. It was a beautiful country. There were banana trees, snow mountains, farm lands, and rivers. They had white sand deserts and the ocean. It was like a bunch of countries rolled into one. The Shrines of Buddha were all over. I didn't like the elephant grass, though. It was about ten feet tall and would cut you like a knife.

When you went to Vietnam were you expecting something totally different? Did it seem like the people back in the United States had no idea what was going on?
The thing is that the news media hurt the troops more than they did good for them. Not like in the wars now, where they keep a lot from the people. In Vietnam, they almost told them that we were coming in for a battle. They went out with loud speakers on planes and told them that the marines were coming in that all of the "friendlies" should get out.

"ONE DAY YOU ARE TALKING TO A FRIEND AND THE NEXT DAY YOU COULD BE CARRYING OUT HIS BODY."

What was the hardest part of being in the war?
The fear of dying and being away from home. There's so much fear inside of you, and you are afraid that it's going to come out. One day you are talking to a friend, and the next day you could be carrying out his body.

Did you have any opinions regarding the anti-war movement back in the States while you were in Vietnam?
Yes, it hurt us deeply. We thought that the American people should have been behind us a lot more than they were.

What kind of reception did you get when you came back to the United States?
Very poor. They called us baby killers, savages, cowards, and losers. They spat on us and threw things at us.

Was there a lot of emotional or physical stress that came upon you?
Oh yeah, seeing bodies everyday.

Did you have any difficulties dealing with memories when you got back?
Yes. If a car backfired or if I heard a loud noise, I would hit the ground. I could not handle it if someone would come up behind me. I slept with a knife under my pillow. If someone touched me, I would turn around and swing at them before I even knew what had happened. I dreamt about being under fire all of the time. Also, taking cover and running out of ammunition.

Are you still having problems with those?
No, when I started talking about it, it seemed to help. I started talking about it when I realized that I could

not stand to look at Vietnamese people in our country. I found myself looking at them with hate. It took me a long time to realize that they were not the enemy.

What do you think that they could have done differently to win the war?
Just go out and win it. Go out and fight the battles, not go after them and then have to stop. There were areas you could not go in, like Cambodia for instance. They would run across the border, and you could not go after them. It would have been nice if we would have had more support from our people back here. When you have the American people behind you, you are going to win any battle. There is not going to be a battle lost when you have the American people behind you. That is what happened in Vietnam.

Could you explain any interactions you had with Agent Orange? How do you think it affected you?
We walked through the areas where the chemicals were sprayed. We ate our food in those areas, and we slept in it. All of the base camps were sprayed to kill the vegetation. Health wise, I had jungle sores and infections, which I still have today. In addition, new problems could creep up at any time. My son has several birth defects and was born five weeks early. My wife had three miscarriages. I also have to live with the fear of getting cancer.

Is there anything else that you'd like to share with us?
When we were in jungles, in the snow mountain area, they had rock apes. At least that is what we called them. If you threw things at them, they would throw it back at you. They were between three and four feet tall. We tried to capture one, but it kicked our butts. We concluded to leave them alone.

Is there any message that you have for young people today about the war?
I do not want to see anybody go through a war, but I believe that this is a beautiful country, and I believe we should keep it free.

Since Zunker's tour of duty in Vietnam, he has worked as a machine tender at the Brokaw Paper Mill for 30 years. He is married to Linda Zunker, who he vacationed with during his period of R &R during the war.

Interviewed and transcribed by Jessica Gelhar and Chelse Radant

RECONNAISSANCE

D.C. EVEREST AREA SCHOOLS

Reconnaissance

In every battle and war since the dawn of mankind, knowledge of the enemy has been important. Scouts were sent out and later cavalry patrolled and provided information about the movement of the enemy. This was no different in Vietnam.

Patrols that entered the field had a "point man" who led the way watching for signs of trouble. Helicopter units had light and speedy helicopters that flew low to the ground hoping to draw fire and find the enemy. The Air Force provided sleek and powerful jets armed with large cameras that took photographs of the terrain in the hope of locating the enemy. Satellites circled the globe hourly taking images of the ground would be studied in great detail. The need for information was vital at all levels of involvement.

In Vietnam, the ground forces usually identified a unit or members of a unit to serve in the capacity of "recon". Many of those individuals were volunteers since the idea and the practice does have risks. Very often small patrols would go out seeking that information, and they would encounter large enemy forces. Later as the need grew, individual companies were designated "long range patrol," and they were assigned to larger parent organizations. These independent "LRRP" companies totaled nine in number according to Shelby Stanton's Vietnam, *Order of Battle* (U.S. News Books, 1981). For example, the 75th Infantry battalion was a parent organization for fourteen companies. Again, as mentioned, individual companies of combat infantrymen would have their own personnel designated when patrols and other activities took place.

Frank Biesel

Biesel, a combat infantryman, served in the 5th Calvary from January, 1968 to January, 1969. He later transferred to a recon outfit and finished his year in country. Beisel re-enlisted four years later.

The "C" stands for company, the "2/5" stands for battalion (2) and the five stands for the 5th Cavalry. It was a regiment but they called it cavalry. Then you have Alpha and Charlie troop (trp) of the 1st squadron, 9th Cavalry, the "Black Hats." I was in Vietnam from January, 1968 until January, 1969 when I went back to the states. I was at Ft. Hood for a few months, and then I volunteered to go back from September, 1969 until November, 1970, and then I got out. I went to college, was on the Dean's list and all that stuff, and then I went back in the service in 1973. I became a military policeman because I could not see myself as an infantryman in a peacetime army, and after that I came to work at D.C. Everest in 1977.

When you go into the service, they train you basic stuff; they train you for conventional warfare. Vietnam was unconventional warfare. It was guerrilla warfare; it was a war of attrition. A lot of people don't get that. We fought the war at first with the Green Berets and stuff. They were sent in to do counterinsurgency. They train small units, and they go out and fight the Viet Cong. Back in 1968 when the Tet offensive occurred, the North Vietnamese really got involved, and that's when the U.S. started bringing in all the troops in 1967 and 1968.

> *"WHEN YOU GO INTO THE SERVICE, THEY TRAIN YOU BASIC STUFF. THEY TRAIN YOU FOR CONVENTIONAL WARFARE. VIETNAM WAS UNCONVENTIONAL WARFARE. IT WAS GUERILLA WARFARE; IT WAS A WAR OF ATTRITION."*

So it was a war of attrition; they fought it like they fought the Indian wars in the old west. They put out bases all around the country, forts and mini forts. Cam Ranh Bay was a main supply base, and Da Nang was a main supply base. Tan San Nhut was the Air Force base outside Saigon. The idea is they have small forts all around fire support bases. At first when I went there, they were called LZs, landing zones. That was their designation because it was a 1st Cavalry outfit, and you landed your helicopters there, and they were secure areas and they were guarded and everything; they had companies there. Then they came out with the fire support base because they had artillery and stuff stationed on them so they could fire support for the infantry units. You would go out from the base.

My second tour there, I was in a recon platoon. Those are the guys that go out and find the enemy without the enemy finding them. Sometimes you mess up, and they catch you, but most of the time you go out, find the enemy, find out who, what, where, when, and why, and they send in more troops to eliminate that, and then they leave. Then they go back and forth, and they figured that if they cause enough enemy loss, the enemy would sue for peace and stop the war, which they eventually did. But, they didn't give up, the Vietnamese. The whole area of Southeast Asia has been in war for over three hundred years constantly, and they had just beaten the French in the 50s. Ten years later we come walking in, and we're going to support the South Vietnamese government, make sure it stayed democratic, because the communists were making inroads in South Vietnam and we didn't want that, so that's why we went in there.

"WE WALKED INTO A HORNET'S NEST IN THE A SHAU VALLEY. THEY WERE BUILT UP, THEY HAD RADAR CONTROLLED ANIAIRCRAFT GUNS, THEY HAD ARTILLERY, THEY HAD EVERYTHING THERE, AND IT WAS MURDEROUS."

When you came to Vietnam you came into one of three places, Cam Rahn Bay, Saigon, or up by Da Nang. The Marines came in through Da Nang most of the time. What you did was spend two days to a week at a replacement center. They assigned you to a unit, and once you got assigned to a unit, you got shipped out to your unit either by helicopter or plane, whichever was available. Sometimes you just stayed right there, and once you got to your unit, they trained you for another week on booby traps. What they mainly did was get you climatized to the climate. It was just humid, and it just drops you. If you have ever been in a hot climate, multiply that by ten, and that will give you an idea of what humidity was like in that country. In the 1st Cav, you learned how to repel out of helicopters. You went through lectures on booby traps and stuff. You have to understand, it takes ten people to support one combat person. Only five percent of the troops in Vietnam were actual combat troops; the rest were all support personnel.

They had ten hundred thousand men there at one time, and just over 50 thousand got killed, but the idea is that it takes a lot of people to support one man. You have artillery support for the infantryman; you have mortar teams that stayed back on the base; you have refrigeration experts, cooks, supply clerks, finance clerks; all these people got sent over to Vietnam. Just because you are not combat arms doesn't mean you're not going to end up in a war. You have to support the combat troops. Once you get through the familiarization course someplace, then they send you to the individual units. I was lucky. I got sent to the 1st of the 9th Cav, the first tour. The 1st of the 9th Cav was a helicopter unit. They had light observation helicopters called LOHs; they had slick ships in '69. Those were UH-1s, hueys, helicopters they were. They fastened 50 caliber machine guns and 3.5 rocket launchers to the skids of the Hueys, and they made those into gunships. The cobras didn't come until '69. The OH-13s were observation helicopters. The LOHs didn't come in until '69 either, and they were still experimenting with the 1st Cav, and they didn't know what they were doing. They didn't know what kind of tasks they would face, so they didn't know what type of helicopter was needed.

My unit consisted of light observation helicopters, OH-13 and slick ships, UH-1s. I was assigned there as a radio operator in the TOC, the tactical operations center. That is the main headquarters for that unit. I was in Alpha troop; so Alpha troop's TOC was at LZ English. I slept through a mortar attack my first night there. Mortar rounds were flying in and I slept right through it. I didn't get to a bunker or anything. Third week I was there we had a ground attack, and I had to climb up on top of the bunker with an M-60 machine gun and shoot anybody that was out there. I watched one VC blow up a bunker with a bunch of infantryman in there, the Blues. The same guy tried to run over to the helicopter, and I just sprayed him with the M-60 and I hoped I hit somebody; it was just flashes in the middle of the night.

You weren't really sure. The next morning we got up, cleaned up, and sent a patrol out. That's the way it went just about every day. You got mortared or rocketed; that was the life of the combat troop. This was located by Pleiku. We were in the central highlands. The 1st Cavalry division sent "A" troop up to the DMZ in March 1970, and we went up for a month because the Marines requested a helicopter unit up there so they could suppress enemy activity. In over a month we killed over 1000 VC or NVA infiltrating there and cut off their supplies. They shot rockets at us, 122 mm from the other side of the DMZ. It was cold up there; we couldn't believe how cold it was up there in that part. It's all mountains up through there, and it gets cold at night. We were in sleeping bags. Until then we walked around in T-shirts or no shirts and shorts and stuff. Up there we could see our breath.

From there we got sent back down, and they opened up a new base, Camp Edwards. It used to be the base of the 101st Airborne. That was around Ta Ninh, which is near Pleiku. Then we got involved with the A Shau Valley. If you have seen the movie *Platoon,* that takes place in the A Shau Valley. We walked into a hornet's nest in the A Shau Valley. They were built up; they had radar controlled antiaircraft guns; they had artillery; they had everything there, and it was murderous. It was bad, real bad. We went to Khe Sanh; I was there for Khe Sanh, A Shau Valley, Tet offensive and the incursion into Cambodia. So I was there for all the significant events plus Ho Chi Minh's birthday, when they hit Camp Evans and blew up the ammo dump.

Camp Evans was the size of a piece of property from Alderson St. to Highway 29 and from Shopko to County J. It took you fifteen minutes to drive from one side to the other in a jeep. It was a huge base. It was a division headquarters, and they had helicopters all over the place. At the same time, they put the ammo dump right next to the fuel dump which was very stupid, but they were saving time because they could reload and refuel and get out of there with their helicopters. The VC fired one rocket. I was standing next to my bunker near the officer's mess, and I was just going to go on top, and I hear this whoosh. I saw the trail of the rocket, and it landed in the fuel dump. They had about thirty guys working, and it went off. I ran to the top of the bunker, and rounds were flying over our heads and exploding. We had a small break room where we could sit down and play cards and whatever, and then we had the main radio room where we had a hugh bank of radios. I went down there because I knew they needed help with the radios, so they said to go to the break room and get more pads, and as I did that, the main ammo dump blew. It picked me up, and I was ten feet underground. The shock wave picked me up and threw me through a plywood wall, and I landed on my back. Another guy was standing over me and asked if I was OK. I said yes, and he told me to get off the floor. And then the fuel dump of 50,000 gallons of JP4 and diesel fuel and all kinds of fuel in these hugh rubber bladders went off. One round hit that, and it blew and it wiped out everything. People a mile away were knocked off their feet. It was horrendous. Everything was knocked over by the blast. Rounds were cooking off for three weeks. You would be driving to division headquarters and a round would go off.

After the fuel blew, we climbed up on our bunkers and decided this was like the fourth of July. We couldn't do anything about it because you couldn't get near it because the ammo was cooking off. So we would be sitting there in our lawn chairs on top of the bunker drinking a beer and watching the fireworks. A round would come in and fly over by us, and we were making bets to see where they landed. This is a fire support base by Ta Ninh just west of the black Virgin mountain, about twelve miles west of there. On Christmas and New Year's Eve they fire off all the rounds from a base on the top of the mountain, and they would have a nice fireworks show.

Could you describe the fire support base?
This is how they create a fire support base. What they do is fly out a basic combat engineer company with bulldozers. First they blow down all the trees in the woods with det cord. Demolition cord looks like a rope, and they tie it around the tree and put a blasting cap to it, put a little timer to it, pull the timer, walk away, and the tree is destroyed and falls down. The bulldozer pushes it away. The bulldozers flatten everything, and they start in the center and they push the dirt out in a big circle. They make a berm, a pile of dirt. That becomes a wall around the fort. In the berm you build firing positions. They are little and big foxholes, with sandbags, about chest high, and you put extra magazines for the M-16, grenades, flares, 40mm rounds in there. You have your claymore mines in there stacked up. From the firing positions in the berm you have a flat area. You put your claymore mines and trip flares in that flat area. A claymore mine has two pegs that are adjustable and a sight. You have two places where you can screw in a blasting cap attached to an electical wire. On the front it says "front" and on the back it says "back." Nobody underestimates the intelligence of the average infantryman. This is loaded with C-4, a plastic explosive. You can whip that up, light it on fire, you can jump on it, you can beat it, and it won't explode. Put a blasting cap in there and it explodes. On the front of it there are 680 double OO buck rounds, BBs, and it will clear out anything from four inches above the ground. It will go out 120 yards and it has a backblast of 120 feet. I saw what happened to a VC who was dumb enough during an attack to crawl up in front of one of these mines and use it as a rifle rest. There was only a small part of the barrel that remained. Everything else was gone; blew him away. There was a 100-foot wire and a clicker. The clicker looks like a box, an electrical clicker. You squeeze the box twice, and it shoots an electrical charge which blows up the mine. It is very effective, and you can use it as a booby trap. You can fix it so that it is attached with a wire across the trail, and you set it low and a person will not see it, and they will touch it with their toe and pull the wire tight, and that trips the trigger and the charge explodes. There were also trip flares which were little cylinders and they were attached to a wire, and when a person brushes the wire, it pulls out the retaining pin and it goes off and shoots a flare up into the air and lights up the whole area.

"YOU BECAME PROFESSIONAL AT FALLING ASLEEP, AND YOU COULD WAKE UP INSTANTLY AND BE FULLY AWAKE."

Did the VC ever get into the base camps?
Yes, the VC could slip through the wire. We would put beer and soda cans with rocks in the can and attach them to the wire so we could hear them if the wire was moved. The VC could slip right through there and come right up to us. They would not make a sound. They also had pho-gas. Pho-gas was a 50-gallon barrel with a claymore mine. It was half sunk into the ground. Pho-gas was a mixture of diesel fuel, JP-4 fuel, and soap flakes. You mix it up in that barrel and put the lid on it and bury it half way into the gound. It was instant napalm. It is an old formula that has been used for years and years. What would happen is that a big force would be coming and pho-gas was one of your last defenses when they attacked the berm. Once you were being overwhelmed by a large force, you could hit the pho-gas. It was instant napalm, and it would make "crispy critters." You usually had two lines of concertina wire called "razor wire." You had an outer line and an inner line, then you had the main defense, and then you had artillery and mortar, and you had a sniper tower, if you were lucky. The tree line was two hundred yards out. It always happened at night or just at the crack of dawn when everyone was still tired. When you first go out at dark, everyone is alert, and you take your shift of two hours on and two hours off and rotate among your buddies, and at dawn you are tired. You can't smoke and you can't play music to keep you awake, so they would attack at those vulnerable times. We had "red lights"

or "mad minutes." The siren would go off, and everybody would jump out of their bunkers and stuff, run up to the berm, and just unload. You spray everything on full auto, everything you had you fired. And they would do that randomly at night. Some nights they wouldn't do it, and some nights they would. They would do it sometimes two or three times in one night.

This is a frontier outpost in the middle of the jungle. The closest help is twenty to thirty minutes away. Closest army base is thirty miles away, which is a main base, so you are stuck out there with the troops. Our strength was between one hundred and two hundred men. We had a company or a platoon of artillery, five pieces plus mortars. Units in the field could call in and get fire support from these bases. Usually the guns were 155mm. You got so used to the artillery going off, at first it made you jump ,and later you could sleep through anything. You became professional at falling asleep, and you could wake up instantly and be fully awake. That is one thing combat would do to you was improve your reflexes 100 percent.

When you went to Vietnam and if you survived the first three months and the last thirty days, you were home free. It takes three months to learn everything you need to know to survive in combat, and if you aren't wounded or killed in the first three months, you will survive your tour. The last thirty days, you start thinking about how "short" you are, a short timer. All you start thinking about is going home, and you relax and you keep your mind on the combat situation. That is when you get killed. We had a guy with twenty-four hours left before he went home. He talked this helicopter pilot into giving him a ride around the base so he could take pictures from the air, and a VC sniper shot him through the forehead when he was 100 feet in the air. Killed him twenty-four hours before he was supposed to go home. His best friend climbed up on the barracks and starting shooting the Vietnamese that were in the camp next to ours. Just shooting them. We knew that there were VC sympathizers in there; we used it for intelligence gathering. We had to pull him off. He had killed five. He was sent to see a psychiatrist.

"YOUR FIELD PACK WEIGHED SEVENTY POUNDS. IN YOUR FIELD PACK, YOU CARRIED A PONCHO LINER, A PONCHO, ONE LINK OF M-60 MACHINE GUN AMMO, A CLAYMORE MINE, TRIP FALRE, EXTRA PAIRS OF SOCKS, GRENADES, AND YOUR RATIONS."

Long Binh was the main jail in Vietnam. This was the main stockade where drug runners and murderers and rapist were sent. They went there before they were sent back to the US. It was as big as Cam Ranh Bay, which was even bigger. You had to salute the officers there, that's how big it was. In a combat zone, you don't salute anybody. When you get to base the officers tell you not to salute them. We went to another base, and it was my first tour, and everyday at 2:00 pm a sniper would come up and shoot at the officers. He fired five shots, and then he would disappear. We went to the berm and looked for him, and all the officers hid. That was his job, to kill the officers. We had this one officer and everybody hated him, and at 2:00 o'clock he was walking down the flightline and every enlisted man in our company saluted him, and the VC started shooting at him. They never hit him, the VC must have been cross-eyed and bow-legged. They couldn't hit the broad side of a barn.

Later in the war the big base camps like Cam Ranh Bay and Da Nang, and Long Binh had a lot of support personnel. They were real strict about uniforms, haircuts, and all that. I went to Long Binh once to see a guy who had been wounded in a firefight. When the helicopter picked us up the platoon sergeant told them to fly us over to Long Binh to see how this guy was doing. So they flew us there. We had been out in the jungle for three weeks and we stunk. In the infantry you do not wear deodorant, after shave, etc: You don't change your clothes, you don't wear underwear but you do wear socks. The heat would give you jungle rot if you wore clothing that was tight. Americans smell different from Vietnamese because they eat rice and fish and some meat. Americans eat a lot of meat so their sweat smells a lot different. You can actually tell the difference. We flew into Long Binh and we got off the helicopter and the pilot said he would be back in two hours. As we are walking toward the hospital, we are covered with mud, blood, and we are all wearing boonie hats and loaded down with all our gear, ammo, etc: This officer walks up and he starts chewing us out for not saluting. You could hear the bolts closing on our weapons. We stated that we were in a combat zone, but he said that on that base we were not. Get those boots shined up he said, and we said, "Yes, sir." In the hospital they made us wash our hands and faces; we were filthy. When we finished our patrol we threw our uniforms away. We took a shower on a platform with a sprinkler system under 50 gallon barrels. We stepped off and a helicopter would fly over and coat us with that red dirt. You would turn around and go back in.

Captured weapons from Cambodian Invasion

What is Recon?
Recon is going out and finding the enemy. Intelligence sources say there are such and such an enemy in such and such area. Recon goes out and finds out who is there and what is going on. We fly out in a helicopter and drop in a small clearing and get into the woods, assemble, and start our patrol. We spend anywhere from three days to a month, and we were resupplyed once a week. If we got lucky, we would get food and other supplies. Otherwise we got LRRP rations which was dehydrated food rations. You see pictures of soldiers with socks hanging from their packs. This is where you kept your C-rations. You put cans of C-rations in the sock, one on top of another, and tie the end. Your field pack weighed seventy pounds. In your field pack you carried a poncho liner, a poncho, one link of M-60 machine gun ammo, a claymore mine, trip flare, extra pairs of socks, grenades, and your rations. The amount of rations depended on how long you were going to be out. We were lucky and after a while we got LRRP rations. It was dehydrated and all you had to do was dump water in there and mix it up. I didn't drink coffee, so I swapped my coffee for hot chocolate tablets. You go out there and you see these guys wearing a towel on their head all the time and that was to take the pressure of the straps off your shoulders, because the heat was such that you sweated a lot. You carried four quarts of water in canteens. You also carried purification tablets so you could go to a bomb crater and get water. We took our baths in bomb craters and every-

body would circle the bomb crater and two or three guys would get in the water. To go to the bathroom, you dug a hole, did what you had to do, and filled the hole up. After eating your C-rations, you flattened the cans, dug a hole, placed the cans in there, and covered them up. You did not want to leave anything for the enemy. The VC were famous for making booby traps with trash we left.

What about bugs, snakes, and other insects?

You had to deal with the snakes and the insects. In my first month, September 1968, I was at An Khe, which was the division headquarters for the 1st Cavalry, and there was a place they called "Hong Kong Row." It had the 1st Cav patch by the side of the mountain. They had a VC attack on my third day, and we were going to division training camp. Six VC made it to the outpost on the top of the mountain and tried to destroy it, and they got all these replacements, and they said that they were going up the mountain, so they said if we run into any VC we were supposed to kill them. We are all armed with M-16s. We all had magazines of ammo, and we went up the mountain, and I got there and looked right in the eyes of a mongoose. It made a shriek, and I screamed and fell off. We got to the top of the mountain and this sergeant told us not to sit on the rocks that were there. We were tired, and it was a nice day and we wanted to get some sun. He told us to look at our feet, and they were covered with scorpions. There were scorpions all over the place. We were kicking scorpions off and brushing them off and people were screaming and jumping up and down. Snakes were bad too.

We were on a mission and this guy got his field pack hooked on a piece of bamboo and he injured his back, so we rigged up a stretcher

"THE GOVERNMENT PAID YOUR WAY TO AUSTRALIA, THAILAND, HONG KONG, JAPAN, KOREA, OR HAWAII. IF YOU WRE MARRIED, YOU COULD MEET YOUR WIFE IN HAWAII, SPEND A WEEK, AND THEN COME BACK.

and we carried him to this field. Bamboo grows on mounds and then they grow out and form umbrellas, and we camped out under them. When you went to a clearing, you sit down and watch out for what is in front of you. I was sitting on my field pack and it was my day for carrying the shovel, and I had my rifle leaning against my right leg and the shovel over my knees, and I felt this pressure on my left foot, and there was a bamboo pit viper crawling across my left foot. A bamboo pit viper will bite you, and in fifteen seconds you are dead. That is how deadly it is. It had just shed its skin, so it was bright pink and green. It was in the shade, and I didn't want to bother him. We didn't wear our boots bloused in Vietnam we left the pants loose cause it was cooler and the snake could have crawled up my pant leg. I was watching the snake, and he looked at me and crawled over my left boot and then over the right boot. I just sat there and wouldn't move. I heard someone call my name and he came over and asked me if I was sleeping. He saw the snake's tail just as it was going off my boot. He jumped back and I jumped up and flew back about twenty feet. The snake crawled up into the bamboo, and I decided it hadn't killed me and I wasn't going to kill the snake. I had two bad encounters with snakes. One time a snake was so fast that it flew past me. It was long and it was brown, and it went past me in a rush. One time we were taking a break and I was leaning on my pack and I had a book and I was reading and my squad leader walked up and said freeze, don't move. I just laid there, and he pulled out his machete and killed a scorpion right near my head. A scorpion will not kill you, but you will get very sick. We also had fire ants and they can sting you and it burns. Lion ants have large pinchers and they will pinch you. They also give you sexual orientation lectures. "Heinz 57" variety lectures about venereal disease in Asia. They still have guys in military hospitals that have contracted these diseases, and they haven't found a cure yet.

What did you do for rest and recuperation?

After six months of service in Vietnam you got R&R, that's rest and recuperation. That was what the military called it. The government paid your way to Australia, Thailand, Hong Kong, Japan, Korea, or

Hawaii. If you were married you could meet your wife in Hawaii, spend the week, and then come back. If you were single, they flew you to Australia or one of the other places. I spent a week in Australia and one in Taiwan. You took a thousand dollars with you. When guys were paid, they asked you how much you wanted. If you were in the infantry, fifty dollars was enough. The rest was put in an account for you. When you went on R&R, you took a couple of thousand dollars with you. You had that much money to spend in a week on women and booze.

The army guarantees you in a combat unit, two cans of beer a day plus two cans of coke. They did not give that to you when you were out in the boonies; they gave that to you when you came back from the boonies. There was one place called "Doc's Place" because he was our medic and the dopers hung out there. The drunks would go to the EM club. I was kind of in-between because I didn't like to do dope or get drunk. I felt that it ruined my senses. I liked to get drunk on R&R, and then I got so drunk they had to carry me. The idea of guys smoking dope all the time was true. You could walk through different areas and smell the pot. Nobody did anything about it. You could buy it right over the fence from the Vietnamese. You could buy a half-pound of pot for five dollars. You could get opium for ten dollars. The guys that used heroin were real echelon guys, and as far as drugs were concerned, I had one bad incident. I was walking back one time, and doc and the other were there smoking cigarettes and stuff and they offered me some. Nothing happened until I realized I was walking about ten feet in the air. We were the ready response group. When you were out for thirty days, they gave the whole platoon three days off. They send you back to Tay Ninh. They had barracks there, with con-

crete and you had three days of R&R. There were bands playing there and steaks on the grill and hugh containers of ice with beer available. It went like that for three days in a row. The first day everybody was bombed and the base came under attack. On the second day we were ordered to pack it up and return, and we were still drunk. We took two cases of beer and picked us up and dropped us off about 1000 meters from the base. We were expected to march back to the base, and if we saw any VC we were supposed to shoot them. We started walking, bumping into stuff and we got to the base just around dawn. There were bodies everywhere. We had this little Hawaiian guy that was part of the mortar team, and he won the Distinguished Service Cross, which is the second highest medal next to the Medal of Honor. He was from Hawaii. He jumped out of his bunk at the beginning of the attack, grabbed a machete, and killed twenty guys with that. He had bodies piled up shoulder high. The place was smoking. We saw GIs picking up bodies, and we were happy we missed it all. We walked in there and the battalion commander saw us drinking beer, and he said you guys are going into the jungle for the next month by coming into my base drunk. We said OK, and we packed off for another month.

Can you tell us about one of your missions?
We got word that there was a VC strike force about battalion size, which is about 500 men in this one area. This was near the Parrot's Beak area. It was near the Cambodian border. There was a peanut shaped area, and we landed there with our helicopters. We looked down, and there was a bunch of South Vietnamese officers and stuff, and they were there to help us with their troops. We set up a defense perimeter and we waited over there. The rest of the battalion was coming in the next morning or afternoon, and we were to secure and check out this area. Next morning we began walking on the edge of the field and we started noticing spider holes. Spider holes are pits dug into the ground with enough room

for one person, and the VC would hid in there, pop up and shoot, and get back down. We started walking into the woods, and we started to see fresh cut trees. The wood was freshly cut, and we knew we were getting into something bad. As we moved through, we noticed a clump of bamboo. We set up a defensive perimeter around it, and my squad was part of that. We went in with thirty-three guys, and my lieutenant set up next to the clump.

"THE LIEUTENANT TELLS THE COBRAS TO FIRE AT THE SMOKE, AND I AM RIGHT NEXT TO IT. THE ROCKET SHRAPNEL CAME AND HIT ME IN THE LEGS."

We had a former VC soldier working as a scout for our unit. My squad was picked first to do a cloverleaf. We made a big loop and then came back to the defensive position manned by the other squads. The other squads did that also. We went out about fifty yards and we saw a trail. I was "tail end Charlie." I was the grenadier, and I was carrying a 40mm grenade launcher. It fires high explosive, shotgun rounds, fleschettes, and flares. I had two claymores with me and a lot of ammo. We got on this trail, and I saw the imprint of a mortar base. With mortars there is a tube and a base that the tube attaches to. I was looking at that because it had rained a few days before, and this was a fresh base plate mark. All of a sudden I saw my squad leader coming back. There is a big tree ahead with bamboo around it. They come running back and they said that we had to get back to the platoon. They said that they had found where an enemy soldier had defecated in the woods and used a South Vietnamese surrender document to clean himself. He left it there. It was fresh. I ran forward and found the big tree. We had walked into an NVA camp of 500 men, and they saw us. We were pinned down, and a soldier named Bob Gilmore was hit and killed instantly where I had been kneeling. Everyone else dropped down and began firing.

I was behind the tree, and I began firing as fast as I could. When the 40mm grenade explodes, everything in a radius of five meters is hit with shrapnel. I just popped out as many as I could. I was told to suppress the enemy, and the other guys dropped back. When I looked around everyone was gone. I was there all by myself. Everything died down and got quiet, and I got up and moved real slow and quiet back to Gilmore and I checked him. He was dead. So I moved back to the tube position, and I ran into another soldier. He had been shot through the hips, and he was bleeding. I put a bandage on him and I was going to move him back to the position because we were only about fifteen feet from our perimeter. As I picked him up, his intestines and other organs fell out, and I set him down and bandaged him again. I told him that I would get the medic. They began shooting at me as I moved back to the perimeter. He started crawling out toward the wounded man. By the time we got back to the position, somebody started calling for "Blue Max" as loud as he could. This was the call sign for the cobra gunships. He wanted them to come in and fire. We had only been fighting for ten minutes. By the time we got there, he had been shot to pieces. We came back and there were big trees. The enemy started firing RPGs at our position. The rockets were full of high explosives. My platoon sergeant told me to shift to the left. As I did, the rocket hit and shrapnel was hitting another guy. A guy named Stone was hit, and I continued to move to the left. Everybody was firing like crazy, and we almost ran out of ammo. I crawled back to my pack to get more, and the platoon sergeant is telling everyone to make the circle smaller. We had to fall back and we didn't have any foxholes. A guy had an RPG rocket land between his legs and fail to explode. The trees were thick and we were between our guys and the enemy. We were pinned down for eighteen hours.

Finally they told us to leave our stuff and start crawling toward our positions, which we did. When we got back to our lines they had foxholes eight feet deep and most of us were out of ammunition. Luckily there was a grenadier there and he gave me a whole bunch of ammo. Once we got out of range, we plastered them with artillery. As the cobra were lining up, I was ordered to pop smoke so I grabbed a purple smoke grenade, and I threw it and it hit a tree and came back to within five feet of me, and I couldn't reach it because we were taking fire. The lieutenant tells the cobras to fire at the smoke and I am right next to it. The rocket shrapnel came and hit me in the legs. I started hollering, and another guy crawls over and helped me. I received the Bronze Star and the Purple Heart.

When you are done with your year, many people don't leave until the day before their tour is up. Up until then, you are loaded down with gear and doing your job. You get back to the replacement depot, they process you in one day, and you get on a plane, and you go home. It takes eighteen hours to get home, so when you arrive in the US, just two days before, you were killing people if you were a combat infantryman. You could have been in a firefight just a few days before. Your combat reflexes are still in action. I was walking down Wisconsin Ave. in Milwaukee, and a truck backfired, and I hit the ground. I rolled over alongside a building and a cop came over and said I must have just come home from the war. He told me I was safe now. It took me a long time to get adjusted. I went to the PX and I ordered a hamburger, fries, and a chocolate shake, and they had trays. Everything was on the tray, and some things fell and I caught everything before it hit the ground because my reflexes were so sharp. I could jump and be on the table in seconds because of my reflexes. I was six foot four and weight 184 pounds. I spent my 20th and 21st birthdays in Vietnam. I told people I was a Vietnam veteran but when I went to college I didn't tell anybody I was a veteran. I lost a girlfriend because I was a vet. We were "baby killers." People spit on us, and there was one World War II veteran who shook our hands in San Diego when we arrived home. I needed a period of time to adjust after I returned. It took me three years to adjust. I went back into the army and became a military policeman.

Biesel returned to civilian life as an welder for the A.O. Smith Company in Milwaukee and is now employed by the D.C. Everest School District.

Interviewed by Ryan Plisch

Mike Foley

Foley was drafted in 1968 and trained in demolitions. When he was in Vietnam, he served in I Corps and ended up a platoon leader performing counter insurgency operations.

This is the last day we were in the lowlands. Behind me is the clouds hanging on the mountaintops. Rocket ridge is the first ridgeline. Our solid green uniform blended in very well with the countryside and all around was better than a multi-colored uniform, ontrary to popular belief.

How did you get involved in the Vietnam War?
I was drafted into the Army.

Did you volunteer for the 101st Airborne?
No, I was allocated. Then I was selected as a replacement troop into B company 3/187 infantry division of the 101st airborne Division. This was the unit to first assault hill 941 known as Hamburger Hill. This unit has existed only three times in American History: once in WWII, once in Korea, and then Viet Nam. I did not go to Viet Nam as most did, with a unit I had trained with. The rest of the unit I trained with was assigned to the 1st Air Cavalry in Viet Nam.

Where did you train?
I was at Fort Leonard Wood for basic, and Fort Polk, and some special training under the MOS 11-Hotel, which included field expedient demolition. There were thirty of us guys who got trained. We were the only thirty guys in the Army at that time that were trained in field expedient demolitions, because they thought the North Vietnamese were going to start using tanks. And they did use seven tanks during the war, but that was all the tanks they used in combat. Did you ever see that movie, "Where Eagles

This is the history of rakkasan.

This is the famous motto of the 3/187. It means "umbrella people". The shape is a Japanese symbol of good luck. In my case that was true.

Dare." That's the 3/187 101st Airborne.

In what year were you drafted?
Must have been December of '68.

How long were you in the Vietnam War?
A little over a year.

The smoke you can see in the mountain valley in the background is a barrage of artillery from our fire support. They "prep" the landing zone prior to our assault. When the smoke cleared we made our descent. Some of us would take a catnap as we circled and waited to go in.

Were you a part of the parachuting group in the 101st?
No, at that time in Vietnam it wasn't parachuting; it was air-mobile. Basically I executed counter insurgency operations against the North Vietnamese. No parachuting involved. On occasion there was a rappel, but for the most part all combat assaults and other operations were onto a pre-planned landing zone. It was airmobile; we'd use helicopters.

The foothills west of Camp Evans. The first ridgeline is known as rocket ridge since the NVA would set up and sight their rockets from there. The lowland on the east is all abandoned rice fields. During the rainy season, much of the lowland you see here was crotch deep in water.

Where were you located in Vietnam?
In the Northern I-Corp, North of Phong Dien, the whole time in free fire zone in the field; in the jungles and lowlands, and the sand flats.

This is the countryside we referred to as the lowlands. It is west of Phong Dien looking southwest.

How did you become the Platoon Leader?
Through attrition, But I had some help. Our company promoted me to Sergeant. Soon afterwards, each company in the 101st airborne selected one combat experienced non-commissioned officer to attend a combat leadership session. I was selected by our company to attend. I was selected as the honor graduate of that course and was told I would be automatically promoted on orders from Major General John Wright Jr, the commanding General of the 101st. I also received a letter of commendation on his behalf. However, I never saw the paperwork for the promotion. They still owe me that one. Whoever was there on the ground, well like everything else, who ever is in charge on the ground, whatever happens more or less revolves around that person, right? So if you worked your way up and became responsible for others in the unit, you normally stayed in charge of that unit until either you messed up or something happens and someone else takes over. Most of thetime I was in charge of a platoon but I also served as a company

When I first arrived at Camp Evans in Viet Nam, there was a battle in which 19 American men were killed. I wondered what it would have been like to be on that hilltop. This picture was taken from that hilltop. It was the most beautiful and peaceful sunset I had ever seen. Yet I realized we were sleeping in the same place those men lost their life. I was devastated and thought "perhaps tonight". But we were fortunate. The next morning we were able to pack up our belongings and continue on a mission.

commander. At full strength our platoons were about 33 men, but usually there were around 19 and much of the time only 9 or 10 men. Others were assigned, and as they came and went, it was the responsibility of these who were constantly in the field to maintain a continuity of leadership. It didn't matter the rank of those who were out there; whenever something happened, every soldier was an integral part of the outcome. And in the absence of commissioned leadership, the men in the field relied on each other for support.

What were base camps like?

I was never in a base camp. I was always moving around in the field. I had an XM-16 rifle and a 45 cal pistol and the field uniform I had on, and would wear that for at least 30 days. Then you have your backpack, your poncho liner, poncho, and your food, eight grenades, 4 pounds of C-4, a claymore mine, four smoke grenades, two concussion grenades, a mechanical ambush device,

These are some of the members of my platoon on their way to a day at Eagle Beach and a steak dinner. They are on an amphibious personnel carrier.

21 loaded magazine clips, 100 rounds of machine gun ammo, a compass, a map, a radio battery, two extra pair of socks, a mess kit, shaving kit, writing paper, binoculars, camera, towel, helmet, flack jacket, jungle cap, machete, some first aid items, and usually 3.5 gallons of water and some iodine tablets and salt tablets. Usually about 5 to 15 days rations, and whatever personal items you had, and that was it. No underwear. No insignias except the screaming eagle. Everything I had when I reported to Camp Evans was taken and reallocated to others. The only time we would enter a limited fire zone was to sign our pay voucher or go in for a stand-down.

I am probably the only person to ever have a 40 round clip for the m16 rifle. I soon found out why we were only issued 20 round clips. The extractor would shear if more than 30 rounds were fired in one burst. Our kit Carson scout grabbed my rifle as we came under attack one night and let go with a burst right next to my ear. I ended up deaf in one ear for several days and a busted rifle.

What were your missions to do?

The last code name that I remember when I was over there was Sparrow Hawk. They'd give you a code word, and that code word was used to report your locations. You would always use your code name when using communications and the codeword for reporting your location. Just out of curiosity today I was looking up hawk, see. Well a hawk kills almost every type of small animal and bird. They eat different things. Hawks capture living animals, kill them instantly for food. They have sharp eyes, swift flyers; they pounce on their prey with lightning speed. They catch, crush, and carry off their prey. Then if you look at a Sparrow Hawk, mainly likes to eat only sparrows, a small bird. The name Sparrow Hawk, it was appropriate. It was basically a lot of the small counter insurgency operations. If the NVA became active in an area, our intelligence would become alerted thru surveillance that there was something going on in that area. So we'd go in and see. If the North Vietnamese were getting a foothold, we would drive them back out and gather intelligence about that unit. We were

This was a bunker complex we encountered on a jungle mountain saddle. The opening of each bunker was constructed in a fashion so even a direct hit would not let any flak in. I was ordered to draw this map and inventory what was left behind. The location of this complex is indicated in code on the middle bottom.

the most combat alert unit in the 101st. On 15-minute notice we would have to go on a combat assault.

Did you know where the enemy was?

This was a former VC company commander. He could talk little English. I later found out he was perhaps the most notorious of all the former VC commanders.

No, they'd shoot infrared pictures or gather intelligence. Where ever existed possibilities of enemy forces. Then we'd go and see what it was. We would also rely on Chu Hoi's to guide us using the information from their interviews. I did not particularly like having a former enemy soldier with me. On several occasions I intercepted cleverly concealed notes they would try and leave as we moved out of our night defensive position. I would send this information into the rear but I never ever received any info back. The chu hoi would be with us only for a short period of time. Their

This is a Chu Hoi that accompanied us on one mission to locate a field hospital.

information wasn't the greatest either. We also would employ Kit Carson Scouts to accompany us and act as advisor and interpreter; they were former enemy soldiers who went to work us. We had the most notorious of all Kit Carson Scouts. I found that out only after knowing him for some time. And then, many times a South Vietnamese interpreter who was familiar with the languages would accompany us.

This is an interpreter that traveled with us in the Street without joy area. He was from Saigon.

Did you fight against Vietcong or NVA mostly?

First part of my tour was in the area of the Street Without Joy that was a mixture of the North Vietnamese and Vietcong. Then the rest was mainly in the jungle, so then the North Vietnamese. At that time they were mostly trying to re-establish infiltration routes from the A Shau Valley.

What was your normal day like?

The normal day was survival. Just surviving the elements was 60%.

Were you involved in a lot of combat?

I was involved in over 50 combat assaults. At the time I had little appreciation for it but looking back I was glad to have control over the situations we found ourselves in. I had the most combat ready unit in the 101st. If some other unit was being overrun, we'd go in and chase them back out. They saw us coming and all the helicopters, and they would di-di mou - that was pretty good; they'd get out of the area. So actually a lot of people would be devastated to be in such a situation but we were always prepared

This is a picture of me in the Dong Ke Me Valley. My uniform is wet with sweat, just as if I had stepped out of a river. We searched this very rapid river for some time before we found this place to cross. Falling in would have meant no return.

and very aggressive. We always had our boots on at night and we always had our backpack in order. I could get any fire support needed within a few minutes except for a B-52 strike.

We went into Dong Ha and then up into the mountains to drive the NVA back off a firebase that had been overrun. My unit landed on a sandbar below the firebase. I led point up the mountain until we came to the trail that had been cut by the NVA. Three company of men participated in that operation. Thirty-eight allied men were casualties on the firebase.

Did you receive any medals?
Among some of the medals I received are two bronze stars and two air medals.

What were those for?
Well, you get a bronze star for basically if you make it six months in a combat zone in the 101st. I also got one for heroism. Here's my second Air Medal Award. There were four of us named on this order. The Air Medal Second Award, it was for twenty-five combat assaults. You get one air medal for each 25 combat assaults. It was usually a high attrition rate, lot of people in and out of the unit. Usually it was because of the elements. Most of the troops would not last long in the jungle because of the elements. They'd get jungle rot or malaria or other types of problems. Whenever I mentioned I was infantry and two air medals to a pilot or other armed forces personnel, they would do a double take.

Copy of orders of Foley's second air medal award.

Was the environment just as bad as the enemy?
Probably worse, the area we were in. If you're out in the elements, it will usually get you first. You actually had to have a high degree of respect for your personal condition in order to survive the elements. Mentally, if you were not in perfect condition, you could not cope. If you missed the smallest possible clue in your surroundings you would be in serious problems. I remember one time going thru the jungle in a perfectly serene area and suddenly my mind processed something I had seen seconds before, and I knew we were suddenly in a critical situation. One small thing out of place in a jungle of information might mean death or survival.

You can barely see the front door to a tunnel complex. To determine where all the openings were, we would use a mighty might, capable of blowing a high stream of air. Smoke grenades would be thrown in, and the hose from the Mighty Mite would drive the air through the tunnels and along with it, the smoke. Wherever an opening existed, smoke would possibly appear.

I got one bronze star for heroism.
It says, "Heroism in ground combat against hostile forces in the republic of Vietnam, July 1970." It says "squad leader", but it was B Company, 3rd Battalion 187th Infantry. (Have you ever heard of the B Company 3rd battalion, 187th infantry Division)? "During operations west of the Song Bo River in the foothills", we were on reconnaissance in force (RIF). "Ambush patrol" - we were on that every night. But we were on a search and clear operation. And "there was spotted some enemy troops along the riverbed". They told us to go in and see what was going on. So we went, actually the next day, to go and RIF out this area. So as we're going in they opened fire on us. We're in a large, abandoned rice patty; we were in the middle of it, got fired on, and got pinned down. We were in a big open field. We had no choice; either lie there and continue to be fired on and perhaps die, or get aggres-

These are four of the members of the patrol that was pinned down by NVA forces in an abandoned rice field. On the left (counterclockwise) is Posznanski, Nitsch who was badly wounded, Heyle who spent his last days in the field as a punishment, and Fisher who was the RTO.

sive. It sank in that this could be our final hour. That picture is still burned in my mind. So I asked who was going to assault their encampment while the rest of the unit work back to our rear and set up machine guns from a higher position we picked out. So I asked this fellow from Nebraska, Nitsch. Then of course, my RTO always went where I went (Fisher from New York). So the three of us would fire and move up on the position while the others would crawl to the rear. Basically that's what we did. It says, "Just crawling within 35 meters of the enemy position, Sergeant Foley threw hand grenades and delivered suppressive fire on the hostile. His actions enabled the squad to find cover and engage the enemy."

So then basically that is the reason I got this, and then after the operation was over, there was a large underground complex. So I called the rear. We didn't have enough demolition to blow it. So I had them bring out some demolitions after this ordeal was over. Nitsch and I went in and set the demolitions in the bunkers. And after we came out Nitsch told me to go back with the unit, he would blow it. I'd always have him blow all this stuff, so I said, "Oh I'll blow it, you go on back with the other guys." So Nitsch went back to marry up with the other guys, and I blew the demolitions. I heard another blast go off; I turned around and saw a big mushroom cloud of smoke. And he got hit by an RPG round, a booby trap. They had the whole perimeter of the complex booby trapped, and Nitsch never saw one. It tore all the flesh off the front of his leg from the instep to the knee; he was all filled with shrapnel, from head to foot. So I ran out with a troop who was from Puerto Rico. We called a Medivac and patched up his leg as best as we could with our field patches, then got him on the Medivac. I put him in for a silver star. He spent six months here in the U.S. hospital patching up his leg. Then, as a result, they gave me a bronze star also, but it was really because

Charles Fisher in his field office. Notice whip antenna, C-rations spread out so he can ponder what he might eat. Machete at hand, ammo box (which we all had one so as to help the machine gunner out), boots off so his feet dry out, sitting on his poncho so slugs won't smell him up, writing paper to his right when the mood hits him, and of course everything else is always in his pack which he is using as a backrest. Radio handset is close by so he can hear if we get a call.

"WE ENCOUNTERED MORE BOOBY TRAPS THAN ANY OTHER UNIT IN THE HISTORY OF THE UNITED STATES. IN ABOUT SIX WEEKS WE ENCOUNTERED ABOUT 250 BOOBY TRAPS."

I put Nitsch in for a silver star that we both got a bronze one. I don't know if Fischer got one, but he should have. I don't know where Nitsch is at today. I did see him once after Vietnam. He got out of the hospital, went up to a street corner, got in an argument with three guys. They beat him up, and he ended up back in the hospital. He was a big guy too, about 6'4", about 220 lbs. Overseas we were allowed two rations a day, so you'd only carry exactly what was going to keep you through the day, mostly water. So like me, I'd have a can of peaches and pound cake, crackers, and mostly water. When I went overseas I was 158 lbs. I came back I was

108 lbs. Nitsch was 185 lbs when he went overseas; when he came back he was 145 lbs. When I saw him he was 220 lbs. It took me about 15 years to get back over 150 lbs. They came in as individuals, and we left as individuals. In our unit, I can show you pictures of 9 or 10 guys I went in the jungle with, and I can't tell you any of their names, except maybe one or two. They'd be in and gone. (Showing pictures of unit Fredericks was with). He was right on another hilltop, another platoon on another hilltop. Basically we were on three different hilltops. (Reading from letter) We set up camp in the late afternoon on a high-saddle ridge. Then about 3 a.m. we were over run by a Sapper Unit. They were all around us, throwing satchel charges. (Talking) Satchel charge explosive that resemble soap, the size of a pound of butter with a blasting cap in it. The blasting cap, they'd usually have to light those. If they had to get through wire fences, they'd put it between their legs as they crawled along. They would get blown up by that satchel charge. They were over run; it was actually the leader's fault, their lieutenant. They never should have set up their night defensive on the L-Z. That night they stayed on the LZ, and the NVA knew where they were. They just went in and overrun them.

These are the men with me in the Dong Ke Me Valley. Slugs and bamboo vipers were very prevalent. There were leeches so small they could get in through the air holes on the boot instep. Everyone is drinking his share of water since it had been some time without. We were responsible to find our own water. While in this valley, we had no radio communication with the rear. The helicopter pilots knew our general location and would make contact with us when they brought in resupply.

I was on the other hilltop, next hilltop over. It was maybe 500 meter across, but 1000m down and 1000m up. They called in ARA and all this stuff, and they said on the radio "We're under attack. I don't think we're going to make it." Then the gun ships came in, firing their guns. After the NVA overran them, an NVA got hold of the radio, we were talking to them on.

"I SAID, 'GOD, IF YOU MAKE ME THE LEADER I'LL TRY TO GET NONE OF THEM KILLED, AMD I'LL TREAT THE VIETNAMESE WITH DIGNITY, AND I WON'T DO ANYTHING TO THESE PEOPLE THAT I WOULDN'T WANT DONE TO MYSELF.'"

Our company was set up in an old French fort west of Ap Pho Trach. A RIF had gone out to scout out the area along the slough to the north. Our snipper set off a booby trap and the most popular platoon sergeant was killed as a result. VC were spotted in that area and the cobra's were called in to provide support. I caught up with locals several days later in the same area unarmed and with some women and children. I told them to didimou as they had nothing to indicate they were doing anything sneaky.

He said, " you got your helicopter in to get your men, but we got your helicopter." A lot of the time they'd probe the perimeter, cut the wires to the claymore mines. When you set up a night defensive, you'd put out claymore mines. They have 700 pellets in it, and they'd blow in one direction. (Reading) we tried to detonate the claymore mines, but they didn't go off. Men were screaming and wounded all around me. (Talking now) This guy, his name was Fredrick; he was the M-60 machine gunner. He was not by his machine gun when they got attacked; he couldn't get to it. (Reading from letter) If I had tried to get to the machine gun, I would surely be killed. To this day, I believe the Lieutenant saved the rest of us from certain death." (Mike Foley talking again)

Then after the gun ships come in, they have rockets, 40mm grenades, and 7.65 caliber gatling guns. When they come in they scare the enemy off.

They come in, long way out, shoot usually three burst of rockets. Whoosh, Whoosh, Whoosh. As they get in closer, swooping down, they shoot their grenades, thump, thump, thump, thump, thump, thump. Makes them duck their head down Then they shoot the gatling guns just before they pull out of their dive. Brrrrrrrrrrrrrrrrrrrrrrrrrrrrrrt. That gives the cobra time enough to climb back out. They can usually make only three passes; that's it. When that's going on, things usually cool down; the enemy troops take cover. But mainly they make a lot of noise, but not too much would happen. All this time I could hear. We're in the jungle; I can see another hilltop. We're on one, and like at the end of the block is the other. There

it is, but if you're going to hump from here to there it would take three days to get there, going through the jungle. We couldn't get there in 10 minutes, it was 3-5 days. We could get 500m a day in the jungle. I've been in the jungle, only getting 300m a day, sunup to sundown. Less than three blocks. I usually had a Puerto Rican with me (they can fight but they don't have any voting rights). Once they volunteered for the military, then they could get in the U.S. This guys name was Angel Santiago. The last time I knew he was in New York City. I don't know what ever happened to him.

Santiago is on the left. When he came with us he could not speak any English. He only had a big white smile. Striplin is next, then Fredericks after he was put in for silver star when his unit was wiped out. Henry on the right, He was later awarded silver star and was seriously wounded after his unit was wiped out.

Did you run into a lot of booby traps in the jungle?

The unit I was in, we went in and cleared out an area called the Street Without Joy. It was the North of Phong Dien, Northern I-Corp. It was Viet Minh stronghold where they defeated the French in the 50's. This area was really heavy booby-trapped; every trail was

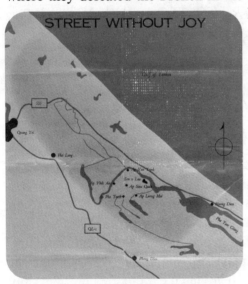

STREET WITHOUT JOY

The area to the right of the sign "QL1" is the area known as the "street without joy", a term coined by the French. It was the Viet Minh stronghold headquarters and was where the French met their final defeat in the 50's. There is a book by the same name.

heavily booby-trapped. We encountered more booby traps than any other unit in the history of the United States. In about six weeks we encountered about 250 booby traps. A lot of them wouldn't be 1 or 2 guys, but 19, 20 wounded or killed at a time. At first we were going to support the engineers as they cleared out the booby traps. They lost so many engineers that the engineers wouldn't go in anymore. They made us grunts do the clearing after that. I was with the first unit that went in the first day, and there were 15 to 19 guys, about 5 engineers. I was towards the front, then the medic (usually they spend three or four months in the field, and then they got to go in the rear). So the medic asked me to wait for him while he went to the bathroom. I was in the front of the unit, so I waited for him while he went. I was in the middle towards the back of the unit. We'd move along, wait for the engineers to clear traps. After half the day, they'd start to get sloppy. See they dig up and dig up and it was nothing. Then just, I think I saw three 105 mm rounds, someone stepped on the triggering device. There was a huge explosion; people blown all over. I had the radio,. I was the RTO at that time, and so I was carrying the radio. I got blown into a bamboo hedge and blacked out. When I came to, I was hanging in bamboo by a necklace, a bootlace, a medallion around my neck. I pulled it loose.

There were two guys behind me, the medic, David Merlo, and then this young guy 17 years old, he volunteered from Tennessee. He had gone into combat shock. I looked around, and I went after the first guy there. There was one guy's leg sitting in a boot. The first guy in line, a young Sergeant, his neck was split wide open on the side, about a third of the way through. Blood was gushing out, his knees in the air, on his back. They were calling on the radio, trying to make contact from the rear, what this blast was. I was ignoring that. I was gonna' help these guys out. So I got down on my knees beside this kid. "Young man," I'd say, and he looked up at me and said, "I'm too far gone. Go help somebody else." Then he just died. When I went to get up, his hand was froze around my medallion necklace. So I got up and pulled his hand off and laid his hands on his chest.

They were still calling on the radio, calling on the radio. So I answered them, talked to them. They said to cut an LZ to get the medivacs in. I had to find somebody's map to give them our location. One of the officers, I got his map out of his pocket, figured out where we were at, called in the location. I started to cut the LZ, and the whole time I'm praying for this guy. And I remembered that, the day before he just showed me a picture of his wife and baby, a picture of that. A newborn son. I was praying that God would give him back his life, preserve his life for the sake of his son. This little 40 foot sq. area, all banana trees in there. I had a machete, just slashing these banana trees down. One slash and each tree went down. About 15 minutes or less I cleared out an area big enough for the helicopters. The first Medivac came in. The rear said they were sending some guys up but they were just coming, not quite there. The machine gunner on the

This is the exact location the boobytrap was set off. Prior to this, it was a beautiful road (trail) along the slough to the east. As we came to this location, there was a sign painted on one of the abandoned French-style houses that said "Repatriation of U.S. troops and peace in Viet Nam". The rounds were on the left side next to a berm. I dug up the detonator and was astounded how it was constructed. As a result, I made sure that my men would leave nothing behind that might prove detrimental. The Vietnamese referred to this road as "bloody Hiway 9".

Medivac and stretchers, they landed and I was talking to them. I pulled on the gunner's arm. The pilot said, "Don't you touch any of those door gunners; they don't get off the Medivac. I saw why they liked to be gunners; you were a gunner on a helicopter, that's where you stayed. They wouldn't get off of the helicopter to help; they wouldn't get off. They wouldn't take the stretchers and load the guys, they would stay on the helicopters to guard, and they wouldn't leave.

Anyway, some support units, guys from the rear came, loading guys on the helicopters. I look, and here's the fellow that grabbed on my necklace; they were putting him on the helicopter. They had an IV in his arm; he was alive. So I said it was impossible that he would survive. It must have been God who saved him. It was way too long. This medallion I had on, it was blessed by a Chaplin before I went out in the jungle. It said, "Our Lady Queen of Angels protect us in combat." If God existed, then he must have saved that man. But I wanted to know if it was God that saved him. Then I wanted God to show me a sign that he saved him, and not

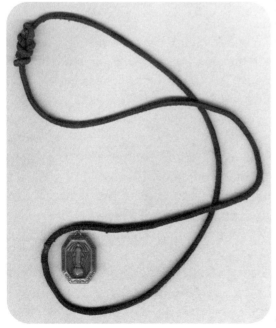

The medallion I was wearing when the patrol encountered the first booby-trap on Bloody Hi-way nine. It turned out to be the first of over 250 booby-traps encountered during the six weeks that followed.

some medics. The captain told me to abandon him; to leave him there and just cut an LZ. The whole time I'm thinking of this, and I get back to the night position, and I take off my jacket, thinking about this. Standing right beside where the medics' shelter is, a big poncho liner between trees. I walked back in the night defensive position, taking off clothes to cool off, and I looked down and my medallion

"I COULDN'T GET USED TO SLEEPING WITHOUT HAVING SOMEONE GUARD ME."

was gone. I thought I lost it in the jungle or something, thought I lost my medallion in the bamboo. I said out loud, "I lost my medallion." And out from under that poncho this hand comes, and says, "Is this it?" And sure enough this medic had my medallion. I said, "That's it. Where'd you get it?" He said, (This man's name was Jim.)" It was clutched in Jim's hand, on his chest. The medic was the one who picked it up. Jim grabbed my medallion off of my necklace; it had been on him the whole time lying in the jungle. I think God really protected that guy. I think he was from Minnesota. Never heard if he lived or died, whether he made it all the way or not. But one of these days I'd like to find out, meet back with him.

That was the first day we went into the Street Without Joy. For six weeks, almost every day, something like that, some unit. And I said at that time I was going to be one just one of the guys. The U.S. government sacrificed everyone there, so I said, I said this to God, "I'm sorry. I just wanted to be one of the guys." Just wanted to be part of the crowd, and if there really was a God, I said, "God, if you make me the leader, I'll try to get none of them killed, and I'll treat the Vietnamese with dignity, and I won't do anything to these people that I wouldn't want done to myself. If he exists, I knew God could do that. In three weeks, I became the leader. I was supposed to be an E-6 when I came back, but the whole time over there, I was usually in charge in every operation that happened. The guy on the ground was in charge; that's the rule of the Army. Doesn't matter if there's a General giving orders, if they're not on the ground, then the guy on the ground made the final decision. And they went by that rule. I can show you picture after picture of guys I was with in the jungle, and a lot of them I can't even tell you their names. Most of the guys that were with me never got overrun or killed. But you saw that there were very few people, at this time only four of us, that were in over 50 combat assaults.

The turnover was tremendous; I always managed to not mess an operation up. When some one was in the jungle behind the lines, after nine months they could get a job in the rear. I never. After nine months people would get too punchy or paranoid. This one time, this guy Ted Heyle from Texas, he had been Company RTO in Camp Evans; we were out in the low lands and swamplands. Ted had about three months to go, he had gone to the rear to Company Clerk. One day a helicopter lands with our supplies. Off the helicopter comes Ted Heyle. I said, "What are you doing out here?" He said Company Commander told him to come out here; he got kicked out of the rear. I said, "You're about to go home aren't you?" He said, "Yeah, only a few weeks to go. They told me I could go with any unit I wanted to go with, so I'm coming out here with you." I said, "Why would you want to do that? We're in the worst area you can be, deepest in the jungle." He said, "Chances are if I'm with somebody else, I'm going to get killed. But if I come with you, chances are I'll live." They kept tract of statistics, who's losing men and who's not losing men.

So Ted was with me, and we were about the third ridgeline in, near the Yellow Brick Road. We'd go Point A to Point B. That's all they told us; wouldn't tell us what's going on. More like a game, they wouldn't tell what's really going on because no one would go on the operation. They'd just say, like a puzzle, you'd figure out what's going on. Even Before Street Without Joy we went on, I can see why something like My Lai would happen. They'd give fire orders; it says there's a village, VC village, "x" number of VC, this kind of weapons, this and that…So it sounds scary. I can guarantee you that anything that would have

NĂM THỨ 5   SỐ ĐẶC BIỆT   SỐ 10

miền nam TỰ DO

TỔNG THỐNG VNCH tuyên bố với báo-chí về cuộc hành-quân Việt-Mỹ trên đất Cam-Bốt

SAIGON.— Tổng thống VN CH Nguyễn Văn Thiệu vừa tuyên bố rằng, khi loan báo quyết định cho quân đội Hoa Kỳ tham dự hành quân hỗn hợp Việt Mỹ trên lãnh thổ Cam Bốt. Tổng thống Nixon cũng nhận định rằng đó là một biện pháp lợi thiết để bảo vệ sanh mạng của đồng bào và các chiến sĩ VNCH lẫn Đồng Minh.

Theo tin Tham Vụ Báo Chí tại Phủ Tổng thống cho biết : Hôm 1 tháng 5 năm 1970, để trả lời báo chí ngoại quốc, hồi Tổng thống nghĩ sao về bài diễn văn của Tổng thống Nixon, Tổng thống VNCH nói rằng :

Hai ngày trước Chánh phủ VNCH đã đồng ý cho Quân lực VNCH thực hiện một cuộc hành quân trong lãnh thổ Cam Bốt để tiêu diệt các căn cứ an toàn của Cộng sản Bắc Việt vì đó là một biện pháp cần thiết và hữu hiệu để bảo vệ sanh mạng của đồng

bào và chiến sĩ VNCH lẫn chiến sĩ Đồng Minh.

Khi loan báo quyết định áp dụng biện pháp 3 trong 3 biện pháp mà Tổng thống Nixon đã nêu lên trong bài diễn văn, bằng cách cho quân đội Hoa Kỳ tham dự hành quân Việt Mỹ trong lãnh thổ Cam Bốt, Tổng thống Nixon cũng nhận định rằng đó là một biện pháp tối cần thiết và thiết yếu để bảo vệ sanh mạng của đồng bào và chiến sĩ VNCH lẫn chiến sĩ Đồng Minh, nhất là trước sự ngoan cố của Cộng sản vẫn duy trì sự vi phạm trắng trợn lãnh thổ Cam Bốt.

Tổng thống Thiệu nhận định rằng, với trách nhiệm của một vị Tổng thống và Tổng tư lệnh Tối Cao của Quân đội, Tổng thống Thiệu và Tổng thống Nixon không thể làm gì khác hơn được để đối phó với sự ngoan cố của Cộng sản xâm lược.

Xem tiếp C trang 2

Quân lực VNCH hành quân tiến sâu vào nội địa Cam-Bốt

SWAY RIENG, CAM BỐT.— Một lực lượng gồm 5.000 binh sĩ VNCH, dưới sự yểm trợ của trọng pháo, thiết giáp, phi cơ, đã tiến sâu vào lãnh thổ Cam-Bốt 10 cây số trưa nay và đã bắt tay được với quân đội Miền ở ngoài tỉnh ly Sway Riêng.

Cuộc hành quân Toàn thắng 42 với sự tham dự của ba chiến đoàn thuộc Quân Đoàn 3 cùng phối hợp với Biệt Động quân, Thiết Giáp, Dân sự chiến đấu, trọng pháo, phi cơ, đã chia làm ba cánh tấn công vào vùng Mỏ Vẹt 36 cây số Tây Bắc Saigon và tiến chiếm quân ly Chipou, (18 cây số Đông Biên giới) và

Prasant (22 cây số Đông Biên giới) nơi mà Cộng sản Bắc Việt đã chiếm của quân Miên vào đầu tháng 4 vừa qua.

Mở đường cho cuộc tấn công, 35 pháo đài bay chiến lược B, 52 cất cánh từ Thái Lan, đội khoảng 1.000 tấn bom xuống các vị trí Cộng quân trong vùng Mỏ Vẹt.

Ngày 29-4, một cánh quân được lệnh tiến vào phía Bắc Mỏ Vẹt đã gặp sức kháng cự mãnh liệt của địch quân vào lúc xế chiều, khi đơn vị này tiến công vào căn cứ dự trữ, tiếp liệu và trại quân của địch.

Một cánh quân khác xuất

Xem tiếp N trang 7

Đây là bản đồ Cam-Bốt. Hiện nay quân đội VNCH và Đồng-Minh đang hành quân để tiêu diệt các căn cứ trước đây Việt-Cộng cho là bất khả xâm phạm.

27 June 70
Phong Dinh prov.

DIỄN - VĂN CỦA TỔNG - THỐNG NIXON về tình hình ĐÔNG-NAM-Á.

Dưới đây là bản trích dịch bản diễn văn của Tổng thống Hoa Kỳ về việc phá vỡ các căn cứ an toàn của Cộng quân trên lãnh thổ Cam Bốt :

Trong hai tuần nay, Bắc Việt đã lột bỏ hết sự mạo nhận tôn trọng chủ quyền và nền trung lập của Cam Bốt. Hàng ngàn quân lính của họ xuất phát từ các sào huyệt đang xâm nhập quốc gia này ; họ bao vây thủ đô Nam Vang. Cam Bốt đã lên tiếng kêu gọi Hoa Kỳ và một số quốc gia khác giúp đỡ.

Nếu nỗ lực này để Bắc Việt có kết quả thì Cam Bốt sẽ trở thành căn cứ xuất quân vĩ đại của đối phương, bàn đạp để tấn công Nam Việt Nam dọc theo vùng biên giới dài 966 cây số, và nơi trú ẩn để địch quân có thể rút về sau khi tác chiến mà không sợ bị trả đũa.

Như vậy, binh sĩ và tiếp vận của Bắc Việt có thể đổ tới quốc gia này, không những gây nguy hại cho quân đội Miên mà còn đe dọa đến sinh mạng của nhân dân miền Nam Việt Nam nữa.

Đứng trước tình thế đó chúng ta chỉ có ba giải pháp.

Thứ nhất, không làm gì hết. Kết quả của biện pháp này hành động này ai cũng thấy rõ.

Đường lối thứ hai là viện trợ quân sự ồ ạt cho Cam Bốt. Tiếc thay, sự chung ta chia sẻ thảm trạng của bảy triệu dân chúng Cam Bốt mà quốc gia đang bị xâm lăng, nhưng quân đội nhỏ bé của Cam Bốt không thể nào sử dụng mau lẹ và hữu hiệu một số lượng viện trợ quân sự lớn lao vào việc phòng thủ đất nước. Cùng với những quốc gia khác, chúng ta sẽ cố gắng cung cấp vô khí nhẹ và quân nhu khác mà quân đội Cam Bốt đang cần và có thể sử dụng ngay để tự vệ được. Mục đích viện trợ của chúng ta về giới hạn này vẫn giúp Cam Bốt bảo vệ nền trung lập chứ không phải giúp họ trở thành một nước tham chiến tích cực theo phe này hay phe nọ.

Với sự hợp tác của quân lực Việt Nam Cộng Hòa, các cuộc tấn công đang được mở trong tuần này để tạo thành những mật khu quan trọng của địch tại biên giới Việt Miên.

Trách nhiệm lớn về các cuộc hành quân trên nỗ đang được các lực lượng Việt Nam Cộng Hòa đảm trách. Chẳng hạn, những cuộc tấn công tại nhiều vùng gồm có những Mỏ Vẹt hoàn toàn do lực quân Việt Nam Cộng Hòa thực hiện dưới quyền chỉ huy của Việt Nam Cộng Hòa mà Hoa Kỳ cung cấp yểm trợ và không quân và tiếp vận.

Tuy nhiên, có một vùng tại đó tôi đã đi đến quyết định là sự phối hợp hành quân Việt Mỹ là cần thiết. Tối nay, các đơn vị Việt Mỹ sẽ tấn công bộ chỉ huy của toàn bộ các hoạt động quân sự cộng sản tại Nam Việt Nam. Trung tâm kiểm soát trọng yếu này đã được Bắc Việt và Việt Cộng thiết lập từ lâu vi phạm trắng trợn nền trung lập của Cam Bốt.

Đây không phải là một cuộc xâm lấn Cam Bốt. Các cuộc tấn công này được mở tại những

Xem tiếp N trang 7

On several occasions, we would assist MACV in their pacification effort. In the days Prior to doing a cordon on a village, they would drop hundreds of thousands of leaflets from a plane over the countryside. These documents would provide information to the people in the region about to become "pacified". It would explain major news items and explain to them how to surrender peacefully (if that be the case) and what to expect for their families, such as medical attention and vaccinations.

come out of that village that night, I would have opened fire Then the next day we went and searched everything; there were no men in the village. All the men are supposed to be in the Army, just women and children, no weapons. The fire orders make it sound like we'd be lucky to make it through the night. So this Ted Heyle, we're supposed to go from Pt. A to Pt. B. I'll never forget the look on his face. A to B was 8 clicks; take us about 15 or 20 days to get there. At this rate, it'll take 24 days to get there. Ted Heyle says he only has a few more days left. Talk about devastation on somebody's face. He was devastated that he would not make it out of the jungle when he was supposed to leave, but he made it out by the grace of God.

This guy, I remember, everyday we'd have to take a malaria tablet, or every three days. Well some of these guys would get the idea they wouldn't take their malaria tablet. See it'd take three months to get malaria. And this guy was from New York, a street savvy; jive talk and all that. Apparently he wanted to get malaria, he didn't tell anyone, so he didn't take his tablets. He was there nine months, so at nine months he did not want to get malaria. He doesn't want to come home and have malaria. So at three months left, he came down with a terrible reaction. So they send him to the rear on a supply helicopter, get checked out. It turned out he was allergic to malaria tablets. If he had taken his first malaria tablet, he would have gotten out right away.

How did you get out of Vietnam?

Well my time was up. I made it for the entire year, but if you had five months or less, you were discharged. When I got back, I had five months left, just under the period I needed. One guy I was with, Stan, he went back with six months and just missed it. We're standing around drinking beer or whatever. Stanley bet all these guys he could drink a six pack of beer faster than they could pour it on the ground. Well Stanley bet them. I thought this was impossible. Put two holes in one side, one on the other, just like a normal can of beer. So they get out a time watch, the guys have their money out betting. Poznanski was all ready, so they started, sure enough; Stanley drank all six cans of beer in less than 19

"THAT'S HOW A GUY SURVIVED, IF MORTARS START BLASTING IN, IF YOU DON'T GET BEHIND COVER FAST ENOUGH YOU'RE IN TROUBLE."

seconds. They couldn't pour the beer on the ground that fast. He won, margin to go. He won the bet. Stanley was a big rough talker; you'd think he'd get your throat or whatever. This one combat, kind of a firefight, they got in pretty close. They cut our claymores, fighting, and after all this, I looked over and saw blood on all of Stan's fingers. Stanley had bitten all of his fingernails down to the bone. You'd think

Page 8

The Screaming Eagle

Fired on point-blank

Fast move saves life

By Sgt. Larry Semenko

CAMP EVANS – 'When the NVA soldier thrust his AK-47 two feet from my face and let loose with a burst of fire," said Sergeant Michael Foley, Piedmont, S.D., 'he thought he had gotten me. But I never received a scratch."

The 3rd Bn. (Ambl.), 187th Inf. soldier was on a company size clearing operation about 10 miles northwest of Hue when the incident occurred. Eight enemy soldiers attacked the unit's night defensive position near several rice paddies and a tree line in the rolling hills south of Camp Evans.

After firing their Claymore mines and producing superior fire power, the 'Rakkasan' squad called in flares and moved forward to sweep the area.

' As I was about to creep over the first rice paddy dike, an enemy soldier jumped up from behind the dike and fired at my face. I fell backwards to my side of the dike,' Sgt. Foley said. "It was a miracle I wasn't hit."

Spec. 4 Reyes Santiago, Rio Piedras, Puerto Rico, the nearest squad member, said, "I saw the sergeant go down--I thought for the last time--and opened up at the enemy."

Sgt. Foley tossed a grenade over the dike and it landed in a rain depression on the wide dirt top of the dike near where the enemy lay. When the "frag' exploded, the enemy got up and ran toward the tree line.

Spec. 4 Charles Fisher Marion, N.Y., the squad member on the far right of the unit, fired at the fleeing enemy. Five NVA then started firing small arms and rocket-propelled grenades to cover for their man, forcing the pursuing Screaming Eagles to fall back and call in aerial rocket artillery.

In the morning sweep, the squad found three rucksacks, four blood trails and six B-40 rocket boosters. Following the blood trail nearest the rice paddy, the "Rakkasans" found an AK-47 and, a little farther on, one wounded NVA.

The unscratched squad detained the NVA soldier. Later, the Screaming Eagles uncovered a bunker complex and found numerous pieces of enemy field gear in the same area.

WIRE TUNNEL - Defensive wire is secured into place at Firebase T by Screaming Eagles of the 2nd Bn. (Ambl.), 11th Arty.   (U.S

Scout dog dies for troo

he was the roughest toughest guy in the world. He came down to where he thought he was going to die, and he chewed all his fingernails down to where they were bleeding. (Showing newspaper) This is on the front page of the Army Reporter and front page of the Stars and Stripes, and in the Screaming Eagle. That night I got shot at about 18 times at point blank range.

Larry Semenko came out in the field and spent a day with us in doing this story. Of the 5 or 6 stories I read, this one is the best factual but overly concise. He does not mention that my men reported I had been killed. Later that night, when I returned to our NDP, and called the rear, our company commander screamed on the phone, "Foley, just what in the hell is going on out there?" He could never remember my code name.

Guys thought I got killed. I got three powder burns, and that's it. I never got tagged for that. To get a purple heart, you have to get tagged for the wound. I got powder burns, shot at 18 times, close as me to you. A whole squad firing at me. I said, "God I don't want to die here." He was like a shield, covered me up.

Were drugs a problem?

Yeah, it was a fine line between the guys and me. It was there, and you'd have to live with it. They'd Court Martial, Article 15 or other Articles for it. This one guy, smoking marijuana cigarettes, he would roll heroin or something, smoke it, and he finally fried his mind. One time when we went in for a stand down, we were supposed to go back out to the landing pad to get lifted out. Everyone is out; we had hooches that were off-limits to everyone else. Left my backpack and weapons in hooch. No one was allowed in it except those people in the unit. We always had our weapons, a rifle and a .45 pistol I always carried. I was a little late, the helicopter pad was waiting. I didn't know anything was going on. Whatever I was doing, I was rushing down to get my pack and get to the helicopter, so I go trouncing down there, open the door, and here's this guy smoking the dope. He's got his rifle there, saying he's not going on the helicopter. Sitting there with all of his combat gear on, sitting in the corner. He's looking over the side with his weapon and smoking his cigarette, higher than a kite. So I got my stuff and got lifted out of there. I got word he got Court Martial. He was held up in the hooch, and no one could get near it. I didn't even know it, but he let me go down there. He wasn't going back out in the jungle. That was the end of him. His mind was fried. They'd take French pills and buy marijuana. We'd go by the villages, and they'd be drying the marijuana in their front yards. I wasn't into that, I never.

Did you have any anti-war movements back in the U.S.? How were you treated?

Well when you got back to the U.S., you were eligible for unemployment benefits. I took a week or two, took it easy, and decided to draw some unemployment benefits. So I went in, and there's this line there, all those government-people treating people like dirt - it was unreal. It was like going through third degree. I said, "The hell with this." I wouldn't take any amount of money to be treated like that. I got one unemployment check and then never went back.

I would have large patches of skin that would peel off my body. I went to the VA Hospital at Ft Meade to get it treated, but they wouldn't treat me because I wouldn't sign a sheet that said I was destitute. I tried to convince them I received this disease in the jungle; it was their responsibility. It didn't help. No one was willing to stand up for the Viet Nam Veteran.

I was classified as 10% disabled since I would not sign a release saying I was A-OK when I was discharged. The last three months in the jungle I could not eat any food and then lay down without it regurgitating. So I mainly drank water. Thirty some years later I was finally able to be correctly diagnosed and treated. That whole time I had a fungus in my stomach and bacteria that previously could not be diagnosed and treated. I will have to take medicine for one year now in hopes my stomach will heal.

There is not a day that goes by that I don't recall the look on my sisters' face when I finally stepped off the plane. There is not a day that goes by that I don't remember the men that served with me in the jungle. I wonder daily about the fate of those that were devastated and mentally defeated in a war they did not want to be a part of. I thank God daily that he gave me the ability to help many under-educated men survive the bureaucracy that otherwise would have devoured them. And I am thankful God was ever present with me when I had nowhere else to turn.

Did you have nightmares when you got back home, hard times remembering Vietnam?

A lot of the guys' names I can't remember. I used to, before I went overseas. I could really play the piano and things like that. After I got back, I more or less forgot. It was months. I couldn't get used to sleeping without having someone guard me. Over there, there was always someone guarding all night long. I could be sleeping in the jungle and hear a twig break and be wide-awake. The unit I was particularly in you had to survive as a unit. Being in a combat situation, you get so that for years, you over-react to simple confrontation. Never got over that. It was like a dog that is always taught to fight; dog comes snarling at you, and you get in your best defensive position and snarl back. You grab them the best place to grab them; that's the way you're taught. It's hard to get over. You can't. Someone on the street walks up and gives you a bad time, you would respond in a defensive manner.

How old were you when you came back to the U.S.?

I had a degree; I had a college degree before I went in. I was going to go in the Peace Corp, volunteered for two years. I got the FBI clearance and everything you need. By the time I got out of the school, it was about a year before I got drafted. There was a kid that was ahead of me in college from South Dakota. His name was Tom McCrall. Tom volunteered for the Peace Corp; would have then been two years prior to me. Peace Corp Tour is two years. Then I went back out to South Dakota. I already got my draft papers; I knew my name was coming up to get drafted, so I volunteered for the Peace Corp. I had done that way ahead of time. I got my airline ticket to fly to California for my Peace Corp training, and I had my draft notice to report for; I got drafted the same time. So I went back out to the Black Hills where I had school, went into the little town of Sturgis. He was out near that town. I was going to see how things were going. I asked someone I met in the town Sturgis, South Dakota. I asked if he's seen Tom, he said, "Tom just got back from the Peace Corp and was drafted." Tom got drafted, going into the military. He spent two years. That was when Jack Kennedy had initiated an executive decree that anybody can spend two years in public service instead of military draft. But then after Kennedy was killed, Johnson took over and changed that. He reneged on that; anyone who was in the Peace Corp was still eligible to be drafted. So I said if that's the deal, two years in Peace Corp and then still two years in Vietnam, then I might as well go. I never flew out to California. One of these days, I'm still going to go somewhere, a couple years, in the Peace Corp.

I got my bus ticket, 450 miles to get my physical, during the winter. I got down to Mitchell, South Dakota, about three fourths the way, and the bus changed. Here's a blizzard; we spent a day or so sleeping at the bus depot waiting for the next bus that's going to Sioux Falls. I went in for the physical, stayed over night. I stayed in a YMCA. They gave you a ticket for meals at a little greasy spoon restaurant with 10 or 15 chairs in it. So I stayed over night in a bunk bed in a YMCA. They were drafting people for the Marines at that time. A guy came in picking everyone he wanted for the Marines. Some how I could tell he wasn't going to pick me. I was surprised at the number of guys that had a lot of physical deformities. They had everyone down to their shorts, four lines of guys. The Doctor came walking through; if somebody had flat feet, knock-knees; he even examined your groin at the same time. They'd look everyone over, and if anyone had a deformity they would tell them to leave.

Is there a certain message you have for young people today about war?

There are several things I would say. Go with whatever life throws at you. Your greatest achievements will come out of hopeless situations. You can always find a way to be of service to others. And never abandon your dreams. I can say that in ones own life, the ultimate challenge is facing death and finding solace with it. War is an easy way out of a frustrating situation. (Showing pictures) This guy here, see, they didn't treat him right in the Army; it's political, there are lifers, and then draftees to serve their time. This Fred (Darrel Fredericks) is from Oregon. They got over run; the NVA threw satchel charges into their night defensive position. The NVA saw them moving from Point A to Point B. Moving from one area to another. When the moment was right, they would attack. First they'd fire mortars in the night defensive. When all the mortars were coming in, he ran out. Everybody got killed or wounded, except him. So that night they brought the medivacs out there, lowered down baskets. He loaded everybody on the baskets, got everybody out of there, everybody that was wounded. They left the dead guys there. There was another platoon that was closer than I was to these guys. This other platoon went over there, and the NVA was still out there. They had to carry all those bodies out of there. None of these guys would have gotten out of there if Fredericks wouldn't have lifted them onto the baskets. I know they got one of the radios, because one of the North Vietnamese spoke English. He got on the radio and said they were shooting, and they shot down one of the medivacs. He said you've got your medivacs in to get your men, but we got the Medivac; and they did, they shot one down. It auto-rotated to another hilltop. They carried the rest of the guys out.

They put Fredericks in for a silver star. The Company Commander, a cocky guy at the time. He was having problems. I know a few times when our unit was with the CP. (command post), this guy, he would lay curled up like a little baby, lay in a ball. So the Battalion Commander put Fredericks in for a Silver Star. One of the guys that got lifted out, (we called cherry, a new guy in the field), he was a Sergeant, instant F-6, he never earned it; they just brought him in. He bad-mouthed Fredericks. They interviewed him in the hospital, and he badmouthed Fredericks for jumping and taking cover in the jungle. I'd always say you have to forgive a guy the first two or three split seconds in combat, because it's an automatic self-survival thing. That's how a guy survived, if you are suddenly under attack, if you don't get behind cover fast enough you're in trouble. That's what Fredericks did. He took cover. When he came back out, this cherry sergeant saw him jump in the jungle and said he was abandoning them. But he was the one who loaded them all on the helicopter and got them all out of there. Because he badmouthed Fredericks, the company commander reneged on his silver star. I spent a lot of time with this Fredericks; I'm going to see what I can do to get his silver star back for him. Actually it was Lieutenant Colonel Chandler (now head of the war college) who put him in for a silver star. I got his letter here from Fredericks; I told him I was going to try to help get him his silver star. (Shows pictures of Fredericks)

This little girl was always very friendly and would ask many questions. She wanted me to take her to America.

This little boy would always come and sit down to observe me as I went about my daily field tasks on our monthly visit to Hiway one. They always knew our position before the paymaster did. He claimed he had no mother or father, and would eat whatever we offered.

Here's a picture of me in the sand flats of Vietnam. I was catching a lizard. See I'd, take a long stick; these lizards would crawl down a tunnel in the ground. You know how to catch a lizard don't you? Take a long flexible stick, stick it down that hole, and crush the hole in. Then you just dig all the sand out, and then there's the lizard. (Showing pictures of himself catching lizards)

What would you do with the lizard?

I'd put him on a string and kept him as a pet. Some guys were scared of lizards. It seems to me

This little boy was a chain smoker. He wanted to know where I came from. We spent 85 days in a row, wet from the monsoon rains.

that a Vietnamese orphan cooked and ate it one cold and rainy day near the Phong Dien River, along with a small sparrow that the machine gunner Scott knocked out of the air. Whenever we went near Hiway One, these orphans would come out and sell us small loaves of bread and warm sodas.

Footnote: Looking back now, I can see this was the first time in American history we were participating in a new mode of operation. I can still remember the first day it was invoked. Everyone in the company refused to break up and go out in self-sufficient units. It was three days before the men in the company were convinced to go on an operation. Platoon Sergeant at the time, Mike Woods, went around and asked every man if they were going to go out. When he asked me, I only replied that I wasn't going to go out by myself. After a period of time, I was confident that it didn't matter the size of the unit. We had supporting us every resource available to the military. I felt a lot of pride when I saw how the units were operating in Afghanistan, knowing I was part of a unit that pioneered the techniques that were being used there. And it was the 3/187 that replaced the marines in Afghanistan.

This information is expressly for inclusion in DCE Vietnam Veterans history book.

Since Vietnam, Mike Foley has taught Computer Science at a Business College, helped develop computer software for the radio and television industry, was a systems engineer for NCR Corporation, and came to Wausau Wisconsin in 1973, where he met his wife Marilyn Etten. He was instrumental in the computerization of Forward Communications Corporation and became a corporate vice-president. He served in that capacity until that corporation was leveraged out by Bill Simon, the former U.S. Secretary of the Treasury, and dissolved. Foley has since traveled worldwide for the companies he started, Realtime Computer and Computer-e-Store. He is also currently helping his wife open an Italian restaurant in downtown historic Wausau, on the square, called Little Italy Brewpub Cucina. They have two adult children, Matthew, an auto technician, and Michelle, who is currently studying Spanish and international business in Spain.

Interviewed and transcribed by Andrew Miller.

Joe Malkowski

Malkowski worked in recon for the Army, serving as a LRRP in the central highlands. He was wounded twice while in country.

Mr. Malkowski, could you give us a little background about your tour of duty in Vietnam?
I'm Joe Malkowski, and I guess I'd like to take you back a few months to my training. I took my basic training, at Fort Carson, Colorado, and that was probably more to teach me discipline as well as conditioning your body. After my basic training I went through Fort George in Maryland, and that's where everything started coming together. They were looking for volunteers for Long Range Patrol. Well, I didn't know what it was at the time, I guess. So they brought their members from the 75th Recon to the western part of Virginia, similar to Vietnam, a lot of trees and woods, and also the 101st Airborne came up there and taught us jump training. Well that ended quickly; then we learned the skills that would keep us alive in Vietnam. So from there I was shipped in 1966 to Vietnam. We landed in Chu Lai, and most of my work was done in the central highlands. As I said, most of the work was done in the central highlands, and we were with recon.

Why don't you tell us a little bit about the goal of recon soldiers. What's the purpose of recon and tell us a little bit about that?
Ok, recon is exactly what it says. You can get this information and turn it into either a reality or a fissile. Most of the time we were flown into an L-Z and we worked from the L-Z. And as you do in six men unit, our strength was actually two platoons, which was 48 men. Six men teams were split up, and that's where we had our divisions. And I was in a bush most of the time; I don't want it to sound like a campout because it was far from that. In war, people die. You look at the person next to you and think that you're going to wake up in the morning and that person is going to be gone. War is finality. And it's real. And I know there are those who said that Vietnam was not a full-scale war, but it was hard to convince me as I was losing friends.

I'd like to hear more about the engagement. You hear this term about firefights and different weapons. You hear that they had trouble with ambushes and Vietcong; others tell us they may have been in larger battles against NVA, the actual enemy and regular troops.
Well, we didn't go out looking for trouble. We were out to get recon, to get information and bring it back to our units. Now and then we did get in firefights, but with six men, you had to try and distract yourself, but it depended on different sizes of units, and you could tell that by the firefights. You could tell if it was a lot or a little. And we would bring that information back home and then go out again. So we'd be out for maybe overnight, maybe three days, maybe six days. And we carried packs on our backs; we were packed mainly with ammunition; we had very little food, but we were taught how to survive in the country.

Did you work out of a base camp?
Well kind of, yeah. Actually the first range was in Chu Lai, and we were worked out and first visited…(looking at map) I see there's Plaiku on there; we were there. Bak To, I heard you mentioned earlier, Paul, Dien Bien Phu. And that was a hot spot, that was a very hot spot. It depends. We never knew. We never knew what was happening in an area until we got there, and that was after we collected information and came back.

Did you call in artillery?
Yes. We worked through the 7th Fleet, Navy, off the shores.

So they fired right off the ships?
Yeah, they could fire 40 miles.

Show me one more time where the ships would be and how far they could actually fire.

> "*…WE JUMPED OFF. SEE OUR HELICOPTER NEVER REALLY HIT THE GROUND, AND WE JUMPED OFF TO THE GROUND, AND I GOT DOWN THERE, AND I GOT HIT RIGHT AWAY WITH DRAG FIRE.*"

Actually, the water right here in the China Sea. And they were shelling us at 20 miles. So they were out in the water quite a ways. We also used the Air Force; had a range and the jets and helicopters. And usually when we were dropped in an area, they would bring us in, drop us and leave us with one chopper circling. We'd work in crews, and six of us would be in one chopper, and the other chopper was there to scout the land and make sure we got on base. Sometimes it's not safe. I was hit twice. I was hit in the right knee area, and also I have some shrapnel in my back and in my chest. So that's two Purple Hearts.

When you get wounded like that, that's very severe. What did they do, medi-vac you to a hospital on a ship?
Yes. Actually what happened here was, it was a six-man team and it was a hot L-Z. In other words, there was a lot of fire going on, and we jumped off. See our helicopter never really hit the ground, and we jumped off to the ground, and I got down there, and I got hit right away with drag fire. So they, we had a radio on the list, and we said to fly back in and get us out of there and the pilot didn't. We're working in six men crews; it's awful hard to send the helicopter; you want to be silent.

When you got hit twice, what do they do? Just patch you up and send you back?
No, I spent about a month in Chu Lai.

And then you got to go right back?
Oh yes.

There's no going home just because you got a wound?
No. Well some of them did, if they tore off limbs and things like that.

If you're well enough to fight again, you go back out?
Right, yeah. And like I said, I had shrapnel in my chest, and I was running on a personal pager, an APC they called it. And I was, they were taking us out to an area to drop us off, with APC, and we hit a landmine. We figured it was a thousand pound bomb. First of all, I was injured on the APC; that's where I got the shrapnel. Shrapnel came down on my head. I was the only one of the six that day.

What did you call that?
A personal cage. APC. (Armoral Personnel Carrier)

APC, are these kind of like, do they look like tanks or something?
Yes, well there's 50 caliber guns, two sixties on the side.

Really the only way the enemy was going to take that out was with mines.
Bombs. They would collect things that we would shell and make there own bombs.

We've heard a lot of speakers down in the Saigon area where booby traps were a concern. Was that a concern in the central highlands as you walked? Were there booby traps up there also?
Oh yes. They had what they called punji pits, where they have bamboo spears sticking down, so if you dropped in you couldn't get yourself back out of there. And they had claymore mines.

They had our claymore mines?
No, no. Most of ours were actual claymore mines. The ones that they made were filled with nails and shells and anything that could hurt you.

How did they set them up?
Some were detonated and some were trip wired.

> "*THEY HAD WHAT THEY CALLED PUNJI PITS, WHERE THEY HAVE BAMBOO SPEARS STICKING DOWN, SO IF YOU DROPPED IN YOU COULDN'T GET YOUR-SELF BACK OUT OF THERE.*"

What's the difference between detonated and trip wired? Do you want that explained or not?
Trip wired means it's usually down at your feet, and it'll be running from the claymore over to a tree, and when you're walking through, you kick the wire and that pulls the pin, and there you go. So we had to be very careful. We were 75th Recon, and we were taught how to handle those problems.

Did you get pretty good at seeing those trip wires? Did you put your best guys out at point?
Yes. I was usually the point.

You were the guy, huh?
They wanted to get rid of me.

You went point a lot and survived?
Yes. You can tell when you get into an area where there might be a base camp of theirs. You can see that the growth would start getting less and less, to give them visibility and see us coming. One experience, I walked into a company sized, which would be about 1500 hundred people, a company sized unit, and they were gone. Where they were, I don't know, but they had a rice stash there, and I don't know how many bags of rice we took from there. But then we ate rice every morning for breakfast, lunch and dinner.

You get to like it then.
Yeah you have to. I guess I wanted to say also, the whole, there were no front lines in Vietnam. The whole country was a front line. It didn't matter if you were in Saigon, down in the Delta, or Central Highlands. It was all war zones.

Did it bother you at all, or didn't you think about it, when you would maybe liberate villages of VC's or NVA areas that were, ok we've been here now, we've burned the rice that was supporting the enemy, and then you go somewhere else, and then maybe a month later, the village that you've liberated is now back in the hands of the enemy. I mean, we've read stuff like that; we've learned about taking a hamlet, leaving it, after losing all these lives. Was that the sort of thing that grinded on the soldiers, that they wondered why, or wasn't that a factor?

No, no it wasn't. We were there to do the job, and we did a job very well. I guess to tell you about the hamlets, most of them were VC controlled. They'd come back to those places during the evening or during the night. There was nothing we could do but liberate the people, since the VC controlled them.

> *"WE'D GET INTO A HAMLET AREA, AND WE'D SEE A SPIDER HOLE WHERE IT WOULD LEAD TO AN UNDERGROUND TUNNEL SYSTEM. THAT WOULD BE UNREAL."*

Is that why hamlets were burned down, and the people became refugees, and you took them people then to resettlement areas?

We didn't.

Not you, but somebody must have.

Yeah. As George said, they were a scared people. That's just the way it was. We'd get into a hamlet area and we'd see a spider hole where it would lead to an underground tunnel system that would be unreal. I mean, there's as much down there as there is on ground. There are hospitals and kitchens; it's unbelievable.

Now I wouldn't assume you ever got that job, to go into a spider hole?

I wouldn't even want to do it. We used to take the small guys out for that, and he'd go in there with a sawed off shotgun or just a .45. And I wouldn't even want to do it.

So did you know some of these guys that were tunnel rats that would go in there? If you did, it would be kind of scary.

Yes, yes it was. Like I said, I didn't want to be in their division, but they enjoyed it, they were taught to do the job.

What was your job as pointer?

Pointer actually cleared the path into the jungle. In the jungle there's actually triple canopies, and what I mean by that is that you go miles, literally miles, in triple canopy; you don't see the sunlight. It's such dense growth. As point, you take a machete, and you open up a trail through this. Of course you got to be looking out for trip wires. It wasn't a fast process; it was a safe one, or I wouldn't be here.

Did you avoid walking down the trail?

Oh yes.

You got off the trails, and those that were lazy and went on the trails were in trouble.

You bet.

They were booby-trapped?

As well as roads. You wanted to stay away from roads. Actually I was trained in mine sweeping as well. Sometimes we would actually treat mines for the tanks and the APC's. This was my own unit; this is the black horse regiment, the 11th Cavalry.

What exactly is mine sweeping?
It's a metal detector, and you sweep the road. Usually you have two; you can sweep where the tracks are. When I say road, roads there are probably from here to a wall away. They're very narrow. It's not, they don't have a freeway system like we have here. To sweep that, the roads, it was a scary situation as well.

What if you found one? Did you call in someone?
No, you took care of it yourself. You take a bayonet and you start folding. And you fold around that mine and cleaned it out very gently. To set a mine off, is pressure. How you step on it depends on what kind of detonator it is.

Sounds dangerous.
Yes it is. Well we were not on a camping trip.

Did one ever go off?
Well actually I can tell you a story about that. We had a Lieutenant who was gung ho. He just got there. He was a second lieutenant, and he always had a knack of getting on ahead of the minesweepers. So one day we were sweeping mines, and he was naturally out in front of us, and all of a sudden they see him jump up in the air and go horizontal, and the mine blew right underneath him. He never had a scratch on him, but he never went out in front of the sweepers again.

So in other words, he knew he had set it off, and he jumped to the side.
He turned to the side and he saw the claymore, and he knew he was in trouble. So he just went horizontal, and he came down and swept the dust off, and away we go.

Tell us a little bit more about how you got into the service. You went into the service in 1966. That's pretty early, for the regular combat troops going in 1965, 1966. Attitudes were pretty good about the war. Did you enlist? Did you get -- actually that early -- would you have been drafted?
I was drafted. The way it was, after high school, I thought I'd go into service. So I went down and signed up. The only thing you had to do was sign the bottom line. And I told the recruiter, I'm going to think about it a day or two. And three days later I got my orders. So they drafted me. The reason I wanted to get in there and get into the service with the Special Forces, Green Berets. That's what I wanted, which, I got a black beret at the same training they took, the 75th.

What's a black beret?
I should have brought it along, I guess. You know what a Green Beret is? Same thing, only it's black. We adopted the black beret as our symbol.

We haven't really talked about the Special Forces. You may just want to mention the type, the training, or what makes the green berets or a black beret more prestigious than the regular soldier.
Well, they're trained. Some have two to three languages they learn. They also, some might be a rifleman and a medic. You always have two areas of expertise, and they're used for advisors, mainly. It's quite a secret outfit. When they're gone, they can't tell anybody.

These kids know so much more about the Navy SEALS through TV and so on, it's probably a similar organization.
Yes. Exactly.

What was an average day like?
An average day you usually wake up, if we were in a base camp situation, about 9 in the morning. And

I want to clarify that. Because we were a night patrol, the night before we got no sleep. So our average day would be up at 9, fill sand bags most of the day for protection under our bunkers, and that night we'd set patrols up out in the bush.

How late did you stay out?
All night. We came back in the morning.

So you went to sleep at 6 in the morning, and get about 3 hours of sleep?
Probably three to five hours.

And you did that everyday?
Not everyday. As I said before, there was eight squads of men, and sometimes we varied that.

You were out in the bush for an expanded period. Now we had a Recon guy in a couple weeks ago who, they'd be out for 20, 30 days.
Right.

They got their supplies by helicopters and stuff like that. When you're out in the bush, are you sleeping in it, or is it war at night?
No.

One guy would come in and say all the action was at night, and they slept in the day. And a different guy who was down in the delta would say something different.
I guess, I was never out for thirty days. I was out for three weeks at a time. Like we said, once you secure an area, you can have helicopters bringing in your food and ammo. And there again, see that didn't leave you off the hook; you still had to go out at night on missions. But the intelligence would tell our superiors where they had thought there was VC activity, and then they'd drop us in the middle of that for recon.

They'd find them, and then they'd find you. What about, how long your tour was? We've been told a tour of duty was one year.
Actually I was there 13 months, actually, because there was nobody to replace me. And I had to be replaced before I left, so I stayed 13 months.

We've also learned there was something called a short timer. What was that?
He reaches the countdown.

One guy said that if you could survive the first month you were there and the last couple weeks, in between you would be ok. Is that true?
No. Well in between really didn't matter, because you knew you were going to be there for 12 months. So I guess your theory is right. If you make it the first month and last month, you've got it made…the short timer, you would see it on his helmet. He'd have little marks with how many days he had left, actually counting down the hours.

So fighting in that time period, 1966 – 67, there was an escalation. How would you rank the American fighting forces? We've read that it was a lot of enlisted, trained professionals, excellent fighting force, and then later on as you get more and more draftees that there was some deterioration at the end. Is that true?
I guess I can't answer that, because I was only there '66-'67.

How was the attitude?

Oh, gung ho. And we were there to set up the recon. We went as a unit, five thousand strong. But we were there just to set up the long range recon for that unit.

How about coming home to America. Did you come back home or did you stay in the service?

No, actually I came back to California, and I visited a friend out there who was in my unit in Vietnam. I guess we partied, but we did for a couple weeks, and then I came home to Wisconsin. I guess what you're getting at is how was I received? Not very well, and it really didn't matter to me, because I knew, in my heart, I did my job, and they had no idea what was going on. The only thing they knew was what the television told them. In terms of any psychological problems, in terms of nightmares, I still have them; they never went away. My war is still going on.

Is it something where you wake up in the middle of the night, or what?

Oh yeah. I find it, when I have a problem I do a lot of driving. I get in the car and drive, and I think to myself.

How is the government in terms of helping veterans after this war? Did they help you at all with those types of things? Were there programs?

I think they did help. There's a clinic over in…Tomah. There's a clinic over there, and I've been there. As a matter of fact that's where my GP is. In Tomah there's some serious, serious cases, and they live right there. It's just day after day after day.

So obviously there are different kinds of stress.

Some of them are out patients, but there are quite a few that live there. And it's not only Vietnam vets over there; it's Korea, World War Vets. It's a tough thing to see, and I guess I don't have it that bad when you compare to other guys.

What did you think about the Vietnamese people? Did you trust them at all?

No, I never really did. I guess I worked with the ARVN troops, but I never was that close where I could really talk to them. I worked with the ROK's, which were the Koreans. They were over there. They're heartless people.

They didn't take any prisoners, did they?

They didn't take any prisoners. No they didn't take any.

So, it's a different situation if you're in Saigon, or if you're in a bigger city and you're dealing with the Vietnamese people. You were more up in the central highlands, out doing your jobs, your missions, and you just didn't have a lot of contact with the people.

Yeah.

I think what she was getting at was, things they read about not really knowing who the enemy was. During the day they might be cleaning your boots, and at night they might be lobbing mortars at you.

Exactly.

I think that's one of the more difficult, having a government in Vietnam that didn't appear to be fully supported by its people is obviously a problem.

Right. In our base camp, we didn't have any for that simple reason. They might be shining your shoes in the morning, and at night, they'd try to kill you. We actually had that situation happen. They had people there helping with laundry and shoes and what not, and we found a little, about an 8-year-old boy with a grenade under him. So it actually happened.

We just looked at a couple other issues. Minorities in the war, we looked at that issue. How, in your unit, in terms of blacks or Latinos, did the groups get along pretty well? Or was it a section of where you're going through a time period of the sixties where there's black power and there's dissention at home. Did that carry over into the war, or were your units pretty solid defending each other?
That was definitely. I'm not going to say it was a problem. I had a lot of black friends, as well as Latinos. But you could certainly tell there was cliques; they had there own little groups. It was pretty much segregated there. When you're out with your six-man team, you got to count on your friend.

Out in the fighting, the combat, it didn't matter what color you were.
That's right. You had to depend on your friend.

What was the hardest part of the war?
Well, being away had some significance. But I guess the hardest thing that I faced and eventually got used to, was the elimination of housing, hamlets, we burnt them down. I'm not going to deny that. And we killed people. So that was pretty tough, at first. But like I say, if it's past your first month, usually you can work it out.

What were some of your missions? What did you have to do?
Most of the recon work is done on six man teams. Now, if you want to search and destroy, you'd have a platoon, which are four squads. That was a search and destroy. But most of the work you did in six.

> *"THEY MIGHT BE SHINING YOUR SHOES IN THE MORNING, AND AT NIGHT, THEY'D TRY TO KILL YOU."*

And what would you do?
Well that was mostly for the Recon work. We used to find out what was in certain areas, take it back to the unit for shelling or whatever they wanted to do with it.

You wanted to avoid fighting?
Yes, with six man teams, you want to avoid trouble.

You didn't want to go up against superior numbers.
Right, you have to keep the odds the kind of the same.

Did you ever get caught in a firefight?
Yes, lots of them.

How do you know when you lost, or when to get out of there?
Well most of the firefights are with the six man teams. So we, there's a method to in extraction, when you pull back. There's always some fire going out there, but when you get back, you want to get back to where you can pull the chopper in and get out of there.

Some people have said these firefights can be less than a minute, where you have this rapid shoot of fire, and then it's over.
Well, if it's that situation, we'd leave the area. We'd take our shit in a different direction.

Did you ever go out on any search and destroys?

Yes. But a search and destroy, like I said, usually you went in to destroy a village. And we did take prisoners, and they were sent back to headquarters.

Do you think that the government tied the hands of the military in the mid 60s? We've heard that there were restrictions on where you could go and what could be bombed and whether you could go in North Vietnam, or could you go here or there. Do you feel that this was a winnable wa, if the government would have let the military make those decisions?

First of all, I guess I'd like to say that I think we won that war. We left; we weren't beaten, we left. And as far as areas that are taboo, there was none for my unit, because we were sent there to gather information. In terms as looking at it as a war that was won, or at least as one where the American forces were never beaten, was it winnable war though in respect of the fact that the civil war stories mentioned that there was always going to be people that were not happy with the Saigon government that we supported? Wouldn't the North continue and continue because they had this cause? Wouldn't this war just have gone on and on like the French phase? Was this going to be a continual war? Even though we could win the battle, could we win the war?

That's one thing I've always wondered. Even if we put in a million men, and we invade North Vietnam and we do all these things, are we faced with a situation where five, ten years later the guerillas are still. you know? The Soviets found that out in Afghanistan, didn't they? When a people really have a cause, they're always going to get that guerilla action, the rebels fighting.

I think you're right. George was there in 1953, and there was a war shortly before there. They've been at war all their lives.

What made you want to get into the war? Why did you decide to enlist?

I guess that goes back to 1965, when I had my enlistment papers made. I wanted to belong to the Green Berets, which is a tough organization. It's like the Navy SEALS. So I guess I wanted it in my heart, I knew I was going to Vietnam, and I had told myself that this was it, and I took the job of training very seriously.

Is there anyone that didn't want you to go over to Vietnam?

Yeah, I suppose my parents, but they never said anything. They knew there had to be a job done, too. They understood that.

What was the worst firefight, specifically, that you were in? You said you were in some, but you didn't really tell any personal information.

I guess the worst one I'd ever seen was Dien Bien Phu. It was, well we were in the bush, and the first marines were on the hill. It was a terrible battle. We had a platoon size for a squad, and that was a tough one. There were a lot of marines who lost their lives there.

Joe Malkowski began working with carpentry, evenually working his way up to constructing power plants. After 25 years of working with the union, he is now retured.

Interviewed by 1st hour American History Seminar Class

Bill Maseman

Masemen enlisted in the Marines in 1963 and served three tours in Southeast Asia. His first tour was as an infantryman in Bravo Company, 1st Marine Battalion, 7th Marines. He entered Vietnam in 1965.

Did you fight against the Viet Cong or NVA regular units?

I fought against both. We fought the Viet Cong on a daily basis because they were the farmers in the local village, whereas the North Vietnamese regulars or North Vietnamese army were regular troops that came out of North Vietnam. When we got into major operations, like the one I mentioned earlier, we fought the North Vietnamese regular army.

Can you describe what an average day was like during the war?

Five o' clock in the morning I'd wake up if I've been to sleep. I went and I had something to eat or I fixed myself something to eat, whichever was the setup at the time. I would then proceed to do my normal duties and go back to where I had started from when I had woken up, which was normally sitting on the line watching the barbed wire fence. I would sit at that barbed wire fence until lunch, have lunch. Again, either they would fix it for me, or I would fix it myself. Go back; watch the barbwire some more. Hopefully nothing happened during the day. I had my evening meal, and I would continue on, up to the night. At nighttime, I stayed awake, get shifts. Maybe I was up for two hours and somebody else was up for two hours. Then I was up for two hours, so I could be up, come five o'clock the next morning while the other guy was sleeping. If I was out on patrol, somebody was awake continuously, 24 hours a day, 7 days a week, 365 days a year.

Did you ever do an ambush? If so, please describe it.

Yes, we set up an ambush outside of Ane Wau, up near the air base, Ane Wau Valley. There were seven of us in the marine recon unit, and we sat there for about eight hours, waiting from a group of Vietnamese to come through. They turned out to be not Vietnamese regular armies, but Viet Cong with one NVA officer. We sprung the ambush, killed all but one of them, took the one prisoner, which happened to be female, stripped the bodies, took everything that was on the bodies, and moved out, smartly, because we'd make enough noise to wake the dead.

What was meant by search and destroy?

Search and destroy was physically moving through an area, whether it be a hamlet or just an open wooded area that might be there, or a jungle area looking for contraband weapons, large caches of rice, anything we deemed the enemy might use. That would be the search end of it. The destroy was us taking whatever we find and make it, render it, unusable for the enemy.

Could you explain any experience you had with body counts, or kill ratios?

Yes. Body counts were normally done as you did these different operations, usually on a company or a battalion size movement. That way we kept track of whether or not we thought we were winning. The war was kept track by the total amount of enemy that we managed to kill in any given operation. Thus you get the body count. The individual says, "Oh, I shot 65 of them," and there's only one lying out there, he still calls it 65, and it was still called a body count of 65.

> *"THE WAR WAS KEPT TRACK BY THE TOTAL AMOUNT OF ENEMY THAT WE MANAGED TO KILL IN ANY GIVEN OPERATION."*

Did you use helicopters to get around?

Yes. I used helicopters extensively, especially in '68-'69 when I was in first recon. We would get on helicopters at our area where we were sleeping, fly out, land 25 miles at Charlie's backyard, run from the helicopter, hide for the next four days, and wait for the helicopter to come and get us.

What was the hardest part of being in the war?

The hardest part of the war was not knowing from day to day if I was going to live or die. A marine only has one object on his mind, and that it to kill the enemy. That's what he's trained to do. That's what he's supposed to do. His only thought was, "Am I going to die doing it?"

Did you have problems not knowing who were the enemies?

Yes, there were a lot of problems not knowing who the enemy was. I have seen five year-old boys with hand grenades strapped to them. I've seen ninety year-old women with hand grenades strapped to them, the same ninety year-old woman or five year-old boy that just sold me a bottle of Coke ten minutes before.

> *"I HAVE SEEN FIVE YEAR-OLD BOYS WITH HAND GRENADES STRAPPED TO THEM."*

Did that bother you at all?

It was a little nerve shaking when I drive down the road in the back of a truck, and the kids were throwing dirt clods at your truck. I didn't know if there was a hand grenade in that dirt clod. What did you do? You shot them. Did it bother me? Yes. Did we do it? Yes.

Was there a lot of emotional and physical stress you had to endure?

As a marine, I don't have the emotional stress that you are looking for. I don't believe it was there. Physical stress, yes. You've got to remember, we were in a combat zone; we lived it every hour of every day for 365 days or longer, and there was no relaxing anywhere in there. That was the job everyday.

Is there one particular experience that stands out in your mind? If so, what happened?
I would say that one particular experience that stands out in my mind would have to be the last kill. That was eyeball to eyeball, him and me, and he didn't have a chance. He had raised his head up about two hundred

> *"THE OTHER KIND OF RECON IS WHAT MOST PEOPLE DON'T TALK ABOUT, AND THAT IS A STRICT KILLER UNIT."*

yards away from us, and we shot him. We went over; he wasn't quite dead. We moved his hand with the rifle in it, and we shot him again, right where he was laying.

What did serving your country mean to you during your active duty and now as a veteran?
Serving my country then as an active duty marine or army soldier meant that I was protecting or providing the freedom that everybody that sat back here in the United States enjoys. Now that I am a retired military veteran, I still believe that the military provides the freedom that everybody enjoys and that includes myself now.

Did you have problems dealing with the memories when you were back?
No. Unlike a lot of others, who got out immediately after they came from Vietnam, I stayed in the military, and worked through the system allowing myself to get reoriented back to a common life. The ones that got out immediately after, they didn't have that chance. They went from military life, to civilian life, from being a hardened combat soldier who could handle anything from a pistol to maybe a tank, to not being able to do anything because nobody wanted to hire the vet.

Could you describe recon operations?
Reconnaissance operations formed into three different brackets. They are all handled by either four or seven man groups in the Marine Corps, four-man groups being force recon, seven man groups being first recon battalion, second or third recon battalion. Recon operations are done on the basis of we go out, we find out the information that the higher head quarters had asked us to find, and we come back. It may be pictures. It may just be our word. Another form of recon is we go out, we find that item that they sent us out there for, and we destroy it - search and destroy. The other kind of recon is what most people don't talk about, and that is a strict killer unit.

Where you ever wounded in action?
Yes. In 1969, on April 16th, I got blown right out of my shoes. We were going out on a predawn ambush from our reconnaissance operations post, and the lead man tripped the booby trap. Of the eight of us that were there, I was the only one that was a walking wounded. The rest were either dead or being carried out.

What was the booby trap?
The booby trap was a device that was placed in a specific area with maybe a string or a cord or something across the trail. As we walked pass it, we would strap the cord, and the explosive would go off. There were a lot of different booby traps. Mine happened to be, we believed, probably an 81-millimeter mortar hanging about six inches above the ground.

Were you ever almost killed?
Yes, at the same exact time. The individual behind me when that explosion happened was killed. We were walking about 2 feet away from each other and in a row, all eight of us, front to back, two feet apart.

Would you ever go back to Vietnam now?

Yes, as I matter of fact, I'm looking forward to it. It's just getting the money and the availability to do so. I would love to go back there and see one of the most beautiful countries in the world. Before the French Indochina war, before Vietnam, Indonesia, Vietnam, all of that area was a prime tourist area; it was a jungle paradise. They used to have large hunting lodges to hunt wild animals from. It is one of the most beautiful countries I have ever seen, and I had seen most of the countries in the world.

Did the South Vietnamese want you in Vietnam?

In 1965, when I got to Vietnam, they didn't want us. They needed us. In 1968, when I went back, they wanted us. In 1972, it had come down to, "Well, we're not sure whether you should be here or not."

Did you go on the three tours because you wanted to?

Yes. The first tour, I went over in 1965. I didn't know we were going to Vietnam. I hadn't heard of Vietnam, but wound up there. The second tour, I volunteered to go back to Vietnam. The third tour, I volunteered to go back.

Why did you volunteer to go back?

There are several reasons to do so. Number one, I was a marine. A marine was trained to work in combat. We go where the combat is. The other one was I had a little brother that was in the army, and by me being in country, he would not be in country.

What kind of reception did you get when you came back to the United States?

The reception I got when I came back to the United States was not what you were looking for. I didn't have people throwing stuff at me. I didn't have people calling me baby killers. I didn't have people spitting on me at the airports. I managed to avoid all that by just simply not being seen.

Do you have any opinions regarding the antiwar movement back in the states or Vietnam?

The antiwar movements were the individual's rights that I was fighting for. Their constitutional rights tell me and tell them that they could say or do basically whatever they want as long as it's not against the law. That's one of the things that I was fighting there for. We were fighting communism, whether they thought it was or not, and part of the freedom that goes along with being able to say and do what you want, somebody has to give up their life for it. I was one of those that were sent to do it.

How was the relationship between the whites and blacks in the unit?

In the units that I was in, there was no difference between white and black. I like to say we all wore the same color. We were marine green. My best friend that didn't come back from Vietnam was black. Some of the best leaders I had were black. I had white leaders that couldn't hold a candle to black leaders. Then again, I had some black leaders that weren't any good. Race in the units that I was in did not exist. Everybody was, again, was marine green.

Do you miss being with your marine friends?

I converse with them via e-mail over the computer. That includes guys that I went through marine boot camp with, guys I was stationed in London with, guys I was in Vietnam with, guys I wasn't even in Vietnam or stationed with. I have friends now or acquaintances strung all the way around the world from London to California, that I converse with through e-mail.

Could you describe what Agent Orange is?

Agent Orange is a chemical defoliant. When it

> *"I WOULD LOVE TO GO BACK THERE AND SEE ONE OF THE MOST BEAUTIFUL COUNTRIES IN THE WORLD."*

is sprayed out, it lands on the leaves or the different material that is there and actually kills it so there is no more cover. It makes green areas dead and brown. It was used to deny access to areas of the enemy by removing their cover. They could no longer use it to move their weapons and people down that area. They had to find new routes. Was it dangerous? Yes. I have a real good acquaintance of mine that is still alive and hospitalized because he was of the spray crew on an aircraft for Agent Orange. Have I had been in Agent Orange? I've been in the areas where it had been used. Do I have Agent Orange poisoning? I haven't got a clue. Agent Orange kills plants, not animals, but as they found out in later years, it does create tumors. It also creates cancer and birth defects in kids. I have two beautiful kids, neither of which have any birth defects.

Did you ever have a friend or somebody that really wanted to get out of the war because it bothered him too much?
No. All of the individuals that I've worked with in the units knew what they were doing, knew why they were there, and they did their job. There were a few people that I saw and met that were the other way. They didn't want any part of it. They didn't want to be there, and it showed on the way they worked. Most of the time, they were draftees. They came to Vietnam. They haven't been "acclimatized" for the heat. They came

"SOME OF THE BEST LEADERS I HAD WERE BLACK."

straight out of marine boot camp, straight out of marine training right straight to Vietnam. No "acclimatization" for the heat, no concept of what they were doing there. They didn't want to be there, didn't want to be drafted, but didn't have a choice, so they thought that a way around this was that "We just won't do anything." Not doing anything got a lot of people killed sometimes.

So what do you think about drafting?
I think that the draft is good, when it is needed, and it may be needed to fight this war on terrorism. I myself am recallable to active duty until I hit 65 as long as I can physically pass the physical end of the military examination. I would go back on duty. I would not go to the combat zone. I would go to some post here in the states to relieve somebody who is on active duty, and a lot younger guy would go and participate in that war. Should it become an all-out shooting war, then it doesn't make any difference. Everybody is going to be involved.

Do you think that the draft was necessary in the Vietnam War?
The draft was necessary in the Vietnam War, yes, without any doubt. We were not getting the enlistment that was needed to keep the troop levels at the level that was needed to fight the war. Remember, during Vietnam, we had people sitting on the DMZ in Korea. During Vietnam, we still had the East Coast of the United States and the West Coast of the United States. The North German plane guarded against Russia, the south mountain area of Germany guarded against Russia; and the Cold War going on at the same time. We had people strung out all over the world, just as we have now, doing just what they were supposed to be doing. Still we had to fight the war in Vietnam, so the draft was needed.

Do you think that the U.S. should've gotten involved in the war?
In Vietnam, yes. Vietnam was a country like North and South Korea that is divided. You had North Vietnam, South Vietnam. North Vietnam was a communist regime. South Vietnam was an independent, legally voted democratic republic. The people had voted for their leaders, and North Vietnam had the intention of taking South Vietnam completely, and turning them it into a communist state, which is where it is anyway. But had we not got involved in that, it might have not stopped in South Vietnam. It could've gotten to South Vietnam, to Laos, to Cambodia, now known as Kampuchea, to Thailand, to India, to anywhere, and by the time it was done moving, you would have had communism spread all through Southeast Asia, middle Asia, Russia, and China.

Did the marines follow the kill, or were they killed?

Kill or be killed…preferably, it was kill, not be killed, but yes, you could say that. We were pretty much young, gung-ho troops. Units that I went over with the first time, we had trained for almost two years to go to Vietnam without knowing it. We had the mental attitude of we're here, we're going to fight. If we die, we're not going to worry about it and, the American military even today, regardless of what people think, had a job to do. We don't like to get killed, but if it happens, it happens. That's our job. It's just like the cop on the street out here. His job is to protect and defend. A military job is to protect and defend. We just do it a little differently.

> *"In 1965, when I first went to Vietnam, anything that moved after dark was shot. It was enemy. That was the classification. In 1968 when I went back to Vietnam, it was they got to shoot at me, before I shot at them."*

Was it difficult to count the number of enemy troops?

Yes, because you never knew who it was. If they weren't physically holding a rifle in their hand, or physically an NVA soldier dressed in NVA gear, we didn't know if he was an enemy or not. In 1965, when I first went to Vietnam, anything that moved after dark was shot. It was enemy. That was the classification. In 1968 when I went back to Vietnam, it was they got to shoot at me, before I shot at them.

What do you think were some reasons that the U.S. had limited success in the War?

The main reason was the American public. They put the pressure on the politicians, and the politicians put the pressure on the military leaders. The military leaders told us how to fight the war. From the day it started until the day it ended, the American military put all of its might behind the war. It could've ended in six months because we would have just started at the South of Vietnam and walked our way to the north of Vietnam. That would've been the end of it, but having said that, that's not the way you choose to really fight a war. Some guys suggested, "Well let's blacktop it, and make it the world's largest airport or parking lot." That meant from coast to Laotian border, to the Mekong Delta, all the way to the DMZ in the north, turn it into black top. Use it as a parking lot or an airport, not conceivable idea, but that was some of its mentality.

How did you think the Vietnam War was different from other wars?

The Vietnam War was different from other wars because number one, we were fighting a people who've never been conquered. They've been subdued, but not conquered. Vietnam was not conquered by the Japanese in WWII, it wasn't conquered by the French during the French Indochina War, and there was no way we were going to conquer the Vietnamese. The best we could hope for in that war was a split like we have in Korea, north and south with militarized zone in between. Now having said that, I will also say that the majority of the people that lived in South Vietnam were glad to see the American military people. Their economy went up, their intelligence level went up, and their durable goods processing went up. They actually made money from the war by us being there.

Do you think the Americans' ideas of U.S. Military warfare from WWII affected their attitudes from Vietnam?

Yeah. World War II was a conventional war. You got out, you went over; you got behind a tank, or got in a tank, you drove down the road, you fought the enemy. You knew who he was; he was standing behind the line at you. He's shooting at you; you're shooting at him. He's in full combat gear, easy to pick out, whether it'll be Japanese or German; they were easy to spot. We went into Vietnam. First time I went I had no clue we were going there until I was two days from being there, and the battalion commander called everybody together. He put his rack of military operational manuals up behind him and shoved them at the back end of the ship, and said, "We're going

"VIETNAM WAS NOT CONQUERED BY THE JAPANESE IN WWII, IT WASN'T CONQUERED BY THE FRENCH DURING THE FRENCH INDOCHINA WAR, AND THERE WAS NO WAY WE WERE GOING TO CONQUER THE VIETNAMESE."

somewhere where these books no longer work; we're going to Vietnam. We going to fight in a country you can't move a tank through." You don't drive tanks through rice patties; they don't work well. One road, north to south, everything else little bitty branch roads. You don't go anywhere. It was a totally different concept that the American military never thought of in actuality.

Have you seen the Ho Chi Minh Trail?

I saw the Ho Chi Minh Trial in many forms. I saw little trails through the jungle, to a two-lane black top road with black lines on it, still in the jungle, so it didn't necessarily mean that it was a little trail. We had a place we called the "Yellow Brick Road." If you went far enough up the "Yellow Brick Road," that's the trail to the banana plantation and the rice country. If you walked up into the mountains and went North of Da Nang, eventually, you would come across a widened off area underneath that triple thick canopy with black tops, white marking on the sides of the road where they would move their heavy equipment down to south Vietnam. To this day, I don't think that you can get anybody to admit that that road ever existed.

Can you explain some activities that you've seen on the Ho Chi Minh Trail?

Most of the time that you saw something in the Ho Chi Minh Trail, you were in the wrong spot. As a recon. operation control leader, we were on the Ho Chi Minh Trail a lot. We would set up our observation posts and watch what came up and down the trail, record it, and take pictures of it. Most of it was what you see in the TV news, the bicycles with the equipment on it, the people carrying it, and occasionally the elephants were walking on the turf. You knew when they were coming. We used to have fun because all you had to do was throw a live round down there, and let it go boom, and the elephants would panic. They would run all over everything, getting out of it, and that was what we called fun.

Did you get to see a lot of Southeast Asia?

Yeah, I got to see parts of the world that most people can't reach. I was in Vietnam, in Thailand, the edges of Laos; I got to see places the average person going to even Vietnam can't see. You go to Vietnam today, it's a controlled tour; you don't get to just walk off into the jungle someplace. There are millions of booby traps out there, still to this day, and some of them work, and some of them don't work. You don't just get to go where you want. You don't get to go look at the things that you think you might want to see. If you have had a relative that was killed in a specific area in Vietnam, and you went there, and you wanted to see it, chances are you not going to see it. They just will not allow you to see it.

Do the booby traps still work?

No, we both put out the booby traps. They put them out; they walked away. They were designed to kill us or kill them. You leave them there; you don't worry about them. If they don't work when somebody walks through, well then that's fine and dandy, and if they did, you got somebody. The idea of attrition by killing is not the way you fight in the world. Attrition by injuring, is the way you fight in the war. You can't kill everybody in the war, but you can injure a whole lot more people. For every person you injured, it takes two to remove him from the battlefield. It takes five, six, seven, to take care of him in a hospital. Attrition by injuring is a better concept then attrition by killing. Booby traps are there, a bunch of stakes are there, the snakes are there, the treeing or rocks, the bears were there, the tigers were there. There's probably still Coca-Cola bottles with acid in it, or glass, ground up glass, sitting somewhere. Some cave where along with two types, three types, or half a dozen different types of weapons that were never found and was totally forgotten are still there.

What was one thing you remembered about Vietnam the most?

 The most vivid thing that I remember about Vietnam was the heat and the smell. The heat on an average summer day would run somewhere around about 130 [degrees] in the shade. The smell is an impossibility to describe. Every country has their own smell; Vietnam had theirs. It's a combination of the terrain, the weather, and the cooking. The smells from the different hamlets would hang in the air, and just like in Wisconsin, you have a fresh, clean smell in the summertime. In the fall, you get to smell the fall because the leaves change. You had the same smell over there, only the smell was unique to Vietnam.

Is there a message you have for young people about the war?

It's over; forget it; it's done with. Look at the pictures, listen to the people who were there, listen to the people who knew what was going on, get the information, put it in the brain in the back of the head somewhere, and sooner or later it will dawn on you that it's over. It's been over since 1972. We now have a new war to worry about, and we're convinced fighting is the answer right now. It's called a war on terrorism, and they just put troops on the ground.

> *"YOU DON'T DRIVE TANKS THROUGH RICE PATTIES; THEY DON'T WORK WELL."*

Is there anything else you want the people to read this book to know about?

Yeah, probably the one thing that has always bothered me in about American public regarding Vietnam, is that it took till the year 1982 before people realize that the Vietnam veteran was a product of their making. They're the ones that said, "Let's have a military," so we went in. They're the ones that said, "Let's go have a war in Vietnam" so we went and fought. They're the ones when we came back that said, "Hey, you guys, we don't even want to hear about you. You guys were doing things that we don't want to know about." In 1982, we had the first Vietnam veteran march in Washington D.C.; we erected the Vietnam memorial. It draws more people to it then the Smithsonian Institute Museums do on a daily basis. Combat veterans, Vietnam veterans, wives and kids, mothers, dads of veterans who died over in Vietnam, and the average person off the street wants to see that monument. Vietnam was a time in the American history that needs to be looked at, remembered, but not relived.

Do you have any ending remarks?

The only ending remember remark I can think of is one of two, *uura* or *semper fi*.

What's semper fi?

Semper fi delas. Short for always faithful. It's a Marine Corps motto UUra is a recon way of saying, "let's go."

Bill Masemen continued to serve his country in the service following Vietnam putting ten years in the Marines and eleven in the Army.

Interviewed and transcribed by Denise Zilch

©2002 D.C. Everest Area Schools Publications

Mort McBain

Mort McBain was born and raised in Glasglow, Scotland, until the age of 16, when he immigrated to the U.S. with part of his family. He was drafted during Vietnam and spent the one year standard "tour of duty" in Vietnam. He served in the infantry, cavalry, and finally LRRP's (long range reconnaisance patrols) of the 1st Brigade, 4th Infantry Division.

How did you become involved in the Vietnam War?
I was drafted. I was 19 years old at that time and living in California when I received my draft notice and my physical.

What were the base camps like in Vietnam?
Well, they were ok; they were hot, humid and very military like in the way they were operated. Going to Vietnam was kind of different because of the humidity and weather; it was a much different kind of weather than what I was used to at the time.

Did you fight against the Vietcong or NVA regular units?
In the infantry I fought against both Vietcong from local villages and occasionally NVA units. I was in a couple of different places while in Vietnam. The first place I was with was the 1st infantry division in the southern part of the country. It was in the Saigon area, Bien Hoa; heavily populated areas. I was an infantryman there, and I was also part of the Calvary. I drove one of the medic trucks, which was sort of an armed pesonnel carrier. It was used to evacuate wounded and dead from the battlefield sites, very often during the heat of the battle itself. The 2nd experience was in the central highlands where I was both in the infantry and then in LRRP (Long Range Reconnaissance Patrol).

Were you involved in any firefights?
Yes, I was involved in firefights, both as infantry, Calvary, and also, probably more times, when I ran into the enemy as a LRRP (Longrange Reconnaissance Patrol). LRRP's operated in small teams, 3,4,5 men on a team. We would be taken out by helicopter very far out into the operating area. We were basically the eyes and ears of the brigade or the division. We looked for things, scouted around and looked for any fresh signs of the enemy. We didn't try to

"I DROVE ONE OF THE MEDIC TRUCKS, WHICH WAS SORT OF AN ARMORED PERSONNEL CARRIER. IT WAS USED TO EVACUATE WOUNDED AND DEAD FROM THE BATTLEFIELD SITES, VERY OFTEN DURING THE HEAT OF THE BATTLE ITSELF."

engage the enemy because when you are in a small unit like that you have to be very careful because chances are that you would run into a unit bigger than yours. We tended to avoid contact as much as possible. We looked for things and we reported information back to headquarters about what we found. We would occasionally call in air strikes, or if we were close enough, artillery strikes on any targets we found that we thought needed to be destroyed.

"FOR US, THE DIFFICULT PART OF THE WAR WAS FIGHTING AGAINST A POP-ULATION THAT YOU WERE NEVER SURE EXACTLY WHO YOU WERE FIGHTING."

Describe what is meant by guerilla warfare?

For us, the difficult part of the war was fighting against a population that you were never sure exactly who you were fighting. It was difficult visually to tell if people were with you or not. That was a great dilemma for American commanders in the field because the enemy could simply fade, after a battle for example, into the civilian population or go back into the village. It was hard to know who was who. It was very frustrating, and we were not used to fighting an un-conventional war or a guerrilla war, and so it became a very difficult and frustrating exercise. As a result of that frustration I am sure many bad things happened. There were some atrocities committed on both sides because it was a very un-conventional type of war.

Did you ever do an ambush?

Yes, we in the infantry frequently went out on night ambushes. Also in the LRRPs we would occasionally do that, but very carefully because, as I mentioned, when you are with a small team you had to be careful whom you took on. You were way out in the unfriendly area and might not be rescued if you got in the hot water too quick. We had to be careful whom we engaged.

Any experience with body counts or kill ratios?

We did have experience with body counts and kill ratios. That was pretty important to the officers and those who were in command because body counts were sort of a sign of success. It was visual documentation of you succeeding in your mission if there were a lot of dead bodies around (hopefully the enemies). So, body counts were used quite frequently to document how well you had done as an officer.

Did you use helicopters to get around?

Yes, we flew everywhere. In fact as a LRRP, that was the only way we would get out was to use a helicopter. We flew quite a ways into the central highland areas. We were frequently in remote areas. Occasionally we'd actually get into Cambodia although officially, of course, we were not there. We knew we were occasionally crossing the line into Cambodia though, because that is where the enemy was and we wanted to find where they were. We got very used to riding around in helicopters. When I was in the infantry in the central highlands, of course, we were supplied and re-supplied constantly by helicopters. The Firebase would be on top of a big hill out in the hills, and everything that came in or out of that base was by helicopter. Then you ran patrols from the firebase and looked for action.

Were you a part of the Tet Offensive?

I was in Vietnam in 1968. I got there the day after the Tet Offensive started, so it was quite an exciting time. I didn't get to see much of the action. We were on call for about 48 hours right after the Tet. I was still processing through the orientation for new in-country arrivals, so I really didn't get to see that much action. I am kind of sad I missed it. As we went around later, we could tell that there had been a lot of things that happened during the Tet.

Were drugs a problem?

Well, they weren't so much a problem, but they were readily available. We had quite a few soldiers that used them, of course. We had un-written rules in the infantry and LRRPs that you didn't use that stuff when you went out prior to a mission or before going out on a patrol. You just didn't do that because if you were impaired in any way, you were not only endangering your own life, but you were seriously endangering the lives of your buddies. That was kind of an honor system that you were very careful with. So, although they were readily available, they were used mostly at the base camp. It wouldn't have been appropriate anywhere else. It was pretty much standard rule that people did not use them in the field because it was much too risky, and you didn't want to be impaired in any way if things got out of hand. In the LRRPs we never used them out in the field, although there was some use in the base camps when we came home, but not a lot. There was mostly a lot of beer drinking that went on.

"OCCASIONALLY WE'D ACTUALLY GET INTO CAMBODIA ALTHOUGH OFFICIALLY, OF COURSE, WE WERE NOT THERE."

What was the relationship between whites and blacks?

In our unit, it was actually very positive. What I discovered personally, and I think this is generally true; under combat conditions the racial distinction frequently becomes less important. In our LRRP unit it was very obvious that mixed race units went out all the time and the team leader, either black or white, was the team leader. For the radio man, it was the same thing. A person had a job to do as part of a team and race was very much secondary, or very insignificant. There were problems from time to time, but not nearly to the extent you would have seen state side. Because of the high purpose of why we were there and the feelings, blacks and whites alike pretty much shared responsibility and respected each other, so we didn't have any problems with race that I could see. We learned to judge people, frankly, on a different kind of continuum based on character, liability, and skill in the field rather than race. Race did not play a significant part in our operations as far as I could tell.

How did you feel about the Anti-War Movement back in the States?

Well, that didn't personally affect me very much. I didn't pay that much attention to it. I still felt at that time that we were there for an appropriate reason. I was a rather un-educated 19-year old. I didn't really have a lot of philosophy to offer. Basically, as a draftee without a lot of personal opinions, which wouldn't have been listened to anyway, I didn't pay much attention to it.

"WE LEARNED TO JUDGE PEOPLE, FRANKLY, ON A DIFFERENT KIND OF CONTINUUM BASED ON CHARACTER, LIABILITY, AND SKILL IN THE FIELD RATHER THAN RACE."

What was the hardest part of being in the war?

I would have to say that just the general conditions of being out in the field were very, very hard. Being in the battle wasn't actually the hardest part. It was so exciting and adrenaline-filled that it was a very exciting time. It was long periods of boredom, and as someone said, "punctuated by a few moments of absolute terror," which would be the actual fire fights that we got into where there were actual bullets flying. That was stressful, but also exciting, and you didn't consciously think about dying or being injured. You were usually pumped up and doing what you had to do, hoping there wasn't a bullet with your name on it.

Was there a lot of emotional or physical stress?

Mostly physical, but there was some emotional stress of course; the fear of being in combat. There is always a negative feeling in the back of your mind that you might be the one that goes next, and there might have been some superstitions that went along with it, a defense mechanism. Each group, each person, developed ways of dealing with that fear of being brought home in a body bag. You didn't talk about it much, but it was always there, and so you just dealt with it the best you could.

Is there one particular experience that stands out in your mind?

There were a few of them that were quite interesting. One or two of them were mentioned in the book that I was part of. The title of the book is *Phantom Warriors Book II* and the author is Garry Linderer. It is primarily written about LRRP units. This gentleman went out to find some of the experiences that LRRP units had. I am in the second book, and I represent the 1st brigade of the 4th infantry division in the Central Highlands.

Do you think the U.S. could have won the war?

That's possible. When I was over there and after I came back, I thought for many years that we could have perhaps done it the same way we did in Korea. But the problem that I saw in Vietnam, and had thought about later, much later, was that the Vietnam War was basically a Civil War. It was not just the North trying to take over the South. There was also a lot of support in the South for the philosophy of the North. I don't think we could have won militarily. We could have fought somewhat differently. Of course, there will be great debate on the effectiveness of the way the war was waged. The generals complained that their hands were tied by the politicians, and the politicians were not sure what they were doing in some cases I think. But there were a lot of questions in terms of how the war was fought. I don't know that we could have won it militarily. Perhaps we could have. There were a lot of restrictions. We could have bombed the North into submission eventually, had we dropped enough bombs in strategic places. But bombing runs were very often confined to politically acceptable targets, rather than military targets, which would have been the choice of the generals. It would have been very very difficult to have a military victory because you would have always had a huge permanent cadre in South Vietnam who were sympathetic to the philosophies in the North. So there remains great debate to this day whether we would have won the war had we done things differently. I don't know the answer to that question.

Did you make any lasting friendships?

Well, not really, just sort of. I have one or two friends that I have had contact with now that I have restarted the friendship with them 25-30 years later; thanks to the Internet. I just got on and made contact with a couple of people I still remembered. We actually have met now and had a reunion a year or two ago with some of the LRRP friends that I had. So I have now a couple friends I occasionally contact. We get together once in awhile.

What kind of reception did you get when you came back to the U.S.?
In contrast to the stories that I've head about people being spat on and treated badly, I really wasn't treated badly at all. I wasn't treated at all any way. It was more like people were not interested. In fact, when I came back I had some slides and home movies. I had given talks mostly to

> *"...IT WOULD HAVE BEEN VERY VERY DIFFICULT TO HAVE A MILITARY VICTORY BECAUSE YOU WOULD HAVE ALWAYS HAD A HUGE PERMANENT CADRE IN SOUTH VIETNAM WHO WERE SYMPATHETIC TO THE PHILOSOPHIES IN THE NORTH."*

my church group, trying to get people interested in what was going on, and frankly, there wasn't a lot of interest in it. I came back in January of 1969 and even though the war was in full swing and thousands were being drafted and shipped over to replace the people coming home, there just did not seem to be a lot of interest. Unless you were on a college campus. I was not on a college campus at that stage in my life. I never really got to experience anti-war movements per se. I did participate in a couple of rallies, but they were more pro-government rallies. I wore a partially illegal uniform. I wore my old LRRP uniform and took all the identification off of it and then participated in a couple of movements that were in support of what we were trying to do. We were opposed to the peace rallies that were against the war. So I did do a little bit of speaking up, but not much.

What does it mean to you to serve your country?
I have always felt, and still feel that as a pre-requisite or as a requirement to the privilege of living in the United States one has an obligation to support the country. When the government calls you, (when I was drafted I was a British subject meaning I legally could have gone to Canada. I decided not to do that. I accepted my draft call, I was drafted, and I was willing to serve. I felt that that was the price I needed to pay in order to become a permanent resident of the United States) you should go. Mostly the intentions of the country and our leaders were honorable.

Were there any difficult memories when you returned?
I don't recall anything. I didn't have any nightmares. I was a very strong person over there. Emotionally and spiritually I could lean on my religion, so I didn't really experience the problems that some veterans did, and I must say, most veterans that I know did not experience problems coming back. But there were some vets that did have problems with emotional stress usually due to things that happened to them over there. Occasional killings of civilians; I am sure a lot of those memories are there for many veterans. Keep in mind that most of the vets in Vietnam were not in actual combat; they were there for support.

Do you have a message for young ones today?
I have mixed feelings about that. I would still advise them that they have an obligation to support, in general, the constitutional principals that made our country strong and great. But at the same time, I think there is a public consciousness that needs to be exercised. When it appears that we are headed for conflict, people certainly have a right under the first amendment to speak freely and make statements pro or con. So while we cherish the ability we have to speak out and have our voices heard, I also believe that we have a obligation to support our constitution and elected government when it makes an official declaration in terms of our intentions including war and conflict. I think we have an obligation to serve the country in some fashion, even if it would be a non-combative roll. I think that is legit, but still, I think that when your country calls, you have an obligation to serve.

Just a few more thoughts I have about the LRRPs; a lot of books have been written about the Green Beret,

Seals, Rangers or LRRPs. Rangers and LRRPs were based on the concept of small units. The two terms mean the same thing. Having an opportunity to work in small teams of highly motivated men- that was a challenge; it was very exciting but scary. My experiences are generally quite positive.

McBain eventually returned to college when 25 years old and received a good education thanks to the GI Bill. He holds a B.S. degree and a M.B.A. from Idaho State University. He has followed the profession of county administration for approximately 27 years and currently is the county administrator for Marathon County, a position he has held since 1987. One of his missions with a LRRP team is chronicled in the book Phantom Warriors, Book 2, by Gary Linderer. He is married, with 5 children, and lives in the Weston area.

Interviewed by Lesley McBain

Peter Nielsen

A volunteer, Neilson was a military photographer serving in Thailand in 1965-66. He flew recon and photographed material for intelligence and then documented many events with his camera.

The Second World War was the war of our parents. In that era there was a much greater respect for veterans following the Second World War than following the Korean War. There was respect for the Korean veterans to some extent, but not as much as the Second World War. When Vietnam broke out and we went in there, it turned into a political quagmire. The military was not able to do its job, there were a lot of restrictions, and then it got into a big political battle. It influenced the people coming back from Vietnam. Most of us were young and we went through a lot, and we came back to a situation in the United States where the feelings were negative toward the veteran.

How did you originally become involved in the war?

I was in the army, and I was sent overseas. When you go in the army, everybody is trained to be a soldier, so you learn to be a fighting machine. You've learned all your skills, and that's the main job of everybody in the service. After that you go into specialty fields. I was a photographer. I spent a year in Korea along the DMZ, and from there I went to Thailand. I did all sorts of photography, ground, air, and I also worked with a classified clearance, so there is a lot of things I never talk about and I can't. I also had the ability to process the pictures. After some of the missions that we flew, intelligence people took the material after I processed them. They had the negatives and the stats and all that stuff. Basically that's where I was sent. They said they needed people in the service, and being a young man, I enlisted.

What year did you enlist?

I enlisted in the army in 1964, and I was in Korea in 1964. In 1965-66 I was in Vietnam and in Thailand. I flew out of Thailand covering the war in Southeast Asia.

Did you take combat photos?

I took pictures of everything.

Were you on ambushes and other rough stuff?

Whatever the needs were for the reconnaissance. I also took pictures of what are called accidents, people blown apart. Pictures were taken of the remains before being put in body bags.

Why did you have to take those photographs?
Documentation.

How long were you in Southeast Asia?
A year.

Are there any events that you can talk about?
Outside of our camp where we stayed was a large city. They had a huge fire. They called us up, and we all went down. Besides having my camera and everything else, we went down and fought the fire. When it ended, the whole city block of homes and businesses were destroyed. The photos that I had taken, since they weren't classified information, were sent down to Bangkok, Thailand. They wound up in the <u>Stars and Stripes</u> because I had photographed a lot of soldiers with their hoses on the flames. That was kind of neat. Also some of the road conditions weren't that great. The trail had a lot of ruts, and these trucks would go bouncing down the middle of the dirt roads.

Did you travel around a lot?
Yes.

What areas did you travel?
I traveled all through Thailand; I went into Laos and into Cambodia. I also flew to Vietnam and back.

Did you go into Vietnam more than once?
I flew in and out, but my main areas were Thailand, Cambodia, and Laos.

Did you experience a lot of combat going on?
No, not a lot, but we did have people that we brought back out of Laos

What was an average day for you?
Everyday was different; you never knew what was going to happen. It was very hot over there, and there were monsoons.

How did you adjust to living in a different climate?
You lost a lot of weight; you did not gain weight. You go into basic training and advanced infantry training and you build up, but during the tour you lose a lot. Stress also had something to do with it.

How was life like for the army personnel that were stationed there?
It was a base camp. The military rules and regulations ruled it "severe." in comparison to the states. In the states you would fall into attention and do other things, but here things were different. You went and did your job during the day. When you finished your tour you came back to the states, and you had to become military again. We had all come back from Vietnam, and we were in this three-story barracks building. They decided we had to have formations. Everybody fell out, and we stood out there, and we

were not "spit and polish;" you lose that overseas. They wanted to get us back in shape again, so everybody is standing down there. The sergeant yells out and one guy replied that he had double timed in Nam and he wasn't going to double time back here.

Did you have opinions of what was going on in the states when you were in Vietnam?
Yes, it was hard. We would read about all the things that were going on, and here we were doing what we thought was right. It was so hard and upsetting that they were taking it out on the troops, but the troops weren't the ones that brought us in there to begin with. The troops were not the ones making the decisions. For myself, being stationed in Thailand, they [the public] didn't recognize that there was a war in Thailand. It's mainly that we weren't in Laos and Cambodia. They didn't recognize that fact until twenty-five years after. They [the government] refused to admit the fact that we were in Laos and Cambodia, but now they do.

What was your personal opinion of the war as it was?
The troops did what they had to do. It was hard; it was rough. Everybody did his or her job. Even though we might not have prevented the Communists from taking over Vietnam, in the long run we did prevent the spread of Communism further. Communists did not get into Thailand. It did not spread any further while we were there, and it did not get farther. While we might have lost South Vietnam to communism, it stopped there.

In your opinion, was the war justified?
No war is justified. As far as I am concerned, you take anybody who wants war; let them go into the ring and fight it out. Leave the rest of us alone. That is my opinion.

What did you experience when you returned to the United States?
We came in and left in civilian clothes, never put our uniforms on. We saw rallies and other protests.

What year did you come back?
I came back in 1966, early enough where I wasn't there till the very end. I was in the reserves at the time.

Did you make any lasting friendships?
There are several individuals that I will never forget.

Is there a message you would like to add for young people?
Be proud of the veterans themselves, but be cautious. When you go into a situation where a war breaks out, and you are called up, this country wouldn't be free if it hadn't been for the fighting veterans. The Second World War was necessary. We had to be involved. We had no choice because we were being attacked. A nation has to have a military. Today we need a military, and you have to roll with the punches. There is no good war, but there

"EVEN THOUGH WE MIGHT NOT HAVE PREVENTED THE COMMUNISTS FROM TAKING OVER VIETNAM, IN THE LONG RUN, WE DID PREVENT THE SPREAD OF COMMUNISM FURTHER. COMMUNISTS DID NOT GET INTO THAILAND."

are times when you have to have a war to protect the free-doms of this country. The Civil War was not a good war, but there are times when a country must go to war. We would not be in the situation where we are if we didn't have the capability to keep people from attacking us, like Saddam Hussein. We must be able to stop aggression.

"WE TRIED TO GIVE OUR-SELVES A GOOD IMAGE; WE WENT IN WITH MEDICAL SUP-PLIES AND SET UP MEDICAL TEAMS WHO WOULD COME IN AND TREAT THE VILLAGERS."

What does "patriotism" mean to you today?
I am proud that I served my country. I am active in the vet-eran's organizations. I'm proud to be an American. You go to other countries, and they don't have freedom of speech, freedom of press, or being able to travel. I am glad I live in the United States and have the freedoms that I have. I feel that I did my part serving this country to maintain this.

What was your opinion of President Johnson?
Since I was an enlisted man, I wasn't really up on political science, and my view was like most army sol-diers. I never looked at the "big" picture; all I looked at was the situations we were in. My whole aim was to do what we had to do and then go home. It turned into a political war that involved the Congress.

Do you feel the United States could have won the war?
It was a civil war, which makes it hard to say; you can second-guess it. Like any civil war, it all depends on the people who live there. The only reason the Communists took over was because the people allowed it. As much as we didn't want the spread of communism, the people themselves let them take over the country.

What were some of your experiences interacting with the Southeast Asians?
There were good people, good culture, and I admired them. They had gone through a lot. I know people who are here today who were refugees. Their parents went through a lot more than we did. We were only there for a few years, and they lived there their whole lives. The ones who are here are here because they were against communism and fought against them. They lost a lot of the family members who are here. Only a very few escaped to Thailand and came out of the camps to the United States.

What was your relationship with the Southeast Asians when you were there?
There were good relations with the people that we worked with. Any time you left, you were always cau-tious because you never knew who the enemy was. You were always watching.

Did you interact with the civilians in the cities and villages?
Not a great deal; we did in respect to helping the villagers because there were a lot of Viet Cong. We tried to give ourselves a good image; we went in with medical supplies and set up medical teams who would come in and treat the villagers. We went down to the village and fought that fire I told you about. We tried to give a good impression of us and what we were after.

What did you do in your spare time?
We had time to relax, but there wasn't anything to do. There were no bowling alleys. We had movies once in a while, or we would sit around and play cards. There wasn't much you could do, so you got bored a

lot.

Was there much drug use by the troops when you were there?
No, it was there and it was part of their culture, but I never got into it.

Did you see other soldiers using drugs?
It was not allowed when we were there, but it was overlooked. It was more prevalent in combat areas; it was overlooked to some degree, but it was not allowed.

You were trained for combat, but did your specialty allow you experience any combat?
I had some experience, but my area was reconnaissance. I would go into areas and fly by, took pictures, and process film.

You took pictures of enemy areas?
Whatever it was.

You flew in helicopters?
I flew in helicopters, fixed wing aircraft; the bubble topped helicopter, the L-19, whatever we needed to complete the mission. We had areas that we went into where we had large cameras and would take photographs.

Did you fly in formation with other helicopters?
No, we traveled alone.

Did you experience anti-aircraft fire?
Sometimes.

Did you experience anything from that activity?
We went down one time and got fixed. The crew chief got us fixed and got us out of there. Some of our crew was injured. We were in enemy territory and in danger. Your adrenaline is very high; your actions are quick and your senses are very high.

Vietnam was described as "guerrilla" warfare. What did that mean to you?
Guerrilla warfare is basically for small units, five or six people, going out into the countryside to do their job. There are not huge formations of troops and tanks to do battle. You are out there on your own to do your job and get out. That is guerrilla. They had the same thing.

Is that difficult?
Definitely! You have no formations; it is hit and run. We were doing the same thing, and I don't think you can win a war that way. There are no large formations so there is no way to tell where they will go. A large formation requires roads and the movement of equipment and material. They can be spotted. Three

or four people can move quickly and quietly. Small groups of people make it rough.

Did you experience "booby traps"?
Yes.

What kind did they have?
They would have "trips" that would explode, and holes in the ground with stakes and things like that.

Was that a daily occurrence?
I didn't see that because I was in reconnaissance. I was mostly in the air, but I saw them a few times. It was rare that I came in contact with them, but they were there.

Did you have contact with snipers?
A chance happening. When you went downtown there wasn't a sniper on every building, but there might be one sniper here or there. You don't know where it is coming from or when. A sniper might fire one shot, and that's it.

How were race relations among the troops in your unit?
We had good relationship on the job. Off the job, they would divide.

How was the treatment of colored troops?
Their treatment was equal in the military. They were fighting alongside you.

Were you involved in any firefights?
Any time you took off and were spotted, we would draw fire. That is why we only went in once and got out. Over the target we would fly low at treetop level, go fast, take the photographs, and come out.

Why fly at treetop level?
They wouldn't see us. If you were way up in the sky, you would be seen. Just a few feet above the trees made you hard to see.

What type of aircraft did you fly?
One was the L-19; we called it a "bubble top," and the other was a "Huey." They have different names for them, but I have forgotten most of them.

Any event or story that you would like to share?
The basic people of the world do not want war; they want to live. When it comes to a war, the people become patriotic to their country and that's why you get into wars. Be proud of the country you live in. When you go overseas and see the conditions of some of these countries, you really appreciate what we have here. The military showed me that. I have seen people living in conditions that were terrible.

Have you experienced any problems with the war since your return?
You put it out of your mind, and I don't talk about. I didn't discuss it with my family. We came back, got

> *"WHEN YOU GO OVERSEAS AND SEE THE CONDITIONS OF SOME OF THESE COUNTRIES, YOU REALLY APPRECIATE WHAT WE HAVE HERE."*

a civilian job, and moved on. Different people had different jobs in the military, and some had more tragic experiences than I had.

Any final comments?
The only thing I would like to say is respect the veterans. They went through a lot, and hopefully we will never get into a situation like that again. Since 1975, we have not had a war of that scale. Hopefully we won't have one, but don't be afraid to stand up for your country.

Neilson as of 2002-2003, is retired from the Army Reserves as a Mastery Sergeant E-8 and the Wausau Paper Mill Brokaw. He is also active in the veteran organizations including the VFW (Veterans of Foreign Affairs) and the American Legion. In the American Legion he is the Commander of Post 10.

Interviewed by Amanda Gliniecki and Kesa Jenks

Ken Niles

Volunteering in 1966, Niles trained for and became a member of Special Forces. He served in Vietnam in 1968-69 as an "A" team commander and an infantry company commander.

You were in the Green Berets; what were they specifically called?
Special Forces.

How did you get started or involved in the army?
I volunteered for the military in 1966 because our country was at war.

What did you start out as?
I started as a private.

Did the military just recruit you?
I went into basic training with a request to go into Special Forces. At the time it meant I was guaranteed to get into every school required for Special Forces. If I failed any of the courses, then the contract was void, but only void on my part. This meant the army could put me anywhere they wanted. I went through basic training, which meant I had to go to Advance Infantry Training (AIT). Then I went to airborne school and airborne AIT. It was a preparation for airborne school. I had to pass the requirements to get into the airborne school. If I didn't pass, I wouldn't get into airborne school. Then I had to pass airborne school; and if I didn't become airborne, I couldn't get into Special Forces. The first requirement for all Special Forces is airborne. Then I would have been sent to a Special Forces school, which would either have been medics, demolition, communication, or weapons. But at that point I had taken batteries and batteries of tests. I had some college so I was being pressured by the military to go to officer's candidate school (OCS). I wasn't going to go at first, but my family, primarily my mother, convinced me to go to OCS. According to my contract, once I chose OCS, they didn't have to put me in Special Forces. I went through infantry OCS. I did have a contact, which I knew when I was in high school, which at this point was a full colonel. Later he became a general in charge of officer assignments. I didn't know that he was watching my progress. When I finished OCS, I had orders for Special Forces Training. That's how I got there.

What were base camps like?
I was in Special Forces, and as such, I had an opportunity to see a lot of different base camps. There were all kinds of base camps - marine base camps, base camps that were in the very southern part of Vietnam, and there were Special Forces base camps. Have you ever seen M.A.S.H. on TV? They were a lot like that. Sometimes they would take over a portion of a town or have one that almost looked like a little west-

ern town setting. It was kind of over a swamp, so it even had a boardwalk to walk over the swamp. They took over a few buildings attached to a town, stuck some barbed wire around it, and that was a base camp. Then there were nice base camps where the brigade and the armies stayed. The third army down in the South had a very nice base camp that the U.S. engineers built from scratch. Most base camps were dirty. Almost everybody, especially in the south, had a fungal infection because clean water was very scarce. Clean water was used for drinking. We washed our clothes and things in fairly filthy water. You couldn't afford to be washing everything and taking showers in drinking water; we just didn't have that much of it.

Could you describe what an average day was for you, being in Special Forces?

Our special-forces base camps were generally smaller and mostly bunker type camps with sand bags and a little bit of barbed wire around them. We didn't take time to build a lot of structures, buildings and things like that. We roughed it a lot more. The average day was that I would get up and have some type of a meeting with the commander of the base, whether the base was just an A-team base or what. I'd get our people together, check out the perimeter, and then we would send people out if there were any roads around. We would send the roadrunner through the immediate area. A roadrunner was two people in a jeep who would drive over the roads to set off any booby traps or mines placed there overnight. What they generally did was get in the jeep and drive about 30 miles per hour faster than the road could possibly handle them. They just kind of flew across the road. Hopefully they would set off a mine before it blew up, and part of the jeep would be over the mine. Then the roads were cleared. We would have some type of a mission that was planned out from the day before. It was generally going out into a surrounding area and looking for enemy activity and then coming back. We had areas of operations that would go out and just look for the enemy. We had an idea of where they were, where they would be, and what type of terrain they would be in. We would sit on the helicopters and look around for them. If we found them, we'd call in contact, engage, and call in contact until help arrived.

Could you explain any experience you had with body counts or kill ratios?

The body counts were a lie. The body counts were a propaganda thing. We had to give a certain amount of body count for every activity. We were supposed to kill a certain amount of enemy every day, and the attitude was if we were out doing our job, we'd be killing people. So if we went out all day, looked all over the place and never found an enemy, then we weren't doing our job. Then we would come back, lie, and tell how many people we killed. It was real interesting that the body count was always so high. We listened to various people report: "Well how many did you get?" "Well we got 3." "We got 6." "We got 7." "How many weapons did you bring in?" "We didn't get any weapons." They must have hauled off all those weapons before. A weapon was worth at least three for a body count.

Did you use helicopters to get around? Describe that experience.

Absolutely, helicopters were the only effective way to get around in Vietnam. You'd run up and get into a helicopter; they would take off and fly you some place. You would jump out. Sometimes the helicopter wouldn't touch down and you would jump out while it was hovering. When you did that, you had to be coordinated because men were standing on the struts of the helicopter ready to jump off. If everybody jumped off of the right side of the helicopter and no one jumped off of the left side of the helicopter, it would immediately tilt. If it tilted, and he [the pilot] tried to adjust it, and he was hovering, his blades hit the ground. This would take out a helicopter and probably a couple of people. So when you jumped off the side of the helicopter, one or more people all had to be coordinated, and you had to both jump off the sides at the same time.

Were drugs a problem for the soldiers in Vietnam?
There was a lot of marijuana used. There were a lot of "downers," barbiturates used. I never noticed it as a problem. There was a lot of beer drunk, and a lot of booze, mainly beer. I had as many soldiers who were drunk when we were off as I had people with a high. I had never had a problem, not in Special Forces, but this was in the regular infantry forces. I never had a problem in combat with anybody I thought was incapacitated because of drugs. But there were a lot of drugs there.

What was the hardest part of being in the war?
The hardest part of being in the war was being responsible for sending men to their death and being responsible for killing civilians.

Was there a lot of emotional and physical stress that you dealt with when you came back or while you were there?
While there, there was a lot of physical stress. It was hard to go out and stay awake. There was a lot of emotional stress being responsible for the lives of sometimes 200 people at a time, making decisions that might require that somebody die, get maimed, or get hurt, and that was fairly stressful.

Do you think the U.S. could have won the war?
Absolutely, because we weren't sent to win the war. We were sent to play games when we would fight. We would find an enemy force and we would chase them. They would get to the border, but we couldn't cross the border. They'd run across to the other side of the border, give us the finger, and set up their campfires and everything right there. They would sit, rest and recuperate. When they got good and ready, then they would come back across. Now, how are you going to win a war like that? The only way we could have won the war was to go into North Vietnam, to go into Laos and into Cambodia, and to go everywhere the enemy was staging. They would stage inside of Laos; they would stage and train inside of Cambodia and inside of North Vietnam. They would get tired in South Vietnam, then run back across the border to rest. We'd go chase them off; then we'd come back, and they'd come back. We'd chase them back again. It was the same thing over and over again. It got very frustrating for the ground soldier because he quickly understood. He understood he was the best-trained soldier in the world and the best equipped, but then when he would have a contact it was easy to spend $100,000 on ammunition on a contact and find out there were 6 or 8 people.

> " *IT SEEMED LIKE EVERY JOB APPLICATION WOULD KIND OF GIVE ME CREDIT FOR BEING IN VIETNAM.*"

What kind of treatment did you receive when you came home?
Well, I heard a lot about how badly we were treated, but I didn't particularly see that. I wasn't expecting a ticker tape parade or anything like that. Nobody came up and spit on me at the airport or anything like that. I didn't have a problem getting jobs. It seemed like every job application would kind of give me credit for being in Vietnam. It was a couple years before I realized how hard I had it when I came back.

What did "serving your country" or patriotism mean to you during active duty and now as a veteran?

Patriotism, we'll put that aside for a second. When I became an officer, I swore an oath to defend the constitution of the United States. The constitution is the law, and the life-blood of the United States, as we know it. That's what it meant to me. It meant doing my duty. My duty was to do as I was told unless it violated what I felt was the law or violated my morality. There were several orders that I didn't obey because I felt they violated my morality. Now, patriotism…I'm not sure what that means. I have been to almost every country in Asia. I spent six years in Asia working in that particular part of the country. I've seen good people, and I've seen

"YOU ARE THE LAW AND WHATEVER YOU DO IS OKAY AS LONG AS YOU ARE DOING IT IN THE NAME OF YOUR COUNTRY. OF COURSE THAT'S NOT RIGHT, NOT MORALLY RIGHT, BUT THAT'S WHAT WAR IS."

bad people. I've seen as many good people and bad people in this country. I do not believe in the phrase, "my country right or wrong," but if they're wrong, they're wrong. So I'm not sure what patriotism means, but whatever it is I paid the dues.

Is there a message you have for young people today about war, especially after this whole Afghanistan and terrorism ordeal?

The reality of it is, regardless of what anybody wants to tell you, war is fun. If you ever watched the movie Pinocchio, remember when Pinocchio got sent to the little island where he could do anything that he wanted to do? He could break windows; he could do all kinds of things. When you're in war, the rules as you were taught don't apply. You can kill, you can harass people, you can bully, and you can burn people's houses down. The guys really liked burning houses down. There was something about burning structures down. You could steal from people; you could demand they feed you their last grains of rice, when here was someone who didn't have any food themselves. You could take their stuff and…. The rules just don't apply. Some people got off on that, and it's kind of fun when the rules don't apply. You are the law and whatever you do is okay as long as you are doing it in the name of your country. Of course that's not right, not morally right, but that's what war is.

War is also ugly. People get hurt; people get killed. You know if an enemy soldier gets killed, or an American soldier gets killed, that's bad. But you know when civilians start getting killed, then that's kind of hard to live with. Even when you know it wasn't malicious. They didn't go out there and find a civilian up against a wall and shoot them. But civilians got killed. You kind of remember the faces and that sort of thing. War is ugly; it's like being in jail. You're sitting there in a dirty, crummy area. Everyday you get up and do the same thing. If you want to go downtown and party, you can't. You're stuck there. The problem with war is that very young people always fight it. When I was with the Infantry Company, the average age of the people who had to go out with me (of the 200 people there) was 17. I had platoon sergeants that were 18 years old. The Vietnam soldier only had to serve for a year, but a year out of a man's time, when he's 18, 19, 20, 21, is a long, valuable time. That is very frustrating. It just seemed like a waste. If we were doing something or accomplishing something, fighting for freedom or fighting against something, that would have been different. Here was the situation in Vietnam—if you had the average farmer who was living out there.

Did you know exactly why you were here fighting?

Oh, I was told why, but that wasn't the reason.

What were you told?

We were told we were protecting the South Vietnamese from communism.

What was the real reason?

Like I told you, this guy we were out there protecting from communism—the only thing we did was harass him, eat his food, and if he gave us any lip, we would burn down his house. He didn't want to be protected from anything. If someone doesn't want to be protected from communism, then it should be his or her choice to have communism. He didn't know what communism was. And we learned real quick from the South Vietnamese the only people in Vietnam who were really against the north were people in south Vietnam who were businessmen and who were making money off of the Americans.

Can you describe any special mission you were involved in being in Special Forces?

A Special Forces mission? One time we had a mission and we were supposed to go into enemy territory. We were going to be sent into enemy territory to find out some information. It was very important, and it was a very secret mission. It just went on and there was just too much planning. It just didn't feel right. There was too much planning. They required that we take three Americans and three South Vietnamese with us. We were pretty skeptical because we had to go pretty deep into enemy territory. We were supposed to go in, and we were supposed to get the information. When we got there, someone told them we were coming. They not only knew we were coming; they knew where the landing zone was, and they were waiting on the landing zone. It wasn't just an accident. We didn't just sit down in the middle of them. They were waiting for us, and the only reason we didn't get shot at more than we did was because they allowed us to get off the helicopters so they could shoot the helicopters down. They shot for the helicopters, and we started to run. Of course we weren't able to accomplish the mission; we had to run for three days and three nights just to get back to South Vietnam.

Describe the Tet Offensive.

Tet, 1968. Generally what we did with the infantry units was search and destroy. In other words, we would go out to try to find somebody. Half the time we couldn't find anybody. They'd be hiding in a little bunker or in the wood line. They might be there and there, and there would be two or three of them in a little bunker. They might have a machine gun and be in the bunker. But think of yourself if you're in a little bunker. There's two of you, and a helicopter lands and 10 Americans hit the ground. You know if you open fire not only do you have those 10 Americans, but you have whoever is supporting them with that helicopter unit because in minutes you're going to have Americans and helicopters and artillery all over you. They didn't take pot shots at us because they knew we were looking for them. If we happened to go in there and didn't find anything, they would hunker down in the bunker, cover themselves with leaves, and things like that. They might have been there, and if we didn't find them, we almost had to step on them. It was kind of like a poisonous snake that just sits there. That's generally how it went.

Tet is a religious holiday, kind of like Christmas. We were expecting them to be taking a break. On Tet in `68, they had this huge offensive. I mean it was like an all out crazy thing. These people came from everywhere. The easiest thing to say about Tet is that everyone died in Tet. It was the biggest bloodbath in Vietnam. The tables were completely turned, and they were after us. We didn't have to go out and look for them. All you had to do was turn around and they were coming at you. They were coming at you in your camps; they were coming at you in the woods. Everything else was just this massive offensive. A lot of us people got killed during Tet. Since they were out in a massive offensive, a lot more of them were killed because the best way they had to survive was hiding and taking little potshots like guerrillas do. Tet was a non-guerrilla tactic. It was as though we were fighting a regular, organized army. It lasted for a little while, but it was very costly for them and confusing for us because we expected them to do that next half. Of course they didn't. But that's what Tet was about.

Are there any other stories that you're willing to share?

There was an interesting thing (not that I'm psychic or anything), but it was like a psychic feeling every once in a while. Maybe it was just a trained professional's feeling, before I ever went to Vietnam. Most of the people I worked with were young kids. There were several times when I saw people and I knew something was going to happen to them. One person I knew - I just looked at him one day, and I just had a real bad feeling. I just knew something was going to happen to him. What really happened was what I expected. When I looked at him, I saw us crossing a stream, and I said, "Now you look up that stream and if anything moves shoot it." I looked at him, and he had his weapon pointed up the stream. He was looking and his head was in that direction, but I could see in his eyes that he wasn't seeing anything. He was back home somewhere. He was distracted. Viet Cong could have walked up in front of him and smacked him in the nose. That gave me a bad feeling. I said to myself, "I'm probably going to have to work with this guy." He got killed a few days later, but the reason he was killed was real hard. I had to write a letter to his family, and this is what happened. We were in close contact with some Viet Cong. We were in a firefight, running around in this wood line. There were a lot of palm leaves and growth, so you can't see but a few feet ahead of you. We were fighting with people who were 20-30 feet away from us. They were shooting and we were shooting. While shooting, we starting moving and were about waist deep in water. This guy was right in front of me. He opened up the wood line and saw a wounded Vietcong. We were in a hot firefight. We're following these people and moving around. If he saw him (a Viet Cong), he should have just shot first. When he saw the guy down, he turned to me to say, "Wounded Viet Cong." He got out the word "Wou-." They shot him in the heart. I believe it was the wounded Viet Cong who shot him, and he fell back onto me. We pulled him out, and of course, we took care of the situation. He never made it to Saigon. He was shot pretty badly. We got him on the chopper right away. I sent a man with him, but he never made it. How do you write a letter to a mother saying her son was killed because he was a good Christian boy? He remembers all the John Wayne movies and that sort of thing. Once a man is wounded and lying there, you don't just kill him. It was what was hard to deal with. I realized I was going to have to teach them, these innocent young boys; and I was going to have to teach them how to be cold, heartless killers in order to survive. Then the problem was, if I teach them real well, what happens when they come home?

Following his return, Ken Niles became involved in sales.

Interviewers: Callie Reger and Kyle Goertz

©2002 D.C. Everest Area Schools Publications

Jim Reesman

Arriving in 1968, Reesman was involved with military intelligence. He served with the 1st Military Intelligence Battalion that was attached to the 1st Infantry Division testing new intelligence methods and equipment.

What was your job during the war? What did you do while you were over there?

At the time I went to Vietnam, I was a specialist 5th class, and my military occupational specialty was 96b, which was combat intelligence. I served with the First Military Intelligence Battalion Provisional, Republic of Vietnam, with the First Infantry Division. We were testing a new concept in combat intelligence support to army units; it was called the BIC/BICC system, which stood for Battlefield Information Center at higher level and Battlefield Information Control Center, at the lower level. We reinforced each headquarters at battalion brigade and division with a team consisting of two officers, two NCO's, and six enlisted personnel. We had some rather esoteric equipment with us at the time that was being tested for the first time. One was called Sniffer. They could mount this on a helicopter, and you could fly over an area. Among other things, it could smell ammonia, the idea being that any soldier still has to go to the bathroom. If there was a concentration of troops in the jungle, and they dug a latrine pit, there would be a strong ammonia odor from the urine in the latrine. The helicopter flying over with the sniffer could then smell a latrine pit, and we could target that area. Unfortunately, the people that came up with the idea did not realize that the North Vietnamese were also intelligent. They proved that when they discovered that monkey urine smelled the same as human urine to the sniffer, and if you hung enough pails of that in the rubber trees, we could fire our artillery all night and never hit anybody.

Most of my time was spent in the base camp. I spent about 5 months in Quan Loi near Anloc; I was supporting a brigade headquarters. On our base camp, we had, I think, three infantry battalions, two artillery battalions, and an engineer battalion. Since the infantry units normally were out in the field looking for the enemy, there were usually about seven hundred troops on the base camp itself. That got pretty dicey for me, because being in intelligence, I knew what it said on the situation map about where the enemy was. North of us, between Quan Loi and the Cambodia border, was a US Special Forces camp called Loc Ninh. In '68 when I arrived there, the famous Tet offensive that had started in January of '68, was over. For the rest of '68 and '69 while I was there, the North Vietnamese Army were moving regular army troops down the Ho Chi Minh trail into the center section of the Vietnamese 3rd Corps. They were replacing the Viet Cong that had been pretty well destroyed in the Tet offensive with the North Vietnam Army divisions. They had a lot of new troops in their divisions, and so they were trying them out. One of the ways they tried them out was to attack the Loch Ninh Special Forces camp that was located north of Quan Loi. They would attack with anywhere from one to three battalions. Three battalions made one regiment. When we would respond with First Infantry Division soldiers, we would have a major battle.

I could sit and look at my map, and there I was at Quan Loi with seven hundred soldiers, and thirty miles north of me was a division of twelve or thirteen thousand men. It got a little scary at times. Something that was very effective at that time was that the Vietnamese had been tunneling for about 40 years in Vietnam. One of the more famous positions was a place called Nui Ba Den where we had a firebase on top of the hill, and in the tunnels underneath them was the headquarters of one of the Vietnamese regiments. We never knew they were there until after the war was over. They were thirty feet down below us all the time we were on top of Nui Ba Den. They did a lot of tunneling.

"WE NEVER KNEW THEY WERE THERE UNTIL AFTER THE WAR WAS OVER, THEY WERE THIRTY FEET DOWN BELOW US, ALL THE TIME WE WERE ON TOP OF NUI BA DEN."

As a result of my position, I spent all of my time either in the brigade headquarters or the division headquarters while I was there. I analyzed information that came from several sources. The first one was from human intelligence. The simplest form is what a soldier sees in front of him on the ground. One of the things that I never understood, but which happened many times in Vietnam, was the higher headquarters and people who worked in government offices simply didn't believe their soldiers. It was also a very political war. After I served my first tour in Vietnam, I worked with the Defense Intelligence Agency in Washington D.C. Later on, I went back for a second tour. One of the things that I learned from open sources when I was in Washington D.C. occurred when they had a congressional investigation about the accuracy of the enemy strength figures. If you remember in, Vietnam there was a lot to be said about body count. Every unit that had contact with the enemy had to report all the bodies that were killed that they could recover so we could count how many of the enemy we were killing. That led to a whole lot of lying on the part of the troops on the field because in order to be a success and get promoted, the commanders had to have big body counts.

While I was at the Defense Intelligence Agency, this investigation occurred and it was interesting to me. It caught my eye because the man they interviewed was the great-great-great grandson of President Madison. He had been the analyst of a certain area of Vietnam at the Central Intelligence Agency. They were asking him questions on how the enemy strength was devised, and he revealed to congress at the time and it was published in the *Washington Post* that the original figures had been given to the US forces when they went into Vietnam by the South Vietnamese. So they started with the set of figures developed by somebody else, which may or may not have been valid because we did not independently derive them. All changes from that moment on were based on that initial set of figures, which was questionable.

I had the experience myself of political influence in counting on my second tour of Vietnam in '72 –'73. I was preparing what was called an Intelligence Estimate, based on the reports that came across my desk from various sources. I came up with a figure for the North Vietnamese division that was down in the Mekong Delta where I was. My figures said they had "x" amount of soldiers, and I was told directly by my colonel to reduce those figures by 50% because they were disagreeing with the figures of the Vietnamese government, and therefore, they could not be published. Any statistics you read about Vietnam, about the strength of the enemy, are entirely questionable, whether it's theirs or ours.

Another thing that happened in strength figures in Vietnam is everybody assumed that the North Vietnamese Army and the VC units consisted only of combat troops, people who carry machine guns, mortars, and just enough ammunition to fight

that day. An assumption was made that all the supply functions were done by supporters in the south who provided the logistics and communications. Thus, they didn't need a supply sergeant and they didn't need this, and they didn't need that. The fact is that any army has a logistic tail, which is 60% of its size. If you look at the North Vietnamese strength figures for 1968, it says 4 million North Vietnamese Army were in the south, which means there's anywhere from 4 to 10 million because they haven't counted the other 6 million. Now that's a fact that I learned in basic intelligence school, when I learned how to estimate an enemy force. It applies to every army that exists. It was true in World War II, was true in the Korean War, and it was true in Vietnam. In any military forces, only 40% of the people in it are fighters. The other 60% drive the trucks, run the radios, and haul the supplies. They may do it on bicycles, but they're moving it, and it takes people. Supplies don't move themselves.

> *"MY FIGURES SAID THEY HAD 'X' AMOUNT OF SOLIDERS, AND I WAS TOLD DIRECTLY BY MY COLONEL TO REDUCCE THOSE FIGURES BY 50% BECAUSE THEY WERE DISAGREEING WITH THE FIGURES OF THE VIETNAMESE GOVERNMENT, AND THEREFORE, THEY COULD NOT BE PUBLISHED."*

I said I was one of the last people out of Vietnam; I left Vietnam on my second tour in April 1973. There was an army personnel unit at the air base in Saigon which processed army personnel in Vietnam and out of Vietnam when I left. They processed me out, and I got on a plane at 0030 hours, which was 30 minutes after midnight. The unit that processed me out left at 3:00 p.m. the afternoon of the same day. I helped close the door on Vietnam.

We have a couple of questions. Well first of all, do you have a message for the young people today? Especially with everything that's happening, people rushing to join the army, and military.

Well I spent 26 years in the army, and I retired. I was a professional soldier I did not go as a draftee. The US army was the best thing that ever happened to me other than my marriage to my wife. I got to see more of the world, meet more people. But I think the thing you have to remember when you're judging whether you are going to support your country by joining the military or not joining the military, is that you have to have some trust in your leadership. Now the problem with that is that every generation makes its decisions on its own experience, and the leadership making the decisions mostly lived through what happened to the previous generation. There is somewhat of a time lag. The decisions that were made that led me to a battle in Vietnam were based on really, truly, honest opinions of our leadership. Our military is dedicated to supporting the will of the nation. You have to understand, war is hell, for whatever reason you go to war. If you're going to do it, you need to accept that your leaders are trying to do the right thing. If you can't accept that or you're unwilling to, don't go. But if you can accept that, give it everything you've got.

What was the most traumatic thing that happened to you during your whole two tours of Vietnam?

> *"I WAS ONE OF THE LAST PEOPLE OUT OF VIETNAM; I HELPED CLOSE THE DOOR ON VIETNAM."*

What's the most traumatic thing that sticks out in your head? Or if there is more than one?

I was fortunate in that I did not have any of what I would call traumatic experiences. Certainly not the kind of thing that would leave you with post traumatic stress syndrome. I think the first time you realize you're being shot at is pretty traumatic, and it doesn't even have to be shot at, just the sound of shots going off. My very first night in base camp when I arrived in Quan Loi, it was about dusk, not quite dark yet, and I went to my cot. It had been a long day, and I laid down, and all of a sudden...BOOM!

A big flash of light next to my tent. I thought, what's going on? It turned out that there was a jeep sitting at the perimeter fence, about 500 meters from where I was laying, and it had a recoilless rifle on it. Now when a recoilless rifle fires, the shell goes out the front, but a whole blast of flame goes out the back, and it makes a huge torch and a big light. That's what I saw. The sound of the gun going off was what I was hearing, not a shell coming in. That was about the most traumatic thing.

Back home, back in the US at the time, there was a whole lot of anti war stuff going on. When you came home, being over there, did you get any unwelcome feelings from neighbors, friends, other people in the country because you had gone over there and fought this war that they were so against?
I hadn't from neighbors because at the time, the business I was in, I didn't get close to my neighbors, and I went directly to Washington DC which was a new surrounding to me. I didn't know anybody, and I was working in the military community where we were very supportive of each other. However, I read the papers, and we did have significant anti-war demonstrations in Washington while I was there, and I did have some unknown person with a squirt gun spray bleach on my army green overcoat. On the other hand, the government reaction to these very large demonstrations got a little bit out of hand too. It got bad enough on one weekend in Washington DC that the Washington police formed a line with big plastic shields and just swept many of the streets, from end to end, picking up everybody on the street and threw them into the local football stadium overnight. They even took people off their front porch who just came out to see what the commotion was all about. They didn't bother to ask what they were doing; they weren't doing anything but looking, but this is what happens when people over react to what's going on around them.

Do you see, because we're talking about one group in power seizing control and wrecking things for everyone else, do you see a connection to what happened in Vietnam to what's going on in Afghanistan?
Well, there is a common thread in something. In Vietnam, it was the people who had been oppressed by colonialism for two hundred years, seeking a national unity. What a lot of people are failing to appreciate, about what's going on in Afghanistan in my opinion, is that the Muslim world, which had been great in the twelfth century, and the eleventh and the thirteenth, has been pushed totally under to second or third class status in most of the world by the twentieth century. They lost their identity, they lost their pride, and in the case of the Palestinians, they lost their nation. What we have in the world today is a group of people who feel disenfranchised with a very strong religious belief and training. Most of what went on in Vietnam was a result of maneuvering between super powers, China, Soviet Union, United

> *"WHAT WE HAVE IN THE WORLD TODAY IS A GROUP OF PEOPLE WHO FEEL DISENFRANCHISED WITH A VERY STRONG RELIGIOUS BELIEF AND TRAINING."*

States, and Great Britain; the NATO countries. Existing nations trying to maneuver for a position of security in the world for their populations. Here we have a different group of populations who are really trying honestly for security for their people.

When you were in Vietnam, did you ever come in contact or work with African Americans?
Every day.

How was the relationship between whites and blacks?
Depends when you were there. Towards the end it got pretty rough because there was an awful lot of drugs in troop units, and the African Americans were probably 40 to 50% of the total combat soldiers in Vietnam. They were pretty angry with us because they felt they were fighting our war for us, and they all recognized that because of the way the war was being fought, there was no way we were going to win.

The relationships were pretty rough. Now a military unit, on the other hand is totally dependent on individuals who rely on other individuals. If you knew how to stay alive on patrol, it didn't matter if you were black or white. If you could help me stay alive, you were my buddy, and that's the big difference.

Was there any drug problems?

The drug problems where I was at were pretty minor. Everybody drank alcohol, and it was readily available. By the time I left Vietnam after my second tour and came back to Fort Hood, Texas, alcoholism among professional non-commissioned (NCO's) officers had become an outrage. They cracked down so by the time I had retired from the army in 1983, they were starting to do breath testing. I came back in '73 and we had regular shakedowns at our barracks. One of the stories I tell is, I came back and I was assigned as a platoon sergeant for the first time instead of a Staff NCO. I reported to my military intelligence unit, and my sponsor told me that as a Platoon Sergeant, one of the things I should do was visit my barracks after lights out to see what the troops were doing. The next night at about 9:00 at night, I walked into the front door, said hi to the Charge of Quarters. I went upstairs, and I walked from one end of my barrack to the other which was about 90 feet long, and I got high. There was that much marijuana smoke in the air. The next day we had a shakedown inspection and took two and a half pounds of weed out of the barracks. Yes, there was a drug problem. As a result, we ended up with involuntary urine tests, and they were thinking of starting breath testing. They definitely cleaned up the military by the time I left. I wouldn't say it was drug free, but compared to what it was in '73, it was a lot better.

Reesman retired from the Army in 1983. As part of the GI Bill, he received his Bachelor of Science degree in Computer Science. He has worked in Information Systems for EDS, Kohls Department Stores, and Wausau Hospital.

Interviewed and transcribed by
Aimee Grosinske and Connie Fell

Bill Tomcek

Drafted in 1967, Tomcek arrived in Vietnam and was assigned to the 3rd Battalion, 39th Infantry of the 9th Infantry Division stationed in the Mekong Delta; his job specialty became reconnaissance.

I graduated from the University of Wisconsin, Stevens Point in January 1967. Once I had graduated, I knew that I no longer had a draft deferment from the army. I had to report to the draft board, and they said, "Okay, if you are not going to go to school anymore, you are now going to be drafted." I was the only 23-year-old in Oconto County that wasn't accounted for, so therefore, I was next to go.

On January 16th, just ten days after I graduated, I was already down to Milwaukee, going through the MEPS center (Military Entrance Processing Station), passing physicals, and that's where I found out that I would be a noncombatant, which means that because my eyesight is poor, I could not be sent into combat. I thought that was great because at that same time I tried to join the Navy, and the Navy rejected me again because of my eyesight. But the Army told me they needed people in supply; they needed people in personnel, payroll, administration, and stuff like that. Since I had a college degree, that would be okay; they could use me, and I thought I had made it.

I was sent to Fort Dix, New Jersey, where I had basic training for eight weeks and then Advanced Infantry Training for eight more weeks. We also took a battery of exams, and of course, being a college graduate, I scored real high on all the exams, and they said I was a good candidate for being an officer. I thought that wasn't a bad idea, to be an officer, so I agreed to be sent down to Fort Benning, Georgia for Infantry Officer School. They told me that after twelve weeks I would be transferred to a noncombatant specialty. After about sixteen weeks of infantry training, I finally asked when they were going to transfer me out of the infantry. I was told, in no uncertain terms, that I was in infantry. They gave me an ultimatum; they said you are either going to be an Infantry Officer, or we are going to send you straight overseas. In my naïve way, a country boy from Oconto County, Wisconsin, I said, "Well, I'm not going to be an infantry officer. You can't make me, and you really can't send me overseas because I'm a noncombatant, and my eyesight is too poor." Maybe one other reason was more important as to why I would not accept a commission. I found out that after completing OCS (Officer Candidate School), I would be discharged for one day and then be required to sign up for two years of active duty. Since I was drafted for two years, and I almost had one year completed, I saw no reason to sign up for another year.

On January 15, 1968, I arrived in Cam Ranh Bay. When I was being processed for overseas, they had to assign me an MOS (Military Occupational Specialty). The clerk wanted to give me 11B10. I knew that was an infantry rifleman, so I objected. He replied that the only other MOS he had to give out was 11F10; I said I would take that as long as it was not 11B10. In addition, since I would not accept a commission, I was sent overseas as a PFC (Private First Class), the lowest rank they could give me. I trained as an officer, and I was a PFC. When I checked into Cam Ranh Bay, I said to the guy, "Look, I'm a noncombatant; I am not supposed to be here." He said, "Yeah, right!" I said, "Open my file and check it!"

Nothing was in my file except orders to go to Pleiku, 4th Infantry Division. The guy looks at the records and says I was a combatant… "I see you are an 11F." I said, "What's that?" He says, "I don't know, but you step aside," I stepped aside. All the 11Bs were lined up on the right and I was the only one on the left. For the next couple of days I was sort of in, like a holding hooch there; guys were going on KP, they were burning crap in barrels, and nobody came and gave me any details. After two days, two other guys show up for morning formation and they stand next to me; I said, "What are you guys?" They say, "We're 11F. I said, "Is that worse than over there?" and I pointed to all the 11Bs. The guys goes, "Ya." I said, "What do you do?" He said, "Recon." Now, being a noncombatant, I had inadvertently volunteered for *recon*. What *recon* means is that you are supposed to be the one who goes out and looks around to find the enemy. Then you call back and they helicopter the infantry in so they can fight the war. My big question always was, "How long will it take you to get here?" They always said about fifteen minutes; it's always about fifteen minutes. Then I would ask, "What are we supposed to do for fifteen minutes while we are waiting?" They would always reply, "Hold your position." Right! How many do we have, maybe two, maybe three people on this *recon* point? I always wondered, "What are we going to be able to do if attacked while waiting for the helicopters to bring in the infantry?"

I never once saw the enemy. As far as I was concerned, everybody that walked by me, everybody that I saw, they were civilians! It didn't matter whether or not they wore black pajamas, or carried weapons. They looked at me and I looked at them. They kept on walking. They let me go; I let them go. I was not going to start a fight because I was a noncombatant.

Six months out of the year it's monsoon season. It rains off and on throughout the day and night and sometimes for days at a time. When it rains, you can't see anything. I wear glasses; wearing glasses in the rain, you can see nothing! So when command would call me on the field radio for a *Sit Rep* (a situation report) and ask, "What do you see?" I would reply, "Nothing…I see nothing!" What do *you* see in the rain? You are just wet and cold and you don't see anything.

The other part of the year is the dry season. As far as heat goes, it's always hot, and when the monsoon season was there, well, then you would be wet, humid and hot. I kept a little thermometer on my shirt, and during the day, all the red mercury would climb to the top and it'd sit there. It only went up to 130 degrees, so I don't know if it got hotter than that. Then at night, I would look at it, like at midnight, and all the mercury would be down to 99 degrees. I never saw it lower than 99; in the middle of the night it's 99, but during the day, if it's 130, that's a 40-degree difference. We'd be sitting there with jackets on and the poncho liner, and just hugging it, trying to stay warm, although it's 99 degrees. You'd look at your thermometer, and say, "99? Why am I cold?" During the monsoon, it would get cloudy and then it would rain, so you'd get soaking wet. Then 20 minutes or a half an hour later, the sun would come out, and you'd be totally dry because it would dry you off that fast. Then a lot of the time it was really a torrential rain, where you would just take most of your clothes off and just get wet, like taking a shower.

It just so happened that when I got to Vietnam on January 15, 1968, I had two weeks of orientation that put me in the field on January 29th. What was January 30th? Tet Offensive, oh, what luck! I get there on the 15th, and two weeks later, I get down to my unit the night of the 29th, the Tet Offensive! I thought it was normal; I didn't know any differently. Everything is blowing up and everybody is running. I was laying on the floor on an air mattress with a mosquito screen around me, just laying down in the corner about three feet high at the edge of the hooch, and I must have been sound asleep! At twelve o'clock when everything started exploding, and I tell you, they just mortared everything and everything was exploding…when I heard those explosions all around me…I just jumped straight up and of course, I hit my head right on the roof! I fell back down, and boy, did it hurt! Then I had to decide what to do. I only knew where one bunker was. I had to run outside the building, down the road, into this bunker. I'm all alone because by this time everyone has scattered. I got in the bunker. Of course there were a lot of people in there, and nobody knew what was happening other than that everything was exploding. We had a system whereby if any of the outlying bunkers around the perimeter identified a ground attack, they would signal what we called the Commo Bunker – the Communications Bunker. They would set off a siren. Then everybody who was sitting in the bunkers inside the perimeter would have to run out there and reinforce the bunkers on the perimeter. They wanted as many people out there as possible; that's why you'd have to run out of the bunkers and run out to the perimeter. The Tet Offensive was a period of time where everything was attacked at once. We didn't know it was the Tet Offensive; I mean, nobody named it, I didn't even know it was *Tet*! It was my first night. I didn't know anything. I thought it was normal, which it wasn't, of course.

After that, we were attacked every night for several months. There would always be mortar attacks. That is when Flegal and I decided we would build a bunker inside of a hooch. We went and got all these ammo boxes from the artillery positions and filled them with mud and stacked them all around the inside of the building. Then we put rafters up above the top of the ammo boxes and stacked sand bags across. Then we hung a light bulb from the ceiling. The light bulb was hooked into the battalion electrical supply. We built an L-shaped entryway, so mortar rounds couldn't come in the front door. It took us, well, we worked on that for a better part of three months. We built bunk beds, which hung down from the ceiling, and then eventually, even though other people laughed at us because we worked all night doing this, we had a real nice bunk bed. Most of all, we felt safe.

L/R Flegal, Wing, and Tomcek are goofing around inside the bunker that they built inside another hooch.

I had to laugh one evening when the mortar rounds were hitting the roof. Picture this...we're inside another building, which is not a great building, so the rounds started hitting the roof and blasting the tiles off, and everyone that was outside started running into our hooch! They were all sitting there on the floor and Flegal and I were laying up on the bunk beds. We decided that even though there was a mortar attack, we weren't going to get out of bed until they blew the siren because we didn't have to run to a bunker, we were already inside a bunker! While all these guys scrambled into our bunker, I started yelling, "Hey! I think I hear a lot of rats running around." Flegal says, "Yeah, they sound like big rats!" They were the ones teasing us while we worked many nights building our bunker, and here they were crawling in our bunker, instead of running out in the street where there could be a lot of danger while getting into a bunker.

What was the average day like?
In the field, we would maintain two or three man reconnaissance positions, mainly at night. We would take turns staying awake at night, listening to our radar set, or just laying there watching. If we suspected any enemy movement in a certain area, we were allowed to call in artillery on those targets. We wouldn't hesitate to get on the radio and contact the artillery units. We would try to sleep during the day, but it was pretty hot, so you just basically slept on and off. Whenever you were tired you'd lie down and take a nap, and hopefully, you took turns sleeping at night if you weren't alone; but if you were alone and went to sleep, you hoped you'd wake up. There were long periods of boredom; people would come by during the day, and we'd haggle over these little trinkets. We played around with a monkey, and we did all kinds of crazy stuff that 19 and 20-year-olds do. Things would happen so fast and furious, and then nothing; then, you'd have to collect yourself and go on. You just hoped nothing bad would happen.

Did you ever do an ambush?
I'm going to say that only one time did I go on an ambush, and it was during the orientation when I first got into the country when I didn't really know what was happening. We marched out of Bear Cat, the 9th Infantry Division base, and went into a rubber plantation where we set up what was an L-shaped ambush,

where, like the letter "L," you set the ambush up so the enemy would walk in and everybody fires criss-cross; they get caught in the crossfire. We set up an L-ambush, and there were four soldiers on my posi-

Preparing for the first ambush from Bear Cat.

tion; two of them were cooks. They made everyone go out to get some experience. The two cooks said, "We're cooks. We're not going to participate in this ambush. We just want to sleep." I said, "No, you can't do that; we have to take turns. We all want to sleep, but we got to take turns." The two cooks said, "Nope." When it got dark, they laid down on the ground and they both went to sleep! To my surprise, they snored just as loud as you can hear anybody snore, both of them! The other guy that was there with me, we looked at each other and said, "This is not good. We're on an ambush. We're supposed to be quiet." While they were sleeping we decided to pick up our weapons and move back about 25, 30 yards. Then we told the other guys on the ambush positions next to us, "Well, if they stop snoring, we know they either got their throats cut or something else happened to them.

So we'll just fire over them." So he and I took turns staying awake that night on that ambush position, and we listened to those guys snore all night. After that, I figured, "Hmmm, this ambush stuff is tricky." You have to have people that are going to cooperate with you. If somebody's going to go out there and goof off and snore, you just can't have that; that'd give you away.

Vietnam was considered a guerrilla war; there were no front lines. In Vietnam, they could be to your right, to your left, to your front, to your back; you're looking everywhere all of the time, and so you never claimed a piece of ground and said, "This is my place." That was part of the problem; that's a guerilla war. Hit and run, nobody owns any ground; you may fight on one piece of ground one day and go away and two weeks [later] come back and fight on it again. That's where the stress comes from, that constant vigilance; you never knew what was going to happen. Every time you'd hear something you'd think, "What is it?"... You just didn't know.

Were drugs a problem?

They were a problem for some people. Anytime I knew that somebody was using drugs or just misusing alcohol, beer or whatever, I would have nothing to do with that, because they were dangerous. I decided that if I knew somebody was doing that I wouldn't go out on a bunker with them. I wouldn't go out on a recon position, I'd just say, "I'd rather be alone," because they were dangerous and you couldn't predict what they were going to do. Basically, I just associated with the other guys that were just like myself. That's what happens, right, everywhere? You associate with other people that are like yourself; we just stuck together that way.

What were the relationships between whites and blacks?

The blacks congregated together and the whites congregated together. I had nothing against them per-sonally. When we were together in the field, it was fine, but if we were in the base camp or people were going to do things, whites and blacks separated.

The other thing is, you always hear about Bob Hope coming and having all these concerts. Well, I never saw any of that. Nobody ever came and told me I could go to a concert. They were always at the big bases. They'd fly these guys into the bigger bases, and then, of course, all the personnel in the base would have a concert. The infantry units were still out there in the bush. While in Vietnam, I didn't even know that the anti-war movement was going on, because I didn't have a newspaper. I didn't have *Time Magazine*, *Newsweek*; I had no TV to watch.

Are there particular experiences that stand out in your mind?

I was in this village, and the river went right by this village, so I wanted to get a good look out on the river. I had heard through some report that the Viet Cong were on the other side of the bank. I wanted to walk out as far as I could and look across. When I went down to the end of the village, I saw all these poles go out in the water with a walkway. I walked out there, to the edge - and I'm standing out there and I'm looking - and all of a sudden, I hear this scurrying of people and talking. I didn't understand it. People were running off, and I'm looking around, like, what happened? All of a sudden, there was a whole bunch of people gathering on the bank, and I'm standing out over the river, and they're all starting to talk and point. I'm standing out there thinking, "Oh-oh, what have I done now?" I've only got 60 rounds, and there's more than sixty people on the bank of the river. I thought to myself, "This is not good!" I'm looking around wondering what to do, and finally an old Vietnamese man from the village came forward and motioned to me and I motioned to him, because I didn't want to go on the bank with all those people there; I'd be mobbed. I was thinking, "I'm going to get mobbed." The guy came out, and I said, "Well, what's going on?" He goes, "Oh!" and pointed. I went over and looked, and then I saw all these stalls. Then I went on the other side and saw there were stalls there, too. I figured out the ones on the outside towards the river were [for] women and the ones on the inside were [for] men. When I just walked out there, all [the] women got up and ran around the other side, and the men that were there got up and left, too. I cleared this bathroom out! I could tell everybody on the bank was in a jovial mood; they were kind of laughing and chattering, so then I decided that I should laugh, too. I started laughing and then the old man that was out there with me said, "Well, let's walk in," and we walked into the crowd. That's when I found out what a bathroom was.

A closer look at the "bathroom" over the river.

One night while I was sleeping in a graveyard alongside some large tombstones, a lizard or snake crawled up inside my pants leg. I'm laying there just as straight as an arrow, and I feel this thing crawl-

The graveyard at Can Giuoc.

ing up my leg. I've got grenades in one hand and I've got my rifle and bayonet in the other. I've got three options. I'm going to shoot it; no, I didn't like the idea of hitting my leg. I'll pull the grenade pin; no, that's not going to feel good either. But if I get bit by the snake, I'm dead anyway, so what's the difference? Maybe this way I won't have legs, but I'll still be alive. I'll grab my bayonet; I'll cut it…that would be okay; if I could grab the snake and cut it, you see. But how do you know you've got the head, right? I mean, really? So as I'm going through my three options that thing crawls all the way up to my crotch. Then it turns around and starts to crawl down. I'm still considering these three options; I'm just laying still, and I'm not moving a muscle. It crawls out of my pants leg, and then that's when, for that moment I felt relieved. But then I started thinking, what if it turns around and crawls back up? My hands are right here, not too far from my feet and my neck. You know, what if it crawls down my neck? As I'm lying there, I say to myself, "Bill, now you got to get up, you got to run, you got to do it on the count of three. Are you ready now? One, two, three, go!" I didn't move; I was frozen there. I said, "Bill, you didn't move! Come on now, you got to go, you have no other choices. It's not on your leg anymore, so you know, you're not going to get bit now. But if you don't move, you might be, so you got to do this again, now, right? Listen up now, you know, one, two, three, you got to go!" On the second try I just had to move. I couldn't just jump up and walk. I had to make sure I didn't jump up and hit another tombstone and knock myself out, right? It was pitch dark. I surveyed the area, jumped up, ran over to another tombstone and knelt down, and tied my pant legs shut. I didn't sleep much that night. It was the only time I forgot to tie my pant legs to my boots!

On another night, the sky was clear, the stars and moon were bright. Everything seemed calm, and I was feeling peaceful and relaxed while sitting next to my 50 caliber machine gun which was set up next to some large tombstones on the edge of a graveyard overlooking some rice paddies. It was about one o'clock in the morning and I decided I was going to brush my teeth. I was carrying my toothbrush as I walked out on the dike down to a road where I met another grunt. He asked me what I was going to do, and I said, "Well, I'm going down to the water wagon and brush my teeth." He says, "Oh, I'm going to get a drink of water." Here it is one o'clock, he and I are walking out in the open, going down this road. He looked over to the right, and you could see the rocket flashes coming right across the rice paddy. He said, "Rockets!" and he jumped to the left side. The rockets were coming from the right, so that was the right way to jump. I'm standing there, still feeling very, very peaceful and I remember saying, "No, it can't be a rocket."

I just stood there, and I looked and I looked, and sure enough, they just came right across the rice paddy, and it seemed like it was right in front of me. That's when I realized, well, this *is* real! I fell straight down on the road, and that's about the same time when the rockets hit! They must've hit the road right next to me because all the chunks of dirt and rocks fell all over me. After the explosion everything seemed to be in slow motion, just absolutely still. I saw this great big cone of white light, and I saw myself floating as a baby, as a young man, and I looked down and there I was! I was lying there and I was looking at myself! I didn't feel scared; I didn't feel anything. It was just the most awesome feeling; it was peaceful, quiet and I was just floating. Then all of a sudden, it stopped and it seemed like this light just came back down. The next thing I remember was saying to myself, "Move your little finger," and I moved it. "Move your little toe," and I moved it. I said, "Well, you're alive!" I mean I'm thinking this, and that's when I jumped up and then took a dive off the right side of the road, and I hit the barbwire fence. It hit me right in the thighs, and I flipped over into the rice paddy, and I fell into the water. Then I realized I'm on the wrong side. We had put the barbwire up to keep the Viet Cong from coming through; now I'm lying on the other side of this barbwire. I know that anybody behind me could shoot if anything moves on the other side of this wire. I know I can't stand up. Then I see two more flashes coming across the rice paddy, and I know that two more rockets are coming. That's when I just took a deep breath and buried myself under the water. I just took ahold of the rice stalks and pulled myself under, underneath the water. Quickly I decided I couldn't hold my breath too long, and if the rockets would hit next to me, it would hurt my ears. As I popped out of the water, the rockets sailed right over my head. Those rockets, I think, went over the road and hit the other side. I then low-crawled over the rice paddy to the edge of the dike. I had to wait until it got dark because by that time, the mortar platoon started shooting out flares to light it up [the rice paddy] because they heard the explosions. Everyone was pretty much awake then, and ready to shoot, but I knew I had to run down the road to the graveyard to get to my fifty-caliber machine gun. I didn't have my weapon with me. If I would've had my rifle, I could've just turned right around and boom! I would've had them; they were just on the other side of the rice paddy. That was the one time when, if I had my rifle, I could've directly engaged Viet Cong, and *I would've!*

When I got back into the graveyard, I crawled up to the fifty-caliber machine gun and grabbed both side handles to pull my face up there to look through the sight…. and, bam! Something just hit me right in the throat and went through my teeth. It hurt bad. I put my hand on my mouth, and there was my toothbrush, clenched between my teeth. Boy, did that hurt! I had hit the faceplate on the machine gun with my toothbrush and drove it backwards, through my teeth, into the back of my throat. My legs hurt and I'm all wet, because I was in the rice paddy and I'm shivering and shaking, frightened. Now I'm there by the machine gun and the flares are going off and I'm looking… I can't see anything. I'll tell you, that was a miserable night and for the rest of the night, I didn't sleep, either. There is an old saying, "Danger makes you think of prayer". That night I learned how to pray.

Tomcek dove through the barbed wire fence and eventually crawled through the rice paddy. Rocket tailfins were found near the road the next morning.

Tours of duty in Vietnam were for one full year. My discharge date from the army was about the same as the end of my tour of duty, January 14, 1969. A guy said he heard that since this wasn't a war, if you could show the US Army that your transition back into civilian life would be harmed because you would stay in for your full tour, you could request to be dropped up to 60 days. Flegal and I wrote letters to all kinds of universities in the states, requesting their catalogs so we could pick a starting semester date within the 60-day drop. For me, that was anywhere between November 14th, 1968 and January 14, 1969. I wrote a letter stating that I was registered at Ball State University, Muncie, Indiana. Ball State was on a quarter system, and I said I had to be in class on December 5, 1968, for my "walk in life," and I would like to leave Vietnam early so I could be in class on time. I sent the letter up the channels. A month or so later my request came back approved. Unbelievable! Great, so then I made sure I had my class list and course schedule. Sure enough, on November 18, 1968 they came down and said, "Well, you got to get going, got orders, got to be in class December 5th. I arrived home on the 25th of November, 1968, and was sitting in the front row of a marketing class at Ball State University on December 5th!

What kind of reception did you get?

There was no reception. It was like, I was out, processed, and let go; that was it. I walked out the door, got a cab, went to the airport, and that was it. I never looked back. In ten days I was sitting in class at Ball State University, Muncie, Indiana. I had the best tan in the whole class, in the whole university. Just think, in two weeks I went from the Mekong Delta to a classroom in Indiana! Wow! What a change! It was wonderful!

What was the hardest part about being in the war?

The hardest part is not wanting to be there. You don't want to be there, but how are you going to get home? You're not! You know you've got a year and you just wait for each day to go by, and you just hope everything is okay. The hardest part is just being there and knowing you don't want to be. All your life efforts then become defensive, like you've got to stay alive, because you know you're not going to leave if you're dead; well, you leave, but not the way you want to. It was even more nerve racking when you were short, thirty days and counting. I remember the dead silence and the knot in the pit of my stomach when the airplane took off from Saigon. When the captain announced that his destination was USA, the plane errupted in a wild uproar.

What did serving your country mean to you during active duty, and now, as a veteran?

Being a Vietnam Veteran actually makes you quite proud. I went through basic training. I went through advanced training. I was sent over to Vietnam. When I came back from Vietnam, I was discharged. I was never stationed at any army base in the United States. I was drafted, trained, sent to war, came back, and then I was done. I have no idea what the army is like in the United States. I would say that I'm very proud to have served my country.

It's not very often that you get the experience of being in combat. When people talk about combat, I mean, I know what it is. I know what to do, and I know how I would've reacted, and I know how others react. I know what I had to do; I did it! From that point of view, I guess you can never take that away from me. I can be proud of it because I'm alive, and I was never wounded. I have no Purple Heart or any-thing to show off. Nobody gave me medals for doing anything great, you know, because how would anybody know. I was out there mostly alone, but I did it; I didn't choose to do it; I just did it.

Do you have difficulties dealing with the memories when you look back?

The answer is "Yes," because when these events happen -- the ambushes, the rockets, the snake, when those kinds of things happen, these memories are stored with emotion. They're right on the edge of your mind and flashbacks are when something triggers off that memory because it's so close to the sur-face, bam! It comes right out. What I have

Injured soldier being treated prior to dust off.

Wounded soldier being loaded onto med-evac.

found out was that as I tried to suppress these memories; they wanted to come out. Even when I went into high school classes the first couple of times to talk about my experiences and showed the slides, I would just click on that picture and say, "That's a rice paddy. That's a picture of a graveyard." I wouldn't want to talk about why I took that picture, like I am now to you. When I was done with that, I hated it because it would bring things up, and I didn't want to remember [those] things.

Do you have a lot of flashbacks now?
No, I saw a therapist who does REM, rapid eye movement, and I've had these memories erased from my mind, from the flash-point aspect. Which means, I still have all the memories, but I can look at them and talk about them, and I don't get totally emotional. There's still emotion there, and I can feel those emotions, but they're controlled.

Is there a message you have for young people today about the war?
My message would be that I would hope that the young people today would be willing to stand up, be patriotic, volunteer, and serve their country. I think everybody should serve their country for two years after high school. It would just give them a concept of war that you're not going to get anywhere else. Go into boot camp, basic training, and then do something for two years. Then when you come out, go to school; you'll be wiser, older and that would mean so much more to you. I know when I went to college after the service, it was so much different than when I went to college before the service; I was much more attentive and eager to learn.

Following the war, Bill Tomcek became a chiropractor.

Interviewed and transcribed by Katie Stewart

HELICOPTER PILOTS & DOOR GUNNERS

D.C. EVEREST AREA SCHOOLS

Helicopters

In the early years of the American involvement in Vietnam, a helicopter unit was dispatched and landed in Saigon. This was the beginning of what would prove to be a massive experiment in utilizing the helicopter as a weapon of war. In the beginning it was seen as an air taxi, transporting the infantry and their equipment to the battlefield. In the early 60's in Georgia, experiments were conducted to create a division of soldiers that could be completely transported by helicopter. That experiment proved successful enough that the unit's designation was changed and they became the 1st Air Cavalry Division with orders to Vietnam. From there, the helicopter war was in full swing.

The helicopter that came to Vietnam changed significantly over the years. The earliest looked primitive when compared to the sleek faster machines that followed. The missions also changed during those years. Aerial reconnaissance was followed by aerial assault, accompanied by aerial bombardment from gunships and cobras. Other types of helicopters delivered cannons to mountaintops, supplies to firebases, men and material to the delta, and airlifted wounded personnel to waiting hospitals and surgical teams. Vietnam truly became the helicopter war.

According to Shelby Stanton's *Vietnam, Order of Battle* (U.S. News Books, 1981), twenty-nine aviation battalions served in Vietnam. Within those battalions were large numbers of helicopter companies that served different functions. One hundred seventeen separate companies served in Vietnam as well, over the years. This number does not include the units that served in the Air Cavalry.

Harold Baker

A career man, Baker served two tours in Vietnam, one in '67-'68 and the second during '70-'71.

How did you become involved in the Vietnam War? Were you drafted? Had you enlisted?
I was career enlisted.

What were the base camps like?
Dirty, dusty, muddy… usually tense.

Did you fight against the Vietcong or the NVA? Describe the enemy.
Very dedicated, believed in what they were doing- probably some of the toughest in the world.

Can you describe what an average day was like in Vietnam during the war?
Usually hot, sweaty, not much sleep; you were always dirty, scared half the time.

Were you involved in any firefights?
Not on the ground; I was in the helicopter unit.

Vietnam is considered a guerilla war. Describe what is meant by guerilla warfare.
You had regular units and you had just the common guy out there. There were women and kids that would shoot at you; just a mix of everything -- not like a regular army -- except for the NVA.

Did you ever do any ambushes?
No - only from the air.

What is meant by search and destroy or search and avoid?
Search and destroy is when you, according to the army version over there, find the enemy and annihilate them.

Could you explain any experiences you had with body counts or kill ratios -- or were they mostly on the ground?

I think some of them are exaggerated a little bit.

You obviously used a helicopter to get around. Do you have any experiences you would like to describe?

No -- we just flew a lot. I went down a couple times. Other than that, helicopters were mainly used to move infantry, med-evacs, and many were (what were called) gun ships -- with rockets and machine guns on them.

Do you think drugs were a problem for the soldiers in Vietnam?

No -- not the first time. The first time I was there in '66 and '67 you didn't see many drugs, but when I went back in '70 and '71 there was a lot of it.

Did you have any relationships problems between the whites and blacks in your units?

A fourth of them were black but we all seemed to get along pretty good. All in the same boat.

Did you have any opinions regarding the anti-war movements back in the United States while you were in Vietnam?

It wasn't much fun being over there while people back home were demonstrating against it. Our country sent us over there -- at least the people could have backed us up or got us out of there.

What was the hardest part of being in the war?

Being away from your family. Luxuries you take for granted over here. It was hot and you were tired all the time -- that was about it.

Was there a lot of emotional or physical stress that you had to endure?

> *"OUR CONGRESS AND POLITICIANS SENT US TO VIETNAM -- AFTER WE GOT THERE, THEY TIED ONE HAND BEHIND OUR BACK."*

Not really, just scared quite bit. Never knew who the enemy was -- they all looked alike.

Are there any experiences that stand out in your mind?

Not really; it's all about the same.

Do you think the US could have won the war?

Definitely. Our Congress and politicians sent us to Vietnam -- after we got there, they tied one hand behind our back and said, "Win the war, but we'll call all the shots from here." THEY screwed up; we didn't.

Did you make any lasting friendships during the war?
Yes.

What kind of reception did you get when you came back to the United States? *Zero.* Nobody ever
knew we came home.

What did 'serving the country' mean to you while on active duty and now as a veteran of the war?
I was proud. I'd do it over again. When I was there the first time I believed in it, and then when I went
back the second time I saw that it was a big waste of lives. It didn't seem like we were fighting for anything. They export rice, and that's about all they got over there, so we don't need that and they don't
have any oil. The only thing I could see was a whole bunch of politicians and some of the big corpora-
tions were getting rich.

Did you have any difficulties dealing with any of the memories when you came back?
Sometimes, sometimes no. Every once in awhile I'll think about it… I'll have a nightmare. Other than
that, no, not really.

Are there any other messages you have for young people about the war?
I guess the biggest thing is, don't believe everything you hear on TV and radio and newspapers as far as
getting involved in a war…. why we're there. It wasn't like WWII where we were attacked at Pearl
Harbor. Like the saying goes, "The old men start the wars, and the young men fight them."

*Baker returned to civilian life as an
insurance agent for New York Life.*

Interviewed by Colin Boynton
Transcribed by Katie Stewart

Gary Berzill

Gary Berzill served multiple tours in Vietnam. As a door gunner on a helicopter, he flew night missions to flush out the enemy.

Were you drafted or did you enlist?
I enlisted in June 1968, and I served in Vietnam from 1968, 1969, 1970, 1972 and 1973.

What was your assignment?
I started in the infantry. First four months I was in Vietnam I was shot three times, and they decided that it was becoming hazardous to my health, so they stuck me behind a desk, I didn't like that idea, and then I volunteered to be a door gunner on a helicopter.

What were base camps like?
Dirty, dusty, unsanitary, hot, and humid.

Did you fight against the VC or the NVA?
When we first got over there, they told us to beware of everybody in black pajamas, but when we got over there, everybody wore black pajamas. It was really hard. It wasn't like World War I or World War II where they had fronts. It went from the tip of South Vietnam in the Mekong Delta to the demilitarized zone up into North Vietnam.

Did you encounter the enemy?
I saw quite a few of the enemy.

Can you describe what an average day was like?
I started when I was flying; I flew at night, what was called "nighthawk" missions. We flew from ten o'clock at night till seven in the morning. We tried to sleep during the heat and all that. Most of my duty was at night. We would fly with two helicopters; we had a low helicopter and a high helicopter. The low helicopter, which I was in, drew the fire to flush out the enemy, and once they started firing at us, we would find their locations and then we would commence returning fire.

Were you involved in any firefights?
I was involved in quite a few firefights. I went through one firefight during Tet, 1968, that lasted almost eight hours.

What is meant by "guerilla" war?
It's hit and run. During World War I and World War II there were fronts, but during Vietnam it was hit and run, city fighting, village, etc. You had no idea when you would be hit or how you would be hit and who was going to hit you.

Did you ever participate in an ambush?
There were various types of ambushes. We got caught in a horseshoe ambush where you are walking into a village and going in straight and they would allow you to walk in and they would be on both sides and the front and they call that a "horseshoe" ambush.

What was meant by "search and destroy"?
Search and destroy is when you are out on recon and you should happen to come across the enemy; basically destroy, no prisoners, make sure nobody gets away.

Did your unit keep body counts?
It was a unit thing; some people did it and some didn't. As far as I was concerned, it was over exaggerated. All of the reports that came back to the United States were so out of line. Basically it was supposed to be more enemy troops killed than American troops killed. There was one body count where we had actually killed about four hundred VC. I was manning an M60, and it was so frantic, so hot, and so fast that I had actually melted the barrels on the machine guns. They were warped and believe it or not, some of the GIs were actually urinating on the barrels to stop them from warping, to keep them cool.

Did you use helicopters to get around?
I was in a helicopter.

What was it like?
It was actually exciting and fun. I spent most of my time outside of the helicopter. We had a pod mounted in front of us because I was a door gunner, and you stood on the landing pod, hanging outside the door held in with a "monkey strap" so you wouldn't fall out.

Can you describe the Tet offensive?
The Tet offensive was one of the biggest offensives during the Vietnam War. That is when most of the NVA regulars were into South Vietnam, and they came from the Ho Chi Minh trail and just commenced raising "holy hell," bombing, and there are things that I don't wish to divulge.

Were there any drug problems after the Tet offensive?
There were drug problems before the Tet offensive and after the offensive. It was so easy for the soldiers to get drugs cheap. Alcohol, drugs, it was there.

How were relationships between the whites and blacks?
During the early years of the war, it was rather tense. I had quite a few black friends and I had quite a few white friends but it depended on the situation. We were in a club, and all the blacks sat on one side and the whites sat on the other. It was very tense.

Do you have any views regarding the anti-war movement back in the states?
I had a lot of opinions, and I was against them. I thought everybody should do their thing, and I would do it again. I would go through the same things I did back then, but I don't think it does any good to complain about it. When they said Clinton was a draft dodger, the comment was made that a draft dodger was in the White House and the Vietnam veteran didn't have a house. It could be a very touchy subject.

What was the hardest part of being in the war?
Wondering if you were going to come home, what you were going to come home to, if you were going to come home. My biggest fear, being that I was so young, was stepping off the plane in San Francisco and wondering if I was going to be shot by a draft dodger, and all of the anti-war sentiment.

Was there a lot of physical or emotional stress?
Yes, physical because of being young; most of the soldiers that were there were young. I was eighteen when I went the first time, not knowing what to expect. Mental stress was just wondering if you are going to make it; what I am going to come home to. I was married on my second tour and I came home to nothing; my wife had left me. The first time I went over, I was engaged, and I came home to nothing. She had found somebody else. There was quite a bit of emotional and physical stress.

Is there one particular experience that stands out?
There are many. I had a black friend that saved my life. We were on patrol and I missed a booby trap, or else I almost stepped on a booby trap, and he saw it and I didn't, and he pushed me away and unfortunately it blew both of his legs off. I was holding him telling him to hang on, but he lost the will and died in my arms.

Do you think the US could have won the war?
The US could have won the war if the politics wasn't involved, because it was a political thing. It boosted the economy, but we definitely could have won. I didn't say we lost because that is one thing you don't say to a Vietnam vet is that we lost. It wasn't ours to lose. The equipment, the training, the men, the lives that were lost, we could have won.

Did you make any lasting friendships during the war?
I had quite a few, but as the years go on, it's been thirty some years, and you lose contact with a lot of them. I had two of my best friends serve in Vietnam, and unfortunately, one was killed in a car accident and the other committed suicide.

What kind of reception did you get when you came back to the US?
It was like the plane landed, we got a steak, and you could go home. It wasn't like the more recent wars where there was a heroes' welcome. My war will end when I get off the plane in Mosinee and had someone there to meet me.

What did patriotism mean to you during your active duty?

I served twenty years, eleven months and eight days in the United States Army. I am a member of the VFW, and I am a member of the American Legion. I am on the honor guard of the American Legion, and I have always been a patriot and will always be a patriot. My whole family has been a fighting family, from World War I to Vietnam.

Did you have difficulty dealing with the memories when you got back?

Yes, still do.

Do you have a message for young people today?

It is just something that I hope young people do not have to go through. It is trying to understand why people were against it, and the people who did their duty did an outstanding job.

Is there any other stories you would like to add?

There was a few funny things that happened. I had a friend of mine, a very dear close friend of mine, black man named Larry. He was about six foot, two, six foot three, somewhere in that vicinity, and he went a good 230-240 pounds, and when we knew that we were going to be mortared or rocketed, it would set off the air-raid siren, and this fool would come on over the loudspeaker and say, "Rockets, rockets, rockets, Da Nang is under attack. Rockets, rockets, rockets, Da Nang is under attack." That is just how it sounded; it was the most aggravating thing. We wanted to shoot him, but I don't think that was legal. Anyhow, we had come out while we were under attack, and we had a bunker position that Larry and I were to man. He was black as black could be, and he had the most beautiful white teeth and white eyes; you have to picture him running out into the area with just his combat boots, his shorts, and his helmet on, and he is carrying around eighty pounds of ammunition and I am carrying an M60 machine gun. We have to make a turn as we are coming out of the hooch, and in front of it was this ditch that was about three foot deep and two foot wide and had the most ungodly stuff running through it. I think sewage would be cleaner than whatever ran through there. But we were running out, and he had the honor of falling into that ditch. None of us talked to him for about two weeks after that because he smelled so bad, and he thought that was rather funny. As I was saying this, I remember the weirdest thing happening. The night before the day before they signed the peace treaty, we knew we were going to be hit; we just didn't know how hard. Right across an open field, I guess about one hundred or one hundred and fifty yards away, was a church, our church that we attended or supposed to attend. We got nailed by quite a few mortars and rockets that day because they knew that the war was going to be over, so they threw everything they had at us, and after the ordeal was done we walked around to assess the damage. When we were walking around the church, there was shrapnel everywhere around the church itself, but not one piece of the shrapnel from the mortars or the rockets was imbedded into the church. We thought that was one of the scariest or weirdest things that happened.

Interviewed and transcribed by Karen Ho

©2002 D.C. Everest Area Schools Publications

Ray Boland

A captain and a pilot, Boland was in Vietnam in 1966 and in 1969-1970. He flew aircraft in support of Special Forces during his first tour and shifted to helicopters during his second tour.

I want to thank you and say how much I appreciate this work you are doing. I am telling everyone around the state about this because I think it is a very important thing to do, and your example dispels the idea I run into some places where older veterans say that students aren't interested in our wartime history. I really appreciate the history projects you are doing here. I found out about your efforts last summer and thank you for the chance to come back today and talk about the Vietnam War. My perspective might be a little different from most Vietnam veterans because I was a career soldier. I wasn't drafted and sent to Vietnam. I was in the army before Vietnam, and I was in the army a long time after Vietnam. I was older than most soldiers were when I went there. I was a Captain and a pilot. I had a bigger perspective of the war because I did a lot of flying. I saw many things that others didn't have the opportunity to see. I saw most of South Vietnam from the air. It is a beautiful country with many contrasts in topography, from a spectacular seacoast and beaches to mountains with lush vegetation.

I was five years into a thirty-year army career when I went into Vietnam the first time in 1966. I went back in 1969. By the time I finished Vietnam service in 1970, I was 33. I remained in the Army until my retirement in 1991, about 10 years ago. My last assignment was Commander of Fort McCoy exactly when Operation Desert Storm was going on. At that point I'd gone full circle from starting my service in 1961 with the call-up of the Wisconsin National Guard. Today, 30 years after serving in the war, I personally believe that Vietnam fits into a fuller historical perspective than Vietnam itself. I am among those who believe that the origins of what happened in Vietnam can be traced to World War II, and the results of Vietnam carry over to the end of the Cold War period. Following the Vietnam War, we saw the decline of the global Communist movement and the eventual demise of the Warsaw Pact Alliance. I think the experience of the Vietnam War played a very important part in these events.

The first time I went to Vietnam, I flew small cargo airplanes to support the Special Forces. I went to many Special Forces camps throughout Vietnam. I can't say I got to every Special Forces camp in the country, but I saw a majority of them. I flew an ugly looking airplane called the Otter. It was designed for bush pilots in Canada and Alaska—many are still flying there. There weren't many of these aircraft in Vietnam. They could carry seven people or about two thousand pounds of cargo. We mostly went into remote Special Forces camps that other aircraft couldn't get into. Mortar and rocket fire were one of our biggest problems. We had more damage from getting hit on the ground than we did in the air. We had to patch up many holes from mortar attacks to get the aircraft back in the air. Then two years later I experienced a big change from flying these slow, bulky airplanes to that of flying Cobra attack helicopters with the 101st Division in the extreme northern area of South Vietnam. Our area of operations extended north to the demilitarized zone separating North and South Vietnam and west to the Laotian border. This included the major battlegrounds of the A Shau Valley and Khe Sanh.

If I had sold an endorsement to Pepsi maybe I wouldn't have needed to work anymore cause I would have made so much money on this picture. This was the only banana tree for miles around, and we planted it. I was sitting under it savoring my Pepsi the day after we had received a major attack at our base camp. At the very end of my career, I had a rare experience during Desert Storm. This doesn't have much to do with Vietnam, except that Bob Hope was very important when he came over there and did the shows for the troops, especially during Christmas time. Bob Hope was a legend through all of the wars. He was here when we were preparing troops at Fort McCoy for deployment to Saudi Arabia. He did a show in LaCrosse and we took 2,000 soldiers to see it. I had a chance to present a memento to Bob at the end of the show. That is my favorite picture because it captures many memories of all of my years of service and all that Bob Hope meant to us and how he brought a touch of home to so many soldiers over the years.

In 1966-67 we saw the peak of the U.S. Forces build-up into Vietnam. By this time we had more than 500,000 troops deployed. That was my point of entry in the war. Looking at it from the air enabled me to see several different aspects of warfare taking place. The Special Forces were involved in helping remote villages defend themselves. Overall, their efforts were pretty successful. That's where you had the Viet Cong guerrillas trying to move through the countryside and actually take control of villages and their resources. Our Special Forces trained people to resist the Viet Cong, and they very actively resisted being overtaken. Some people think that the Viet Cong insurgency was a popular uprising among the South Vietnamese people. I don't believe that. I believe that it was a movement created and directed by the North Vietnamese with massive support from Russia and China. In general, the fight for villages was a lower level of combat. During that time frame, in other areas such as Pleiku or farther into the highlands north of Pleiku, there was more of the North Vietnamese Army regimental forces presence. In the south you had primarily the Special Forces and military advisory team operations, as well as main force US units facing Viet Cong elements. Then the farther north you went toward the border between North Vietnam and South Vietnam, you found the heavier force type fighting. By the time I got back in 1969-70 and went to the Northern I-Corps area, we fought almost entirely against very large North Vietnamese regimental forces coming down from North Vietnam. They mostly came down the Ho Chi Minh Trail, through the Khe Sanh area or down through the A Shau Valley. In 1969-70 the 101st Division, during the time of Vietnamization under President Nixon, began turning the majority of the ground war over to the South Vietnamese troops. Between November 1969 to November '70 I started out firing attack helicopter missions for the 101st Division, and by the time I finished, it was all in support of the 1st ARVN Division, the army of South Vietnam. Most of the 101st forces had been pulled completely back at that point. It became more difficult to communicate with forces on the ground; however, most of the Vietnamese units had English speaking Australian advisors with them. We would talk to them on the radio, and they would tell us where they wanted us to shoot and what was going on. It was always fun to talk to them because of their accent. It just seemed sort of weird in the middle of fighting a war to hear these very jovial, Crocodile Dundee sounding characters who always had cheery things to say even in the middle of a huge firefight. The attack helicopter mission was unique because it filled in between all of the other firepower such as artillery, jets, and ground fire. There was a special role for attack helicopters that is worth telling about. Artillery was the main source of fire support for the troops on the ground, and most ground troops never want to stretch beyond their artillery support capability; that was very key. On the other hand, artillery can only fire so close to the units on the ground without endangering the friendly forces. Our mission was to fill the gap in between which meant most of the time we were firing rockets within twenty-five meters of our own friendly forces. This was very difficult and stressful.

"A VERY FAMOUS BATTLE DURING THAT TIME WAS FOUGHT AROUND THE AREA CALLED FIRE BASE RIP CHORD; WE SUFFERED A LOT OF CASUALTIES THERE BEFORE WE GOT TROOPS OUT OF THERE."

One thing you never wanted to do was hurt your own people, so it took a lot of practice and training to be confident and proficient in what we were doing. Often the troops on the ground were screaming for our help and were literally in a survival situation because the enemy was a very close distance away. Usually we didn't get involved unless it was a very close contact fight. Then things were at a point where we were the only kind of supporting fire that could help them win the fight. Usually we were on standby 24 hours a day and flew a lot of our missions at night. The unit I commanded had to have the first

two aircraft off the ground within two minutes after being called. That meant that you had to have crews and aircraft ready to go. All they had to do was jump into the cockpit, squeeze the trigger that ignites the engine, and within two minutes they were off the ground on the way to the target. The next two aircraft had to be off within five minutes, the next in 15 minutes. We had to be able to sustain that and rotate, as each team would return to refuel and rearm. We just kept replacing each other for as long as the engagement continued. This went on all of that year, and the summer of '70 was very difficult during the last major battles of the 101st Division. A very important battle during that time was fought around the area called Fire Base Ripcord. We suffered a lot of friendly casualties there before we got our troops out. From that point on, the South Vietnamese pretty much were responsible for the area and there continued to be a lot of very heavy fighting. I must admit, I had it relatively easy compared to people on the ground. We were shot at, hit, and sometimes shot down, but in terms of what the people on the ground were facing every hour, of every day, our mission was a lot easier. Our whole purpose was to try to help them accomplish what they had to do on the ground.

I would like to make a couple comments about the South Vietnamese Army. Again, there are different opinions about them. The 1st Division that I worked with happened to be one of the best units they had. They fought very well, they were very organized and, they planned their operations very well. I enjoyed supporting them, and they did a good job. Later, in 1975, when South Vietnam fell, the 1st Division was over run, yet they fought very hard until the end.

When you were in air combat what did you do, specifically?

As a U.S. Army pilot in 1969-1970, I flew the Cobra attack helicopter. It is a tandem seat aircraft (front and back) that was designed so the weapons could be fired from either seat location. The back seat station had better controls and weapons capability than the front seat. As you can see in the pictures, it had rocket pods mounted on small wings on the side. Our aircraft had a total of four—two on each side. Each pod could hold nineteen rockets, so fully loaded, you would have 76 rockets on board. In the nose of the aircraft was a flexible turret that had a machine gun and a 40mm grenade launcher. These weapons could be moved up and down and from left to right. Typically the pilot in the back seat did most of the flying, and the front seat would navigate. The better site for firing the rockets was on top of the rear instrument panel, so we fired most of the rockets from the back seat. The pilot in the front did most of the operating of the nose turret. On a typical attack you would engage a target that had been identified by somebody on the ground. The back seat pilot, who also was the aircraft commander, would fire the rockets, and as he would break away from the target, which was the most vulnerable time, the front seat pilot would open fire with the turret and try to suppress the target area with a machine gun as you tried to circle around and come back in again. The Cobra at that time was very new. It was designed specifically for the Vietnam War requirements. Prior to that we had mounted rocket guns on Huey helicopters and used them as gun ships. For its day, the Cobra was a sophisticated weapons system that was pretty accurate but took real team effort between the front seat and back seat crewmembers. Usually we would always have at least two aircraft on a mission. I found that depending upon the size of the enemy force and the type of weapons they had, you were really much better off with three aircraft. With three you could really sustain suppression of the target area and protect each other while you were turning around to come back in again. We mostly used the technique of diving on the targets, which is a pretty exciting thing to do with a helicopter. The steeper your dive was, the tighter the shot pattern would be on the ground. The more slant you had with the dive angle, the more the explosions would stretch out across the ground which increased the risk of endangering the friendly forces. The more you could come in right over the target and dive on it, the better chance you had to get the maximum accuracy. So we worked and trained hard to be very good at this. It was very difficult work. If you can picture being in the back seat in a steep dive, controlling the aircraft, firing the rockets, keeping the rotor system in control, listening to three or four radios going off in your ear at the same time and trying to keep track of where the other aircraft were—you can imagine that after about an hour and a half you were pretty wiped out. Fortunately, within an hour and a half you had to be on the ground refueling and rearming anyway, and got to take a break.

> *"WE USED A TECHNIQUE OF DIVING ON THE TARGETS A LOT, WHICH IS A PRETTY EXCITING THING TO DO WITH A HELICOPTER."*

Were you ever shot down?

Only once. I received hits to my aircraft several times where I wasn't forced to go down and could make a normal landing. On the one occasion when I was forced down I was able to land the aircraft without crashing. We took a number of hits and lost our hydraulic systems which made it difficult to control the aircraft. We were lucky to get it down and walk away unhurt.

What is it you were vulnerable to -- are they rockets fired from the ground or gunfire from the ground and AK-47's?

The shoulder-fired, rocket-propelled grenades (RPGs) were a serious threat but machine gun fire, the equivalent of 50 caliber, was probably overall the most problematic. I have seen aircraft hit by an RPG and go down. If an RPG hits a helicopter, it's usually not survivable. Small arms fire you could take and usually make it on home to fly another day. Machine gun fire more often would take you down. I had 12 Cobra aircraft assigned to my unit. Of the 12 I started out with, we lost ten of them during the eight months I commanded the unit. One of the remaining two original aircrafts survived the war and actually turned up in another unit I commanded in Texas three years later.

Was there any single battle that was partiularly large where the firefight that you engaged in was so big it was in the textbooks?

I can recall a couple of battles like that, that really stand out in my mind, but not as the biggest source of our own losses, our aircraft losses. The biggest event in terms of losses was a night I will never forget. It was the third of May in 1970 when we got

"THE BIGGEST SOURCE OF AIR-CRAFT LOSSES IS A NIGHT I WILL NEVER FORGET. IT WAS THE THIRD OF MAY IN 1970."

hit with a barrage of 122mm rockets at our base camp. Fortunately, five of our aircraft weren't there as they were out at other missions overnight. We otherwise were pretty much wiped out. We had to rebuild our camp area and replace the destroyed aircraft but were able to continue. Sadly, the next night, we lost one of the few remaining aircraft and both pilots. One of them was from Oshkosh, Wisconsin. The battle at Ripcord was the biggest that I was involved in as well as a couple in the Khe Sanh area that I mentioned before. One of the questions provided to me for this interview had something to do about stress. As a commander, one of my most difficult jobs was to try to know and monitor the condition of each of my pilots on a daily basis and know when they were at a point of fatigue and stress whereby I had to pull them off missions. This constant strip- status- alert we had, a lot of other units didn't have. I had pilots who never left the flight- ready shack next to the aircraft for as long as two to three weeks. Food was brought to them, and they just stayed right there because they had to be ready to take off in minutes. Fortunately, most of the pilots were a lot younger than me. Their average age was 20. We had several

young Warrant Officers who went right from high school, to flight training and then to Vietnam. They had a lot more stamina than I did, but there were still times that you had to rest them for a day or two before they could go back in the air.

An area of certain controversy and study that I'm sure you're getting into was the way the war was fought overall. Most of us who were there found it hard to accept the fact that there were so many limitations in place that restricted what might have been done and could have been done. We felt like we were going out and flying these missions; then we're sitting ducks at our base camp for rocket attacks. After a while you start thinking maybe this isn't the best way to do this, and we were kind of trading

shots. You'd go out and shoot them up and then come back to the base camp and wait for the next rocket or mortar attack. The situation was much too static for helicopter employment. This is part of what I'm thinking about Afghanistan now and how that's going to work. We likely could use a lot of helicopters before that war is over. I'm trying to picture how we will operate, where they will stage the aircraft, how much distance they are going to travel, and how much forward positioning they'll do, and so on. I hope we don't repeat any past mistakes.

One of the hardest parts of our mission was to go out on night operations, which we did a lot of. The firebases would often get hit at night, which made it even more difficult to bring the artillery in. So they'd call us. We didn't have the capabilities that the aircraft have now. Before I retired from the Army, I had a chance to fly the Apache. The difference between the today's Apache and the Cobra in 1970 is hard to describe. We have a true night capability now. Most of the work helicopters are now doing in Afghanistan is probably at night. We have the ability to see, operate, acquire and engage targets; it's a vastly better capability. But being tied down the way we were in 1970 and then having to do so much at night with very limited night vision technology, is what I remember as the hardest part of it.

Towards the end of the war, we supported a major attack into Laos by South Vietnamese forces. This was not a very successful operation, but at that point many believe it may have been too little, too late. Most experts agree we could have changed the outcome of the war only if we had cut the Ho Chi Minh Trail in Laos. I agree with those who believe the war could have been won. Now we are going to get into the same question with Afghanistan. Can we really win in this place? I will tell you from my 30 years of Army experience that wars can be won any-where and any war can be won if you have the commitment and resolve to do it. To win requires the attitude that you're going to do whatever it takes, and you are going to pay the price to win. This is not unlike what win-ning is about anywhere. Any team that is going to win, whether it's in sports or on the field of battle, has to be so fully prepared and capable it not only knows it can win, it has what it takes to do it. You can't do that half-heartedly. You can't say you're going to fight but then don't really want to throw your best punch. We want to win the game but we're not really ready to win. It's the same basic principle. I would predict that before we get through we are going to see a big war in

Afghanistan. I believe we will fight to win. The question we have to ask ourselves today is easier to answer now than it was 30 years ago. Why are we going 10,000 miles away to fight a war? What did they do to us? That was a hard question in Vietnam. You thought of that question every day that you were there. But today we have only to think about the thousands of people that were killed right here in the U.S. at the World Trade Center, the Pentagon, and in Pennsylvania. It's a whole different ballgame. I think we should not have a question of resolve. Never has anything like this been done to this country. This is different than the other wars. It's not only different, it's much worse.

As you compare the two situations, do you think we learned something from the Vietnam War in regard to our media?

It seems like it's always a challenge to keep the media from becoming more negative than positive toward a war effort. We must do a better job of restricting media access to the war, but that is controversial also. We should not walk on the freedom of the press, but does the public have a need to know certain things versus not. This happens to be an area that I have had the opportunity to look at in depth. During grad-uate study, I focused on the effect of media and public opinion particularly during war times. Someone you might want to have come visit with you is Don Heiliger who is in Madison. He is a member of our Board of Veterans Affairs. Don was a prisoner in Hanoi for six years after being shot down flying a jet mission. He will tell you about how they heard the press talking about the raids they were about to go on. The enemy knew they were coming and when they were coming. That kind of thing clearly needs to be more restricted. Generally what we're doing in war should be reported, but exactly when and how should be restricted. I'm uncomfortable for example, when it is reported that a thousand soldiers from the Tenth Mountain Division are getting ready to move into a certain area—we don't need to know that.

Do you think in Vietnam that was a problem -- that the media helped to turn the American people at home against the war, and they contributed to the downfall of the whole thing?

Yes, I think so. However, I think our policies were more at fault than the press. I would not place primary blame on the press, but I believe our press reporting strengthened the resolve of our enemy and weakened ours. When we miss the bombing target and we hit the Red Cross warehouse or cause some civilian casualties, it should not be sensationalized. What about the intentional killing of U.S. civilians on September 11? I don't want to forget about this here. If people in the U.S. are saying, "Oh those innocent civilians over there got killed today," the same news reports should remind us about all of those who lost their lives here in the US due to deliberate terrorist attacks. I can tell you from my own experience, and I know it remains the same today, we have a tradition in our US military forces of not endangering or wantonly hitting civilians or civilian targets. I went through that. There were times that I would not fire even though someone on the ground was asking me to because I knew that it was an endangerment to civilian non-combatants. That is the rule. Accidents happen, yes, but as a military force we are very careful. Our capabilities today are more accurate, but things can happen where civilians and innocent people are going to be affected.

Can I bring you back to your first tour of duty when you protected special forces on the ground? Tell me about the special forces.

It's a good thing to talk about because we're starting to use them now in Afghanistan or at least that is what's being reported. The meat and potatoes of the Special Forces are called the A Teams. They are a 13-person detachment that has a mix of people that include a medic, a communications specialist, and a variety of other skills that form a combined team. Their mission is to go into a local setting, normally in a remote area, and assist organizing local people to be able to defend themselves. That is what they were doing in the back country in South Vietnam. Often there were limited roads and very primitive conditions. What I did was resupply them and bring them anything they needed. As I said earlier, many of the small dirt airstrips could only be reached with the type of airplane we had. On any given day we would deliver anything from food, to ammunition, communications equipment, to mail—whatever they needed. I got to know a lot of these soldiers as I moved around, and they asked you to bring this or bring that the next time you came. I have to tell one true personal story, and this is when I first started flying in Vietnam. I had not flown the Otter aircraft until I got to Vietnam. After a very short training checkout, I was told I was all set to fly a mission the next day! I was sent to the Saigon area and told to report to a Special Forces Major. He would tell me where to go from there. When I found him he said, "Okay, we are going to go to several remote camps. You just take off, and I'll tell you where to go." So, away we went, and I'm just learning how to fly this airplane. We came to a place that had a dirt runway that wasn't very long and had a big dip in it. As I was trying to figure out how to land, I misjudged it, and I stalled at about 50 feet off the ground and we hit really hard. It didn't damage the airplane, but it made our teeth rattle. Everything fell down from the overhead storage areas. Once we shut down and got out of the airplane, this Major came stomping over to me and I could tell he was upset. He pulled out his pistol, pointed it at me, and said, "That was a terrible landing." I quickly agreed. He said, "I've got some guys at the next camp that have been out there a long time, and we're taking these supplies to them. There is some beer in there. If you land like you did here and you crash and ruin that beer, I'm going to shoot you." He seemed serious enough that I knew I had to do better. So you talk about the best landing I've ever made in my life. I lined up on final approach for about 10 miles. We came in with a rate of descent of about two feet a minute. It was a very soft landing, and I lived to fly another day.

My feelings about my experience in Vietnam are with me forever. I can never forget the terrible loss of so many Americans. I continue to tell myself these losses were not in vain and that we convinced the Communist world that we would not be defeated on the battlefield. I was in Germany 15 years after leaving Vietnam commanding a helicopter brigade two years before the Berlin Wall came down. The Germans were telling us that Communist control of Eastern Europe was about to end. We didn't believe it. We still had a border mission, and I was flying border patrol. I am convinced now that the continuum of events that started in World War II passed through Korea and Vietnam and then on through the rest of the Cold War. I think what has brought us to this day is that as a nation we have given hope to the rest of the world that they too can be free.

Can you reflect about the Ho Chi Minh Trail and the significance of the trail, and what we were trying to do?
Well, that is probably the most controversial part of the whole thing. Because we wouldn't make a commitment to go into Laos and Cambodia in earnest, the enemy had this unrestricted supply line that came right down the side of Vietnam, and they could enter into Vietnam at any of a number of points off that trail and continue to re-supply their forces. For any war you might study, you can find that if you shut off the enemy's supply and support capability you win. General MacArthur was a master at this in the Pacific. It is particularly true when the enemy is at great distance from their main base or homeland. So in order to win, we would have had to shut down the Ho Chi Minh Trail and stop all forms of supply coming down into South Vietnam. What we did instead was monitor how much was doming down the Ho Chi Minh Trail. This was nice to know, but it didn't do anything to help our cause.

Did your division ever do anything to try and shut down the Ho Chi Minh Trail?
As I said earlier, Operation LamSon 719, in January 1971, was a late attempt to do it. I think it was not the right kind of force with the right kind of capabilities at the right time of the year to accomplish the mission. To succeed would require a blocking force that could remain in place as long as required. One of the problems in that area is that when the inland monsoon season arrives, it is very difficult to do much flying. Roads were poor, and the trail, essentially, was just a trail. So sustaining a force out there would be very difficult. The 101st Division, while I was there, did not try to do that. We went into the A Shau Valley a couple of times, but again, without the resolve to stay there on a permanent basis.

Ray Boland returned to Wisconsin and became the current Secretary of Wisconsin Department of Veterans Affairs.

Interviewed and transcribed by Zack Zeihen and Mike Wanzerski

Ed Bruner

Ed Bruner enlisted in the service and was trained as a helicopter pilot. He initially flew medivac flights but later transferred to the 227th Assault Helicopter Battalion and flew gunships.

What do you do as an FBI agent?
We investigate federal violations of law. There are over 300 of us, and we cover nine counties out of this particular office for North Central Wisconsin.

Were you drafted or enlisted?
Regarding my military service in Vietnam, I enlisted.

What year?
I enlisted in January of 1966.

And how old were you?
I was 19.

Did you go to college before or after your involvement in the war?
I went to college, partly while I was in the military. I had returned from Vietnam at that time but was still in the military, and then I finished college after.

What was your job in Vietnam?
My job specifically, I was a helicopter pilot. I served in the army with the 1st Air Cavalry Division. I initially was assigned to the 15th Medical Evac., flying medical evacuation for actual combat pick-ups in the field. Then I was transferred to the 227th Assault Helicopter Battalion, and I flew gun ships.

How were you received once you came back to America?
It was unusual. There was animosity and friction with society, and I don't think we were held in high regards as far as going to a war; at that time, unbeknownst to us, a political-type war.

Did you ever have any nightmares?
Yes, I think anybody that's been there has. There are some things there that you don't mind remembering that were good, and there were things that were bad.

Do you think that talking about the war helps in any way?
I think it does. I don't think keeping anything bottled up inside you helps you, so I don't mind talking about it.

Did you get wounded at all?

I was wounded, not seriously…fragmentation and white phosphorus burns when one of the places that we were stationed at completely blew up and was destroyed.

Did you ever receive any medals for your services?

Yes, I received numerous medals. The Bronze Star. The highest medal I received was the Distinguished Flying Cross, called the DFC.

Can you describe that and what it looks like?

The Distinguished Flying Cross; it's like the 4th highest medal that you can get in the military. The way I got - several of us, our crew - got that was because we were flying a mission in which one of our helicopters had been shot down. This was just prior to the Tet Offensive of '68, and it was a night operation in which we, as gun ship pilots, would fly escort for six other helicopters that are carrying troops. Because one of our own aircraft and crew had been shot down on a rice paddy at night, a scramble mission was called for and launched, and we flew escort infantry into this downed aircraft to provide security and protection for it. As we were approaching the landing zone, (LZ), there was machine gun fire with tracers coming up from the ground. We had not seen that before. We used tracers, but in this case, there were tracers coming from the ground. We knew this was a different type of situation because the Viet Cong — you couldn't tell where they were at when they shot at you. So we engaged the target for protection on the flight and returned fire with machine guns and rockets, but sustained numerous hits and were shot down.

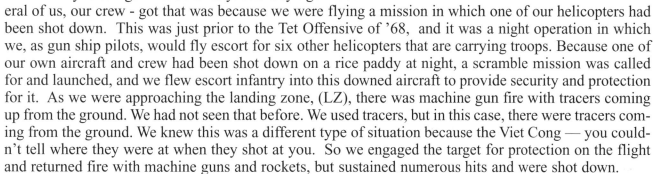

Was there any discrimination or problems with blacks or Latinos?

Discrimination, as far as treating them unfairly, you mean?

Right.

No, I don't think I knew what the word discrimination was.

Were there any problems with the freedom riots going on in America? Did you see any of that?

We would hear of draft dodgers. We would hear of resistance against being drafted into the military because of the fear of the feelings perceived in the United States at that time against the political individuals that were manipulating the war. We learned of that through news broadcasts and various things, and our initial impression was that these were just draft dodgers, or people that resisted and didn't want to really fight for their country. We learned more after.

Do you have any interesting stories or memories that you'd like to tell?

I think I just told one of the more interesting ones of getting shot down. I was shot down twice, once in a medevac and once in a gun ship. The gun ship one that I just alluded to was probably the scariest because we were being shot at after we got on the ground, so it was close to being captured. We had another helicopter break away from the formation and discover that we were in trouble. That helicopter came in and rescued my entire crew and got us out of there. It sustained hits from gunfire at the same time, but we got out. The entire crew got out, basically in one piece without any serious wounding. My co-pilot had been wounded in the foot when we were initially shot at when we engaged the target, but I don't know of any other particular stories that would be interesting. I mean, every mission, every day was interesting, something was unique, something different. Going to different LZ, seeing Vietcong in waves and trying to overtake one of our military artillery posts that was on the verge of being overrun, that was about as close to being right smack in the middle of chaos as I've ever seen.

Where were you trained?

I was trained with the Army Primary Helicopter Flight School in Fort Walters, Texas, and after that, we graduated from Primary Helicopter School and we went to Advanced Helicopter School, Fort Rucker, Alabama. Then from there, Vietnam.

How was the morale of all the soldiers?

Morale would go up and down. It would be down when you'd lose one of your comrades, obviously. It was counting the days, one by one, trying to get to the end of the year. We had a tour of one year, and we wanted to get out of there. It was a terrible thing that the government did — at least with Washington with manipulating the military. The military should have been left to do it on its own. If you put military generals in charge of a battle, of a war…they're the ones trained on how to do it. They should not be told what not to do because it's politically incorrect, or politically correct, I don't think. We were there for one purpose, and it's not to fight a political battle.

Do you think that the American government was right into coming into this war?

That's a good question. If my memory serves me correct, Vietnam had to ask for assistance from the United States because of a losing and an ongoing problem with wars that dated long before the Vietnam conflict that we got involved with in the middle '60's. There were problems in North Vietnam, and they were assisted by the French prior to that. But if another country asks the United States for military assistance, should we ignore it? I think not, if it can be resolved and the rules defined ahead of time. So, I don't know if I'm qualified to answer whether we should or shouldn't have been involved with Vietnam in the first place, but we went over there, thinking that it was to help the South Vietnamese.

Did you think you were a better person for going to Vietnam?

I think coming out, virtually unscathed, I'm better for it. I would hate to say anybody would have to go into combat, into war, if you didn't have to absolutely do it, if it wasn't necessary. Whether or not another conflict occurs around the world and we turn it into a Vietnam would be a mistake. But on the other hand, I think if NATO, a unified group of countries such as NATO, were to try to protect another country that is in trouble, that is probably the ethically correct thing to do rather than ignore it. There are ramifications for that; there are negatives and positives for everything that we do. Somebody smarter than me has to figure out what those impacts are and if we can live with them.

Ed Brunner followed his Vietnam experience by continuing to fly and later served as a police officer and a special agent for the FBI.

Interviewed and transcribed by Tabitha Strong Gehl

Mark Holbrook

Holbrook served as a platoon leader in A troop, 7th of the 17th Air Cavalry. He flew light observation helicopters performing recon. He arrived in October 1968 and left October 1969.

I entered Vietnam at Cam Rahn Bay and was immediately sent to Nha Trang, which at the time was II (spoken as "Two") Corps headquarters. Vietnam was militarily broken into four quarters called corps. For most of my tour I flew outside of II Corps for administrative purposes only once or twice, but from a combat perspective, I operated almost exclusively in the II Corp area. My unit belonged to the 1st Aviation Brigade but was under operational control of the 4th Infantry Division at Pleiku for the entire time I was in Vietnam. Much of the time my unit's missions were around an area called the tri border area, where Laos, Cambodia, and Vietnam came together. The Ho Chi Minh trail came in just south of Dak To and followed a valley called the Plei Trap valley and then the Ia Drang valley. The Ia Drang is where the 1st Cavalry got into one of the first major battles of the war in 1968. Late in my tour my troop was sent to An Khe (formerly 1st Cavalry Division headquarters) to support American troops working in that area. An Khe sits between Pleiku and Quin Nhon.

When I got in country, my unit (Troop A, 7th/17th Air Cavalry) was located near a town called Ban Me Thout. Prior to the Vietnam War this area had been a major rubber producing area, and remnants of French rubber plantations was evident whenever you took off and flew in the immediate area. The Ban Me Thout area is a relatively high, fertile plateau in the central highlands of Vietnam. The area to the west of Ban Me Thout that was north of a line from the Ia Drang valley to Pleiku and then east toward Quin Non was a fairly heavily mountainous area. The mountains were not so much like the Rockies but were more similar to the Appalachian Mountains in the U.S.

The job of the air cavalry in guerilla warfare was primarily intelligence gathering. We did some support activities for infantry as well, but most of the time we were out in an assigned area of operations (AO) looking for signs of enemy activity. I would say we were split from about 85% intelligence gathering to about 15% troop support that may have included inserting long range reconnaissance patrols, providing fire support for units in contact, and assisting in insertions of infantry units in force. Occasionally we would do convoy support, but that was usually a very poor use of our resources and equipment. Units composed almost entirely of gunships were more appropriate for that kind of a mission since it gave the ground commander a very quick source of firepower when he needed it. Our helicopters were occasionally used in that type of a mission, but it wasn't a mission we liked to participate in since it left other resources, ie., our scout aircraft, under-utilized.

Air Cavalry squadrons are composed of three Air Cav troops and one mechanized troop. The Air Cav troop is broken down into a scout, gun, lift, and infantry platoons. The job of the scout team is to fly very low and slow right on top of the existing vegetation looking for enemy activity. The guns flew cover over the scouts at about 1500 feet above the ground (to stay out of range of small arms fire), and the lift ships typically sat someplace waiting for a call from command and control aircraft to insert the infantry. The infantry and the lift always worked together until the lift dropped them off.

Typically, a scout pilot was a busy guy. He had four radios in his aircraft that had to be monitored on a regular basis. He had an FM, VHF, UHF radios, and the intercom that he communicated with his observer on. A light observation helicopter (LOH) flew with two people inside: a pilot and an observer. The responsibility of the pilot was to fly the aircraft and give the observer a platform by which he could see the ground. The observer's job was to sit with an M16 or an M60 leaning out over the skids to observe what was going on below the aircraft, directing the flight path of the aircraft to put him in the best position by which to observe, and reporting to the pilot what he was seeing. A wire strung from the console of the aircraft to the bulkhead on the side, and on it hung a variety of grenades. Sometimes there were concussion grenades, but most of the time there were red smoke and white phosphorus. If the aircraft drew fire, the observer's first responsibility was to mark the area with smoke and then return fire to suppress the enemy fire as the aircraft got out of the area. The aircraft also carried a six-barreled electric Gatling-type gun called a minigun that fired either 2000 or 4000 shots a minute. It was seldom used but could be helpful under certain circumstances.

"SOMETIMES YOU JUST HAD A SIXTH SENSE FEELING THAT THERE WAS SOMEONE DOWN THERE, AND YOU WOULD JUST MOVE, TURN AND PROBE, TRYING TO SPOOK SOMEONE AND GET THEM TO SHOOT AT YOU."

Each person in the aircraft wore a type of protective vest called a "chicken plate" and a survival vest that included an emergency radio, a red smoke grenade, and other survival type gear so that if you got shot down, you could be seen. The seat you sat in, in the helicopter, was armor plated with about one half-inch of thick, highly compressed ceramic armor plating. The armor plating would stop a gun direct hit from a 30-calibre machine, but it was not supposed to stop a whole lot more than that. The "chicken plate" worn by the pilot and the observer was in a holder, and it protected your vital organs. Your head and your legs were exposed, but the rest of your body was fairly safe behind armor plating.

Our troop flew, in what the terminology of the day called, a red team. Some air cav units flew pink teams composed of one LOH and one gunship that worked as a team. Because of our area of operations, which included triple canopy jungle, we flew red teams composed of two LOHs and two gunships. The lead scout would basically fly a relatively straight line across the AO or as the terrain demanded until he spotted conditions that signaled enemy activity. His flight path would then be dictated by the nature of the intelligence he was developing.

Each day we were given an AO, and based on the shape of that AO, we might pick out a corner to begin our reconnaissance in, or if there were some intelligence about enemy activity, we would start there. Typically, the job of the scout team leader was to fly a pattern until he saw something that led him out of that pattern. It may be a trail that was freshly used; a bunker complex or any kind of fresh sign that led him to believe there was enemy activity in the area. If it were a trail, he would begin following the trail, hoping to intercept whatever was on it. If it was a bunker complex, he would sniff around trying to determine if the enemy was still in place. Sometimes you just had a sixth sense feeling that there was someone down there, and you would just move, turn and probe, trying to spook someone and get them to shoot at you. When that happened, you had a confirmation of enemy location and a target for the gunships.

The role of the wingman was to constantly fly circles around the lead to provide additional eyes for the recon or to provide suppressive fire if the lead drew fire from enemy locations. Similarly, if the wingman drew fire, the lead could turn and suppress fire.

The gunships usually (except during the monsoon season) flew at 1500 feet, and the scout team monitoring radios and passing on the intelligence information gathered when the Command and Control (C&C) had to leave to refuel. They were, of course, also available to attack targets should the situation warrant it. At 1500 feet the gunships were out of the range of AK-47s that could hit you if you were below that level.

What worried you below 1500 feet?

AK-47s. I had one RPG fired at me during my tour there, and luckily, it missed. It was hard to hit us with machine guns because of the short exposure time that an enemy soldier had when you flew directly overhead through triple canopy jungle. The OH-6A was probably the best scout aircraft ever made. I am, of course, very prejudiced when I say that since it saved my life on numerous occasions. They were very forgiving and took a lot of hits before they went down. They were very crashable. I had guys go through two hundred foot trees and walk away from the crash.

We were operationally controlled by the 4th Infantry Division. My unit belonged to II Corps, but II Corps placed us under the operational control of units that were operating within II Corps. In A Troop's case, this was the 4th Infantry Division. The 4th might further give us out to one of their brigades that would give us to a battalion that was operating out in the field. A lot of times we would go out, and there would be a hilltop, and up on top, a firebase that might be occupied by a brigade, a battalion, or a couple of companies. We would be given to them, and they would say, "Here we are on the map, and we want you to do a reconnaissance all around us and tell us of any enemy activity." So, they would have a place where we could operate out of for the period of time we were assigned to them. It would include a location for petroleum, armament, and an area secured by infantry to park the aircraft that were not in the AO. If we were operating, let's say in Plei Trap Valley, there was a Special Forces firebase located at a place called Polly Klang where they had a runway and an area secure enough for our aircraft. Chinook helicopters would come in and lay down POL (petroleum, oil liquid) bladders full of JP-4, and another would come in with a pallet of rockets, machine gun ammunition, and grenades that were used to rearm and refuel our aircraft and troops for the day.

Sometimes you work all day and you may see nothing at all. At other times you may see a bunker complex and put some

A day off at the hooch on Camp Enari, 4th Infantry Division Headquarters near Pleiku.

artillery on it. And on other days, all hell would break loose, and you would be giving and taking fire all day long. The team also flew with a command and control aircraft that flew about 2000 feet. They had radios and were always in contact with people we were in support of, so they had access to support from those units. We were also always in contact with a forward air controller (FAC) who was our main contact for air strikes. They flew a single engine fixed-wing aircraft, and they would always be in the area if we needed them. When we contacted them, they would be our liaison for coming up with airstrikes, whether they were F4s, F100s, or even by diverting what was called an "arc light," a flight of three B52s. So we had a lot of resources that we could call upon if we needed too.

How successful we were as a military unit was dependent upon the aggressiveness of the commander of the unit. If we found some enemy activity and we wanted to develop it, air cavalry was a very aggressive unit. The idea is to find it, engage it, and destroy it. That is, conceptually, what air cav is designed to do, and the kind of people that get into those units are trained to aggressively pursue the enemy. They are people who want to engage and destroy it. On the other hand, you may have an infantry unit that was concerned about casualties. So you find something out here and you say, "Let's start dumping on," and they say, "Well, let's see what happens." That would be frustrating for the air cav. Air cavalrymen liked engagement, liked a good fight. Why risk losing men and equipment if you aren't going to inflict casualties?

Describe a firefight.

During a firefight when air cav is called in, you might find an infantry unit on the ground establishing a perimeter and fighting a defensive action. Or you might be inserting infantry in an LZ, lift helicopters coming in, dropping infantry off, who then spread out and set up a perimeter. They will push out when their numbers increase and move toward the enemy. The whole situation is really controlled chaos. Lift helicopters are coming in on an axis with gunships on either side firing rockets and machine guns and suppressing fire. You may have scout aircraft operating under this lift umbrella, trying to find anything that is down there so that these lift ships can stay as protected as possible. You may have airstrikes going in, put in by the red teams. So this combined arms force is a busy field of action. The guy who is taking the biggest brunt of the action is the guy who is down on the ground. He is one guy with an M16 and taking fire, so everything else is designed to support this guy and destroy as much of the enemy force as is possible. As things slow down and this lift gets in, the idea is to pile on as much friendly forces and supplies as you can.

Which helicopter pilots face the greatest risk?

I was an LOH pilot. The lift pilot faced the greatest risk. Helicopters will travel about 120 knots. Most of the time the lift helicopter with soldiers in is above that 1500-foot ceiling, but when you come off that 1500 foot ceiling, and you head for that LZ, one of the things that happens is that you come into small arms range, and you start slowing down. Lift helicopter would come in, and by the time he hit the LZ, he would be doing about 5 knots and be about 10 feet off the ground. When you see these things on TV where the helicopter comes in to a hover and the soldiers jump out and walk away from the helicopter, those are training films or lifts into secure areas. In reality, a lift helicopter in combat may never get closer to the ground than 4-5 feet. As the helicopter zeros out its airspeed, it immediately begins to rotate forward to begin to pick up speed again. The infantry jumps out and

"SO, YOU WERE SITTING THERE, AT FIVE TO TEN KNOTS, FIVE TO TEN FEET ABOVE THE TREES AND ALL OF A SUDDEN YOU HEAR AN AK-47 GO OFF; THE OBSERVER WOULD THROW SMOKE AND THE PILOT JOB WOULD GET THE AIRCRAFT OUT OF THE AREA..."

heads for cover. Believe me, infantry want to get off the helicopter as fast as they can, because if it gets hit or they lose an engine, nothing is predictable. They want to get away from it as soon as possible, so as soon as they think they can hit the ground safely, they are off the helicopter and are moving and looking for cover.

Typically, a lift helicopter is coming in, and the minute it flattens out, it's close enough to the ground that you will see guys jumping off the side. Then they will just rotate through, pull pitch, pick up speed, and get out of there. The helicopter crew is trying to get up as fast as they can. Radios are going nuts, you hear machine guns going off, your talking to you're co-pilot or your gunners on the side, you're monitoring a VHF radio and maybe talking to someone in your lift on the FM radio, and you can hear command and control up here on your UHF radio. All these things are going on, and you kind of selectively listen to who you need to be listening to or talking to. It is, literally, chaos.

Typically, during an insertion, we would be flying a mission some distance from the point of insertion looking for the enemy positions. We would probably be about 5 or 10 feet on top of the trees, and if it was elephant grass, we were within 20 feet of the ground. If it was triple canopy jungle, we might be 200 or 300 feet in the air. You would fly slowly, and your rotor wash would go down and part the vegetation, and the observer would be out standing on the skid with one foot, looking down. If he spots something that's hot, he would throw a red smoke out to mark it, and then the gunships and the C&C aircraft would plot the coordinates and listen to our description of what's down there: maybe a trail that's fresh or a bunker complex, any number of things. If it's a bunker complex, you might want to put some artillery on it or air strikes to destroy or just try to see what you can shake up. Most of the time when we found the enemy, it was because they started shooting at us. So you are sitting there, at five to ten knots, five to ten feet above the trees, and all of a sudden you hear an AK-47 go off; the observer would throw smoke, and the pilot's job would be to get the aircraft out of the area, because the minute that smoke is seen by the gunships, they would roll in on the target. They are coming in from wherever they are in their orbit, so you needed to clear the area of the smoke.

What are Cobras armed with?

They could be configured in a lot of different ways. They have stubby wings called pylons on the side. A Cobra is 36 inches wide in the fuselage, so when they're diving on a target, the guy that is out there with an AK-47 has a very slim target to shoot at. Each pylon had the potential for two rocket pods or two minigun pods on each side or a combination of the two. The 2.75" rockets can have warhead types that are either high explosive, anti-tank rounds, or fleschettes. A fleschette round is a 2.75 inch rocket-

Special Forces and strike forces on the Ho Chi Minh Trail, West of Polei Kleng.

head that carries nails in it that have fins instead of a nail-head. When you fire a pair of rockets from 1500 at the right angle of attack, it will put one nail in every square foot of a football field. There are 23 rockets in each pod. If you were to "salvo" a pair of pods, you can imagine the anti-personnel effect going into an area. Those little nails will penetrate an awful lot of leaf; the trunks will stop them, but the nails will continue down to the ground.

How many days were you out, and how many days were you at your base?

I was a platoon leader after three months, and I flew about 5 out of 7 days. It sounds like a lot, but you can't lead from the ground.

Can you describe the Ho Chi Minh trail?

There was one main trail that ran just inside the Laos and the Cambodian border and then split off into minor trails as it entered Vietnam. In some places it was a one-lane dirt road, and in other places it was just a foot trail. Along the trail you might find bunker complexes where soldiers rested on route to their destination or revetments where they parked and camouflaged trucks.

Did you enlist?

I was drafted out of my freshman year in college; they forgot to send my deferment in. I went to the Registrar's office, and they said I was supposed to have a deferment and not to worry about it; they would take care of it. Basically, I was majoring in sheepshead in college. I was basically failing everything. I was going to UW-Sheyboygan Center, and I went to college because all of my friends did. So I went home that weekend and thought a lot about what I was doing. I came to the conclusion that if I went into the Army, in a few years I would be older, have the GI Bill, and maybe some direction in my life. On Monday I went back to the Registrar's Office and told them to forget about sending in my deferment. I was drafted in February of 1966.

I was a typical 18-year-old at the time. I had no concept that I might die. They drafted me, and as a come on they offered me a chance to enlist. They gave me an option. If I enlisted I might get to go to Germany or choose my MOS (job type). It was really a trick though. If you enlisted for a specific location like Germany, they would train you, send you to Germany for six months, and then ship you to Vietnam. Since they also said you could choose your MOS, I chose that option. There were a lot of different jobs. I knew about Army Intelligence Agency, which was a communication intelligence unit, and they hardly ever went into combat. For three years I figured I could do that. When I got into basic training, you take a whole series of tests. When I got halfway through basic training and they said I qualified for OCS and they needed officers, I realized that officers made more money, so I opted for that.

I went to OCS at Ft. Knox, Kentucky, for six months. It was very intensive military training. When I got there the first day, I reported to duty in my dress greens. I was carrying my duffel bag, and it's full of everything I own in the military. They placed us in formation, marched us, and made us crawl on our arms and knees all the way back to the barracks. They said not to worry about our green uniforms, because we will not need them again. By the time you get out of here, you will be officers. That's how it started. When I was halfway through OCS, they said I also qualified for flight school and I could be a helicopter pilot. I thought that would be exciting, so I signed up for that. During the course of my time in the Army, I flew Cobras, LOH's, and Hueys. Most of my time was in light observation helicopters: they are the sports car of aviation.

How long did it take to learn how to fly?

Eight months. Four months of primary flight school in Texas and four months of secondary flight school at Ft. Rucker, Alabama, where they transitioned us into Hueys (UH-1s), instrument flight, formation flying, reading maps in the air, survival courses, etc. A helicopter is truly a sports car. You get in a fixed wing and you can trim it up, and it will basically fly in a straight line until the wind knocks if off course. Helicopters are hands on. You can rest the collective on your knee, and you can fly with one finger, but you essentially have to have your hands on the controls at all times. They have pedals for directional control (yaw), the cyclic that controls the pitch and roll, and then you have the collective, which changes the angle of attack on your blade. Angle of attack on the blades determines vertical speed (rate of climb) and horizontal speed (rate of acceleration and airspeed).

What was your tour of duty?

One year. I got in country on the 13th of October and left on the 12th of October. I went on R&R to Australia. I went into Vietnam pretty much "pro" Vietnam. I left pretty much against it. By the end of my tour in 1969, the military was starting to ship guys home because of the Vietnamization policy and because there were a lot of protests at home. We didn't have the political will at home to win the war. Once the military realized that politicians were not going to unstrap the arm tied behind their back, they began to fight a war that inflicted upon them the least amount of damage. We jokingly said that the motto of the 4th Infantry Division must be "Seek and Avoid." We would come up with good intelligence, and they would say, "We are going to think about this for a while." We were not able to pin them down and put enough force in to destroy NVA forces we discovered.

Many times we were looking for units that attacked us and then retreated to Cambodia where we couldn't go. We were shot at from units in Cambodia. The Cambodians could not stop the North Vietnamese. The NVA knew how to use their resources, and they were politically smart.

"WE DIDN'T HAVE THE POLITICAL WILL AT HOME TO WIN THE WAR. ONCE THE MILITARY REALIZED THAT POLITICIANS WERE NOT GOING TO UNSTRAP THE ARM TIED BEHIND THEIR BACK, THEY BEGAN TO FIGHT A WAR THAT INFLICTED UPON THEM THE LEAST AMOUNT OF DAMAGE."

Overall today I am more anti-war than I was before Vietnam because it seems like such a futile exercise. From the time of recorded history, wars have never solved anything. The Israelis and the Palestinians have been waging war for decades, perhaps a millennium. The Irish have been fighting the English since the 13th century. And if you look around the world, you'll find many other, similar groups of people who hate each other as a result of long standing feelings of revenge. Wars do not solve problems; they create more in most cases. We have not learned the fine art of compromise, so we kill people to get our way. Believe me, when I say "we" I mean humans, not just the U.S.

Did you ever see any evidence of "Agent Orange"?
Not as part of usual duties. The only vegetation that I saw removed was removed by explosives. I did see some area while doing administrative work near Phan Thiet, but none around Pleiku. Around Phan Thiet you could see rectangular areas where it was apparent that chemicals had removed the vegetation, but nothing like that around Pleiku

How were you treated when you came home?
My experience was not a bad one. I landed at Ft. Lewis, Washington, and took a bus and got my orders for my next duty station. I changed into civilian clothes and got on an airplane to fly home to my family. When I arrived at my next duty station, I lived on Ft. Knox, a fairly protected area from anti-war protesters.

Mark Holbrook is a vice principal in the D.C. Everest School District.

Interviewed and transcribed by Ashley Geisendorfer

Albert Kovatch

Kovatch was a maintenance officer and pilot serving two tours in Vietnam. The first was in 1968 and the second in 1971. He flew lift helicopters in the Delta, supporting ARVN and American units there.

Could you describe what you did in the army?
I was a pilot and a maintenance officer. I test flew aircraft. I watched and supervised repair. I was a parts officer for aviation parts supply and averaged between twenty and sixty million dollars of inventory. I personally signed for three million dollars of inventory for awhile.

How long were you in the war and when did you get there?
I got there in January of 1968 and left there in January 1969, first trip. Second trip -- I got there in January of 1971 and left in December of 1971.

Were you enlisted?
I had enlisted in and then went to flight school. I was an officer.

What were some of the base camps like in Vietnam?
Ours wasn't too bad. The first one was basically an old Japanese World War II airbase that we occupied. The second time was near the airstrip built right next to the town of Can Tho, which is a big town in the Delta.

Were any of your camps ambushed?
We were mortar attacked.

What kind of helicopters did you fly?
UH-1s and CH-47s.

What were they: observation or reconnaissance?
No, lift- aircraft.

Were you ever fired at while dropping off troops?
I was shot down a few times.

The plane just went down?
Yes, I took it in the engines easily and lost power and just landed.

Could you describe what an average day was like?
An average day would start anywhere from three-thirty to four-thirty. Six-thirty is when we would take off. You would fly out. Our flight area, usually you could fly across it in two hours. It was almost a hundred and fifty miles, two hundred miles. We'd fly out and land. At that point if you were working with a group of aircraft for an assault, they would tell you where the troops were. Usually they'd land at an airstrip that had been set up because re-fueling was easier to set up that way. We would re-fuel, go wherever the troops were going, lift them in. We could be doing that all day, lifting troops in, or in a lot of cases, we'd lift them in and we'd go into standby status. Then some of us would go out on individual shifts, doing different missions, usually hashing trashes as we called it, carrying supplies out. On a day we didn't go out with the company as a group of ships, we had individual ship missions, which were basically hashing trash for the advisors. You'd go work for a province, a province would be similar to a county in size, pretty big area but similar to a county. You'd work for whoever was the main advisor in the county, the main American because most of the area we worked in, there wasn't a lot of American troops. We were supporting ARVNs and the American advisors. The advisors would advise the ARVNs, and then they would do the work. We would go out to support them. They had little base camps all over. At least once a week each province had a ship. They needed that. That's how they got their rations, got their ammunition, and stuff like that. We'd haul them out.

Were you there during the Tet Offensive?
I got there in the middle of it.

Can you describe what it was like during that time?
Consider what happens at the Mardi Gras, and then picture that half of those people were shooting at you. That's about everything; everything broke loose. Every little brother that could carry a gun was out shooting, whether they were celebrating or shooting at you. Tet started out as a celebration because that's their big New Year's party. From there it got real nasty.

"IT WAS ANYWHERE FROM 85% TO 99% PURE HEROIN, SO IT DIDN'T TAKE A LOT. I KNOW A LOT OF THE GUYS TOOK THE EASY WAY OUT OF THE WAR WITH HEROIN."

Were drugs ever a problem during that time?
No. The drugs that we had a problem with came on in '71. That got to be more of a problem when we weren't flying as heavily as we did in '68. In my own mind, the Chinese pushed the drugs because the heroin that the guys got, a little vial about the size of a thimble, a sewing thimble, it would cost you maybe four dollars. It was anywhere from 85% to 99% pure heroin, so it didn't take a lot. I know a lot of the guys took the easy way out of the war with heroin. You take one of those vials, you snort it, and you take a couple good swallows of whiskey, and that's it. You're dead. It kills you.

Were you discharged right after your tour of duty?

No. I stayed in nine years, nine months, and fifteen days. I got out over some discrepancies that the army was having over promotion policies. I wasn't going to stay in any longer. I said the heck with it. I got out.

Were there any racial problems between black and whites in your divisions or camps?

My first tour we didn't really have any racial problems. My gunners and crew chiefs, a lot of them were black, and you didn't think about color. You supported each other because most of the time if you went out on a sailor ship mission, you didn't worry about color because when you landed out there you were the only Americans there. You supported each other. My second tour there was a little bit of black power stuff going around. That was a little bit of a problem, but our area wasn't as bad because it wasn't a main American area. There wasn't a lot of ground troops and stuff, so you had to watch your back and everything else. Everybody watched each other.

Was there a lot of physical and mental stress out there?

Always mental stress. I'll give you an example of mental stress. You land in a ten ship going into an assault; nobody's shooting at you. You think you're going to have it made. You look down through the chin bubble and you see the trip wire going right across the top of your skid to the bomb that you can see right over there that you didn't see on landing. Talk about mental stress, that happened.

So you flew pretty low then to the ground?

That was when we were landing. That was only when we were landing. If we'd been flying, I'd have been dead and it would have been no rod and trip wire.

How did you pull out of that one?

I had to pull out. Called the ground advisor and told him to send some troops over and disarm the damn thing. I wasn't going anywhere until it was done because when I landed easily and stuff like that, you don't just set right down. You kind of slide a little when you touch down because you're maintaining position on the other aircraft or the helicopters. It slid underneath the wire, and there was no way I could fly backwards.

What would you say was the hardest part of the war for you?

Probably when the orders came out that if we got shot at we couldn't shoot back. That's the hardest part. You start being shot at from the ground; we could not return fire.

> *"YOU START BEING SHOT AT FROM THE GROUND. WE COULD NOT RETURN FIRE."*

Why was that?

Because you might be shooting at some friendlies.

It was just a mistake?

No, it wasn't a mistake. A lot of times a lot of the VC would be wearing the same uniform as the ARVN troops. A lot of ARVN companies had VC in the company, and these guys would shoot at you hoping you'd shoot back. We'd figure if somebody shoots at you, he's not friendly. It don't matter how many of them there are.

Did you make many very close friends over there?
Yes.

Did a lot of them die?
A lot of them did not return. My classmates. This is my group at Fort Walders, (looking at picture), the company I was in. I started putting Xs on the people, and I realized I would have to about erase half the photos to put enough Xs on there, my classmates that didn't make it.

Then people were just replaced? As soon as someone would die, a new one would come in?
Yes. For awhile at least it went that way. I'll give you an idea of this "esprit de corps" and stuff. This guy "Pops," Gary Allen, he didn't have to be there. He'd already retired once. He came back in because it was an opportunity to fly, and he wanted to fly.

What kind of helicopter did you fly?
A TH-55A, a civilian thing. That was our primary trainer.

What was the standard base like for the helicopters and everything?
The main heliport out there was at the Downy Heliport. A lot of these guys wanted to fly, and this was the easiest way to fly. I almost went into the navy out of college, but the navy tried something and they lied, and I caught them at a lie, and so I went into the army. At the time I had caught them in a lie, I had already taken the army test and everything and had it in writing from the army that I was going to flight school, and it was just up to me to get through it. They couldn't guarantee getting through it, but I got through it.

Where were you stationed when you first got there?
Soc Trang. It's down in the delta about two hundred miles south of Saigon.

Did you go right into combat?
You bet. The next day I got there. For pilots, you're already trained when you get there. They have orientation but we were in the middle of Tet when I got there. Your orientation was that you grabbed your helmet the next day, and you took off with whoever they assigned.

Did you stay at this one camp the whole time?
Yes. I was in an aviation unit not associated with a division or anything like that, so we stayed because everything in our operation was easy to fly to.

How many helicopters did you usually fly with?
Ten to fifteen unless it was a double company effort.

Mainly lift helicopters?

Yes, lift helicopters, and if you had guns, you had maybe four guns in our area, four or five maybe if you were lucky.

Were the Viet Cong pretty heavy through that area?

Yes. Southwest of our base, right off the end of our runway, we had what was called a tiger's tail. We called it that because we were Soc Trang and our nickname was Soc Trang Tigers 121st Assault. This tail was a wood line with a creek through it. The main road coming from further south up through this thing was only about a quarter mile wide, but it was five, six miles long. At night some nights the gunships would go out there straight for you, and a lot of times when they'd go straight for you, you'd get secondary explosions from a VC kind of move, missions and stuff up through the area. Whenever you could catch them like that and blow it up, you'd always blow it up.

Were you ever involved in any ground attacks? Did the Viet Cong ever ambush your bases?

I was never involved with it, but I was an airfield duty officer a lot, which is main officer of the guard at night. You're responsible for the whole damn place. They give the keys to the office and tell you to make sure you open up in the morning if it's still there. A few of them disappeared-- got the hell blown out of them.

Bases?

Yes, especially when they're out in the middle of the jungle up north.

In the highlands?

Yes. We were mostly in the delta with the rice paddies, so it was a lot clearer and you had groups of trees. We had the U Minh forest part of it along the West Coast. That's where the VC got started against the French and there were a lot of factories. You go in there, thirty-foot high trees, thirty-foot high brush, and it had pathways cut through it and all the brush wired together so that it wouldn't leave holes, so we got a lot of stuff out of that.

How were you treated when you came back to the U.S.? Did you get a lot of negative treatment?

Spit at, called baby killers, you get a little of everything. Yes, negative, quite a bit of negativity.

Did you have a lot of trouble with memories and stress when you got back?

> *"HE WAS SUCKED INTO AN AMBUSH, AND THEY JUST SHOT THE BOAT TO HELL."*

It took me a long time, and every time somebody, something went off loud behind me, to get from wanting to jump on the floor. When a siren went off, I'd jump. Now and then once in awhile I still have that problem.

Are there any stories you could share with us, such as combat stories you have?

We had a scratch mission one day. They called in about ten of the aircraft, whoever they could get together because the navy ran swift boats, which were basically thirty and forty foot craft, high-powered boats. The river patrols usually mounted a couple of fifties and a forty millimeter canyon and some of them had horizontally firing eighty-one millimeter mortars. They work in twos, as units, followed some sampan and went off the main river just west of Mai Tho and basically disappeared in the middle of fire. He was sucked into an ambush and they just shot the boat to hell. They called us in, a scratch mission, which means they just call on the radio and start reading off call signs and tell us where to go to. They had ten, twelve, of us grouped. We loaded our troops that they had, and what they told us, that they were coordinating an Arc Light, which is a B-52 strike. They figured we should be probably three or four miles away when the bombs hit. If they would have had any more coordination and figuring we'd have probably been on the ground when the bombs hit. But we were five hundred feet in the air, and the aircraft just goes and starts shaking. We landed, dropped the troops off. I don't know what we put them in

"ONE OF THE BOMBS WE DROPPED, 750 POUNDERS HADN'T GONE OFF AND IT WAS LAYING ABOUT TWENTY FEET AWAY."

there for. It just looked like if you took some chocolate pudding and whipped it up. That's what the ground looked like. I mean the trees disappeared; there weren't even stumps. The main shocker was when I landed and looked down and about, excuse the French, shit my pants because one of the bombs we dropped, 750 pounders hadn't gone off, and it was laying about twenty feet away. We both, my pilot and me, about shit our pants. You didn't know whether this bomb was dropped on purpose with a delayed action fuse in it or dropped with a booby-trapped fuse or if it was just a plain dud. All bombs are good. It's the fusing mechanism that might be the dud, but the VC were good enough about taking these and making land mines out of them, putting command detonate in. That's why we fixed a few of them up so if they started carting them off, it'd blow up in their face. Here I'm landed from it, and I've got basically hurricane of wind coming off the rotor system beating on this thing, and I'm wondering is the son-of-a-bitch going to blow up in my face. If it blows up I'm not going to know it.

What was flying in monsoon season like?

Hop in the pool, get on the bottom, and try to cross it. It can come down that heavy. I flew into it one day in probably September, October. We were out supporting doing this hash and trash single ship, and it started coming down so damn hard. We weaseled our way in and got down on the ground, but the area I am in is the most beautiful blue-green you've ever seen. There was only one problem, I was fifty miles from the gulf, and I couldn't tell that because the rain was coming down so heavy. This looked blue-green, that looked blue-green, everything looked blue-green. I had no idea, so we landed. Had to let down a place to land and let stuff fast because it's coming down enough that it's enough to turn an engine out when you got into the heavy stuff.

How low did you think you'd probably be flying during that time?

Easily if it's coming down that hard, you don't fly. You land because if you're really trying to sneak in you're taking a real awful chance of going low. The lower you are the more chances are you're going to be shot down.

How many troops would your helicopter carry?

We usually took on ten ARVN. If it was Americans, anywhere from four to six.

How are they different?

Weight. Average American weighs two hundred pounds plus eighty pounds of equipment. Average Vietnamese soaking wet is a hundred pounds, hundred and ten pounds, big difference.

Did you ever have to lift any injured soldiers out? Kind of like a medical helicopter?

Son, I've carried more injured and more dead then you could ever think about. We carried so many one day I called in landing coming back and asked

"I HAD BLOOD ENCRUSTED ON MY DECK. WE QUIT COUNTING BODIES ONE DAY. WE JUST FIGURED TONNAGE."

for the fire truck. And they gave me a little bit of static, but they sent it out. And the fire guys reported back and never had any trouble after that. I had blood encrusted on my deck. We quit counting bodies one day. We just figured tonnage.

So did they just get lifted back to base then?

Yes, we just lifted them back and let the mortuary have them. I didn't handle too many Americans; most of these were all ARVN. And some of them were good. The ARVN marines were excellent as far as I'm concerned. I saw them one day-- we had ARVN marines in one operation and ARVN soldiers. Marines are one group and ARVN is the Army of the Republic of Vietnam. The marines, they are the same part of the government, but to me it's a different level of troop. Put in three hundred or four hundred ARVN in the morning in a tree line like from here to there about this distance. They were taking firing. They didn't advance they stayed there all day. Early afternoon we put in an insert of ARVN marines. Their first sergeant company commander got up, stood up, and took fire. The first sergeant blew his whistle, all the marines got up. He blew the whistle again. They pulled the bayonets out, they fixed bayonets, and they walked into the tree line. Ten minutes later the tree line was secured.

So they were like the elite then?

Yes. They knew it. They were cocky but they knew they were good, and I always supported them.

Did you ever lift in any American Special Forces or were they just basically all ground troops?

Special Forces are ground troops. Yes, I did work with the U.S. Special Forces.

How?

I supported them out of their area of operation. I wished I'd have a map, I could show you. All this is in my mind, but I can't reference it to you because you have no idea. And they worked this one group out of the Mekong. They were within six thousand yards of the border, six clicks, four clicks, click is a thousand yards. Right across the border of the Cambodian outpost was a VC base camp. After a flag of truce the Special Forces guys went over and talked to the Cambodian troop commander and told him that they had a four-deuce mortar, which is the same as a 105 howitzer, except it's a mortar, pointed at his camp. And it would always be pointed at his camp. And if a ground attack ever came from over there, they were not going to fire on his camp. And they never got a ground attack from that area.

How many times were you shot down?

I was shot down once. Shot up quite a few times. But we had one mission one day in late afternoon. It was an order to pick up some ARVN troops, and we were pushing trying to get as many on as we could because we wanted to get done. We'd been eight, ten hours flying that day. You get damn tired and it's hot. And I had a strong aircraft and I had ten or eleven on, and what we did we call a hover check. You load up, you pull up to three feet and see if you can hold yourself at a hover without losing power. Well, I pulled up to three feet. I held and I called lead and said I would go. And we started taking fire and everybody scatters. I pulled in power, I pulled in to take off, and I didn't go anywhere, and I told the crew chief start throwing off ARVN troops. When we get to the point that we can move this bird, I say we'll take off. We got down to, I think, five. We threw half of them off before I could slide the aircraft. I took a chance on the land mines and I started sliding. With the helicopters as the same as the fixed wing, there is a point when the plane starts to fly and a fixed wing is when you lift up and take off and a helicopter. It's the same thing where you're going forward fast enough that the fuselage develops. This is called translational, and I just started sliding until I could hit that. And I had about a five-mile run, but it didn't have any trees over four foot high. I would say at a quarter mile I got the aircraft flying. Then it took me another probably two miles going straight out to get enough height that I could turn to get over the trees about the height of that little oak over there. Talk about a weak airplane. Turned around and went and landed at the compound just northeast of Can Tho field but about five miles across the river, and I stayed there till almost dark before someone remembered we were still out there and come got us. We got the troops off, and they headed for town because it was near a little town where they were from. And we took and put the machine guns out, two machine guns, took them off the airplane, set them down, loaded them up other than what we had and prepared to stay there.

What were your helicopters equipped with, as far as weapons?

Two machine guns, one on each side.

You'd have two gunners on there?

Yes. Your crew chief would be one of the gunners, and then we had a door gunner. The gunner was responsible for the maintenance on the guns and loaded ammunition, and when he was done with that, then he helped the crew chief maintain the aircraft. These things take about an hour. For every hour you fly, it takes about thirty minutes of maintenance, so if you flew eight hours you usually spent four hours on it.

So, did you guys fire very much on your helicopter? Did you have to fire at the enemy very much?

A lot of times, a lot of times. Anytime you're going in for an assault and anybody starts shooting at you, you automatically return it.

Did you guys do kill counts or anything?

No, half the time you couldn't see if you killed anybody. Some guys did, tried to. I just wanted to stay alive.

Did you ever have any rest and relaxation periods?
I had one R and R on the first trip. I went to Tokyo. On the second trip I came home for two weeks leave. I had an R and R I could have took, but I didn't even think about it. I should have took it because I wanted to go to Sydney, Australia.

How was Tokyo?
Nice but damn expensive. I was sitting in a bar one night in the hotel talking to a Tokyo businessman, and he said what did you come here for? He says, I was born and raised here and I'd rather be in New York City. It's cheaper.

How much money did you make?
Three hundred and ten dollars a month.

And how much did you keep out for personal expenses?
I spent just about all of it. I bought a lot of camera equipment, some high-fi stuff. I still have all the camera equipment and most of all the high-fi stuff.

Were there a lot of people trying to sell things to American soldiers?
Oh yes. You had people in black market all over the place. Hell half the time the black market had more cigarettes, pop, and beer than PX did.

We had a speaker in earlier in our class, and he said all he bought was cigarettes and beer.
See now that's the difference being with an American, totally American unit in an American area. You went to a base camp, and one there is no place to spend money and two, a lot of this stuff was if you were out in the boonies, out in the base camp this stuff was automatically given to you. You didn't have to buy it. Usually you had a beer ration of one or two cans a day if you were out in the sticks. I don't know how some of them drank it because I can't drink hot beer.

What was the weather like down there? Really hot all year round?
Yes and what was really cute, (I call it cute because one time we had a cool spell come in.) it got foggy like it does around here and got down to about 55 degrees and you would have thought it was 55 below zero the way the people dressed. They were cold. They're not used to it. What you've got on for a shirt is heavier material then most of them wore with three or four pieces. So any cool days, there is no central heating or anything like that. If you're lucky you're in a decent building maybe you'll have an overhead fan. That's all.

Is there any personal experiences that really stick out in your mind?
I was almost done for the day and I had a Vietnamese officer turn around and hand me a note on which he wrote "thank you." The only Vietnamese over there that ever said thank you. You appreciate the help.

Were a lot of the native people pretty negative against you guys or did they cooperate pretty good?
They cooperated pretty good. I didn't know anybody that really at least in our area that did not enjoy Vietnam immensely. You could have a girlfriend or two or three if you wanted them with no problem as

long as you didn't run out of money. I won't say any more about that.

Did you ever get any diseases or jungle rot or anything like that down there?
I'll do my standard thing here. That's a memory from Vietnam.

What were the insects like or reptiles and all the animals and stuff down there?
A lot of rats, a lot of birds. You didn't see a lot of cats and a lot of dogs. The main reason is cats and dogs are food. Rats -- we had a standard joke that if you went downtown and bought a sandwich from a street vendor it was a rat sandwich. It probably was. Well, it didn't taste bad. The rats over there are different then rats here. Most of the rats over there are vegetarians and they'll also be bigger then a cat. I was officer of the guard one night my first trip over there, and some shooting started on out of the line inside the perimeter area. I went out there and the crew chief had got scared and he turned around and saw this big damn thing there and he thought he was a feral cat or maybe there were some like bobcats around. He thought maybe he'd been stopped by that, and he turned around, and what he did was he shot a big rat with a 45, did not

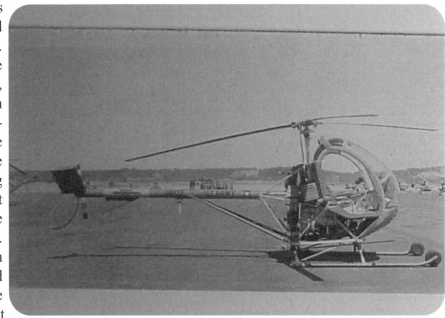

kill him. You're talking an eight, ten-pound rat. These are big. But we didn't have trouble with snakes in our area. I never did see a snake. The only snake I saw was a python that our first sergeant had as a pet. And that old boy he was about 20 feet long. And when he died they had to bury him just inside the minefield. You had the outer fence of the minefield and the inner fence, and they buried him between the inner fence and the minefield to keep the people from town from digging him up.

They eat them?
You bet. They wanted him to be brought downtown and sold. It was good food.

How close were you to town?
Ah, our first, well both bases. The first base, town was tiger's tail was this end of the base, town was that end of the base, and right there. Second time around we had this base we were on, was built between Benhoi Air Base and Can Tho. I would say we were probably a quarter mile from Can Tho and a half-mile from Benhoi.

What was sleeping like? How much sleep do you think you probably got on an average day?

Oh shoot that depends on what you were doing. Some days you got a lot of sleep because you'd go out, do the insertion and go on standby status, (which was wait till something happened, then you could sleep). I went downtown and bought a hammock. You could buy hammocks that were basically made from nylon fishing line. They could ball up to the size of your fist. I'd hook one on the back of the cargo compartment and bring it over the top of one of the pilot's seat and hook it down on the seat belts. Lay out there, I'd lay there and there's room on the cargo deck for two there and usually the crew chief would flip down the first set of troop chairs and he would lay on that, and so we'd all be asleep in the aircraft.

What did you all have for equipment? What was standard equipment that you would carry during a flight?

Standard equipment: survival radio, chicken vest, your 38 or 45, and anything that would contain liquid that you could bring. I carried a quart thermos with me all the time. We tried to keep an insulated can they use for hauling meals or liquid in and then with ice if we were lucky to get ice. You'd carry that with you all the time and whatever rations you had that you could beg, borrow, or steal.

How many people do you think were probably in the camp?

First trip-- probably four hundred to five hundred.

So pretty small then?

Yes.

Has talking helped you recover from your emotional scars?

A little bit, but I get so pissed off at things, excuse the expression, but things had happened that didn't need to happen. Like we landed one day; I got out of the aircraft and was shutting down. The turbine engine had a mandatory two minute cooling down where you turn it down to idle and let it run to cool it down. It makes the engines last a lot longer, and I was out and I walked back. I had ice in my thermos. I was the only guy who had a thermos in the crew that day, but we had no water, and I was going back trying to find some water, and we got hit by a mortar attack. The VC made one mistake. They didn't let the aircraft shut down before they fired, so it was in idle. The guys, whoever was in the cockpit wrapped the throttle and took off. I dove in a bunker. I looked out and two GI's were crossing the runway and got hit by a mortar blast, and I ran out. I gave first aid and the first guy that saw me flying down with the two guys landed and we picked them up. I tried to get a bandage over the guy's hole in his chest about that big. The other guy had a slice in his neck and he was throwing up and I was trying to hold him so he could throw up while holding something on this guy. And we were five miles from the medevac hospital in Meitoe and we dove into there and I helped carry the guys off and I held the guy's foot down. I was holding his feet and a couple of other guys were holding his arms while the doctors stuck a chest tube in and drained three quarters of a gallon of blood out of his chest and then called for a chest kit to cut him open and try to save him. I don't know if they saved him or not.

Vietnam ended with the fall of Vietnam because out Congress would not own up and live up to the contractual agreements that we had with Vietnam. We were supposed to supply ammunition and spare parts, and Congress would not vote the money to buy the stuff. The biggest problems over there with the fighting was it was too political. They would not let the military run the fight.

Could we have won the war?

We had enough power over there to win it but...we could have. We even had one country that volunteered to finish the fight and terminate and we would not allow that. Chiang Kai-Shek (Nationalist China) volunteered his army to come and finish the war and, he would have done it. He would have killed a lot of people. An example was given by a friend of mine that was with the first cav, and he supported the tiger division of the Republic of Korean Army, the Koreans that were over there. They were in a joint exercise. The First Cav walked through a village and found nothing wrong. This unit, the First Cav, tried to take in whenever possible to have the pilots and crews go out for a day with the ground troops so they have an idea of what was happening. When you have an idea of what was happening, it's a lot. You try to help them a lot more. The Americans walked through. He was with the ARVNs or the ROKs, the Koreans.

> "*THEIR COMPANY COMMANDER KILLED A SEVEN-YEAR-OLD KID AT A COMPANY FORMATION OUT THERE. SHE CAME WALKING UP WITH A CLAMORE MINE STRAPPED TO HER CHEST AND WHAT WE CALL A CLOCKER IN HER HAND, A DETONATOR.*"

The Koreans walked through the village, looked around, the same things the Americans did, walked on out of village till they were out of sight, and they put a perimeter up around the village. And they said why? Why are you doing this? The Americans said the village was okay. This is where an Oriental's outlook makes a difference. With no refrigeration, most of these villagers didn't have, you didn't cook any more than you can eat at one meal. The Koreans looked into the cooking pots and there was too much rice being cooked. They said these people are expecting visitors shortly. They bagged a VC company coming through. But things like that stick in a lot of people's craw that they don't understand what happened like at My Lai. There were civilians killed, but in combat in this type of guerilla warfare anybody that can pull a trigger is an enemy soldier.

A friend of mine...we were together in between tours. We rented a house together where we were instructor pilots at Fort Rucker. His friend was in the Marine Corps. Their company commander killed a seven-year-old kid at a company formation out there. And she came walking up with a clamore mine strapped to her chest amd what we call a clocker in her hand, a detonator. She wouldn't stop. What happens is that the VC tells these kids to do this and will give them fifty cents worth of candy. Well, fifty cents to a kid or equivalent fifty piasta when you're working maybe daddy's working for a hundred piast a day. Actually the international exchange rate was something like five hundred piasta to the dollar even though we supported their economy by an exchange rate of a hundred and ten piasta to the dollar. Whether they made us exchange, we couldn't get the international rate; we had to do the rate to support the economy. And so you figure you give a four or five year old kid, seven year old, ten year old, something like the equivalent of a half day of a father's income to go buy candy, they'd do anything for you. They don't realize it's going to kill them. There ain't going to be a piece of candy. And he shot them. The government in order to protect him, court marshaled him and collaterally investigated him. A collateral investigation means they figure the cost, and you have to pay for it. They figured it costed 39 cents for the bullet that he shot the kid with and charged him that. By doing that, nobody could sue him in civilian court. That was protection for him.

A friend of mine, another friend, had a GI go wacky and highjack one of their aircraft. He wanted to get to Saigon, get out of the country. A huey might make it to Saigon, but it ain't going to get out of the country. They stopped to refuel it and he got distracted and the pilot shot the guy. They did the same thing to him to keep the parents of the soldier from suing the guy for wrongful death. They collaterally investigated him and charged him 39 cents for the bullet. Weird things happen. Some things ain't weird; it's just the way they happen.

So do you really think this war was really necessary?
Yes, but the problem is it wasn't necessary for us to lose. The main country that's communist now is China. In this country, it's half of Congress. Your liberal Democrats if you look at the way communism runs and what they want to do and look at what the liberal democrats want to do, you will find no difference. They want to tax the hell out of me to give it to the person in town who don't want to work. He won't get off his lazy ass and go do something and there is work out there. And in this town when you can get a job turning hamburgers at McDonalds for seven dollars an hour that's called opportunity to start. You've got to prove yourself someplace and these people say, I can't get fifteen dollars an hour; I don't want the job. Well they ain't going to give anybody fifteen dollars an hour the first time around unless it's a government job you lucked into until you prove yourself. There's too many of these people; they're too lazy, a good example of laziness, and the people on welfare. I'm a postman walking around in town. My old people, my retired people, and some of them are working, and during a snowstorm they'll be the first people to clean their walks, their steps. And the other people they can be home; I have seen them at home sitting and watching the snow come down and letting it build up three or four days until I drop their mail off before they will clean that walk. They have no pride; why should they have pride? They don't have to do a damn thing. Their money is given to them. This is wrong. I have found fault with Congress allowing the people who ran to Canada to avoid the draft, to allow them to come back. Most of these people that went to Canada you'll find out, quite a few of them are relatives to people in Congress or relatives to a politician or kids of rich people. They could afford to support them in Canada. I think it's mockery to everybody that died in Vietnam to allow these bastards back into this country.

Did your views change like before and after?
No. Communism had to be something to be fought. Just because Russia supposedly turned capitalist and the wall came down, doesn't mean anything. They're still out to get us. In 1991, China couldn't loft a missile out two hundred miles and because of eight years as liberal democrat president, China can now put a missile here in this state. Prior to Clinton, they couldn't do it. They couldn't loft a missile and target it. He allowed one of his friends, and it's proven it was a friend of his that owns a large private company, that put satellites up to use China as a launch platform, their missiles as launch platforms. They crashed one of our missiles and it was six months before they allowed an American inspection team to that missile, into that satellite. And the satellite navigational chips weren't in that satellite and that had decoding in them for how we do it. And that's how they learned it. Those chips never had been returned just like that naval plane that they got last month. The plane hasn't been returned yet either. Nowadays there's a way to handle it if they had gumption. Plane lands, China won't give it back, you immediately lock all Chinese ships up that are in port in the United States and they are not allowed to unload. They are given orders to sail. You cut off the trade to China. What makes it bad is that most of the clothing that the U.S. soldiers wear now is made in China. Law requires it to be made in this country, but they got away somehow with that stuff that's being made over there. Next time you go through buying stuff, try to find something that's made in the U.S.

It's hard.

It's very hard. We are losing our manufacturing capability, and I think before you young fellas get my age which I'm 55 now so you've got what 30 years, 35 years, you're gonna be fighting another war for independence in this country, and it may be with sticks. A lot of these people might say I'm going off the deep end, but I don't think so. You won't have any manufacturing capability left in this country. If you can't manufacture it, the country that's manufacturing it can set the price or say no, you do this, you surrender. There's a problem coming up with the United Nations. It has to do with human rights. We won't pay the bill. They kicked us off the Human Right Commission. They don't want an American on the Human Rights Commission because most of the countries don't look at human rights like the way we do. You have no rights in most other countries, and that's one of the reasons they don't want us on that commission, and the day that somehow they get together and vote the United States out of the Security Council, mark that day with red ink because that's gonna be the start of trouble because anybody on the Security Council can veto anything that happens. Once they vote that if they want to ship troops in here, they can. Ultimately, if you ever look through the U.N. charter, you will find there is no mention of human rights in their charter. It's just something we brought up. It started with, there's no rights like in our Constitution you have the first ten amendments which is basically human rights. There's nothing in their charter like that. It's just wrong stuff. They'll be fighting again.

Following his return, Albert Kovatch was in the vending machine business, hotel maintenance, and was in the postal service.

Interviewed by Mike Brown
Transcribed by Vicki Karcher

Richard Marquart

Drafted into the Army, Marquart served as a crew chief on a helicopter in the 187th Assault Helicopter Company stationed at Tay Ninh. He served in Vietnam from September 1969 to October 1970.

How did you become involved in the Vietnam War? Were you drafted?

I was drafted. I was drafted in the army when I was twenty years old. I went through basic training at Fort Campbell, Kentucky. Then I went on to Stencil Helicopter Training in Fort Eustis, Virginia. From there I went to Vietnam, and that's where I was stationed, 187th assault helicopter company. My main duties were inserting troops into the war zone and extracting them. We also had other duties. I was mainly a crew chief and had a pilot and co-pilot, and you have a crew chief and a helicopter. Other duties that we had were flights everyday. You would pick up troops or drop them off, and they were called LZs or PZs. Then also they would split. You would rotate one helicopter; that crew would be designated for that day to deliver mail, pick up mail, neighboring fire support bases, and then you would just rotate it. You would rotate it. I can't remember exactly how we rotated it, but it was you rotate it. In a flight you were a lead helicopter; you were tailer in between and then you were also on these mail runs.

Do you remember the day that you were drafted? What all happened?

No, I really don't. I was twenty years old. I did go back to school for a half of year at the tech, and then I went to work at Wausau Motor Parts which is where I went back to work when I came back home. I was kind of expecting it in a way because I was right at that age that I could have slipped through or not. I was kind of expecting, but it was a shock because you thought you might slip through, but no, I didn't, and I accepted it. I have no regrets for going as far as the war was concerned; it was a different type of war over there than fighting for our country. You were fighting for another country. You didn't know what all the facts were, but you were willing to go over. I'm sure you heard of other kids going into Canada or whatever, and I never resented them because they did what they had to do and I did what I had to do. I didn't want to go over there, but I went over there. I wasn't going to be a draft dodger or flee the country, but I never resented any of them that did do that.

When you first got over there, what was going through your mind?

I think I was like just about any other young guy that went over there. We were scared. You got off a plane that was air conditioned and right away the heat and the smell. We are very lucky in this country to have what we have, and you could just sense the smell, the heat over there and everything else. Over there you appreciate what you have over here. They had at that time, I don't know what it is like now, but they had nothing. It was just a sad situation over there.

Did you fight against the Viet Cong or NVA regular units?

Yes, but our job mainly was to get the troops in and out so we weren't involved in actually fighting other then maybe taking fire, going in or out of an LZ, which did not take while I was over there. I was very lucky. I can remember there were at least two times that we took fire. There was one time where I can explain how hard it was to infiltrate the Viet Cong. We had dropped off a load of troops. We had a nine ship lift. It was an LZ, a landing zone, where you didn't have a lot of room to land so you went in maybe three, four helicopters at a time, dropped off troops and another three, four were behind you and dropped off more. I remember we put 'em in. I remember seeing a village; apparently it was an abandoned village. I don't know exactly how many troops we did put in at that time, I forgot, but I happened to be with them when they did pick them up three, four, five days later. Later on I found out that they found nothing in there. It just so happened when we took them out, our helicopter was the last helicopter out of that LZ. We took fire coming out of that LZ, and they said they never found nothin' in there, so that's how these Viet Cong were buried in and they could not find them. That's the way that war went over there. You didn't know who you were fighting. You couldn't get at them; it was that type of war over there.

Could you describe an average day during the war?

An average day would be getting up early in the morning, probably anywhere from six to seven or in that area, sometimes later, depending upon your flight plans. Then you would get your helicopter ready. You would check it out, and make sure that it was ok to fly. The door gunner would get all the guns out and mount them; we would mount them probably together and go do our run around with the crew chief. Then the pilots would come out and they would do their daily checks on the helicopter. Then we'd get our orders, the flight would get their orders, and we would fly to a particular area depending upon whether you're inserting troops or extracting them. We would sometimes wait around for hours for our next movement. Sometimes you'd do it right away. Sometimes it would only take you a couple of hours and you were back home. There was a lot of waiting in between picking up troops and dropping off troops depending upon what was allocated for the troops to either stay in the area for a day or two or come out right away. My duties as a crew chief was to tear down the helicopter and do my dailies, and it would be logged in a book, do any repairs or report any repairs to maintenance that had to be done and make sure the helicopter was clean, and get it ready for the next day. That was the way it was. There was a lot of waiting. There was a lot of waiting in between.

How were the guys that came on the plane with you? I mean were they just pretty silent when they came?

Yes, in a way. Mostly the troops, the infantry troops that you picked up were pretty silent. There was a difference between picking them up and letting them off. You could tell; there were expressions. They were scared when you were going in and dropping them off, but when we picked them up you could tell in their face they were a little relieved to go back to a bed for a change. It was two different things. We were used as a medevac from time to time depending upon what had happened. I fortunately never had to be used as a medevac, as far as that's concerned. That wasn't too bad.

You weren't involved in any firefights?

No, not really. There was one time where we had come in, I was in a single ship where we were delivering mail, picking up mail that day, and we had come back home. I was already started to tear down my helicopter, and our unit had gotten a scramble that some infantry troops pinned down, and they needed to get some more troops in. I did go on another helicopter with another crew chief. I don't remember taking very much fire. The fire that we saw was tracers that were either coming at you or you were firing the tracers. We didn't fire a lot of rounds going into the LZ. It was a scary situation. It was the only time I remember that. There was another time where we were also coming back from another mail run, where it was our day and we got a may day, which was our unit had been further north picking up some troops or dropping them off. We just heard it over the radio, and so what happened was one of our helicopters had picked up what they call cache, and that's where they had picked up some wheat or food or whatever it was, some ammo that was buried that they had found that the Viet Cong had stashed. They had two helicopters, and they were transporting this. One of the helicopters had an engine failure or something, and they had gone down and they had gone down in the jungle. As we were listening on the radio we decided to fly up there because we knew where they were. In that time at least two other helicopters tried to get the troops out because all it was was the two crew chiefs or the crew chief and a gunner and the two pilots. There was nobody else but the helicopter that was in the jungle; they could not get to them because of the dense jungle. One of them had a rotor blade strike on the terrain or the trees and they couldn't get out. We were on route and we knew where they were, and we got to them, and I'll never forget the expressions on their face because there was a big knoll and we motioned because they saw me and I motioned to them to come our way. I'll never forget their expression; they were never so happy to see somebody that could get them out, and we got them out. That was really a rewarding incident. They tried twice and they couldn't get them out, and we got 'em out. Later on before it even got dark they had gotten somebody in there to sling load the helicopter out of the jungle because you don't want the Viet Cong to get a hold of any of our radios, but they had taken out the radios, and they had brought them with 'em. You don't want to let them get a hold of anything that they can possibly use. That's one of your first concerns when you get out- you destroy your radios and whatever you think that they can use. I do remember that, and that was kind of a scary situation.

> *" ONE OF THE HELICOPTERS HAD AN ENGINE FAILURE, AND THEY HAD GONE DOWN IN THE JUNGLE."*

Did you have any experiences with body counts?

No, I did not. Luckily, because I was in a helicopter and I never was right up front. All I saw was a couple times tracers coming at you. Other than the heat and the discomfort over there, it was like any other day, even at home. You had guys played cards, and you talked and you drank. When anybody ever had asked me, even firing the weapons over there, it was like going hunting here. When reality sets in is when those tracers start coming back at you. Then you know it's not a game again. During the day it wasn't that bad. I was in a helicopter unit. I was always in a bed every night so I didn't have it as bad as a lot of the grunts there, the so-called grunts, the infantry. I was very lucky in that aspect.

> *"I'LL NEVER FORGET THEIR EXPRESSIONS; THEY WERE NEVER SO HAPPY TO SEE SOMEBODY THAT COULD GET THEM OUT, AND WE GOT THEM OUT."*

What about drugs? Were they a problem at all?

Yes. Marijuana was. I never saw any, where I was. I never saw any hard drugs, but you could walk through our company area and smell the marijuana in the air, so yes, there was marijuana over there. I never encountered any hard, but marijuana was there. You knew the guys who smoked it, and I had tried it once, but I didn't have any interest in it.

How was the relationship between whites and blacks?

I never saw, as far as I was concerned, anything where you were confronted on a daily basis. I mean for the most part the blacks hung together and the whites hung that way. I didn't see it interfering with any of our jobs or in my unit as far as that's concerned. The blacks stuck together.

In an infantry would blacks be together?

No. In our unit, in the helicopter unit, when we were in our hooches, they hung together and we hung together. We did intermingle at times, but it wasn't on a real buddy-buddy basis. We talked and then we didn't talk. I never saw anything where we didn't like each other. We might have inside or had a grudge, but I never saw anything like that in my unit.

When you got back from the war did people have opinions about you? Did you have to face anything?

No, I did not. I was very fortunate there, too. I came in through California, and I just wanted to get home so fast that I processed through within twenty-four hours. I got to the airport, and I never really paid any attention if anybody had given me any dirty looks comin' through, coming home. Nobody ever said anything one way or the other, you know. When I was actually home here, they might have asked me a few questions. I know you hear a lot of stories where some of them were criticized and everything else, but I never was. I never saw that, and I think you see more of that in the bigger cities. Wausau is a small town. I don't think you really see a lot of that. I might be wrong, but I didn't see that.

Did you make any lasting friendships during the war?

No, not really. We had good friends over there, but I just lost contact and never followed up on the friends that I made over there. I probably should have. And they never followed up 'cause I know we exchanged addresses. I remember doing that with some of the guys over there, but they never followed up, and I never did, unfortunately, so that's the way that goes.

What was the hardest part of being in the war?

I was a year in a helicopter unit, and I don't know if I was just naïve or just wasn't scared enough to think I wasn't gonna die 'cause I didn't think anything was going to happen to me, and I don't know why. For what reason, I knew there were times that I was scared. There were a lot of times I was scared, but for whatever reason I never thought I wasn't going to come home. Not being home was the hardest part, being in a strange place and being in war. That was probably the hardest part. It was a good experience. I don't want to say war was a good experience, but being away from home was a good experience. Being away from home and being in the service was a good experience. Not necessarily being in a war was a good experience although it did turn out to be, I guess, a good experience for me. Fortunately, I made it back home all in one piece and alive. There were a lot of soldiers that didn't make it home or didn't make it home all in one piece, so they're going to tell you no, it wasn't a good experience. They experienced some horrible things, so it's not a good experience. I would say for the most part, the ones that did not experience some horrible things, they would say it was a good experience for them.

Do you think being in the military has just helped you with everyday life?

Yes. I think it is a good experience. I think it is a good experience for guys and girls just to get away from their parents and their home, and I think service is a good experience for everybody. Some discipline. I think it is a good experience for everybody.

Is there a message you have for young people today about the war?

I've talked about it with my children, as far as Americans are concerned, how good that we really have it. I mean the Vietnamese had really nothing. What we take for granted is just amazing for what they had at that time. I don't know how it is over there now, but I would say that unless you are living in Saigon or some of the bigger cities that they don't have much. It doesn't necessarily have to be material things either, I don't think. It's just that their way of life is just so poor. It was so poor, and that's only one little small country in the world. The only message that I would say would be to appreciate what you have in life, to really appreciate it because it's so hard to look at them children and everything over there. Everybody wants to live in the United States, and you can't. Everybody isn't going to live in the United States. They've also got to help themselves too, and we can help them. This country can help other countries, to a certain extent. We can't have everybody coming over here.

Did you have any difficulty dealing with the memories such as how the men reacted to things when they came back from the war?

No, not really. I guess I say luckily, I didn't see that much that was horrible about war other then a few disturbing things. What I did see, I just blanked it out, and didn't think about it. I was just glad to be home alive to get on with my life. There are some, especially the infantry, that did see some horrible things and experienced horrible things, and it was hard for them to blank that out. It was just a thing of the war. I would imagine it was hard for them. I was lucky that I didn't have to experience that.

What did serving country mean to you during active duty and now as a veteran?

As far as active duty was concerned, I just thought of it as being drafted, a young person just being drafted, and I just had to do it because I was drafted. I probably didn't think of it at that time as serving my country really. I think I probably just thought of it as just a duty that you're doing just to be a citizen of the United States, that our elected officials thought that they were helping out another country get rid of communism, and that we had to try to stop it. I guess I never really thought of doing it, per se, "for our country." I just thought it was the right thing to do that I was drafted. I wouldn't have thought either way if I wasn't drafted. I had no desire to go into the service after school, but just at that time there was the draft, and we knew we were fighting with a communist country to rid communism. As far as afterwards, I really never cared to be a part of any post service as far as the legion. I did eventually join the legion, but I know I probably should participate, but I don't even participate in, I don't go to any meetings or anything as far as that's concerned. I know I have been approached. "Why don't you?" All the World War II Veterans are starting to dwindle, so they want to keep it up. I just have no desire.

When Richard Marquart returned home he went back to work at Wausau Motor Parts.

Interviewed by Vicki Karcher and Jacalyn Schultz
Transcribed by Vicki Karcher

Mike Siegel

Mike Siegel has been President of Williams Realty in Wausau, Wisconsin for the past 20 years. He has a wife, Carmen, and one daughter, Katherine. Mr. Siegel also has three grandchildren.

During my college years I met a friend who was taking helicopter training through the navy, and he spoke highly of it. I became intrigued, so I enlisted to go to flight school. I entered the service in June of 1966. After basic training, I started flight school. I finished flight school in the early summer of 1967. Due to a car accident, I did not go to Vietnam until September of 1967. I served in a 3-quarter cab of the 23rd infantry division in Chu-Chi, Vietnam. My primary job was flying delta model hueys, which carried troops. Although a portion of my job was just hauling supplies back and forth places, the more interesting part of my job was working with long-range recon patrols, Special Forces, and inserting a squad team into an enemy-filled area. I also did the insertion and extraction of those troops. If

> *"I ACTUALLY WENT THROUGH 3 HELICOPTERS IN ONE DAY. THE FIRST ONE WAS SHOT UP PRETTY BADLY; THERE WERE A LOT OF BULLET HOLES."*

they were found, then we had to get them under somewhat hostile conditions. I also did a lot of medical evacuations, or medevacs and I am happy to report I hauled out well over 200 injured people and never lost a man on board. I received several medals while I was there. One was a Bronze Star, 25 awards of the air medal, and I won the Distinguished Flying Cross three times. I returned to the United States in September of 1968.

What was your average day like?

Typically the average day started… About every other day I was on dawn patrol…that was at dawn, obviously. We would do a low-level reconnaissance of Highway 1, which was the major artery in Vietnam and some of the other roads too, in an attempt of assertion. If the bad guys had done any damage to the road by either blowing holes in them, setting mines, or anything along those lines. That sometimes got interesting because the bad guys put claymore mines in the trees and aimed them at us when we went through. That took about an hour or so. We'd come back, have breakfast, then what we would do what we would call "hash and trash" which is more of the routine type of flying. I talked about earlier when we would haul more supplies out to the outpost, or we would haul people. That was the boring part of the job. Periodically, every two or three days I was on medevac alert, which means I laid around, and did nothing until I was needed, and then of course everything was in a big hurry. Generally, when you are on that program, you are on for 24 hours.

Did you mainly do reconnaissance work, or were you on stand by for medevac helicopters?

The type of helicopter I flew, we did a little bit of everything. The reconnaissance work could have been done in any type of helicopter. The type that I flew they call them an Iroquois, but everyone called them a … mine was a Huey UH1D, that is set up and designed to carry about 6 combat infantry men that are fully equipped for battle. On board is an aircraft commander, and a pilot, (pilot and co-pilot) and we had a crew chief and gunner in the back with hand and machine guns. We did not fly specifically marked medical evacuation with the big red cross on them because that became a target, and we didn't want to go un-armed either. Basically, I worked with small patrols that I put in and took out in the medical evacuation. The helicopters were designed for different things; one was a LOH, which stands for light observation helicopter, which was a two man aircraft, a pilot and a gunner, and they would typically go out and do the observation reconnaissance functions. There were two different kind of gun ships that we used. The slang word I used for the one I flew was called a "slick" which as opposed to the fun models which mean that it had helicopter (mini-guns) hatlet guns, if you will, and rocket pods that hung out from the side, because we didn't have that, so that is why we were called slick because we were slick-sided. I also flew a little bit of guns, and was the first group in Vietnam to fly corporate helicopters, which were a more advanced gunship.

> *"IT IS NOT LIKE YOU ARE FIGHTING EVERY DAY, BUT YOU NEVER KNEW WHEN IT WAS GOING TO START."*

You were in Vietnam from 1967-1968. Did you make any lasting friendships while you were there?

I got married about two weeks after I returned from Vietnam, and during the periods of time I was there, I determined that some of my closest friends were those people that I was serving with. And as a result, four of them stood up for my wedding. We all went our separate ways afterward, but about a year ago, because of the Internet, not all, but many of us have gotten back together, exchange e-mails, and went on a web site. We are planning a reunion in September of 2002 in Chattanooga.

Did you have any difficulties when you came back with people giving you a hard time?

Sure, almost everyone did. Many of the people that I was similar in age to were anti-war. Some of us became anti-war later, but there was lack of acceptance and certainly a lack of appreciation amongst the general population.

When you were doing evacuation were you ever under fire?

Yes, all the time. I had a co-pilot who received 3 Purple Hearts. I never got a scratch, and I was very fortunate. We flew in the big fancy of the Vietnam War, which was called the Tet Offensive that happened in very late January of 1968. I actually went through 3 helicopters in one day. The first one was shot up pretty badly; there were a lot of bullet holes… 38 or 50 holes in the helicopter. I did receive fire about a dozen times, lost tail rudders and engine hydraulics. You have to understand that the job we did was in many ways like the job everyone else had in that you had hours and hours, perhaps days and days of sheer boredom. This was punctuated by seconds and minutes, perhaps an hour, of sheer terror. It is not like you are fighting every day, but you never knew when it was going to start. The first day of the Tet Offensive, our helicopter was shot down; that happened to me more than once. Some days were worse than others. Essentially, I was very fortunate in every case. The first time I went down on the particular day I just mentioned, there was an airport in Saigon called Tan Son Nhut (1ˢᵗ day of Tet), and the North Vietnamese would come down, and prior to that time, we were fighting the Viet Cong who were the indigenous bad guys. As a result in this operation, right at the end of the runway this was happening, so when I tried to take off on Highway 1, I was shot up pretty badly. As a result I landed on Tonoinhute Airport. That happened to be the only plane in traffic that day because they shut the airport down because of the war going on. I was very fortunate.

Do you have any other interesting facts about looking for the enemy?

Yes, if we were looking for something suspicious we would venture out of the highway to see what we could see. I did very little of that. Most of the guys that did were the LOH's (light observation helicopters) that would fly very slowly and low on an attempt to not only see something but to draw fire. There was gunship flying on top-they called them a 100-killer combo-that would hopefully come in and take care of everything.

Was the war winnable?

No, we did not think the war was winnable while we were there. Obviously, everyone has his or her own opinion. A lot of the time we would be shot at from a village, and we were not able to return fire. We were fighting a war that didn't have anything to do with land. The war was very mobile… good use for helicopters.

> *"WE COULDN'T TRUST THE KIDS EVEN -- THOUGH THESE KIDS WERE CUTE AS A BUG'S EAR. ONE OF MY FRIENDS BOUGHT A COKE FROM ONE OF THEM, AND IT ENDED UP HAVING GROUND GLASS IN IT."*

Did you have a lot of contact with people in the villages?

Only occasionally, but for example, we'd have a couple of heavier artillery pieces taking hours to set up, and during that time there were kids coming around trying to sell you stuff. There was prostitution that went on. We couldn't trust the kids even -- though these kids were cute as a bug's ear. One of my friends bought a coke from one of them, and it ended up having ground glass in it. Therefore, you quickly decided what you wanted to do and not deal with indigenous civilians personally. You don't know whom to trust; we didn't know for sure who the bad guys were. It wasn't easy. The guys there were happy all the time while they were there; we were worried about them. There was a guy we nicknamed Crazy Bruce. Many were excellent while they were there, but not always gung-ho all the time.

What kind of influence did drugs have on the war?

Drugs were openly available. They were a problem. They were used recreationally and sort of as a help-me-through-the-day kind of thing. Many of the troops were using them.

Do you have anything else you would like to say?

Medevacs were extremely rewarding because of what you were doing. I took more pride in the LRRPS (Long Range Reconnaissance Patrols), the Special Forces, and the Green Beret men. When they got in trouble in many cases, I was the lead ship that would go get them. I had a backup in case I got shot down. There were two teams of helicopter gunships, two ships in each team, four total. We then would have two Air Force fighter jets above them. Then say on top we would have the C and C (commander and control) and he would tell me where I needed to go since I was going right in the tree tops. He would tell me where to land, and these guys would cover our butts. The trick was that the Vietnamese allowed us to take off, and then they would come out in the clearing and shoot us in our bellies because that is where we had fluids, hydraulics, and gas. So we learned, and they would throw a rocket right into the place we took off from. Those were the seconds that got pretty exciting. Military had an expression, "Hurry up and wait," because of the times you wouldn't do anything. Everything was ho-hum. Low and slow…not a good combination when dropping troops off. Low and fast…was ok.

Interviewed by Ryan Fasula
Transcribed by Jacayln Schultz

Gary Wetzel

Congressional Medal of Honor Recipient

Wetzel served in the 173rd Assault Helicopter Company as a door gunner. Seriously wounded during an insertion, Wetzel was cited for his gallantry in that action and awarded the Congressional Medal of Honor.

Where did you enlist?

I enlisted in the service here in Milwaukee, Wisconsin. I took basic training at Fort Knox, Kentucky. Then after you got done with basic training you go through what they call AIT, which stands for Advanced Individual Training. I had my orders to report to Fort Leonardwood, Missouri, in construction and heavy equipment. Prior to the service I worked a little bit of construction, so I had some knowledge; I went down there and right away I was an instructor in heavy equipment. I taught a lot of different classes. I had a lot of guys who were coming back from Vietnam, and they were telling me stories… "Sooner or later you're going to go over, so..." The army has what they call "10- 49s" to request your next duty station, so I put in a request to go to Vietnam. I figured, I'm in the service for three years- go and get it over with so I can come on back. They turned down my first two 10-49s because where I was at, it was critical to be an instructor. Then we had a lot of overflow of people coming back at that time, so in September I got my orders, and I believe 36 days later I was in country.

When you got off the plane, did it all kind of 'hit you'? How different it was to actually be IN country?

Yeah, it was different. I remember I spent, back in those days we flew in a turbo prop going over— which was 26 hours of airtime sitting on a plane, facing backwards with a bunch of other guys and a couple bags. It wasn't the world's most pleasant flight, but we were on our way—anticipating the excitement to go over. Not necessarily to get in a war-type situation, but, "I'm in the service. This is where I will serve, do my duty, and then come back." We landed in Saigon early in the morning (this is in October). I remember- of course the aircraft was air conditioned, but when we opened the back of the plane up we felt that hot, humid air.

How old were you at the time?

I just had turned 19 in September.

Lifting weights in Lai KHE

Did you have two tours or just the one?
I did two tours in Vietnam.

On your first tour, what types of things did you participate in?
My first orders, I was attached to an ordinance outfit, which was okay, but I've always loved flying. After you're in the service for a year and one day, re-enlisted, and then I went flying. I was on the 173rd helicopter company, the Robin Hoods. I was pretty good with the M-60 machine gun; I modified them and knew the weapons; when I got to the outfit I knew what I was doing. I didn't really know what I was going to get involved in, but I loved flying. I had aspirations back in those days, to eventually become a helicopter pilot. At the time, in the early sixties, they needed a lot of pilots, so a lot of gunners and crew chiefs were getting what they called "stick time," a chance to sit in the seat and fly a helicopter. I had all of my paperwork then that went all the way up to battalion. After I got shot down the third time, I extend-

Gunshack

ed my tour, came home. I was home for X amount of days, went back to Vietnam, and then had my paperwork- Company, Battalion, Brigade- however they do it. I had aspirations of becoming a pilot. Everything was approved up until that point, and about ten days before I was coming home from my second tour was when I got shot down for the fifth time. I was severely wounded, plus the loss of a left arm kind of curtailed that aspect of my life, being a pilot. In a helicopter you do need four limbs to fly the helicopter.

Could you continue with your memories of that last time you were shot down?
What we were doing that particular day was what we called "eagle flights." You get two sets of five helicopters with an average of seven to eight GIs inside. (These are what you called slicks (showing photo). I sat here- pilots here.) So what eagle flights were... you just flew around like an eagle, and if you'd see something that's suspicious, you fly on in, drop your troops off, check out the area. If there's nothing happening, you come back and pick them up and then go find another area. On this particular day they were aware of some unfriendlies in a certain area. We were brief on the LZ (landing zone). We had to prep it with 105s, with jets and then- normally, when you come in on what they call a 'hot LZ' you had two sets of gun ships. The first set of guns comes in and what you do is try to blow up the LZ and keep the bad guys out- at least their head down. The second set of guns are about one hundred yards in front of you, so when you're coming in with your troops you try to eliminate the least amount of casualties as possible. On this particular day, of course, we were briefed before the operation. I knew where we were going, and I looked, and the air strike was on the other side of the river—so right away you figure that there's been a mistake. I had been on numerous, numerous operations. I knew there had been a mistake. When I looked back, the gun ships were about a quarter of a mile behind us- they're supposed to be in front of us, at about treetop level. That's when all hell broke loose. We went in with 14 helicopters, 10 Americans and four

Infantry leaving helicopter on operation.

Australians. Mine was only the one that got shot down on the LZ. We got hit in the left front of the helicopter with an RPG- what they call Rocket
Propelled Grenade. It blew the front of the
ship apart, and it came skidding to a halt.
We had two guys that didn't even leave the
cabin. The cross-fire was so bad that they
were killed right there. It was like July 4th,
but it was on the ground. My immediate
concern is to try and get my buddy out. I
ripped the door off, and my crew chief came
from the other side. He was on the inside of
the radio pedestal, we were trying to lift
Timmy up to push him out on the other side.
From the waist up he was okay, but from the
waist down he was nothing but chopped
meat. I tried to pick him up and get him at
least half way through the radio pedestal,
and that was when a homemade grenade went

Ap Dong An Republic of Vietnam Jan 8, 1968

off behind me. When I say homemade grenade- anything you can put in an explosive device: nails, glass,
and whatever—that's what I got hit with. It landed about four feet behind me and caught me pretty good
from my shoulders on down. It blew my whole upper arm out, but from the elbow down there wasn't a
scratch. It was just hanging on by some skin and bone, and later on I took what was left [of my arm] and
tucked it inside my pants and just kept on fighting. When you get in situations, you'd be surprised what
the human body can take or will stand. Of course we have choices, but I figured at that time I was going
to die, and I figured I'd take a few more of the bad guys with me. Knock on wood though— I'm still here!

***What was going through your head when you first took the shot to your arm? Did you think you were
finished right there?***

Well, you had the initial pain and you
yell. There were a lot of things happening, and I still had some spunk left in
me, so I tried to do the best I could.
Later on, we had one medic who was
shot in the back—he couldn't move, so
what I tried to do was grab the wounded and slide them across the rice paddy.
It was a lot of mud and slop. They used
a lot of human waste. It didn't smell
nice. I was trying to drag the wounded
to him so that he could try and patch the
guys up. I passed out various times from
loss of blood.

Fueling Helicopter

***How much time had lapsed now since
you were shot down?***

I don't know. We fought for 10 or 12 hours before we got any help. Later on, I found out through other
sources, that we had been surrounded by an estimated 800 to 1,000 V.C., and we only went in with about
14 ships and probably in the first couple minutes I think 52 to 56 of these guys got killed, so there were

just a handful of us that were capable of doing anything. There was such disarray. We were just trying to do the best that we could. I figured, "This is it!" What they eventually did was drop some troops about half a click away, and they eventually worked their way towards us on the one side, and that's how we later got the wounded out.

That was obviously your last mission. How long was it between being on the field and back in the states?

I spent seven or nine days on what they called the Super Critical list. When I first got pieced back together, they used stainless steel stitches to cut down on infection. I want to say nine days in country at an evac hospital until they stabilized me somewhat better so that they could transport me to a better facility. From there I went to Tokyo and they made a revision. They cut another inch and a half off my arm because of all the infection. I was there for I think about a week or ten days. From there I went to Travis and then from Travis to Ft. Simmons, outside Denver, Colorado. I believe I spent about five months in the hospital. I had various skin grafts, and I had to learn how to walk again and get adjusted to using this thing [prosthetic arm] and civilian life.

What other injuries had you sustained that you had difficulties walking?

When the frag landed behind me, I had some spinal damage. I got hit with a machine gun, with 38s, and later on I got stabbed in the right thigh with a bayonet.

I imagine that your rehabilitation was really difficult. You were in for the long haul.

I accepted the loss of my arm because I knew it wasn't going to grow back. What I could do is make a better tomorrow, try to get on with life, get adjusted and do things. It probably took about three years to get used to the prosthesis where I did things naturally rather than thinking you had to do things with two hands. A lot of times I'd grab for things with two hands, but "Ok, Gare—let's figure how we're gonna do it different!" so environmentally- about three years of work. Now I tie my own shoes, tie my own tie~ I don't wear snap- ons. I can flip bacon, and I don't burn my fingers. I ride my Harley and my bike isn't any different than anybody else's. I just taught myself how to do it.

Collage done by Karl M. Rupert, 1989

Are there any other setbacks or things that are difficult for you?

I'm not afraid to ask people for help. If you get frustrated and stuff, it's like, "Gary, you can't do it!" There are things you cannot do, so why get an attitude? I just ask someone for help or do it a different way.

When you came back to the states, you didn't know you were going to be a medal recipient at first. How did you find out?

I finally got a job at Laddish Co. I was working in the office. I had a Colonel, Major, and a First Sergeant that came to the office where I was working at, and they asked me to come down to the office. "Hi, how ya doing"—they didn't look like military— which, at that young age you don't know much about military law but I had done my time, I gave you my arm. "what the hell else do you want?!" They were like, "You're going on

Standing by helicopter.

trip." And I was like, "No, I'm not." It took them about two weeks to convince me that I was going down to get the Medal of Honor because I had gotten the Distinguished Service Cross in country which is the second highest medal. Who figures you're going to get the Medal of Honor. To go back a little bit about the Medal of Honor—when I was in Tokyo and they took out over 400 stitches, tubes that I had had everywhere were all taken out- some of the guys that I had pulled out were recovering from their wounds and found out that I was there… They would walk up to the bunk and here I am, a skinny little piece of meat, and they'd say, "Are you Gary Wetzel?" and I'd say, "Yeah," and then they would pull out their wallet and show me pictures of their wife, kids, or girlfriends. "Hey man, because of you- THIS is what I got to go back to!" and THAT's what the Medal means. Those were the guys that put me in for it. I don't know if I should thank them or whatever, but there is a lot of responsibility that goes on with that blue ribbon and people think you're Superman, but you're not. You're just a guy doing his job.

Did you have the chance to keep in touch with the guys and their families when you got back then?
When you first get out of the service you get a lot of the Christmas cards and stuff, and then, throughout the years it tapers off. They have their lives and I have my own. I'm sure when our paths cross, we'll know it.

When you returned to the states, there were a lot of anti-war demonstrations going on. Being a Medal of Honor recipient, how did you feel?
Yeah, we would have demonstrations going on down here in Milwaukee, and I'd come down incognito. And I believe in freedom of speech, say what you've got to say- fine. But don't burn my flag. I've seen too many guys die for it; too many guys get hurt for it. I remember guys who were just a year younger than me that were waving this Vietcong flag and I'm like, "Don't do it or I'm gonna have to take you down!" – which I did a couple of times! I didn't care if I was outnumbered 200 to one. You're not going to fly that flag, and you're not going to burn the American flag. I guess we and this civilized society take certain things for granted. You're outside and it's hotter than heck, and then you come in here and we've got air conditioning, lights, hot and cold running water- we tend to forget that we should look back in the past once in awhile and just kind of reflect on the sacrifices men and women had given for the right for you and I to be here today. We have SUCH a freedom; we need to reflect on what it's all about.

The Congressional Medal of Honor

And that's exactly what we're trying to do. Us being able to do this project here means SO much more than reading in a textbook.

It's like when I go around talking to young high school people. In the book it's maybe a page to a page and a half — Kennedy and Johnson got us involved, Nixon got us out, there's some stats, and that's it! It doesn't say what happened. Normally, when I speak to young people I have two to four other vets and my story is different than his and his different than his. I try to bring along C-rations and give all a little P-38. Of course, nowadays you got to give each kid a plastic spoon with all the crap floating around. But the rations got all the good stuff — ham and lima beans all the good stuff! I go, " Here, taste some," because it sounds good, but then they spit it out and I go- "Well, that's the stuff we had to eat. You know — its protein!" Think of the sacrifices. People shouldn't look at war as a John Wayne type of thing or a male testosterone thing because war is horrifying. It's not manly, and it's sad when we get in situations where we have to use human beings and there's a life lost or people getting wounded. You ask- why? I can look back and say, 'I lost an arm for my country.' But why did I lose it? What did we get accomplished?

I have read that some soldiers made statements that they did not feel like they were fighting for their country, they were fighting for each other. Did you feel the same way?

At first, being a young guy, I was so proud for being a young service man that here I am taking part for my country and helping another nation get a little kick in the butt to get started. Boy I was prouder than a peacock! Eventually, when I got to the Robin Hoods, my big thing was I had a 45 Western Style, kind of like ad-lib like Jesses James, and I was big bad-ass, which ya think you are, but you're not! Here I am, a 19-year-old punk kid and a PapaSan would come down from the village. We would sit down, and he'd get this razor and lather you up and it's like any other cowboy, "Wow, shavin' with a straight edge — that's big time!" Of course, you got peach fuzz and… Then we got hit one night. We had about 20 choppers on a flight line, and there are sandbags between each chopper. It had to be two or three in the morning and the V.C. started coming across the air strip so we couldn't get the ships up. We pulled out the 60s and just leveled what was coming. We eliminated a lot of the elements. When the sun

Presentation of the medal.

comes up and everyone and all the dust starts settling down you go out and look for a body count. This guy that used to shave me [a PapaSan] was laying about 40 meters to my right with a satchel charge! So he was coming there that night to kill me! So here you think you're doing things for a country, and you trust these people and this guy's is trying to blow me away. Then it was like, "brother for brother": you know, we'll do our job, but I'll watch your butt and you watch my butt. If you look at Korea or World War Two, the vets came home- All right! Handshake! When the Vietnam guys came home we were brothers! Black, brown, purple, pink, whatever, we're brothers! No one can take that away from us.

Going back a little bit, what was it like the day you were in the White House, receiving your medal from the President? What were some of your emotions?

We were all young and growing up. We look in this constitution and look at the President as a God-like type figure. I mean, "THERE is the President!" It was kind of neat in this society because when our fore-fathers sat down and put together this thing called the Constitution, and that's that, the majority of us — under this umbrella that we support that Constitution and what it stands for. You've got a leader that's guiding you or showing you the way. You've got your House and Senate and a bunch of other people, but meeting the President.... It's hard to describe. It's a great honor. It's a great respect. Fear. I mean, here he is. Before the ceremonies we were just in this room in the White House with some of the President's staff informing how they answer things. "Yes, Mr. President. No, Mr. President" – there's proto-col. Then he came in the room, and we were all shaking. He sat right down next to myself and put his hand on my leg and said, "How ya doin', Son?" and I'm all, "Fine, Mr. President." It was a trip! I liked him for who he was. The next day we went to Arlington, and I met the Kennedys. I think it was the five-year anniversary of the assassination of President Kennedy, and I met Jackie, Teddy and Bobby all down there. There were a bunch of Secret Service guys, and I got the Medal of Honor.

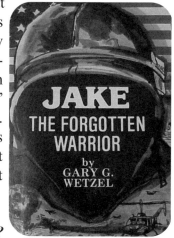

Emotionally and mentally, what got you through all of your rehabilitation? Any person or thing in particular that kept you going?

It was mostly me trying to make the better of who I was or being who I was. But looking back to some-thing that was inspirational.... When I was in Tokyo, recovering from my operation, there were a bunch of football players that were on the U.S.O. Tour. Of course I'm a Packer Backer from way back.... I think I was the only one in that ward from Wisconsin, and they say, "Is anyone in here from Wisconsin?!" and I said, "Yeah, what's the big deal?" "Well we've got some football players and Bart Starr." (That was the last year that they played in the Superbowl) I think I had a nine-foot arm on at the time! So they came over and covered me up with a nice clean sheet so I wasn't bloody and didn't look like crap and what-ever. Then Bart came over and we chatted for a while. I had been really down, and he really picked me up! Now when he came back from his tour, there was an article I've got some place that was in an American Legion Magazine that they had asked him [Bart Starr] what was his memorable thoughts about his tour, and he says, "I met a little 'ole red-headed guy that lost his left arm from Wisconsin." So, he made an impact on me, and I must have made an impact on him! It was kind of neat!

A proud recipient and his Harley

Do you have any last thoughts or advice for young people today- maybe headed towards the service?

Well, we look at the service nowadays compared to the service in my time, and they're all special because you're putting time in for what the flag stands for. But we'll say nowadays, in the computer era there are so many programs in the military that will transition with you into civilian life, plus you're getting paid good! There are innumerable educational benefits and you're in that 18-20 year stage where you're full of all types of stuff and go out and party, get drunk and stupid, whatever. But what's wrong with going out and serving your country for a couple of years because you'd have a good education. Give something back instead of "take,

Other medals he's received.

take, take!" In this time, in society, we take everything but give something back! So you can say, "Yea, I cared." With the service's whole touring process you get to travel a little bit, you grow up, you get educated. There are different types of the service, however. If you want the bang bang, shoot 'em up or be in infantry, you can, but it's not meant for everybody. In this day and age, now that we have the all-volunteer service, the people that are going in are good, quality people, and they're going in because they want to go in. They want to serve their country and be part of it. Years down the road they can look back and tell their grandkids, "Yeah, I took part. I was a little pea in the pod, but I did take part!"

Wetzel has gone on to meet five different Presidents, multiple celebrities, and other distinguished persons. Wetzel feels it is his duty as a Medal of Honor recipient to inform students on the war history of Vietnam. He is actively working for the return of our country's POWs and MIAs.

Interviewed and transcribed by Meghan Casta

MEG HAN.
Best of Everything
Gary G. Wetgl

The President of the United States of America, authorized by Act of Congress, March 3, 1863, has awarded in the name of The Congress the Medal of Honor to:

SPECIALIST FOUR GARY GEORGE WETZEL
UNITED STATES ARMY

Citation: For conspicuous gallantry and intrepidity in action at the risk of his life above and beyond the call of duty. Specialist Four Gary Wetzel, 173d Assault Helicopter Company, distinguished himself by conspicuous gallantry and intrepidity at the risk of his life, above and beyond the call of duty. Specialist Wetzel was serving as door gunner aboard a helicopter which was part of an insertion force trapped in a landing zone by intense and deadly hostile fire. Specialist Wetzel was going to the aid of his aircraft commander when he was blown into a rice paddy and critically wounded by two enemy rockets that exploded just inches from his location. Although bleeding profusely due to the loss of his left arm and severe wounds in his right arm, chest, and left leg, Specialist Wetzel staggered back to his original position in his gun-well and took the enemy forces under fire. His machinegun was the only weapon placing effective fire upon the enemy at that time. Through a resolve that overcame the shock and intolerable pain of his injuries, Specialist Wetzel remained at his position until he had eliminated the automatic weapons emplacement that had been inflicting heavy casualties on the American troops and preventing them from moving against this strong enemy force. Refusing to attend his own extensive wounds, he attempted to return to the aid of his aircraft commander but passed out from loss of blood. Regaining consciousness, he persisted in his efforts to drag himself to the aid of his fellow crewman. After an agonizing effort, he came to the side of his crew chief who was attempting to drag the wounded aircraft commander to the safety of a nearby dike. Unswerving in his devotion to his fellow man, Specialist Wetzel assisted his crew chief even though he lost consciousness once again during this action. Specialist Wetzel displayed extraordinary heroism in his efforts to aid his fellow crewmen. His gallant actions were in keeping with the highest traditions of the U.S. Army and reflect great credit upon himself and the Armed Forces of his country.

November 19, 1968
THE WHITE HOUSE

Leonard Zilch

Entering the Army, Zilch trained to be a helicopter mechanic. He served in Vietnam in 1966-67.

How did you become involved in the Vietnam War?
Basically what happened was I was going to a technical college, and I decided I didn't like the program that I was in. And at that time there was pressure to either enlist or to get drafted, and I decided I had a better option if I enlisted instead of waiting until I got drafted.

What area did you go in?
I went into the army because I had better options going into the army than I did going into other fields.

Why did you become a helicopter mechanic?
Well I initially went into the service to become a helicopter pilot, but I had a certain problem with one of the tests that deals with hand eye coordination. Therefore, I wasn't allowed to go into the pilot end of it, but then I was elected to be a mechanic, a helicopter mechanic.

With all the deaths of pilots were you later glad that you only became a helicopter mechanic?
At that particular age I was interested in flying and I was interested in excitement, and I can tell you that being a helicopter pilot you received both.

What kind of helicopters did you fix?
I fixed the UH1, UHB model huey; basically it was the huey helicopters.

Can you describe what an average day was like during the war?
For me it was to get up early. Then after we had chow, we would come back and straighten our area in the barracks, and then we would march off to our work and be given assignments in various choppers that we were working on, to replace particular parts that got shot up or take off parts that got out of time. In other words, they only fly certain parts in the aircraft for so long. Then they would have to replace those parts to get them flyable again.

What was your perspective of the war?

My perspective of the war was relatively narrow. I really didn't see particular action. It was just my little world, one of fixing helicopters and living the life in the barracks and going downtown occasionally. Also pulling some guard duty at times, but I was not in a combat zone.

Were you in Vietnam in 1968?

I was in Vietnam in 1966 and '67.

Were drugs a problem for the soldiers in Vietnam?

I didn't see them around. They may have been available, but I wasn't a druggie, so it never crossed my mind. Alcohol was a problem. Other than that I'm not aware.

How was alcohol a problem?

Well, basically you're bored out of your mind when you get off of work. You basically have nothing to do You can go downtown, but it's dangerous downtown because you never knew who your enemy was, and the fact is, you didn't really have anything to do. So the only thing you do is go down to the club, and the only thing there was to drink.

How was the relationship between whites and blacks in your unit?

At my particular time it was a little strained, but no real particular problem. Although we did have a black individual that hit and threatened a sergeant before we came to Vietnam. What happens then? In this case he got transferred out because they were not going to send that individual to Vietnam because there could be a problem with fragging.

Did you have any opinions regarding the antiwar movement back in the states while in Vietnam?

Yes, I had some opinions and my feeling was this: That we were trying to fight a war we could not win because they would not let us win it. The fact is we were sticking tremendous amount of money into the place, and yet it just seemed to me that we were getting nowhere at all.

What was the hardest part of being in the war?

Boredom. Another thing for example is the business of not knowing who your enemy was. I had to guard a PX facility where they stored PX items downtown. You never knew if the kids around you or the people who were around you would attack. You just didn't know who your enemy was, and that's very difficult.

Was there a lot of emotional or physical stress you had to endure?

There is always emotional stress in whatever you were doing. It was different over there because you're isolated and confined, and your world is relatively small, and there was always the thing of desiring to go home, to get away.

Is there one particular experience that stands out in your mind?
There are many, but one particular one was when I was on a ship. When I got into Qui Nhon they put lights over the ship at night so that that would deter anybody putting satchel charges up against the ship and try and sink it. It was the feeling that when I went into Qui Nhon that was a beautiful peninsula. The palm trees and white sand and it was really gorgeous except that it had an overwhelming smell of urine.

Do you think the U.S could have won the war? Why or why not?
I think the U.S could have won the war, and the war could have been won not so much with guns but with policy.

Did you make any lasting friendships during the war?
You make all kinds of friendships, but it's like when the wind blows and the dandelion seeds fly off the head of the dandelion and go hither and yon. They're just gone. I didn't have any lasting friendships.

What kind of reception did you get when you came back to the United States?
I received a pretty good reception. I never felt in the small town that I lived in that I was oppressed. We did not have a lot of anti-Vietnam business where I lived.

What did serving your country mean to you during active duty and now as a veteran?
I'm glad that I did it because I learned many things that I could have not learned otherwise, but at the time it was not particularly an enjoyable experience.

Did you have difficulties dealing with the memories when you were back?
Not me because I was not involved in anything that would cause that problem, but I can tell you what the problem was. It's like this guy went into the village, and they suspected some VC were hiding in a clump. So we threw a grenade in there, and basically what he did was killed two children. That type of thing plays on a guy, and not knowing who your enemy is. You never know where it's coming from. It is a real strain.

Did you ever kill someone personally?
I never did.

Could you describe the worst damage that you have ever seen inflicted on a helicopter?
Yes, I can quite easily since I was a helicopter mechanic. We had a condition that's called a red X. A red X would mean if it had that particular damage it would down the helicopter, and in other words, nobody could fly that helicopter till it was fixed. We had an individual fly a helicopter in and land it on an air strip that had five red X's on it. In other words, that helicopter should not have been flown in. To give you an idea, up on the rotor blades that go around there is a device called a push-pull tube, and it changes the pitch on the blades to give it lift or neutralize it. It had a bullet hole through that tube, and basically

it was only being held on by about a half an inch of metal. If that individual knew that, if that would have broke, that ship would have come down.

Did you ever hear any reports of battle from anyone?
I have had battle around me, but I have not seen it. In other words, I was out one time. We had a detail that came up every now and then where you had to take the garbage out, and you would guard some Vietnamese people who did the actual work, and as we were washing the deuce and half, on the way, just before coming home, there was a firefight some place around me where I heard guns going off, but I did not see any myself.

Have you ever seen casualties in war?
I've seen casualties in war, and I have seen both the living and the dead. One particular individual that I knew ran into a tunnel. He ran into a bayonet into his stomach, and he showed me his wound, and he lived from it. Lucky the guy didn't pull the trigger, which is usually standard policy.

Is there a message for young people today that you have about the war?
War is just plain no good. It is no good for anybody. If it can be avoided, it would sure be nice, but some times it just can't be avoided. I would say if you're going to be in a war situation and you do not want to be in conflict, actually doing the fighting, get yourself a particular skill like a helicopter mechanic or some other job that will keep you away from the front lines.

Do you have anything that you want people to get out of your interview?
I can't see a conflict that cannot be resolved with understanding of each other's cultures and with love. Apply those particular principles when hate and greed and prejudice sneaks in that causes problems that are just unfixable some times.

Following the war, Leonard Zilch was a mechanic and truck driver.

Interviewed and transcribed by Denise Zilch and Mary Vang

ARMOR

D.C. EVEREST AREA SCHOOLS

Armor in Vietnam

When American units were destined for Vietnam, armor was downplayed because of the terrain. Jungle and delta areas can be difficult for the movement of heavy armored vehicles. In many cases, that proved true, however, it also became evident that armor could and did provide useful support to many infantry units that encountered the enemy.

There were a small number of independent armored units incountry. One notable unit was the 11th Armored Cavalry Regiment, which was the largest independent armored unit in Vietnam. Convoy duty and patrols became a part of their daily routine. Armored personnel carriers provided useful security to convoys. Ambushes were not uncommon, and the availability of armor provided relief.

In the I corps area, Marine armor was available and used with effectiveness. Road patrols and convoy duty were part of their routine as well.

The VC and the NVA did introduce and use small numbers of tanks during the conflict and after the United States withdrew. In 1973, larger numbers of tanks were deployed and used against the South Vietnamese forces.

Scott Andrews

Andrews trained in tanks and served in the Chu Lai area through most of 1970 and early 1971. He served on APCs in an armored squadron performing recon and ended his tour in charge of radio traffic in the command post .

Could you explain the different things you did in Vietnam?

Before going to Vietnam, I worked at Best Bakery in Schofield, so when I got to Vietnam, I worked in a mess hall baking for about a month. When they realized that I was supposed to be a tanker, they sent me out to the field for about five months. After that, I started to work with a friend of mine who had a command post (CP) track, which was set up halfway between our living quarters and the field. We would take all the information the troops sent back and put it on a map. We kept track of where they were anytime they'd engage the enemy. We would write the coordinates down, and that went to our squadron headquarters, where they kept it as intelligence. We were in a reconnaissance platoon, so we drove around in personnel carriers and tanks and looked for the enemy. When we got close to them, they would shoot at us, and then we would engage the enemy. I was in charge of the CP track. I had three people that worked for me, and we ran the radios on a 24-hour basis taking any information that came in. We made sure the troops got the re-supplies that were requested each day, and they usually got one hot meal a day. The supplies and meals were flown in by helicopter, and we would coordinate that. We'd also coordinate any type of big movements with our squadron headquarters. There were three troops in our squadron - Alpha, Bravo, and Charlie troops, (A, B, C) with about 150 people in a troop.

How did you become involved in the Vietnam War?

I was drafted in May of 1969, and I went to Milwaukee in August for my pre-induction physical. From there, I was sent to Ft. Campbell, Kentucky for basic training and testing to determine my military occupational specialty (MOS). I ended up as a tank crewman, so I was sent to Ft. Knox, Kentucky, to train with their armored unit. I came home on Christmas, and in January, I flew to Vietnam. I was stationed in Chu Lai, 40 miles south of Da Nang, on the South China Sea. It was pretty, with really nice beaches. In January 1971, we moved much farther north and stayed there until I came home in March.

Could you describe what base camps were like?

Our rear area was Chu Lai, which was like a small city. It had a PX where you could buy things like electronics, clothing, and candy. We had movies at night, and we had our squadron headquarters and payroll there. We had motor pools, which were big garages. We had about 10 Sheridan tanks, 25 armored personnel carriers, and our support group, which was a tank retriever, spare personnel carriers, other track vehicles, and the CP, which was an oversized personnel carrier. They had other troops there also, and a big motor pool where they fixed damaged tracks. They had a USO on the beach. You could swim on the beach, and they had shows there. Some Korean businessmen made suits, coats, and jackets that you could buy and send home. The landing zones were different though. They were small base camps. The one that we worked out of quite frequently was called LZ Hawk Hill, about 25 miles north of where we were and

about two miles off of Highway 1 (probably the only blacktop road that ran the whole length of South Vietnam). The LZ was a big mound of dirt with rows of concertina or razor wire around it, and in between that there were trip flares. The smaller landing zones were just concertina wire and bunkers. You'd dig a hole, put a metal culvert over it, and pack sand bags on it. Hawk Hill had pre-made guard houses. They were on stilts with sand bags on top and around the inside. They had machine-gun posts around the perimeter that were manned night and day. They were really dirty. It was all sand and dust in the summer. In the monsoons, when it rained, it was mud sometimes 6" deep. We were in the low land along the ocean where

L-Z Hawk Hill

there were all rice paddies. The LZs had their own little infrastructure. Ours had large bunkers for the squadron headquarters. It was a tactical operations center (TOC). The walls were covered with maps to plot out where they saw enemy and where each troop was stationed. They had mess halls there. When I worked in the CP track, I lived with 10 people in a big wall tent about 20 by 12. Hawk Hill had an artillery outpost. They had 155 artillery pieces set up right over the top of us, so it was very noisy. We would take cigarette filters apart and stuck them in our ears for earplugs. One of the artillery places made a crude pizza and we had soda, coke, and beer. Once a month we got sundry packs with shoestrings, pens, tobacco, cigarettes, writing paper, and candy bars. We'd get one box

"WE DIDN'T REALLY SEE THE ENEMY BECAUSE THEY WERE SOMEWHERE IN THE WOOD LINE. SOMETIMES WE WOULD GET TOO CLOSE; AND THEY WOULD SHOOT AN RPG, WHICH WAS A ROCKET, AT OUR TRACKS."

to split up per group. Most LZs had a small village right outside of it, and kids would sell you Popsicles. You seldom saw a car. People traveled by foot, bicycles, motorcycles, Lambrettis, or busses. They could pack 3 or 4 people on a motorcycle. On the busses they would put everything inside they wanted to protect, like pigs, chickens, anything that was of value, and the people hung on the outside going 35 or 40 miles/hr. How people never fell off and got run over is beyond me.

Did you fight against the Vietcong or NVA regular units; and could you describe them?
Most of the time we didn't see more than 4 or 5 people traveling in a small group. The Viet Cong wore the woven straw hats and black pajamas, but doing reconnaissance, we didn't really see the enemy because they were somewhere in the wood line. Sometimes we would get too close, and they would shoot an RPG, which was a rocket, at our tracks. Then we would search the wood line and shoot into it. If they

shot back, we would try to find them, get them out of their holes, and try to take prisoners to get intelligence information. We had so much firepower shooting into the wood line that once they stopped shooting, they either retreated, or they were dead. If we actually killed anyone, we would take a body count. I never witnessed anyone being killed, but I saw dead Vietnamese.

Can you describe what an average day was like for you during the war?

In the field, we would sleep in the tracks or dig a shallow hole and lay on a poncho with a blanket on top. We would get up by 5:00 AM and have cans of C-rations and coffee for breakfast. We also had soda and water. Every track was self-contained. The whole floor of the track was ammunition, and on the walls we hung hand grenades and flares. We'd go out for about 3 weeks and then come in for a week. In the morning we would meet and go over the day's activities, and then each platoon would go in a different direction. There were 4 people on a track, and in the morning we would ride through the jungle. We would take routes that weren't traveled very much because the Viet Cong would plant mines near the heavi-

"WE CALLED A COUPLE GUYS JOHN WAYNE BECAUSE THEY WERE REALLY BRAVE, BUT I THINK THEY WERE REALLY NUTS."

ly traveled routes. Usually the mines didn't injure people severely but would damage equipment. However, Charlie troop had a personnel carrier that ran over a one thousand pound bomb, and 10 people were killed. In the afternoon you could sit for an hour or so, go for a swim, or wash clothes, but someone always had to keep watch. From 2:00 PM until 6:00PM we would search more areas. At night we lagered. We would form a big circle with our 9 tanks and 21 personnel carriers. We would find an open area, not real close to the jungle, so no one could sneak up on us. We would put Rocket Propelled Grenade (RPG) screens (cyclone fences) across the front of our tracks, so they couldn't disable our tanks with any RPG's. An RPG was made to hit the outside of a tank, burn through the metal and explode on the inside. By putting up the screens, it would burn through the screen and explode on the outside of the tank. A helicopter would bring us great things to eat like instant potatoes, chicken, and ice cream if we were lucky. We had iced tea and powdered milk. We would draw straws to see which platoon would eat first and which one got the cold food at the end. In the evening, we would take inventory of our supplies.

Bravo Troop Command post track

If we needed any rounds or hand grenades, we'd call that in and get resupplied the next morning. In the logger at night we would have a meeting of the lieutenants and the sergeants to plan different strategies for the next day and whether or not we would be involved with the South Vietnamese Army. We would call back to the rear and inform them of our plans. We had a secure unit, which we could set different codes on and push it into a radio. It made the radio like a telephone, but it scrambled everything that went out, so the enemy couldn't understand what you were talking about. You didn't salute lieutenants in the field because that was a good

way for them to get shot. Nobody wore any brass on their collars or anything on their helmets to show rank. Everything was Olive Drab color (OD). If you weren't part of planning for the next day, you were on guard duty.

We had two-hour shifts from 11:00 PM until 5:00 AM. That was a typical day unless you were shot at. If anyone was hurt, an area had to be set up for a helicopter. Most of the people that I saw hurt were those that hurt themselves with hand grenades they threw too close to themselves. We called a couple guys John Wayne because they were really brave, but I think they were really nuts. They would run down these areas and say, "Come on, let's get them!" No thanks, let's do it the way we're supposed to. While I was there, we lost maybe four people. They weren't from our platoon.

As my tour came to a close, I was in the CP track. We moved up to the demilitarized zone. The operation was called Operation Dewey Canyon. We road marched with all of our tracks down to a port, and we put all of our equipment on a LST (Landing Ship Transport). The front end opened, and we put all of our tanks, personnel carriers, and equipment inside, chained it down, and went out for three days in the South China Sea. We ended up going to Quang Tri, which was just south of the demilitarized zone at the North Vietnam border. Then we road marched into the Khe Sanh Valley,

Bravo Troop- 1st squardon, 1st clavary

which was where the Tet Offensive took place in 1968. In February of '71, we were set up for over a month and nothing happened. It was really spooky because we knew people were there, but nothing happened. Our people were getting really complacent. They'd go down to the river to go swim, and they'd take a radio and a towel, rather than a helmet, flak jacket, and a rifle. It was spooky because you could watch bombing going on at night. Off in the mountains you could hear the B-52s and helicopters with mini-guns working over the mountains. We were a mile away, but nothing ever came close to us. I watched on television after I got home on St. Patrick's Day 1971. Our whole troop got spilt up. They usually worked in a group a little ways away from each other. The NVA split squads apart from the platoon. They got in between them so they couldn't get back together. When I found out it was the troop that I was in, I turned off the TV because I didn't want to know about it. I don't know how many of the guys that were there when I left are still around because I never really checked into it.

Were drugs a problem for the soldiers in Vietnam?
Yes, a lot. You could buy heroin and marijuana in the streets of Vietnam. They used to sell bottles of diet drugs. There were guys that took tablets that were called downers. They were just like sleeping tablets. A certain number of people did drugs, but it wasn't the majority. However, wherever you went, drugs were there.

How was the relationship between whites and blacks in your unit?
Our unit was pretty good. I think it was more of a problem when I was stateside than overseas. However, the black guys still hung around together. It was pretty much integrated. In a platoon, you'd have about 10 black guys with 25 white guys. You had to rely on each other, so the guys became friends. I had a couple of friends that I haven't written to since I got out of the service, but I was close to one guy that was Puerto Rican. You met all different nationalities, which was a good thing. Myself, being from Wisconsin, I was not exposed to different minorities. You never saw any other culture than Polish or German. Guys partied together at night. We had a club you could go to. We never really saw any fights. Most of the people got along well, and if they didn't, they just stayed away from each other. They didn't really try to provoke anything.

Do you have opinions regarding the antiwar movement back at home while in Vietnam?
When I came home in 1971, most of the protests were done. I guess that people have the right to protest because we live in a free society and have freedom of speech. I felt I had an obligation to serve my country. My dad was in the service. That's one of the reasons I went in. I knew people who went to Canada and stayed there. My cousin's husband went to Canada, and he's lived there ever since. I guess that's his choice. There are choices you make in life, and you have to live with them. I wasn't against protestors. I didn't have any experiences coming back where I was picked on because I was in the service.

"...THIS GUY AHEAD OF US WENT OVER A RICE PATTY DIKE AND CAME DOWN ON THE BACKSIDE. A MINE WENT OFF AND BLEW ALL OF THE ROAD WHEELS OFF."

What was the hardest part for you being in the war?
The hardest part was being away from my family. I had mixed emotions on why I was there. I really didn't want to kill people, but I was there fighting for my country. After a while I wondered if it was really for my country or not. What was happening over there wasn't affecting the United States directly. Indirectly, it may have affected the United States in years to come, but as we can see now it really hasn't. At first you did everything they told you, but the longer you stayed there, the more you questioned why you were there. I was born and raised Catholic, so it was a question of religion too. You know you're not supposed to kill, but yet you were there for the United States. Fortunately for me, I came back in one piece. The closest time I came to getting injured was when a guy ran over a mine with a track that was right next to ours. That's about it.

Was there a lot of emotional or physical stress that you had to endure?
Not for me, but there were a lot of other people that did. I think that's why the drugs were so prevalent for some people. Most of the stress that I saw was in the people that were in the field on a daily basis. I was fortunate because I was in the field for only four or five months. I wasn't really involved in a real stressful situation when I was in the rear. It really took its toll on the people who were in a number of firefights. They were heavily into drugs because I think they were afraid and didn't know what to do about it.

Searching wood line in personnel carrier

Is there one particular experience that stands out in your mind?
The experience that I remember the most was going to the field the very first day with three personnel carriers. We were just outside of Chu Lai in a little town called Tam Ke where there was a helicopter landing strip of perforated metal. We went out to the field to meet up with the rest of our group, and we weren't more than 50 yards out when this guy ahead of us went over a rice paddy dike and came down on the backside. A mine went off and blew all of the road

wheels off. The driver got a concussion out of it. They had to come and fly him out. That was my very first experience five minutes into it, and I thought, "Oh my God." I was sick for about two weeks after that. I had an upset stomach, and I couldn't eat. I just didn't know what was going to happen. Then the next day, it was the same type of a situation. We got out into the field and everybody was just sitting down to eat. They had just flown the helicopter in, put all the hot food out. The Vietnamese shot two RPG's into our lager, hit one screen and hit another tank a little ways away from us. We took off back into the jungle chasing them. Like I said, I was sick for two weeks. I figured, "Boy, if this is what it's going to be like for the rest of the time I'm out here, I'm not going to make it." Eventually, you get somewhat used to it, and things calm down a little. You go for longer stretches without action, but after those two days I thought a whole year of this is going to drive me nuts. Fortunately it didn't.

Do you think the U.S. could have won the war? Why or why not?

From what I know now, I'm kind of skeptical that they could have won it. When I was there, fewer and fewer shipments of our re-supply came out. If you'd order 50 boxes of .50 caliber rounds, you might get

Andrews in a personnel carrier

25. By the time I left, a lot of the tracks didn't even have full loads of ammunition. Another thing that was tough was that they had free-fire zones and friendly zones. They were getting more and more friendly zones and less and less free-fire zones, so you had to call in before you fired. If you saw Viet Cong running across a rice paddy carrying rifles or RPG's you couldn't engage them. You had to call into the rear and tell them where you were. Then you had to get an approval to either fire or not fire. If it were in a friendly area, they'd say there's a friendly village a couple hundred yards away. You can't engage them. So you got to the point where they handcuffed you. You couldn't fight a war the way you were supposed to fight a war. When I left Vietnam, I was upset because I thought that if they bombed more and had more ammunition they could have won. Now as I look back on that after a number of years, I'm kind of skeptical. I've read a number of articles that have talked about what a sophisticated tunnel system the Vietnamese had, how they traveled, and the way that they fought the war. I really don't think the United States was ready to fight a guerrilla war. It wasn't the typical line them up on both sides and keep marching together until whoever had the most people left won. The strategy was shoot and hide and shoot and hide. I read an article on one landing zone in Vietnam. It was a large hill and the United States was stationed all over the hill, but the Vietnamese had tunnels all through the whole thing, and they were living right underneath them. I don't really think we could have won a war like that, because to find the enemy is really almost next to impossible.

Did you make any lasting friendships during the war?

I thought I did, but I haven't talked to people from Vietnam since maybe three years after I got out of the service. It was kind of hard to make friends with people because they were only there for a year. I know there were a number of people who became life-long friends. You were saying that when you were there, but once you got back and got into society again, I'm not sure how many of those really lasted. I did talk to a guy about 5 or 6 years ago. I picked up a copy of a Vietnam veteran's magazine, and they have a locater in there that locates people by company that they were in. One guy was looking for people who were in my particular company, and he was there in 1970. His name was Rick Cassidy. We wrote back and forth a couple times just to say hi. We never really stayed in touch, but that's the most recent contact I've had with anyone.

What did serving your country or patriotism mean to you when you were in active duty?
I was brought up to listen to my parents and do what they said. I never really questioned them a lot. Patriotism to me was fighting for my country. If you had to go off and fight, you did what they said and listened to what you were told. I felt I had an obligation to my country. You were not sure what would happen if you said, "No I'm not going." There was a little bit of fear there also, but to me I felt that it was my duty if I lived here, to fight for my country.

Is there a message that you have for young people today about the war?
If they should have to make a decision regarding fighting in a war, let their value system guide them in their decision. There will always be people willing to volunteer for duty. If you feel you can't bring yourself to fight, volunteer in another way. In times of strife the country needs everyone's help. You don't have to be in uniform to make a difference.

When he returned, Andrews worked as a welder for Central Fabrications and then as a heavy equipment operator and supervisor for Wisconsin Public Service Corporation.

Interviewed and transcribed by Jessica Dabler and Travis Kozlowski

Tim Mero

A Marine tank officer, Mero arrived in Vietnam in October 1967 and departed October 1968. He was stationed in Hue and served on staff duty and then commanded a tank platoon. He did participate in the Tet offensive of 1968.

Just to begin, can you just say when you were there and were you enlisted or drafted?

1966 I went on active duty, 1967 I had completed three formal schools and went to Vietnam in the fall of '67. I was a school teacher, so I volunteered and went on active duty as an officer in ranking.

Were you drafted or enlisted?

No, I was not enlisted, so when I went into the Marine corps, I went on a program where I was commissioned as an officer. I had been teaching in St. Paul and already had my master's degree, but thought it was something I had to do, and I did it.

Where did they put you in active duty in what kind of area?

When I was on active duty, I was trained and became a tank officer; I was in combat arms in the marine corps.

Can you describe what an average day was like?

Every single day was different, and I had many jobs when I was there. The jobs were so different. When I was working as a staff officer at the tank battalion, I had responsibilities. I was S2, which would be intelligence; I did a lot of work on my own. I worked with a couple that assisted me, but I spent a lot of time out with villagers and with small Marine units that were living in security compounds in certain villages. I worked with them on civic action projects, and I did that for the first three to four months. I was very much involved in working with the civilian population, helping them.

What were the enemies like?

Not everybody did see the enemy. I think that's a misrumor. A lot of people that are in support positions often do not see the enemy. They do a lot of security in that, but I had the opportunity in January of '68 just as the Tet Offensive was beginning. I was in language school; I was studying the Vietnamese language in Da Nang. I was put on an airplane, a helicopter, and flown up towards Khe Sanh and then to Dong Hong. They were forming a special task force, and I became part of that task force for the remainder of the time I was in Vietnam except for the last three weeks.

What were the base camps like?

I lived in a base camp the whole time I was there. Initially, I was in one down below Hue City. There also was an ARVN or South Vietnamese army unit that had a lot of their training facilities right around there, so it was relatively secure until the Tet Offensive. It was quite comfortable and very good living. If there could be, it was as good living as you would get. We could take a shower every day and had clean clothes and lived in a plywood hut with a metal roof and had screens so it was as good as it ever got. In January of '68, when I went up just below the DMZ (demilitarized zone) in those base camps, my first day when I walked into the one called Camlow Hill, I lived in a culvert for a few weeks until some people had moved out, and then I finally was able to find a tent. The camps--if it was a dry day, it would be dry; there would be a lot of dust blow-

M67 Flam Tank

ing. We weren't being shelled all the time, so it wasn't that bad, but it just wasn't clean and you lived kind of below ground, lots of sandbags if you had some type of a tent. Part of it would be above ground, and you would have a trench right along the side where you had your cots so that you could roll into it when you were being shelled. As we got into the months of February and March, I had a special assignment; my unit was very much different than most. I did-n't stay in one place. I was on about 15 to 17 minutes alert, so if the call came, I had to be able to move my people that were at three different base camps. I had to get them all together, and then if somebody was in trouble, then it was my job to take my tank unit and the people that were a part of that unit and go to that base camp and reinforce them, and that's what we did. We did that all over the northern part of the DMZ. We also did operations with others, from those base camps. We'd go out on operations for up to a week, and then we'd eventually come back to that base camp and continue to live.

You were there during the Tet Offensive. What was it like because it was a big turning point during the war?

I was in Hue just before the Tet Offensive. It was a very beautiful city and the walled city was unique. I used to go there quite a bit. I remember a Catholic cathedral in Hue City, and that cathedral was absolute-ly beautiful. That survived the Tet Offensive, but some of my tanks were involved in a lot of the fight-ing right near there. I wasn't there myself. I was pulled out and flown up north, so from that point on, there were lots of action. The North Vietnamese were much more aggressive and planned a lot bigger attacks. There were quite a few battles where I was involved. Unlike a lot of other units where my pla-toon of tanks, another platoon of tanks, and a company of infantry that frequently happened or would be with a battalion. They'd be up against two or three battalions of enemy and some very large units and it was not necessary like some of the others where it was hit and run.

Vietnam was considered a guerrilla war. What is meant by guerilla warfare?
Well, in guerilla warfare, some of the things that we did, even though I was in a tank unit, some of the things that we did were in a guerilla type operation, but the enemy for the most part would not necessarily become decisively engaged with an American unit. They would hit, inflict as much damage as they could, and then disappear so you frequently never saw the enemy. I remember at Dong Hong combat base, that was a very large base just about three to four miles south of the DMZ and on the Camalow River. That particular base had a huge ammo dump, and there are a lot of pictures of that thing exploding. When they hit that ammo dump with rockets, they were fired from somewhere near me. We saw them launching the rockets and firing them at Dong Hong combat base, but from where they were firing was a no fire zone. We were not allowed to engage the enemy even though they were firing rockets and blowing up this very large compound about six miles east of us. That was some of the real frustration with that particular war.

Did you ever do an ambush on the enemies?
Yes, I did. Again it was unlike most. I was not in an infantry unit, but there was one night that an enemy battalion was moving against a bridge that I was responsible for guarding. I had four tanks and there were some other units attached to me, and I had four of my seven tanks. The call came in that night that this battalion was moving to blow up the bridge, to knock it out, and a South Vietnamese unit was on patrol and spotted them. They told headquarters, but when I got the word where they were at, I had some mortars that I had acquired that I wasn't suppose to have. I had mortars and I had lots of mortar ammunition, so I cross trained my tank people to operate these mortars, and we did ambush them. We knew exactly

Tanks in support

where they were, and so we took them under fire with those mortars and spoiled their total attack. This was a very large unit of about four or five hundred people that were suppose to take this bridge, but we caught them long before they got there, and so it was an ambush. It wasn't the type of ambush where they're coming down the trail and you're right off the side of it, but it was an ambush.

There are certain things where you search and destroy. What is meant by search and destroy?
In some of the operations that were done where they would search and destroy, it might've been a village; it might've been

where they were looking for a particular compound, an underground complex and command post. If they found it, then it was to be destroyed, and that's the way I understood it. I know that some involved villages where they would go in, clear all the people out of the village, and go through to check to see if there was military equipment, arms, ammunition or whatever and anything they got. It was destroyed, so I was involved. There was one free fire area, designated free fire zone to the east of Camlow Hill that ran up the coast. I did a lot of operations in that area from Camlow River up to the military zone, and that was a free fire zone. So if you caught people in that area, civilians weren't suppose to be there, and they knew it. There were a couple of villages, and the enemy had occupied them. They were abandoned and had been occupied, and we would search them and find the enemy unit and then go through a search and destroy type operation to weed them out and destroy all of their equipment.

Some of the groups kept body counts or kills. Did your group ever do that?

No, we reported our casualties and we reported the number of enemy that were killed. I remember in one particular day I was supporting a battalion. They had just been flown in from an area called a rock pile, and it was up in the mountains. They were flown down to where I was; I had been ambushed the night before, my platoon and another tank platoon. We were trying to go over to the Constrain force, a unit that was in trouble, and so it was around seven or eight o'clock at night, and we got ambushed. We fought for five hours before we could disengage and get out. The next day, a battalion came in, and I was support-

A tank named THOR during Operation Thor

ing that particular battalion, and we went back in operation. The first day they had missed in action, lots of casualties. I had quite a few with my tank platoon and two tank commanders that were shot in the head. They both survived. When we got there, we were fighting a unit, and on the second day of that battle--it would have been three days after we were ambushed-- on the second day of that particular battle, there was an old cemetery, and we normally wouldn't fire at the cemetery or you wouldn't do anything except that particular cemetery, the enemies hid. That was their stronghold; and we were coming across a rice paddy area. They killed a bunch of marines, and we had lots of casualties; everybody was pinned down. If you stood up, you were above grass level, and so you were under fire. So the only people that could move were my tanks and so we took the offense in that case and routed the enemy. It was company, there were lots of people killed that they were responsible, at least 90 of them in that company that were killed. I captured two people and put them on the back of my tank, and those were the only two that I know of that were captured. We reported to our superior (in that case, it would've been the battalion commander) and told him it was easy to tell they were laying all over and there were airplanes flying over us, spotters trying to direct artillery and that, so it was easy for them to do a count and report that count. As to whether that was inflated by somebody afterwards or something, I have no idea, but if you did have an engagement, you did report how many people had been killed.

Did you use helicopters to get around?

No, I was a tank officer. I didn't use them. Helicopters supported us though. The night that I mentioned there was an ambush, we had some. I had some really serious casualties; I had one tank commander, and his particular tank had been hit. We were ambushed. I had 27 people; the other platoon leader had around 15 or 18 people. We were ambushed by a group of about 400, so this was a very large ambush that we were in, and as I said, it took us five hours to get out, but right in the middle of that ambush, everything was chaotic. I had several marines that were badly wounded, and we had to get them out. Some helicopters came in right in the middle of the fight. They came in, and we were able to abstract those casualties, and two of my tank crew men, they both survived.

How long were you there?
I was there for 13 months.

How was the relationship between whites and blacks in the unit?
We were a really small unit. In the seven months that I was up there, my platoon was not part of a tank company that was a part of the tank battalion. My platoon had a special assignment. I had to, I was under direct orders, there was a colonel that was in charge, but we were under direct orders from the commanding general of the division. We had to be able to respond whenever we were needed if anybody was in trouble, and so I always had to have five gun tanks with a main gun. It would have been a 90-millimeter main gun, and I had two flame tanks that were part of my unit. We had the only flame tanks that were in Vietnam, and then I had a squad of combat engineers, and I had at one point some army and some other people. We were a real small special unit, and we had to rely on each other for everything, so we got along extremely well. African Americans that were in the unit, there were some Hispanics, we all got along great. We ate, slept, did everything together, and it was unbelievably strong. It was nothing like what's depicted in the film *Platoon*. A good friend of mine that was in the unit that depicts, and except for the way they portrayed all of the drugs and all of the alcohol, it was pretty realistic. They're just over drammatizing something that wasn't as big of a deal. But the people that I was with were very close and some of them died for each other. It made no difference what nationalities or ethnic backgrounds; there was no difference. It was a good deal.

So did you develop a friendship between the guys that were in your group or was it strictly just they are part of your group?
That's a tough one. In the marine corps, I was an officer. I had no staff NCOs, I had no senior enlisted that were part of my unit. I had lots of young enlisted people, and we got along, we talked, I mean we were together all day long, and there was lots of times that you're not involved in fighting, I mean lots

The old swimming hole Cam Lo River

and lots of times. It becomes boring, and there was a certain code that is in the marine corps. I was friends with them. We went on first name basis because I was the lieutenant and they knew that if I had to tell them to go some place and fight, they might die, and that's the way it was. But we had a great relationship. They would've done anything I asked them and we frequently went on patrols together, on foot patrols. We did lots of that type of action, but we were good friends, but it wasn't, I didn't have a lot of other people that were my rank a lot so I didn't have other lieutenants and officers, and that. I was pretty much alone. The people that I was responsible for, and that, we got along very well, and we were not, we were pretty ragtag looking. We were pretty grubby looking, but they were good people and they fought hard.

If I had a tank that had mechanical problems, I had to call to headquarters, and I had to get permission from the general staff in order to take that tank apart and repair it. If it was going to be out of commission more than 15 minutes, then I had to have their permission to do that. So frequently, when I had one or two tanks that had major mechanical problems and needed some big work, work that might take two or three days normally, we would get it done in two or three hours, but we might have four tank crews working on it and a maintenance unit would come out from the battalion headquarters with everything that we needed. We would take no more than two tanks at a time, but we go through and do all of the repairs that had to be done and get everything fixed and get them back on line. Then as soon as that was done, because it had been just very strenuous work for several hours, we'd horse around and we had absolutely nothing. I mean we don't have anything like baseballs; we have nothing of that stuff. There were games, but we entertained ourselves.

What did you do doing your free time?

We had no place where we could go buy candy or soda or anything like that. That didn't show up. We were not part of a regular unit, so it was very infrequent that we got any kind of beer. We went about two or three months. I mean there was no beer, there was no candy, there were no newspapers, there was nothing, so what do you do? It was hard, and so we spent a lot of days, we reinforced all of the barbwire and the fencing stuff on our position. We did lots of work because we had to do something, and that was about it.

Did you have any opinions regarding the anti-war movement back in the states while in Vietnam?

While I was there, no, I didn't understand it. When I went to Vietnam, I didn't have any grand ideas. I understood exactly what I was getting into. I understood the type of war that it was. I was really impressed with the marines that I was involved with and the army that were in our area. It use to amaze me that they could be in such heavy combat and suffer such casualties. It would be after five, six days of continuous with very little sleep and then all of a sudden you have-- they'd be disengaging, and they travel one

Truly combined arms

or two hundred yards, maybe a little bit more, not very far, and they'd come to a village where in one moment, they would've killed anything they saw. There would be no animosity; they were very kind and very friendly to the local civilian population, so I mean they really impressed me.

What was the hardest thing about being in the war?

I think the hardest thing about being in the war was knowing that there was an absolute lack of support back in United States. That was tough. We didn't get newspapers very often. There was a newspaper that used to come, but from early January until late April or early May, that four or five months period, I never saw a newspaper. They never showed up. We didn't have it, and so there was an absolute lack of news. I remembered that I had, there were some packages of things that were sent to me by my family for my birthday, and my birthday was in the early part of January. When the stuff finally arrived, it had been aboard a boat, a landing craft, coming in off of a ship that had been blown up, so eventually I got the packages in late April, and it was kind of neat getting the things, but it was really screwed up. There was no news, and you didn't know what was going on back in the states, not for us. For some of the people that would've been in the larger built-up areas and that, I'm sure they had regular, daily information and it might've been different, but where I was, you just didn't know. I didn't know that Robert F. Kennedy was killed, and I didn't know that Martin Luther King had been killed. When I got a letter from my youngest sister, who is a year older than I am, and her comment was "What a shame that these two people had been killed," which it was a shame but I remember at the time, I didn't feel anything one way or another. It wasn't from my environment, seeing people die a lot, and I didn't think that much more about those two people than I did of the other people that I knew that were dying. I mean there was no news; you just didn't get much news. Anyway that was kind of tough.

Tim Mero at Con Thien

I think the other thing that was tough was that when an enemy was in a no fire area and they were shooting at you or they were shooting other marine units, you couldn't do anything about it. They wouldn't allow you to do anything. I had a good friend, I didn't know him at the time, but this guy came by, he was in a two and a half ton truck, standing in the back. He was a lieutenant. He was from my battalion, but I had never met him before. I saw a tank battalion truck stop at the bridge, and so I ran over and talked to him, and his name was John Gully, and later on we became good friends, just before I came back. John was on his way up to pay some of his people. They had been made part of our unit, and he was on his way up Cantian to pay some of those people. He got just north of us a little ways, and he was in a small convoy, but his particular truck was hit with this direct, large caliber direct fire weapons. John and the truck were destroyed. I have pictures of it being hauled out later, and the whole front end was gone from the truck from this round that hit it, and John was blown off the back. He was wounded, and it was kind of sad because later that afternoon, here came that same truck being hauled by a wrecker and taken out and the driver and the assistant driver were both killed, and John had been blown out of the truck but he survived. Anyway, there were lots of things like that where you meet people and then you didn't get too close. You didn't want to get too close because then you would get hurt too much if they got killed. There was nothing you could do about it when people were being hurt, and that was sad.

Was there any physical stress like a hard working day and tired?
Yea, there were lots of days; days were long. Normally I would not go to bed till around midnight. We were very undermanned and my people would be in bunkers and on tanks and stuff like that. In addition to my platoon, I always had ten extra tank crewmen assigned to me to help with security and as replacements if somebody got hurt. There were lots of stressful days. Everyday was like that. I'd be up late in the evening, sometimes one or two in the morning, and then I would try to get some sleep, and then frequently it would be 8:00 in the morning before I would finally wake up. I'd be lying on top of one of the bunkers or lying out on some sandbags or something, and it would eventually get hot. There was a lot of

stress like that. I think some of the other things were exposure. Are you going to ask me about Agent Orange? No. There were quite a few of us who were exposed to Agent Orange. In fact, it got dropped right on top of us in one battle and so I had areas on my body. I had three areas that, there was nothing, no indication, all of a sudden, within a couple days after that, you had these big holes; there was no tissue left. Everything had rotted away, and so you had these big holes. They're open spots, and nobody knew what it was. Nobody could tell us anything about it. Eventually, they healed and I never left because of that, but there was just lots of filth. There was lots of disease in the water, lots of malaria and other stuff. I'm trying to think, there was other things you could get from the water, and so that's what we had to bath in. We didn't have fresh water. Living conditions were not good. That was very stressful.

Was there one particular experience that stays in your mind?
There were lots of different things, lots of different battles, things like that, and I think probably one of

the neat things I remember, there was a young corporal, Aguilari. He was Mexican and he was from Mexico, but he was in the US Marine Corp. He actually was raised in Texas, and his parents came up from Mexico. He was in my platoon, and it was one particular serious fight that we were involved in. We were supporting a battalion that were assaulted, and all of a sudden, this young guy comes walking up the path behind me up a road. He had gotten back from R and R. I had been able to arrange so he could get back on rest and rehabilitation, back to Hawaii, so he got back and got to his wife who was expecting a child. She was very close to giving birth to the child, and we were able to get him back to Hawaii. She flew to Hawaii so that they could have a week together just before she gave birth to the child, and mainly he came back. He was all happy and everything. That was really neat, so there was lots of humor; there was lots of fun, lots of jokes, and lots of things that we did.

I think if there was one thing that really stood out as a great time, but then it became a bad time. One of my people had a friend who was a cook in the general's mess, and so one, I had to send people back and I sent one tank back with the road sweeps, everyday that went back to Dong Loa. This guy told me that if he went back, he could probably get some fresh food. Well we hadn't had any fresh food. We'd been eating C-rations for months, and so I sent him back and he came back with an unbelievably amount of fresh frozen food. Of course when they got it all, it all had to be eaten that night, but there was so many steaks, and so many different types of meat and dehydrated shrimp and other stuff so when he showed up at about three or four in the afternoon, there was all this fresh meat, so we set up. We got all of the tank crews, got everybody in the compound together. There was a company of infantry with us that night. We got all this food ready; we got the fire ready to go, and everything was ready. We were just going to start cooking all this food, and there was a reaction. I had to go over to camp Carol because there was an assault taking place around three in the afternoon. I left, got my tank crews, we all got on, and off we went, and we left all of that fresh food that this guy had got for us sitting there. Of course the infantry ate it while we were gone, and when we got to camp Carol, it ended up to be just a drill. We weren't there very long, and so then they just released us and then we had to come back.

When we got down into this valley known as Death Valley, there were lots of vehicle and tank holes there that were all burnt out. We got right in the middle of all of those vehicles, and one of my tanks broke down. The final drive broke, and the battalion commander, or this task force commander wanted me to destroy the tank, blow it in place, and I didn't want to do that, so it was just that dusk. It was getting dark, and so my tank and my crew, we stayed with this other crippled tank, and we took some toll cables and other things from the other vehicles, got the parts that we needed, and we disconnected the final drives. We got everything ready, and then we had to hook up our tank to this one that was crippled, and then we dragged it. Pulled it all the way to the base camp, but that was two tanks. We were all by ourselves; we didn't get back until about 11:00 at night. Headlights couldn't do anything, so it was absolutely dark. We made it back and were not engaged by the enemy. No one knew. I don't think the enemy understood how few of us there were, but I really felt kind of left out there, empty, like I said. There were two tank crews. There were eight of us total and we were just kind of all on our own but we got back. I remember that night very very well.

Do you think the US could have won the war?

Now I got to tell you my side, my politics come into this. I wasn't there to win a war. I was there to make sure that the South Vietnamese had the chance to choose and if they want the freedom and the type of society or the type of government that the South Vietnamese were trying to develop or whether they wanted to be under communism. That was their choice, and it honestly didn't matter to me whether they chose our style of life or whether they chose to live as communists, as long as it was their choice, that it wasn't forced upon them. Could we have defeated the enemy or defeated the North Vietnamese? Sure, we could have, but that would've taken a tremendous commitment and for what? There was no reason to invade the North and to try to kill all of those soldiers. It wouldn't have served any purpose. It bothered me that we eventually withdrew. I almost went back to Vietnam in '73, right towards the end of the war. I was on an airplane, and when I got to Okinawa, they were going to send me to Vietnam again as an advisor, but then it turned out I didn't have to do that. I stayed in Okinawa.

What kind of reception did you get when you came back to the United States?

There was a lot of deep grieving when I got out of Vietnam. When I got on the airplane in Vietnam, and it a was large 747, it was a big airplane, and I had eaten pretty good that night because I flew on Air America, the CIA type airplanes. I flew on one of their planes from Pine Tri down to Da Nang and with a bunch of goats and chickens and stuff like that. It was really kind of funny, but that night when I got on the airplane to fly to Okinawa, it was really amazing to board that plane. I mean everybody was cheering and stuff. It was just such a relief to be out of there, and I hadn't slept in a long time that I remember. Instead of sitting in the seat, I was near the window. I crawled under the seat and laid on the floor so I could sleep. I couldn't sleep sitting up, so I laid on the floor and then they woke me just before we landed in Okinawa. When we got ready to come back into the states, there was a lot of deep grieving at the place, about what we might expect, and I was really concerned about harassment. I didn't want to be spit upon or anything like that, so I delayed going to the airport. I got a flight out of California that left around 1:00 in the morning, and I didn't arrive at the airport until about an hour before so it's after midnight so there weren't a lot of people around. I didn't see anybody, but there was real concern about being mistreated, and I was quite anxious about that and that bothered me. Later I ran into a lot of that type of sentiment because I was stationed at Great Lakes and there were lots of problems after that, but I was concerned about it.

Are there any friendships that you kept in touch with now that survived?

There were some people that I became friends with over there. One guy changed his next duty stations and joined me at Great Lakes, Illinois, and then we lived together for a couple years. I was probably a very crude person when I first came back. I was very callous and there were things I probably did that I'm not all that proud of. Not nasty things, but I didn't treat people well, and I was very indifferent to a lot of the things and concerns that people had in the United States, anti-war and anti-government and I remembered the Black Panthers. That was a big deal at that time, but I was very cold. It took me awhile, I would say probably a year and a half or two, before I really got all of that stuff behind me.

Well what did serving your country mean during the act of duty?

I was a schoolteacher, and I had already been called up for the draft four times, and I was about to lose. I lived in Minnesota at the time and they were going to terminate the teaching deferment that kept you out of active duty, so I volunteered and I went. I don't regret it. I feel very proud about what we did. During the whole period I was there, I was involved in civic action, helping the local people. I did that up in the DMZ area, all over, so I did a lot of things. My experiences are very different from what other people might have had because I got very involved with the local people, and I'm glad that I helped. I didn't like the way it turned out, and I feel sad about that. I haven't kept a lot of close contacts. There were opportunities to keep a lot of those relationships. This fall in October, there is a Vietnam tankers reunion in St. Paul, and I'm going to go to that.

Is there a message that you want to give to the young people today that want to learn about the war?

War is not a good experience. If you have to do it, you've got to do it a hundred percent. You can't go into it halfheartedly. If you've got to do something like that, you're in a war. It's no license to break laws, and there are laws even in war on when you can and when you can't kill someone, and I would hope that nobody has to anymore. Somebody will. There's a lot of people that fought in Vietnam that we don't remember being there. We don't think about the Hmong. We don't think about the Montanyards who fought. There were lots of Australians who were there. There were a lot of Koreans who fought there, Korean marines. I lived with, right near, a battalion of Korean marines for a while, and there were people from lots of different places that were there and did a very good job. There were a lot of civilians that were there, and I don't know if I want to go back or not. I have flown over the area on my way in the mid '80s. I flew from Okinawa to Thailand, and there were several times flying over Vietnam that I look out the window and I knew exactly where we were. I had been there, on the ground in those areas, and I knew exactly where we were. That brought back a lot of memories, but I'm not so sure that I need to go back and rewalk or go to the places where I was.

Tim Mero remained on active duty until 1987. An educator before he joined the service, he returned to that field and is an administrator in the D.C. Everest School District.

Interviewed by Karen Ho

Dennis Pritzl

Assigned to the Armored division, Pritzl served with "D" troop of the 17th Cavalry. When that unit rotated home, he was transferred to the 11th Armored Cavalry Regiment where he completed his tour.

It was the last of the draft. I graduated from high school in '69 and began working in a paper mill in Park Falls: July of that year I got a notice I had to take my physical for the draft. That's when you know that you're going. I was in shape. I enlisted. Let's get it over with. So technically I was IA enlistment. From there I went to Ft. Bragg, North Carolina, took basic training. From there I went to Ft. Knox, Kentucky, and went AIT, Advanced Individual Training for tanks. From there I went right to Vietnam.

Can you describe what an average day for you was like during the war in Vietnam?
It was always hot and it stunk. The whole country smelled terrible. It was the first thing you noticed when you got off the plane. Later I found out why. They had no sewer system. Everything was done anywhere. That's when you grew up in a hurry, when you were sitting down on a toilet and a woman sits down right next to you. I'm not in America anymore. The realization comes in a hurry.

If there were any blacks in your unit, was there a difference in relationship between whites and whites and whites and other blacks?
Big. A lot of racism. Blacks always stuck together. There was all the handshaking, they had this ritual that went on, you know, the slapping hands. It was irritating to me. I was never racist until I was in the service. I became one.

Did you have any opinions regarding the anti-war movement going on in the United States while you were in the war?
Yes, it pissed me off. I was over there thinking I was doing the right thing for the country, and there were people back home saying I was wrong. To this day it bothers me.

What was the hardest part of being in the war for you?
Coming back and not being recognized as a soldier, somebody who wanted to do something for the country. They thought I was a baby killer, doing wrong. That was the biggest thing, was coming back, how people treated you.

When you were in Vietnam was there a lot of emotional or physical stress that you had to endure?
Emotionally, yes. Physically, no. I was in good shape, so it didn't bother me. Just the stress of every day, wondering when you're going to get shot at. You never knew where they were.

Is there one particular experience that stands out in your mind from the war?
Yes. I was with General William Bond when he got shot right next to me. He was about three feet away from me. He was the only general in Vietnam to get killed. And I picked him up and threw him on the chopper. April 1st, 1970.

Do you think the U.S. could've won the war?
Oh, yes, no doubt.

And then why or why not?
Because it was a political war. It wasn't run by the generals. For instance the Gulf War. President Bush said do what you have to do. They did it in a week, two weeks. If the government would've said do what you have to do, it would've been over with.

What kind of reception did you get from people back in the States when you came back?
None. That's what pissed me off. To this day, I don't think people know what we went through.

Did you make any lasting friendships during the war?
You want to hear a story? About five years ago I got a call from someone who's been looking for me for thirty years. It was a guy who got shot that I went to the hospital with. I thought he died. I didn't know. He's now living up by Park Falls. His name is Larry Lawver. You can call him sometime. He got shot pretty bad over there.

"I WAS WITH GENERAL WILLIAM BOND WHEN HE GOT SHOT RIGHT NEXT TO ME. HE WAS ABOUT THREE FEET AWAY FROM ME."

Could you describe a firefight?
The firefights; I was in every one. We were ambushed, because you never knew where they were, you know. We're going down the road and the all of a sudden all shit broke loose, and we just defended ourselves. That's what happened to the general. We had just got done with a firefight, so the general comes in; he wanted a body count. So he's walking alongside me, and we're getting body counts, and someone shoots. He got shot by a sniper.

So would you say when you were in Vietnam that the enemy initiated most of the attacks on you?
All of them were. Every one. But you didn't know when or who or where.

What were living conditions like for you?
Like living in the woods. The only time you got a hot meal is when they would bring you one in, maybe once a month. Otherwise it was C-rations all of the time.

If there was one mistake you think that the United States made in the Vietnam War, what would you say it was?
Going there. We had no business there. I see that now, but at the time, you know. My dad was in World War II and helped stop communistic aggression. We've got to stop this, you know. At that time I thought I'm doing the right thing, we're stopping communistic aggression.

How much combat time do you think you actually saw?
I was in three major firefights.

So most of the time there was really nothing going on?
No, most of the time we were just out on missions. We were looking for them, waiting for them.

If you enjoyed anything in Vietnam, what would you say it was?
Going to Hawaii. I got married in Hawaii. I've since then been divorced, though.

When you got back, were there any major family changes for you in your life?
Not really, no. Other than I don't think anybody in my family knows what I went through, or if it ever meant anything, so we just don't talk about it.

A tactic used in the war was called either search...; well there were two tactics. Search and destroy or search and avoid. I was wondering if you knew anything about these?
Search and destroy. Everything I was in.

So you were involved in firefights?
I was one of the first tanks. Yes.

Vietnam was considered a guerrilla war, obviously. Describe what you think is meant by guerilla warfare.
Killing people who live in the jungle, who live there. They always have the advantage. Always. Except once the firefights started, and we called in the gunships and stuff. Then we did.

Was your unit ever a victim of any booby traps?
Yes. We hit a landmine once. It killed the driver. Flipped the tank right over.

Did that happen often?
That didn't happen a lot. Very few.

What were the base camps like in Vietnam?
A lot of fun. We were out on missions maybe thirty days at a time. When we came in it was just a big party. One thing the government did was take care of us. We had all the food and beer and everything we could drink. They had strip shows going twenty-four hours a day. Those were good times. They'd call them stand-downs. We'd stay for about three days at a time. The government gave us everything we wanted.

You mentioned a difference between the VietCong and NVA. Did you fight against the VietCong or the NVA?
Both, but mostly the NVA.

Can you describe the enemy a little bit?
You know what NVA means, North Vietnam Army. They were well-trained, well-disciplined, tough. There were civilians that went to the Communist side.

Did you ever use helicopters to get around in Vietnam?
When I moved around sometimes.

Do you think drugs were a problem for the soldiers in Vietnam at all?
Yes and no. Some guys, yeah, were marijuana hustling. You could buy a coffee can for a dollar. Yes, I tried it, but I never touched it after that. I learned how to smoke over there, and I'm still smoking.

Did you have any difficulties dealing with memories when you got back?
PTSD. I just put in a...PostTraumatic Stress Syndrome.

Can you explain any experience you've had with body counts or kill ratios?
We always were on top. The worst one I was in was with General Bond. I think we killed about seventy-five. We lost three.

Did you think that the body counts were in any way incorrect?
Well, yes. The only body counts we got were the ones we saw. How many blood trails were out there, we don't know.

We read about counting a gun as five people, if you shot them down and got their weapon.
No. I do have a weapon here (referring to picture). I personally wanted to take home. That's an AK-47.

That was from an NVA soldier?
Yes. Nice weapon. Brand new. I was going to send it home, but my CO decided he wanted it more.

Was there a lot of conflict between you and your authority?
If there was one nice thing about Vietnam, there wasn't much military discipline over there. What are they going to do, send me home? If that was our answer…that was one good thing about it. Everyone knew what he had to do. We didn't need the rules of discipline. We went through basic.

Did you ever feel you were put in a dangerous situation by fighting in a war? Can you describe that?
We had one lieutenant that didn't know what he was doing. This was a ROTC graduate, a guy who went all through college on the army, so when he graduated from college he went into the service, but he was a lieutenant now, an officer. He didn't know jack shit. He got us lost. You know, went in there like John Wayne. No, you know. We refused to go. We'd been there.

Did you know anyone back in the United States that dodged the draft?
No, thank God.

When you were in Vietnam, what were some of the missions that your unit was sent on?
Search and destroy. All of them were, but we used to have certain areas we tried to control, like we'd take eighty acres every day, or mile, or grids, or whatever they were called. We tried to control certain roads, make sure they were always open.

When you were in Vietnam did you feel the United States was winning?
I didn't know. I was just enlisted; I didn't know what the hell was going on. Christ, I didn't even know what Vietnam was until I got drafted.

Did you feel that it was unfair that America sent troops over there to fight for something when the kids didn't even know what they were fighting for?
At the time, no, but I do now. My hindsight is 20/20.

What were your thoughts at the time?
When I went in I thought this is the right thing to do. My dad did it, my grandpa did it.

What were some of the hardest memories that you had from the war?
Losing people.

Friends, people you knew well?
Yes.

So you were mostly involved in tanks?
Yeah. Tanks and communications.

Were you driving?
I did everything. Everyone starts out as a driver, because that's the first person that gets killed. They don't want you to drive around with those tanks. If it stays there, it's going to be in a firing zone, in a kill zone. There is one picture of a tank in there that got hit by a RPG. Right here, this is the RPG one. Right through where the driver sits. It burns a hole through, and after it gets through it explodes. That's about four inches of steel it burns through.

So you were fortunate enough not to get hit by one when you were a driver, obviously.
I was a driver for a couple of months. The more time you have in the country, and then you get the better position. Seniority rules.

I didn't know anything could pierce a tank.
It melts right through.

Were you ever involved in an ambush of the enemy?
No. They ambushed us all of the time.

So you basically had to defend yourself then?
Yes. A couple of times when we were patrolling the highways we had people on the highways that weren't supposed to be there.

So would you say often times when you were attacked that it was very unexpected?
Yes, all of the time it was unexpected.

How long were you there?
I was there ten months. I got off early. Here's what happened: I was with D-troop 17th Cavalry. I was there six or eight months. The war was winding down, so they figured they would start taking units away. They took my unit away, but I didn't have enough time in to go home, so they sent me to 11th Calvary division, where I stayed there for another three or four months. Christmas came and I had enough time in to go home early, so, ten months I was out of there. I left Christmas Eve in the morning and I got home Christmas Eve. I flew for eighteen hours.

> *"EVERYONE STARTS OUT AS A DRIVER, BECAUSE THAT'S THE FIRST PERSON THAT GETS KILLED."*

How did you defend yourselves during firefights? Was there really anything you could do against missiles and weapons?

Most of the time I was on a machine gun. We would just shoot and they shot back. And then we'd call in air strikes, helicopters, and artillery, whatever we could bring in.

Did it take very long for air support to get there when you called it in?

It didn't, but it seemed like a long time. I imagine they were there in half an hour. It seemed like all day. Once they came in, that was it. Their ass was ours then.

Can you describe an experience where you thought you were going to die, if there was one?

I thought I was going to die on that April 1st one. But when the helicopters came in, then I knew I was safe.

Do you know exactly in Vietnam where you were?

I was in Ben Hoa. Then I went fifty, sixty miles north of that.

You said you were off of bases for a month at a time. Were physical conditions hard for you?

Not for me, no.

For other people was it?

Maybe for some of the older people that were out of shape. It was always hot. You could die for a cold beer. We would give anything for a block of ice. If you could get a beer and ice and start rolling it and in a couple of seconds it was ice cold.

When you were in high school were there any anti-war rallies going on or anything?

No. I grew up in a small town, secluded from anything.

When you got back from the war was there anybody that you kept in touch with right when you got back?

No, that's something you kind of push away, I guess. My best buddy in high school and I both went into the service together. We lost touch. He got involved in drugs and was in some bad shit. That's what I really miss is that I lost a good friend over there.

Do you think the war changed a lot of people's lives in that way?

Yes.

How would you say it changed people?

Well this guy, Tom Pepper, he was the jock of the high school, good all around guy, and when he came back, he was so screwed up you couldn't even talk to him. I know he's getting help now, but he's still not the same. I lost friendships from high school. I think those two years I lost a lot of friendships, you know, like today people out of high school... You know there's something you can't relate, something that's missing there of what I went through and what they've never experienced. I mean I didn't even go to my fifth class reunion because of that war. I thought there was no way I could associate with these kids anymore.

With the recent events of the tragedy in New York, what would you recommend? Would you recommend military action or...?

Yes. I think we should blow the son of bitches. Take the country over.

So you believe that the bombing we're doing now is right?
We're not doing enough of it. They killed 5,000 of ours; we don't have that number yet. After Vietnam let's do it right.

So you feel that Vietnam was a huge mistake for the United States Army?
Oh yeah. I do now. I didn't at the time.

Do you have a message for young people today about the Vietnam War? What they should think about what happened?
I don't think they can imagine what it's like.

Can you explain what you mean?
I think the biggest thing is like what I did. I can't even relate to my friends in high school. That two-year gap was too big of an experience of what I have done and they didn't.

You felt that you were changed from the war?
Yeah. I still do. You know what happened September 11th? You know it's terrible to say this, but this country needed that.

It's amazing how people are showing their patriotism.
That's the way it was in World War II, World War I, how you feel now.

People didn't have the same sort of patriotism?
You and I could both be brothers. I could come back and you would say, what the hell were you doing over there? Killing babies or what?

What do you think the difference was between the other wars and the Vietnam War?
Maybe because we didn't have something like September 11th happen. It was so spotty; there was just so few killed every day.

The Tonkin Gulf incident, where the Vietcong apparently attacked our boats... which is how we got involved in the war... President Johnson got us into the war because he said that we were attacked by the Vietcong in the Tonkin Gulf and instead of—
We were in before Johnson though. Kennedy was the one that sent advisors over there. Johnson escalated it. He didn't know what the hell he was doing.

Instead of formally declaring war, he used the Gulf of Tonkin resolution to really get people over there and get the draft started.
Johnson was our biggest problem in this country. He was a Democrat. There I go now.

Do you think Johnson had a reason for taking military action so quickly and drastically?
I think Johnson had a lot of money based…he had a lot to do with helicopters and stuff. A lot had to do with money to keep the war going. More helicopters, more money. All politicians, I think, had their hands into something.

We read that out of all of the politicians, senators' children that had gone over to Vietnam, only one had gotten killed. Well, a lot of them didn't even go just because they were the children of—
They got deferments and all this other bullshit.

Do you think that was fair at all?
No.

Do you think that had any effect on what was happening in politics in the United States?
No I don't. But you never know. Politics nowadays.

Did you find anything in the tunnels (referring to a picture)?
Remnants of food, clothing, stuff like that.

You never found any people hiding?
No.

Was there a lot of confusion about who the enemy was during the fights or anything?
During the fights there wasn't.

During the day like when you went into a village or something?
They all looked the same. How would you know?

Was there anything else you would like to share?
Not really. If we do go to war, I hope the nation isn't divided like it was.

Following the war, Dennis Pritzel became a mechanic.

Interveiwed by Melissa Peter and Ben Simmerman

Mike Zeimer

He served in Vietnam from June 1968- June 1969. He was with "The Black Horse." 11th Armored Cavalry Regiment, as the S-1 Clerk. He worked at the regimental headquarters. His rank at discharge was Sgt.

How did you become involved in Vietnam?
My hometown is Shawano. When I graduated from the University of Wisconsin-Stevens Point, in the heart of the Vietnam conflict in 1967, they were already drafting teachers with two children from my hometown. I decided that I was going to go anyway, so when I graduated, I enlisted in Officers Candidate School. I got fed up with O.C.S. because I was going to have to put in a hitch four years after O.C.S. I decided to drop out of O.C.S. after about eleven weeks and went to Vietnam. I was busted back from an E5 to an E1. I went over and got assigned to the 11th Armed Cavalry Regiment.

Could you describe your job in Vietnam?
My job was like a "Radar O'Reilly" in my unit. The 11th Armored Cavalry regiment was the smallest independently standing regiment in the United States Army. We were more like a glorified company smaller than all the regiments. I was the S1 clerk which is the administrative clerk for the colonel. How I got that job was interesting. They had a whole bunch of us that came in as replacements off the airplane, and they set us outside the personnel hut and one of the questions that they asked was who could type. A couple of people went in ahead of me, and I don't think they did very well. They got to me and told me to put paper in the typewriter. I started asking questions like what size of top margin did they want, what type of side margins, and the sergeant said: "Just type." I asked if they wanted double spaced or single spaced, the sergeant said, "Just type." I started typing, and I was never really fast, but I could type accurately. I was looking at the material that I was to copy, not at the keys. The sergeant came up and asked me why I wasn't looking at the keys. I asked him if he wanted me to look at the keys. He asked, "How can you type without making any mistakes and not look at the keys?" I told him I was a typing teacher and my college degree is business education and I was qualified to teach typing. I got the job. My job was running the colonel's office, but probably one of the most important reasons they wanted me to type accurately was I also had to type the KIA letters and MIA letters. They didn't want any corrections or errors, and some of the letters were very difficult to type because I knew the person that was killed or missing. One letter took me forty-one attempts until I got it right. Otherwise, I handled the office business.

One of my colonels was very unique. For the first six months I worked for Colonel George S. Patton II, the World War II general's son. He was just as unique as his father, in regards to what his father did in World War II. George S. Patton II had stag handled .357s as his sidearms. He would hang out standing on the runners of his helicopter and shoot his pistols. He had a work ethic that went twenty-four hours a day. He would give a lot of speeches, and he would want them typed on the 3x5 cards, not just written on them, so I got many opportunities to type 3x5 cards at weird hours of the morning like two or three a.m., or

"For the first six months I worked for Colonell George S. Patton II, the World War II general's son."

whenever the colonel got the inspiration to wake me up. He was very good to me in return. There were chances for me to sleep in and he wouldn't wake me if there was nothing going on. Colonel Patton was very protective of the people who took care of him.

There was this cocky young lieutenant that came in the office and very often insisted that I light his cigarettes. I am now a non-smoker. At that time I smoked a pipe. When I got to Vietnam, I couldn't keep my pipe clean, so I starting smoking Filipino cigars. I had two cigarette lighters. One I used for lighting people's cigarettes in the building. Also I had my blowtorch which was a Zippo lighter that I had the wick pulled up above the cage. I used the Zippo when I was driving convoy in the wind. It had a huge flame. This guy caught me in a bad mood. It was the third or fourth day he came in the office pestering me about lighting his cigarette. I was typing when he came in. This man had a handlebar mustache, and he bent over to get a light, and I reached in my desk and got out the "flamethrower" and whipped that up by his face, and I snapped the wheel and he let out a holler. He now had a short mustache on one side. Colonel Patton came out of his office and asked me what was going on. I told him that the lieutenant demanded that I light his cigarette for the sixth spare time this week. George lit into him. I think his tail was still burning when he left the base.

I was never in combat, but I did go into the field with the convoys, and I worked in these forward base camps. I was a clerk, and I did a lot of typing, office stuff, guard duty, and I was a driver, not just the colonel's vehicle but a two-and-one-half ton truck with a box office on it. It was not a combat vehicle but a mobile office, and when we went forward it became the colonel's office. My office was in a tent. In the base camp, I was in a building that had slatted sides. Everything was open because you wanted the air to move through.

Did you enjoy your duties or did you have favorites?
Since I went over there as an infantryman, which would have been out in the swamp with a high potential of getting killed, yes, I appreciated the fact that I wasn't out there. Did I enjoy it? No, not always. Like many of the other people over there, I didn't see a purpose as to why we were there. I looked forward to going home. I was there one year and one day. I enjoyed it more than some other people. The people in the field who came back to the base camp couldn't handle the mundane activities of the base camp, and they often asked to go back to the field.

Where in Vietnam were you located?
"The Black Horse," 11th Armed Cavalry base camp was southeast of Bien Hoa at Long Giao. We also had a camp at Bien Hoa, and we operated out of there when we went out on convoys. You didn't have to be in the field to be in danger. Our tent got blown up in the base camp one night. The enemy shot some rockets at our base camp, and fortunately, they didn't hit the large tree that was in our camp. If the rocket had hit the tree you get what is called an air burst like a fireworks display and metal goes in every direc-

"THE KNIFE WAS JUST A FEW INCHES FROM HIS HEAD, AND FORTUNATELY, WE HAD ALL ROLLED ONTO THE FLOOR."

tion. If the rocket hits something on the ground, most of the explosion is sent in one direction. When there is an air burst, the shrapnel goes in every direction. The two rockets came down on two vehicles outside our tent. Both were destroyed. One of my friends in our tent heard the rockets' whistle which they made as they came in. We all rolled on the ground face down. We did have a bunker, but we did not have time to use it. My friend had a Buck hunting knife which he wore on his belt. The knife was in a sheath, and it was unbuttoned on his duffel bag so if he heard something at night he could reach over and take his knife out. There was no place that was safe. The VC could creep through the perimeter into the base camp, so he kept the knife by his bunk. The shrapnel had destroyed the handle of his knife. His pants were there, the sheath was on his belt, and the blade was in the sheath, but the handle was gone. Can you imagine the force of the impact to remove the ebonite handle and the steel shank off of that knife and leave it there in its position? The knife was just a few inches from his head, and fortunately, we had all rolled onto the

floor. If the rocket had burst in the air we would have all been dead. That was as close as I came to personally being killed. My only injury was a leg injury caused by a tent stake. Nothing from combat. I don't think I ever shot anyone. Sometimes on guard duty you would see movement or think you saw movement, but it could have been anything, and we would lay down machine gun fire in the general area of the movement. I do not think I personally shot anyone. That isn't to say that I wouldn't have fired because you get in a different mindset. You see people that had been shot, and it changes your whole mindset. That may be why I don't hunt anymore.

What were the base camps like?
The base camp is a clearing basically in the jungle. They got in there and defoliated it with bulldozers and chemicals to make a safe area. Our base camp at Long Giao was an open space, and in our case, a few miles from Xuan Loc, which was where we would go to attend church. There were people from Xuan Loc who worked in the base camp, and you didn't know whether they were enemy or friendly. They would clean or mow yards. The base camp was either muddy or dusty. It was either raining everyday or it didn't rain for months. You would be full of mud. Electronic equipment or cameras would be muddy or dusty unless you had a good zip lock bag. Our base camp had a few permanent buildings made out of wood. Most of the building had a wooden floor, two by four frames and a roof made from a tent. Some of the tents, by the time I got there, were in bad shape, and during the rainy season, you did not stay dry.

One guy, Cooper, in our tent had a father that was Mexican, and his mother was Irish. The Irish sent him potato whiskey and the Mexicans sent him peppers. One day I asked to try one of the peppers. I ate the pepper, drank my beer, finished his beer, and went outside to get some water because it was so hot!

Cooper did not control himself when he drank. One night after drinking way too much, he lit up his M16 and shot holes in the roof of our tent. Cooper was a PFC when I arrived, made it to Spec 4, and then back to PFC. He extended because he wanted to get out. If your term was short and you didn't want to serve the remaining time in the states, there was a formula where you could get out in less than two years. When I left he was still there, and he had been reduced in rank back to PFC again.

What was an average day like in Vietnam?

For me it varied a lot because my day might start at three in the morning. I was on call twenty-four hours a day, but my normal day was to get up, eat breakfast, work, eat lunch, go back to the office and do the office routine. The colonel gave a lot of speeches, and I typed a lot of notes for him. Then, every so often, there was guard duty. I didn't have a lot of kitchen police (KP- mess duty) in Vietnam. Back in the states I pulled a lot of KP. Guard duty came up, and I didn't really have a day off. One day just blended into the next. I did have a Christmas tree at Christmas time. I had a dog, but I don't remember its name. You never knew what time in the night you might be awakened by incoming; incoming rounds that aren't close to you will still wake you up. A bunker was a big culvert, a big metal culvert that normally goes under a road with layers and layers of sandbags. You couldn't stand up in it. You went in and sat down and on each end there was an opening that was surrounded by sandbags. I spent a lot of time in bunkers. My shower was a barrel on a rack above me, and the truck came and filled it with cold water. Hopefully you didn't shower just after the truck filled it. The barrel was painted black so the sun would heat the water. Toilets were outdoor toilets over a barrel. The barrels were pulled out and fuel oil added and the contents were burned.

What was your clothing like?

Because I wasn't out in the field, I didn't carry much. I wore very light-weight fatigue long pants, the cloth sided jungle boots, and a fatigue shirt. You carried an M16 all the time and a few clips of ammo. I didn't carry a pack. You would have to clean your ammo and your weapon because we didn't use them much and sand got in the action. For guys in the field, in the mud, it must have been something trying to keep your weapon clean. When we were off duty, you could wear other stuff, but I didn't have a lot of civilian clothes.

What were meals like?

I can't remember much about the meals. You lived through them. They fed us. Sometimes when we were on a convoy run, the kitchen would send food out, and if you were a coffee drinker, a big stainless steel urn would come, and you had different types of coffee every day. Every fourth or fifth day you would get coffee like you enjoyed. One day it would come black, the next day it would come with sugar, the next with cream, the next with both cream and sugar, and the next day it was black again. The water didn't taste real good. It was drinkable, but it had a bad taste. We would cover the bad taste with Kool-Aid. I don't remember the food being that terrible. If you went off base you had to be careful of what you were eating. It was not uncommon to eat dog. There were certain things that were better not eaten.

Did you have any experiences with kill ratios or body counts?

When I did the KIA letters, I knew what our losses were.

Did you use helicopters to get around?

I was on a helicopter one time. Our whole regiment was oriented around tanks and helicopters. We had regular helicopters and Cobra gunships. I only rode in a regular Huey one time. The staff sergeant put me on the helicopter and told me to go back to base camp from a field location. I only had a few days left before going home to the US.

Did you travel around much in the country?
I drove on convoys as the driver of the headquarters truck. I was on five or six convoys that varied in distance. We went to one of our many forward camps which were much smaller than our base camp.

Were drugs and alcohol a problem with the soldiers?
Yes, I stayed clear of the drugs. I would have a beer or two, but I didn't do drugs. Alcohol could be controlled by the Army to some degree, but the drugs were a different issue. A lot of young people were over there. I was older because I was a college graduate, but a lot of these people had just completed high school. They didn't want to be there. I had a guy in my unit that contracted a social disease after going to town.

How was the relationship between blacks and whites?
We really didn't have any problems that I know of.

What were your feelings about the anti-war movement back in the US?
My personal feeling was that I was going to serve, and I didn't have any issues with those people. They had their ideas and I had mine. I didn't want to be there any more than anybody else. I just hoped that one day I would be able to go home. I was married when I went, and the war changed me, and when I returned we divorced. My wife said I was not the same person when I returned. Maybe I wasn't.

Did you endure a lot of physical or emotional pain?
Physical, no, because I was in a base camp. Emotional, some, because you are away from home.

What was the biggest difficulty that you faced in the war?
Giving up part of my life. On a day to day basis, accepting the fact that I was there. I had no control over that. The emotional part was not knowing if you were going to be there tomorrow. Even if you weren't in the field, there was still danger. PFC Cooper could have awakened that night and unloaded his M16 into us instead of the tent ceiling. Not everybody died over there because of enemy fire, and I'm not saying that people intentionally killed other people, but accidents happen in that type of environment. It wasn't just rifles either. You had hand grenades, claymores, etc. There were a lot of accidents. People got infections and wounds didn't heal. Then you start getting short (little time left to go in Vietnam) and the mental thing really begins. At a short timer's party I drank too much and could have been injured that night. I came home very skinny. When I stepped off the plane in Milwaukee, my parents and my wife didn't even recognize me. Missing what you could have been doing back home was hard. I don't regret doing that. It is part of my past.

Did you make any lasting friendships during that time?

Yes, I made many friends over there. However, none that I have kept in touch with.

What was it like returning to the US?

I got out because I had served enough time. When I went to Vietnam my tour gave me enough time in the Army that I was discharged immediately. I used my GI Bill for a loan on a house. I had my bachelor's degree already so the education part I didn't use. I used my military experience on my resume, and I think that it helped me get a job after I returned. There was a time when some employers valued that.

Do you remember what kind of reception you got when you came home?

Yes, my mom, my dad and my wife. As far as with people in general I didn't experience anything negative. I never observed anything negative. My home town is Shawano and that was different than Chicago or Philadelphia or New York.

What did it mean to you to be serving your country in Vietnam?

I guess I felt the obligation. I felt that I didn't want to be a draft dodger. My father had served in World War II and was discharged because his eyes were bad. I served in Vietnam with eyesight that was worse than his. I felt that I was obligated to serve my country. Somebody has to do it. If you want a safe nation, somebody has to step forward and serve.

What recognition did you receive for your time?

The typical ribbons that they give you. My job after the war made up for any other recognition not received.

Do you have a message for young people today about the war?

I think that it was a phase that America went through, and you have to accept all the good and bad that comes with it. It was the hot topic of the day. I don't know why the protestors didn't want to serve, and I can't explain why we were there. Somebody decided that it was good for the United States. I am not a politician, and sometimes you have to follow the leader. I survived, but I know that many people didn't. Their families might have a different opinion from mine. The young people of today need to understand that someday there may be a conflict, and they will be expected to step forward and serve.

After Vietnam, Ziemer taught Business Education in high and middle schools, sold insurance, and called on doctors, pharmacies, and hospitals selling pharmaceuticals. He is currently semi-retired, selling insurance on a part-time basis.

Interviewed by Philip Beck

COMBAT SUPPORT

D.C. EVEREST AREA SCHOOLS

Combat Support

According o Shelby Stanton's Vietnam, Order of Battle (U.S. News Books, 1981), combat support elements are composed of engineer, military police, and signal units. These units provided direct support to the combat units that were responsible for engaging the enemy.

Engineer units totaled 47 battalions and 62 separate companies that served in Vietnam providing a variety of services from land clearing to float bridge construction. Directed by larger units, they were assigned to such tasks as road construction, airfields, petroleum facilities and pipeline construction.

Military police units fell under the overall control of he 18th Military Police Brigade that was based at Long Binh. The units provided normal police functions as well as security, traffic control and involvement with detainees and the civilian population. There were seven military police battalions and 26 separate companies. The military police battalions normally served as part of a military police group that was responsible for a two corps area in Vietnam.

Signals, the largest of the three groups mentioned, were responsible for the reception and transmission of communications at different levels of command and using different networks and equipment. Thirty-three different battalions operated at one time of another in Vietnam and 67 separate companies. Some were support elements to divisions, and others had various responsibilities for corps areas or telephone line construction and supervision. Units on the ground, in the air and offshore needed signal support, and that responsibility of maintaining the network fell to these units.

Sid Bouldin

Bouldin was in the 1st American Cavalry Division, 1969 and 1970. He served as a chaplain's assistant.

When did you serve?
I was in the army from 1969 to 1970, and I was in Vietnam the last part of that two years.

Were you drafted or enlisted?
I actually enlisted, but for two years.

What did you do in Vietnam?
I did a couple of things. I was trained with an infantry M.O.S. The chaplain's assistant was a bodyguard for a chaplain in the field or at a firebase area. We also helped the chaplain with worship services, but while I was in the Old Guard in Washington D.C. I picked up the chaplain assistant M.O.S.

So did you protect people?
Chaplains are not allowed to carry weapons, so the assistant is like a bodyguard.

Why weren't they allowed to carry weapons?
Chaplains are never allowed to carry weapons.

What were the base camps like there?
Not good. I was in a forward firebase called "Buttons" near Song Bay, which was along the Cambodian border. I was in the first air cavalry in late '69 and '70. That's where most of the action was at the time. You slept in tents. We used mosquito nets at night, not to protect us from mosquitoes, but to keep the rats off of us.

> *"WE USED MOSQUITO NETS AT NIGHT, NOT TO PROTECT US FROM MOSQUITOS, BUT TO KEEP THE RATS OFF OF US."*

What was a typical day like for you?
I don't think there were any typical days. Some days we'd go out to the field to do services. Other days you'd fill sand bags to put around the tents. Some days we would have services there; just a variety of stuff. We would normally go in helicopters. The first air cavalry division used helicopters regularly.

How old were you at the time?

I graduated from college in '68 and went in shortly after, so I was 22 to 24. While I was there, I was 23 and 24.

Did you move around a lot?

Yes.

Where were you located in Vietnam?

I was along the Cambodian border, and then towards the last few months of my tour, I got moved back to sort of a medium area, which was somewhat safer.. We had better food and safer housing.

What was the hardest part for you?

Being there. Mainly everyday you counted one less day you had to be there until you got to go home. I was not married. I was single at the time.

Is there a particular experience that stood out, that you enjoyed or didn't enjoy?

On the night of December 23, 1969, we came under heavy rocket attack from the enemy. Everybody went to his or her particular area where you were assigned. Some of the enemy actually worked at the firebase during the daytime and then became the enemy at night, but you didn't know who was who, obviously. And so they knew where everything was, and they were able to set the rockets up to do the most damage. And that particular night

> *"...THAT PARTICULAR NIGHT WAS REAL, REAL BAD. WE CARRIED AN AWFUL LOT OF WOUNDED AND DEAD THAT NIGHT."*

was real, real bad. We carried off an awful lot of wounded and dead that night. And then oddly enough, there was a three-day truce, the 24th, 25th, and 26th for Christmas. I felt called into the ministry at that time. Then it was interesting because on Christmas, we had a Christmas party for the village children. And the soldiers gave gifts to the little children, and provided them with some Santa Claus; typical American type things. But then on the 27th, the war started again. That was my worst individual time.

What was it like to ride in a helicopter?

Noisy, depending on what type of helicopter you were in. They would have machine guns on the side. They would drop you, and then they would leave.

How did you get your food and clothes or did you carry it with you?

Everybody had a certain amount of clothes and food. If you were out in the field for a period of time-- of course you'd have rations. But in the forward firebases, they would try to give you hot meals. My family sent me Hickory Farms packages, and that's what I lived off of. Some of the food wasn't too bad though. On holidays they would try to give you better food. It wasn't too bad.

How physically draining was it?

I was in terrific physical condition at the time. I probably weighed 150 pounds. Just like being in a sport where you get in top physical condition, and that's what you're in.

What kind of training did you have to go through?
I went through basic training, and I went through advanced infantry training. I was fortunate because right out of advanced infantry training I went to Washington D.C. and was in the Old Guard which was the ceremonial unit. I stood along the side of the road for President Eisenhower's funeral. My company did not do the Tomb of the Unknown Soldier, but we were in that same battalion. There were five companies and one of them did that. We mainly did funerals and parades but also riot training.

Do you think that the Vietnam War has changed you as a person?
Sure. Yes, I wouldn't be in the ministry. It was a total change.

What had you originally gone to college for?
Economics.

Were there any special problems?
If you've ever seen the movie *Platoon*, you can see the type of racial trouble everyone dealt with. That was pretty typical. And it wasn't all whites and all blacks; there was some mixture.

Is this a hard subject to talk about? When you think about it, does it bring back mostly bad memories?
Yes, I probably wouldn't have done the interview fifteen years ago. You needed to come to terms on where you've been. Every time I do communion, I still think about that night. For some reason it flashes back.

Are you happy with the effects it has had on you, like going into the ministry?
I enjoy the ministry. I really love it. It's easier for me to say because I came out without any physical wounds. I didn't get shot. I didn't get Agent Orange or any of the things that could have happened. I was one of the fortunate. At the time I was there in '69 and '70, if we would get back to Long Binh or Saigon ,it was like a night you knew you were going to make it. There were 100,000 American troops in that area.

What were you doing before the war?
College.

Did you ever think you were going to go into the war?
Well, the war dragged on and on; every year you had to get your college deferment, so you knew when you graduated that you were going to have to go into service unless there was something wrong with you.

At first, did you want to go?
Not really. In 1968, *Time* magazine ran an article that it was the worst year to graduate since 1943, and by the next year they had the lottery, so in '68 you still had to go unless there was something wrong with you.

When you were in Vietnam, did you travel along the rice paddies on the ground?
I didn't beat the bush everyday, no. Most of the time I got to come back at night. I wasn't in the rice paddies. I was in the jungle area.

Did you ever consider not going in?

No. My father served in World War II, so I felt obligated to go as well. I never considered not going, and if my son had to go, I would want him to go too.

Would you like to describe the items you brought?

This is just a patch of the first Cavalry. This is a letter I sent home to my parents; this is a map of Vietnam that they had given us. This was the general orders for me to get the Bronze Star. This was when I left the service; what awards I had gotten. Honorable, discharge etc. This is just some of the places and various orders I had gotten to go different places. When I got home I also got an award that nobody else that you interview I guarantee will get. The United Daughters of Confederacy gave me an award for having been in the service. You had to have a direct descendent who fought in the Civil War on the southern side to get that award. I doubt anybody else you interview will have a direct descendent on the southern side. That was this medal. That organization is dying out. It's a nice thing, mainly elderly ladies now. That's the honorable discharge and Bronze Star. And then these are just pictures. That was a picture of me while I was in the army and with my cousins before I went overseas.

Metals earned in service.

What was it like to come home?

Obviously, you were extremely happy; you had made it and you got out. They didn't want Vietnam veterans hanging around the bases, so if your time was anywhere close to up, they would let you out. There was a lot of prejudice against Vietnam veterans. You got to the point where you just didn't tell people; you didn't talk about it.

Did people think you were wrong to go there?

Yes. There were a lot of protests against the war, and at that time the majority of the country had decided the war probably wasn't a good war for Americans to be in. It was a time of civil unrest, probably like no other in our history or at least in many years.

While you were in Vietnam, were you aware of the secret wars in Laos?

Mostly in Cambodia since I was stationed near Cambodia. Technically, Americans could not go into any other country, but the North Vietnamese and Viet Cong could attack you. Then when you got your strength, you could not go into those countries to pursue them, so it was like a safe haven for them, the fact that they could shoot rockets into where you were and you really couldn't go after them. I guess you could fire back, but you couldn't really pursue them across the border until 1970.

What year did you come home?

June 24, 1970.

And at the time were you living in Wisconsin?

No. I was living in North Carolina. I had never been in Wisconsin until I came up here to start the church, which was in '87.

What was one of the first things you did when you came home?
I went back to the Presbyterian School of Christian Education and then took some time off and went to Carolina Beach.

So you basically just continued your life?
Well, started it over.

Has ministry helped you get through it all?
I think so. When people know you're a Vietnam veteran, you tend to meet a lot of other veterans. I have several in my church. We're the fortunate ones who got back.

Is there anything else that you would like to talk about?
I would encourage you to go the Vietnam War Memorial if you're ever in Washington, D.C. I've been there once, but I was with a lot of people. I really didn't stay but a few minutes.

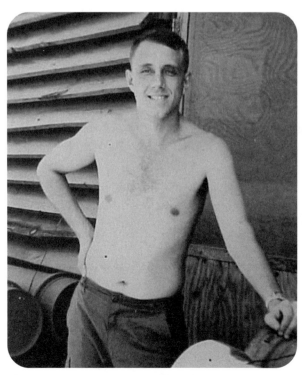

Sid Bouldin states that his Vietnam experience led him to became a minister. He is currently a pastor in the Schofield, Wisconsin, area.

Interviewed and transcribed by Pader Moua and Matt Boland

Outside Divarty Chaplain's Office

John Coppens

Coppens was an officer before he went to Vietnam and served on a General's staff as S4 which is responsible for reporting on combat readiness. He served over there during 1968 -69. The General and his staff were stationed near Saigon.

Could you tell us a little bit about if you were drafted or enlisted?

No, I was in the Army at the time that I was sent to Vietnam, so I was already an officer at the time I went. When I came back, I was a major.

What were the base camps like?

The first base camp I was at was in Phu Bai, which is up in the mountains. I got to Vietnam; they said it was going to be warm-- hot, most of the time in the jungle. It wasn't warm and hot. It was cold, wet, and lots of rain. Hurricane Agnes, I think, was about at that time. We slept on the side of this mountain, and you could see the paperwork-- people that were working on papers down the river and things like that. It was cold, and nobody was prepared for it.

Could you describe what an average day was like during the war?

I was on a general's staff most of the time, so I got up at five in the morning, seven days a week, and prepared for the general's briefing which was at 8:00 in the morning. I had to gather all the information together from everybody-- all the maintenance and service people. I told the general in the morning his S4 or G4 briefing, which was what his combat readiness was-- which means whether or not all of his tanks, guns, helicopters, and all that were ready and how many were not ready; if they had enough ammunition, if they had enough food, and all of those types of things to sustain combat operations. Then after that briefing, which was usually about 9:00, if I didn't have anything that the general said to take care of right away, then I would normally go out to some of the locations that we had. We were near Saigon most of the time that I was there. We had different locations that were supporting the guys in the field, and I would go to those locations to make sure that things were ready such as maintenance and that type of thing. I would also go out to the field once in awhile to make sure the guys were getting along. I would talk to the headquarters of the companies or battalions, and they would tell me what it was like. Regularly, I would go out and talk to the troops to make sure that they were getting food, that they had enough ammunition, and that their weapons were working right. I would usually get back about five in the after noon. Usually at six the general would have another briefing, which was a little bit shorter. We'd tell him what type of operations he had during the day; different people would tell him different things. The S3, which are the combat guys, would tell him whether or not we had any contact during the day, how many prisoners we had, had any killed, or that type of things. Then I would tell him whether or not we had any other helicopters that got shot down, whether we had some tanks that had problems, and that type of thing. If the general said something, which he usually did, to make sure that things were ready for the night because nighttime was the main time that combat was happening in Vietnam, especially our part; we would go back and make sure that things got fixed or were ready for nighttime operations. I'd get done about ten.

Could you describe the Tet Offensive?

I wasn't there for the Tet Offensive. The Tet Offensive happened before I got there. If you were around at that time, you would have seen the President go to Fort Bragg, North Carolina. The President said that one of the things he was going to do to straighten out the war after the Tet Offensive, was send part of the 82nd Airborne to Vietnam. That's what I was in, the 3rd Brigade of the 82nd Airborne. They sent that group, which is usually considered in the lead part of the Army, to Vietnam to shore up the defenses. Initially, up north by Hut Phu Bai the 101st had some difficulty. They won't appreciate this, but they had some difficulty protecting Saigon during the Tet Offensive. They sent us down to secure the area around the airbase there and around Saigon. That was our main mission for most of the time I was there-- security of the site.

Could you explain any experience you had with body counts or kill ratios? Do you know anything about that?

We got involved a lot in body counts for some reason or other. A lot of people, especially American newspaper people, wanted to know how many people we were killing and how many people we were losing; so the body count thing got very strange. I'm sure everybody's heard stories about how various people counted bodies. One night, just kind of a funny aside, we had a new weapon that we fired one evening when they had some ruckus, and we had a body count of something like 250. Fortunately, they weren't 250 Vietnamese…they were 250 Vietnam ducks. But that was in the general's briefing that I was talking about at eight in the morning. We had 250 body counts; unfortunately, it was ducks. There was a lot of pressure in body counts, and that was why that particular story came up. A lot of people don't think that people got questioned or reprimanded or got in trouble for making bad body counts, but I know of at least two or three officers that did. Various times they reported, as an example, like body count two, and the way they counted that was two pieces of a body. I know those types of things seemed like they were common. The paper wrote them up a lot, and it seemed like the Army was doing it; but that wasn't true. Some individuals

were, but when it got to a certain level they did pay attention to that.

What was the hardest part of being in the war?

Hardest part of being in the war was leaving. I had two little daughters. One was two and one was three. I left my family in Green Bay. Getting on the airplane was the hardest thing to do. A lot of people went back to Hawaii or came back to the states. You got five days R&R, and you'd go almost anyplace. You could come back to the states, except that took a lot of time; so most people went to Hawaii or Australia. I decided that I would not see my wife. I couldn't see myself getting back on the plane. I said, "Nope, once was enough."

Did you make any lasting friendships during the war?

Yes, I did. I made friends with some really nice people. I met some nice people. It was a really strange place. People that haven't been in war wouldn't understand it. I used to be an artist of some sort. I used to pay lots of attention to sunsets, pretty flowers, beautiful buildings, and things like that. I cannot remember one sunset, flower, and beautiful thing about Vietnam. I cannot. Didn't recognize it then, and I don't recognize it now. It's a strange thing. Friendships were different. Friends are friends, everybody's got 100s of friends. You guys are in school, you got 30 people in class, you think that…but, real friends, it's really difficult to find real friends in great quantities. I think if you can find one or two a year, you are doing pretty good.

Is there any one particular experience that stands out in your mind?

In Vietnam? No, it really kind of runs together. There were some funny things that stick out in my mind. When I first got to Vietnam, was the first time I got shot at. We were sitting at an outside theater watching a movie, and somebody shot up the movie screen. I started running towards the bunker that we had off to the side. I was new and had only been there a couple of days. The guy that was next to me was crawling faster than I was running. I said, "Boy, I've got to do something else here," because I was trying to run to this bunker, and this guy was crawling faster than I was running. That was my first experience of being shot at, so that kind of stood out in my mind. Some of the things that you see in movies were true, like when you took the flight over to Vietnam and the plane. On the flight, there was a guy with a guitar playing music. On the way home, there was another guy on the plane with a guitar playing music on it. Some of the songs that were popular at the time were "I'm Not Going to Vietnam," "I'm Staying Away from Vietnam," or something like that. Some of those things come back when you watch movies. I don't know what's stuck out in my mind. I saw a whole bunch of people without hardly any cars in Saigon, but Saigon was supposed to be the Paris of Southeast Asia. I didn't find Saigon to be very pretty. It was interesting and had lots of people, very few cars. You'd drive by a churchyard and see a graveyard. It looked like they had swastikas on all their graves, but they weren't swastikas. They were the other way around; they were crosses actually. The next Tet was kind of interesting because these Vietnamese had big meals and helped us celebrate Tet, which was kind of unusual. I liked helicopters before I got to Vietnam. After I got there for awhile, I stopped liking helicopters. One thing that stuck out in my mind when I got back, I never saw anything that I thought was pretty. I'm sure there was, but I didn't see it.

Can you describe what it was like to be on a helicopter?

When I first got there, I liked airplanes. I had flown on a lot of airplanes and in helicopters before I went to Vietnam. It was just that you flew in them so often, and they just seemed to get noisier and noisier the more you rode on them. It just was some of the things that happened to me on helicopters weren't very good. I had to accompany a body one time that had drowned and been in a river for probably a week or two. That was terrible, and everybody got shot at. I never got shot while I was in Vietnam.

Is there a message you have for the young people today about the war?

Not that war. I really feel that wars are real attacks on men's souls. If you don't go, you feel like you should have. If you do go and you see someone get wounded, you think that you're really lucky that you didn't get wounded, but you feel guilty. If you get wounded and see someone get killed, you feel like you're guilty because you didn't get killed. The only people that come out not feeling guilty about something, are the guys that get killed. Wars are terrible. They are just really terrible. I think that I felt when I went that I should go. I think if I hadn't gone, I would have felt guilty about not going. I know a lot of people didn't go and say they don't feel bad about it. I cannot believe that that's true. Ladies, you have a little bit better choice because most people don't expect you to go to war, so you don't have that inside of you thinking that you should. If you want to, you can. If you don't want to, you don't necessarily have to feel guilty about it. With this thing that's going on, a lot of people if it came down to people having to go to war, would probably try to avoid it. If they weren't successful at avoiding it, they'd probably be mad. If they were successful at avoiding it, I still think that they'd feel guilty. I think that stays with you.

Do you have any opinions on the anti-war movement that went on in the U.S.?

Yes. I didn't like it at all. I felt like I should go. My family would have liked it if I didn't have to go. My wife went to religious service one day with my two little daughters, and they talked about the bad guys that were in Vietnam killing all these poor little kids. I didn't like that, and my wife didn't like that. I didn't like the newspapers. I didn't like the reporters that were in Vietnam. If you were in Vietnam, and you told them something, they would say, "Well can't you change that? Can't you make it a little bit more graphic or little bit more reality?" No, you tell them the truth. If you saw something happen, they tried to blow it out of shape. When they reported stuff in Vietnam, they a lot of times left it open. When my wife was watching TV, or my daughters were watching TV, they would say that a bunch of people got killed in this particular location, which happened to be where I was, without giving details about it, and there was nothing really going on. A lot of people felt that if they didn't go that they had to say that there should be peace so that nobody would go. I think that caused a lot of problems with U.S., and I think it is causing a problem right now. I think a lot of the rhetoric from the President right now is very strong, emotional, and I think he's doing that because he doesn't want what happened now to be like what happened in Vietnam where the President wasn't really emotional, especially the first two, Eisenhower and Kennedy. Everybody thinks that the war started with Kennedy, but it didn't. It started with Eisenhower, but neither one of those were really strong behind the war. Before the American people got talked into the war, they got talked out of the war.

Was there a lot of emotional or physical stress you had to endure?

The emotional stress was getting on the airplane. I did volunteer. Because I was in the service at the time, I could have gotten out before I went to Vietnam, but I knew I was going to go to Vietnam, and so I said I would have felt really guilty not going. If you went right now, you feel bad for your Mom and Dad and all those people that love you. They feel guilty about going, and then they feel guilty about not going. War is just really bad. Not that they shouldn't have wars, 'cause sometimes they're necessary, but they're terrible.

What kind of reception did you get when you came back to the United States?

Everybody talked about that. A lot of people were told at the time I came back, which was 1969, "When

> *"YOU SEE DEAD BODIES OR DEAD PEOPLE OR HAVE TO TELL FAMILIES THAT SOMEBODY'S DEAD OR SOMETHING, YOU FEEL BAD ABOUT THAT..."*

you get back to the states, don't wear your uniform," and some of those things. I said, "Like hell. I'm going to wear my uniform. If I've got to wear it over there, I'm going to wear it over here." There was a lot of that stress. I didn't get hurt physically. I didn't notice too much. I never got shot. I got one leg a little bit messed up because of the war. I worked a lot of hours. I got up about 5:00 in the morning and got done probably at 10:00 at night. Then at 10:00 at night, I didn't do anything else. Once in a while you would read or something like that. The guys that were in the field had it much worse. I know a friend of mine while I was there had malaria and was in a forest, but they couldn't get him to the helicopter. He had malaria for almost two weeks but couldn't get him out because of the Vietnamese and a bunch of other things. He was in there for about two weeks without any medication. Those guys had it much harder and that kind of stuff. People were shot and a lot of physical stress for the average person over there. GIs that didn't get wounded would go out at night on an ambush, sit out at night and set up some type of an ambush. Generally, they didn't get hit or didn't get involved in action. If they didn't get shot, they would get back to their base camp and spend a couple of days of rest. The system, only being there a year and having the base camps where you pull back to rest for a couple of days, physically it wasn't that bad.

Did you have any difficulties dealing with memories when you came back?

No, none. I'm not sure why that is except for the fact that when I got back I said, "Geez." I did not recognize anything as being pretty or beautiful. I did what I thought I should do when I was there. I went because I thought I should. I think inside, I just didn't feel bad. I saw some killed and some things like that, but I'd seen that before Vietnam as I was in bomb disposal. I had seen quite a few people killed, what have you, back here in the states. You see dead bodies or dead people or have to tell families that somebody's dead or something, you feel bad about that and you remember that and you have visions of that, but that wasn't anything that wasn't back here also. I didn't have any bad memories.

Do you have any other stories or experiences you would like to share with us?

No, the questions on your questionnaire were about what was my job after I came back. I just said what I did after I retired. When I came back, I was, because I was a Vietnam veteran, because I was an officer, I got involved with a lot of burial details, people coming back from Vietnam. I got involved with notification of next of kin, and that was absolutely terrible also. You drive up to somebody's house, and they knew exactly why you were there, that someone was killed. Then you have to go in and explain that to them. That was very difficult. Some people did that for a long time.

> *"YOU DRIVE UP TO SOME-BODY'S HOUSE, AND THEY KNEW EXACTLY WHY YOU WERE THERE, THAT SOME-ONE WAS KILLED. THEN YOU HAVE TO GO IN AND EXPLAIN THAT TO THEM. THAT WAS VERY DIFFICULT."*

I did that for about a year. I was in Alabama when I came back. That was kind of a long period, except that being in Alabama, there weren't as many, I don't think, to notify; but that was really difficult to cope with the family. Some people got angry and some people felt like they should thank you for coming and talking to them. It is not something that's appealing.

John Coppens stayed in the Army until 1983 when he retired and became a restaurant owner/manager.

Interviewed by Steph Orzel and Jenny Reuter

David Gajewski

Gajewski volunteered for the Army in 1963 and trained in radio signal interception. He worked for the Army Security Division in Saigon as a Morse Code Intercept Officer.

Were you drafted or did you volunteer for the Vietnam War?
I volunteered.

What was your attitude going into the war?
I volunteered before the war was really going heavily. I was in from 1963 to 1967, so when I went in we didn't know much about Vietnam. I was in the Army Security Agency. That is what I signed up for. I had to take four years instead of the normal three that a guy would take if he signed up at that time. The reason I did that, I guess, is that I wasn't too keen on doing any fighting, but I thought I should go in. I ended up at Fort Devens, Massachusetts, after basic training in Fort Leonard wood, and I learned Morse code. I was a Morse code intercept operator, and I had a top-secret crypto clearance. They had to check us all out when we were in the security agency. They came back and asked a lot of questions and did some background work on us. Anyway, when I was done at Fort Devens, I went to Panama for two and a half years. When I was in Panama, I was hearing a lot about Vietnam and what was going on, so I volunteered to go to there. Right away they took me — they figured, "Well if he's dumb enough to volunteer, we'll send him over," and so they did.

I guess on the way flying over, I remember this pretty well, things were pretty quiet on the plane. Nobody knew what to expect. When we were coming in to land in Tan Son Nhut Airbase near Saigon (now that's called Ho Chi Minh City), it was sort of like the Fourth of July. You saw flares going up and fire fights going on. They turned the lights off on the plane, and we landed. I knew I was in a pretty good unit because when I got there, most of the guys were in what they call replacement outfits, where you went and waited. They just took infantry to different outfits. When guys got killed or went home, they had to replace them. When I got there, a Jeep came and was looking for me, so I knew that I was in pretty good shape. We were stationed right in Tan Son Nhut. They picked me up and took me over there. A funny thing was that the first guy I met when I went in the mess hall, which was where you eat, was a guy I knew at Fort Devens. He was also one of my best friends from Brooklyn. I went home with him — Stan Joyia. It was just unbelievable that I should meet him right there because he went to Turkey, I think, and I went to Panama. Then it ended up that he was the first guy I met from our outfit in Vietnam.

What were the base camps like?

I was in Tan Son Nhut, which was the main airfield for Vietnam. After about four or five months there, they sent us up to Ben Hoc and Long Binh. Those were base camps where the infantry would come in after they fought for a little rest and recuperation. We went out to fields where they had antennas. Of course that's what we had to do; we had to copy code. That's where we copied our code from little trailer houses that were air-conditioned. We copied the Viet Cong. They'd send messages back and forth; we'd listen, and we'd try to pick up what they were sending – whatever was going on.

Could you describe what an average day was like when you were in the war?

There was no such thing as an average day. When I was in Tan Son Nhut, we didn't pull any guard duty or anything. We were strictly security. As a matter of fact, they didn't call us security over there; they called us the 175th radio research group, so they really didn't know what we were doing. Nobody was supposed to know what we were up to. Our camp was right next to the airfield. Tan Son Nhut was the busiest airport in the world at the time. You heard helicopters taking off, jet planes taking off, planes bringing troops in and out, bombers going out, and jet fighters going out. You had to get used to it in order to sleep. Between the airfields and us, there was a big corrugated tent (probably about ten feet high and solid) you couldn't see through. The jet fighters and bombers were each in their own separate stalls. They sandbagged them, so if one blew up, the other ones didn't blow up. That was kind of the way it went. Well, this one night in December, about one o'clock in the morning, all hell was breaking loose. We didn't think too much about it because we weren't involved. It was the air force who was doing perimeter guard, and they had mine fields.

Gajewski riding an elephant while on R&R.

They had barbed wire fences, and the Viet Cong were coming in. They got through, and they killed I think four of the air police and two of the dogs. There were five or six of them that got in, and they brought satchel charges in. They'd go up to an airplane, sit under it, and blow her up with them going with it. When this was all happening, we were right next door. At that time we weren't carrying weapons, and they said, "Go get your weapons." We said, "What do you mean – we don't have weapons." We should've had the weapons. So we were down in the trenches with our helmets on, and this stuff was raining down on us every time they'd blow up a plane. So after that, we started carrying weapons. Anyway it got pretty hairy there for a while, but the air force boys handled it. We didn't have to worry about it, so that was probably the most exciting deal that happened to me. I never had to shoot anybody. I had to copy code and sit in an air-conditioned building when I was working.

What was the hardest part of being in the war?

I guess the hardest part was just being there; the country stunk. It was hard being away from home. We were in somebody else's back yard, and they didn't want us there.

Did you make any lasting friendships during the war?

Not really. No, I mean we were pretty good friends when we were there because we were all in the same boat. You know, I did have a guy come and see me from Chicago – he stopped over to see me.

Did you have any opinions regarding the anti-war movement back in the states while you were in Vietnam?

Oh you bet I did! I didn't like that at all. I thought they ran the war all wrong. They "handcuffed" us; they wouldn't let us fight it the way we should've been able to fight it – like they're letting them fight it now [war in Afghanistan]. You know, you bomb where you have to. We couldn't go over the 17th parallel, we couldn't go in Cambodia, we couldn't do this, we couldn't bomb on certain days, and blah blah blah. That was all coming from Washington, and they were all wet. Then there was Jane Fonda, who went to Hanoi and degraded our pilots in
the Hanoi Hilton who were prisoners of war. You know she wanted them to apologize to the Viet Cong, who were murderers murdering their own people – terrible, terrible, terrible. They didn't let us fight the war right. Otherwise we would've won that war.

How was the relationship between whites and blacks in your unit?

Very good. We had no trouble. As a matter of fact, one of my best friends was a black guy, and one of the guys I disliked most was probably a black guy. They were just like us. I mean we didn't have any racial problems – in our outfit anyway. But I wasn't in infantry. Infantry might have been a little different; there were a lot of drugs going on. I'm going to tell you something about drugs in Vietnam now. I knew everybody in our outfit. Out of the couple hundred guys, I only knew one guy who smoked pot. That was it – one guy! As a matter of fact, he was from Milwaukee. That's all I knew.

> *"ALL OF A SUDDEN THE LIGHTS FLASHED AND THE SIRENS WENT, AND THAT MEANT THAT THEY WERE GOING TO HIT US."*

I'll tell you a little story about when we were in Ben Hoa. When we were there, we played a lot of cards, drank some beer, and this and that. We were playing poker one night, and there was a nice big cash pot – over a hundred dollars I'm sure. All of a sudden the lights flashed and the sirens went, and that meant that they were going to hit us. We all had to get our flack jackets on, get our helmets, and guns, and go out to the perimeter. I said to the guys, there was five or six of us at the table, "I'll take the pot." I raked the money in and put it in my pocket. When we got out to the perimeter and we were all in the ditch; there's shooting going on. Down the line come the guys saying, "Where's Gajewski, where's Gajewski?" The first sergeant looked down, "Why the hell are you looking for Gajewski?" They told him, "He's got the pot." So they didn't want me to get shot because the pot would go. They were worried about the pot – not Gajewski!

Is there one particular experience that stands out in your mind about the war?

Well, I don't know. I suppose the way it ended was terrible. We walked away from those people. A lot of the people who fought with us suffered and died after we left. We left them sitting, and that's not good – that's terrible! We did a terrible, terrible thing by walking out on them.

Do you think the U.S. could've won the war? Why or why not?
You bet we could've won the war! We could've won the war if they would've let us fight it the way the generals wanted to fight. It was a political deal all the way down the line. L.B.J. and Kissinger – they were all, I don't know how to say it, terrible. I don't know what to say about it, but the generals and the army and the air force should've run it.

What kind of reception did you get when you came back to the United States?
I'll tell you this deal. When I got out, I went to college at Stevens Point. I only stayed one semester because I couldn't handle it. There was a lot of protesting going on about the war. The professors were teaching protesting; they were very liberal professors trying to influence young kids coming out of high school. I was at that time 22 or 23 – an older guy. I couldn't take it. Every day they were preaching to these kids, "Now that you're in college, you're on your own. You don't have any responsibility." They told them that the war was all wrong. I guess the war was all wrong – the way we handled it. It was wrong, but to go run and hide and not serve was worse because you had guys over there fighting. If you didn't go there to relieve them, then who was going to? This was not a deal where you were going to save the world, but somebody had to relieve the boys that were there. Somebody had to take their places.

What did serving your country mean to you during active duty, and what does it mean to you now as a veteran?
I guess I was kind of patriotic. I thought I was going to do something and I should. As a matter of fact, I've got a son who's in the service, and I think he's a little patriotic too.

Is there a message you have for young people today about the war?
Well, that war's long gone. That's a war you don't want to forget, but you don't want to fight that war over. That war could've been won but wasn't, and that's water over the dam. I think young people should have to serve. I think going in the service is not a bad deal – two years, if they drafted you. You would only have to serve two years, and you wouldn't have to fight if you were a conscientious objector. They'd make you a cook or whatever. You wouldn't have to fight, of course. One of the favorite sayings of one of the generals was, "You don't have to carry a gun, shoot anybody, or fight. Just come along, and once the shooting starts, maybe you'll change your mind. You never know how you're going to react. Luckily I never had to kill anybody because I didn't want to. That's why I joined what I joined. I don't know how I would've handled it.

Was there a lot of emotional or physical stress you had to endure during the war?
There was some stress, but everybody had it because the stress was the unexpected. You never knew. You could be walking down the streets of Saigon, and there were so many times that guys would leave bicycles with packages on them that were bombs. They would blow up and maybe kill five or six guys. Then

guys were shaking in their boots for about two days. After that they kind of forgot it and started going about their business again. Then another one would come along and put a bomb under somebody's chair or something. There was a lot of that going on. Of course there was a lot of stuff going on in Panama too, when I was there – "Yankee go home," and a lot of stuff like that.

Do you have anything else to say about the war or any other stories?
I'm not disappointed or anything. I don't feel bad that I went into the service. I think that it was a very good experience for a young man like me to go into the service and find out what it was all about. After being in the service, you remember 99% of the good times and 1% of the bad times. But really, 99% of the times were bad, and only 1% was good because you had to put up with a lot of bull. That, I think, builds a little character because you had a little responsibility, and you had to have a little discipline.

David Gajewski works as a plumber for Gajewski Plumbing. David is married to Trudi Gajewski, and they have three children.

Interviewed by Michael Wodalski and Drew Krueger

Gary Hall

Hall was a recovery specialist in the Army, trained to recover vehicles. He served in an artillery outfit. Hall was stationed just south of the DMZ from July 1970 to July 1971.

What station were you in? Were you in the army, on ground, or in the marines?
I was in the army on the DMZ most of the time. We moved ten times while I was over there.

In Vietnam?
Yes.

What was your station?
I started out at Dong Ha. It's four miles south of the DMZ.

What years were you there?
I got there the third of July, 1970, got home Fourth of July, 1971.

What was your unit and department?
I was a recovery specialist. Over there I was a wrecker operator, but the army taught me how to drive any-

thing they had at that time. If it broke down, I had to get it back to the shop, whether it be on the back of a semi or on the wrecker or if it was a track vehicle, like a tank. We had a track recovery vehicle, which was a wrecker with tracks on it so you could go through the woods with it. I was with an artillery outfit, which were eight-inch guns. The bullets weighed 150 pounds, and they'd fire depending on if it was an eight-inch or a 175mm it'd go 20-30 miles.

So what was the hardest part of being in the war?
Being scared, real scared.

Back door of an 8 Inch Gun
Courtesy of Members of 2nd 94th Artillery

Do you have any specific stories?

I should've died fourteen times. We had to change the barrel on one of these guns, and my outfit had one wrecker. The shop had to take the barrel to the gun on a semi and supply the other wrecker, and I was the first one that went out to the firebase. I drove over the road just ahead of the semi that hit a mine. I was only a minute or two ahead of the semi. I drove over the mine, and the guy in the semi hit it. I had to tow his truck back. He died.

How old were you when you went there?

I was twenty when I got over there. I turned twenty-one in 'Nam.

Was there a lot of emotional or physical stress that you had to endure?

Yes, being scared. I just tried to stay alert. They said 70% of my outfit was on drugs, but I didn't want to be messed up if something happened. I was four miles from North Vietnam. If something happened, I wanted to be alert, so I could take care of myself.

175 mm Howitzer during a fire mission

Was it harder being on the border?

No more than any place else. During the day we had civilians working in camps and maids washing our clothes. We called them hooch maids. Local barbers, and in the ten times we moved, four times the barbers were caught coming back at night through the barbed wire to blow us up.

So you couldn't really tell who the civilians and who the V.C. was?

No. During the day they'd be your friends; at night they'd be coming to cut your throat.

Can you describe what an average day was like during the war?

Hot and/or rainy. When it got down to about 85 degrees, we had to put our jackets on. It was 110-115 degrees where we were constantly.

How did you get past the heat and everything and still be able to fight and work?

You just did it. It was a part of life.

Was there really poor nutrition? Did they have enough food supplies?

They had enough supplies, but we always ate C-rations. I remember the date on one. It was packed in December, 1944, and I was eating it in '71.

How was the relationship between the whites and the blacks in your unit?

In my unit it was pretty good. I put some movies on video. It shows the guys wrestling, but they're just playing. Just trying to get through the day. We were like brothers.

Did you make any lasting friendships during the war?
Definitely. I lost a lot of them too. The ones that are still alive, we got to be better than brothers.

Was it hard to keep in touch with them? Did you see them often while you were fighting?
Yes. We were side by side continually.

"THE THING THAT REALLY BOTHERED ME MOST IS I FLEW INTO MOSINEE AND A HIGH SCHOOL FRIEND OF MINE, THE FIRST THING HE SAID WAS, HOW MANY DID YOU KILL?"

Did it help to have friends that you could come back to at night or was it distracting worrying about them?
I don't know that I ever thought of that. I know I didn't like it while I was out, but it wasn't like coming home to my girlfriend or my wife. No it wasn't. It was just a real good friendship.

Do you think the U.S. could've won the war?
I know we could've. It was the politicians that lost it.

So you think if there were less riots and people were more supportive of the war that we could've won?
Yes. The support that we weren't getting was helping the politicians drag it on, but the tire and oil companies were making money and lobbying Congress to keep it going. They didn't want to pull out because they'd lose money.

What kind of reception did you get when we came back home?
I was lucky enough to hear what went on before I went over, so when I came back they gave us a new uniform. They called them "greens"! When I got on the airplane, that came off; so when I landed in Chicago I just had a brown shirt on and some dark pants. If you were in uniform, you were a soldier and people got spit on. Blood was thrown at them, paint was thrown at them, but I was lucky enough to hear this before I came back. I knew I had to disguise myself. The thing that really bothered me most is I flew into Mosinee and a high school friend of mine, the first thing he said was, "How many did you kill?" Not "Hi, how are you?" but "How many did you kill?" He could have hit me in the nose with a two by four, and it wouldn't have hurt any worse.

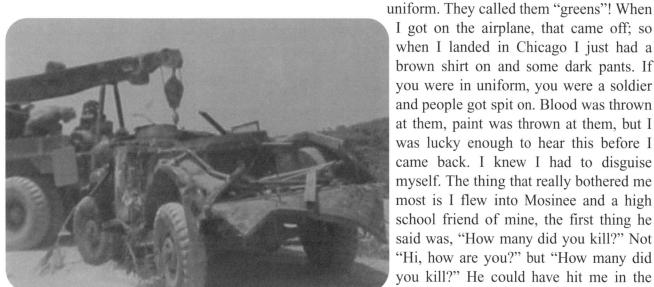
3/4 ton pickup that ran off a cliff

Could you describe some of the traps they used? Did you come upon any?
I didn't see any personally because I was on the road most of the time, but I've got pictures of them. One

8 Inch Gun at Dong Ha
Courtesy of the members of 2nd 94th Artillery

of them was one of our rounds that apparently didn't go off or they got ahold of it some how. They dug a hole in the trail, put it in, put a different trigger mechanism on it, and if somebody would've tripped that trigger, it wasn't just the one that tripped it, the whole squad would've gone. When we fired them, there's a 300-meter kill radius. 300 meters from where this went off, everything's going to die. If you're within 600 meters, you're going to get hit with something. So they were big booby traps.

Do you know if the U.S. had anything like that?
We'd tie lines across the trails to set off flares, and we'd have claymore mines that they'd set up to go off when they tripped them. We didn't use them that much other than to save ourselves. It was more of a defense mechanism.

Who do you think had a more efficient way of fighting, the V.C. or U.S.?
We had a more efficient way, but they were so ingenious. Our mortars were steel tubes with sights on them, and you could pinpoint where they're supposed to go. They were using hollowed out bamboo shoots, and they'd just stick them between their legs and sit and drop. It's really ingenious what they used.

What did serving your country mean to you during active duty and now as a veteran?
Well, if it wasn't for the military and the jobs we had to do, we wouldn't have the rights and privileges that we have today.

Did a lot of people that weren't for the war still go to the war?
Yes. We had this guy in our outfit, he was a hippy against the war, but he wasn't willing to go to Canada to get out of it. He protested every day, told off his boss every day, but he was there doing the job that he was supposed to be doing. Yes, there was some people there that didn't do their job, and that's why they had to put them in jail.

When you were fighting and you saw something happen to your friends, how did that affect you? Did you ever experience something like that?
Yes. When I had to get this equipment back, on the way out there I saw what I thought was a stump burning, a tree stump. And it was right along side the road and everything was cleared away from the road and I couldn't figure out why that big tree stump was right there on the side of the road. When we passed it, I looked back, and it was the top half of a guy I knew.

Filipino floor show on Hill 52

What happened to the people that did take drugs?

One of them is in jail for 40 years for bank robbery. Most of the people that were on drugs in my outfit were on marijuana. I had a local guy come up and offer to sell me a kilo of heroin. I told him he better leave before he dies.

Memorial at the Wall on Nov. 1984

Is there any one experience that stands out in your mind about the war?

There's more than one. I still have dreams about it. Some of them are really silly dreams, but some are nightmares. I still think about Eddy Reed. I still think of the sniper that shot at me while I was going down the road. The guy that hit the mine that I drove over. The RPG that was meant for me that blew the guy's left hand off. The guy on his left got his throat cut on the right side, and I took the guy with his neck cut to the first aid vehicle. I was going back to get the guy with his hand, and he was just staring at his hand and it looked like a bunch of wires just hanging out of his arm, and he was screaming at the top of his lungs. We went out with no protection and these guys were a tank outfit and their boss said, "You ain't going out there without us." So he turned his group around. He was coming back from where we had to go.

How is everyday life like now? Do you think about it everyday?

At least once everyday. Sometimes it's two or three hours. I get done with this interview; it'll be about three days before I come back to straight. I've been talking to school kids for ten years, and every time I do it I have two or three bad days before I straighten out.

Do you think anyone that was there really recovers from it completely?

I don't think so. I work with people that forgot what day they came back. They know what month, but they're trying real hard to forget about it. It's a whole year out of your life, and it's a bad year. You remember parts of it.

Like what you said about Asians, what other viewpoints have you changed because of what you went through?

I can't stand kids. Three kids, and the oldest couldn't have been more than fourteen, threw a grenade at me. I lost the hearing in my right ear, and it blew me out of the truck on the other side, and I took the door with me. Broke three ribs on the left side. I don't know how I raised my two kids because I don't care for little ones. With my four grandchildren, I have a hard time. They come in, say hi, give me a kiss, ten minutes later I have to leave. I just don't care for little ones.

Do you have any regrets of anything you did there or before you went to the war?
No. I was going to get married before I went, and I decided not to because I didn't want to make anyone a widow at age eighteen. When I came back, I was not the same person, and I know that I told my wife before we get married, I said, "I don't know if I love you. I've been killing people for a year." But I've been married for thirty years.

Was it easy to keep in touch with your family?
No. I moved ten times. The address changed ten times. My girlfriend wrote pretty much every day, but there were times when it took two or three weeks to get the letters. And then you'd get a handful at a time. I'm not a writer. I was lucky to send one letter a week.

"THREE KIDS, AND THE OLDEST COULD-N'T HAVE BEEN MORE THAN FOURTEEN, THREW A GRENADE AT ME. I LOST THE HEARING IN MY RIGHT EAR AND I T BLEW ME OUT OF THE TRUCK ON THE OTHER SIDE, AND I TOOK THE DOOR WITH ME."

What did you talk about in the letters? Did you say what was going on, or did you avoid it?
I lied a lot about what was going on. I tried to avoid it. You told them how much you were thinking about them, how lonely you are, wondering about people back home. They didn't know anyone over there so it's hard to talk about your friends. I made audiotapes. It took about three days to fill up a 60-minute tape. I asked all the drunks to say something so I could finish up the tape.

Did you ever hear of any soldiers fighting civilians?
We didn't know if they were civilians. They all wore the same clothes. They were the guerrillas. We didn't know if they were the civilians or not. They'd strap explosives to the kids and send them into a crowd of G.I.'s because they knew all the G.I.s would play with the kids. They got a group of G.I.s around, and they'd blow them up.

Is it true that a lot of soldiers didn't even know why they were fighting?
I didn't know why I was fighting. To me it was a big swamp. You got off the airplane and the smell of the place just made you sick. Death. They didn't have any plumbing so you'd just go to the bathroom any place. It stunk.

Was it kind of a culture shock when you came back to the U.S.?
Yes, the world changed completely in the year I was gone. Unit patch XXIV Corps Arty., National Defense, and Bronze Star
Before I went, I had blue jeans and black jeans. They called them H.I.S., the manufacturer, and Levis. When I came back there was tan, black, blue, green, the psychedelic colors were really in then. Things changed so much. That's when they started sales tax. The sign says $5 for a pair of pants. When I went to pay for them, they wanted $5.10. What the hell you talking about? The sign says $5, here's $5. And my wife had to drag me out of a couple of stores because I was fighting with them.

Does getting awards help?

No, when I came back, I was in Fort Benning. I only had a month left in the service when I got my Bronze Star. It was three months after I came back, and this started out being a court martial because, like I said I was a wrecker operator. I went out on some kind of mission to pick up a truck or something. When I came back the rest of the guys were on their way out with the track vehicle, and I was the only one trained to run that certain piece of equipment. The rest of the guys were mechanics. They could have run it, but it would have taken longer. I had just gotten inside the compound and these guys are going out. The boss was in the track and I got out and asked the driver, Gil Menzer, where were they were going. He says, "B battery is over run. We have to go get the guns." I said, "Wait for me." I ran over and grabbed my weapons, flack jacket, and helmet out of the truck because I never wore them. I jumped on the outside of this armored vehicle and we went out there and got our butts kicked. Before they started up, I got on, the boss said, "You can't leave your truck there." I say, "Why not?" He said, "What happens if the enemy gets it?" I said, "If the enemy gets that inside the fence, they'll have a hell of a lot more, they're going to want before they get that." He said, "Well you gotta stay with your truck." I said, "No, I'm the only one trained on this thing. I'm going." "I'll give you a court martial." I said, "If we come back you can." And that's

Hall repairing a wrecker

the last I heard about it until I got back to Fort Benning, Georgia. I was called up in front of the formation and given me a Bronze Star.

How did it feel to receive that?

I felt like an idiot. I'm in front of people who mostly haven't been to Vietnam, and they're giving me a medal for saving some iron. I just did my job. At the time, I thought, if those guys get killed out there doing my job, I wouldn't be able to live with myself. So I got on and did my job. The boss went out one trip. "Too hot for me." Then he made me the boss. So I'm sitting in the tank commander's chair inside this thing. I went out there four times. We literally got our butts kicked, but we didn't lose any people.

Because we were defeated, did you still feel a sense of accomplishment?

We were not defeated. The politicians told us to leave. If it was up to the people fighting there, we would have started down in the Mekong Delta with B52's and gone till we hit China. As long as we were there, let us do our job!

If something happened to your family when you were there would they let you go back?

Immediate family. Brothers, sisters, mother, father. Both my grandparents died the year I was over there. I spent a lot of time with my grandparents. I could have come back for my grandfather's funeral. They buried him three days before I got back. They would have let me come home for that one because they were pulling a lot of people out of Vietnam at that time. But then I would have had to go back and clear post and give back all my equipment they gave me for Vietnam. I'd have to go back and have somebody sign for it to say I turned it back in.

Do you have any stories or anything else you want to share?
Just the things I think about daily. The RPG's and getting sniped at. They shot at me as I was going down the road. A round came through the windshield, caught me just above the brim of the helmet. For some reason I had my helmet on that day. The helmet weighs thirteen pounds, and driving down the road, that'll just pound your head into your shoulders, so I always had it on the seat. And I got hit. It snapped my head back, and it caught the guy that was standing in the back of the truck. He had a machine gun on the roof. Caught him just below the knee. We were driving back to Dong Ha, and there was a kid with a water buffalo plowing the field, and I heard him shoot and it scared the hell out of me. I said, "What are you shooting at?" "Oh, I never shot, a water buffalo before." I glanced over there at the water buffalo. You could see the bullets bouncing in the water near the boy and his buffalo; he hit the buffalo in the shoulder.

Gary Hall is now a Mail Processing Equipment Mechanic with the U.S. Postal Service at Cedar Creek. He has been a mechanic most of his civilian life.

Interviewed by Erin Lukensmeyer and Morgan Klarick

John Krukowski

A career serviceman, Krukowski served in 566th Transportation stationed in Cam Ranh Bay delivering materials to all parts of Vietnam. He arrived in Vietnam in January 1966.

How did you become involved in the Vietnam War? Were you drafted or enlisted?

I enlisted in the service in 1962. For three years I was in Germany, and I got elected to go to Vietnam, just like all the rest of them did. I went during January of '66 and came back in January of '68. Actually, I spent twenty years in the service; I'm retired from there.

About how old were you?

I was twenty-four. I was married and had a child already. Of course, as soon as I came back, I had another one. I didn't enjoy it there too much. While I was there, I was on a road in a transportation company delivering bombs for the Air Force, which was quite a chore. We worked fourteen to sixteen hour days, and it seemed like it was just basically around the clock. I also did repair on the trucks that we used to haul the bombs. It was the type of thing that I basically went there as a mechanic but ended up doing everything just like everyone else did. Everybody pitched in to do whatever had to be done. Then after doing that for three or four months, I got elected to be on an inspection team because of the good service record I had. Then we had a twenty-one-man inspection team that went around to all areas in Vietnam. We made sure that everybody had what he needed to fight the war. Basically, I did that for about eight months.

What were the base camps like?

All tents, there was no solid buildings. It depends what part of Vietnam you were in. My home station in Cam Ranh Bay was probably the safest part of it. We were quite secure because it was a peninsula and we could protect ourselves pretty well. Aside from that, every place you went there were tents and holes in the ground. Every tent had a deep hole. Where possible, they had the complete unit surrounded by fence, machine guns, artillery, whatever was available to them, or what they needed. There were a lot of helicopters. When I was on the road, I traveled from Saigon up to a town called Da Nang just short of the DMZ. So I traveled basically the whole part of Vietnam. They only had one road.

You mentioned helicopters. Did you ever use any to get around to places, and what were they like?
Oh yes, we used the old style ones they had and also they had what they called a "flying boxcar." It was a real light plane; it was a cargo plane that could take off on a short runway. That's why they used it. We mostly used that plane because it was real versatile and light. I don't think it cost as much money as the chopper did either. We mostly used that because we could haul all of our cargo and everything that we needed in that plane with us. We did a lot of on-ground travel, too, in small vehicles. Most of it was actually on the ground. The only time we used planes was if we were going to an area that didn't have road access or was surrounded by Viet Cong and we weren't able to get through, so we'd fly in. Otherwise we were mostly on the ground.

"WHEN I WENT THERE I MADE UP MY MIND THAT I WAS COMING BACK. ONCE I LEFT, I THOUGHT ONLY OF MYSELF, SINCE I WANTED TO COME BACK HOME."

Can you describe what an average day was like for you during the war?
Long. It was very, very hot. Temperatures got up to 130 degrees, and it was humid, very humid. They had what they called the monsoon seasons there, which were terrible. It was raining all the time and hot. It was very hard to sleep that way with a bulletproof vest on and a helmet. I have to say I think I wore mine every day for that whole year. I don't think I ever took it off. I'd hate to smell it now. That went to the shower with me too. They were hard, long days. I guess regardless of how it was, when it came to sleep time, there was no problem there. You could sleep anywhere if you had to, even standing up.

Were you involved in any firefights?
Technically, no. We did run into quite a few hostile fires where other groups were fighting. I do know what bullets sound like when they are close. Whether any of them were shot at me, I don't know. I kind of doubt it. I guess if I did know, I would be more scared, but as it was, I never was hit. I had some friends that were. They never made it home, but I feel fortunate because I did.

What was the relationship between whites and blacks in your unit? Was there a difference?
No, I think we have more of a problem today than we did back then. I think in the military you have a lot less of that than you do any place else. This is because everybody, when they go through basic training, is basically trained as a group of people. When it comes down to it, the level of everybody is identical. There really was very, very little discrimination whatsoever.

Were drugs a problem for the soldiers in Vietnam?
I hear it was. I don't know of any. I didn't ever see any. But I did hear there was a lot of it going around, a lot of selling and buying and that type of thing. I didn't get involved with it, and I know nothing about it, mainly, because I was on the road all of the time. I was very seldom at Cam Ranh Bay. I was just basically there to get reorganized to go someplace else. It was a day or two and back on the road. I really didn't get involved with a lot of people, you know, as far as in other units or anything else.

What was the hardest part of being in the war?

Having to go. It's leaving the family, actually. It's something that you don't want to do. I don't care what anybody says, everybody is scared. They may say they're not, but they are. You know, I think a single guy has got a lot less stress on himself. When I went there I made up my mind that I was coming back. Once I left, I thought only of myself, since I wanted to come back home.

You kind of touched on this, talked about the family, but was there a lot of emotional or physical stress that you had to endure?

With me it really wasn't, but with my wife I'm sure it was. It was really hard on her. We had a little girl that was born in Germany. She was six weeks old when we came, and she was about eight months old, I think, when I left. My wife was German. We got married in Germany. She never was to the United States, and I forced her to stay with my folks. She wanted to stay in Germany, but I felt she was safer by my family. She didn't really care for that, but she put up with it, and I'm sure she had a lot of stress there. It was something new for her. I'm sure it was hard on her.

Is there one particular experience that stands out in your mind?

One thing today that I kind of feel sort of sore about is everybody says that the Vietnam War wasn't a war that we should have been in. For us, who had to go, it was a "legit" war, and I kind of feel real sore about that. The bigger part of the population doesn't think it was worth anything. It really was for the lives that it cost us.

Did you make any lasting friendships during the war?

No. I kind of forced myself to refrain from that. I knew what it was like, so I didn't want to become too close to them, to any particular people or persons. I was only worried about myself.

Do you think that the U.S. could have won the war, and why or why not?

Sure, hands down. They could have won it if they would have just let the generals run the show. I think it would have been a piece of cake. I think they could have handled it with no problem. You hear it was just a political thing, but I don't think we really know the true story yet.

When you came back to the United States what kind of a reception did you get?

None. The only reception I got was my wife. That was it. I came home and I was on a thirty-day leave and I went back to my new station, that was it. The first recognition I got for being a Vietnam Vet was last week. I went down to Fort McCoy. I got a ribbon.

What did patriotism mean to you while you were serving and now as a veteran?

I guess that's a hard one to answer. I was a dedicated soldier. I wanted to always make sure that I had done everything right, and I didn't really have a problem going and fighting the war. It was something that I knew that had to be done. I feel today the same way. You know, I wouldn't want to do it, but if I had to, I would, even at my age.

People say that Vietnam was considered to be guerrilla warfare. Could you just tell us what it means to be guerrilla warfare?
Guerrilla warfare is something that's kind of basically like we are doing now, with the small groups of people going in and infiltrating undercover and search and destroy type thing. They're basically well-trained men that aren't afraid of the dark, so to speak. They're not afraid of anything. They can live off the land; they can do just about anything. They're paratroopers, they're fighting men, they're everything. I guess what you'd call a fighting machine. You've heard that expression? That's basically how that war was fought. The air force dropped a lot of bombs. They dropped 250-pound and 500-pound bombs, which I don't think had the potency that ours have today, but they were powerful. They dropped what they called napalm bombs, which were firebombs. Those were huge. They dropped a couple of them, and that would start the forest on fire, but that was to assist the guerrillas and the people back down on the ground that were running through the jungles.

Were you able to communicate with your family back home?
Yes, letters, and I had a tape recorder for a while. Tape recorders had just come out, and I got one, and I was able to send a few tapes home. We had to be careful what we said. We could only say certain things. We could not discuss anything military or what was going on, so it was a sort of a thing that you wanted to not do if you didn't have to. But it was possible. We communicated some.

If you ever had time for yourself, what did you like to do?
I never thought about it. There was one time during the war that usually was at mid-time that you could meet your family somewhere. They had picked three or four places in the world that they would ship the family, and you could meet. Our place that we selected was Hawaii. I could have met my wife in Hawaii, but due to our circumstances, we just let it pass. I didn't want to start something with meeting the family and then not want to go back. I decided to just continue on and get it over with. But that was about the only free time anyone had. They ended up being able to take two weeks of rest and recuperation, what they called "R & R." That's about as much free time as anybody had.

What were major differences between the United

States and Vietnam?

There was a big difference. There were very few places that had buildings, solid buildings. Most of the homes that people lived in were all straw. Those were built right in the wet swamps – rice paddies.

Basically, that was the home for those people. That's all they had. Some of the big towns like Saigon and Da Nang, had solid buildings but they were put up and owned by the French people. Vietnam was– years and years ago – populated with the French people. They put a lot of them up, and there were still a lot of French people there yet.

What did you think of the South Vietnamese people?

They're people just like we are. I'm not a prejudiced person at all, none whatsoever. There are a lot of people that degrade the Hmong people that are here, but they fought right alongside of us. I'm not a prejudiced person. I think everybody's alike.

Did you ever have any experiences with the Viet Cong?

That's an unknown question. They were all over. Everybody dressed the same, and you never knew who you were talking to. You could have been talking to a Viet Cong and never know it. So whether I did or didn't, I can't answer!

Is there a message you'd like to give to young people?

I would like to say one thing. If we do run into a conflict like we have right now, I think everybody should be concerned.

Following his return, John Krukowski became an auto technician.

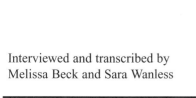

Interviewed and transcribed by
Melissa Beck and Sara Wanless

Dwight Nelson

Dwight was in the Military Police and was stationed at Long Binh from December of 1970 until January 1972.

At the time I was drafted, July of 1970, I was teaching at Wausau High Senior High School; this was before the split into East and West High Schools. I was drafted in 1970, sent to 'Nam in December, and came home in January of '72. Teachers were supposed to have automatic deferments, but President Nixon decided to give some of us a "vacation" over there, and I was one of those who were chosen to go. At first, I was trained to become an infantryman, but when I got over there, my MOS (military operating status) was changed to Military Police because they were trying to deescalate the war. At least that's what the statisticians were telling the world. Fewer infantrymen in the jungle; we must have been winding down the war. Another indication that they were trying to get out was the media attention on the number of soldiers that were now being sent home. I was given a two-week crash course when I got to Vietnam to become an MP and so was no longer an infantry soldier.

A buddy of mine, whom I had trained with stateside, was a battalion clerk, and he had information that the group I trained with was being sent to the DMZ (demilitarized zone). I asked him if there was anything he could do for me. He spoke to his personnel sergeant, and I ended up as a clerk right across the street from his group. I spent my time in Vietnam typing morning reports, applications, and letters that the military needed typed and shipped…stuff like that. While I was there, I did not fire a weapon; well, I take that back. I fired a 45 caliber pistol at a 55 gallon drum, emptied the clip, but that's about as much experience firing a gun as I had.

Long Binh post, where I was stationed near Saigon, was the largest military base in Vietnam at the time. Soldiers reported there for their orders to be shipped out to the different places. The year before, 1969, during the Tet celebration (their New Year), the base was almost overrun by the North Vietnamese even with its size and the number of Americans there. While there, maybe one rocket hit this place, but that was it. I went sometimes out to outposts by jeep, but basically we carried sidearms and we didn't encounter much action. Mainly it was uneventful. The post that I was on had open-air theaters, restaurants, bars, entertainment, and even a golf course on it, but that was only for officers. Other than the fact that something *could have happened*, it was a "vacation" given to me by Nixon; as for hostile action, I didn't encounter much.

Were you paid for this job?
Yes, I think it was $100.00 a month and up to $125.00, plus a few other benefits; so, about $1200-1400 a year. I think you got $12 a month for overseas and hazard duty pay was $15.

Can you describe what an average day was like?
An average day usually started at 6:30 a.m. We didn't have morning formation when I first got there, but then we did towards the last couple of months. Basically, we got up, showered, did whatever we needed to do, and then I reported to the office between 7 – 7:30 a.m. I typed the morning report which included who was on base, who was on leave, who was injured, who was sick, and who was on duty at certain locations or off post, and so on. The morning report could have no typing errors. If you screwed up, you had to start over again; that was a pain in the butt! Once I got that done it depended on who and what the lieutenant wanted me to do. I usually typed up some applications for medals, did some filing, and other kinds of reports. Sometimes I went up to the main headquarters to get things run off, and whenever we decided we were done for the day, we quit! That was usually around 3:30 or 4:00 p.m. After that, we would hang around in the hooch, have some beer, go out and get something to eat. I didn't work Saturdays or Sundays. We used to play handball, tennis, go swimming, and a lot of times in the evening, we used to get drunk.

"YOU NEVER KNEW WHAT WAS GOING TO HAPPEN; WHERE I WAS, YOU JUST NEVER KNEW WHAT MIGHT HAPPEN."

Did you have any drug problems?
Yes, I had an alcohol problem. The first night in the post, I met these five guys that decided to welcome me in, and one guy was going home the next morning. He was a scotch lover and so was I. We split a bottle of Kent Scotch the first night. We drank a lot, and some of us got very drunk. Some of us not so much; but we didn't do it every night. Some of the people I hung around with were drinking more than I was. In our hooch, I knew probably four guys that had been busted because they were using drugs. I stuck with alcohol. That was probably our biggest problem.

How was the relationship between blacks and whites?
It was pretty separate in my unit. Blacks hung together and whites hung together. There was a little crossover, but basically they split up in separate groups. For anyone recommended for a medal, applications had the name, a description of the incident that took place, why the person was recommended, but no mention of race.

Did you make any lasting relationships?
There were a couple of people; one lives in Madison and one lives over in Minneapolis that I keep in contact with off and on. The one who's in Madison is the one that put me behind the desk; the other company clerk and the other guy worked in the motor pool.

What was the hardest part for you in the war?
The hardest part for me was just the fact that I was over there, and you never knew what was going to happen. Where I was, you just never knew what might happen. After the Tet of '68, the base was very quiet, but there was always that uncertainty.

What kind of reception did you receive when you came back to the United States?
I know some people that had a hard time coming back, but at the time I came back, I was married to a woman that worked at the University of Stevens Point, WI. When I came back, nothing was mentioned; we had a big party and everything. No one ever said "murderer" or anything like that. It didn't gain you anything to be a veteran. If you told someone you were a veteran, compared to World War I or II, they patted you on the back. For us, people just said, "Oh, okay," then they moved on. If they were also involved in Vietnam, then you got a different kind of reception.

Was there one particular experience that sticks out in your mind?
The feeling that I had when I went over as an infantryman was the scariest feeling I have ever had. Once I got over there and ended up in the position as a company clerk, I felt better about being there. Still, just thinking about *what could happen* was most outstanding in my mind. The North Vietnamese fired on us about four times that year, but that was near the perimeter and I was far away from that. I was located near the city of Saigon, a very heavily populated area.

In the hooches, there were fairly good-sized cockroaches, and at night while you were sleeping, you'd just unconsciously flick them off. There were certain reactions I picked up while I was over there; that was one of them. I was on the top bunk, so it wasn't as bad for me as the guy below me had it. In the morning, you'd be sure to check your boots for roaches before you put them on, too.

"I BELIEVE WE WOULD HAVE HAD TO DESTROY THE ENTIRE NORTHERN COUNTRY IN ORDER TO HAVE MADE A DIFFERANCE. THE MINUTE WE LEFT, THE WAR WAS LOST."

What would you say to young people today about this war?
The people that govern our country make you go to war, so in a way, I was there because I was an American citizen and that is what you do for your country. You serve your time whether you were drafted or volunteered. I'd say that you should be proud to be an American and that you live in a society that has a high standard of living, a large enough country with a range of occupations, a variety of places to visit and things to do. Most importantly, we have our freedom. Just be happy you are in America.

Do you think we could have won the war?
No, there were strategies and military tactics that only the North Vietnamese knew of that we were not capable of doing. The minute America pulled out of the war, it was lost to the Communists. We were just *there*, that's all, and nothing was accomplished by our presence. I believe we would have had to destroy the entire northern country in order to have made a difference. The minute we left, the war was lost.

Dwight is currently a mathematics teacher at Wausau West High School in Central Wisconsin

Interviewed by Jacalyn Schultz

Jim Palmer

Jim Palmer served in Vietnam as an Ammunition Technician from 1969 to 1970; he was also trained in infantry.

How did you become involved with Vietnam and were you drafted or did you enlist?
That's a very good question. I had already gone to college, and I tried to get a job with my bachelor's degree. I just couldn't do it because my draft status was such that it was just about the time that I was going to be drafted. So knowing that I couldn't get a job and knowing that I was going to be drafted, I went and joined the marines for two years. As an enlisted person, I was an officer.

Could you describe your enemy? Were they Vietcong or NVA regulars?
Most of the people that we contacted I would have to guess were Viet Cong. NVA regulars regularly worked in large groups, company size battalions, and I was up in the I Corps, which is in northern Vietnam. And most of what we saw, most of what we took prisoner, and most of which we destroyed were the people in black pajamas, which were the Viet Cong. Once in a while you would see NVA regular but not very often.

Can you describe the average day and what it was like?
I was trained as an infantryman, which means that I was assigned to an infantry company that runs controls, gets security work and ran operations. So once I got over to Vietnam they were short an ammunition technician. Since I had large knowledge of guns, being raised in northern Wisconsin, I guess it was natural, I suppose, and I took a liking to guns and that. The fellow who was an ammunition technician was not trained. That's a military specialty, but neither he nor I were ever trained for that. We were self-taught. It was on the job, or OJT, on the job training. He was from Minnesota. He was due to rotate back to the world. The Marines had to do 13 months over in Vietnam, and his term of enlistment was getting short, so they asked me if I would help. When he left, I took over. Our duties, responsibilities, were primarily to take care of all of the weaponry and the ordnances, all the rounds, the hand grenades, machine gun ammo, tear gas. We did that for a headquarters company on Hill 55, which is in the I Corps just out of Da Nang. Our job was to take care of all of the weapons, disperse the weapons as they were needed, disperse the ammo, keep track and log in all of the ammo. In case we had bad ammo,we would dispose of it in the ammo dump. Then we ran security, we ran controls, we would run patrols, and then at night we would deliver all of the special weapons: the M-60 machine guns, the 50 cals, the starlight scopes

which were night vision scopes, and all of the ammo to all of the bunkers surrounding this big hill. This was taken to all of the people who were going to be on guard all night, and then we would take a position on guard as well. The next day, if we didn't have a patrol to run or if we didn't have an operation, then we would spend the day cleaning the weapons and getting them back and logging in new ammo and ordering out more ammo, and so forth. So that was kind of the typical day.

If we ran a patrol, we would run it down to the river or we would run it through a mil, and we were basically running patrols to keep the Viet Cong from gaining too strong of a foothold in the local area. We would get in firefights, and we would go out and sit in what we called observation positions all night. Three Marines would go out and sit in the dark back to back. We were out mainly to observe if there was any traffic, foot traffic, or Viet Cong in large numbers. Or we would go out on killer teams and set up an ambush. If we received word that there were large movements of troops, then we would set up an ambush team. Any time we went out, and we positioned ourselves for an all night stay, we would call in our coordinates. So if we needed some artillery backup or some mortars, people knew where we were, and we could direct it so we could keep the enemy off of our backsides. Any time you went out in the field you would have to let the big guns know where you were so if you needed their help, you weren't scrambling at the last minute trying to determine your coordinates so you could call in the artillery.

So that was kind of exciting sitting there all night watching for people. If you were on a claymore observation team, then you were not supposed to engage the enemy. If you were on a killing team, then you were supposed to lay down claymore around your position (which is an anti-personnel mine), and then you were to kill them if they were enemy soldiers. One night three of us were on an observation team and sitting out just trying to gather intelligence. One stayed awake and two slept. It would be hard for three of you because you couldn't talk and you couldn't smoke cigarettes. I wasn't a smoker anyway, and you couldn't do anything other than just listen. You were a listening post is what you were. I looked up and saw an enemy soldier coming; I could tell because of the clothing he had on and the type of headgear. He had one weapon, an AK-47, slung over his shoulder, and he was silhouetted against the sky, so I had a pretty good view of him. We weren't supposed to engage the enemy, but I was kind of anxious to get my first kill, so I woke up the others. All I had to do is poke them. They woke up. I made motions that I wanted to shoot him and they waved their hands no. I indicated that this would be my first kill, and I was looking forward to it. They wanted to

> *"WE WEREN'T SUPPOSED TO ENGAGE THE ENEMY, BUT I WAS KIND OF ANXIOUS TO GET MY FIRST KILL, SO I WOKE UP THE OTHERS."*

know if there were anymore coming. I indicated that I didn't think so. I didn't shoot, and 32 more came. We could have killed a half a dozen or a dozen, but we were outnumbered. So it is a good thing I held off. We could have called in artillery to dispose of them, but all we were out there to do was to listen and measure troop movement. Later on that night they hit some gunships work over in the area not too far from there. We did call in the information after they left. We obviously wouldn't call in the information when they were there because we would have brought in all the small fire in the world. That was pretty exciting.

Once in awhile we would get word that some of the grenades were short fused. Whenever you handed out grenades you had to keep record of whom they went to, not by individual, but by squad or platoon. We got word back that we had a couple of crates of grenades with short fuses. If they would have a real short fuse, they would go off in your hand after you pulled the pin, which would blow you arm off. So it would have been better to have a long fuse. The only trouble with the long fuse is you pulled the pin and threw it into an enemy area, and they'd pick it up and throw it right back at you. So you didn't want a long fuse either. We got word that we had some short fuses, and I hadn't dispersed any of that type of grenade. They were in one of the bunkers that were sand bagged and protected. So Buddy and I decided we would take the grenades to a bridge instead of blowing them up in the dirt pit which is what we were supposed to do. We decided we would take the grenades and go fishing. We would pull the pins and throw them in the water, and they would go boom, and then all the fish would float to the surface. The Vietnamese would run in the water and grab them, then run back. They didn't have to use a hook or a net or anything. The concussion could just make them float, and they would grab them. The Vietnamese would go to shore and wait for more grenades. We got rid of every grenade that way. We were pretty stu-

"WE WOULD PULL THE PINS AND THROW THEM IN THE WATER, AND THEY WOULD GO BOOM, AND THEN ALL THE FISH WOULD FLOAT TO THE SURFACE."

pid as I look back on it because we would pull the pin and see how long we could hold them before we dropped them. They were short fused grenades, so we were just guessing that they were a second or two short. Sometimes they would get just under the bridge and blow up. The bridge protected us. That was the kind of thing you do for fun because there wasn't much recreation except for that.

In our area there was a basketball hoop on sand that you could shoot on, and you could knock a volleyball around on. There really wasn't much to do for entertainment. We would race snakes, and we would line up ammo crates maybe 100 feet long. The ammo crates are wooden. We would make a long row of ammo crates, and we would turn loose some snakes and bet money on them. We would play cards and cribbage. We did a lot of sandbag filling. We were always rebuilding bunkers. I kind of looked forward to patrols because they had action. One time we discovered a big collection of rice, and evidently, what happened is it was transported there with intent to feed Viet Cong in the area. The rice was stashed in an area where they could come get it. They would divide it up amongst themselves. A lot of the Viet Cong worked in small groups rather than a big group or platoon. We decided we were going to booby trap the rice. Well, two days later we went back, and the rice had been moved. They had taken the booby traps too. They had moved it to another area where, in fact, we found it. We were thinking we would booby trap it again. One of our guys inadvertently touched off one of their booby traps while we were setting ours. They had booby trapped their own rice. Luckily, no one got killed. Those were the crazy things you would do. You would booby trap this and that.

If you had to go through a gate to get into another village, (sometimes they had gates to keep the animals out or animals in, guess), if it were a gate that swung open, sometime Charlie would... (of course the villagers knew where the mines were. Sometimes the villagers were hostile towards us and friendly towards the Viet Cong.) So when you would open the gate, a mine would go off, and it could kill you. So we became pretty shrewd and decided to tie a rope to the gate and go back 75 feet so we would open the gate and no one would get hurt. Then Charlie got smart. The villagers must have told them what we were doing, so they would set the traps back so they would be where we were pulling on the rope. It was hard to stay ahead of them; they were pretty shrewd. Then we could have gone right next to the gate because the mines were back. Those were the things people didn't talk much about, but certainly kept you on your toes. Any time you would walk through a village, you kept in mind that all of the kids that were waving at you and the mothers that went about cooking and cleaning, probably didn't like you being there, and they probably had husbands or sons in the Viet Cong. You just had to assume that everyone you came in contact with was not as friendly as they seemed. I imagine that it is a lot like what the fellows in Afghanistan are putting up with now going into a village and not knowing who your friends are because you can't tell; they all look alike.

Were you part of an ambush?

We set up different ambushes and triggered them. Very rarely would you find dead bodies. They dragged their dead off. You would find blood trails. My first kill, I shot a guy in the water. We were on a patrol along the river. Across the river was known as Charlie County, and that was not a safe place to go, but our side of the river we kept relatively secure, we thought. We were running a patrol and we came across three young boys. They took off running right away, and they had to be 14 or 15. We came around the corner, and they were in the river swimming. We hollered, "Come here. We want to talk," in Vietnamese. They saw us and then they took off. We hollered stop or we would shoot. They kept going, so we just opened up on them. One of them made it to the other side. The other two, the one I shot and the one that Sergeant had shot. We saw the water turn just boiling red. There is no question that they never came up. Then we went back and went through their articles that they had left on the riverbank. They had an American GI T-shirt, they had a 7-millimeter Chinese pistol, a transmitter radi, and of course, they had their black pajama clothing, and I can't remember what else they had. They definitely were Viet Cong, or they would have talked to us.

We picked up their gear and we came through their village. Earlier in the morning the kids would run up to us and ask us for gum. They could say gum. I flipped a kid a stick of gum, and he walked alongside of me for 40 or 50 yards telling all of his friends that I was number 1. He kind of marched alongside of me. But that night we went through the same village, and I was carrying one of the hats, and I had the 7 mm. pistol, and I had some other piece of his clothing. We walked through the main street if there was such a thing. The little boy came running over, and when he saw the hat and the gun he spit on me. He spit on me. We kind of assumed that he was his brother. We never could prove it, obviously, but to that kid in the morning I was the number 1 Marine, and that night he recognized something I was carrying, and he was pretty angry. There was some connection, but we didn't know what. The village was close enough to hear the firing. We unclipped a magazine each. We sprayed the river down pretty heavy. It bothered me for a long time, and we would go through the village everyday, and I never saw the kid again. When I had the chance, I was in the rear one day, and I went and saw the chaplain. He said, "That's what you do in a war, you know." He said, "that kid was 14 or 15, so how many American GIs could he have killed or did he kill?" So I couldn't feel too bad about it. That little guy that in the morning I gave the stick of gum to made me into the number 10 GI, which was the worst you could get. Number 1 was good, number 10 was bad. It was kind of an unusual situation. I turned the pistol into intelligence, and they were supposed to log it and give it back, but I never saw it again. So from then on any souvenir I took, I would never turn it in because somebody would keep it for themselves. I brought home a pistol, an M1 cut off, and grenades. I brought things like that. If I had turned them in, I would have never gotten them back. I learned my lesson pretty quick.

Did you ever use a helicopter to get around?

Yes, we did a lot. In fact most of the ammo that I was responsible for lifting up to different observation posts, we called them OP's -- those were mountain top bunkers. Like on top of Rib Mountain there could have been as many as 40 or 50 of them all spaced out. There would be a big sandbag area of bunker dug into the ground. Some of them you could put a helicopter on, and some of them you could just load onto a deck while the chopper was hovering in the air. Anytime we made ammunition runs, or had to run large numbers of troops, we used choppers. The Marines used CH-46's and CH-53's. We didn't use too many of the Hueys that you see the army use in Vietnam war pictures. We used the bigger ones. Of course there were cobra gun ships. I got to see one. I wish I could have flown in one. Those were the ones with all of the high-powered explosive devices. They were all pretty light because they were a one or two man aircraft. I spent a lot of time in choppers, and to this day when I hear a chopper, it sends a reminder to me, those memories.

I missed a chopper one time. We had spent an entire morning loading a CH53, which was a big twin-engine diesel chopper. We put quite a bit in it, and we spent the entire morning loading it with fuel oil in 55 gallon drums. We would use that to burn out human waste. The outdoor privies are what you would use if you had to go; you would use one of the privies and drop it into a barrel of the fuel oil. Once it got to a certain point, you would pull the barrel out and pour it into a hole and you would burn everything up. You never had a stink really. We had the fuel oil and a bunch of new plywood for the bunkers up on the post. I had a buddy up there, and I would go and spend a couple of nights up there once in awhile. It was really beautiful. You could see a long ways. You could see the South China Sea. You could see the Da Nang River and a lot of the mountain area installations around Da Nang. It was really a pretty picture, and it was great sitting up there on top. I went up there a couple times.

One time I was up there sleeping in one of those bunkers. I was in there; there were three men to a bunker. One person would stay on watch, and the other two would sleep. We were right on the peak of a mountaintop, so there was no way that Charlie could have gotten to us. He would have to crawl up a very steep mountain to get to us. We were just up there to keep an eye on things. I woke up and crawled out of the bunker in the morning, and there was a big cobra snake, dead. My God, it must have been 6 feet long. It kind of startled me. I said to one of the guys who happened to be a Pima Indian from Arizona. That is the same tribe that Ira Hayes was in. Ira Hayes was one of the Marines that raised the flag at Iwo Jima. Johnny Cash sang a song about him years later. It said whisky-drinking Indian the Marine that went to war. He was a hero. This kid that we called Chief. All of the Indians in the marines are called Chief, and they weren't offended by it. This Indian was in the bunker with me while the other guy was on guard. During the night he felt the snake crawl over him, and he just picked up his collapsible shovel, and he killed the snake. Then he threw it out of the bunker. I said, "Where did you find that?" He said, "In our bunker last night." I said, "Chief, what time did you find it." He said, "I don't remember. I felt it crawl over me. It must have come from where you were." He said, "I just killed it." I said, "why didn't you tell me?" He said, "I knew you wouldn't stay in

> *"DURING THE NIGHT HE FELT THE SNAKE CRAWL OVER HIM AND HE JUST PICKED UP HIS COLLAPSIBLE SHOVEL, AND HE KILLED THE SNAKE."*

the bunker the rest of the night." I said, "You're right, I wouldn't of." So he put it on the spit that day and he cooked it. He said in his tribe that they eat snake. It didn't taste very good to me. He skinned it out and put it on a stick. All I could taste was the burnt wood.

Anyway we were loading the chopper, and we loaded the oil and plywood, and we were going up to the same observation post. It took us a couple hours to load. The pilots weren't ready to go, and we got tired of sitting around. Then I went to a buddy and asked, "Can I borrow a jeep for a couple of hours, we are going to run into Freedom Hill," which was a big Air Force PX complex. We would get a cheeseburger there which was a real treat. We knew we were going to be eating C-rations for the next week. I took one of the guys with me. The observation post was visible from where we loaded the chopper, and it was up a couple of thousand feet. You could walk up there, but it was dangerous because it was steep and Charlie may have mined the trail for you. It was probably a six-hour walk. We decided to go to Freedom Hill and started talking.

We got back a little after two. We were a couple of hundred feet from the pad, and the chopper lifted off.

"FOUR GUYS WERE KILLED, AND THE OTHER FOUR SOMEHOW SURVIVED. IT HIT THE GROUND, AND THE ROUNDS WERE GOING OFF."

I was like, oh shucks, now I have to walk up there. We had to go up there because it was a duty assignment. As soon as the chopper got up 200 feet, it flipped over on the side and crashed right in front of us in the rice paddy. Four guys were killed, and the other four somehow survived. It hit the ground, and the rounds were going off. Every fifth round is a tracer round. Every fifth round left a red flash. The ammo was blowing and the grenades were blowing; it was all a mess. Probably what happened is one of the engines died out, and it could be flown with one engine, but the weight shift of all of the fuel oil and plywood shifted and pinned the four guys behind it, and they couldn't get out. The guys who died got pinned in behind the plywood. They called the fire department in that area. The airport had a fire department for airplane crashes. You couldn't get near it because the rounds were going off over your head. One of my buddies was in a hooch 75 yards from where the chopper landed, and one of the props came right through the cabin and landed along side of his bunk. Corporal Jackson woke up, and there was the prop from that chopper. He came out of there, and it was the first time I had ever seen a black guy that looked white. He was scared, and he didn't know what happened. It was like a Fourth of July celebration. Then the next day we had to go in and try to salvage what we could. Basically, we were on a body search team. There were no bodies; they were fried. I remember one boot sticking out of the mud and I though it was a boot. I pulled it out of the mud, and it was a leg that was burned and toasted. Inside of the boot was someone's foot. I called someone over and they bagged it. I don't know how they could find out whose it was. The bodies were burned, and you couldn't recognize anyone because it was a pretty hot fire with all the fuel and the ammo. It was pretty disheartening because one of the guys that got killed was Shortround. He must have lied to get into the Marine Corps because he was 18 and on his second tour, so we figured he came into the Marines when he was still 17. He was a wise cracker boy, and he was real small, but it was his second tour. I have pictures of the scene the next day, and I got pictures of the memorial service for the four guys that got killed. The Marines put sandbags on the ground with a cross and take a rifle with a bayonet and stick it in the sandbags with a helmet on the end. And then you just go back to work. You don't think much of it, 'cause everyday you hear of someone getting killed, and after awhile you just say, "Oh well. He was a nice guy," and what do you do now.

I was supposed to meet a buddy in Hong Kong once. He and I were friends. He was on bridge duty, so anyone that wanted to cross Liberty Bridge had to go through an MP station or a Marine station. He would check the ID cards of all the villagers, and he and I agreed to meet in Hong Kong on our R & R. He never showed up. We had the dates set aside, but he never showed up. I was pretty mad, 'cause I went and checked all the hotels. They would send you on Rest and Relaxation to Hong Kong, Taipei, Australia or Hawaii, and you would get a week off. They would fly you there and you would get to dress in civilian clothes and go to shows and eat. We called it I & I, intoxication and intercourse, but that was our interpretation. Carpenter never showed up; I was pretty mad, 'cause I had looked all over Hong Kong; there were six hotels that they brought the GIs to. I cursed him all the time I was there, 'cause I spent a lot of time looking for him.

When I got back to my unit I was waiting to take a chopper out to where my unit would be, and I ran into a fellow that I knew, Negro kid from Detroit, and I said "You know Carpenter?" and he said, "Yeah I know Carp." "Well the dirty SOB was supposed to show up in Hong Kong, and he never showed up." Then the guy kind of dropped his head and looked away, and I said, "What's wrong?" and the guy said, "You don't know?" and I said, "No, I don't know. What was I supposed to know?" He said, "Carpenter got killed two weeks ago." I said, "No crap, I didn't know that. What happened?" He said, "Well they were running patrol up in the rock pile, big rocks, some as big as a room, whole series of them, and there were tunnels and caves, a lot like what I assume Afghanistan is like. They were piled, and Carp might have been running point at that time, and he stood up and got shot and fell down into a rock crevice. It might have been 20 or 30 feet down in there, and he couldn't get out cause he was shot, and they didn't have enough rope, so by the time they got a chopper in with the equipment to get in there, he bled to death. Of course the people in his unit knew that, but I didn't know that till I got back from Hong Kong, so my anger turned to a different type of anger, I guess, 'cause I couldn't be mad anymore. Now I knew why he didn't show up. Kelly was the kid from Detroit. Funny how names will come back to you every once in awhile; he was the one that told me how Carp had died.

> *"SO BY THE TIME THEY GOT A CHOPPER IN WITH THE EQUIPMENT TO GET IN THERE HE BLED TO DEATH."*

Was there a lot of drug use, like in the movie _Platoon_?

Well, you know I sat in circles where guys would smoke marijuana and pass it around, but I never wanted anything to do with it. Shortround was a good one for smoking, but he was a goof ball to start with. There was a French liquid that some of the guys drank; they got it from some of the Vietnamese women. We called it speed; I don't know what its name was, but I suppose the Vietnamese women used it to keep their bellies down, either because of the water or food they were eating. A lot of the women seemed to have a big belly, like they were pregnant. I never paid any attention to it, but after awhile I said to one of my buddies, "Everyone of the women over here is pregnant." He said, "They aren't pregnant; it's something in the water or the food." They would take it, but it wasn't a laxative, but it had some way of ridding the body of the moisture. Some of the GIs would take it, and it makes them higher then heck. I never tried it. I saw one of the guys that took it, and he crawled up into one of the towers at night, and he wanted to jump out of one of the towers because he thought he could fly. He made a hell of a time. His name was Johnson, and he was a neat little guy, but he got hung up on something, and I think it was that speed. We called it speed. I don't know how he got up there. It was a big tower, like 40 feet in the air, and there were three of us in there. We had a M50 machine gun, and we didn't like tower duty because you kind of stuck out. If you had a sharpshooter up in the hills or someone with good cover, they could pick you off real easy. Johnson got up there, and we had to sit on him because he was convinced that he could fly out of the tower and land on the ground. I don't think he fooled with it after that.

You could never tell what kind of drugs you were getting. I could see that, and I didn't use them. Things were not sterile, so you couldn't really trust anything. You couldn't even buy a Coke. Kids would run away and set up little roadsides stands right out in the middle of nowhere, and they would be selling American bottles of Coca-Cola. You couldn't even risk buying it from them. It was warm, and a lot of times they would drill out the bottom or put a peg in the bottom and fill it with some kind of acid or something. You had to be careful with the villagers because it was probably tainted in some way or another. Some could have been good, but I never fooled around with that stuff. I got goofy enough with the little bit a beer that we had access to, but we never got around to whisky or anything. Someone said that you got two cans of beer rationed a day. We never got two a day; you were lucky if you got two a week. If that was a common ration supply, someone was ripping us off, 'cause I never saw that much. Yes, there was drug use there, and I never saw the drugs used in such a way that drugs caused someone to lose their life, although I am sure it happened. You hear lots of horror stories where a guy on one of the three man listening posts, where the guy on duty, remember there is only one guy awake at a time, and the patrols would not come back, and they would go looking for them. They would find all the guys with their throats cut, and you know what happened was the guy on duty fell asleep, and Charlie came and cut the throats of all three of them. You would hear stuff like that. How much truth to that I don't know, but it sounded reasonable to me. A guy falling asleep on posts was a court martial. That's the difference between living and dying. Most of the people that I knew who got killed were killed by friendly forces or by accidents, like tripped a land mine or something. As far as the chances of getting shot, directly by the enemy, it might have been 20 or 25 percent. I am just guessing. More people were killed by hidden devices like mines, and there was a sizeable amount of Americans shot by other Americans, not on purpose, but maybe mis directed artillery fire. You might remember the scene from *Platoon*, when they were dropping the artillery right on top of them. When you drop artillery right in on top, that means Charlie was right in your back pocket. You may as well call it in and die taking your chances. That way you take your chances in hand to hand combat or being shot in your bunker or trench. If they were that close to call in artillery on your own troops, that means they were pretty close to you.

> *"MOST OF THE PEOPLE THAT I KNEW WHO GOT KILLED WERE KILLED BY FRIENDLY FORCES OR BY ACCIDENTS, LIKE TRIPPING A LAND MINE OR SOMETHING."*

Did you have any opinions about the anti-war movement back in the states?
I hated it. It was the worst thing that ever happened to American soldiers. What we would hear about it was terribly demoralizing, and you would hear about it from your military newspaper or if someone would send a clipping from home because we didn't have TV. We had Hanoi Hannah on radio; she was a woman that was speaking broken English that would send out her messages about, "Give up, American soldiers. Go home; you're not wanted here." She would say stuff like they are protesting in Madison, WI and Cincinnati, OH and Hanoi Hannah would go on and on about how the war effort was failing and how the soldiers were being made fools of, and so forth. Any of the protesting that was done stateside was publicized by Hanoi Hannah, or the U.S. newspaper would get in the hands of an American soldier, and he would read it and share it. It was pretty bad.

Jane Fonda was really, really hated by the American troops 'cause she went over there. On one particular instance she was visiting an American POW camp where Americans were being held, and one of the soldiers slipped her a note. They were only showing her what they wanted her to see, obviously. The story goes that the soldier gave her a hidden message that he got to her and she turned it over to an NVA colonel and he tortured that soldier. Instead of her taking the message, (it said something like we are being mistreated, please investigate more thoroughly,) she read it and gave it to the colonel, and a couple days later that guy was killed by torture. The soldiers really hated her. I marched in the Welcome Home Vietnam Vets Parade in Chicago one time, and it was a big parade like 500,000 American vets and probably one million people watching from downtown Chicago, and they had a big placard with her picture on it, with a big diagonal line through it. I can't think of anyone that American soldiers hated more. They never had much good to say about her. The protests that were going on over here did a lot of harm to the morale of the soldiers, and I think it gave false hope to the NVA and Viet Cong. Madison, especially, because it was a hotbed of protest, and if the other GIs knew that you were from Wisconsin they would kid you a little more. They would say, communist buddies in Madison are up to it again. You had to take a little bit of kidding I guess.

What would you say was the hardest part of being in the war?

The hardest part, I think, was recognizing that the military was not in charge of the war. I think a lot of us had that feeling that the politicians were really running the war. They would call it a stand down or a sit down or a cease fire period on a holiday, and that's when Charlie would move the most. They wouldn't allow us to run our normal patrols; they wouldn't allow any flight recon. We pretty much pulled back during holidays, and that's when Charlie went crazy. That's when we should have been pounding the hell out of them, and that's why we should have continued to bomb the North because the supply routes that came out of the North is what were supplying the soldiers in the South. They ran it down what they called the Ho Chi Minh Trail. I think that we could have done a better job of closing those supply lines, and that was the life-blood of the NVA and Viet Cong. They were so easily supplied because we couldn't shut off the supply routes. We couldn't go into Cambodia; we had soldiers go in there and get lost or mis-directed, and sometimes illegal operations were run in Cambodia, but we were not supposed to be in Cambodia. We just had the feeling that the military was just listening to someone else. The politicians seemed to have control over the war efforts. I don't think that it was the same in Desert Storm.

I really think that the hardest part of fighting in Vietnam was not seeing anything good come out of the effort. In the end we had to accept that we didn't win. You would take some territory today, like taking over CWA in Mosinee, and hold it for a couple of months and find out that it didn't meet a military objective that was critical, and leave it. The Viet Cong would be back in there the next day, and maybe it took 200 lives to take it. They talk about Hill 825 and 810; they lost hundreds of lives to take those hills, and then two or three days after they were on those hills they left them. They didn't see a need for them. If you are familiar with history- the only reason we took Iwo Jima and we lost several thousand Marines there, (I want to say we lost 7000 Marines killed and 30,000 Japanese killed) was that it was a strategic airfield on the Coral Islands. That had some purpose, even though we lost many lives. But in Vietnam you would do something, and two or three days later you would move somewhere and Charlie would move right back in. I think they are seeing that with Afghanistan. If you follow the news, we clean up an area and then leave. The Taliban moves right back in. We would do operations, and they would tell us that there were no Viet Cong in this sector. They were all removed, and there were no villagers. We would run a patrol out there about a week after, and there were all kinds of signs of recent human life. There were people in and out of the so-called secure areas. The hardest part was fighting and not seeing anything positive come out of it and seeing your buddies being hauled off to the hospital or worse yet, being body bagged. Seeing those guys being carried out, for what? What did we gain by all this?

Was there more emotional or physical stress?

Physical was tough. The first day I reported into Vietnam it was like 114 or 115 degrees, hotter than heck. Then when monsoon season came in, it rained everyday. You were wet from daylight to end; you never dried out. It rained for seven months. The physical strain was bad enough. Guys would get trench foot, 'cause their feet would never get dry, and they would never have socks. They had some serious foot problems. Mentally, the only real strain was wondering when your ticket was going to get punched maybe.

The guys would talk about that. The guys would go out on patrol and laugh and say, "Hey is it your turn today Williams?" "Nope Smith, I am going to make it through the day." They would kind of kid about it, but deep within it kind of bothered you a little bit. Guys would say that they were not afraid, but if you looked at them at the time they were exchanging fire or we were waiting for artillery to be dropped into some hot zone of some kind, you could see fear on the faces. I am sure that I was no different. Now remember, I was 23 or 24 years old, which was pretty old. They called me Gramps, when lots of the kids were 17 or 18, right out of high school. There were a lot of poor kids; you didn't see kids from rich families. They were in colleges, getting some kind of deferment. Some of them may have gone over the border to Canada, or someone

> *"'TILL THIS DAY, WHEN SOMEBODY SLAMS THE DOOR OR DROPS SOMETHING BEHIND ME, JUST THE NOISE OF BEING STARTLED, IT SHAKES ME UP."*

ended up in a desk job. I will say this, that Lyndon Johnson, who was President during part of the war, his son-in-law was a Marine Lieutenant, and he was exposed to some battle. I mean, he could have been protected. Lyndon Johnson could have had him sitting in some rear area in a secure location, but he was out with the ground troops. I don't know for how long, but it wasn't like they took him over there and hid him in some rear area and made him drive a Jeep for a General.

When I first came home from Vietnam, I did not talk much about Vietnam. In fact, till this day, when somebody slams the door or drops something behind me, just that noise of being startled, it shakes me up. If I know someone's going to slams the door, or I see him going to drop something, it doesn't bother me, but if it happens behind me and I don't see it, it is like the chopper blades. I can hear them coming. So I didn't talk a lot at first. Then some of the problems that Vietnam vets have had, is that they don't talk about some of the experiences, and as a result, they have all those feelings inside, and it eats away at them. I figured I would talk to my family, but my kids don't know much about it. I give talks to schools and that, but I haven't shared a lot with my family. I think it has been good, from my standpoint, to get rid of some of those feelings. If you get them in the open, you can deal with them.

So you did have difficulties dealing with the memories when you got back?

You have to remember that Vietnam is a lot different than other wars. You didn't have the front lines like you did in World War II. When we took Germany and marched across France, we had clear lines of distinguishing conquered areas. We didn't have that in Vietnam. What area you took today, the next day the Viet Cong would be running loose in it again. That made Vietnam different from other wars. You could leave a war zone in Vietnam and be back in the states in your hometown in 24 hours. World War II they shipped most people by boat. In fact, the early days of Vietnam, most of the troops went over and back on a boat or ship, so it took longer. But you could leave an area where you were getting shot at, and in 24 hours you could be sitting in the living room of your home. That's a pretty quick transition, and a lot of guys had trouble making that quick of an adjustment.

My mother would tell you the story that she woke up the first two or three nights that I was back home, and when I came back I spent a couple weeks in California before I came back to Wisconsin. But she can tell the story about waking up in the morning and going into my room, and I'd be under the bed. Something happened during the night, and I just dove because it was safer. We had some bunkers in some of the areas of Vietnam where I would not sleep in the bunker. They were sandbagged and very safe. They even had RPG screens that they used to deflect the rocket away. The bunkers were pretty secure on some of the line positions, but I wouldn't sleep in them 'cause the rats were bigger than house cats. They were just filthy places 'cause GIs would throw their candy wrappers and whatever in there, and it would attract big rats.

Couple of months ago I got a phone call from a gal in Indiana. She asked me to return her call. I looked at the number and the name, and it didn't mean anything to me. Laura something. I have it written down. So I called her back and said this was Jim Palmer, can I help you? I thought it might be about my work out at the Tech. She said, "Did you know Bob Ellis?" I said, "Jeez, over the years I might have met a Bob Ellis. Where would have I known him from?" She said that he was killed in Vietnam, and I said, "Oh the Big E." She said what do you mean, and I told her that he was a tall guy that played basketball. She said that he was my brother. Another Marine shot him accidentally. She went on to say that when they shipped his body from Vietnam, they crated up all his clothing and personal effects and sent it to his parents. Well, they were in such chaos; his mother was having heart surgery the day that they got notified that he was

> "SHE WANTED TO KNOW WHAT I COULD TELL HER ABOUT HER BROTHER, BECAUSE BOB WAS KILLED WHEN SHE WAS EIGHT YEARS OLD. SHE WANTED TO KNOW WHAT HE WAS LIKE AND IF HE SUFFERED..."

killed. The family was in turmoil from that point on. They got the box weeks later with all his personal effects. They were in such shock that they didn't open it and put it in the attic. Thirty years later they come across that box. They open it up, and they go through the stuff, and they come across my name and phone number, but I was raised 100 miles from here. Somehow through the Internet, they found my hometown, where I haven't lived for the last 30 years. They found out I was in Wausau and got a hold of me through information, and they called.

She wanted to know what I could tell her about her brother, because Bob was killed when she was eight years old. She wanted to know what he was like and if he suffered and things like that. Well, I didn't want to tell her too much about how he got killed because I was there; I was standing a few feet away. She said that she didn't have any pictures of Bob from Vietnam; we thought they might send some of that home. I said, "I have pictures; I'll share them with you." So I am going to Indiana the week after next, and I am going to look her up, and she asked if I would go to the cemetery with her.

We were really good buddies. Bob and I and another guy by the name of Big Red decided one Christmas that we were not going to go see Bob Hope, who was putting a big show on in Da Nang. We decided that we were going to get into this three-man basketball tournament in one of the rear areas that we heard about it. Well, Big Ellis played at Notre Dame for a year or two before flunking out; he could really shoot. Big Red was a bulk of a guy at 6 foot 4 inches, 240 pounds, just a hell of a rebounder, and I was a pretty good guard, so I could get the ball up the court. In three-man basketball you really needed a guard and two scorers or a rebounder and a scorer. We decided that we were going to enter this tournament, and we won it. We beat the Blacks and the Hispanics. We went through the tournament like nothing, even though there was some good ball players that entered this tournament. We just happened to win game after game. They couldn't stop Ellis cause he had a fall away jump shot that was beautiful, and Big Red controlled the boards, and I could get the ball up the court. The Blacks would pressure you pretty heavy. They'd bump you all the way up the court, but I hung on to the ball enough. We won the tournament. Well ironic as it might be, Big Red was the one that shot and killed Ellis. The other guy on the basketball team shot the other one. I didn't tell her all that. She wanted to know as much as she could about her brother, and I am going there in a week or two, so I will drive about 45 miles past my son's house and spend a day with her and tell her what I know. I won't tell her about the details of the killing. He was a good guy, her brother.

I think the thing that I regret the most is I had an address book of all the names and the hometowns of the guys that I served with, and somehow it has gotten misplaced over the years, and I can't find it. I have lots of scrapbooks and slides, but I don't have the names, but sometimes nicknames. I don't remember all the states they came from. I think if I can get into the Marine's records on the Internet, I might be able to find some of the guys.

"I HAVE HEARD OF PEOPLE THAT LOST THEIR LEGS. THEY STILL THINK THEY HAVE THEM, EVEN WHEN THEY COME TO, AND THEY STILL THINK THEY HAVE TOES TO WIGGLE."

I would like to know what happened to some of them. Some might be dead or in prison or others like me and schoolteachers. You meet some nice people. In other wars they sent people over in units. In Vietnam, people would go over individually. Fifty Marines might come into Freedom Hill on this day, and they might go to 30 different units, where in the old days when they sent groups over to a war, they went as a whole unit and they came back as a unit. That made Vietnam different than other wars. Some guys were really reluctant to get too close to other buddies.

People got shot and wounded, and if a person got wounded bad enough, they might be transported out of country and they end up at a hospital ship out on the South China Sea, or sometimes they send them to Japan. I remember going into a hospital to see a buddy in what we called a First Marine Hospital. It was very rare that they kept you in country, but he had some disease. I went in to see him, and the guy in the next bed had no arms or no legs and a bunch of bandages over his face. He asked me if I was a Marine, and I said yeah, I am too. I looked over and I could just cry. He had stubs for legs and wrists missing. I had heard about these eight Marines that had accidentally tripped a big bomb that Charlie booby trapped, and he was the only one that lived out of eight. He had lost his legs and arms, maybe just came out of surgery. He said, "I am going home." "Where you live?" I asked, and he said "Chicago, Illinois." I said, "Great Lakes." He said, "I'll be there in a couple days and won't my family be happy to see me." I don't think that he knew his arms and legs were missing, or he was so pumped up on drugs. I thought to myself that his family won't be happy to see him like this. I could not believe that he thought he was normal, 'cause he wasn't. That was pretty hard to see, and I looked at my buddy on the bed, and he just shook his head, like he was just goofy. I have heard of people that lost their legs. They still think they have them, even when they come to, and they still think they have toes to wiggle. This guy had nothing. My age may have made it easier to adjust cause I was 23 or 24; a lot of the guys were 17 or 18 years of age.

Do you think the U.S. could have won the war? Why or why not?
Yes I think we really could have. I kind of got to that subject before when I said that if we would have

cut off their supply routes, the Ho Chi Minh Trail. Even then our B52's could have blasted the trail so that they couldn't have shipped anything over it. They used elephants on the trail to transport the stuff up and down the trails. There were some places that you could not have wheeled vehicles, so they used elephants. I think that if we would have kept the politicians out of it and hit them hard when they were down. There was a time when we had the upper hand, but winning the war, what would that have done? If we would have gotten a truly democratic government in place, perhaps that would have fulfilled our goal of being there, but everyone was so corrupt over there. Very much like the leaders in Afghanistan,

at least the warlords anyway. Winning the war would have meant to really knock out their army and to really have kept them from re-supplying. The villagers were really caught in between a rock and a hard place. The Viet Cong would come into the villages and take their males out young and old, at gunpoint and say that they are going to fight with us. If you resist, we will shoot you. The villagers wanted no part of the Viet Cong, but they didn't like us either because they saw us as intruders. Very similar, I am guessing, to what they are seeing in Afghanistan from the locals. They don't like the presence of the American people. There were pockets of places that you could win acceptance, but you really had to put in a government that was going to be honest and truthful and truly democratic. With all the politics, even if we would have won, I don't know if we would have won.

Do you have any messages for young people today about what happened?
I have a boy in the army right now, in the army reserves. I think the military still provides a viable option for young people; it's a great area to get into. You are taught discipline, and I think that you learn how to get along with other people. I think that there are far more benefits to serving in the military than not. But my advice would be to take advantage of the many opportunities that the military has. I mean you can go to college today after you have been in the military, and they will pay a great share of the college expenses. You get to meet people and experience some different things. I encourage everyone I know. Only one of my boys ended up in service; the other ended up getting married after he got out of college. If you are single and have a desire to at some point later in life maybe take advantage of some educational opportunities rather than sit around and work at Kwik Trip or a window factory, I think the military is a good place to go. I think it serves a lot of good needs. I would never discourage anyone from going into the military. Even if we were to get into a big confrontation, I wouldn't discourage it. The people that are fighting in Afghanistan, a lot of them are career soldiers and have been preparing for the ultimate, for battle, for years. I can tell you that when they were given the word go, that they were going to engage the enemy. For some it was a relief, 'cause that was what they were trained for. I would be very surprised if someone came home and they regretted the experience or they were afraid of dying. I think that most of them, because they were career soldiers, were looking forward to practicing what they were taught. Certainly there will be some that regret it. It does disrupt lives or careers, but nothing to the point that you can't put it together again.

Do you think that the people that went over to Vietnam knew what they were fighting for or why they were there?
No, we were not really tuned into what we should have been told, not like the soldiers in Afghanistan. They knew they had a purpose and that was to route the enemy out of their holes and give the country a chance to return to a more democratic state. I don't think the people in Vietnam knew; remember the soldiers were a lot younger. If you look at the average age of a soldier versus Desert Storm or Afghanistan, I think that you would see quite a difference. I don't think the young soldiers knew why, and I didn't

know as much about it then. I had not seen a map of Vietnam till I got there. I knew where it was, but I hadn't seen a map of the country itself. It could have been square for all I knew, but I knew that it was long. If you would have asked some guys if it was near Australia or Germany, I think a lot of them wouldn't have been able to tell you. I think the communication is a lot better today. People have better expectations because they know more of what's going on. Look, you could be engaging in a battle in Afghanistan and the family could be watching it on the TV live. We didn't have that kind of technology back then. I think the soldiers today are better prepared for what they are going to get into. We were not taught anything about the customs or any background or the religion or disease. We were given little training in jungle warfare. The soldiers that have trained for Afghanistan have trained for that kind of fighting and in many cases because they are career soldiers, for many, many years. It was not unusual to go into the Marines and spend three or four months in California, come home for a week, go back to California for two weeks, and be in Vietnam. We only had five or six months of training. That wasn't nearly enough. I think the people today are better prepared. I think they have a better awareness of what they are fighting for. I don't think that we had any idea like we should have.

Jim Palmer has been teaching at North-Central Technical College as a Traffic Safety Instructor for the past 29 years. He is married to Deborah Palmer, and together they have 3 children.

Interviewed and transcribed by Eli Jackson and Tyler Derby

Charles Pufahl

Charles Pufahl was drafted into the army and became an image interpreter. He was in the 219th military intelligence detachment, and was located in Bien Hoa. Pufahl returned home after being in Vietnam for over 13 months.

How did you get involved in the Vietnam War?
I was drafted.

What were your first thoughts when you were drafted in the Vietnam War?
As soon as I was drafted, I knew that's where I was heading. It was just that time in the war.

What were the base camps like in Vietnam?
They are hard to describe. When I first got to our site it was very primitive- all tents, no permanent buildings, wooden floors. Very primitive, I would say. It changed by the time I left, but initially it was just tents for everything.

How did it change?
By the time I left thirteen months later, about 90% of the tents had been replaced with metal building on concrete floors.

Can you describe what an average day was like during the war?
I didn't have any average days. I was very lucky. I was an image interpreter which meant I read aerial photos. The aerial photos that we got to read were so old that they were of no value, so I didn't do what I was trained to do. Most of the time I was there, we worked as carpenters, building the permanent buildings, so there were no average days. For some reason I became my boss's chauffeur. About three times a week he would ask me to take him into what was then Saigon and then pick him up there the next morning. We had to attend guard duty around our camp at night, and every other night we were on guard duty, so if you were on guard duty all night, you didn't have to get up and go to what we called the office until noon the next day. So every day was really different.

How long and how much training did you need to have before going to Vietnam?
After basic training I went to the Army Intelligence School in Baltimore, Maryland for nine months of training as an image interpreter. Then just a month or so after, I was shipped to Vietnam.

What was your ranking during the war?
The day I left I was a specialist fifth class or E5 pay break.

How was the relationship between the whites and blacks in your unit?
We were all the same. We treated each other the same, and there was absolutely no problem. We had a number of Hispanics, and I did not see any hatred like that at all. We were all just there together, and everybody the same.

How was the relationship between the Americans and Vietnamese?
Where I was, it was great. We had it so well that we didn't clean our own tents. We hired Vietnamese to do it for us, wash our shoes and wash our clothes and all. We were just friends. They got to know when our birthdays were, and they would bring us gifts. Then we would find out when their birthdays were and would bring them gifts. They would even help celebrate our holidays like Christmas and stuff. We got along really good.

What was the hardest part about being in the war?
Just being away from home and the weather was so different. I grew up in Wisconsin, and it's hard to spend Christmas where there isn't a bit of snow, where the low temperature at Christmastime was 80 degrees. It was really hard to adjust.

Where were you located or stationed at the beginning of your time in Vietnam?
While I was there, I was at the 219th military intelligence detachment, which was part of second field course headquarters. We were located in Bien Hoa. That was about thirty-two miles from Saigon.

What were some of the things that you missed the most from home?
To be honest, I can't say that I missed the beer, 'cause we had our share of beer, but the thing I missed the most was just being gone from home. Just everything about it.

How did you feel after your return home?
I have known people that I have worked with for fifteen years that never knew I was there because I don't talk about it. I don't talk about it, not because I'm ashamed of being there, or my feelings on whether or not we belonged there. It was just that I was so fortunate; I saw no battle, and it was almost like a vacation. In fact I had it so good that I could have left there six weeks earlier then I did, but I stayed an extra six weeks because I had it so good. It felt like it wasn't my doing, but I didn't accomplish anything there. The photos we got were so old and had no value, so we didn't do what we were trained to do. I saw people that were in battle and came out and are having nightmares now. I have had none of that, so I don't brag about the fact that I was there. Not that I'm ashamed; my situation was just different. I even wanted to go back when I came home. I had an uncle from town who worked with the refrigeration company. He had just come back from a year in Vietnam. This is 1966. As a civilian, he

made $40,000 a year. I said, "Uncle, I want to go back with you for a year to make that kind of money." Had I been like the typical Vietnam soldier, there's no way that as soon as I came home I would want to go back there. I guess I was really fortunate. I'm not sorry I was there. I'm proud of the fact that I was there, but I felt it was unnecessary, so why talk about the fact that I was even there. It was just different for me, and I wish everyone could have had it like that, but that wasn't the case.

"I HAD IT SO GOOD THAT I COULD HAVE LEFT THERE SIX WEEKS EARLIER THEN I DID BUT I STAYED AN EXTRA SIX WEEKS BECAUSE I HAD IT SO GOOD."

With the extra six weeks you were there, how long were you there in total?
I was there for just shy of thirteen and a half months. The only reason I stayed six weeks longer was because as soon as I left there, I got out of the army. I had said I wanted out of Vietnam after a year, or actually 364 days was your assignment there, one day short of a year. Had I said I want to leave, I would have been reassigned someplace else for four and a half months, so if I stayed there for six weeks, when I left Vietnam I would be discharged. It was selfish, and I would not have done that if I hadn't been so lucky or had it so good.

Is there one particular experience that stands out in your mind from when you were there?
You don't forget the entire experience. The biggest thing I remember was the weather and the rains. When we got there, it was dry, and it stayed hot and dry for I don't know how long. Then one day we had a short downburst. It lasted five minutes at ten o'clock in the morning. Every day after that we had that same downburst at about the same time of the day. Each day it would last a little bit longer, from 5 minutes to 7 minutes to 10 minutes for awhile. Then it would start in mid afternoon. There would be another downburst, and they kept getting longer and longer. Soon the point came when both the morning shower or downburst, they weren't showers, got to the point where the morning one and the afternoon one met each other, and it rained for two to three weeks straight. It never stopped raining, and then just like it started, it stopped. There would be a break sometime in the afternoon and then the break would get longer and longer until the afternoon showers stopped, and it was dry again. I had never and will never again experience weather like that. I guess that's one of the biggest things. When we had the showers in the morning and afternoon, it would rain so hard that everything turned to soup. It was just mud all over. The sun would then come out right after that, and it would get so hot that by the time we had the next shower, everything would be baked hard just like the table top. That was something to experience, and that would be the thing I remember. My kids still can't believe how humid it was even when it was dry. A couple months before we had rain, it was so humid that we kept 25-volt light bulbs in our metal lockers to try and keep our clothes dry, just so the heat from the light bulb would try to keep your clothes dry. Otherwise it was like they just came out of the wash, they were so wet.

"...IT WAS SO HUMID THAT WE KEPT 25-VOLT LIGHT BULBS IN OUR METAL LOCKERS TO TRY AND KEEP OUR CLOTHES DRY."

Did the weather have any effects on your duties or make it hard for you to use the equipment?
No, not really. It's just being in the army, or any branch of the military, you're trained, and the weather doesn't stop what you had to do within reason. You can't paint a building in the pouring rain.

Did you make any lasting friendships during the war?
No, not really. I communicated with two people, one from Idaho and another from Milwaukee, and we were together from basic training all the way through Vietnam, probably about six months after I got out.

Is there a message you have for young people today?
I really do not have any idea of the political reasons for being there, but I just hope that I do not have see us, our country, do something like that again.

Is there anything else you would like to add?
I think what the school is doing with this project and the others similar to it are fantastic. I also thought that I was very fortunate in Vietnam, and I am very thankful for it. I wish everybody had it as good. I am not ashamed of it, but after nine months of school, training, where we only had to go to school and not have any other duties we trained very hard and with intensity. Iit bothered me that our information did not help anyone.

Pufahl was a police officer for 31 years in the Everest Metro Police Department. He has a wife, Cathy, and three children.

Jerome Ravey

Serving in Vietnam from '67-'68, Ravey was in Marine aviation. Stationed in Chu Lai, he serviced the safety equipment of jet aircraft.

How did you get involved with Vietnam? Were you in the Marines beforehand?
Yes.

Could you describe what you would do?
I was in an air-wing squadron; I used to work on jet aircrafts. I was in North Carolina and then sent over to Vietnam. I was in the advanced party. We worked on safety equipment, oxygen tanks, and ejection seats, making sure everything was safe on the aircraft.

What would you do in an average day?
On an average day, we would service the aircraft before flight and made sure that the pilots had oxygen. There were small tanks that we had to make sure were full of oxygen. We checked over all of the equipment and made sure they had all of their survival equipment in case they were shot down.

"TWO WEEKS BEFORE I WAS SUPPOSED TO COME HOME, THE VIET CONG ATTACKED OUR BASE. IT WAS A LITTLE ON THE SCARY SIDE."

Where were you located?
I was in South Vietnam in Chu Lai. In the North, if you ended up being in Viet Cong territory, then you were in trouble.

Do you have any opinions regarding the anti-war movement back at home?
A lot of people just didn't know what was going on over there.

What was the hardest part about being in the war? Did you see war or were you rather isolated from it?
You couldn't help not seeing it. When we arrived in Chu Lai, they told us that we had to go on work detail. We loaded a bunch of dead bodies in body bags on a plane.

Do you have any stories of your time in Vietnam?
Two weeks before I was supposed to come home, the Viet Cong attacked our base. It was a little on the

scary side. A rocket was fired at our hanger but missed. It hit the bomb dump behind our hanger. You could feel the concussion five miles away.

Was there a lot of physical or emotional stress that you had to endure?

The emotional part was going over there and that you really couldn't do much about it. Working on the base was this Vietnamese woman with her little girl. Some Viet Cong came to her village, and she lived off the base from where we were. One night they came to her house and told her that if she didn't stop working on the base, she'd be sorry. She came to work the next day, and the Viet Cong took her daughter and cut off her head. Those were the things that were going on in Vietnam that people didn't realize.

Many of the soldiers that were in Vietnam had apathy; did you have any negative opinions about the whole ordeal when you were there?

No, mostly I was there because it was my job. You were hired to do it, so you did it. A lot of guys were drafted and sent over there, and that's where a lot of the problems came from. They didn't really want to be there.

When you went back, how did people treat you, knowing that you were in Vietnam?

When I first came back, I went back to North Carolina where I started out from before I went to Vietnam. It was a military base, a military town, so it wasn't really a factor how people treated me.

Is there one particular experience that you lived through in Vietnam that you'll always remember?

One thing that sticks in my mind is that there was a guy who flew a lot of missions into North Vietnam and never got shot down. When we went back to Carolina, he died in a plane crash. All that time he was flying missions into North Vietnam, and he came home safe. Once he got home, he died.

Do you think that the US could have won the war?

I think the United States could have won because the United States is a very strong power. It was just that there was so much pressure from the people in the United States that it forced a lot of pressure on the military to get out of Vietnam.

Did you have difficulties dealing with Vietnam after you got back?

No, not really.

Did you make any lasting friendships with anyone after the war?

I became a pretty good friend with a guy that I had met from Arkansas. When we came back, I was on one base. He went to another base about five miles away.

Do you have a message for young people about war and what it's like?

Sometimes I think that kids today don't really understand what's going on, but what can I say? It's part of being on the world. Countries are always going to fight with one another.

Do you think there are parallels with what's happening today in Afghanistan and Vietnam?

There'll always be war. There's always someone who wants to rule the world.

How were the relations between the whites and blacks?
I don't really know what it was like for the infantry, for the guys out in the jungle. Where I was, we were working alongside of one another. He's another Marine. He might be the guy that ends up protecting your backside.

Did you see much racial differences between the American soldiers in Vietnam and the Vietnamese they were protecting?
I didn't really see it, but from what I heard when the Vietnamese and American soldiers would go into a battle, the American soldiers would start to attack and the Vietnamese would turn around and be running away. They were scared. They weren't trained like the United States' soldiers.

Were drugs ever a problem where you were?
I don't know if it was a real problem. There were some around, but I don't think anyone around my area was addicted or anything.

Do you think it was a mistake going into Vietnam?
I think the only mistake was that they didn't finish what was started.

Do you have any feelings on the outcome?
I just feel we should have finished what was started.

Ravey now owns his own handyman business. He and his wife, Penny, are foster parents.

Interviewed by Jenny Priebe and Melissa Martindale
Transcribed by Melissa Martindale

Dennis Reno

Dennis Reno was in the Army 8th Division in the 945th detachment. He served as a medic (91A). He served from June of '68 until April of '69.

How did you get involved with the armed forces? Did you get drafted or enlisted?

I believe at the time the enlistment was for three years. When I was a freshman or sophomore in college at those times, and when you're young and you're wild, you don't think too much about anything. My grades were about a "C" average, and so, consequently, I received a notice from a draft board saying that I would be eligible for the draft. So I decided that I'd better do something about it because I knew what would happen if they just drafted you right out of college. They throw you right into the front lines, and so I went down and I talked to the enlistment officer, and I signed up for three years. I had a choice of what I would go into at that time, and I picked the medical area because I had a minor in biology from college, so that worked well for me.

What was day-to-day life like personally for you?

Well, that's a big question, what life was like. It had its ups and downs. I was an E5 over in Vietnam, which is a NCO (non-commissioned officer), so I had responsibilities to other people, and I had other people under me also. I had leadership roles as well as the role of performing my general duties within the operating room over there. There were days when it was long, and we worked long hours. Our primary concern at the time was caring for the patient. We received all the injured patients there, and working in the operating room we had a chance to work right along with the surgeons as well as the anesthesia providers at the time, and that's where I got my interest in anesthesia. After I came back to the states, I went back to school and got my degree. The average day would be get-up, do the usual army things that's expected of everyone, and then take care of the patient and try to survive without getting killed. There were times at our hospital when we were mortared a few times and shells came in, and we had designated areas to which we would go called bunkers. We never really thought of that as happening to us. Our primary concerns were to take care of the patients, the boys. At that particular hospital we also took care of the North Vietnamese captured soldiers, and that's probably one of the reasons why we weren't bothered a lot because the NVAs weren't going to bomb their own guys, and they knew that we kept some of their troops there. It was more of a political play somewhat, too. We had our good times, too. We were off duty at times, and they had entertainment for the enlisted men.

You were in Vietnam in 1968; do you have any insight about the Tet Offensive?

Yes. In 1968, I had arrived over there just as it was finishing up. I got into a little bit of the tail end of it there. They had a couple Tet Offensives I believe. The first one was totally unexpected. That was the big one where we lost quite a few troops. I was not involved in that one at all, but the other one, I was there and it wasn't as bad. It has been a long time since, and my memory has gotten old as I have forgotten things, or I just choose not to remember a lot of the things that I've seen.

Did you ever use helicopters to get around, or how did they help during your stay in Vietnam?

Yes, we used Huey Helicopters for transporting the wounded into the hospital and that. The detachment that I was attached to was a small medical attachment, and we had capabilities of moving around Vietnam as a small unit. We had one surgeon, an anesthesia provider, a tent, a small operating room, and a huge helicopter called a Chinook Helicopter that would move us around. We had a jeep, and all of our sterilization

> *"YOU MADE A LOT OF FRIENDS IN THE SERVICE, AND THAT'S HOW YOU SURVIVED."*

equipment was all completely mobile surgical type of hospital, but they were very small. We did not have to leave a field hospital. We were basically stationed there with the capability of moving around. They basically kept us there because they needed us there, because they were short of manpower at that place, so that's where we provided most of our services. The choppers were very useful and always handy when they were needed.

Is there any one particular experience that stands out in your mind while you were over there?

That's where I met my wife, which was a good experience. That's something that I will always cherish. My wife was an army nurse over there, and we fell in love there, and we came back to the States and got married.

Did you have difficulties dealing with the memories after you returned home?

Not really. That has not been a huge problem for me. However, about ten years ago, I was painting around the house, and there was some program on Public Radio or something where they had interviewed a bunch of Vietnam Vets, and they were playing some songs, and that kind of struck a bell with me. I sat down and shed some tears for a few minutes, but that cleared up, and it has never bothered me since.

What do you think the hardest part of being in the war was for you?

At that age, my early 20's, probably just being away from my family and being away from all my friends and loved ones. That was probably the most difficult part of the war at that age.

How do you feel about the people who were in the US that were anti-war people?

While I was over there, we had very limited access to the media. We would listen to the armed forces radio, and that wasn't necessarily played up to us. We didn't have a lot of access to the so-called marching over in our country against the war because they just didn't want to show the troops that. When I returned back to the States, I was basically ETS, which means Enlisted Time Served, and I came back, and I was out of the service from Vietnam. I was a little angered for a short time, because I went right back into college, back into school. I met people that were somewhat antagonistic to the war, and I did voice my disapproval over that. I didn't march or anything, but I did voice my honest disapproval. I became a member of the Vietnam Vet's Club at the university, but that club was basically a club to support one another for the guys that came back.

What did patriotism mean to you while you were serving in Vietnam?

Back then it was a different time, a different period than what you boys have now. In other words, I was going to college and then basically taken out of college to serve. Initially I was a little upset from being taken out of college, but once I was amongst the organization with the troops, that left me, and I became a member of a large family, a large unit within the military; you became not one, but one of many people. You were always looking out for your buddy, your friend. You made a lot of friends in the service, and that's how you survived. Those who didn't have friends or buddies generally had psychological problems or they just had a very rough time. So you counted on your buddies to get you through.

Did you keep any lasting friendships from the war other than your wife?

A couple years ago I had a guy call me who I met in basic training, actually, when I first went in. He was a guy from Mexico who could speak very little English; he came from Milwaukee. He had got my name somehow. He was active in the Veterans of Foreign Wars as was I, and he called, and we talked on the phone for a while. Every once in a while I'll see somebody at a restaurant or something that I recognize, and we'll talk, but I don't go out generally, socially, with somebody all the time.

Is there a message that you have for young people today about the war?

Well, I always told my son, "Dad went to war so you wouldn't have to go to war." But I told him that if there is a war during your time, it is your obligation to be patriotic and to do what your country wants you to do. I've had uncles that served in the Korean War and WWII, and myself and my brother served in Vietnam. But we did our duty, and we do our duty so those who don't want to go to war may not have to -conscientious objectors. I always felt that if that was their belief, so be it; I wasn't going to criticize that.

Dennis Reno has a wife and two children, a son, Keith (28), and a daughter, Carry (31). When he came home from the war, he completed his degree in nursing. He has practiced anesthesia for 27 years.

John Rhyner

Enlisting in the Army Security Agency in 1969, Rhyner arrived in Vietnam in August 1970. He was assigned to the 509th Radio Research Group and was stationed in An Khe with the 374th Radio Research Company.

What were the dates of the beginning and end of your tour of duty in Vietnam?

I arrived in Vietnam 4 August 1970 and departed on 3 August 1971. I was then assigned to the U.S. Army Security Agency in Europe until my ETS on 21 December 1972. I separated from the service for three years and have been in the National Guard ever since November 1975.

How did you become involved in the Vietnam War?

I graduated from Everest in '67 and graduated from the Marathon County Technical Institute in '69. Not a lot of jobs were around, so I decided I might as well put in my time in the military, something different, a new challenge. I enlisted in the U.S. Army Security Agency on 6 October 1969. I went active 22 December 1969 and left for basic training on 5 January 1970 to Ft. Leonardwood, MO. After basic training, I was sent to Ft. Gordon, Georgia, for communications training. After thirteen weeks at Ft. Gordon, I graduated, took a one week course in jungle survival and was sent home on thirty days leave. I report-

ed to the Oakland Army Base at Oakland, CA, on 4 August 1970. We had about three days at Oakland before being bussed to Travis Air Force Base, CA, for our flight to Vietnam. We flew with a commercial carrier (Airlift International) on a "stretch DC-8" which holds about 250 people. We flew the "northern route," Travis to Anchorage, Alaska, which took about 4 hours, then to Japan, another 8-9 hour flight, and finally to Bien Hoa Air Force Base, Republic of Vietnam. In total, about a 21 hour flight.

Military Assistance Comand ID card

After you arrived in Vietnam, where did you go?

We stayed overnight at the Long Binh Army Base, which is about ten miles from Bien Hoa, and we were part of the group assigned to the 509th Radio Research Group. In order to become a member of the Army Security Agency, you needed to have a Top Secret Security Clearance. You had to receive special training, and you were very much separate from everybody else. So when our plane landed in Vietnam, there was only a few of us who were actually from the Army Security Agency. The majority were regular army people. When we got to Long Binh Army Base that night, the sergeant said, "First off let me get one thing straight. I can send you guys anywhere I want to." Now I'm already thinking, oh no, this is not what I had in mind. But then he said anybody going to the 509th Radio Research Group or some other MI (MI being military intelligence), you can fall out. We were given our barracks, fresh linens, a good night's sleep while everyone else was getting tested and processed. In the morning we were bussed to Tan Son Nhut Air Force Base and the 509th Radio Research Group.

Aug.31, 1970. Operations 375th RR. Laundry from next barracks hanging on barbed wire.

What was your typical day like in Vietnam?

Once I got to my unit, it was probably three weeks after I first arrived. My first unit was the 374th Radio Research Group. We worked a rotating shift at a communications center. As I recall, a typical day (if we were on day shift) we got up usually around 5:00 or 6:00 a.m., went to the mess hall and had breakfast. We were at the Operations building by 7:00 o'clock. I worked an eight hour rotating shift. You would go to the Comm Center and be briefed on the current situation. We would type and send messages. If there weren't any messages, we would just joke around and find out the news that's going on, talk to some of the analysts. When dinnertime came, you went to dinner. When the end of your shift came, you went back to your barracks or went down to the shower and then changed clothes. You didn't have much variety; they were green. You went back to the barracks after supper. We had a club at our site and would go down for a couple of beers. If there was a show that night, we'd go watch a show. We were back in bed by 10:00 or 11:00 o'clock at night, and everything started over again. Now my type of duty was totally different from most people who went to Vietnam. I wasn't allowed to go to combat because of our security clearances and our training and experience with encryption devices. The smallest unit you could be assigned to was a brigade, and that was only a handful of people. And we were not let out of sight, literally.

So they didn't want you guys to get into the hands of the enemy?

They didn't want us to be captured because of what we knew. We worked in the Radio Research Group, which is a cover name for the Army Security Agency. The name Army Security Agency was classified during the time I was in Vietnam. Their parent unit was the National Security Agency, which up until 1967 had been in existence for twenty years, and most people in the government didn't even know it existed; yet it took up probably a third of the defense budget. To this day, it is probably the most secret area in the government. The CIA isn't even close.

> *"TO THIS DAY, IT IS PROBABLY THE MOST SECRET AREA IN THE GOVERNMENT. THE CIA ISN'T EVEN CLOSE."*

What type of messages would you send?

The messages we would send when I was at the 374th at An Khe would have target information. We had a group of people known as "Leftbank." "Leftbank" were helicopters (choppers) that would have large antennas out from the front of the chopper. They would fly quite high and would detect a radio signal. They would take a reading as to the location of that radio signal. They would record that, and they would bank the chopper to the left (hence their name). They would go fly to a different part of the sky, and then they would turn around, come back, and try to fix onto that radio signal again. They would crosshair to get an exact location. They would radio that information back to our unit, and we would attempt to identify the unit and try to translate a lot of the information that was being transmitted as to its use in intelligence. If it was just a unit ready for a fire mission, we would call in our artillery or an air strike. That type of message would be sent as a flash message. A flash message, you would have about one to ten minutes to get out of the site. Usually within about five minutes you would have either an air strike coming in or artillery fire going out.

Did you guys have better conditions than a lot of the other non-combatant units?

Yes, very much so. Our mess hall served meals nearly 24 hours a day. Our mess people would usually trade rations with the general's mess. So many times, especially during holidays, we had it better than a lot of people. We had four barracks, a mess hall, a motor pool, senior enlisted officers' barracks. We had our own perimeter with people manning the post. It was manned in the evenings to prevent sapper attacks. A sapper is a Viet Cong that would carry a satchel of explosives. Their big thing was to throw the satchel into the back of a barracks. When it exploded, people would come running out the front and   Viet Cong would shoot. So sappers were a real threat to any of the

Nov. 1970, Camp Radcliff.

units in Vietnam. But in our instance, we had our own perimeter and guard stations. Each person on the station would have about 140 rounds of ammo, so we were quite secure.

Did any sappers ever attack your base?

Not in our area, but it happened in the vicinity. I was stationed at Camp Radcliff in An Khe. It was about 33 miles around. Roughly, it was about the same size as the city of Wausau. We were in the Central Highlands.

Did you consider the Central Highlands to be a pretty secure area at that time?

No, not at all. If you go back to the World Wars where you had front lines, you were here, all of your people were behind you, and the enemy was in front. In Vietnam you didn't have that, because there were no lines. What you went in and took one day, later that night belonged to the enemy because you weren't there. You could not necessarily trust the civilians or housemaids that worked in the barracks during the day. They may be your enemy at night. So who to trust and what to trust and when, was very difficult.

What type of civilian contacts did you have?

In our case the only civilians that would have been around would have been the civilians that worked in the compound during the day. The house girls worked in the front of the barracks doing laundry and

Looking at "golf course" (chopper pad or helicopter port) hoist helicopter behind telephone pole. Left is Operation 374th.

things like that. A papa-san would be doing the dirty details that are necessary to maintain life. Beyond that we did not have any civilian contact. If a civilian wanted to enter the operations compound, he or she would have an armed escort.

Did you talk to any of the other soldiers from different bases?

We did not run into that situation very often just because of our uniqueness. We did not have visitors other than high-ranking officials.

What was the hardest part about being in Vietnam?

I guess being away from home is always tough. I mean, we were very well occupied and we were on a real world mission. And those of us in the Army Security Agency, whether you were in Vietnam, in Europe, or anywhere in the world, you had a 24-hour mission seven days a week. There was no such thing as weekends off, unless you were scheduled off. I guess being away in a strange area is hard. When you're in a situation where there is so much that is new to you that you have to learn in order to survive, it makes it difficult. The most news that you had was a couple days old. You just weren't exposed to that. It was very much word of mouth from people in your unit and what you could get off the teletypes or radio.

Sept. 2, 1970. Taken out back door facing NW toward motor pool.

In your communications department, did you ever have to intercept messages from the enemy?
In communications, no. What we would do was take the information that the intercept operators and Leftbank gave us. The analysts would interpret that information and we would pass it on to Fort Mead, Maryland. Fort Mead, Maryland, is the Headquarters of the National Security Agency. I would go so far as to say that 98% of our messages were sent to the National Security Agency.

Did you have any connections to the CIA?
Well, it depends how you interpret intellegence agencies. We were not part of the CIA. We were a part of the National Security Agency, which is far more secret than the CIA was and ever will be. The National Security Agency is the code breakers. If you go back to the 1970s, I guess one way you could equate it was large companies at that time compared each other by how much computer equipment they had in square footage. NSA in the early 1970s had thirteen acres of computers. The NSA would generate the codes that the military used, all of the different classifications or levels of codes. We worked totally separate from the CIA. I guess the way you look at it is the CIA was usually more involved with person to person type contacts. The National Security Agency was involved with electronic spying.

Did you feel safe in Vietnam because of the way you were protected?
Yes and no. I mean you're safe. Well, it depends on how you determine safe. Are you immune from being hurt? No, you're not. Your buildings are quite thin. I'm talking, at best, plywood. I guess your biggest threat was enemy rocket attacks because when the Viet Cong fired a rocket, it went in a specific direction. It had no guidance in it, so wherever it fell, it fell. If your number was up, your number was up. The closest hit we had was close enough that we had debris from the blast fall on our roof. That's close enough; that's all the closer I want to be. But beyond that, no. The security, we felt pretty secure just because of how we were located. We were somewhat in the center of the perimeter. The people that worked for you during the day were your enemy at night.

Did you get used to the climate in Vietnam?
Well, I'm not real good with hot weather because I sweat easily. I went to school in Georgia and had Vietnam training in Georgia, which is quite comparable to what the climate was like in Vietnam. It's hot and it's humid for the most part. The Central Highlands, on occasion, would get some snow. You would have very huge temperature swings. It would be quite hot during the day and would be quite cold at night. You were there, and you didn't have a whole lot of choice, so you might as well adjust to the climate.

Did you move to any other bases?
Yes, I was at An Khe from about September to December 1970. At that time the Fourth Infantry Division was standing down or going home, so to speak. And really what going home meant was the flag went home, but the people who weren't done with their tour were reassigned elsewhere in Vietnam. Very few people actually went home. The Fourth Infantry Division was from Ft. Carson, Colorado. When the 374th Radio Research Company left Vietnam, the company became the 374th ASA Company. The majority of us went to the 330th Radio Research Field Station in Nha Trang, and some personnel were reassigned elsewhere.

Camp McDermott- Nha Trang RVN. Chinese Mercenaries Barracks.

Were your conditions better at Nha Trang or worse?
They were much better. Number one, it wasn't so far to get supplies. You were right on Highway 1, which goes from Saigon to Da Nang. You were literally right on the South China Sea. You could go down to the beach, spend a half-day off laying on the beach. It was much nicer.

How many people were at Nha Trang?
It is hard to say. Now just talking my unit, probably 200. There was a post there. How many people were actually assigned on it? It's hard to say. There was an airstrip. You had a Military Region 1 and Military Region 2 headquarters.

So did you have to decode any enemy messages?
Enemy messages, no. That would have been done by the analysts. We encrypted and decrypted friendly messages.

So was there any chance for the enemy to intercept your messages?
Those sent from our hands they could not. Your main way of encryption now is scrambling the message, but then you're also jumping across the entire frequency spectrum.

Looking east to the South China Sea. Camp McDermott- Nha Trang.

Were you involved in any major military operations?
I was not involved in the incursion into Cambodia in June 1970 by the 4th Division. I arrived there in September. So other than calling in, typing, and sending the message to determine the targets for the air strikes and artillery strikes, no.

Did you have to learn about the Vietnamese culture?
We did go through a two day training session at Fort Gordon. It was a combination of classroom and learning about their culture, climate, and country. And then you had one day where you learned tactics. They were making the assumption that you were going out into the field even though you knew you weren't. But how to defend yourself and take care of yourself in the types of situations that are most likely, such as an ambush. Things to avoid, but if you were in the unfortunate position to get caught in an ambush, what you would have to do to survive.

When you went out to town, did you ever carry a firearm?
If you carried a firearm, you are in the position of showing force, and you are inviting the action. So firearms were never visible.

Have many of the messages or information been declassified since Vietnam?
In our case, no it's not. It will never be declassified. The classification categories we used were: unclassified, confidential, straight secret which was downgradable, secret code word which will never declassify, straight top secret which is degradable, and top secret code word which is not. 95% of our messages were code word which will never be declassified. And most of the classified messages, even if you were to see them, would mean absolutely nothing. They usually have something to do with another country or it's going to have something to do with our country that would be of use in combat to another country. A lot of our traffic that we sent looked like gibberish. I have no way of even interpreting these messages. It's the value for intellegence purposes. Pictures were always classified. Any information on a personal nature about a person would be classified.

Did you commonly look at the pictures or messages that you received or sent?
Sure, you read everything that goes past you. The only exception to that was if it came in "eyes only." That's not a classification, but it's a handling instruction. In that case it would only be the Comm chief or the operations sergeant that would see it. At that point it would have a cover sheet over the top and would be delivered to the addressee by courier. Have I ever seen one? On occasion, but as far as regular classified messages, sure. If you were working at a relay station, you could take the time to read the holes in the teletype tape, or it could just come out of the monitor and you could read it coming off as it is. You still had to know what the classification was because some sites that we had communications with did not have top secret storage capability.

Do any messages that you received or sent stick out in your mind?
Sure, I guess some of these situation reports. I won't tell you what the classification is, but they would refer to ships in the South China Sea. You would get the name of the ship, a by-item list of everything that was on that ship, and wherever it was going. And in intelligence, we knew everything that was going in the harbor and everything that was coming out of the harbor. We would get 7-8 messages like that every week. Other than that I can only think of some messages pertaining to a Vietnamese general and his movements throughout the country. We'd receive a message from the analysts and interpret that message back into English.

"Lynn" house girl- commo 374th RR.

When you went to town, what exactly did you do?
If you wanted to seek adult pleasures you could seek adult pleasures. If you wanted to go to a movie theater, you could go to a movie theater. If you wanted to see the sights, you could do that. Whatever GIs wanted. If you just wanted to go lay on the beach, you could do that to. A ride into town cost about 100 Piasters. At the time I was there, the exchange rate was 450 Piasters to the dollar. You could go down to the vegetable and fruit market and buy fruit if you wanted to. You never knew where it came from. Do you want to take that chance? Probably not. A lot of people went down to the bars at night. You were drinking warm beer. Very little ice was available.

How often did you get to go to town?

Usually when you had a day off. Now in my case working shift work, I worked 18 days on and one day off, like all other shifts. We had literally everything we needed right there. If you wanted to go to a movie, we had our own outdoor movie theater. It consisted of about 20 benches set up and four big sheets of plywood set up and painted white and all covered over the top with parachute silk so you could watch movies in the day as well. We would take a can of Pepsi and drink half of it down and fill it up with Crown Royal and go watch a movie. The concessions there were better than back in America. You made the best out of what you could.

How did the civilians treat you?

That is kind of hard to say. I think a lot of the Vietnamese shunned us just because of the aura that a GI has. They are looking for ways to profit from you. I can remember on convoys we would cross a railroad bridge, and most railroad bridges would have planks on that you would drive on. So it was a one way bridge. While you were waiting on one side, you would have kids running up to you and trying to take C-rations and things like that off of you. While they were distracting you, they were also undoing the straps that held the gas can in place. I mean everything was free for them to take off. You really had to watch the security of your vehicle. For the most part, if you were in town, people wouldn't come up to you very often. They would keep to themselves. One reason people would go to town was the girls. The going rate was 500 Piasters for 15 minutes. We haggled over the prices. That's like a buck ten.

Do you have memories of a worst day in Vietnam?

Not really. A person tends to remember the good things, unless the bad things were really important to them. I can't remember one. You made the most of what you could because there was a lot of unknown, and you didn't know what would come.

Did you get news of the protests that were going on about Vietnam?

I don't remember much about the protests. We would get news through the *Stars and Stripes*. As I remember, it was published in Hawaii. Everybody read it. It was a real reliable newspaper. Beyond that our only source of information was the radio station AFVN. Like in the movie *Good Morning Vietnam*, that was basically the way it was run. I remember the call sign for the station was: "This is AFVN serving the American fighting man 24 hours a day from the Delta to the DMZ, with transmitters in Quang Tri, Da Nang, Qui Nhon, and Nha Trang with the key network station in Saigon, Vietnam." That was broadcast about every hour.

330th Radio Research Field Station at Nha Trang

How were you treated when you came home from Vietnam?

It was different only because you actually had to go out and find a job. Once you got back to the civilian populous you weren't wearing a uniform so no one could tell the difference. You really weren't treated any differently than anybody else unless you made a spectacle of yourself.

Did you make any lasting friendships during the war?

Yes, I had a friend from Cincinnati, Ohio, one from Minnesota, and one from Detroit. Two out of the three I have stayed in somewhat contact with. But when you went to town, you would go with them. You felt safer going with someone you knew than someone that you don't know.

Overall, how did you feel about US involvement in the war?
You look back at it with hindsight. At the time you were fulfilling a mission. In our case we were providing real intelligence back to Washington. How they wanted to interpret that intelligence was up to them. Our primary mission was to gather information. We had to get all of the messages sent and secure and prevent them from being intercepted.

John Rhyner has continued to serve his country in the National Guard. In November 2002, John will have 33 years of military service.

Interviewed and transcribed by Matthew Nohelty and Andy Kryshak

Keith Weller

Drafted into the Army, Weller was trained in artillery. He began by working with the guns and later became a forward observer. He finished his tour by working with the MARS radio. Weller served from May 1970 to July 1971.

When did you first realize or when did they tell you that you were going over to Vietnam?
The war was going on when I was drafted, and I expected I would go over there because of the activity that was going on. When I was drafted, I went through the basic training and all of that, and as I progressed, through onto the Advanced Individual Training. They trained me for artillery, and as it ended up, I did go over there for about 13 months.

Did you have many friends that went with you?
Most of the people in my platoon ended up going over there.

What was one of your major jobs when you were over there?
I had three different jobs when I was over there. One was working on a 105 Howitzer group in which we set up a firebase and provided protection for the platoons out in the field. The next job that I had was out in the field along with the platoon. I was a forward observer for the artillery group that I had back at the base camp, and the last job that I had over there was running a military affiliated radio station, or MARS station. Basically that was a short-wave ham radio connection between Vietnam and the United States so our soldiers over there could talk to one of the bases here in the United States. From there they made long distances calls to whoever you wanted to call or talk to in the United States, so it was only a long distance call in the United States, rather than an international call.

What kind of experiences did you go through while you were over there?
I saw everything from way up North by the demilitarized zone up in the northern part of Vietnam all the way down to the Saigon area. We got moved a lot when I was over there. The United States was pulling back out of Vietnam at that point, and we slowly progressed into the

"I SAW HOW THE PEOPLE LIVED THERE, THE RICE PADDIES, LITERALLY PAPER SHACKS, CARDBOARD SHACKS THAT THEY CALLED HOME, BUILT OF AMMO BOXES THAT WE HAD LEFT BEHIND."

South. I saw everything from the DMZ area. I saw how the people lived there, the rice paddies, literally paper shacks, cardboard shacks that they called home, built of ammo boxes that we had left behind. You can't appreciate what we have in the United States until you see something like the way they live over there. From there I continually moved South into the Cam Rahn Bay area, which was a more developed area that was more modern, and then down into the Saigon area, which was the old part of Vietnam. That particular area had many, many really nice homes, very ornate in the central part of Saigon. Once you get on the outskirts, it's just like you're out by the DMZ again. That's how dramatically things changed from the true ghetto, so to speak, to the upper, high-class people. It wasn't uncommon as you went through some of the towns. The mayor of the town had a car. I saw many cars, like a '55 Chevy, '57 Chevy that were in mint condition over there. They were the vehicles of the mayor of the town. Nobody else in town had anything, and nobody else in town really owned anything of importance. What they had literally on their backs and their really little huts and shacks was all that they owned.

On duty at the MARS station.

What kind of horrific things did you see over there? Did you go into battle ever or anything like that?

The closest I was to any action myself was I had a rocket land about 100 yards from me one time, which sent up a cloud of smoke. The closest real action that I ever saw was when I was out as a forward observer for the artillery. One of our platoons out in the field ran into the Viet Cong out there, and they kind of both saw each other and ran in opposite directions, so we called in artillery to where we thought they were. You could see the bombs exploding as they hit around our guys out there. We could land some of the rounds within 100 yards of our guys without hurting us, but at where we thought the enemy was, at that point. That's about as close as I had to anything happening to me.

How long were you over in Vietnam?

I was over there for 13 months. I started up by the DMZ zone, continually moving south. I was only in one spot for maybe two or three months at most, and then I was off and moving to different spots, setting up a new base and everything.

Were you ever furious with America for sending you over there because it wasn't really America's battle, as some people say?

No, I really didn't feel that way myself. I was not involved with the thick of the battle. I was not involved with horrific things, and there weren't many instances of that which I heard about. I had no first hand knowledge of a lot of that stuff. For me, it was something that I had to do for my country, and I felt that it was my duty and obligation.

Did you lose many friends while you were over there?

While I was over there? No. I did have an acquaintance from my home town high school. He was in a class ahead of me. He did get killed over there. There were several from the area that I knew but didn't know personally.

We were fighting with the South Vietnamese. Did they help you in any way, like food or in battle or anything like that?
Yes, they did. It was really hard to tell because sometimes these people were your friends during the day,and your enemy at night. It was hard to tell one from the other, but we did have a lot of the women come in and clean the hooches and everything and do dishes, things like that on the big base camps and where there were accommodations like buildings. Out in the field, you never saw any of the Vietnamese people at all. In the base camps and the major base camps they were in there working along with our guys, providing support for us.

> *"...SOMETIMES THESE PEOPLE WERE YOUR FRIENDS DURING THE DAY AND YOUR ENEMY AT NIGHT."*

You didn't feel like they just wanted you to fight for them?
I didn't have any personal contact with the guys or anything because they were on their separate own compounds and areas, fighting the battles themselves. It was hard to tell who your enemy actually was because during the day they were your friends, and at night they were fighting against you, and you really didn't know it.

While you were over there, did you have any physiological problems from being in the war?
Personally, I did not. I do know of many people that came back with a lot of flashbacks and things. They were probably in the thick of the battle, being in enemy fire and everything like that, where I never was. I have a cousin that still to this day suffers flashbacks from that. If there is a loud noise, he screams and jumps, especially unexpected noises like if something happens behind him. I've already seen him take a swing at a policeman once because of a loud noise that happened behind him, and it was just a reaction. I didn't see any major battles.

> *"IT REALLY OPENED MY EYES UP AS TO HOW OTHER PEOPLE LIVE IN OTHER PARTS OF THE WORLD. WE REALLY TAKE A LOT FOR GRANTED IN THE UNITED STATES."*

The closest I was, was a mile away. Personally, I don't think I suffered at all from the war. It was a great experience for me. I think that it really opened my eyes up on a lot of things, on how parts of the world survive and live compared to the United States. It really gives you an appreciation for the United States of America.

If you had the chance, would you go back and fight?
Yes I would, without question.

Is there anything else you would like to add to that?
It really opened my eyes up as to how other people live in other parts of the world. We really take a lot for granted in the United States. We have a lot of freedoms that many other countries aren't able to have

Vietnamese village made from "war scraps"

Ornate home near Saigon

because of either the government they have or just the way they happen to live, like where they are, if it's a very poor nation or something like that. The United States is very lucky to be positioned like it is to help everybody else to upgrade themselves.

If you had to tell a young man who might have to go fight for the United States, what would you tell them about your experience and how to react to things?
I think it's a duty for everybody to fight for the freedoms that we have here in the United States, and I think it's a true obligation that every person, not only guys, but girls also, do what they can to preserve those freedoms for the United States.

How old were you when you came home from Vietnam?
I was over there for 13 months, so I was about 24 or 25 when I came back. I was 22 when I joined the service. I was in there for about three years, so I was about 24 when I came back. Because we were pulling back out, I got an early out from the service and did some time in the National Guard for the rest of my tour.

Did you notice any big changes with the people, the United States, or just with yourself?
I guess the biggest thing I missed was that we didn't have any contact with what was happening back here. One of the biggest things to this day, I saw the movie about Apollo 13. I never knew that was a true experience that happened until I saw the end of that movie and it explained it. I always thought it was a fictional movie, and this was something that I never even knew happened while I was over there because

we did have a radio, we did have our local stations, but they didn't have a lot of world news on. Everything over there, even when we were calling home from the MARS station, we couldn't give our location. We could say we were in Vietnam, but we couldn't tell where we were. We couldn't really tell what was going on over there. It was more secretive that way. There were a lot of things that I missed or that I just didn't know about that was happening back home. Even a lot of the riots and stuff that were going on back here against the war; we were really cut off from that, and we just didn't hear about it.

Building a firebase near Cam Rahn Bay.

Did you kind of adapt American ways over there? We see videos now in classes like on them bringing beer for the people that were fighting. Is that something that happened a lot, adapting of American ways?
Yes. The American way of life was very prevalent over there. I wouldn't say that it was completely American, but we did bring a lot of our Americanisms over there, so to speak. When I was over there, I went through a lot of Coca Cola. I drank a case of Coca Cola a day because it was so hot, and we needed something to drink. We did have beer there too, but we did not have hard liquor, mostly beer. I wouldn't say it was brought to the front lines or anything like that, but when the guys got out of the front lines

and back into their base camps, it was available back there. Most of the creature comforts of home were available. There were places in the base camps where there were TVs you could watch a lot; this was all run by the government, provided by the government. In the South Vietnam area, they really don't have any TV stations as we know them today here. All of the programming was pre-programmed and pre-set. They really didn't have a newscaster or anything like that. Everything was regimented sitcom, so to speak, just one right after another. That's why we had no idea that some of the stuff was happening back home.

Did you ever come to a place where there was a battle and you couldn't believe your eyes?

Most of the land over there is pretty mountainous, and then there is the flat stuff where the rice paddies are, but a lot of the stuff when I was over there in '71 and '72, where the bombs hit, there was nothing left. I've got some photographs here of some of the hillsides that we were moving artillery through. They'd bring in the big bombers and everything, and they had bombs that were called daisy cutters that would literally clear off and just flatten within 100-yard radius of where the bomb hit; there would be just nothing there but dirt. A lot of the stuff was just completely blown away, and you just did not see it anymore, very little rubble left, very little activity. What you really saw was the act of battle. It wasn't a battle like you saw in World War II, or in battlefields and buildings demolished and things like that, although I did see some of that. But most of the places that I saw were again, these paper shacks and just shanties and some of the things that were made from our leftovers. Our ammo boxes were taken apart and re-nailed together into what they called a house, and it was a six or eight foot square hut or shack put together, and that was their home.

For 13 months, being over there, what was a day like?

One day ran into the next; they were all the same. You never knew if it was Saturday or Tuesday or Sunday or Wednesday. One day was like the next. There was nothing separating out like we know it here. There was no weekend; there was no time off. We were over there for a reason. It just ran from one day to the next like that. Daily life depended on where you were at. Normally, it was rise early in the morning and you had your jobs to do, and normally there were other people that would fill in like when you were sick. You'd go on like a 12-hour-shift or something like that, where you were on for 12 hours and then the other guys would come in and they'd take over. When something was happening, everybody was out; everybody was doing what they had to do to take care of business.

Do you sometimes think about things that you did in the war? When you came home did you feel different?

I guess early on I had a lot of thoughts about what was happening back there or not happening. We were pulling back out without really winning the war. It never was called a war. I don't know what it was called, a scrimmage? That's one of the things-when we went over there, we didn't go over there with the purpose in mind to win, I don't think. We had the capability to do it, but we just didn't follow through with what we should have. That's the most disappointing thing with the whole war. I saw so many lives lost over there without achieving a cause, and then turning a country back over to the North Vietnamese. To me that was a big sacrifice, and I couldn't figure not having made it.

Do you have anything you'd like to tell the people, like what war is about, and what it feels like, and how you think they should feel about it?

It comes down to serving the country. We have a lot of freedoms here that we take for granted, and I think it's everybody's duty to do what they can to help their country and their cause. We take the pledge of allegiance everyday, and if you listen to what the words say in that, I think that it speaks for itself. It's really just an obligation to protect what we have here because it's very precious.

Following the war, Keith Weller has worked in sales in Wausau area businesses.

On duty near Cam Rahn Bay.

Interviewed by Jenni Marcell
Transcribed by Kim Anderson

SERVICE SUPPORT

D.C. EVEREST AREA SCHOOLS

Service Units

According to Shelby Stanton's *Vietnam, Order of Battle* (U.S. News Books, 1981), service units comprised units of adjutant general, composite services, maintenance, medical, ordinance, quartermaster, and transportation. These units provided logistical support to other units of the American army in Vietnam. Control of those units came under the 1st Logistical Command located at Long Binh. From there, operational control was transferred to command units located at Cam Ranh Bay, Da Nang, Qui Nhon, an Saigon.

The adjutant general branch in Vietnam was concerned with the processing of replacements and returnees to and from the country. This task included equipping, feeding, housing and transporting thousands of men into and out of Vietnam. Two battalions and twenty-five independent companies handled such processing.

The supply of equipment and material was the responsibility of the composite service units. Most of the major ground fighting units had a support or service battalion assigned to them specifically. Forty-two different battalions have been identified that served in Vietnam. Sixty-three independent companies provided a variety of services during the years in Vietnam.

Maintenance had to be made available for all the various fighting and support vehicles and equipment. Units either provided direct support to an operational unit or general support for units in a geographic area. There are twenty-one identified battalions that served in this capacity. Forty-eight independent companies provided similar services where they are stationed.

Medical services were classified according to services provided. Some medical battalions were integrated into a divisional structure, and many were independent. Some medical units set up MASH's in the field, and many provided the personnel for field hospitals. Field hospitals were large facilities located at major military bases. One unit even provided a hospital for POW's. Seventeen medical companies served independent of the above units or hospitals.

Ordnance units were responsible for the supply and maintenance of ammunition located throughout Vietnam. There were four battalions located at major bases throughout Vietnam. Plus, there were eighteen independent companies.

Quartermaster units in Vietnam were responsible for petroleum distribution. There were five battalions organized for this effort and fourteen independent companies.

Transportation was involved in the movement of personnel and equipment. besides trucks, units handled aircraft and provided maintenance for their own vehicles. A total of twenty-four battalions served in Vietnam over the period. One hundred eleven independent companies provided services above the ground, on the ground, and on the water.

Jack Flaker

Jack Flaker served in Vietnam from December of 1966 to December of 1967 as a Psychological Operations Officer in the city of My Tho, which is about 40 miles south of Saigon.

How did you become involved with the Vietnam War?
I was a reserve army officer, and I planned on staying in for 20 years. However, I was released from active duty in 1972 which was after my tour in Vietnam. At that time all military people had their chance at a tour in Vietnam, at least the army people did. For me it was not an unpleasant experience or a tough assignment. I was a Psychological Operations Officer and worked with a counterpart who was a captain in the Provincial Government. We dropped leaflets that asked the people in the surrounding area to support the local government and not to side with the communists. We also handed out commodities to people in need. Some of the things we gave them were cooking oil, rice, flour, and items such as that. We would go into the countryside with a group of soldiers and give the people those things and show them what we could do for them. There were some loudspeaker broadcasts from airplanes. The airplanes were based in the city of Can Tho. Can Tho was a large MACV(Military Assistance Command, Vietnam) base in the Delta. I had to find out when the planes would be available and coordinate when we could get them into My Tho, make sure that they were getting targeted to the right locations, and to where we thought they would do the most good.

> *"WE DROPPED LEAFLETS THAT ASKED THE PEOPLE IN THE SURROUNDING AREA TO SUPPORT THE LOCAL GOVERNMENT AND NOT TO SIDE WITH THE COMMUNISTS."*

What were the base camps like?
They started to build a base camp in the Delta during my time there. At that time it was just a construction site with some soldiers protecting it, and they had large civilian machinery. But I lived in a French Chateau that was taken over in the city of My Tho, the capital of the Province of Dien Thong. I really don't have that great of an idea as to what was going on in the Northern part. I was out on the Delta which was a large rice growing area.

What was the French Chateau like?
It was obviously built by the French, a large turn-of-the-century building. It had modern amenities installed in there. It was just like some of the large turn-of-the-century homes here in Wausau.

Did you stay there with other Psychological Operations Officers?

No, I was the only Psychological Operations Officer. I was there with the other people that would have worked with the Provincial Government. For instance, my boss was a colonel, and his counterpart was a Provincial Chief that ran the Province which was like a state in the United States. The place that I stayed, which was in the same compound, had beds for four officers. The other officers were two Air Force pilots

and one Army pilot. They would fly over the Province looking for possible enemy locations. When I would have time, I would fly along with Dick Pribnow. It was just something to do because my job was one of those that didn't take 40 hours to do. One of the things I did do, however, was when they had military operations to search for the enemy, then a radio operator and I would go along in case we needed air support. The air support usually would have been the Air Force jets or army helicopters for fire-power. I probably went out on about 100 of them, about two a week, in the time that I was there. At other times, I'd have time on my hands, especially on weekends. We wouldn't have operations planned during that time, so we'd have those days off. I'd go flying with Captain Pribnow just over the province to see what it was like and try to find enemy forces.

Were you involved in any firefights when you found the enemy or not?

I was not in any firefights at all. There were probably less than 100 shots fired on all 100 operations I went on. The only casualties we had were from booby traps, but that was only four or five soldiers wounded in the time that I was there. My experience in Viet Nam was not a nerve-racking experience. The one thing that I would do was I'd fly with Captain Pribnow. He had a little plane, and I sat behind him. He would allow me to fly the plane back to My Tho because he had to fill out his paper work of what he saw. That was kind of fun, and I enjoyed that. We did that on weekends, too, when we had time off.

What was the hardest part about being in the war?

Being away from my family was the hardest part about the war. It was tough. I had a brand new daughter. When I went to Vietnam, my daughter Anne was less than one year old. One of the neat things about the war was that I got to go on rest and recuperation in Hawaii. There, my wife Yvonne and Anne met me so I could spend a week with them in the middle of my tour. I wrote home just about everyday (about five days a week). It was just another thing to do. For me trying to stay busy was the toughest part of my job there.

> *"WE GOT UP AS HIGH AS WE COULD IN THE PLANE IN A HURRY, AND WHEN WE GOT BACK, THERE WERE A COUPLE OF HOLES IN THE PLANE."*

Is there one particular experience that stands out in your mind from when you were over there?

Yes, one did. It goes back to flying with Captain Pribnow. His airplane could carry four rockets under the wings. The rockets were supposed to be smoke rockets for marking on the ground where we'd find enemy so we could bring in helicopters to support the area. He put high explosives (H.E.) like little bombs under his wings, and he'd go try to shoot enemy, and you'd hardly ever see anybody, but you'd see boats on these many canals that were there. We called them sampans. We'd go sink sampans with the little bombs in enemy territory. He'd do a dive bombing type strategy, go high in the air and then come down when he had it in the sights. The airplane didn't really have sights; he'd put grease pencil on the windshield, and he'd shoot at the boats. After doing that for several months, we found a sampan at a canal crossing, and we were coming down at it almost ready to let go of the rocket, and there was this 50-caliber machine gun shooting at us. I guess they had enough of us going and sinking their sampans. A 50-caliber machine gun is a pretty big gun, and every fifth bullet is a tracer, and you could see these yellow things going by the windshield of the airplane. We got up as high as we could in the plane in a hurry, and when we got back there were a couple of holes in the plane. So that was as close as I wanted to get to combat in Vietnam. It was boredom that got us into that. After that we didn't do that anymore.

Do you think the U.S. could have won the war?

I think there's always a possibility that we could have won, but I don't think we were destined to win the war. I think there would have had to be changes, probably too many changes that the American people and we, as military people, wouldn't have wanted to do. The way it was set-up, obviously, we couldn't have won. I think that probably the government we were backing wasn't good enough to win for anyway. I think it was probably very unlikely that we could have ever won that war.

"THEY WOULD TAKE THE FEATHERS OFF AND CLEAN THE CHICKENS, AND THEY'D START CHOPPING IT UP UNTIL THEY GOT TO THE TOENAILS..."

Is there anything that you liked about being in Vietnam?

I liked the people that I worked with. The country was nice. I enjoyed photography and took some nice pictures while I was over there. I was walking around in Saigon, and I had my nice Omega watch stolen from me. This guy ran, grabbed it, and dove into the Mekong River. I never saw him again. I enjoyed the times that I was in Saigon, and the people there were nice. I think it was interesting just to go out and see banana trees, pineapples, and stuff like that growing that you can't see in Wisconsin.

Did you meet any interesting people while in Vietnam? Did you get to know the Vietnamese people very well?

Surprisingly, not outside the Provincial people that I dealt with. I'm not that good at languages, even though I did take some Vietnamese before going over there. I wasn't able to get into conversations because my counterparts could speak and understand English. When we went out on operations, at times some of the Vietnamese officers wouldn't be able to speak English, so we had an interpreter. I found the food interesting. We had chicken on almost every operation we went out on. They'd purchase chickens from the local people. I called it chopped chicken. They would take the feathers off and clean the chickens, and they'd start chopping it up until they got to the toenails, and they'd throw it in a big pot and that was our meal along with rice and a soy sauce made from fish.

While we're talking about food, did you eat any-thing gross while you were over there?

Not really, although this one time they brought in paddy rat. I watched where it went, and I decided not to eat it. In that town I met this guy that had a housekeeper that was a Vietnamese cook, and rather than eating the Army rations, she'd cook for the two of us. She'd go down to the market and get us lots of fresh fruit to go with the meal. That was real nice, and I paid her to cover some of the cost of the food.

How did people treat you when you returned to the U.S. after serving in the Vietnam War?
I was still in the military. I stayed in for five more years. As far as I was concerned, people treated me well. Many times I was living on base with people in the same situation as I was. There were no hard feelings between my family and I. I found it hard to figure out why people were protesting and doing those types of things. But looking back now, they probably had a point. We obviously didn't win the war, and we wasted time there.

What did "serving your country," mean to you during active duty and now as a veteran?
I traveled a lot in addition to just being in the military. While I was in the military, I spent three years in Germany, a year in Korea, and a year in Vietnam. I was in California, Texas, and North Carolina. I love traveling. Since then I've been to China on my own. I've traveled again throughout Europe. You find that the best country in the world is the United States. It's nice to go and visit, but one of things you enjoy is that we've got the best country. We have the best people, and we have a good way of life that is worth protecting. I'd hate to have other people telling us what to do. I think we have a good system where we can voice our disagreements and most of the time they are respected, and in the end you'll usually come up with the best results. Vietnam is a good example of this freedom; it was obviously good that we got out when we did, and I think that it takes people to be willing to sacrifice and protect our country. I am proud that I served my country, and I would have liked to stay for my 20 years, but I am glad that I am in Wausau so that my daughters could get to know their grandparents. When you're in the military, that's a problem because you don't get to have much of a family life, and I've got a great family.

Is that one of the reasons you moved to Wausau after your military service was done?
Yes, my wife Yvonne is from Cecil, so I looked for employment in the Fox River Valley and Wisconsin River Valley area, and I just happened to end up back in Wausau where I grew up because there was a job opening at Marathon Electric when I went to apply. They needed an accountant, and I had a degree in accounting so that just happened to work out. It was a good choice because I have three great sisters, brothers-in-law, cousins, nieces, and everyone that make these miserable winters fine and easy to put up with.

Did you have any difficulties dealing with the memories when you were back in the U.S.?
No, none whatsoever. I was not in a difficult wartime situation where I could have been killed, like during that one plane incident with the 50-caliber machine gun. My biggest problem was boredom while I was there. Occasionally, there was some mortar fire that landed in the town of My Tho. It never really threatened our compound. For me, there were no real scary war situations.

Would you want to go back to Vietnam today?
My wife, Yvonne, has said for the last 20-25 years that she'd like to go to Vietnam, and I never had any interest in it. But in the last couple years I think yes, I would like to go back. I'd like to show her where I was and to see what changes have taken place there. When I first left Vietnam I didn't want to go back. I thought of it as I've done my time, and I was ready to go home. It wasn't a happy time for me while I was there; it was pretty boring. Now, I would definitely like to go back.

Are you still in contact with any of the people that were in your group?
No, none at all. I lost contact with most of the people in my group real quickly, like within a year or so. The biggest reason for that was because we were all in different branches of the Army. I still am in contact with people that I know from Air Defense but not from my Adviser MACV job.

Is there a message you have for young people today about the war?
I wish there were no wars. I think that having a strong military organization helps prevent wars. People should not think that military people are out there looking for a fight. I know they're not. I think a country that would want to get into a war with the United States or our allies might have second thoughts if we are strong enough and may seem overwhelming to them. I think that we are a strong country, and I support our military.

Since Jack Flaker's tour of duty in the Vietnam War he has worked at Marathon Electric and Able Distributing Co. as an accountant.

Interviewed by Jessica Wolf and Jamie Theisen
Transcribed by Jessica Wolf

Ray Knippel

Knipple joined the Army in 1951 and was sent over to Vietnam in September 1967-February 1972. He was the head of the MACV(Military Assistance Command Vietnam) the Chief Administrator of the NCO (Non-Commisioned Officers), and belonged to the CORDS organization (Civil Operation Rural Development Support) which assisted Vietnamese government in passing the Pacification Plans.

My name is Ray Knippel. I went to Vietnam in September 1967 and ended up in Saigon at a replacement center. I was supposed to be assigned to a particular unit in Military Assistance Command Vietnam headquarters (MAVC). When I went out to the headquarters for my interview, I found out that the job was no longer available. I was concerned about what would happen to me. I spent several days in Saigon before I was finally assigned to an organization in the headquarters called Civil Operations and Rural Development Support. It was a group of Army, Navy, Air Force, and Marine people and included people from the American embassy and from the United States Agency for International Development. We were a liaison organization to the Vietnamese government to assist the Vietnamese government in planning for the secession of hostilities and the redevelopment of the countryside into an agricultural status that it had been before the war.

I lived in a building about three or four miles from MACV headquarters. I was bussed back and forth on a regular basis to and from the headquarters. We worked an average of twelve hours a day, seven days a week. My job was on the administrative end of it. I took care of a lot of paperwork; I took care of classified documents. I did just about anything administratively that needed to be done. Most of the people that I worked with were directly in the headquarters building. We had one small group of three people that worked in the Vietnamese Ministry of Rural Development. They would call me periodically whenever they needed supplies. I would go to the supply office and get whatever it was they needed and contact them when I had everything, and they would send their secretary out to pick it up. Other than that isolated group, we were all located in the headquarters building which was located at Tan Son Nhut Airbase in Vietnam. I got there in September 1967. The normal tour of duty in Vietnam was twelve months. I think that this was probably the most interesting job I had all the while I was in the military. I originally enlisted in the Army in February 1951 and decided to stay in. When my tour in Vietnam was half over, I talked to my boss, who was a civilian, about extending my visit to six months in Vietnam. I could provide a bit of continuity in the administrative end of it and I thought that I was doing something worthwhile. He agreed, so I applied for a six month extension which was approved. The same thing happened later on. I finally ended up staying in Vietnam until February 1972.

Did you support American involvement in Vietnam?

We were involved, and I was in the Army. I supported what we were doing in the office I was in. It was called the pacification of Vietnam, and it was different from the fighting end of it. The fighting end of it was concerned with eliminating the effectiveness of the Viet Cong. The part I was involved with was trying to enhance the effectiveness of the Vietnamese citizen, the farmers and peasants who tilled the soil, and trying to build up their economy. We had a varied assortment of people from different agencies as I have already said. The lowest ranking individual in the office was a PFC. The highest ranking military member was a full colonel. The highest ranking civilian member of the organization was the equivalent grade of a US ambassador. So we had a lot of different folks of different political persuasions, educational and working backgrounds, a very diverse group which made for some very interesting conversations at night.

There were interesting work situations when we disagreed on what approach we should take on something. Somebody would bring up what they thought was a good civilian point of view, and somebody would counter with what they thought was a good military point of view. Then we would hash it out to see what we could do. Some of the officers worked very closely with the Vietnamese military and civilian government in order to work up the pacification plan. The plan was intended to eliminate combat activities in the

"WHEN I ARRIVED, AND SEVERAL OF THE OTHER GUESTS STARTED ARRIVING, HE INTRODUCED ME TO THE AMERICAN AMBASSADOR TO VIETNAM, THE PRESIDENT OF VIETNAM, AND TO GENERAL LUAN, WHO WAS THE CHIEF OF POLICE."

four corps areas in Vietnam and what to do to rebuild the country economically, commercially and agriculturally. The people who worked in the Ministry of Rural Development for the Vietnamese government were dealt with by me on a regular basis on the telephone.

I didn't know the extent of the involvement with my office with the Vietnamese government until the man who was the senior liaison with the Vietnamese government called me up one day and said that the following Friday he was going to have a little get together at his villa, and because of everything I had done, he wanted to know if I would be willing to come. I said yes. I arrived at his villa expecting just a small group of people, probably that I knew, and it didn't quite work out that way. When I arrived, and several of the other guests started arriving, he introduced me to the American Ambassador to Vietnam, the President of Vietnam, and to General Luan, who was the Chief of Police. He traveled in a much higher circle than I did. I didn't feel that comfortable around all of these high powered people, so I kind of gravitated over to the bar, and as people came up I started mixing drinks for them. Mark appreciated the service that I provided because he frequently invited me over to his functions as the resident bartender. I got in on some interesting parties and met some interesting and influential people while I was there.

Did you experience the Tet Offensive?

I was in Vietnam during the Tet Offensive in 1968. I lived in a building on Plantation Road. Just about a half mile from my building was the Phu Tho race track. Vietnamese Tet is the equivalent of our New Year, a lot of celebration, a lot of gun shooting, and fireworks. During the Tet of 1968 there was a lot of firing and noise and rockets in the air. There was a military bus stop near my building where I would be picked up and transported to the headquarters. Nothing seemed to be happening, and I was not riding the bus at that time. I had acquired a motorcycle, which is another story. I was surprised there was so little traffic on the highway. I finally decided that it was due to the Tet celebration that people were sleeping late from the night before. When I got to the airbase, there was a string of Vietnamese soldiers stretched across the road, and they all had machine guns. All the machine guns were pointed in my general direction, so I just raised my hands and they let me through. When I got to the headquarters building, I found so few people there I was informed that the VC had attacked the city the night before and they had captured the Phu Tho race track. My building was about a block from some empty fields, and the VC were in the fields. I finally got home that evening, and we were told to remain in our billets until further notice. Most everybody in the billet, that lived there had a refrigerator in their rooms and some food stashed away. We did not have dining facilities in our building. I was the senior occupant and responsible for the safety of the people in that billet so I called a meeting and we kind of canvassed our food supply. We decided that we would dine jointly instead of separately, so we pooled all the food we had. I set up perimeter guards around the building, on the building, and the Vietnamese guarded the building on the outside. We organized our self defense and had our own counterattack plan if anything happened. There were strings of Vietnamese refugees going by and evacuating to get away from the VC. We were under siege for three days. We ran out of food, and some of the people came to me and wanted to get permission to go out and find some food for us. I was hesitant about this, but they ended up with three people who were armed with a sub-machine gun, a rifle, and a .45 pistol. They were willing to go look for

"WE RAN OUT OF FOOD AND SOME OF THE PEOPLE CAME TO ME AND WANTED TO GET PERMISSION TO GO OUT AND FIND FOOD FOR US."

food. They were planning to go to Tan Son Nhut airbase to see what they could get there. I finally said it was all right. They took off, and they were gone for several hours. They came back, and I went down to see what kind of supplies they were able to obtain for us. Unfortunately, they didn't have any food, but the jeep was loaded with beer. Leave it up to the Americans!

Do you keep in touch with any of those people?
No. I mentioned the motorcycle. I used to have to make periodic trips down to the American embassy, and I usually got a staff car to do this. Traffic in Saigon is not like anything I have seen outside of Tokyo, Japan. It's absolutely horrendous, even worse than Washington, D.C. It used to take me several hours to make a round trip, and it was about four or five miles. One of the American civilians who left had owned a 90cc motorcycle that his wife still had in her possession and she didn't drive it. She was the secretary in my office, and she mentioned it one day, and I decided to buy it. I bought it and drove it around the parking lot for several days until I got familiar with operating a motorcycle. I would take my motorcycle down to the embassy when I had official trips to make and I could make, it in about thirty minutes when it had taken hours before.

Ray Knipple Master Sergeant Vietnam 1969

During the Tet offensive, when I was on my way to the headquarters one morning, between my billet and the airbase was a little Vietnamese compound that was a radio station. I don't know who they communicated with but it was there and I said there was a block between the field and the buildings. The VC had occupied the field. This morning just as I got by the radio station, they started a fire fight between the people in the station and the VC in the field. I didn't think I could turn around so I leaned over the gas tank and sped away safely. I didn't get hit by any bullets.

While the Tet offensive was on, in the field just north of us, I don't know how heavily the VC had infiltrated, but they sent out helicopter gunships. Helicopters had the ability to hover and they had gatling guns attached to the skids, and they used tracer bullets in the guns so the pilots and the gunners could see where the bullets were going. They would get three or four helicopters hovering over there, and they would saturate the field with thousands of bullets. I never went over and looked, but I am convinced that nothing could have survived such a devastating attack.

I used to go periodically to a Vietnamese cemetery, primarily because it gave me an opportunity to get away from the noise and the bustle and gave me a place that was secluded and peaceful. Unfortunately there were times that people would be coming in to bury one of their casualties. The wailing and the commotion of a funeral like that was something I had never experienced. It was very unique. I cannot explain the sounds that they made or the impact that it had on me being in the same vicinity and witnessing the event. I got to know some Vietnamese people in the time that I was there, but I never got to learn the language. Each one of the billets that I was in had a Vietnamese who served as the desk clerk, acted as a liaison between the military and the Vietnamese, and took care of the maids and the houseboys. I was in my second billet, and I happened to mention to the desk clerk one day I had to make a trip to the Vietnamese Civilian Personnel Office and talk with them about something, and she asked me who I was going to see. I told her that I was going to one of the ladies in the office and the desk clerk said that she was her sister. When I arrived in the office, I met Miss Hong and told her that I knew her sister. She confirmed that she was her sister, and we became good friends. They took several of us to a Catholic mass one Sunday morning, and that was an experience. I didn't know that there were that many Catholics in Vietnam, but the crowd was incredible.

We went downtown one day in a jeep for dinner in a Vietnamese restaurant. There was an enclosed area that had a guard on it, and we parked the jeep in there and went in for dinner. When we came back out, the jeep was gone. We called the transportation folks and told them that the jeep was stolen, but they said they had the jeep at their facility. The transportation people pointed out that where we had parked the jeep it was in an unsecured area, and so they confiscated the jeep. They kept it for two weeks. I can understand that because there were guards that would inspect the undercarriage of the jeeps to check for bombs.

Everybody used to talk about Vung Tau. Vung Tau was apparently one of the nicest places in Vietnam. I had never been there, so my boss told me one day to make plans to go and see Vung Tau. They let me take one of the staff cars, and I found a few people who wanted to go, so we went and spent half a day on the beach. It was the worst time of the day because the sun was at the highest point. I learned that it was an R&R place for allied soldiers and VC. It was a neutral zone, and neither side messed with the other. It was there for relaxation and swimming, and the war was off limits while you were in the area.

Did you travel off the base a lot?

I used to make periodic trips, deliveries and stuff, to second corps. Saigon was in third corps. Fourth corps was the Delta, first corps was up in the north, and second corps was between first and third corps. I did make some delivery trips into second and fourth corps, but I never got up into first corps area. If you have ever seen any movies of Vietnam or seen newsreels about Vietnam, parts of the country are very lush, very tropical, beautiful places to be. Saigon's temperature varied between seventy and ninety-five on an annual basis. We had two seasons, a dry season and a monsoon season. During the monsoon season you could almost set your clock at 2 o'clock in the afternoon when it started raining. When I first started traveling on my motorcycle, I used to wear a poncho to keep the rain off, but in that kind of temperature when you are wrapped up like that, you start to sweat a lot. You'd get as wet as if the rain hit you, but you wouldn't smell as bad if you got wet from the rain. You would get soaked to the skin, and an hour later you would be dried off. During the Tet Offensive my building faced an access street that led to Plantation Road. On Plantation Road there was a billet that the officers lived in, and their building and my building formed an "L" shape, and in the billet behind the officers were four generators that supplied power to the officer's billet. I had a small generator out in front of the billet I lived in. During the Tet offensive a rocket came in and missed both of the buildings but hit the generator behind their building and blew out the power. We were fortunate there were no casualties, but they wandered around in the dark until they could make arrangements. Vietnam had its own power system. It was not up to the American standards, but they ran forty to fifty cycles, but the American equipment wouldn't operate with that standard. That is why American buildings had their own power supply.

"I MAY HAVE BEEN THE ONLY SOLIDER TO BE ORDERED OUT OF VIETNAM."

I was scheduled to remain in Vietnam until June or July 1972, but a message came in from the Department of the Army to issue orders to send me to an assignment in Washington, D.C. We sent back to the department that I had extended for six months, and I had taken the thirty days leave that we were authorized, so I was obligated to serve, but the Army said that they knew I had been there long enough and to send me home. I may have been the only soldier to be ordered out of Vietnam. If you extended for six months, the military services gave you thirty days leave to anyplace in the world. Your leave would not begin until you arrived at your destination. We had an enterprising young man who picked out an island south of Hawaii, so he flew from Vietnam to Hawaii, He must have had this figured out because once a month there was a ship that went from Hawaii to the island. He arrived in Hawaii one day after the ship left. He spent almost thirty days in Hawaii waiting for the next ship. He got to the place where he was supposed to go, and he had his thirty days there, and the ship left the day before his leave ended, so he was there for an extra two weeks. He was gone for about three months before he returned to Vietnam.

What kind of reception did you receive when you returned to the states?

I was assigned to an agency out of the Pentagon, and I guess the people in that area were connected with the military or the government, and I didn't have any problems.

Did any protestors bother you?

No, about the same time I came back they were negotiating with the VC to release the prisoners being held in the north. You received a hash mark for six months overseas, and I had about ten of them. At Ft. Myer I was in a club and people were sending drinks over my way seeing all the hash marks on my sleeve. I appreciate what you are doing getting these stories out.

Knippel retired from the Army in February 1981. He also worked for a non-profit organization for 11 years, then retired. He did volunteer work for a Catholic Church. He is now a Sacristan at Resurrection Parish in Wausau. Knippel has extended family in Wisconsin and California. His hobby since high school has been to repair clocks.

Ray Knipple Master Sergeant U.S. Army

Interviewed by D.C. E. Junior High students

Gerald Kort

Kort was a chaplain in a VA hospital for fifteen years, serving from 1982 to 1997. He was involved with many soldiers with Post Traumatic Stress Disorder (PTSD) and other problems.

How were you connected with the Vietnam War?
My connection to the Vietnam War came through the veterans that served there where I worked as a Chaplain in the VA hospital for 15 years from 1982 to 1997.

What was your job there? What did you do?
I was a Chaplin.

Were the people pretty bad, or were there different degrees? You helped them through post-traumatic-stress disorder, correct?
Yes, we had a PTSD program there. I worked with that, and I did one-on-one with individuals as well.

Without saying names, could you tell some of the stories?
Yes I could. Most of them are rather gruesome. I don't know if you want the stories. One that I've used before, an individual who came into the hospital periodically, just was depressed. He was using drugs and alcohol to an excess. Periodically he'd come into the hospital and get dried out and get put back on his feet and would leave and it wasn't long before he'd be back in. I worked on the intake ward. The psychiatrist, the nurse, the social worker, the psychologist and the Chaplain would meet and go over the patients' symptoms and try to work out a treatment for them. When he came in, this young man was angry. He was extremely angry when he was sober and dry. His language was bad. Anyhow, he wanted one on one. That's what he kept asking for. That means individual counseling, not just stick him in some group, or fill him full of drugs. Well, the team had talked and nobody wanted to take him. The psychiatrist said they didn't have time and the psychologist was scared, didn't want to meet with him. Nobody wanted to meet with him, so I said I'd meet with him. The next team meeting with the man, he came in, and the nurse said, "You'll be meeting with the Chaplain." The patient said, "I don't want to meet with any God d*** Chaplain." That is what he wanted, but the psychiatrist said, "It's him or nothing; you take your pick." So eventually he said, "Okay, I'll meet with him," and the first few meetings were difficult. He was angry and we had to work through that, get past his anger at the whole world, the VA, everything, and everybody. I sensed underneath the anger there was a lot of hurt there, so we stuck it out and eventually he came to trust me enough where he told me this story. In 'Nam he had been in this firefight, him and his platoon, and they were getting overrun. His best buddy was injured by shrapnel that had cut across his abdomen

and his intestines were coming out. This was not just a buddy. This man had also served best man at his wedding, so they had a close relationship. His friend had said, "Don't let them take me. Don't let them

take me." They knew that often torture awaited those that were captured, so the patient, let's call him Jim, Jim picked his buddy up and tried to balance his rifle over his shoulder and picked up his buddy and tried to run through the woods, the jungle. Periodically he'd have to put him down and push his intestines back into his abdomen, and the guys eyes were glazing. He was dying, but he kept saying, "Don't let them get me. Don't let them get me." The Cong was getting closer, so eventually Jim had to make a decision. He took his rifle and killed his best friend, which was a humane thing to do, because he didn't want to be captured and whatever life he had left,

to be tortured. But it was something that bothered and ate away at Jim for all those years. He had never been able to let it out, so we did a lot of crying, and we did a lot of talking about forgiveness. Eventually he was better and he left the hospital. I can't say he was cured. I don't know if he'll ever be cured, but he was able to function without running back to the hospital for drugs, or without always turning to alcohol. I've seen him in years since then, and he's adjusted as well as can be expected. That's one kind of situation -- when they had to face that choice. One that isn't told very often, and for good reason, at this one particular camp, I'll call this one Jim too. Jim was telling how there was this one big black soldier who periodically would go off to the nearest Cong village and would rape a Vietnamese girl. He'd come back, and they would shell or morter the compound where the guy was staying. Well, they got sick of this, so one night when the black man came back to camp, Jim was on guard duty and he shot and killed him so they didn't have to go through this. But what happened was that it angered the black members in the platoon, so they had their own war going on inside, as well as facing the Viet Cong. There are some that are too gruesome to tell. One other one, so often when our troops came back they were called baby killers, and they were spit on. In some cases they were, but I had one young man that came to see me, and he was fighting ever since the war. He grew up respecting life and learned that children are precious and you never do anything to hurt them. In 'Nam he had killed a Vietnamese child, but the reason being that the child was coming at them with a grenade. You look at it from the outside, and you say that you were justified, that even though this was a young person you would've been killed, but he couldn't get over it. Part of his mind knew this was justified,

> *"THEY KNEW THAT OFTEN TORTURE AWAITED THOSE THAT WERE CAPTURED."*

kill or be killed, yet it was a child, and so he faced that and will always face that agony for the rest of his life. Many of them went into deep depression. They used drugs and alcohol just to try to numb some of these experiences, going against their morals and what they had been taught.

Did you have any women or girls that came to see you, or was it all guys?
Through the years I had a few female patients, but they weren't directly involved in battle, so it wasn't that kind of problem. A lot of the Nam vets wouldn't come to a Chaplain; they didn't even want to be in the VA, they didn't trust the VA. That was one underlying thread almost universally in the PTSD patients.

They didn't trust the United States government, and there were some good reasons, but they erected whatever kind of defenses they could psychologically, to battle this, and in most cases, they were poor defenses. Through the program some were actually helped. There are other stories, problems that we worked through, but some of them are too gruesome to tell. Vietnam was just not like the other wars in which you had a definite enemy and you knew who it was. You were fighting soldiers, but in Vietnam in the villages you didn't know who was Cong and who wasn't. You never knew where the danger lay. Drugs were rampant: uppers, downers, narcotics. They sensed it was a futile war. Having to face women and children, having to face a country that was divided, having to face jeers, spitting, there were some I talked to that when they embarked they walked through crowds, and people spit on them and called them names. That didn't happen in other wars. There was more need for counseling in Vietnam.

Were most of the people you counseled draftees or had they enlisted?
I knew both. Enlisted men had PTSD too. There were guys who would be reliving these experiences in their sleep. They'd be in bed, and many of them would end up hitting or choking their spouses. That was one of the reasons we needed them to come into the program. They couldn't get rid of the nightmares. They were hurting their families, their loved ones.

Do you have anything else to say?
We shouldn't have been there. It created pains, upheavals, that have marred families from that point on.

Could this happen today?
Oh sure, because politicians guard their turf.

Interviewed and transcribed by Kristy Isberner

Larry Krause

Krause served with the 3rd Marine Air Wing which was stationed in Da Nang. He arrived in Vietnam in 1968 and served in finance in that unit.

First of all I think we should just get your story and then ask questions. What did you do, and how were you involved in the war?

I was in the Marines and was stationed in California for two years. At that time I got orders to go to Vietnam and was assigned to the 3rd Marine Air Wing, a division of the Marine Air Force. After receiving my orders, I flew back home to visit my friends and family in Wausau, then flew to California to a staging area for those military personnel that are going to Vietnam. On the way over, our plane stopped in Anchorage, Alaska. It was the middle of winter, the beginning of February or late January. From there we flew to the island of Okinawa which is another staging area. Military bases occupy nearly the entire island. I was there for a day or two, and then we boarded planes that took us to Vietnam. A couple hundred thousand troops were stationed in Vietnam by the time I arrived, which was early 1968. No one was there to meet me when I landed in Da Nang. You just get off the plane, and it's hot, and it's dusty, and there are dirt roads. I showed someone I met my orders, and he said, "I think it's down the road." I started walking. Eventually, after walking and hitchhiking about 10 miles, I reached the location of the unit I was assigned to, which was right in the middle of Da Nang. I located the building I where I was assigned to work, and as I walked around the corner, there were all the guys, having a steak fry. Not exactly what I expected for my first day in Vietnam.

The barracks were old, French barracks made of stucco. We lived right there in a small compound which was about the size of Marathon Park. Right outside the cyclone fence bordering the area where we lived, was the village. The Vietnamese lived right in our backyard, about 20 feet away. I worked in an office that controlled supplies and finances for this Marine Air Wing. Most of the people in the Marine Air Wing were pilots and flew planes. There weren't too many of us that didn't do that. We were in a support role. What most people don't know about Vietnam is that for every person that was in a fighting role, there were at least ten that weren't. They were supporting them in various ways, whether it be what I did, which was keep records, or people that were cooks, jeep drivers, delivery people, medical, or auto repair personnel. There were people that worked in the morgue . . . all sorts of jobs just like you would have in a typical city. Various branches of the military were stationed in Da Nang including the Marines, Army, Air Force and Navy. However, Da Nang was predominantly occupied by the Marines and the Army. Da Nang was the I-Core, which was the northern-most sector right below the DMZ (demilitarized zone). This was an area between South Vietnam and North Vietnam.

I got into the country the day after Tet. Everything was disrupted, or at least the military wasn't quite as organized as they had been, and that's probably one of the reasons I was sent there. It was the Tet offensive. I was fortunate to get there after the Tet as opposed to the day of the Tet. In those days a "tour of duty" (active duty) was 13 months. I was a three-year enlistee who had already had two years in, and all of that time had been in Palm Springs, California. In hindsight, Palms Springs, California, was a pretty nice place to be, but I had volunteered to do my 13 months in Vietnam. I had arrived in Vietnam about February 1st, so my "tour of duty" would have me scheduled to get out the following January. But the Marines had an "early out" program, that if you were due to get out within a month of Christmas, they let you go home early. So I got home December 1st. I was only in Vietnam about 10 months.

What was an average day like?

We lived in a barrack probably a little larger than 15 feet by 15 feet. They were stucco, built when the French were fighting the Vietnamese back in the early 50s. We'd get up in the morning and shower, but we didn't have any warm water. You never get used to a cold

"WE WORKED SIX DAYS A WEEK. SUNDAYS WE WENT TO CHINA BEACH."

shower, no matter how warm it is outside. After showering, we could go the mess hall. I usually went directly to my office. We had coffee and our computer printouts. It was like an office anywhere. A colonel ran the office, but he was rarely there because he liked to fly, so he flew whenever he could. Pilots don't really want to work in the office. There were about six of us in the office, and I ran the office for the enlisted people, similar to what I did back in the United States. We usually worked until about 4:00 p.m., and then we went to the Sergeants' Club. The Club was nothing more than a bar with an area where they could bring in some bands. That would be a typical day.

We worked six days a week. Sundays we went to China Beach. The only difference between China Beach and a beach in the United States is that helicopters were flying over for protection. It was different than a lot of people think; there was less danger for many people than most people realized. Other than going to China Beach, there was no place to go, so we stayed right in the compound. We had television, but it was Vietnamese television. We had some shows from the United Sates, but just a few. It was all controlled and all censored. We didn't get newspapers from the United States, so we really didn't have any idea of the protesting going on. We knew it was going on before we left, but while over there, you're basically limited to the *Stars and Stripes*, which is the military newspaper.

I went to Okinawa two or three times on what's called a courier run. This was to get their documents or to take my documents there. It was our headquarters. You'd go down to the corner where there was a helipad, where helicopters land. The helicopter lands and you ask where he's going, and if he's going to the airstrip, you hitch a ride. No tickets necessary. So you'd helicopter hitchhike to the airstrip. When you get to the airstrip, you'd sit around waiting until a plane came through that had some room, jump a plane, and you'd go to Okinawa. You'd stay there for two or three days, as long as you could before you had to go back, of course, because this was like R&R. I did that about three or four times. I went to Hong Kong for a couple days. I went to Malaysia for a week. So it wasn't as if I had it much better than any people actually.

Our base was a very tame kind of operation, not very dangerous at all. We'd get rocketed sometimes which was our only fear. The Viet Cong would try to shoot rockets at the airstrip to get the planes. If they had what's called a short round, they miscalculated; then we could get hit. They'd have no reason to direct their fire at a bunch office people. Why would they want to hit us? They wanted, of course, to get the planes. They never really hit us while I was there, although after I got back to the United States, the office I worked in got hit by a rocket, and some people were killed. It was a very unfortunate thing, but it was an accident. They had missed their target.

Were there any African Americans in you unit?

Sure. We had some, and we had some racial problems. When I was there, we had race riots. Not too severe, but one day when we were coming back from China Beach, there was a large group of blacks (more than 40) running up through the center of the highway. They were chanting anti-white phrases. We were kind of nervous, sitting in a jeep with a pistol when a bunch of guys not too pleased about your color are coming through with automatic weapons. Nothing really happened, but that kind of racial problem was unusual. The black guys I worked with in my office were not racist.

Were you enlisted in the army or were you drafted?

I was going to college in Madison, and like a lot of people my age, I wasn't ready to go to college. I was bored or lonely or whatever you are when you are 19, so I enlisted in the Marines. I dropped out of college, enlisted in the Marines, and went home and told my mother. She was not happy at all with that decision. She didn't think that was too smart, and she was upset. At the time the Marines hadn't been drafting yet, so I enlisted, which meant I was in for three years. The Marines eventually started drafting people.

> *"WHEN YOU ARE IN VIETNAM, IT'S A DIFFERENT CULTURE. THERE ARE VERY FEW RULES."*

Did you ever see a problem with drugs in Vietnam?

The only drugs were marijuana and a lot of alcohol, more alcohol than anything else. All of the units that weren't in the bush were in combat. We all had beer and any kind of alcohol, pallets full of it, and every drink was 20 cents regardless of what it was.

Was there a lot of emotional and physical stress?

Not where I was. Certainly not physical and not emotional to the extent that people would have in combat situations.

Can you describe more about what you did in the office?

I was called the fiscal chief. Our group kept the records that relate to what is purchased. This is very similar to a budget for school, recording how the money is spent and what items need to be requisitioned. We kept records for the entire air wing and produced reports from the records. The colonel needed to make sure the records got to his boss who was in Okinawa, and I was usually the guy that was lucky enough to take them.

What do you think was the hardest part about being in Vietnam?

I didn't think it was that hard. Probably the hardest part was adjusting to very few rules. In the United States military there was a rule for everything, and certain people that go in the military get comfortable with the fact that you had to do this at this time otherwise you get in trouble. When you are in Vietnam, it's a different culture. There are very few rules. For example, if I wanted to go somewhere, I just figured out how to get there, and I could go. I had to work at not becoming bored. I read, and I played a lot of bridge.

Did you get to fly any of the airplanes?

I didn't fly because I wasn't a pilot, but I was on a number of them because that was our mode of transportation. C-130s, which are still in use, were cargo planes used to go back and forth to Hong Kong and Okinawa. Helicopters were like our taxicabs. That's how we got around the country. They never had windows because they could get shot out. They built the window opening without a window, so when we flew you could put your arm out the window like you would in a car, and it was a good way to travel.

Did you learn anything that you didn't know before you were enlisted in the Marines?
I think I probably learned independence. In the Marines, they treat you badly if you don't play by the rules. They can put you in the brig (jail), or they can send you to Vietnam. Once I came back, there's nobody in my life that could ever put me in jail without a trial or send me to Vietnam. In the military you don't have the same rights that we do right here. The military has a different code of justice, and they can put you in jail without a trial for certain infractions.

Did you make any lasting friendships during the war?
There were four of us that played bridge regularly. We came back to the Unites States, and each of us went our own way. We had a lot of things in common, but when you get back here, life goes on and you tend to forget about it.

Was there one particular experience that stand out? One memory?
I discovered that a friend of mine from Wausau was stationed on Chu Lai. I caught a helicopter going in that direction. You can do that on weekends, ask for the day off. He worked in supply, and he found something on the floor of their supply warehouse. He took it to his captain, and it turned out this thing was a gyroscope for a fighter plane, which is an extremely expensive item. It was worth $100,000. The captain said, "Where did you find this?" "It was just lying in the middle of the warehouse next to a shelf," he replied. The captain said, "Take it out and bury it. It's not on my records, and I don't want to explain to anybody why it's here." That would be a classic. The military didn't care what it cost just so you don't look bad. This officer didn't want to have to explain how you could possibly find something that wasn't on his records, so the easiest thing to do was just go bury it. There was a lot of waste.

What kind of reception did you get when you came back?
I went to California, which at that time, the late 60's, already had an antiwar movement going on. I was there for a while because I had to wait to get "mustered out." During these few weeks I attended a quiz show in Hollywood hosted by Bob Barker.

Did you have any opinions regarding the antiwar movement that was happening back here while you were in Vietnam?
I didn't know a lot about it because the media was so controlled and censored our news. When I did get back, I was involved in the antiwar movement because I thought after being there, I saw how ludicrous the war effort was. I knew it wasn't going anywhere. There wasn't ever going to be a victory. Once you are there, you recognize that. You just hunker down, put in your time, and come back home.

Do you think the U.S. could have won the war?
They probably could have if they were willing to treat it like a full scale war. If they implemented heavy bombing, I'm sure they probably could have won. The Vietnamese have a history of fighting with other countries, so even if you won, that wouldn't have stopped the fighting. You'd win and discover you didn't win anything.

Do you think Johnson or Nixon could have done something differently that would have ended the war more quickly than it did?
Sure. They could have pulled out. Either one of them had that option, but neither one would do it. Lyndon Johnson was very close to pulling out. From what I've read, that's one of the reasons he didn't run again. He didn't want to face the decision and be the first president to withdraw from a war. Nixon could have done it earlier. Basically he bombed North Vietnam to the peace table, but it would have saved an awful lot of lives if he would have just walked out. His ego and pride wouldn't allow him to do that. Instead he prolonged the war two to three years.

When did you hear about the Tet Offensive? When you were on the plane going there?
I didn't hear about it until I actually got in the country.

So you weren't involved in any way?
No. It was over.

Did you ever see or have any encounters with the Viet Cong or NVA?
No, never saw any, but did see a lot of ARVN which is the South Vietnamese army.

Did you learn to speak any Vietnamese?
No, just pigeon English which is a way that GIs communicate with the Vietnamese. Basically it is a form of English that is simplified for some basic communications.

Do you have a message for young people today about the war happening?
War is not a very glamorous thing. It's necessary, but anyone that wishes to join the military should recognize that war is a horrible experience. They'll lose good friends, and they may be injured themselves. It's a dirty job, but somebody's got to do it. You probably won't be appreciated when you get back. So many Vietnam veterans weren't.

Following his return, Larry Krause served as a chief financial officer.

Interviewed and transcribed by Megan Bahr and Jennifer Graham

Jim Weirauch

Enlisting in the Marines, Weirauch served in Vietnam as a cook. He served his tour in Vietnam in 1967.

How did you become involved in the Vietnam War? Were you drafted or enlisted?
I enlisted in the Marine Corps in 1966.

What were the base camps like when you first arrived?
When I enlisted in the Marine Corps, I went to San Diego for basic training, and because of the activities in Vietnam at the time, they were very busy and there were a lot of troops at those bases, a lot more than you planned on.

Can you describe what an average day was like during the war?
Basically, when I was in Vietnam, I was stationed at a base that was about 20 miles away from the main base. I happened to be a cook in the Marine Corps, so the basic day would consist of getting up at four in the morning and working all day, and basically, at night we would spend some time maybe having guard duty or perimeter duty. This means we had a perimeter around our base that we were stationed at, and we would stand guard duty at night. So basically, you worked about seven days a week, mostly the whole day. Of course there were guys that were in the infantry that would go out and patrol, and there were armor tank divisions so everyone had different jobs.

Were you involved in any combat?
Not directly in any hand-to-hand combat. I was involved in a lot of mortars and rockets and that kind of thing dropping in on where we were stationed. A mortar would just make a bunch of holes in a normal sized house, and a rocket would take a normal house and completely flatten it. So when more would start dropping, we would run to bunkers, which were mainly big holes with sandbags all over the top and around them, and try and get out of the firing zone.

Can you describe what the camp was like where you were stationed? Were there medical areas there or near by?
Most of the housing would be made out of wood floors and tin roofs and screen all around the side. Yes, there were medical facilities and mess halls and places where you could buy your basic needs as far as your toiletries. In most places they actually had a place where they would show movies at night, and they would make it possible to have a beer available even though you were in Vietnam. Unless you were in a

very heavy war zone like up in Khe Sanh, it would be pretty much like a military base in the U.S.

Were there any problems with drugs where you were?

I would say that there was a certain amount of guys that smoked marijuana. That was pretty common because it was so easy to get. But as far as drugs when I was over there, it didn't seem to be that big of a problem, but as far as smoking pot, there were a number of people who did that.

How long were you in Vietnam?

I was there from January until October of 1967. The reason I was there for less than a year was because when I went over with a whole regiment, there were several thousands of us that went over at the same time, when ordinarily a lot of men would go over for a full year and stay over there for one reason or another.

Did you ever get hurt or wounded in any way?

No.

Could you describe the relationship between blacks and whites that you saw?

I think there was a little discrimination both ways when I was in the military, but I don't think it was more prevalent in Vietnam than it was any place else in the U.S. Part of that is because you have such a diverse group of people that get together in the military. A lot of blacks are just being around whites and whites are just being around blacks for the first time, and they learned knowledge about the cultures of each other, but overall, I don't think Vietnam was worse than it was anywhere else.

Did you feel people back in the states knew what was going on in Vietnam?

I think they knew more about what was going on in Vietnam than the soldiers in Vietnam knew. I think the civilians in the states had a better knowledge because of all the news media and because, I think, most of the guys that were over there that were in the military didn't believe they were fighting communism. As far as the anti-war movement, I guess you didn't really pay much attention to that when you were in Vietnam. You were over there for a reason trying to do your job, and I don't think it was a big issue with the soldiers.

"I THINK THE HARDEST PART WAS KNOWING WHEN YOU WERE GOING OVER THERE YOU MIGHT NOT BE COMING BACK..."

Do you think the U.S. should have gotten involved in the war in the first place?

I feel that everybody is entitled to their own opinion. At some point some of the things that came out later on as far as the political motivation to continue to fight the war might have been validated, but I still think that there is a difference in opinion as to if we should have been there. But I think that history will prove that there was some reasoning and protesting about how we could have ended it a lot sooner and won it.

What was the hardest part of being in the war?

I think the hardest part was knowing when you were going over there you might not be coming back, but then when you were over there that fear kind of went away. Then when it was close to time to come home again and it was near the end, you got a realization that you only had a couple more days, and if you made it through then you could come home. It wasn't like a fear of death. It was just one of those things that when you were young, you kind of wanted to live a little longer. It was not like you were having a constant fear of death.

Do you have any experiences that stand out or were harder than others?
Not really, I don't really think much about it, and I don't really dwell on it. It's not even clear in my mind. There are certain things I remember. I can remember going over there and being activated and landing in Vietnam and wondering if right when you got off the plane you would start getting shot at, which really doesn't happen because even though you are in a country where there is a war, there is not fighting everywhere, but I don't have a lot of memories about it. I am kind of a go-with-the-flow guy.

Do you think you made any lasting friendships during your time in Vietnam?
I don't communicate with anybody that was in the military; I don't know where anybody is. I had some buddies over there, and I came home. I can't say that I really had any lasting friendships, but I am sure that did happen to others.

When you came back, were you happy to be back or did you feel like you didn't stay long enough?
No, I was happy to be back and to get out of the military. When I came back, even though you had people protesting and that sort of thing, that's not how I was treated. I was treated like, not a war hero but someone who was respected. I remember never being treated like I was a killer; I was always treated very nicely.

Was it hard being there and seeing men just being killed and men killing men?
Yes, it was something that was hard to accept, like when I might be having a normal day and then next I might step on a land mine and you're gone. That's not something you get used to, but it's all part of being there.

Do you have a message for young people about the war today?
Well as a father, obviously, I don't want to see another war, but I still believe that the U.S. is doing what is right. But the type of war that we are fighting is different than Vietnam or any other war. I do feel that the military in general is a good experience for young people, and if they have to represent their country, then so be it. I wouldn't want to volunteer my son to do it tomorrow, but if he did do it, I would think that he was doing what was right and to go ahead and do it.

Do you have any other stories?
No, I don't have a lot of recollection of a lot of the things that happened over there.

So it wasn't really emotionally hard?
No, I think that the toughest part is knowing that you might not come back or that you could get blown away the next day, or the same day, or even 10 minutes from now.

Interviewed and transcribed by Sally Merckx and Kristina Burrows

NAVY

Naval Support

In 1956, the Vietnamese government asked the United States to assist them. A portion of that assistance was devoted to the Vietnamese Navy. Consequently, over several years, naval forces of the United States would provide a large presence in Vietnamese waters and in the South China Sea.

American naval efforts began by training and supplying the Vietnamese with a basic force that could patrol and guard the extensive shoreline of South Vietnam. The movement of mean and material on the water from the North was ongoing, and patrolling was necessary to stop the supply. Supply ships began to unload American men and material in the late 50's, continuing into the early '60's with helicopters and other equipment.

As our efforts grew stronger, so did our naval presence. Destroyers patrolled the South China Sea even moving closer to the waters of North Vietnam. In 1964, the Gulf of Tonkin Incident allowed the government to get a resolution enlarging the war effort. American carriers were on station providing aerial strikes against the North. Other American naval assets were located at Cam Ranh Bay and other ports. Destroyers and smaller craft operated near shore to stop the infiltration of enemy supplies and to provide gunnery support to land forces. Small patrol boats moved up and down the rivers and waterways of the South in the hopes of stopping the movement of the enemy. Other naval units were stationed near shore Hospital ships provided extensive medical services, and many older vessels were converted into barracks ships for the riverine force in the delta. The "Brown Water Navy" took obsolete naval vessels and converted them into monitors and other armored craft for river patrols. The Navy provided an extensive and military support for the many years that the United States was involved in Vietnam.

George Flynn

Flynn entered the Vietnam conflict after serving in the Korean War from 1951 to 1953. As a part of Tom Dooley's humanitarian effort, Flynn was involved in the movement of Vietnamese people from the North to the South following the French defeat.

Could you explain your role in Vietnam during the 1950's?

My name is George P. Flynn, retired Executive Vice President of SNE Enterprises. I served in the Korean Conflict from late 1951 to mid 1953. In 1953 the Korean conflict ended, and the French were losing their war in Vietnam. So from late 1953 through 1955, the US Navy performed humanitarian duty in Vietnam. We helped the Vietnamese people flee south so they could be free. The move was most difficult for the Vietnamese people since they had lived on their little plot of land for centuries. Many of the old people did not want to move, but they sent their children south to be free. The country had been controlled by the French, and therefore, a strong Catholic presence influenced the Vietnamese people. The Church said: "Communism is bad. Go south," and that they did. The people of Vietnam were used to occupational forces. Before the French, the Japanese were there, and they viewed this new force as just another occupier. Past occupiers had a unique system that controlled the people. They did not educate them nor did they let them rule themselves except for a select few that were the puppets of the occupier.

So we offered to help those seeking freedom from this new occupier to flee south. In late 1953, I joined a team with Dr. Tom Dooley, a U.S. Navy medical doctor, to carry out the assigned humanitarian mission by moving people South on board U.S. Navy ships. In preparing the people to board our ships, we treated them with chemical spray to kill various types of bugs, particularly lice. We had to treat ourselves with kerosene baths to remove the lice acquired on our daily duty assignments.

We arrived in the city of Haiphong in December 1953 and experienced the enemy first hand. We met Vietnamese pilots that couldn't hear because the Communists drove bamboo slivers into their ears. We learned that the Communists didn't kill the people; they controlled them with fear. They would only kill the mayor of the city and the Catholic priest, thereby removing figures of authority. They started this process in the North and continued it during their drive southward. They used the system of previous occupiers to control the people. They knew that once they had their leader in place they controlled the city. So community-by-community they took control.

During the time period that you were there, there was an open window where people could move south?

Yes.

And your role was to help people move to the South of Vietnam?

Yes, we moved people south, moved them to freedom. In that process, the US Navy, as a humanitarian force, moved people to Saigon, now Ho Chi Minh City, and helped them with the democratic government of the South to set up little farms along the rivers and the coastlines of the Mekong Delta. They were free. But like any other people of any nation, they wanted to govern themselves. So a man in the North, Ho Chi Minh, built on that premise to drive south, to control the country, and to be the only leader. In the end, it was a very vicious war.

Did you see any combat in Vietnam?
No, it was a humanitarian unit. We saw the viciousness of the Communist regime that was coming in. They were very mean to the people.

Could you briefly reflect on your attitude towards the Vietnam War, having served as a humanitarian unit in the '50s and helping move people from the North to the South for freedom, and then seeing how this was escalated; what did you feel in terms of the Hawks and the Doves and all the stuff that went on in the 1960s?
At that point in time, in the 50s, I was very sympathetic to the cause of the Vietnamese because we saw a people fleeing from terror and aggression. We were a humanitarian force, helping people to be free. But in the mid 60's, our government became involved in their government. So our political leaders believed it was important to send our young men and women to defend those people against the communist aggression. From their desks they became warriors, and that's dangerous. I personally disagreed with the war because it was a civil war. It was Vietnamese fighting Vietnamese. Our young people were called to defend the freedom of another people, and they served honorably. I have the greatest respect for all of our forces that answered the call to serve. They honored this country, and we need to honor them. We also have to remember that in the mid '60s, when the politicians got involved, industrial millionaire giants profited from the production of weapons of war. That, of course, produces jobs, and living standards changed, but at what a price. Stand at the Vietnam Memorial in our nations capital, and you will sense the tremendous cost of a freedom that we defended and lost.

"THEY HAD STRIPPED HIM OF ALL HIS CLOTHES AND HAD TAKEN BAMBOO STICKS TO BEAT HIM OVER HIS ENTIRE BODY."

Did we make the same mistakes the French made?
No. We didn't make the same mistakes. We established a new level of individual freedom through education and technical training of their citizens and military to defend themselves.

What was your toughest experience?
Being part of a humanitarian force was not a tough or bad experience. When we first got to Vietnam, we patrolled along the coastline to the village of Da Nang. One evening we were called out on a night mission because a Catholic priest was being tortured by a group of North Vietnamese. We found the priest hanging over the main altar of his church. They had stripped him of all his clothes and had taken bamboo sticks to beat him over his entire body. He was rescued and did live. There were many events that showed the savageness of Communist warlords. I never understood how they could be so mean to their own people.

What was your opinion of the anti-war movement?
I wasn't in agreement with it. I didn't agree with the process of the government in the war, but I didn't

like the anti-government movement, anti-war movement. That is not being patriotic because what happened is they ended up taking it out on the soldier, you know, and they were just doing their duty.

"OH, YES, I HAVE NIGHTMARES. YOU KNOW, YOU WAKE UP AT TIMES VERY SHOCKED."

When you returned home from the war, what kind of reception did you get?
I got a very good reception. You know, first of all we weren't really in the war because I was there as a humanitarian unit and so I-- there were no parades like World War II, but they also didn't spit at us. For instance, my basic military service was in the war zone, was in the Korean War zone during the Korean conflict. That is a forgotten war. They don't realize what happened in that war and as an indicator look at D.C. Everest, they did World War II to Vietnam. They are going to do Korea but that's it. They skip over Korea. Korea cost a lot of men and women's lives defending someone else's freedom. That is what they did in Vietnam too.

Did you make any lasting friendships during the war?
Most of my friends are now gone. I still belong to an association of people that, are not from Vietnam, but from Korea. I used to have some shipmates; everybody has gone their own way.

Do you have any memories of the war?
Oh, yes, I have nightmares, You know, you wake up at times very shocked. Not from Vietnam, but from Korea.

Any stories you want to share?
No. Dr. Dooley was the type of person who could do things that I couldn't do and others on the team couldn't do. He would take babies who were covered with sores and puss, and he would literally hug them and hold them. It is very difficult for a Westerner to do, but that is why he endeared himself to those people. They loved him.

Would you like to leave a final message about the war?
I figure pretty much that it is included in what I said. It ended being when politicians become warriors; it cost lives, and that's what happened in Vietnam.

George P. Flynn is a retired Executive Vice President of SNE Enterprises.

Interviewed by Ben Lindsay and Andy Miller

Tom Lawrence

Lawrence enlisted in the United States Navy. He was mainly on the South China Sea and stopped ships to search them.

This interview was conducted with Tom Lawrence and Dave Schilling.

How did you first enter Vietnam and the draft? Did you enlist?
I enlisted. I wasn't drafted; I enlisted.

What branch?
United States Navy.

Where did you receive training?
I went to boot camp at Great Lakes— down by Chicago. I volunteered to go into the nuclear area, so I went out to San Francisco for 'nuclear power school' they called it. It was kind of odd… In the Navy, you volunteer and you go for four years; if you're going through a nuclear program, you volunteer to go for six years. In my particular station, I went through basic nuclear power school and I graduated, but they cut the program by 10 percent. So the lower 10 percent of the graduating class did not have to do that extra two years after. So from there I was assigned to a destroyer section. They called it Tin Can, and it operated out of Long Beach, California. From there [Long Beach], I did not go individually to Vietnam. Dave Shilling (being interviewed with me) went to Vietnam as an individual, and when he got to Vietnam was then assigned to a unit. Our whole unit went as one unit to Vietnam. There again was the difference between the Army and the Navy; the Army went in for twelve months, and the Marine Corps went for thirteen months. The Navy, generally speaking, was assigned six months; they were then withdrawn and later went back for another six months. My first tour was 1966 through '67 and then I went back for my second tour in February of '68— through the end of September of '68.

So the attitude towards the war was still pretty good then?
It was really odd. The big change came in 1968 with Tet. Prior to that, I don't think there was quite the reaction to it here in the States. There was a lot of protest and stuff, but it was never… it was different after Tet. It got meaner; it seemed like it got more personal with more directed at the soldiers and the service people. Prior to that it was just kind of amorphous, anti-government thing, but after Tet it seemed like it became more directed towards the service men themselves.

How much fighting did you see? I mean you were probably on the ship.

A destroyer is not a big ship; it's a fairly small ship. It doesn't draw much water, and they were running a program when we first arrived called Sea Dragon. The mission of the ships that took part in Sea Dragon was harassment and illumination, shore bombardment, and interdicted shipping. If the army was pinned down, they would call for supporting fire, so we'd provide that. We did numerous things.

So basically you sat in the water and shot at shore most of the time?

Yeah, pretty much. When we got into interdicting ships, you know the VC and the NVA were not stupid by any stretch of imagination... If you tried sending supplies to the south at sea, you would get stopped. A lot of ships stop you and you don't get supplies through; obviously you're going to change your tactics. So they started running in shore. They figured the larger ships could not get in shore to stop them. That was where the destroyer came in because we did not draw a lot of water. We would go into the estuaries and the river mouths and up rivers and stop anything that floated. We'd search it, looking for contraband, ammunition, supplies, anything. The first tour I was in, we did that a lot. We'd search junks.

So were you all around Vietnam? All around the coasts? Where exactly?

I was aboard the *Picket*. The *Picket*, generally speaking, operated out of Dong Ha and up by, it's all up in I Corp around the DMZ. We also did quite a few firing missions in North Vietnam itself. We went as far north as Vinh, which is about halfway to Hanoi, but the rest of the time we stayed down around Dong Ha... well between Hue and Dong Ha. We operated in that country mostly.

So you, being in the Navy, did you carry standard weapons on you?

No we didn't. The only time we carried a standard weapon or a personal weapon was when we went aboard a junk to search it. The first time I went aboard one, they gave me an M-16, and honestly, we had no training whatsoever with an M-16. When we went through boot camp, like I say, I went to Great Lakes, and it was the wintertime, and our part of practice and qualifications with weapons was with .22 rifles. I never even loaded an M-16 until I got in country, and I had no idea. An armorer loaded it, he showed you the safeties and all that stuff and then gave it to you and said, "Here, take it, don't shoot nobody on our side." The second time I went aboard a junk, I told the guys I didn't want an M-16; I wanted an M-10 shotgun. At least I knew how to load the thing; I knew how to fire it, and I was comfortable using it… and it was much more impressive. The barrel was that big around, and if you put it right here, they understood English a lot better.

So did you have many encounters with the NVA or Viet Cong?

No, we searched probably less than ten Sampans and junks. The rest of the time was pretty much off-shore. We'd stand off 5-7,000 yards, just pound the hell out of whatever we were told to pound the hell out of. We didn't get a lot of return fire because they didn't have really good shore batteries. They had some recoilless rifles that could reach out. We got hit a couple of times but nothing serious.

What was your average day like as a person onboard?

It was more like a job because I was in the engine room. We made the water, obviously made steam to make the ship go and all that stuff. So we took three shifts, three watches. We had a morning watch, an afternoon watch, and an evening watch, and we rotated throughout the day so there was someone on 24 hours a day. Then every Friday we'd dog the watch. Like you'd get up in the morning, 8 o'clock in the morning, and go down to the engine room. You stand a four-hour watch; you'd get off at noon. Then from noon until four-five o'clock you'd work, fix, repair, grease, and then you went and ate supper. There was generally a movie, usually the same one for months on end. You'd hit your rack about, well if you were working the morning shift, you worked from 8 'til noon. Then you were off until 8 o'clock in the evening. Then you went back down to the engine room for four hours watch. You got off at midnight; you went to bed, got up at eight the next morning. You did that for a week. Then Fridays they'd dog the watch. You'd rotate a half a watch. So you'd go from the day shift, and then you'd work from 4 to 8. No, you'd get it from 4 to 6 and work 4 to 8, and then the next Friday you'd change it again, and you'd work from 12 to 4. So it was like a job; it was like taking a lunchbox and going to work.

Like a swing shift?
Right, right. Except at two o'clock in the morning when you had to re-armour and refuel, they'd come get you out of your rack, and you'd have to take on stores, take on fuel oil, take on ammo. That was another job we did called plane guard. We'd follow behind a carrier, and if one of their planes crashed, you were expected to go bail the pilot out or at least go there, and that was kind of boring because carriers go pretty fast and they're way the hell out, way the hell out. They're 25 miles out, can't see land, and all four boilers on the line, and that poor old tin can would just be cranking it out about 25, 30 knots trying to keep up with a carrier while they ran flight ops. They ran flight operations sometimes twenty-four hours a day.

Did you ever see any man to man firefights?
Yeah, I can remember a couple of them where we got pulled into Quang Tri. We were way in shore by Quang Tri and a friend of mine and I were back on the fantail just smoking a cigarette and relaxing. They had the whitest beach at Quang Tri, just beautiful, beautiful beaches. We noticed a bunch of people running around on the beach; we weren't paying much attention to it. He was looking through binoculars at it, and I went down to the compartment. I had just purchased a scope for my rifle at home when I was in Japan, and I was looking through the scope. Here were all these people running around on a beach, and you'd hear splashes and splats in the water and stuff. The guy I was with, David Roberts said, "I think maybe we should go below." I said, "What's the matter?" "Those are bullets— they're shooting at us!" So we did that, and another time at Batchchant River, the Army was running an operation. They called it a hammer and anvil. We got into this estuary, and the Army was going around, and they'd land on this peninsula of land to meet up across it and start moving back toward the estuary. The destroyer, the tin can, would be anchored right there, and they would drive anyone in that area down towards the water so they would have no place to go. Then we'd cut loose. We'd start with five inch— five could reach out pretty far, and then we would switch down to three-inch guns because you could really depress those, fire point blank into the jungle. Then from there went down to the fifties on the wing bridge. That was Batchchant River; we got a naval commendation for that one.

Were drugs a problem with anybody on the ship?
Usually not. Like Dave Shilling said, our drug of choice was alcohol. There were a couple of guys that were kill heads, potheads, but not a whole lot of them. There was one guy aboard that I would have liked to throw off the side.

Was there any anti-war movement stuff that you knew about when you were there?
Not when I went on the first tour. That was another major difference in the Army. Everybody else was over there, they'd get their tour, they'd go back, that was it. We went, we came back from the first tour,

we'd have to go back for the second. When I came back in '67, we landed; our whole corp was at Long Beach, California. We landed just up from Los Angeles. They had one of the biggest anti-war demonstrations that happened on the West Coast there that summer, and we walked right into the middle of the darn thing. We didn't know what in the hell was going on. We came off the ship, and there were bunches of people waving at us. The next thing you know, they were screaming "baby killer" and making spitting gestures at us. We had no idea, no idea that it was happening.

I would assume you didn't like the anti-war movement. Your opinion of the anti-war movement, what was it?

I figured that most of them were there for the girls. That was about it. I mean, I don't know. Its kind of amorphous feeling of distaste for. It never occurred to me, it never occurred to me to avoid military service. It never would have crossed my mind to get out of it.

Do you think the United States could have won the war under the circumstances?

I guess you would have to define your term of winning. No, I don't think, there was no winning, there was no winning. They weren't in it to win.

It was a political war?

It was a political war.

Did you develop any lasting friendships?

Yeah, amazingly we did. There again, the difference is most people flew in by themselves. They were with a unit for awhile, they flew out by themselves, and came back to the States by themselves. We went over as a unit; we stayed together as a unit all the time when we were there; we came back as a unit. Several good friends, some of them I keep in contact with, not a whole lot of them, but some of them. As a matter of fact one guy in there introduced me to my wife.

Were you sent anywhere else after you were in Vietnam? Did they send you directly home from there?

No, that's one thing about the Navy. We operated mostly out of Subic Bay, the Philippines. We would go- it was about 8 or 900 miles to Vietnam from there- we would go in country; we would do our turn on the gun line, or do whatever we had to do for anywhere from 2-6 weeks. Then we would return to the Philippines to be rearmed, re supplied, and we also showed the flag in Hong Kong. These guys got R&R after they had been in country for six months; they'd get R&R somewhere. That was our R&R; we got sent up to Hong Kong. For 38 days we were up there; just laid around, didn't do anything, just had fun. On the way in, because obviously ,the ship doesn't fly, we stopped at Japan, and then on the way back when we came back to the States, we also stopped at Japan; we stopped in Okinawa. The second tour we did our R&R down in Singapore, so yeah, we got around Southeast Asia quite a bit.

How exactly were you received when you returned to the United States? You must have returned twice right? The first time versus the second time maybe?

The first time we hit the States we walked into that big peace demonstration, and the only thing I was interested in was getting back here on leave. The second tour I had met my wife just before we went over seas, and I got back there, got back to LA, the only thing I was interested in was getting up to her place. I didn't come back to Wisconsin after the second tour. I stayed out there. When we got back after the second tour, my wife met me, she wasn't my wife then, but we were engaged. She met me at the ship, and we went up together. She lived up in the valley so we went up there. It was mostly family things.

You seemed happy to have served your country? You don't have any anti-war feelings or anything?
I didn't. I didn't get involved at all. I just wanted to forget it when I got back. Shortly after I was discharged, which was Friday the thirteenth, my wife and I jumped in her car and headed to the Valley where she lived. I proceeded to get drunk that night, and I don't think I sobered up until 1971.

Did the war have a lot of emotional effect on you?
I denied it. I didn't think I had a problem because I wasn't a combat man. I never looked at myself as a combat man because I wasn't on the ground, I didn't carry a gun, I didn't get shot at. Yeah, it had a very deep, long-lasting effect. You denied it and denied it and denied it and blanked it out and blanked it out and blanked it out, yet I was continually, I would get angry for no reason whatsoever. I'd fly off the handle. I refused to make friends. I would isolate myself. That's one of the things that my wife and I came very close to war over, because I didn't want anyone around me. Anybody I met, I didn't care who they were. I had no people skills, whatsoever. Finally she put her foot down, and she said, obviously, you're having some problems. You have some hang-ups; you've got something wrong. Let's find out what it is. That's when I met a bunch of guys. There was something in the paper about Vietnam Vets, and they said they were going to have a meeting, so I went to the meeting. I don't know why. I still don't know why. I went to the meeting, and here it was the Vietnam Veterans of America, and I met a whole bunch of guys that were pretty much in the same boat I was in. I started to put two and two together and realized I can have some real, long-term effects from that war. It's hard, really hard to define. My wife's father served. My dad was never in the service at all, so I have no idea. My wife's father was in the service. It was always amusing to her... they're from Colorado. He said what he wanted to do when he got there (this was like fifties) was buy a place on top of the Rocky Mountains and surround the place with howitzers. If anybody was coming up there he didn't like the look of, they wouldn't make it to the top. That was funny; that was amusing to her. That was her dad. When I said I wanted to move into a middle of a swamp somewhere and be guaranteed that no one would get in there, then it wasn't funny because that was her life. That was her dad's life; this is her life. She wanted friends; she wanted relationships; she wanted to go to movies; she wanted to go out to eat; she wanted to walk down the street. How can you do that when your husband says I don't want to meet a bunch of assholes?
I didn't want to... you'd get to a restaurant and somebody would drop a tray, and you'd dive under the table. You also have problems with authority figures. I used to have a lot of trouble with police officers. I never liked police officers. I got stopped for speeding once on the freeway. Actually, it wasn't speeding— it was going too slow. When I got out of the car, the cop pulled a gun on me. The next thing I know, I'm laying in the god damn gutter with him standing on the back of my neck trying to put tie wraps on my hands because he was going to arrest me. He was going to arrest me because I threatened to kill him. Things like that, the results, the aspects of PTSD that I displayed was anger and distrust of authority figures, any authority figures, police, doctors, doesn't make any difference; they were assholes. You ask most Vietnam Veterans, and they would say they have no trouble with results of the war if the bastards would just leave me alone. I just don't want to be messed with. That's a very telling aspect of PTSD.

[David Schilling]: Actually none of us talked like this probably for six, seven years. No one cared to talk. You learned quickly to keep your mouth shut, and if you ran into somebody you know, "Gee, haven't seen you for a long time. Where've you been?" There are people who would rather say I'd been in prison than to admit that they were in Vietnam.

Did you go to the any of the emotional, war- effect centers— like Tomah?

No, because I refused to admit I had a problem. I didn't have a problem. If the bastards would just leave me, I had no problem. Just leave me the [pause] alone. Since then I got involved with the group Dave mentioned. I'd do a lot of work and a lot of self-examination and a lot of learning; you learn how to deal with things. I would say five years ago there would be no way in hell that I would sit here and talk about it. I would not do it. I wouldn't do it. I'd refuse to do it.

Any other interesting facts that you would just like to share?

[Dave Schilling]: I think it's neat that you young people do want to know and that hopefully learn from our mistakes. I always told my son, "I wish you wouldn't make the same mistakes I do," and yet I knew that sometimes he'd have to make the mistakes to learn. Once I realized that, we got along better. But still, I'd hate to see us go to war under the same pretenses we went, and I think Desert Storm wasn't perfect but it was better. A lot of Vietnam Veterans went to Desert Storm, but they wouldn't come back and have a victory parade with the other troops because they still had that stigma of Vietnam. For years, we didn't even care to be recognized. Now there's a bunch of us go to parades, and we really don't care what people think. We're just going to try to piss and tell how we feel. I think society is maybe making a turn for the better. I'd like to think that. If we get into another war, we'll see. When I went through school, (I graduated in '62) WWII was just ancient history. Korea was over, had been over long enough in the past to be of totally no interest to me whatsoever. It was history and it wasn't current events, so it kind of got ignored completely. I don't know. Obviously your instructors and I don't know what your take on- is Vietnam ancient history to you? Or is it… it is certainly not current events by any stretch of your imagination…

No, but the tactics of it will apply to a lot of situations we're in today, in our government. It's important to learn about it too— what happened back then, what the whole war was about. That's just what our teacher is trying to stress.

[David Shilling]: The final failure of diplomacy is war. Unfortunately, old men make war, but young men have to fight it. I think that's one thing that really angers me the most about it is that they don't realize what the effects are. It's easy to say, it's almost easier to start a war, fight over something; it's macho. They don't realize, apparently don't seem to realize, what the long-term damage to the generation that has to fight the war…and it is long-term.

[David Schilling]: It's not only the damage to us; it's our kids. I know my son is definitely got authority problems. He's twenty-eight and he still does. It makes you wonder, does some of this go into genetics? We can have big arguments but could it be that Agent Orange chemicals do strange things? I know chemicals have definitely altered my body to the effect that I got to take other chemical pills to fight against what they say didn't happen. My diabetes is the result of injury, stress, and other stuff. If Uncle Sam would just admit it and give us the validation that we need, that's all we want. I want them to salute the flag as if it was high, wave, and say thanks. That's all you got to do. That would be overwhelming to me if they just do those three little things. But there's people out there who don't even want to respect the flag, and Tom and I, really, the flag tears us up when we see a ceremony with a flag. It still rips right into me. I guess that part of it, the Army did teach me right, and the service, because we were taught, drilled in ceremonies to respect and all that. I think it's neat that I give talks at Newman because I know the history professor from Marathon, and what amazes me even more is how less timid the Asian people have gotten. They will ask questions now. For years, they wouldn't ask a question; they wouldn't approach us;

they'd probably thought we'd kill them with a slingshot. I was just telling Tom in Minneapolis, there's a gal going to be a doctor in two months in psychology; she's full-blooded Vietnamese. Ten years ago, I wouldn't have had any Vietnamese work on me, and so I'm breaking down, too, with time. I think time heals, but they didn't really give us all the tools to heal with. One example I'll give you-I was in Japan and we had this doctor, and I have respect for doctors. There's no way I could be a doctor, and I'm amazed at some of the things they can do. And this doctor, he was just one of the glorious doctors I've ever seen in my life. He comes in and he says,"While you were on the table and I had you all cut up and parted and everything else, I took 36 pictures. I would like you to send them home to your fiancée." And I thought, "You asshole, get out of the room." But then I was thinking he might have done that so that you would fight. See a lot of times they would use reverse psychology so that you would turn around and get so angry that you fight. It taught us to be angrier. We were already angry. To this day I'll bring it up with some doctors, and they said that's unethical. That guy should have lost his license. That's just not humane, but strange things happen in service that don't happen in civilian life.

[Tom Lawrence]: Service is a different, entirely different culture.

[David Schilling]: I went to the seminary for five years, so I do closed culture; that was as closed as it gets. They had a convent in St. Asions. Every chance us young dudes had we were over there trying to talk to the future nuns. That's the way service was; it almost kept you locked in. You didn't know what was going on in the rest of the world. And that's where we think at times lost two, three years of our life; that we could have been here with a hot car and hot babe. Instead we were in the old man's Army.

I was older. I was twenty-one, and most of the people in the service, I think, were, on average in Vietnam—19. These kids never had a chance to grow up. They never grew up; they never had. You went into the service and if you went to 'Nam you came back here an old man. Emotionally speaking, you were an old man, and a lot of these people, they just never had a chance to grow up and have fun. They went right from high school right to old age.

After Vietnam Lawrence worked for Wisconsin Public Service and was also a Marine Mechanic. He was married in 1969, had a daughter in 1970, and now has two grandaughters.

Interviewed by Eric Doescher
Transcribed by Vicki Karcher

Lyle Pemble

Volunteering in 1966, Pemble joined the Navy. He served initially on a transport ship that carried Marines to Vietnam and later transferred to a destroyer. The destroyer was assigned guard duty for aircraft carriers that were stationed off shore.

How did you become involved in the Vietnam War? Were you drafted or did you enlist?
I enlisted.

How old were you?
I was eighteen, and I originally tried to get into the Army. I took my test to get in, and they got some things goofed up and delayed me, so that's how I got involved in the Navy.

Did you know when you enlisted that you'd go to Vietnam?
No, I had no idea.

What year did you go to Vietnam?
The first time was 1966.

What were your jobs through the war, and what did you do?
I was a machinist's mate requiring me to work in the engine room, about ten feet under the water line of the ship. I was a throttle man. I operated the throttles that moved the ship forward and backward. We had 60,000 horse-power engines. That was a lot of horsepower at your fingertips. I liked my job because they graded you on your performances. I got very high grades on my performances because I liked the job, and it was challenging. I had a lot of power in my hands, and that was an ego trip, I guess. When we weren't out at sea, my job consisted of a lot of maintenance. It was all steam valves, and we had a lot of leaks to repair, a lot of pumps to repair from the constant running they required while you were out at sea. Every time the speed of the ship changed, it taxed steam lines and pumps. Every time it came down in speed, it cooled lines off. Each and every time we did something like this it was a tax on the machine, the pumps, and steam lines. So, we had a lot of repair to do. That was my job.

Do you remember the name of the ship and what it was like on the ship?
The first ship I was on for two years. It was a transport ship. It was the APA 27, the *George Clymer*. We took it over to Da Nang with 2,500 Marines. We trained the Marines how to get into their boats, how to get down the side of the ship, and how to get into the boats. Then we'd beach them on an island, stay over night, pick them back up to bring them back. They'd have to climb back on the ship. That's what I did for two years. I was stationed out of San Diego. Then we got a change of orders, and I was transferred to a destroyer (a DD 449), the *USS Nicholas*. It was the fastest destroyer in the Seventh Fleet at the time. It

was one of the oldest and still the fastest. It was designed to go 38 knots, and we could still hit 32-33 knots if we were pressed. A knot is about 1.8 miles an hour, so it was a pretty fast ship. My job was the same as it was on the transport ship. I was the senior throttle man in the after engine room. On the transport ship we only had one engine room; there was an engine room and a fire room on one side and a fire room on the other side. These fire rooms supplied the steam for us to operate and maneuver the ship.

What were the other parts of the ship like?
The ship was very tight. It was somewhere around 300 feet long and probably 40 or 50 feet wide. There were almost 400 guys on it. The compartments were very crowded and not very big. Our compartment had about 90 racks. Racks are basically just an aluminum frame made out of pipe with canvas hooked on it and a little two-inch mattress over the canvas. It was your bed. There were four of them about 2 1/2 feet apart. This was tight quarters; not like what you have today.

Were you ever on a base camp on land or anything?
No.

How long were you there the total time?
In Vietnam, I went on six-month cruises. We did lot of different things in six months. I would say five of these months were in Vietnam. We had two basic jobs. One, we guarded aircraft carriers. We followed the aircraft carrier approximately a thousand yards behind. We were there when the aircraft carriers launched their planes to attack the different targets. If one was lost while taking off or while landing, we picked up the pilots. We had to do this a number of times. We had one incident about three o'clock in the early morning. A plane was taking off, and something happened that wasn't supposed to happen. The pilots went down with the plane, which disintegrated. We picked the plane up in pieces, but the two pilots went down with it.

Did you ever fight against the Viet Cong and the NVA units?
The other part of our job was to go up rivers, basically the Vong Tau River, a very narrow river. You could shoot a slingshot off the ship and hit the land. We drove up it, but we couldn't turn around and drive back out. We had to back out because it was that narrow. We went up rivers like that and bombarded for the troops. Before our troops went in, they would find spots where the Viet Cong held camps. The different spotters we used would radio telling us where to go. Then we would line up our guns and bombard about seven to eight miles. We hit their camps and different things on the shoreline.

So you never really got off the boat?
No.

Did you ever see them, or were they inland?
We never really saw them. Vietnam was a very, very thick green jungle. It was not like our hard woods. It was very thick. At night we saw fights going on from helicopters which drove over VC camps. They (VC) would shoot up at the helicopters. You could see the bullets because they were tracers. There were many thousands of rounds you could see when there were surface to air fights. We could see the jets when they dropped their ordnances and their bombs. You could see the explosions. But other than that, no, we didn't see them. Another one of our responsibilities was to do a lot of patrolling for people in boats, what they call sampans. We would send a boarding party to get on to these sampans. They would search them, and if they were found to have any weapons or anything that could aid the VC and be a detriment to us, we would destroy them. We would get back on our ship, and our ship would sink the sampans.

What exactly are sampans?
They were little boats.

From Vietnam?
They were boats like a little sailboat, very crude. They had little diesel engines and just putted along. Most of the time they didn't have anything in them to worry about. We just let them go. If they did have something on them, we destroyed them. I believe we destroyed maybe a dozen or so. There was anywhere from three to maybe five people on them.

What was an average day like? Maybe there was a certain day that stood out?
An average day for me was to work in the engine room. It was a regular job, and it was very hot. The average temperature on the destroyer was about 115-120 degrees. The bottom of our engine room was where the fire room was. All the boilers were down there, and one level up is where I operated throttles and different things, but an average day consisted of doing repairs and whatever needed to be done. Then we stood four-hour watch. When I wasn't working, I had a little time to sleep, eat, and lounge around on the deck a little. Then we had four-hour watch, which required me to go back to the engine room. We wore a set of headphones which communicated to different areas of the ship. I talked to main control, which was the forward engine room. I also talked to the bridge where the pilots, the cap-

DD-49 USS Nicholas, DD-450 USS O'Bannon, CVA-65 USS Enterprise

tains, and whoever, was up there were. We had opportunity to communicate throughout the whole ship with these headphones. They were plugged into the whole communication network on ship. We had chow time and there wasn't really much time to do anything else because we worked in the engine room, were on a watch, or we were eating or sleeping.

How long exactly were you in Vietnam?
I was on four cruises (on the plane guarding, and on the rivers about four or five months out of a six-month cruise). I was in Vietnam maybe four and a half months or so.

How did your family react to you going to war, and how did you react going to war when you found out you had to go to Vietnam?
I don't really know about my family; they were concerned, I guess. I was scared because I didn't know what was happening over there. Then, I can remember it like it just happened yesterday, I can remember my first night setting out on the fantail of the ship watching the planes drop bombs, watching bombs go off. They were big, bright, balls of orange fire that just would brighten the sky. It was miles away, but it was just awesome. All I could think about was people dying. I wasn't against the war, and I had no problems with being there because I loved my country. I felt I had an obligation to my country. I didn't agree with the principles of the war. It was a political war. It was totally different than Desert Storm, where the

United States wanted to win it. Vietnam could have been won if they would have allowed the military to do what the military could do. It could have been won.

How are your opinions about the war different from when you first went to Vietnam, or are they the same?
I still believe there's a time for war. I believe that is the situation our country is in now. Yes, there's a time for war. We protect our country; we protect others if we can. I guess I'm just a firm believer that if one nation tries to over-power another nation that is friendly to us, that's what friends are for. I'm not a war-monger, but I am a person who believes in defending what is ours, what has been given to us by God.

Could you explain any experiences you've had with body counts or kill ratios or anything else?
There were little boats called RPBs, river patrol boats. These boats might have been 20 and 30 feet long and had lots of guns on them. They had machine guns in the front and in the back. They had grenade launchers and all kinds of goodies because their job was to go up rivers and take out the Viet Cong or catch them going across the rivers. The people on these little boats suffered a lot of casualties. The people in the jungle could see them on the boats, but they couldn't see into the jungle. A lot of them came up to our ship all shot up. The guys in the front of their boat would sit in a little hole in the boat. In the front of him was a half inch thick of armor plating, and it was a half moon protecting, or supposed to protect, the gunner in this hole, sitting. He had either a twin 30-caliber machine gun or twin-50. I remember this one time when they brought the boat up next to us, the man in the front was shot up. Sometimes the bullets went through the armor, and sometimes they didn't. I can also remember another time when we were shooting, and there was a tremendous explosion. I believe it was the *USS Jenkins*; but I'm not sure.

At times, when shooting a lot, we would get what they call a hot shell. I believe it was called that. We had X amount of seconds to get a water hose down the barrel of a gun to cool this off. This would prevent an explosion. They don't know if it was either that or if they took a hit from a shore battery, but it exploded the ship and cut it in half. Half of it exploded and went down. Believe it or not, the other half of the ship, I believe it was the front half, stayed afloat and was towed in. We didn't see a lot of the stuff that shore people saw or what the *PBR's* or the swift boats saw. We were out at sea and away from that. There were times when they would send us in and tell us real nice things like, "Where you are going you will be within range of our guns," but we'd be out of range because our guns would only shoot about eight miles.

> *"I CAN REMEMBER MY FIRST NIGHT SITTING OUT ON THE FANTAIL OF THE SHIP WATCHING THE PLANES DROP BOMBS, WATCHING BOMBS GO OFF. THEY WERE BIG, BRIGHT, BALLS OF ORANGE FIRE THAT JUST WOULD BRIGHTEN THE SKY. IT WAS MILES AWAY, BUT IT WAS JUST AWESOME. ALL I COULD THINK ABOUT WAS PEOPLE DYING."*

Were the ships you were on ever attacked by anyone?
Yes, we took some hits. It's pretty hard to hit something moving all the time. It was easier to hit a bigger ship moving slower than ours was, which was moving faster. We did a lot of shooting while we moved. A destroyer is very maneuverable. When 7-8 miles away, the electronic guns would lock on a target that was pretty accurate, but with shore bombardment to the ships they would come close at times. When they did come close, it would be loud in the engine room because we were below the water line, and it was very, very scary down there at times.

Did anyone ever get killed or hurt from them?

No, no one ever got hit--just our ship. We were lucky, much luckier than some. We had a close call. Once, I remember it was a Sunday afternoon, and a friend, who happened to be the throttle man from the forward engine room, and I were playing cribbage. All of a sudden the ship sped up. I looked at him and he looked at me. I said, "Mike, something is wrong." We all went to our battle stations. We only had X amount of minutes to get to our battle station because once they lock the doors and make watertight integrity in the ship, you can't get out of wherever you are. Some guys were there in their skivvies (underwear); some guys were there dressed. You had to get there fast. We apparently got very close to some of the Viet Cong with our artillery, and they were going to try to take us out. They launched six of their MIGs to come after us, and we didn't have any weapons to shoot down jets. We had 4-inch gun shells and torpedoes because we were an anti-submarine ship. We had to get out and move away from them as fast as possible. The captain came over the intercom and told all the people the *USS Enterprise,* the aircraft carrier we were with, had launched a dozen Phantoms to intercept these MIGs. They did get three of them, and the other three got away. That was probably the scariest moment for me and for our ship. It lasted probably an hour, but during that hour, I'm quite confident that there was a lot of praying going on. Nobody was joking; nobody was laughing. Everybody was very serious because in the engine room there are super heated steam lines. They are 850 degrees, and all I could think about was a rocket or a shell coming through our hull, which was only like a quarter of an inch thick, and penetrating a super heated steam line. That would boil you like a lobster, and you'd have less than five seconds to live. Everyone in that engine room would be taken out if that were ever to happen, so a lot of things went through my mind. It was a very scary moment.

While you were over there, did you have any opinions regarding the anti-war movement at home?

I was very upset with it. Disgusting. Some of the T.V. was disgusting and the personalities and the way they handled themselves. I mean the military, the majority of the men fighting, didn't agree with the war either. But we served our country, and we never talked bad about the country. We had a job to do, and we did it. The American people let us down. I came across a lot of these people when I got out of the service. I just didn't have any time for them. Some people don't have anything better to do, I guess. They're good enough to live in this country, but they're not good enough to give their life for it. Or, they would rather see their fellow neighbor die than themselves. I did not and do not think very highly of draft dodgers and things like that.

> *"We had a job to do, and we did it. The American people let us down."*

What was the hardest part of the war for you?

Probably going up the rivers because they were dangerous and they were scary. It took a couple of hours to get up to them where we would do some of our bombarding. If we got attacked while we were in the river, we had to back out of it as fast as we could. We never knew from one second to the next what was going to happen or when it was going to happen. I did not like going in the river; we were too vulnerable.

Did you ever get attacked while you were on the rivers?

Once, yes. We got hit once, but other than that we were very lucky.

Was there a lot of emotional and or physical stress that you had to endure while you were there?

I guess stress to one person is different to someone else. I liked my job, so it didn't cause me any stress. Some of the situations we were put in, you know, like the rivers, were more stressful for me, knowing that people were getting killed. But I think the most stressful thing for me was the people back home not supporting us. That was the biggest, saddest time of my life, coming back and getting treated like we got treated.

Did you make any lasting friendships during the war?

Oh yes. I had a real good friend. In fact my best friend was a black man from Philadelphia, Philip Braxton. He was a fellow machinist mate with me. We worked together. We did a lot of things together. You just learn to be a family, you know, when you're living that close together; when you sleep together, and eat together, when you shower together. You do everything together. One of my real good friends, Dixon, wanted me to go into the PBRs with him. I don't know; for some reason I didn't want to, and he did. He went, he got transferred, got onto his PBR, and I believe it was his second mission out on a river where he lost his life. Their PBR got taken out. I guess the Lord knew better for me, stopped me from going to certain places that... I guess if I was a glory seeker, like sometimes I wished I were, it could have got me in trouble. When I was going to go into the Army, I wanted to be a paratrooper. That would have required you to be on the ground there, and that could have caused problems too, so, the Lord knew everything, and he worked it out, so I'm happy about that. We all had our job to do, and we just do it the best way we can.

Do you remember there being conflicts between blacks and whites?

There were very few times. I could count on one hand how many times I saw a problem amongst some of the guys on my ship. There was not a problem really. The only time it got to be a problem was when somebody started drinking. When there was no drinks involved, it was one happy family.

Were there any drug or alcohol problems?

Yes, I had a very good friend from Fort Worth, Texas George. He and I were very close because he loved hunting and I loved hunting. He loved fishing and so did I. We did a lot of things together. When we came off our cruise, we were stationed in Hawaii on a destroyer. These guys went to the back room and started taking the cover off the water heater and pulling some of the insulation out. Then they took some drugs out. That's where they hid their drugs. They had marijuana and LSD. What the other stuff was, I don't know. George came to me and offered me LSD. He wanted to know if I wanted to try it. I can remember saying to him, "If you want to be a friend of mine, you won't ever ask me to do that again." I said I didn't want anything to do with this. In fact, I said I was not going to stay for the weekend as we had planned. Then I just left; I just got away from the situation, and George continued to play with the LSD and marijuana. I got a letter from him after we got out of the service, and he told me he was starting to have eye problems from something he was taking. I don't know if it was the LSD or marijuana. I don't know what that does to people, but I was really scared. As far as I know, he gave up the drugs and went clean because of the eye problem he was having.

What happened when you came back home?

There were a lot of demonstrators that would block bridges. They would block a lot of places, and when they saw people in their military uniforms, they'd make comments. There would be a lot of verbal bashing. Some of the riots got pretty violent. I can remember a friend who used to be on the Arlington Police Force, and his job required him to keep bridges open from these demonstrators. They would block the bridges so no one could drive across. He was concerned because they carried weapons and things. At times it would get out of hand. It was not only the military they bashed; it was law enforcement also. They were trying to do their job and stay out of harm's way. The larger cities saw the majority of this. Going back to my little town, I was a war hero, but coming back to the U.S., you were a bad guy. You were the enemy.

Is there one particular experience that stands out to you?

If I were to pick one memorable experience, it would be that time we were attacked by those six MIGs. Yes, I'll never forget that time, never forget that day or forget what I was doing. It was very memorable.

That day was the scariest time of my life up until then.

Did you have any difficulties dealing with memories when you came back?
No. Probably because, again, we were not involved in the real dirty shore fighting like the Marines and the Army people are noted for. That's much different.

Is there anything else you just want to add; a particular story or anything that stands out?
You've got your different branches of the military, you got your Army, you got your Navy, you got your Marines, you got your Air Force, and some jobs are a lot of... Take, for instance, your Marines; they don't like the Navy. The Marines are a branch of the Navy. They think they've got a rougher job than the Navy. The Army thinks they've got a rougher job than the Navy. My opinion is one is just as important as the other. You can't get along without any one of them. They all have their special jobs to do. I mean, look at Afghanistan right now. It's

Standing by the throttles where I worked.

airplanes that are fighting the war. A lot of things have to be taken out of harm's way before the ground troops can go in. That's the job of the Air Force, and that's the job of the Navy. Sure, the Navy gets treated a lot better. We had better chow and sleeping conditions, instead of these men on the beach doing the fighting and what they have to sleep in. Their standard of living is like an animal when they are in those conditions, when it's raining, all the mud and all the infections to contend with. I can see where there is bad feeling between some of the Marines and the Army compared to the Navy or the Air Force. But when the truth is known, we have to have all of them. They all have their special jobs, special duties. One is just as important as the other is.

When you said that you enlisted, did you enlist because you thought you would be drafted, or were you looking for a particular job that you wanted?
No, I guess I'm just a believer; I have always been a believer that every American man should have to serve four years in the service. I believed it then, and I still believe it. I believe you learn respect and values. In Israel today, every one has a military obligation to serve, even the women. The United States isn't like that, and I'm glad it is not; but I am a firm believer that every American male should give four years or at least three years to active duty in the military.

Is there anything else?
I'd do it over again. I would do it over again without a second thought, if our country had an emergency where they needed people my age and it was for the defense of our nation. I would be the first one to pack my bags and go where they want me to go. I could truly say that nobody loves America like I do. I just have a love for America.

Is there a message you have for people who don't really know about the war, like our generation?
America got her freedom not by sitting down. They got their freedom through wars. I think a lot about the Alamo, what went on there, and the odds against the people in the Alamo. They knew their lives were going to be taken, but they knew what it would do for the country. Nobody likes war, saying that you are against war or against the military because of religion... I definitely believe that when certain things happen especially to our own nation, like (September 11th). We have evil people in this world who would just love to try to take away from you what you have. I believe there's a time for war, and I believe that what we're doing now is proper. I do not believe that the Bible is against war. There is a story in the Bible when God told Moses to number all the people from 20 years old to go to war for Israel. They did not

have any opportunities to say they didn't believe in war or anything. It was a command from God to Moses, and that's my belief today. God doesn't like war either, but He knows there are certain times and certain cases and certain things that happen in our world where these things are necessary. There is even a verse where it says, "You're going to hear of wars and rumors of wars." These things have to be. That's human beings. War will be here until we're gone, until the Lord comes back, and even He will have a war against this world, against the nations that go against Israel. He will wage that war Himself. I just believe every American should be ready to defend our country and should be ready to give his or her life for our country.

I have one more question for you. How do feel about how America handled the war? Do you think the war could have been won?

Vietnam? I think, without a doubt, the war could have been won if it wouldn't have been political. It was very political. They would send us in places and would want a compound taken out, for instance. We would start firing, we would destroy half of it, and they would say, "Cease fire." To me, if you're going to do something, you want to do it all. You don't want to cease fire until you destroy everything you went there to destroy. There was one case I can remember, where there was an estimated 300 people; we destroyed about half of them and the other half got away. You could set-up the shells from our guns to explode either on the impact on ground, or you could set them up to explode so many feet up in the air. We shot the first shells in, and they exploded on the ground. Then we waited. The other shells were set to explode above the ground so the shrapnel would flare all over the ground. It would do the majority of the damage. So this airplane, this spotter plane, told us when to send this salvo of shells and when these people would start coming out of the huts running for cover. Then that's how we would get the majority of these people. It was a very wide area where the shells would explode. I believe if the government would have allowed the military to do what they wanted to do, we could have won that war. But, when the government tells you when you can shoot and when you couldn't shoot, what you could shoot, what you couldn't shoot, you cannot win a war by being selective. To win a war, it has to be like when the atomic bomb was dropped on Hiroshima and Nagasaki. Many innocent people got killed, but it ended the war. That's the way it is in any war, in my opinion. If we want to win a war, if we're going to put our lives at stake in a war, then we have to win it. We have to fight it to win. I believe that there should be no holds barred to win a fight. Anything to protect the American fighting person, I'm in favor of. The faster we get a war over, the better.

Were you involved in the Tonkin Bay incident at all?

I was in there during the My Lai massacre and those different things.

What was that like?

I've got my own opinion about that, too. Our government trains people to kill; every military man is trained to kill, especially the

> *"I AM A FIRM BELIEVER THAT EVERY AMERICAN MALE SHOULD GIVE FOUR YEARS OR AT LEAST THREE YEARS TO ACTIVE DUTY IN THE MILITARY."*

Army and Marines. That's their job, I can remember Lieutenant Calley. He had these men under him, and he was responsible for them. They went in there, and they killed many people. America went on the defensive because it was a lot of women and a lot of children; but American people don't realize that the Viet Cong used numerous women and children to kill our people because the Viet Cong knew the majority of our people wouldn't kill women and children. You didn't know who your friend was over there because the ones that wanted to be your friends were your friends for a while; but when the Viet Cong would come through, they were caught between a rock and a hard place. If they weren't our friends, we would kill them, and if they were our friends, the Viet Cong would kill them. So they had a rough road but a lot of times our people got betrayed by who they thought were friends. That is why there's a lot of hatred today in America towards the Hmong people and these people living here. We didn't know if they were our friends over there then; we don't know what they're really thinking about now. This I can see causes much resentment in the hearts of the military people that were in Vietnam. I work with some Hmong, and they're very good workers. They're very good friends of mine. I get along just fine with them. I don't have a problem with it, but a lot of people do.

Lyle Pemble has worked at Weyerhaeuser since 1976.

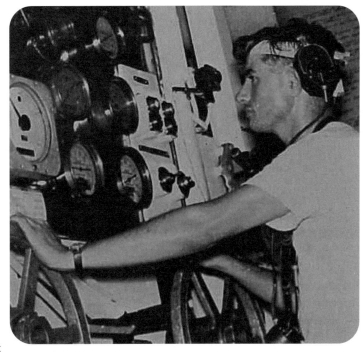

Interviewed by Elizabeth Novak and Kim Marquardt

Jim Rowlette

Enlisting in the Navy, Rowlette served on a destroyer off shore of Vietnam providing fire support to ground units. He also served a tour on a hospital ship.

Were you enlisted?
Yes, enlisted, then assigned to the service.

What were the base camps like that you were at?
Base camp would not be the appropriate word. I served two tours of duty on the *USS Inseron* destroyer and fired support off the coast of Vietnam. I served one tour of duty on the *USS Sanctuary*, a hospital ship providing medical aid to the wounded, and one tour of duty in naval support activities in Da Nang, providing combat information support.

Did you fight any of the Viet Cong or North Vietnamese, and if you did, can you describe anything?
In the naval gun support, I destroyed many suspected Viet Cong villages, just took a significant amount of human life, wounded, casualties. In my time, there were activities where a perimeter was overrun. That was all the direct combat, taking of lives as well.

Can you describe an average day in the war, what it was like?
It depends on which place I was at. On the destroyer, an average day was boring and routine until we went into combat. We learned to provide gunfire support. It was very straining, strenuous, and stressful. On the hospital ship an average day was very sad. You would see wounded Vietnamese, American soldiers, children, and women, coming in time and time again, decaying, dying, sometimes in front of me. It was very, very difficult. Ku Chi was pretty much providing combat information for air support, those kinds of things.

Were you involved in any fire fighting?
Yes, in reaction to perimeter strikes at naval support activities in Da Nang, trying to protect the base itself. Usually pretty short lived. It could be a rocket attack followed by croogs trying to break our perimeter, and the way you'd react to them. That would be about the size of it.

Vietnam was considered a guerrilla war. Can you describe what was meant by guerilla warfare?
I'm not exactly sure I'd call it a guerilla war. I know what is meant by that. It was primarily jungle fighting, no fixed lines; same turf was fought over and over and over again. I would describe it as a civil war, within which we got involved, for reasons that never have been very clear to me.

Did you ever do an ambush?
No.

What was meant by search and destroy?
Search and destroy was basically find the enemy and pursue and eliminate.

Can you explain any experiences you had with body counts or kill ratios?
At the age of nineteen and twenty, the body count was kind of a thrill, to know how much you destroyed. It fluctuated, of course, and that is no longer true, but we ultimately too, kept body counts for the gun fire support. So that is the only way of knowing what we had accomplished. The longer I was involved in the Vietnam War, the more and more disillusioned I felt with the body count. It seemed to me just a way of trying to provide a number to signify some kind of progress that wasn't taking place.

Did you use helicopters to get around, and if you did, can you describe your experience?
We used helicopters quite often. We used helicopters to transport the wounded to or from the hospital ship when I was with the hospital ship. Very often we would take our medical services to the villages. We would travel to and from villages by chopper. At one point, when I was at naval support activities in Da Nang, we flew in a chopper in a medical support mission, and we were shot down and landed in a rice paddy. Fortunately, no one was injured.

"WE DIDN'T KNOW EXACTLY WHAT WAS GOING ON, BUT WE KNEW WE WERE GETTING OUR ASS KICKED SOMEWHERE. AT THAT TIME WE DIDN'T KNOW THAT LATER THIS WOULD BE CALLED THE TET OFFENSIVE."

Were you in Vietnam during the Tet Offensive?
Yes I was.

Can you briefly describe that?
At the time of the Tet Offensive, I was on the hospital ship, *Sanctuary*, and we were at active quarters for about 100 hours straight receiving wounded; overloaded, treating the wounded, not only in the surgical units and medical floors, but treating them directly on the flight deck. We didn't know exactly what was going on, but we knew we were getting our ass kicked somewhere. At that time we didn't know that later this would be called the Tet Offensive.

When you were in Vietnam were there any drug problems with the soldiers?
Absolutely.

Can you describe that?
The places that I was at there was a lot of use of marijuana. There were some soldiers, sailors, that were on some heavier stuff than marijuana, but for the most part it was marijuana and alcohol. I knew there were other folks using harder drugs, but they weren't the larger percentage of folks.

What was the relationship between whites and blacks in your unit?
Actually, in the units I happened to be in, they were pretty good. I don't recall a lot of overt racial tension in the particular units I had to serve in.

Did you have any opinions on the anti-war movements back in the States when you were in Vietnam?
When I was in Vietnam, I very much, at least in the beginning of my time, disagreed with what they were

doing. The longer I experienced the war myself, I realized that they were making sense- that we needed to get out, that what we were doing was wrong. It was harmful to the people, and by the time I came back to the States, I did not like the government.

What was the hardest part about being in the war?
I think simply being away from home and being away from life as I had known it to that point in time.

Was there a lot of physical or mental stress that you had to endure while you were in Vietnam?
In time, I experienced a whole lot of guilt. There were times of anger and rage, and sometimes just the day-to-day ins and outs.

> *"IT WAS HARMFUL TO THE PEOPLE, AND BY THE TIME I CAME BACK TO THE STATES, I DID NOT LIKE THE GOVERNMENT."*

Was there one particular experience that sticks out in your mind?
There was a chopper pilot by the name of "Dust Up 47." He used to bring casualties to the hospital ship, *Sanctuary*, and we developed a relationship in a way. I was an air controller for the hospital ship. After about four weeks I noticed that his number wasn't recalled anymore. I asked about it, and they said he had been shot down and disappeared somewhere in the Ku By area. I felt very, very sad that particular month.

Do you think the U.S. could have won the war? Why or why not?
No, we had no moral grounds to justify the harm we would have created, the harm we would have had to create to win the war. As long as we had to fight it on the Vietnamese's terms within the context of American realities, we lost our chances of winning. And a victory would not be a victory. It would only be a loss of our integrity.

Did you make any lasting friendships during the war?
No.

Can you go into detail on why you didn't?
Depending on where you were at the hospital ship, naval support activities, artillery, we flew in as strangers and flew out as strangers. I never saw these people again.

What kind of reception did you get when you came back to the United States?
None.

Were you spit on?
No, I was discharged in South Carolina, went home, stayed drunk for a few months, and then that's all.

What did serving your country mean to you during active duty or now as a veteran? By the time my active tour of duty ended, I was ashamed to wear a uniform of the United States. I've never participated in Veteran activities. I'm not a member of any veteran clubs or anything like that, and I would never choose to take part in any celebration that glorifies the military service.

Did you have any difficulties dealing with the memories when you came back?
Not in terms as anything I would recognize as flash backs, but it was a number of years before I was able to gain sobriety.

How long were you in the war?
Two years.

Is there any message that you have for people today about war?
The only message I have is that you take a life, you waste a life, and it's not necessarily the one you've taken. I have a hard time finding justification for what we call "war."

Can you go into detail on what your jobs were?
On the *U.S.S. Henderson* my job was a number of things, providing information for gunfire support for my own unit and land based artillery. We worked to provide gunfire support to various targets. I also was an air patroller and just stayed and helped air seat pilots. For the hospital ship, *Sanctuary*, my primary duty was air traffic control of the incoming and outgoing choppers to make sure it was clear and safe. Naval Support activities in Da Nang was a lot of air traffic control, providing perimeter defense, going on night cap missions to provide support to the Vietnamese people. When I was aboard the *U.S.S. Enerson* we also got a lot of surveillance of the Chinese coast. We went inside territorial waters of China, around the island of Tai Minh, the same island that we had a fiasco regarding an American spy plane. We were doing that in 1967, taking our ships inside their territorial waters, and triangling to find out where their artillery was, where their missiles were set, those kinds of things; nothing new really. My job primarily was to be a part of the gathering of information, assess it, and distribute it to the appropriate resources.

Can you describe what your training was like and how much time you spent in training?
Boot camp was pretty simple. It was mainly physical and learning nautical terms and coming to understand what it is like to be aboard ship. My training in my specialty, which was the use of the great art of gathering up combat information and assessing it, was a 38 week school in Great Lakes, Illinois, where we learned everything from the electronic make-up of radar and those kinds of things, to combat assessment and navigation, air control. I can't remember all the things we went through.

> *"THE ONLY MESSAGE I HAVE IS THAT YOU TAKE A LIFE, YOU WASTE A LIFE, AND IT'S NOT NECESSARILY THE ONE YOU'VE TAKEN. I HAVE A HARD TIME FINDING JUSTIFICATION FOR WHAT WE CALL "WAR."*

Were there any other things that you remember about the war that you would want to share?
I guess it's not an experience that I talk a lot about.

Can you go into what the ships did?
Destroyers, their primary job was gunfire support. It might be a suspected enemy movement along a path within our gun range, about 5 to 7 miles up. The Army would call us, the gunfire support, and they would give us the coordinates, and we would put that into our computers and then point our guns in that direction, and we would fire support for land based troops. Sometimes it would be just a suspected enemy movement. Sometimes it would be in the middle of a fire fight; we would be providing support directly, often over the heads of the troops, to the enemy, trying to stop their attack. We often also did search and rescue missions for pilots. We would be part of a search and rescue team, picking up pilots that were going down in the South China Sea. When I was on the hospital ship, *Sanctuary*, our primary job was to treat those casualties that were needed beyond the capabilities of land based MASH units, so these people would be brought out to us for surgery and those kinds of things. Treating a lot of victims of Napalm.

How old were you when you were enlisted?
I was 18. It was 1961.

When you said you thought the U.S. couldn't win the war, do you think they could have done anything different so they could have won?
Given the political limitations of the time, I don't think anything different would have happened or been allowed. They only way of winning militarily would probably have been the use of nuclear strikes, and that is intolerable. I don't think we could win a land based war in Vietnam. I also don't think we had the heart to win a war in Vietnam against an enemy that had a much firmer moral agenda on why they were battling.

> *"I THINK THE MENTALITY THAT WE CAN NOT BE DEFEATED IN THE BATTLEFIELD CAUSED US TO BE DEFEATED."*

Do you have any feelings on whether Johnson and Nixon did the right thing for the war by sending more troops in?
I think that every buildup was an episode of madness, but I don't hold Johnson and Nixon responsible because this war began under the office of J. F. Kennedy, and it began to grow from there. I think the mentality that we cannot be defeated in the battlefield caused us to be defeated. We were defeated in the battlefield in Vietnam.

Do you think that part if the reason it took the U.S. so long to come out was because of their pride?
Exactly. I think pride. I think military pride, and I think political insanity. Leadership that did not have the courage to recognize a mistake and own it, be responsible for it, and change it. When the war first started, Johnson was not telling the citizens what was going on.

Do you think he did the right thing by doing that?
No, I don't think he did the right thing. I think he did the politically astute thing, but people have a right to know, and they were not given that opportunity in the beginning.

How much did you know about the anti-war movements while you were over in Vietnam?
Quite a bit, because I got *Time* and *Newsweek* and those magazines. We had an armed force radio. We got some mention of it from that. We were quite aware of what was going on at that time.

Was there anything that you remember from the fight?
No, I just really remember the perimeter strikes that I was involved in. It was dark, there were sounds, flashes, the screaming of rockets, noise, chaos.

Most of the attacks were at night then?
Yes.

Do you know why that would be?
I think that when you are trying to attack a compound, it's easier to approach with the cover of darkness.

When you were in the helicopters, were you ever shot at or hit or anything?
No.

Following the war, Jim Rowlette has provided services to people as a family therapist and an AODA counselor.

Interviewed by Jess Long
Transcribed by Kristy Isberner

David Stachovak

Enlisting in the Navy, Stachovak served on a destroyer that was providing offshore bombardment to ground units in Vietnam. Following that experience, he trained as a corpsman and returned to Vietnam.

How did you become involved in the Vietnam War?

I would have been drafted. I had worked at a dairy after I got out of high school for about a year and a half, and I got my draft papers in the mail. I went down and talked to the recruiter, and I joined the Navy instead of being drafted into the Army. Then I came home, and I never even opened up the Army draft papers. I probably opened them up, but it didn't mean anything anymore because I had joined the Navy already.

Could you just tell us how it was going over, and when you got there, what you were thinking?

I went over there twice. The first time after boot camp, being in the Navy, I went to a ship, the *USS Osbourne*, and we were home ported in Long Beach, California. I was there for about a month, and then we sailed across the Pacific Ocean. We stopped at all the little islands, Midway, Guam, Hawaii, on the way over. Then the ship was home ported for the next couple years in Yokosuka, Japan. We didn't stay there very long because we'd only go back there about once every six months or so, and then we would spend the rest of the time in the waters in and around Vietnam. Aboard ship it was different because you didn't get into firefights or anything like that. We would just go offshore and then do what we called a shore bombardment with the Marines or Army, or somebody needed assistance, they would call on our ship. Then we would just anchor off, but not necessarily anchor, but we'd be offshore, and then we'd shoot missiles inland.

Our ship had five what they called five inch 38s; the shell is five inches around, about this long. The projectile was about that long, and it weighed probably about seventy pounds. They would put a canister of gunpowder, about this big around and about that long, behind the shell in what they called a lower handling room. Then when that powder ignited, it would send that shell up to like fifteen miles inland, and we could drop that bomb on any target they wanted. So we were there for about a year. At that time, when we first got aboard the ship, I was the gunner's mate missile. My specialty was working with what they called an ASROC. It was Anti-Submarine Rocket. So, that was my onboard experience or responsibility. Then about half way through that, I decided to become a corpsman, which was a medic, a navy corpsman. So, I spent about a year and a half aboard that ship in Vietnam, and we did shore bombarding.

We were anchored. I had stood watch that night, and about six-thirty, seven o'clock in the morning we were anchored just off the shore of Vietnam somewhere, and they started shooting at our ship while we were anchored which is not a good situation. So we had to quick pull the anchor up, and we got two direct hits. The ship got hit by some kind of what they called recoilless rifles, which is a big gun that's mounted on either a truck or on a railroad car, and then they could shoot big shells at us. Then they could quick run the vehicle into a cave and hide it so that we couldn't destroy it with our guns. Unfortunately, they did hit us, and they hit our rocket storage area onboard the ship. It put a big hole about that big through the bulk head. It went right straight through the ship actually, and they also hit our radar control room, which put us out of commission as far as firing back within accuracy. We could lob shells there, but we couldn't lock on any target because it wiped us out. Well then it started a fire in the rocket storage room which is not a good place to have a fire. So, one of the guys went in with a hose, and he was the first one there, a fireman they called it. He went in spraying, and he was able to get the fire out before it blew the ship up. Had he not done that, we probably would have sunk, but he was able to do that, and we had no major injuries from that. I think one guy probably bumped his head falling down the steps or something like that.

Then we went back to the Philippines for what they call dry dock in which they bring the ship out of the water and put it up on a kind of water filled port storage. Then they let the water out, and the ship is sitting up out of the water, completely out of the water, and then they could do the repairs on the ship. So we were there for a couple months while they repaired the ship, and then we went back to Vietnam. Then about a couple months later I got orders to come back to the United States to go to school. I went to corps school. From corps school, I went to field medical school, which was all at Camp Pendleton, California. I was stationed for another year at an orthopedic ward as a senior foreman. I mostly had, I'd say, motorcycle injuries, and guys wounded in Vietnam were the primary patients that we had. I did that for a year, so that would have made my third year in the Navy.

Then I got orders to go with the 2nd Battalion 9th Marines 3rd Marine Division. I went back to Vietnam, this time onshore. That was a little bit different experience than being out at sea because you were actually on land where most of the action was. I spent about six months in the bush, as they called it. That's where you're actually out in the jungle and making contact or trying to make contact with the enemy, or the guys would probably not want to make contact. Then, we were around the end of July of 1969, and they started drawing troops back out of Vietnam, and because we were the 2nd Battalion 9th Marines, we were one of the first units over in Vietnam, and one of the first ones to get pulledout. So they pulled us back to Okinawa, and I spent the next about five months until December of 1969, and then I got out.

When you were over there the second time, what were the camps like?
Well, our rear area was Quang Tri, and we didn't see that very much, but it was dusty and dry and hot primarily. These are just tanks that they set up, and they do firing missions from inside. This is somebody out in the bush. During one of the first ambushes we walked into, a couple of these got killed, I think, and then some other guys were wounded. But I have been able to keep in touch with them. I haven't found out where he is yet, but this guy e-mails me every once and a while. He's doing real well. He works for the general, some big wig in Washington. I can tell you more about these if you want to know about the firefights and stuff like that. But the rear area was pretty much all open because they would blast it with Agent Orange. Quang Tri was a pretty good sized base. They destroyed everything with Agent Orange, and of course that makes everything die, and then everything gets totally dry. So it's either totally dry with maybe six inches of dust everywhere you go, or it's totally muddy because then it would rain. So you had your choice of totally dry and dusty or totally mud. It was hot, always hot like this or hotter because it was always probably ninety to one hundred degrees.

Did you fight against the Viet Cong or NVA regular units? Describe the enemy.
It was hard to say who we were fighting. I guess the Viet Cong probably, and we also fought against the

North Vietnamese Imperial Guards at one point. These were supposed to be their elite troop, and the only difference that we noticed from the bodies that we would find is that they seemed to be taller. And we

thought, we suspected, that they might have come from China, some of them. Some of them were almost as tall as us, which is kind of unusual. They were kind of big people, but of course we only saw what was left of them, the dead ones.

Can you describe what an average day was like during the war?
We'd get up in the dark, usually about five o'clock in the morning, and you'd make yourself a cup of coffee. What we would do is take a little bit of what they call C-4. It's plastic explosives. We would just roll it into a little ball like this, and then just squeeze it so it came to a little point. We lit it on fire with a match. We'd take like a sea ration can and empty it. After we cleaned it out, that would be our coffee cup and underneath kind of a handle on there. We'd use the cover for the handle, and that would be our coffee cup. From then on you'd always save that one. We'd make ourselves a quick cup of coffee because if we'd light this up, it burns real hot and real fast. We could bring this little cup of water to a boil in about a minute, it was so hot. Then we'd have coffee. Then we would open ourselves up a C-ration of some sort.

Usually what would happen is that we would go either on a company size patrol movement or else we'd go on a squad size. There's three squads in a company depending if we were going to be coming back there that night or if we would keep on moving. Usually it was a squad size with about fourteen guys. We would go out, and there were two corpsmen for every three squads, so the corpsman would go every other day, and then the marine squad would go every third day. We'd go out with a different squad every other day, and we would have certain checkpoints that they would want us to investigate and maybe seven or eight checkpoints. Sometimes they would send more than one squad because there would be more than one company. We'd be checking out one area while another company was checking out another area. As we got to each of these checkpoints, we would radio in and tell them what we found. Of course, they would know if we made contact with the enemy because we would radio that in right away. We were usually pretty lucky; we never did. We came close, but we got lucky. We would call in at each of these checkpoints, and we would just work our way around. The whole time we would either be going up a hill or down a hill. We would have quite a bit of equipment on our back, maybe a hundred pounds of equipment as you were on this. Then we would usually get back into the perimeter just before dark. We would set in and fix ourselves something to eat for supper, and then we would go to bed. The Marines would have to stand watch beside us. It would get dark, and then they would have to stand about a two hour watch. One of the Marines would have to stay awake while the other people slept. Then his people would keep relieving each other all night. The Marines were lucky if they got five hours of sleep uninterrupted a day. We were pretty tired and always on the go from morning in the dark until we set in at night in the dark, even if we were company size. The only difference is that if we were company size usually we were going to a destination. They would pick another hill out, and then if we went there at night, then we would have to set up what they called a hayseed perimeter. We set in just before dark, and then we'd set out our antipersonnel mines, claymore mines they called them. We would set in for the night. Usually our mortar guys would set in coordinates. Just before it got dark, they'd fire a few shells, so they knew where the shells would land later on in case there was movement in that area. They'd set up the perimeter, and then we would set in on another hill that night. We would be all ready for the next morning. Whether we went on a company size or on the squad size, that was about the only difference. The average tour, we called that being in the bush, and the average tour in the bush was seven months. Then they would rotate us. Again, the Marines were about the same as the corpsman. They tried to bring us to what we called the rear area, which was Quang Tri in our case. The corpsman would spend the last six months of the thirteenth month tour in a rear area running the battalion aid station and things like that. That was a typical day.

Were you involved in any firefights?

Several. The first one was probably the worst one on a personal level because they were actually able to wound and kill a couple of our guys. I had just been in the country for about three weeks, three or four weeks, and this particular group of Marines hadn't made any contact with the enemy. The closest to that point was about a half of a mile away. Actually, a couple of the guys had seen some gooks, as we called them then, running. I don't know if they even fired at them, but they were pretty comfortable in thinking that we wouldn't make any contact. I was on one of my first squad size patrols when we walked into the ambush. We were walking along following a dried out riverbed. The guys were stopping and filling their canteens up with water after we crossed this log. I was even able to stop here and take pictures of these guys crossing this log. It was real nice; this was a dried out river coming down the mountain here. We cut across this, and these guys were farther down the trail here. This guy is taking a drink of water with this other guy. They were best friends from back hom;, they went through boot camp together on what they called a buddy plan where they both enlist at the same time into the Marine Corps, they go through boot camp together, and then they give them their first active tour wherever they had to be, together. Then, after that they would break them up.

What happened right after I took these pictures was, I was walking across this log, I had just got to the end. The point man, which I believed to be this guy here, which is the other guy's best friend, got shot in the head and killed. Then shrapnel wounded the two guys immediately after him, this guy here and San Miguel. Then we returned fire and were able to crawl up and jump in a bomb crater and pull the wounded guys up, and we treated them. There was another corpsman with me because I was still new in the bush. He was supposed to be teaching me the ropes, but he kind of went in shock because he had never seen anything like that before. I gave the one guy a shot of morphine and the other I couldn't because he had a lung problem. He had a piece of shrapnel in the lung, but they both survived. We finally were able to convince the gooks not to hang around. Then, they brought in medevac choppers, and we got these guys out.

That was our first firefight after I was in the country. The rest of them usually didn't involve our squad directly. We supported other squads that had gotten pinned down in firefights, and we would come up on them. We were just lucky enough not to walk into another ambush ourselves. We had a couple of ambushes that we set up ourselves, that our company did. I was fortunate I didn't have to participate because I was a medic, so I could just sit back and wait for the action to get over and take care of the people who needed Band-Aids or whatever.

Did you have any experiences with body counts or kill ratios?

Not directly, no. They would probably have asked us, but it was kind of hard to be truthful about it because the Vietnamese would drag their wounded and killed bodies out of there as much as they could, just like the Marines really. Most of the time, if we were in a position that we could let them, I don't think we cared if they did or didn't. They were pretty good at getting them out, and then they would bury most of them on site, wherever they could. In a few areas we probably killed more of them than what was left. Then of course, they couldn't always drag their people out. We would in some cases bury them, but most of the time we would just leave them lay wherever they would have gotten killed.

We were in one area that probably had quite a few bodies around. We didn't count them, but we were there longer than what we would have wanted to be, like a couple of weeks. After two weeks in the hot sun, these bodies were pretty well decomposed. If this is bad, that was as bad as you could imagine, considering they'd go from a full body that looked normal, almost healthy other than maybe a bullet hole. In a matter of two weeks it was actually pretty well rendered to a skeleton because the flies and everything had a pretty good picnic over there. The heat was so favorable for decomposition; it would be pretty foul smelling whenever that would happen. In reality we could smell a decomposing body a mile away. You could imagine that if you were set up just a couple hundred feet away from the bodies, it was pretty rank.

Did you use helicopters to get around?
Oh yeah, it was the number one transportation. It was either helicopters or walking, and we preferred helicopters.

Were you in Vietnam during Tet?
That was 1968, right?

'68 yeah.
No I wasn't. I was in part of '66 and '67 and '69.

Were drugs a problem for soldiers in Vietnam?
No, there it wasn't as big a problem as I hear about and read about in our areas because we were pretty much always in the bush. In the rear areas some of the guys would get a hold of marijuana and stuff like that, but had they been caught, they would have been court marshaled or something like that. Of course, we didn't want anybody to be stoned when they're supposed to be standing watch because that's not very good for our environment either. It wasn't probably as big a problem for us as, apparently, it was in some areas.

Was there a problem between whites and blacks that you saw?
Not so much in the bush. In the rear area when people had a little more time on their hands, not to sound prejudiced, but the black people were just getting into the Black Power back then, and they got jobs in the rear area like running the mail. We'd call them poke jobs, which were the easier jobs. They would steal a lot of the mail that came into the country and some of it going out of the country. For example, if somebody got a package from home or something. Some of our mail was stolen, but we had more of a problem with that Black Power. That was kind of predominant when we got pulled out of Vietnam and spent four or five months in Okinawa. The black people were coming of age, I guess, and would gang up on the white people that were on liberty and beat them up and stuff like that. It was kind of racially tense back then, but while we were actually in combat there was none of that. We were all real supportive of each other. It's just when we had time, when they had time on their hands, that the problems would happen.

Do you have any opinions regarding the antiwar movement back in the states while in Vietnam?
I don't know. It was kind of confusing. I didn't become a Jane Fonda hater as much as a lot of people. It

was kind of hard to understand why we weren't being supported. I married a hippie. My wife protested on the streets of Madison. If I would have understood it a little more, I probably would have joined them. At the time, while we're in the country, we didn't think of that being like they were against us. We were just more interested in surviving. People can say what they want about the war, but what it is, is trying to survive. If you happen to get into a bad situation where people are shooting at you, you shoot back and try to get yourself out of that environment. It wasn't like a Second World War or a First World War where they had definite lines and trenches and you held your line and trenches. We would have minor, minor situations like that where for whatever reason they would want to take a hill.

> *"PEOPLE CAN SAY WHAT THEY WANT ABOUT THE WAR, BUT WHAT IT IS, IS TRYING TO SURVIVE."*

Then we would take the hill, and then once we got the damn hill, we'd go onto the next hill. It didn't matter. We might come back two months later and take that hill again. It was kind of stupid, but that's what we did.

What was the hardest part of being in war?
The hardest part was probably dealing with the bodies. The wounded ones were one thing because you always had the hopes that they would be alive, but having to deal with getting the dead bodies out was probably the worst.

Do you think that the United States could have won the war?
Sure.

Why do you think that?
Because we had superior firepower, and we had air support which they didn't have. Had we gone at it to win the war, I believe they wouldn't have had a chance, but we did more skirmishes.

Did you make any lasting friendships during the war? Do you keep in contact with them?
Yeah we did. Probably the best friends I'll ever make. What is it? Baptism by fire. We don't realize it at the time. We try not to form friendships there because there was always a possibility that we would get killed, or they would get killed, and then we would feel bad. We tried to remain independent and aloof, but after we'd been there and spent months and almost up to a year in some cases with the same people, helping each other survive, we definitely establish a life-long friendship.

> *"I THINK EVEN IF WE'RE DOING THE RIGHT THING OR WE THINK WE'RE DOING THE RIGHT THING, WE SHOULD HAVE A BETTER IDEA OF WHY WE'RE THERE AND WHAT WE'RE DOING THERE."*

What kind of reception did you get when you came back to the United States?
I didn't have anybody spit at me or anything like that. I was happy to get out, and I left my Marine's uniform even though I was still in the Navy. I refused to put my Navy uniform back on. I was discharged in the Marine uniform, and of course, then once I got out, I took the uniform off as fast as I could and hid it. Then I came back and I pretty well tried to start-up life normal, and I won't say I for-

got about it, but I just didn't think about it anymore than I had to.

What does serving your country mean to you during active duty and now as a veteran?

Back then we really didn't think about it; it was just something that we were taught. We just did automatically without thinking. That was your duty, and everybody did it. We had good examples from WWI, WWII, and even the Korean War, so if they said that's what we had to do, well then that's what we did. Now I question it more. I think there's times that it's probably good to question it because I don't think we are always right. I don't think we always belong in getting involved. I still feel that we have some responsibilities to serve our country. That hasn't changed. I think we should be proud to do it, but I think especially the people who aren't in the service should question whatever they want us to get involved in. We should know what's going on. I think the Vietnam Vets were pretty ignorant about history and about what we were doing there. We just did it because we were told to do it, and I don't think that's good. I think even if we're doing the right thing or we think we're doing the right thing, we should have a better idea of why we're there and what we're doing there. We still should follow orders without thinking because that's part of surviving, but as to why, why we're there, we really should question that, be involved, and know what's going on.

Did you have any difficulties dealing with memories when you got back?

Not difficulties. I mean just about every veteran, I think, suffers from some amount of post-traumatic stress, PTSD, Post-Traumatic Stress Disorder. I'll always have the recurring dreams, but I don't think I woke up too many times choking. I think it's more normal than not because it's just a person's body and mind having a tendency to block things and then come out when they're sleeping. I don't, I try not to lose sleep.

Is there a message you have for young people today about the war?

It's not a glorious thing like you see in the movies. It might be necessary at times; you do the best you can, but I would certainly try to avoid it whenever possible. Other than that, we're not the ones that make war. If there's any way we can prevent it, I would recommend that way.

Is there anything else you want to add?

I made myself a promise because I had seen people... we would go to Sturgeon Eddy, here in Wausau, and visit people that were old and sick when I was a kid, somebody my parents knew. There would always be a couple of these guys running around at the hospital. We would always call it the end of Sturgeon Eddy because it was like all the nuts were there. There would always be some little guy there running around, and he'd be real shaky and you know kind of weird. I would always say, well what's wrong with him? I was not even a teenager probably, and then somebody would say, "Well he's shell-shocked. He's shell-shocked. He got that in war." I always pictured that you'd see these movies where a big shell would land. It would blow him up, and he'd fly up in the air, but it wouldn't blow him to pieces. He would just get tossed head over heels. I thought that was shell-shocked, when he got shocked by the shell. Actually it was just a form of Post-Traumatic Stress. Some people would actually go nuts sort of. I said that I made myself a promise that I would talk about it to anybody that was interested in hearing anything about it and try to be as truthful as I could without fantasizing. My biggest thing is memory. I do kind of lose chronological order of things and would block things, so it's kind of hard to be real. Some people have a gift to remember details of where they were and what they did, but I was never privileged to it. I never knew where the hell we were most of the time anyway. It was all jungle, and it was just talking to other guys sometimes that I would even know where we were. A lot of that information I forgot, but I do have memory of some of the things that happened. I know of some of the places where we were.

Do you have anything further to add?

Two guys would go out on a listening post. That's all they did all night with the radio was just sit there very quietly. If they had any movement at all, they would call back on the radio. Usually they would already have it coded out that if they hit their button that's all they would do. They wouldn't even talk because that would give away the position. If they had any contact, maybe they had worked it out before that they would push the button once, the microphone button once. Then they might talk back or they might not, to ask them what's going on. If they could tell them, they would radio in that, "Hey I have movement here," or something like that. Then they also had an ambush, which were usually four or five guys. They would go out and actually set up on the trail somewhere while it was still light. Then they would take turns sleeping. That was the whole idea... that if the enemy would come in, they were set-up in such a way that, hopefully, they would wipe out the enemy. That would be an ambush. That'd be four or five guys.

I was only invited along once on that because I snored. They kept waking me up, and they'd say, "Doc, quit snoring," and then I would. Finally, I was sleeping on the side of a steep hill. I'm back like this against the hill, and I woke up. I'm thinking, why did I wake-up? I could feel something warm on my lap. There was something on my lap, and as I sat up, whatever it was jumped off my lap and ran off into the jungle. To this day I don't know what it was. I don't know if it was a rat or a monkey or something trying to stay warm. I stayed awake. I was never invited back on an ambush. I was listening close in the ambush. That's about it.

> ### *"THE WILL TO SURVIVE IS PRETTY STRONG."*

Then they would have your normal watches all along the perimeter. Guys would relieve each other all night long, and those, people of course, would stay awake too. These two guys were coming back from a listening post in the morning and bumped into some enemy. There was a firefight over on a bridge. This guy, Bob, went out to help these guys, and he got wounded. He's lying there, and any time they'd send another Marine out to try to save him, they would shoot him again. He's lying there, he'd been shot once or twice, and then they shot him a couple more times. This one corpsman went up to try to save him, and the corpsman shouldn't have done that in the first place, but the corpsman got shot. He said he can remember he didn't know who it was, but he can remember in slow motion seeing this guy get hit. He got shot in the head and tossed backwards. It dropped him back down on the ground. Of course this corpsman got killed. Then Jim Beaman, who was my partner, was the one who finally crawled out there, grabbed him and dragged him down into a ditch, so he was out of fire. Initially, I think he got shot in the legs. Then periodically he got wounded in a few other places as they would take another shot at him. Jim patched him up and stopped the bleeding. They got him on a helicopter, and after he was in the helicopter, the helicopter got shot. He got hit through the floor of the helicopter. I don't know where he got hit that time, and he says he was lying there. They told him later on that he said, "Stop shooting me!" He had been shot so many times already, the poor guy. He walked without a limp. The guy walked without a limp, and I finally after about the third or fourth day I said, "Bob do you mind showing me any of your scars?" He opened his shirt, and he was just scars like patched up holes all over his body. He raised up his legs, and he's got holes where he had bullet holes in his legs, just like in the cowboy movies. I mean the guy had bullet holes all over him. Some of these guys were amazing, the damage that you would see to the individual. He is joking all the time, but I think that helped keep him sane.

I had one black guy, I think he was a sergeant, a big black guy got shot. He was pretty shot up too. When I was working on him, his legs were shot, his arms were shot, and one of his testicles was shot off. He's lying there all bleeding, and I wondered if he was going to live. I think he lived; I don't know for sure. We stopped the bleeding, got IVs going, and he's lying there. He's so shot up I think he's going to die at any minute. He says, "Doc, will I still be able to have kids?" I said, "Yeah you still got one testicle. It works real good." That was his only concern. He's lying there practically dying, and he says, "Am I going to be able to have any kids?" It kind of struck me funny back then. The will to survive is pretty strong.

Do you have any other stories?

You hear these stories of where they use the expression of baby killers, and you hear about the My Lai Massacres and stuff like that. We went into villages where there were friendlies. This was very common to go into a village of friendlies, and we just didn't go in and start shooting people. That was very unusual. It may have had real good reason for starting shooting because there may have been weapons that were suddenly exposed. It was very common for us to come across a group of friendlies and bring them back into our perimeter. They would interrogate them, like ask them questions about movement in the area. Sometimes they were a little reluctant to tell because their lives were at stake, too, if they would squeal too much on the Viet Cong.

One time, for whatever reason, they left me alone with three or four other Marines. They went to check out. We were on a squad size patrol, which are about fourteen guys. About nine or ten of these Marines leave us sitting and waiting for them to check out some movement on this hill. All at once I can hear Vietnamese voices coming closer and closer. They look at me because I'm the ranking person. I had the highest rank of the Marines. I didn't know anything about, but I played Cops and Robbers when I was a kid, so I knew about setting up. They're looking at me, so I said, "Ok you go up on that hill, and you go..." I set up this ambush, and I hid behind this big rock. I dug out my 45, loaded it, and got it ready. I hear them coming around the bend, and I could see them coming. They didn't look too dangerous because they're all carrying baskets. I didn't see any weapons or anything. Now I'm laying there thinking, "What am I supposed to do?" I waited until I could take them by surprise, and they were right up on top of me. I jumped out in front of them, and there was about fourteen of them. Of course they all screamed and they stopped. Now I've got them surrounded, and I didn't know what to do, so I stood there. They had IDs. Why would they in the middle of the jungle have these, but apparently all the friendlies have these. They're showing me their IDs, and of course they all look alike. I'm going, oh yeah, like I could really tell. Meanwhile, they knew they were surrounded by these other four Marines. Ok. they all looked pretty good, and they even had kids with them. I just had them sit down in the shade, and we waited. When the other Marines came back I said, "Hey I captured us some Vietnamese." We took them back to the rear area. I was good at Cops and Robbers, and we played Cowboys and Indians when we were kids, so I knew how to set up an ambush. We captured them single handedly, some innocent villagers. We didn't just go in there blasting like you hear these stories about that. It didn't happen.

If you saw the movie *Platoon*, it's interesting. That was a good movie because it showed you what it was like. That part of it was really true, like when you remember when he landed and everything, the dust and the dirt flew up. That's how it really was. It's really dry and hot, and that was very realistic. Any segment of that movie could have been realistic, even the massacre in the village and all that. But there's not one squad in Vietnam that would have ever seen all that excitement onto one squad because 90% of the time it was boring, routine, and nothing was happening. Any one five minute segment of that movie could have happened to one squad or maybe two or three, but all that happening to the same squad in Vietnam, no way. They say like 10% of the Vietnam Veterans saw any action, 10% of them were in a firefight, and the odds went down and down and down of that happening. We weren't under fire the whole time. That was just a small segment of your thirteen months or however long you spent. If we happened to be in the 10% of 10% of 10%, you could have gotten killed in those few minutes. That would happen, but that was just a quick segment; just like a snapshot of your whole time.

While it was happening it was bad. We had a situation where two of our platoons crossed this river before it set in dark. We weren't able to cross that night because it was getting too dark, and the river was too deep and too fast. They didn't want to chance us going over in the dark. We set up perimeter on the same side of the river, and these other two platoons went on. They walked right into an ambush, and they just got wiped out. Not everybody, but a real high casualty rate of those two platoons. We could hear the shooting, scream-

> *"OUR PLANTOON NEVER GOT A SCRATCH, AND THESE GUYS WERE JUST ABOUT WIPED OUT."*

ing, and the carrying on pretty much all night long. At one point they were calling for a corpsman, so I'm climbing up, crawling up closer to the river thinking it was on our side of the river ,when one of the sergeants jumped on me. "Where the hell you going?" I said, "Well they're calling for a corpsman." Here it's on the other side of the river. They're still in the firefight, and this guy had been injured in the head. He was delirious. There was a corpsman with him at the time, but I didn't know that. The sergeant said, "You just stay behind a rock where you belong." The next day we went across there to help them. That was pretty bad because we would have a cargo net pretty big, maybe 12 by 12. Then when the helicopter would come, the four corners would fold up, and that's how we'd carry cargo. We had that heaping, heaping with flack jackets, helmets, weapons, and stuff from the guys that were wounded or killed in those two platoons. Our platoon never got a scratch, and these guys were just about wiped out. It's just your timing. That's all happening a hundred yards away, and we were perfectly safe. That's why I said the movie is believable, if you just remember that it couldn't all have happened to the same group of people in the thirteen month period. A couple of segments, but not everything. The guy getting shot at the end where he was running and every time he'd get up they'd shoot him again. That was pretty interesting. Generally speaking, if you get shot at the end of your finger, you'd probably be down and out.

In the rear area, they still had French mines set-up where nobody knew where the damn mines were. They would just put a fence around the old French quarters where they had the French mines. These three or four Marines one day would take their C-rations and they'd throw it over this fence trying to hit a mine to set if off. It's pretty stupid because you still could have got fragments. But these Marines decided that they were going to go in and get some of these C-rations, cans of food that were out on the mines. Why? Some of these Marines weren't the top of their class. They were starting to climb the fence. One guy got over the fence, the other guy was climbing up, and the third one was getting ready to climb up. The second guy decided this was stupid, so he decided to go back down. Just about then, the first guy stepped on a French mine. It went off, and it killed him. I don't know if it killed one of the other guys too. The third guy, it hit his hand, and it amputated his hand. Of course he's screaming, and it sounds gross, but all that was wrong with him was that his hand was gone. He screamed, and he went into shock. He died

"WHEN I WAS CALLED TO TREAT SOMEONE, I'D IMAGINE THE WORST POSSIBLE THING. ANYTHING LESS WAS A RELIEF."

of shock just because he lost his hand. The next guy can be all shot up, and another guy can just have an amputated hand or a finger. It's such a shock to him, that he dies of shock. That's what happened to this guy. Had he just calmed down, and if a medic could have gotten to him quick enough, it wouldn't have been a real big deal other than losing your hand. I've seen bullet holes in the back of the hospital a lot worse than that, so it's kind of ironic some of that. That just kind of became common place.

You know you're going to see things like that, but it's not going to be everyday, unless you have to be one of these poor guys that had to do the bagging of bodies. They put them in what they called a body bag. Those guys probably mentally were worse off than the guys out in the bush. They would deal with those bodies everyday, put them in the plastic bags, and put them aboard a plane back to the States to be buried. They would see that day in and day out. I think those are the guys that really had a lot of mental problems. We dealt with it. When we were in Laos, we had to walk back into Vietnam. There were too many of us because it was like a huge operation, and one of the last days we were there, we took a few casualties. We were socked in, and the helicopters couldn't come in and get out wounded and killed because it was too foggy. We had to carry a couple dead bodies out. That was kind of emotionally bad. It was just like a whole string of guys spread out, a hundred feet between guys, and a thousand guys walking along the road. You could see for miles ahead, and here every so often would be a couple Marines carrying a body hung in a poncho. Whenever they stopped to rest, they'd set the poncho down. Of course they'd stop bleeding, but there would always be a puddle of blood where they'd stopped to take a break. We're walking along, and we'd see that puddle of blood. It was a human being; it wasn't a deer or something. We were kind of happy to get them on a helicopter and out of there. That's very depressing to the troops when you're carrying a dead body for a day or two.

What was your biggest fear?
My biggest fear was that in spite of all the training I had, I wouldn't remember what to do to treat an injured man. I feared that the injury would be so gross, I'd freak and not be able to help the injured man, or possibly put him in shock because of my reaction. When I was called to treat someone, I'd imagine the worst possible thing. Anything less was a relief.

Following the war, David Stachovak became a cable splicer for GTE/Verizon.

Interviewed and transcribed by Vicki Karcher

WOMEN IN NAM

D.C. EVEREST AREA SCHOOLS

Women in Vietnam

Near the Lincoln Monument in Washington D.C. the Vietnam Wall occupies an area of the Mall. After the wall was completed, a statue of soldiers was added to complement the memorial. After that addition, one more was made. That final addition was a statue to commemorate the involvement of thousands of women who served alongside the soldiers honored by the wall. This statue is one of nurses aiding a wounded man.

Nursing was and probably is the one specialty that people think of when you mention the role of women in the Vietnam War. Many women served in the field hospitals that received the wounded from helicopters just in from some landing zone. Others served in modern facilities located in a motor city in Vietnam, and still others served on hospital ships anchored off-shore.

Nursing was only one of the specialties that women performed in Vietnam. Many soldiers only remember the stewardesses who were on their flights to and from Vietnam. However, women worked in the embassy and in many clerical as well as medical specialties. Their services were seen and felt throughout Vietnam.

Diane Carlson-Evans

Evans volunteered for Vietnam as a registered nurse in the Army Nursing Corps. She was first stationed at the 36th Evacuation Hospital, in Vung Tau, and on the second half of her tour was moved to the 71st Evacuation Hospital, in Pleiku.

When were you sent over to Vietnam?
I arrived on August 1,1968.

How old were you?
I was twenty-one.

Did you get drafted or was this something you wanted to do?
Women volunteer for the military, and some of us, like me, also volunteered to go to Vietnam. Women have never been drafted (conscripted) in the history of the United States. No law has yet been passed conscripting women into the Armed Forces. However, once in the military, you are under their command. Many women did not choose to serve in Vietnam but received orders to go there.

A group of Army Nurses courtesy of *Celebration of Patriotism and Courage.*

Where were you stationed in Vietnam?
I was assigned to two different places. My first six months was at the 36th Evacuation Hospital in Vung Tau, near the South China Sea and the southeastern delta area. The second half of my tour I spent at the 71st Evacuation Hospital. This was further north in the central highlands, about thirty kilometers from the Cambodian border near a mountainous area called Pleiku.

What was your main job?
I went to Vietnam as a registered nurse in the Army Nurse Corps. The corps has different specialties such as operating room, emergency room, medical/surgical, and so on. I was considered a medical/surgical nurse, so my first assignment at the 36th Evacuation Hospital was as a staff nurse taking care of wounded soldiers. The unit was an open ward with sixty patients in it at any given time. I cared for soldiers who were being prepared to go into surgery and those returning from surgery. It was a very busy time; this was 1968 and the height of the Vietnam War. At an evacuation hospital we received and treated patients, stabilized them as best we could and evaced out the most seriously wounded to the United States or to other hospitals along the air-evac chain, for example to Guam or Hawaii. If they were not severely wounded they may have stayed on at our hospital until recovered, or transferred to an in-country rehabilitation/con-

valescent hospital. Then the soldier went back to the field, or to his or her unit assignment. Later in my tour, I also worked in a burn unit, and while at the 71st Evac. Hospital served as Head Nurse on a surgical unit.

What was it like when you first arrived?

That is hard to put in one sentence. I will just give you the immediate sensation. It was hot, extremely hot. We landed in the evening at the Tan Son Nhut Air Force Base near Saigon. It was kind of frightening; as the door opened there were armed guards with bandoliers of ammunition across their chests. They escorted us out to a bus that had windows covered with chicken wire, the glass was black so you couldn't see in. We had armed guards with us on the bus the whole time to the 90th Replacement Center. This is where they took us for a few days to give us orientation to Vietnam and to assign us to where we were going on the first part of our tour. It was a reality check. I am here now; I am in a war zone, and it hadn't really struck me yet as to how dangerous a place it was. I knew it was dangerous for our soldiers because I knew they were being wounded and they were dying in Vietnam, but I was not real sure of how dangerous it would be personally for the medical personnel. I was eager to get started with my work, but I also had the reality that I was in a war zone.

When you said orientation, what was that like?

It was pretty basic. They gave us a handbook for U.S. Forces in Vietnam and told us to read it. They advised us to take our malaria pills, be careful about drinking the water unless it was from a lister bag, or first putting tablets into it. They told us if we left the hospital and went down to the village, we shouldn't eat the food or drink their water because we may get sick. Nurses were advised not to travel by convoy, helicopter or anyplace unless on official orders because it was too dangerous. I remember being told about getting an "Article 15"—that something negative would go on our records, or we would go to some military jail or something if we broke the rules! Orientation was basically regarding our safety, acquainting us to the country, where things were, the layout of various hospitals, the kinds of hospitals that we would be assigned to. When I received my assignment to the 36th Evacuation Hospital, I was told where it was located, what kind of patients we would receive, and that kind of thing. We also received our supplies such as a poncho liner, jungle fatigues and boots, flak jacket and helmet.

What was it like during a push?

A "push" meant that lots of casualties were coming in at the same time, and we were really pushed to get all the work done that needed to be done. It was very tense, and people's lives depended on us. A lot depended on how smart and how quick we were, how brave we were, how awake we were, and how vigilant we were. All of our senses were heightened. I am sure you have heard of an "adrenaline rush"; adrenaline is a natural hormone that can result in a fight or flight mode, and our adrenaline was pretty high. I think for the entire year it kept us alert, hyper vigilant, and awake.

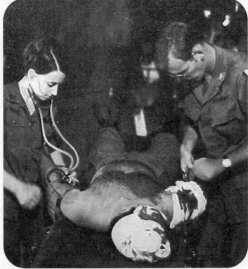

National Archives photo courtesy of *Celebration of Patriotism and Courage.*

Was there any certain times that you can remember that you would like to share?

I cared for a young soldier at the 36th Evacuation Hospital who had shrapnel wounds but not seriously wounded enough to be sent back to the U.S. He waited three days to have his wound stitched up. Most wounds were not closed immediately because they would get infected, so the policy was to have a "delayed primary closure" or DPC about three days following the injury. During that time we could irrigate the wound, give the patient antibiotics and intravenous therapy if necessary, and make sure nutritionally they were doing OK, plus see that they didn't have any other problems like malaria, typhoid, amoebic dysentery, or an "FUO" which was a fever of undetermined origin. So, this young man had his delayed primary closure, and after another week or ten days for the healing and removal of stitches we sent him back to the field. He was from Minnesota, and I was from Minnesota, so we struck up a nice friendship because we talked about Minnesota things. He was such a wonderful young man; while he was up and about recuperating he assisted other patients with their crutches or wheelchairs, fetched supplies, always asking us what he could do to help out. That is what patients often did when they became ambulatory and were convalescing. They would do anything they could to help the nurses and their fellow ward mates. Before he left to go to the field, he asked me if I would write to him, and I said that I would. But I never received a letter back from him. Later while I was serving in Pleiku, I received a manila envelope with a letter in it, my letter, which had been returned to me. It had never been opened; it was from a commanding officer telling me that he was sorry but that Eddie had been killed. So, I learned from that. We patched them up, cared for them, we did everything we could to save their lives, and we sent them back to be wounded again or killed, and it was just so tragic. I remember sitting on my bed sobbing, and that was the last of that. I quit crying because crying didn't do any good. It did-

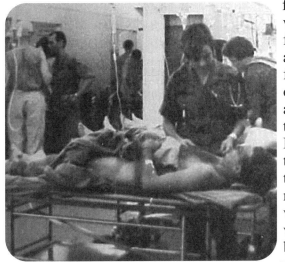

Patient in a hospital courtesy of *Celebration of Patriotism and Courage*.

n't help and all I could think about was his mother and how sad it was for his mother to get the news. It was hard for nurses to get close to patients, because if you got close to them it was very painful to know what happened to them and think about their grieving families. Part of our way of coping in Vietnam was keeping our distance from the emotional pain and being able to sort of anesthetize oneself to get through our days. We couldn't feel the tragedy and heartbreak while doing our work, it would become toxic. We had to be positive for the responsibilities in front of us each day. Yet, I know that I never lost my compassion for my patients. I have never forgotten Eddie, and always touch his name on the "Wall" when I visit there.

"WE PATCHED THEM UP, WE DID EVERYTHING WE COULD TO SAVE THEIR LIVES, AND WE SENT THEM BACK TO BE WOUNDED AGAIN OR KILLED, AND IT WAS JUST SO TRAGIC."

Any other stories you would like to share?
When I was at Pleiku, in the central highlands, it was much more dangerous than Vung Tau. We were closer to the Cambodian border, and we were in the jungle. Our hospital supported the 4th Infantry Division, which was really being hit hard that spring of '69. So our casualties were coming to our hospital directly from the field by helicopter or ambulance. If they were lucky, they got to us in ten to fifteen minutes. If they were trapped in the jungle or the hills somewhere, it could be days before they got in to us. These were fresh casualties coming in to us in great numbers. We would stabilize them as best we could and ship them off to other hospitals, but sometimes they were so severely wounded that we had to keep them. It was really traumatic with the seriously wounded men because we couldn't do anything to save them. To see them deteriorate and know that their families couldn't come and be with them was really hard for me. In the United States we are so accustomed to being surrounded by the people we love

when tragedy like car accidents or terminal illness occurs. In Vietnam, the patients, the nurses, the doctors, and medics weren't family, but we became family to the wounded and dying, and we were the last people in that person's life. We became very important to them. I have thought about that a lot over the years since I have had my own children. The pain isn't just about witnessing the terrible wounds from guerilla warfare and the various assorted weaponry of rocket and motar blasts, land mines, bouncing betties, punji sticks, grenade shrapnel, napalm and white phosphorous burns, multiple penetrating gun shot wounds, it is also about people's mental suffering. War is a terrible thing, and we have to at all costs do what we can to prevent war, learn from the lessons of our past wars. But it seems like we don't; we just repeat the same mistakes.

Being a woman, did you ever feel that you were treated different from the men?
We were different in Vietnam. There were so few of us. There were approximately 10,000 women who served in Vietnam. There are no exact figures, and there were also American civilian women serving in Vietnam. Of the military women, about 90% were nurses, so the majority of American women in Vietnam were nurses. I felt, personally, that among my peers and among the soldiers and among my patients, there was a lot of respect for us. We had to be careful of course, very careful, use good judgment and common sense about where we went and who we were with. We were young, so we didn't always use good common sense. We didn't always use good judgment, and we went off to places where we shouldn't have. One day I wanted to get away from the hospital compound and see the neighboring village of Pleiku. This was not a safe area. Our hootches and hospital was rocketed and mortared from time to time, there were sappers that found their way in, it was not a safe place by any stretch of the imagination. The hospital was surrounded by concertina wire. This is like barbed wire, all rolled up, rolls and rolls of wire to prevent enemy sappers from penetrating the compound. Also, the hospital base perimeter was surrounded by four guard towers. The guards, armed with bandoliers of ammunition, provided us 24 hours surveillance, and occasionally they were targets for the enemy. Anyway, one day, two other nurses and I decided to sneak away. We found a willing driver with a jeep who took us downtown to the primitive village of Pleiku and dropped us off. We shouldn't have been down there, but we were curious about our surroundings. Somebody must have told the military police that there were nurses in downtown Pleiku, so pretty soon we noticed that we were being followed, and thought OK, we're in trouble! They left us alone for awhile, and then finally one of the MP's came up to us and said they would escort us back to the hospital. They actually let us sneak back in so we didn't get into trouble! They were watching out for us, respectful of us, took care of us. I think there was a lot of respect for the women there.

> "IN THE UNITED STATES WE ARE SO ACCUSTOMED TO BEING SURROUNDED BY THE PEOPLE WE LOVE WHEN YOU ARE IN A CAR ACCIDENT OR HAVE CANCER. IN VIETNAM, THE PATIENTS, THE NURSES, THE DOCTORS, AND MEDICS WEREN'T FAMILY, BUT WE BECAME FAMILY, AND WE WERE THE LAST PEOPLE IN THE PERSON'S LIFE."

When I talked to Lynn Kohl she said the guys had a place where they could go when under attack and the nurses had to go underneath their bunks.
That's right. We didn't have bunkers available in all places. At the 71st, the nurses were told to get under their beds during attacks.

How did that make you feel?

I didn't feel very safe, but didn't spend much time worrying about it. We had helmets and flak jackets hanging right by our bed. I would grab my helmet and put it on and put my flak jacket over me and curl up in my poncho liner under my bed. This was our protection. I know that some nurses had bunkers in other parts of the country because they told me of time spent in them. Our particular hooches and the hospital were heavily sandbagged. Now that was fine if the shrapnel was coming at the angle of the sand-bag, but if the rocket or mortar was going to land on top of the hooch, which some of them did, that wouldn't be any help at all. Hospitals were attacked over there, rocketed and mortared. Patients were wounded and killed as they lay in their hospital beds; it happened in Pleiku as well. The Geneva Convention outlined that wartime hospitals were declared safe zones. Well, the rules go out the window in war time. Most of our hospitals in Vietnam had big red crosses on the top of them. We used to laugh that those were the targets for the VC because they loved targeting the hospitals, but that was part of their psychological warfare. They did it on purpose because they wanted to diminish the sense of safety and security of the troops, including the medical personnel.

What did you do with the patients if there was a mortar attack?

Our SOP, standard operating procedure, when we under attack, was to get all of our patients under the beds and throw mattresses on top of those who couldn't. The first time that happened I grabbed my helmet and flak jacket and put them on first, because if we are dead we can't help our patients. We didn't have to tell the patients to get under their beds.

They had been out in the field, and they were under the bed in a second. Everybody was on the floor except for the patients that were attached to intravenous therapy or other hook ups. Some had blood lines, transfusions, catheters, tracheotomies, and were on the respirator. I put mattresses on top of them. I remember, I was in a forty-four bed unit at Pleiku, and every bed was occupied with a wounded soldier one of the nights we were rocketed. I also had wounded and burned Montegard children in my unit. We cared for civilians injured in the crossfire of war. It just so happened that one of the doctors in my unit was a pediatrician. Everybody knew that, and they would bring all the sick children to us. Now, I have all these sick babies and children, so I am running all over the place making sure that mattresses are not only on the wounded GIs, but

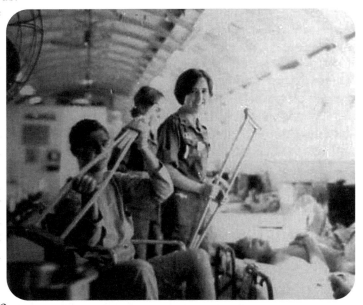

Lt. Diane Carlson at the 36th Evacuation Hospital, Vung Tau Vietnam, in 1968

the children as well. They are terrified, and don't know what to do. We had this one little girl who was burned by napalm from her neck to her ankles and was in terrible pain all the time. I couldn't do anything for her; I couldn't touch her, put anything on her, or put her under a bed. If you touched her she would scream. She is in this crib, and because I couldn't do anything physically for her, I just sat by her so she knew somebody was by her. Then she became so terrified that she began screaming. So this little girl, this tiny little girl, is screaming at the top of her lungs. There is the noise of incoming; it's crazier than heck, it's noisy, it's dark, and it's like a hallucination. I am trying to give you this picture so you can understand what this is like and what it was like for the patients because it was awful to hear this little girl cry, because this reminded the guys of home. Like somebody's kid sister crying in the night, but not the same. It was bizarre. We are an American hospital for wounded GIs, and none of us knew we were going to be caring for children. That is one thing I was not prepared for when I got to Vietnam. There has been a lot of controversy about whether or not women should be in combat. Some believe that women should not be in combat, because all the men will be taking care of the women and going to their rescue and providing aid, comfort, safety, and security for the women. Picture that scene that I just shared. I was the only woman on the ward that night, and I was the only woman who was doing everything, providing the comfort, security, and safety of all the men on the unit and all the children, and I never ran for safety. I did not get under the bed; I didn't run to a bunker. I stood there by that little girl that was crying because I couldn't do anything for her, and I wanted her to be able to see me. I was holding her hand, and I wanted her to have a little comfort, that she wasn't alone. So this whole philosophy about women being shrinking violets in a war zone is pathetic. It just didn't happen that way. Women are strong. They are maternal and they are caring, and they will carry their load, rise to the occasion, and do whatever it takes to be part of the team. I saw women do incredible things, in the combat zone, in Vietnam.

> *"I WAS THE ONLY WOMAN ON THE WARD THAT NIGHT, AND I WAS THE ONLY WOMAN WHO WAS DOING EVERYTHING, PROVIDING THE COMFORT, SECURITY, AND SAFETY OF ALL THE MEN ON THE UNIT AND ALL THE CHILDREN, AND I NEVER RAN FOR SAFETY."*

When you came in contact with the Vietnamese, were you ever scared that they may be the enemy?
You were cautious all the time, because often they were. We had Vietnamese women working on our wards who were doing general housekeeping duties, cleaning the floors, making the beds, washing the laundry, that kind of thing, and you didn't know if they could be the enemy or what, because they all dressed alike and looked alike. On my unit we discovered things were disappearing like medications, medical supplies, and dressings. We decided it had to be the "mama-sans" who were stealing it. So we started stripping them down before they could leave the compound, and we found (this is what women will rise to) that yes, they were stealing from us. They were taking from us for their men, their people, they were fighting their own war, and they were doing all the things we were and surviving, being resourceful, being strong, finding ways to help their people. (Years later we found out that there was an underground hospital for the VC not too far from Pleiku.) They were stealing our supplies to take them to their hospital. Then of course, they all got fired, and here we had been paying these people with United States money, and they steal our supplies and take them to the enemy's hospital. But can you blame them? Wouldn't you do the same thing? We were very careful with what we said around these people. We were always kind of watching our back. I have to tell you a funny story. At 5'5" I am tall compared to the Vietnamese women, who were about five feet or less. But because I was thin I had small undergarments. The women stole all my underwear because it fit them! I would send out my laundry and they would hang it out to dry in the sun and it all disappeared! I had to have my mother send me all new underclothing, and then I had to keep it under lock and key. Can you blame them? Why wouldn't they want some nice, pretty American woman's underwear? At the time you are angry. I was angry at the Vietnamese. They were stealing our supplies, our belongings, personal stuff like perfume, but now years later, when I look back at this, what would we do if we were in their situation. They wanted the things we had.

What about the children? Were you ever concerned that they could be helping the enemy?
Not while we were in the hospital. I never had any fear of the kids. Now I know that our men in the villages and out in the jungle where the troops were had to be very careful. The children could have been the booby-traps, and they might have been sent out to be the distracter, and they had a grenade on them, but in the hospital I was never afraid of the kids. I loved the kids. Kids were just kids. That was one area

that was hard for me. It was hard to build up a wall between the kids and me.

U.S. Army photograph courtesy of *Celebration of Patriotism and Courage*

Did you ever feel that you just couldn't do it anymore, that you just wanted to stop?

No, I never got to that point. I can't remember that I thought that I just wanted to quit and go home. It was not an option. I remember though being surrounded by so many people, yet feeling very lonely. It was a very lonely year. I don't know why, when there are so many people around you, but there were times that I felt very lonely and very sad. I knew that it was a year that I had to get through; there was such important work to do. You don't think much about yourself, you have people depending on you to do your job.

How long were your shifts?

Twelve hours. The assigned shifts began either at 7:00 am or 7:00 pm. I was head nurse on my unit at Pleiku, so I wanted to get to the ward early, about 6 or 6:30 am, to be sure everything was in order for the day, and sort out what had happened that night. Shifts often turned into thirteen, fourteen, fifteen, sixteen hours, and during pushes, during casualties, maybe it would be around the clock, especially for the operating room. Though we worked in shifts, there was no real escape from the 24 hour a day mission. The nurses on duty just had to keep going. We worked six days a week.

What would you do on your day off?

While stationed at the 36th Evacuation Hospital I joined other medical personnel to go out on "Medcap" (Medical Civic Action Program) to the local villages. We went together in jeeps, bringing medical supplies and our goodwill. We were limited by what we could accomplish, but the villagers were incredibly grateful for anything we did. We administered medication for worms, did vaccinations, pulled teeth, treated small wounds. Once in awhile, the surgeons would find something they thought they could fix, and brought the patient into the hospital. On other off days, I would visit a nearby orphanage and help to feed, bath, and tend to any injuries or illnesses among the hundreds of abandoned and orphaned children.

Were drugs a problem?

Yes, they were. Drugs (and alcohol) were very available in Southeast Asia, so some of our troops used them. War is a terrible thing. People do whatever they need to do to survive and get through the days. When I was there in '68 and '69, drug use was not as bad as later. Drug use became worse as the war wound down and morale diminished. Troops began to feel the lack of support from our government and our country. The troops that arrived later wondered why they were there. The war was winding down and they had the possibility of losing their life, and there was a lot of tension around the whole morality of the war. The troops were not given a purpose, an objective, a reason to fight.

Lt, Diane Carlson at an orphanage in Vietnam, 1968

What did you do for fun?

Well, I don't remember a lot of fun in Vietnam. I did some risky things, just to get away from the hospital and see some of the country. I'd go up in helicopters — when I wasn't on orders to be in one. Some of us nurses would say, "Let's find out what an Article 15 is." Then wonder, "what can they do to us, send us to Vietnam!" One day a pilot took me out when he thought it was pretty safe—there hadn't been any activity in the area for a while. I have some incredible photographs from the air of that little trip. Most of the time when off duty, I would go back to my hooch and tape music on my reel to reel recorder. Music was my saving grace—sometimes I just wanted to be alone and music was a good friend. When you are on a ward all day long with forty or fifty or sixty patients, and so much going on around you, you have to get away from it. In my tiny little room, I could get away from all the chaos, noise,

"FROM MY ROOM, I COULD GET AWAY FROM ALL THE NOISE AND RESPONSIBILITY AND CRAZINESS THAT WAS GOING ON AND LOSE MYSELF IN MUSIC."

responsibility and craziness that surrounded me and lose myself in music. It helped me a lot. I'd go to the O Club (Officer's Club) once in awhile to find people to talk to, or listen to one of the bands that came in and played some music. There was a lot of drinking for some. I don't remember talking about our patients or decompressing, or debriefing; it was just chit-chat. There was volleyball, and we would get up a game, or baseball or softball once in a while.

What kind of medical staff did you have in the hospital?

When I got to Pleiku, I was told that there were supposed to be seventy-five nurses there, but I don't know the actual number. It was a 400 bed evacuation hospital; that is not a lot of nurses for all those shifts and all those patients. The intensity of the wounds and the injuries was high. These were sick people, and we

didn't just have wounds. We had Typhus, plague, and malaria, and fevers of unknown origin; from the jungle we have snake bites, tiger bites, monkey bites; and we have all the accidents, vehicle crashes, all kinds of fatalities in wartime that doesn't come from weaponry. And we had lots of injured civilians, especially children. When I was head nurse in a very busy surgical unit there were usually only two registered nurses to take care of that whole unit. We had probably four corpsmen on duty, they worked incredibly well. We couldn't have survived without our corpsmen, they were fabulous. We had surgeons, and medical docs of various specialties, radiology technicians, dentists and other support staff. We even had a pediatrician on my unit.

Lt. Diane Carlson in Vietnam in 1968

Did you receive any medals?

I received the Army Commendation Medal when I left.

What was that for?

It didn't mean a lot to me at the time. It just meant I did a good job. Lots of people deserved medals and didn't get them. Lots of people received medals and didn't deserve them. They didn't give nurses many medals. And most of them certainly deserved them. Some of the officers made sure each other got medals because it was good for their career. Sometimes it was about who knew who and who wanted to help whose careers. I have a tainted view about medals and Vietnam. I don't know if it was like that in other wars. There was a head nurse at Pleiku who actually said nurses don't deserve medals and wouldn't give any, as we were just doing our job.

What was it like when you came home?

It was hard when I came home. There was a lot of anti-war, anti-soldier sentiment in the United States, and we felt that. Many of us too were anti-war by the time we came back. We could see the war was not taking us anyplace and wondering why we were fighting with no clear objective, but we couldn't understand why the country had turned on us. We were just soldiers there—given our orders, and we did our best just like any soldier had done in past wars. The country didn't separate the politics of the war from its soldiers, and that was very painful; not only painful but it made me very angry. I didn't know what to do with my anger, so I kept it inside. I didn't talk very much to people about what I did, and eventually I didn't even want people to know that I had been there. It often just set me up for humiliation or put me on the spot to answer, "What was it like in Vietnam?" How can you explain to somebody who was never there what it was like, especially when you felt they probably weren't that interested anyway. I was discharged out of the service when I returned from Vietnam and started a nursing position in a Minneapolis hospital. I discovered though that I was still in Vietnam mode. I was still hyper vigilant, and I heard noises around me, I was hyper-alert, and I was not sleeping well at night. I was feeling guilty that I shouldn't have left Vietnam just when I was getting good at what I was doing, and that I should have stayed. Back in the States, I am angry that people around me are taking their anti-war views out on the soldiers and then I find that I am not satisfied with civilian nursing. I couldn't find a lot of compassion for those who were in the hospital for routine surgery. I quite that job after only three weeks. I went to Madigan Army Hospital at Ft. Lewis Washington because my hooch mate from Vietnam was assigned there, and we decided to be roommates. I went to work at the army hospital there as a civilian nurse, and that is when I decided to rejoin the Army Nurse Corps. The recruiter asked me if I had a preference for assignment. When I asked for Brooke Army Medical Center at Ft. Sam, Houston, Texas she assured me I had it. I guess there is a reason for a lot of things, and it was at Ft Sam that I went back to nursing Vietnam veterans and soldiers returning home from the war. I worked as a head nurse in the Intensive Care Unit and Recovery Room; applying the nursing skills I had developed in Vietnam. I found that I was really happy in what I was doing, it also helped me decompress because I was in a military community, not a civilian community, and I really needed that decompression. I was not thriving very well in the civilian sector. At Ft. Sam I met my future husband; we have been married now for thirty-three years. We have four great kids. The main thing I feel about having served my country is that I did something worthwhile. I would do it again. I met wonderful people and I even met a wonderful person to spend my life with.

Did you suffer from PTSD?

Yes, I was pretty depressed for a lot of years. I didn't know why, and I wasn't connecting it to Vietnam.

Did you receive any help for that?

Finally, I went to a Vet Center because I was really, really depressed, and it was kind of scary. Here I have these four kids, and they needed a mother. I was losing my will to live. I had heard of Vet Center's opening across the United States to help Vietnam veterans readjust. So, I called the one in Minneapolis and found the people there very helpful. I started working with a counselor and he said to me, "You are so angry," and I was shocked. I said, "No, I'm not." I didn't think I was angry because I wasn't hitting anything or anybody, and I didn't appear to be an angry person. Then we started talking about that, and he said anger turned inward is depression. Of course, I had to admit that I was angry at our government, the politicians whose misguided policies caused the deaths of so many people. I was angry at our country for sending all these young people to Vietnam, and then not backing them up, not accepting and honoring them when they came home, not supporting, not caring about the fact that they were committing suicide in large numbers as well as suffering from other things like agent orange poisoning. I couldn't comprehend the betrayal. I couldn't condone it. It was wrong, it was unjust, it was unfair, and it was a tragedy. We have more than 58,000 names on the wall, and thousands of veterans who commit suicide and are dying from complications of their war time service. I had seen the courage; sacrifice and suffering of so many young men and women while I was in the military then saw them come home and suffer the aftermath of war on the home front. My life took a turning point after I attended the dedication of the Vietnam Veterans Memorial in Washington, DC in 1982. It was following my visit there, that I began seeing someone at the Vet Center to sort through my Vietnam experience. I realized that I needed to talk about it, and over time I found that I needed to do something with that experience, in a healing and educational way.

I guess I took the anger and used it constructively. I recognized that I could not forget the soldiers, especially my patients and what they had gone through. I also recognized that I wasn't thinking about how we women had suffered too and that the women didn't receive recognition or acknowledgement that our service was worthy— that we contributed a great deal. This is what precipitated my idea to honor the women in a meaningful way. Instead of letting my passions and anger tear down my life, I could rebuild and put it to good use. I believed that our nation would honor and remember the women if they only knew the truth But never in my wildest dreams did I think that it would take almost ten years and be as difficult as it was. There was a lot of opposition to the whole idea.

It is a great thing that you did and I am sure a great number of women are happy that you did it,
They are, they really are. Some women veterans told me early on that they didn't need a memorial and did not want to help with the grassroots efforts. They wanted to put Vietnam behind them, and were not even acknowledging their veteran status. That turned around too; more and more women have stepped forward. It's been a long healing process. I can't tell you how many women wrote to me after the dedication saying that they didn't realize how important a memorial would be for them. They are grateful. And our brother veterans are grateful. They have supported us all along. We women share the tragedy of the spilled blood of our brother soldiers

I was going to ask you about your involvement with the memorial but you have answered that.
You know that I am the founder and the president of the Vietnam Women's Memorial in Washington, DC.

Did you ever have any problems with Agent Orange?
Not that I am aware of.

Anything else to add?
The Vietnam Women's Memorial portrays a mortally wounded soldier; he is suffering and the women who surround him render courage and strength; they reveal the anguish, the despair and the futility of war. There is no winner. There is only comfort in the knowledge that wherever men and women are sent they will do what they are trained to do and they will put their lives on the line for one another. Meanwhile, the Congress and the citizens who send them to war must support them, for their orders are mandated by the people. But a patriotic country will do everything possible to prevent sending its own people into harm's way in the first place. A patriotic country will pay atten-

Women's Memorial courtesy of *Celebration of Patriotism and Courage.*
© 1993, VWMP, Inc.
Glenna Goodacre, Sculptor

At the Vietnam Women's Memorial in Washington, D.C.

tion to the details of all its previous wars—the details of death, destruction, suffering and repetition. For in repeating wars are we solving problems? We will find out what a great country we are, not in flexing our military power, but in our power to refrain from using it.

Diane worked several years as a registered nurse and is the founder/president of the Vietnam Women's Memorial in Washington. Diane has been a nurse educator, veteran advocate and activist. She lives in Montana with her husband and her four children. Diane returned to Vietnam in 1998 and bicycled 1200 miles from Hanoi to Ho Chi Minh City (Saigon). She visted local Vietnamese people and other Vietnam vets from both sides of the war. (Sponsored by World Team Sports)

Interviewed by Jenni Marcell

Penny Kettlewell

Penny Kettlewell served two tours in Vietnam where she was a nurse. In her first tour in Vietnam in '68 she worked in the intensive care unit and Receiving/Emergency and in her second tour in '70 she was head nurse of the intensive care unit.

What was your term during the Vietnam War?
I was over there from Sept 1968 and I went back again in July 1970.

How old were you?
Twenty-four.

Being a woman, did you get drafted or was this something you wanted to do?
In those days, you had three year nursing schools. In my third year I joined the Army, and they would pay for that year. I owed them after that. I did volunteer for Vietnam.

What was your main job when you were in the war?
My first tour over there I worked in the intensive care unit and Receiving/Emergency, and my second tour over there I was head nurse of an intensive care unit.

What functions did your job have?
I took care of the patients. In intensive care in the receiving area we took the patients when they got off the medevac chopper, and we stabilized them as best we could. Then we separated the ones in triage, the ones that were salvageable from the ones that weren't, and we tried to find out who everybody was and get them sorted out. In the intensive care unit we took care of them either immediately after surgery, or if they couldn't be operated on, we took care of them then if they were not salvageable.

Did you find your job pretty hard?
Beyond anything you can imagine.

Emotionally?
You would dream, and you drank a lot.

Did you get treated differently than males?
Yes, over there we got treated better than most of the guys. The guys took very good care of us because we were doing everything in our power to take care of them.

Were there many drug problems when you were over there?
On my second tour, it was more by then, because it was so frustrating for the guys and they knew the war was never going to be won and we were playing political games. Yes, they took a lot of drugs. On my first tour over there, there wasn't as much, mainly marijuana. Mostly people were just trying to do their jobs.

Was it mostly nurses or were actual GIs doing it more?
The guys did it out in the open and had it available. I would say the majority of the nurses drank.

Did you deal with many Vietnamese?
Yes we did. Whatever the guys brought in, if they had room on their choppers for the injured Vietnamese soldiers or civilians and they also brought in the POWs and they also brought in groups of Montagnards, like native Americans, they brought them in.

Did your unit work on POWs before our GIs?
That happened occasionally. People in intelligence tried to and were able to interfere occasionally. Ninety nine per cent of the time that only happened if they had somebody who had information that could save lives. They were never put ahead of the GIs for other reasons other than that.

Did you have a problem with that?
Of course we had problems. You could only argue so much and get your point across so far. You get all these big shots, and they are telling you what is going to happen. Tempers were very hot in those days, and in those days nurses did what they were told. Things began to evolve later when nurses were given the control to make decisions. We started taking over triage, and we decided which patients would go to surgery, and this was something we always wanted. I would say that we brought nursing into the twenty-first century, and of course the doctors finally looked up and saw that nurses had brains capable of making decisions.

How did you deal with large numbers of casualties?
Like I say, you walk in and did what you could do. You survey the area and pick out something that is not being done, and you started working there. As long as you were working, you didn't have time to worry about anything else but taking care of patients until everything was done. When things were over, you got cleaned up, and then you thought about it.

Did you have mama-sans?
Yes.

Did you have any problems?
I didn't have any problems. You did realize that the Army told you to have them. Then you knew most of them were VC at night, and that was probably the worst thing about the war was the blatant politics. It was just games that were being played.

Did you receive any kinds of medals over there?
They gave me a Bronze Star when I left.

What did you get that for?
They were handing them out.

What did you do for fun over there?
We made our own fun; we partied a lot. It was sort of like MASH. You invent games. We would string something up and have a volleyball game. You would do what you could think of. It was very inventive. You can be very inventive when you are trapped in a small area.

Do you have any special event you would like to share?
My best friend was one of the nurses killed. She died November 30th. They had a big push in Pleiku, and patients were coming in faster than they could deal with them, and they called us and wanted us. They took a surgical group from each hospital, and it included a nurse and another technician and when they shipped them back, the plane went down (according to the government due to weather), but the corpsmen who found the airplane said it was full of bullet holes. I have a hunch it was probably shot down. All were killed, and our chief nurse did not choose to recognize the fact we lost two nurses. She wouldn't let us have any kind of service. We had to go to the other hospital. Then the Army sent her mom a telegram saying they were sorry to announce the death of her son. Her mother is still bitter about that.

Did you ever date the GIs?
Of course when I left I was engaged, and when you got back to civilization, things were not the same as they were over there. Almost all the nurses found some guy that they were comfortable with; it was sort of protection. You had people hitting on you all the time because you were the only "round eyes" that they saw. The doctors, who were officers, didn't want you messing with the GIs. GIs were more your age, and you really wanted to have more fun with them.

What was it like when you first came home?
Sort of a nightmare. I came back in '68, and I got off the plane, and then there was a strike of some sort going on and I couldn't call anybody and I had to go out and hail a cab. Out in the front were all these draft dodgers and anti-war people, and they were yelling at us and calling us all kinds of names, threatening us, spitting at us and all kinds of things like that, so this other guy who had gotten off the plane with us, -- I didn't know what was happening. But he lived in Oakland and I just wanted to see my folks. So I went with him until I could contact my family in Salt Lake City.

How did your friends and family treat you when you first got home?
My dad was career Air Force, and he was proud of me. Nobody wanted to hear anything. They wanted you to get on with life. They didn't want to see anything from the war, hear anything bad, and they wanted you to get back to the way you were before you left.

Did that hurt when you couldn't talk about the war?
I was glad I didn't have to say anything. I really felt guilty about coming home. As much as I wanted to come home, I felt really awful for leaving my friends there who were still working hard. As things went, I broke up with the guy I was engaged with and went back in the Army and back to Nam.

Did you suffer for any post traumatic stress syndrome?
I did just fine until 1990. Then my world fell apart.

Anything else you would like to add?
I think there is one thing. When we went through the treatment at the Minniapolis Veterans Hospital we were very, very fortunate that they had nurses in the branches of the military, and they were finally able to deal with the ways nurses dealt with PTSD which was different from the guys. Nurses have horrible guilt that they didn't do enough. The guys who have PTSD, have different guilt. It is something that is almost indescribable. Being somewhere where there is nobody that you know, where your resources are totally out the window, where the mores and values are totally different, where the events cannot be described. After you are there for a while you can't believe what you have become accustomed to. It was a time when everybody was rushed into something they didn't understand, and it was awful.

What was your unit?
I was with the 67th Evac. We were in Qui Nhon. My second tour was the 24th Evac at Long Binh.

"NURSES HAVE HORRIBLE GUILT THAT THEY DIDN'T DO ENOUGH."

If you had a choice to do it again, would you?
Probably.

Did it mean that much to you inside?
It made me a more capable person. It made my realize that I can do anything. Under the situation you think that all the guys in your age group and younger are being shipped over there, and someone, as a nurse, needed to do that. You get a bit of a high when you are doing a job well and you save one of these guys. You do something that is so positive, and it is a high. When I came back after my second tour, I went to Ohio State and went into nurse anesthetist, another special job, and did that for thirty years. I was finally able (inn anesthesia) to relieve pain, at least in others.

What would you say to young people going into the service?
Trust your instincts.

Penny Kettlewell is now a CRNA (Certifed Registered Nurse Anesthutist). She has two brothers who are both in the navy and her father is a retired career officer from the Air Force.

Lynn Calmes Kohl

Kohl was a nurse at the 71st Evac Hospital in Pleiku, RVN, serving in the operating room. She arrived in Vietnam in June 1969.

What was your term during the Vietnam War?
June 12, 1969 - June 11, 1970

How old were you?
I was 22 years old.

Being a woman over there, did you get drafted, or was it something you wanted to do?
Neither, I was lied to.

How so?
I was in my last year of nursing school, and it was in the spring. We were ready to graduate, and one of the girls (it was on a weekend and there were three or four of us in the lounge) came in. I forgot if she had just talked to a recruiter or if she started dating one, I can't remember; but she came in all excited and she told us all about this wonderful opportunity in the Army. We would go in as officers because we would be graduating, and we would have our choice of duty stations. Well, we decided to go down and talk to the recruiter, so we did. I had some friends that had just gotten back from Vietnam, and they said, "You don't want to be over there. It's not what you think it is, so you don't want to go there."

> *"I WENT BECAUSE I WAS LIED TO."*

So, I asked him about my chances of going over and he said, "Absolutely none unless you volunteer; since you're a female, they cannot send you unless you volunteer." So, we told him we would think about it. About a week later he called and said that that weekend they were going on maneuvers to Florida, and he asked if we wanted to go along. It was four girls and a hard decision. So we flew down to Florida with them, and they wined and dined us, and we thought this would be great. He kept on telling us about Ft. Ord, wonderful Ft. Ord in California, right on the beach. He just made it sound so glamorous. So again, I asked about going to Vietnam, and again he said, "Absolutely no way unless you volunteer." The other three

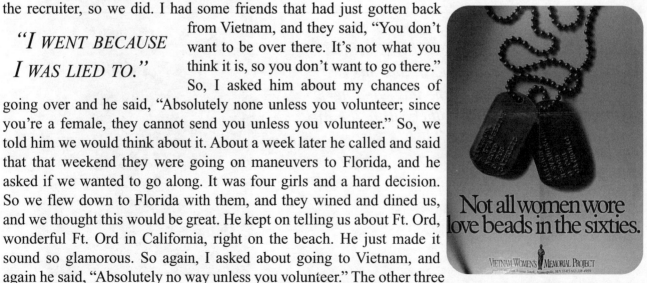

girls joined. I had reservations yet. I still wasn't sure. I waited and talked to him some more, and he kept on insisting that there was no way unless I volunteered, and I knew that I wasn't going to volunteer, so I finally joined.

We went to Ft. Sam in San Antonio, TX for basic training, and then we went to Ft. Ord. The four of us went to Ft. Ord. They kept telling us about it. We thought, right on the beach and everything; it sounded really nice. We went, and within a month I got orders for Vietnam. So I went to my commanding officer, and I explained the situation and said there had been a mistake. She just sat there grinning and said, "Do you have that in writing somewhere Lieutenant?" No, I didn't. Within another month the other girls all had their orders, too. Then the girl who talked all of us into joining went AWOL, got pregnant, and was out of the service. The other three of us were sent to sunny Vietnam, and she was out! I went because I was lied to, and I thought I was the only one until I went to the dedication of the Women's Memorial in Washington D.C. in '93. I ran into several women, and they were from all over: from California, from Florida; they were from all over, and several of them had the same story. We decided that the recruiters all go to the same recruiter school, and they were told how to tell the same lies.

So when you finally made it over to Vietnam, where about were you stationed?
Cindy and I went over together, and Sharon came over later. We thought that at least we would be together, but when we got over there they separated us and sent us to two different places. I was sent to the 71st Evacuation Hospital in Pleiku, the Central Highlands. The first thing I remember is before even getting off the plane, when they opened the door, there was this smell. It was just a horrible smell. Then we started going down the stairs, and there was this POP, POP, POP and people started running all over. People were pushing us down, and hollering and screaming…telling us to run over to this one building. We were under small arms attack. It hit us; this was for real.

We had to stay overnight at Nha Trang. We talked to the nurses there, and they were telling us all this horrible stuff. The next day Cindy got sent to one place, and I got sent to the other. The chopper in front of me got shot down (Cindy wasn't in it). When I got to Pleiku, it was too late to get my orders. I had to wait until the next morning. They took me to my hooch, which is a wooden structure. There were seven of us, and then there was a little room that had a shower (cold water), a sink, and a toilet. Some of the girls were talking to me and said the 71st started out as tents and then went to a wooden structure. They realized that they would be there longer, and they became more permanent with sidewalks and stuff. We were sitting out (there were some little steps) talking and the next thing that I knew, I heard this whistle and a thump. Everyone was gone. I was there by myself. Where did everybody go? Then one girl, Lynda Van Devanter (who wrote the book *Home Before Morning*) came out, and she grabbed me and pushing me says, "Get under a bunk, any bunk, it doesn't matter. We are under rocket attack."

The next morning I went to get my orders. My M.O.S., which is your military occupational specialty, was post-op nursing. I had a whole three months orientation to that, so I thought that was what I would be doing. They told me that I would have to go to surgery because they needed somebody there. Well, in order to be in surgery in Vietnam, you were supposed to have had at least a one-year OR course in the military for combat nursing or have worked in an OR for three years in a civilian hospital, and I didn't have either. Besides that, I had had a very bad experience in nursing school in surgery. When they said I had to go to surgery, that was traumatic right there. When I got there, I was told to put on a mask and gown and just watch this case. It was a real bad case. He had already lost a leg and an arm; he had over 100 pints of blood already. There was a surgeon working on his stomach, and one was doing repair on the leg, and one was working on his head. He was a really bad case. So I was just supposed to watch and see how they were doing things. I was there about five minutes, and the surgeon looked up, and he saw

me just standing there (I was in a mask and gown, so he didn't know who I was, and he didn't know that was what I was supposed to be doing). He threw a scissors at me and just
hollered, "Don't just stand there. He is going to lose that arm anyway, so cut it off." It was just hanging there by a tendon, so I had to cut it off. That was my first five minutes there. It was probably my first forty-eight hours that gave me post-traumatic stress. It was down hill after that.

What was your main job?
I was an operating room nurse. I started out doing circulating. As a circulator, you set up and tone down cases, got the case started, and ran for needed supplies, etc. We often had "pushes" where a chinook would land carrying 100 or more patients. When you heard one of those coming, you might have just put in a 12-hour-shift and were on your way back to your hooch, you turned right around and went right back. We didn't have enough surgeons, so when that happened, during the "push" the nurses and even some of the techs had to do some of the minor surgeries by themselves.

What are techs?
Operating room technicians (corpsmen). We had to do some of the debridements, some of the minor cases by ourselves. That for me was very hard because I really didn't know what to do. I knew my basic anatomy and physiology, but I often wondered if I did more harm than good...if someone's walking around or not walking around because of something that I did.

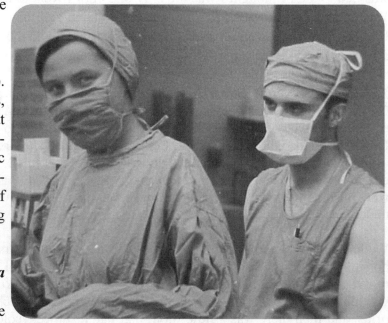
Gowning up for a case.

Did you have to decide whether or not a patient was going to make it?
No, I never had to do that. That was done in the ER. Nurses and doctors there had to make those decisions. When we had a "push," they had to divide patients into three categories: the most critical that they felt would make it, the less critical (who would make it), and then the ones who were so severe that they didn't have a chance. They set them over in the corner. You only had so many staff available, and it was impossible to save everyone.

How many nurses or technicians did you have working in one unit?
During the day there would be maybe three or four nurses and a tech for each one. At night you were always by yourself as the charge nurse, and you had a couple of techs. That was it.

Do you remember any certain patients?
We got the patients right from the field. They came from the field to us first. Then once they got stabilized, they would go to a safer area. Then from there they usually went to Cam Ranh Bay. Then from there, if they were stable enough to travel, they would go to Japan, and then from Japan, once they were well enough to make the trip to the States, they went to the States. The hardest part was we never knew if they lived or died...if our hard work was a success or in vain. We got everything! There were a lot of burn patients, (a lot of choppers shot down) and they would be really bad. We had to make up names and

make a joke out of it in order to deal with it. So like we would say, "Oh, a crispy critter's coming in," or a "horendoplasty." It was just a way to stay sane. Then we got casualties that were Montagnards (the Montagnards are the mountain people of Vietnam). They were in the Central Highlands by us, so we often had to deal with a lot of the civilians around the area. We also had camp Enari by us (the 4th Division), we had an Air Force base by us, and a MARS unit, and we had to take care of those patients. Periodically we would get POWs (prisoners of war) that we would have to do surgery on.

Was that hard for you?

It was hard because there were a couple times during a "push" they made us stop working on the GIs, our guys, to get this guy in because they wanted to be able to interrogate him, so they wanted him done first. Then when they got done interrogating him, they killed him anyway. In the mean time, we had guys who died because they couldn't get in because we were operating on him. Some of the people refused to stop working on the GI's and they were threatened with court martials. It was hard. It was very hard.

"THE HARDEST PART WAS WE NEVER KNEW IF THEY LIVED OR DIED...IF OUR HARD WORK WAS A SUCCESS OR IN VAIN."

Vietnam Womens Memorial Project, Washington, D.C.

What was it like being a woman in the war? Were you ever harassed or anything like that?

There were times when some of the nurses and the Red Cross girls would be. The General over in Camp Enari decided that it would be a nice thing to have a couple of nurses come each weekend. They would give us steak, and he thought it was a moral booster for his men. We had to dress up, wear a dress or a skirt and wear heels. Basically, we were to be their entertainment for the weekend. We thought that was horrible because we needed to be back doing what we were there for. It got to a point where people were refusing. Then we were threatened to be court martialed if we didn't go. We had that to contend with. The weekend that I went, George Goble was there. He was an entertainer, and his son had been wounded, and his son was receiving a Purple Heart. He had flown over to be there when his son got the Purple Heart. He was there with us, and he ate with us. The trailer that we stayed in was next to the trailer that he was in, and he came and talked to us. That was a plus for our weekend. There were guys who tried to make passes, but on the whole they were really pretty much gentlemen. They were just so happy to see what they called a "round eye," an American.

Did you get treated any different than say a male nurse, or even the GIs?

Well, not in some things, but it's really interesting. They had bunkers for the male officers and the enlisted men when under rocket or mortar attacks. But they didn't have any for the women. All we could do was roll under our bed. Besides that, they had our hooches up on the top of the hill, and they had a big red cross painted on the top of our hooch. It was like, here we are! There were things like that. Plus we were not allowed to have a weapon. The male officers and the enlisted men had a weapon, but we were not allowed to. We were over-run one night. They ended up getting all the sappers, but when I opened my door the next day, right outside the door was a dead NVA. Had he gotten through the door, my room was the first one. I would have been the first one he would have gotten, and we had nothing to protect ourselves with. They wouldn't allow women to handle weapons. We also did not get combat pay. Men did, but women didn't because they said that we weren't in combat. Pleiku City got renamed "Rocket City" because we got hit so often. It was close to once a day. The day that I left we got hit three times, and I was sure that that was it. You always hear that the last few days, that's when a lot of people get killed, and we got hit three times, and I was sure that I was not going to get out of there alive. Actually, through the whole thing, I didn't think that I was going to. I sent a will to my friend in Milwaukee, and had her hold it just in case. I didn't want my parents to be worried.

Do you have anything that you want to tell about?

Well, you do some stupid things. We had a Special Forces team that was in the area, and I started to "date" one of them. You don't really date when you're over there. We had a movie theater and you were usually under what they called "red alert" because we got hit so often. If you were on "red alert" anytime you went out, you had to wear a flak jacket and helmet. I have some pictures of me with my dress and flak jacket and this helmet on going to the movie theater with this guy. They never played the movie straight through. They would have the second reel first, and then they would have the third, and then first. They never quite got it right, so you never saw the movie from beginning to end. I was dating this Special Forces guy, and he had access to a jeep. One night he says, "Come on. Let's go for a ride." I said, "Well, I will only go if my friend can go along." My friend Sharon said she would go with me. I had on this bright orange dress, and it had rained and everything was muddy. When we hit some puddles the mud flew up, so we were laughing. We had a great time, but the next day it hit you. Here you were in the middle of the night, out in this jeep, Vietcong out there and land mines, and a bright orange dress on, and you're laughing. I never did that again! We had some fun times like that. People's birthdays were special. We tried to make a cake or something. We went to the mess hall and asked for a cake mix. Well, you know we were thinking "cake mix," but their supplies are for hundreds of people, and so they gave us huge proportions of things. We got this huge container that we found. We cleaned it out, and we started to try to mix it all up and get a little bit out of it to make a cake. So we did things like that that were really silly.

On a "date" donned in flakjacket and helmet.

Did you ever come in contact with any Vietnamese children or civilians?

Yes, we had a lot of the civilians. This woman came in who was pregnant, and they were real busy in the

Have Things Really Changed?

Things have changed, so they say
Vietnam Veterans can be proud now
But they had a parade for us
And nobody came
Except a few scattered here and there
Mainly out of curiosity, it seemed to me

Things have changed, so they say
I thought so, but now I'm not so sure
Except, they were right about one thing...
I WAS PROUD!

© Printed with permission from:

Lynn Calmes Kohl
5/2/84
Written after marching in the Oshkosh parade for Korean/ Vietnam
Veterans on 4/29/84

ER, and we hadn't gotten patients in surgery yet because they were in the ER waiting to come to surgery. They told to me sit there and watch her. So, I was staying with her. They're very stoic over there. They don't make a sound. I thought she was just in early stages of labor because she was just lying there very quiet. Then all of a sudden she made this tiniest little sound, kind of like "umph." I thought I should check her, and there was the baby.

They usually have the children out in the fields when they are working, and they will take a stone and hit the umbilical cord to break it. Then they just tie it and put the baby on their back and go right back working in the fields. That's how life is over there. They have a lot of children because they usually don't have very many that last after five years of age because of diseases, their way of life, and lack of food. When you have a patient in, the whole family comes into the hospital. The whole family camps down their hallway. So it might be the mother, the father, or the child who needs head surgery or is in the medical ward, and the hall is filled with the whole family. They stay there until that person either dies or leaves. They have mats they lay down and sleep on. They bring a couple of pots to do their cooking in, and that's it.

When you saw a patient, did you ever feel like you couldn't do it anymore? Did you feel like you needed to stop?
Early on, probably the first week, probably after I cut off the arm. You learn very early to shut off your emotions. You did such a good job at it that most of us have not been able to bring that back. It's really hard to try to reverse that once that has happened. So you had to totally shut down that part in order to do your job. You had these GI's dying, and they are asking you if they're going to die, and you say, "Oh, heck no. You're going to be just fine," and you know that they're going to die. You have to be able to have a smile on your face. At Christmas, I felt I couldn't take it anymore, and I took an R&R to the Phillippines which turned out to look just like Vietnam.

Was that hard to do at all?
It was real hard. It was real hard. Often you felt like you couldn't go on, but there was nothing you could do about it.

Did the nurses get anything for it?
After this one big push we had our head nurse put several of us in for a Bronze Star. Then shortly after that she left, and they hadn't

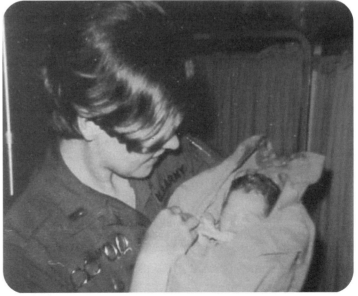

Just delivered!

come through yet. When the new head nurse, came she was reviewing everyone's records. She saw that we had been put in for the Bronze Star. She said that only the guys in the fields deserve medals, not some-one that was just there doing surgery or just what they were supposed to be doing. So she took them away from us. Then during a rocket attack one nigh, she cut her knee on a cocktail glass, and she accepted the Purple Heart for that, and yet she took all of our medals away.

Did you ever get any medals?
Just the usual ones. If you were there you received a Vietnam Campaign Ribbon.

What was it like when you came home?
I took a delay-in-route. I didn't come home with the other people. The people that I knew, all my friends, had been there a week or two earlier than me, and they were given drops. So they got an early out. They got out a month early because they had just made it, but I was on the other side of the time limit. So all my friends that I knew left, and that last month was really hard because I didn't know anybody. All these new people came (FNG's), and I lay in my hooch. I was very depressed. That last month was really hard.

My parents had never had a vacation and it was their anniversary, so I had saved my money and I sent money to my friend in Milwaukee. She got airline tickets for them, and I met them in Hawaii. That's

In Dress Blues

another story. All year I saved my money for this trip, and I told my dad not to bring any money along because I wanted to show them the best time. He only brought a hundred dollars or so along. When you

"YOU HAD THESE GIS DYING, AND THEY ARE ASKING YOU IF THEY'RE GOING TO DIE, AND YOU SAY, 'OH, HECK NO. YOU'RE GOING TO BE JUST FINE,' AND YOU KNOW THAT THEY'RE GOING TO DIE."

first get to Vietnam, they take your American money and they change it into what they call MPC (we called it funny money). Then right before you go back, they change it back into American money. American money over there was worth lots and lots and lots. I slept with it in my pocket, and I went to work with it in my pocket. So I didn't leave it around because our mama-sans stole stuff. We had mama-sans working for us. I had one more day, so I was just changing my uniform into a clean uniform, and I had just taken my pants off and laid them on the bed. The girl down the hall screamed. I ran down there to see what was going on, and all of a sudden we saw mama-san just go tearing out. I went back to my room, and she had all of my money. All of my money for the whole year, and all the money I was going to use on the trip. I was going to go island hopping, go to a luau, and have a fancy hotel for my parents. So I slipped on another pair of pants, and we going running after her, and we were screaming at the MP at the gate to stop her, and he's going, "What, what?" And she goes running right by. She got all my money. I got to Hawaii, and my dad had a hundred dollars or so, and that was it. My friend had given me a little bit of money, so I had maybe a couple hundred dollars. That was it. So we ended up in this raunchy hotel, and we couldn't do half the stuff, but my parents didn't care. They were just happy that I was coming home and that I was alive. They didn't care, but all my money! It was probably a good thing that she got away because I really think that if I had caught her I would have strangled her to death. I really do. I really do think I would have killed her. I had a ring stolen and jewelry and different things were stolen. We paid these mama-sans to do some ironing, to wash our clothes. How they washed our clothes was they put them in this tub, put water in, and walked on them, and that's how they washed our clothes. If you had anything good you did it yourself by hand, but not your uniforms. Then we even bought her an ironing board, but they squat to do everything. They sit there and do that, and we had bought our mama-san an ironing board thinking we could make life easier for her. She never even used it. One night they caught all these mama-sans setting up rockets aimed at our hospital. They were all these mama-sans that we were paying, and we found out that they really weren't South Vietnamese, they were NVA. You couldn't tell. I was glad that I didn't work in the emergency room because after so many things were disappearing, the commander said that the nurses in the ER had to do a vaginal test on them. That was how they were getting stuff out. You would not believe what you could get in a vagina!

Mama-san washing our clothes.

What kinds of things were stolen?

Well, linen. They got, I don't know how many sheets out of one woman. Multiple sheets plus she had jewelry, and she had someone's gun. They have so many kids that they stretch. You would not believe what they found doing vaginal checks. They would steal our stuff, and then they would put it on the black market down town. They would sell it. We went through a period of time where we started running out of bandages, so we started ripping up sheets to use for bandages. Our drugs disappeared. We had GIs die because the drugs they needed were in Pleiku City on the black market. We didn't have them; they never even made it to us. So we lost GIs because the drugs were stolen that they needed if they had a cardiac arrest.

What exactly is a mama-san?

A mama-san is a Vietnamese woman paid to do tasks for the unit. We had one who worked in surgery. We really liked her, and she wasn't one of them who got caught, so we're hoping that she really was South Vietnamese. She was very good and she was very intelligent. She really learned to put the instrument sets together and autoclave them. She learned to do a lot of things for us. She worked hard.

Were they mostly women?

Yes, there were some men, but mostly women. We had to pay the ones we hired in our hooch out of our own money. Everyone in our hooch got together, and we would pay a set amount for doing our uniforms, etc. You worked minimum 12-hour shifts, six days a week. That was your minimum. Like I said, if you see one of those Chinooks, you just turned around. If there was a "push" you were there for days, so we didn't have time to be doing washing and things like that.

Do you remember any unusual incidents on the job?

When you had to shave someone, they didn't have the disposable razors like they have now. They had the

...BUT I WAS

You were not there when your loved one died...
But I was

You were not able to hold his hand...
But I did

You could not tenderly cradle his head...
But I did

You could not smile and whisper, "it's okay"...
But I did

You were not there to comfort him at the end...
But I was

You did not tell him softly good-bye...
But I did

You did not see how brave he was...
But I did

You did not get to cry at his death...
But I did

You were not able to grieve for his soul...
But I was

You did not know that he was gone...
But I did

You could not cry on the way to the morgue...
But I did

You did not know that someone was also crying for you...
But I was

© Printed with permission from:
Lynn Calmes Kohl
5/1/90, 9/10/90

straight edge. We had this really bad case, and they needed to work on this guy's head. He had been out in the field for a long time, so he had a big scruffy beard. The anesthetist told me to shave his beard so that he would be able to tube him and have a place to put the tape. I had never used one of those before, so the very first sweep I made a big gouge in his cheek. So he wrote down on the chart, "First incision made by Lt. Calmes." Then after the case they gave me a straight edge razor and said to go home and shave my legs. I came to work the next day with Band-Aids everywhere, but I knew how to use one after that.

Did you ever have any patients that just died on the bed?
A lot. I made a lot of trips to the morgue.

What did you have for a morgue?
It was a wooden building. They go in to do identification, get cleaned up, and put in black body bags. Then a plane comes and takes them home.

Do they bring them home?
Yes. When we had pushes, we lost a lot of patients. A friend of mine in the hooch had been dating this chopper pilot, and they were engaged. One night he came over, and they were going to go out. She wasn't back from work yet, and I was the only one in the hooch. I had seen him a lot before. We began talking. He had a real sense of humor and he was always cracking jokes and stuff, so we were just yucking it up because he was so funny. The next day when I got done with work, I noticed outside of the building there was this great big stack of body bags. I had seen them before, but I had never ever in my life gone over and looked at one, and I never did after. For some reason I was drawn over there, and besides the regular stacks there were little ones. They would be from a chopper crash - really burned or something that would be just ashes. There were these three small ones, and I looked down, and there was the chopper pilot's name. It's just like time stood still. It seemed like I was standing there for years. I was just in shock. Finally I was able to walk away, and I never ever went back again. Then we had a nurse, and she was having so much trouble. She was begging them to send her back to the States because she just couldn't deal with it. She only had one more month to go; she had already been there eleven months. They should have sent her back, but they refused to send her. One of the corpsmen found her in her room. She had taken an overdose of Darvon, which is a painkiller. It didn't kill her. She is still alive, but they never could bring her around, and now she's is a vegetable. That's how she went home to her parents, a vegetable.

Did that happen a lot, not just to nurses, but others too?

Not too often. On our compound people got into drugs because they were forced to. Corpsmen worked a minimum of 12 hours just like we did, and then they also had to pull guard duty. We had this commander who was an "old timer," and he had been in the "Big One," World War II, and that's all he ever talked about. He was always making us do things like have our boots shined and wear our boonie hats, and everything had to be just perfect. This was a war zone; we're doing all we can to keep people alive. Who's got time to shine your boots and to worry about everything being perfect? The 4th Division had offered to send some of their guys over to pull guard duty so that the corpsmen could be doing their job. He refused. He said, "We can take care of our own!" These corpsmen either had to start doing their guard duty shift, which is a three-hour-shift, then try to get a little bit of sleep before they went back on duty, or they would have to quick get some sleep, go back to guard duty, and then go back to work. They would be so exhausted, so if they had to go on guard duty right away, they would take an upper to stay awake. But if they had to go on second, they would take a downer to try to get some sleep. After a while they would need two, three and it started going up, and pretty soon they were shooting up. It was all because of this idiot who was too proud to accept help from the 4th Division. Our corpsmen got hooked on drugs because of him, because they had to survive. They wouldn't have been able to do it without some kind of drug. It was not their fault.

Downtown Pleiku

Did you try any drugs to stay awake or go to sleep?

No. They would come into surgery sometimes, and they would be so high on drugs, and they would think they were super techs then. "We can do anything," and it was like, "No, you can't. You're screwing up here." It was really bad. They tried to get me to do marijuana. It's really strong stuff. The Vietnamese start their babies on marijuana. When they have these newborns, they give them a puff of marijuana and that keeps the baby quiet while they're working in the fields. I have a picture of a little kid (a small boy) with a joint, and he is just a little kid. It is really powerful stuff over ther. It's very strong, but it doesn't bother them, because from little on they're raised on it. So to them it's not strong or anything, but to our guys who aren't used to it, it's really powerful. It's part of their culture. It takes care of pain and things. It keeps the kids quiet.

When you went out of the compound did you ever go to downtown Pleiku?

Yes, our address was Pleiku, but the city was a little ways from us. I went down a couple of times. It was interesting. There were Coca-Cola signs and a Shell gas station amongst all the other stuff. But it was dangerous to go there, and after awhile, it became off limits.

Was it weird to see what you believed to be a South Vietnamese person but was actually North Vietnamese?

The mama-sans were, but you never knew. They all look the same. It was frightening. The whole thing was frightening. I really didn't think I was going to come back alive. Like I said, we got rocketed and mortared so often. I really didn't think I was going to come back. I didn't.

Do you suffer from Post-Traumatic Stress Disorder?

Yes, I have that. I was the first woman to go through the PTSD program at Tomah, and they didn't know what to do with me. When the fellows go they all stay in this one huge room because they figure that if they wake up with nightmares, the other guys are there to talk to them. But they didn't feel that they could put me in with them. They only had one unit that actually had women veterans, but because they only had one unit in the whole hospital and they got every type of patient, including psych patients, it was a locked ward. So when I first got there, they put me on that ward. When my family started walking away, and they closed the door and the nurse locked it, and I couldn't get out, that was horrifying. The room that I was in had two beds, and during the night this woman came in that had overdosed, and nobody came and checked her all night. So I'm sitting there all night with one eye open making sure that her chest was still going up and down.

DEEP INSIDE ME

Where is the key
That will set me free?
That will unlock the door
To the Vietnam War
I store deep inside me?

Where is the day
It will be okay
To unleash the storm
Of the misery borne
Deep inside me?

When can I cry
For the men I saw die
And lay them to rest
Along with the pest
That lays dormant deep inside me?

I watch others' pain
From the "dragon" they're slaying
And I envy them...
Isn't that insane? But...
That's what's deep down inside me!

© Printed with permission from:
Lynn Calmes Kohl
2/20/90

The guys raised such a stink because they said that I needed to be on the PTSD unit, that it was not a good thing for me to be in a locked ward. They raised such a stink that they moved me over there. Right outside their big room was a supply closet, so they cleaned that out and put a bed in there for me and that was where I slept. Then they didn't know what to do about showering. The guys had a shower down the hall that was on the alcohol/drug ward. The guys offered to stand guard because they didn't trust the alcohol/drug patients. They would stand guard while I took a shower. The staff finally decided that they could trust me, so the nurse gave me the key to go down to the nurses' shower. I could shower in there. Then I found out later that when I applied to go to the program, the head of the hospital just went bananas because he didn't know why I wanted to come there. Why did a female need to? He didn't understand why a female would have post-traumatic stress. Why did I want to come? Was I a women's liberator and just trying to cause problems, or did I really need some help? Or what? They didn't know. So, then they didn't even know if they should accept me or not. Then they thought if they didn't accept me I would go to the press. I stayed there, not as long as the guys because they have it down pat what to do with the guys, but they really didn't know what to do with me. I had the same symptoms as the men, but women think and feel different, and my experiences were different than the guys. They never quite knew what to do with me. I got what I could out of the program, and then we mutually agreed that

it was time for me to leave.

When was it that you were in there?

December '82- February '83. I have been seeing a counselor until recently. I have been to a program in Minneapolis for VN nurses. There is nothing in the state of Wisconsin for women. So I had to go to Minnesota, but then that got shut down after three years. I had to stop going to that. There is not a lot out there for the women.

Countdown to DEROS, Date of Expected Return From Overseas.

When you came home, was it hard for you to get back to the normal routine?

Backing way up, I went to Hawaii, and Lynda Van Devanter did also. We both came back, and that's a big thing over there, coming back and seeing the Golden Gate Bridge. That was the big thing. We had pictures of it up, and you looked at it everyday, knowing you're going to see this some day. Well, because we took the delay in-route, we had to get a military hop. So instead of taking a plane back that had windows, we were in a cargo plane that had no windows, and we didn't even get to see the Golden Gate Bridge. When we got there, I had some friends up in Oakland, and they came and picked me up. They had me stay there a few days, which was wonderful. They kind of debriefed me. He had been in Vietnam, so he helped with some things. First they told us to take our uniforms off. We asked why. They said, "You can't go out there with uniforms on. There are people out there that are going to stone you and throw tomatoes at you and everything else." We had to take off our clothes and throw them in the trash and put on civilian clothes, which was stupid anyway. Anyone coming through that door, they knew had just gotten back from Vietnam. So we got tomatoes thrown and got stoned - people were against the war. If you're against the war, fine. We were against the war, too, but don't take it out on the warrior. Lynda had hitchhiked to the airport. She refused to take her uniform off. She still had it on, and people would go by and they would roll down their window and spit on her and did all kinds of stuff. I was lucky because I stayed there, and they had me send all of my military stuff home early. When I got on a plane, nobody knew.

OUR BABIES ARE DYING

Our babies are dying
It's not from the war
But from what they sprayed on us
Twenty odd years before

I listen in horror
To stories I'm told
Of beautiful children
Who'll never grow old

Their symptoms are varied
Yet still they're the same
Why must our government
Play this sad game?

Our babies are dying
Does anyone care?
Wake up out there people
We've no children to spare

We fought for our country
What price must we pay?
For standing up proudly
That swearing-in day

We had no idea
The paths we would pave
Would be a death sentence
Sending children to their graves

Wake up out there people
Before it's too late
Our children to their graves

Wake up out there people
Before it's too late
Our children are dying
Don't seal their fate

Our babies are dying
Let's settle the score
Stand up to our politicians
Tell them we won't take ANY MORE!

© Printed with permission from:
Lynn Calmes Kohl
9/11/90

Not very many people knew that women were in Vietnam. There were a lot of women who did a lot different things in Vietnam. Once I got home, no one knew, and most of my friends had moved away, so I just was forgotten. The interesting thing was I wanted to tell my family and my parents about my experience, but I didn't want to upset them. I thought that I would wait until they asked me something, and they were dying to ask me some questions, but they were afraid that it might upset me. So for years and years, nobody ever said anything. We never talked about it for years. Then finally, I said something to my mother. I asked her, "How come you were never interested in what I did or what happened?" And she said, "Are you kidding? We were afraid to ask you." My family has gone through a lot. One of the symptoms of post traumatic stress is rage. It just comes upon you. You don't even know that it's going to happen, and it's always over some dumb little thing. The dumbest little thing, and all of a sudden this rage comes. My kids, my husband went through a lot. Then there's Agent Orange. They say that breast-feeding is the best thing

THE MONSTER INSIDE ME

I go through the day
In the usual way
Or so I would like it to be

But without warning
He comes out storming...
That horrible monster inside me

He rants and raves
And hurts in so many ways
Those who are closest to me

My God, will this end?
Will the lives destroyed mend?
Once rid of that monster inside me

But what price must I pay
To put him at bay
Am I stuck with that monster inside me?

© Printed with permission from:
Lynn Calmes Kohl
4/90

that you can do. Well not for us that have been exposed to Agent Orange. Agent Orange stays in fatty tissue, and what's fatter than the breast. So I nursed my two kids, and they both have a lot of medical problems. We have been to doctors and doctors, and they never can find out what exactly it is. It's like this or it's like that, but it doesn't complete a picture. I'll mention Agent Orange, and they'll say, "Well, that doesn't exist, and if it does it's not <u>our</u> problem. It's a government problem." The government of course says that Agent Orange doesn't exist, so they won't do anything. It's very frustrating. My grandson has been sick since he was born. He is four years old and has been sick since day one. He has been in the hospital. He has never had a normal bowel movement. He gets all kinds of things like rashes that they never can figure out what they are from. They come and go. They tell you that Agent Orange doesn't exist. They will just wait until we are all dead. Did you ever look in the obituaries with the little flag in the corner? Look at all the ones in there around my age in the 50's. Cancer. I don't know how

Lynn is one of 26 women in Keith Walker's book, " A Piece Of My Heart" which has also become a play.

many of my friends are already dead from cancer or brain tumors. Brain tumors are very common in Vietnam vets.

"WHAT A SHAME THAT AMERICA CONFUSED THE WARRIOR WITH THE WAR."

When did you marry?

I married a corpsman actually. I came back in June of 1970 and we were married in November of 1970.

You didn't have any programs when you came home for help?

There was no debriefing when you got off the plane. You got out of your uniforms, and you were back home in hours. No debriefing, no nothing after being in Vietnam a year or so.

Any final comments?

Yes. I remember...

- long hours and the endless stream of gravely wounded casualties.
-working on our knees in surgery during rocket attacks.
- rolling under my bunk when the siren went off because the women didn't have bunkers to go to.
- the feeling of terror when I discovered the body of a dead NVA soldier just feet from the hooch following an attack, knowing that my room was the first one through the door.
- the look on a young soldier's face when he clutched at my arm begging," Please don't let me die!"
- the despair and anger when we went without medications and supplies because they were being sold on the black market.
- the never-ending feeling of isolation and loneliness.

And I will NEVER forget looking down at the tag of a body bag and seeing it was a young chopper pilot I had just joked with the night before. And I will NEVER EVER forget crying all the way to the morgue everytime I had to take a body up......crying not for the young man inside, for it was too late for him....but crying for the family left behind who would be without him forever!

In closing, I would like to say how very proud I am to have served with all the brave and courageous men and women who gave 110% for their country in Vietnam. What a shame that America confused the warrior with the war. Hold your heads high and **WELCOME HOME!!!!!**

"For those who fought for it, freedom has a taste those protected will never know." (WW2 Vet.)

The Timberframe
I stood there and looked at the building
A shell, almost naked
But even then, it beckoned me inside
I peeked around the corner of the door marked
"Do Not Enter" and tip-toed in
A friendly face smiled and said, Come on in
and look around," and introduced me to one
of the many volunteers and craftsmen who
have lovingly made you a reality.
I gently touched your beautiful wood and
marveled at the pegs that hold you together
I went upstairs and peeked out of every window
and explored every nook and cranny
As I did, I felt you gently encompass me
and I felt safe and secure.
I stepped out onto the balcony and when
I looked out over the Highground for
as for as I could see, it took my breath away!
And such a peace and calmness came over
me that I almost wanted to cry for joy!
And then I knew, that just like the land,
you are yet another healer of the Highground.
And when you are completed, as hundreds
of people walk through you, each one
of them will be offered your strength
and beauty, your peace and calmness,
and know that they are "HOME."

Rest peacefully, Dennis.

© Printed with permission from:
Lynn Calmes Kohl

After the war, Lynn Kohl worked as a nurse(mostly OB) until 1990 when she decided she had seen enough death and dying to last the rest of her life. She became a Massage Therapist and body Worker. Her husband, Ken and her children Tracy, Michelle, and Kristy, are the important things in her life now. She is a Lifetime Member of Vietnam Veterans of America, DAV, and VFW.

Interviewed by Jenny Marcell

At the Wall, Washington, D.C.

Kathy Mero

Mero served as a nurse aboard the USS Repose, a US Naval hospital ship, off the shore of DaNang, Vietnam. She served on board for three months and then rotated to the United States Naval Hospital, Guam, where she completed her tour.

What position did you have in Vietnam?
A Navy nurse.

What forms of education did you have before you left?
A Bachelor of Science in Nursing and immediate training at the Navy's Women Officer's School in Newport, Rhode Island.

What made you decide to enter the war?
Actually, I wanted to be a military nurse from high school on, and it had nothing to do with war. I don't believe in war, but I just wanted to be a nurse, and through some personal experiences and investigation I had decided that I would like to be military nurse. When I went to my first duty station, I requested a hospital ship.

Was there anyone who tried to persuade you not to go to Vietnam?
No.

What year did you go to Vietnam?
Actually I was stationed aboard ship for three months until the ship was decommissioned and members of the ship's company were either rotated back to the states or completed their tour of duty at another duty station. In my case I was sent to the US Naval Hospital on the island of Guam. Guam was considered as direct support of military operations in Vietnam.

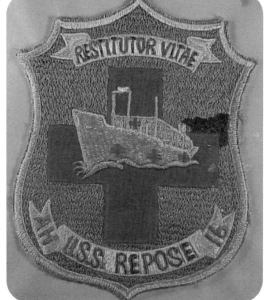

Patch from *U.S.S. Repose*

When you went to Vietnam, where were you sent?
To the *USS Repose*, the "Angel of the Orient," a US Naval Hospital Ship. The ship was "on station," anchored off DaNang, Vietnam, for three months and then cruised for three months up and down the coast of Vietnam. After the three month cruise, the ship would

again go "on station" for three months.

What were you doing on the ship?
I was a charge nurse on the orthopedic ward.

Did you usually deal with soldiers who had been wounded pretty badly?
Yes, most of the soldiers, sailors, and Marines who were sent out to the ship were badly injured.

So, it wasn't just emergencies?
In most instances we dealt with emergency situations, individuals dying from their injuries and others who were shot up pretty badly. All were taken care of as quickly as possible. We also received individuals with medical situations like malaria, dysentery, even the flu. We cared for Vietnamese adults and children in a civilian ward and North Vietnamese military on occasion.

How many people were on this ship? Do you know a number?
The *Repose* was a 750-bed hospital ship. I don't actually know the complement of officers and enlisted who kept the ship operational.

Do you know how many other nurses were there?
I believe there were about 29 of us.

Could you describe a normal day?
A normal day would depend on the shift that I worked. There were three shifts, seven to three, three to eleven, and then eleven to seven. Periodically I "pulled" duty in the triage area. Triage is an area where injured individuals were brought directly from the battlefield via helicopter. As the wounded were brought up the ramp on the way to the triage area, the staff would check to see if they're alive, if alive what were their injuries, and then a decision was made as to who received care first, second, etc. Usually I worked the day shift on the orthopedic ward. On my own ward we would receive patients from the recovery room after their initial operative procedure was completed. A regular day would consist of reporting to work on the ward, taking report, and then directing and working side by side with the corpsmen to give care to thirty to fifty patients. The corpsmen were highly trained in patient care and great to work with. On the ward the patients were in racks or beds that were chained to the walls or the bulkheads. In an orthopedic ward, the racks were usually two high, and in the regular medical ward, where a patient might have malaria, the racks were three high, and so you had to climb to get to the patient.

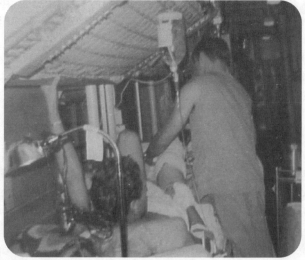
Orthopedic Ward

After the routine care of our patients was completed usually lunch would follow. Then came chores like cleaning up, dressings changes, and medications to dispense. Before three o'clock I would give report to the next charge nurse and return to my space in the nurse's quarters. Because there are not many places to go on a ship, my time off was often spent writing letters, walking the decks, or getting exercise on one of the top decks designed for this purpose. Actually exercise was a favorite off-time activity for many because you could get out of your uniform into sport clothes. Otherwise we wore one form of uniform each day, every day. Often we would just go back and help on the ward because there was too much free time or back to the ward to help out if there were a lot of casualties on a particular day. Mealtime meant getting back into your regular uniform and going to the officer's mess for a meal, and then in the evening, if you didn't have to back on duty, there were movies, books to read, people to talk to, and more letters to write.

Would you say overall that it was a good experience?

It was a difficult experience in the sense of the number of casualties, long hours, sadness, and grief. Yet there were wonderful people to meet and a sense of adventure in so much of what we did. A lot of my time aboard ship I remember as FUN.

Do you still keep in touch with people from the ship?

No, not really.

16,000th Helicopter Landing

Did you try to at all after the war?

There were a few people that I kept in contact with from other duty stations but not from the ship. Actually, I came home and was stationed at the Naval Hospital at Quantico, Virginia. I married my husband, who was a Marine. While we were on active duty as a couple, we did occasionally meet people we knew from this period of our lives. On the whole, I did not write many letters to people and lost contact soon after the experience in Vietnam was over.

I've been researching the war, and I know that there have been reunions. Have you ever considered going to one of those?

No. I guess I got busy with life, and frankly, reunions wouldn't have interested me. In the early '90's, I went to a presentation by a former Army nurse and Vietnam veteran Diane Carlson-Evans. Diane spearheaded, if this is the correct word, the Women's Memorial. From discussing the women who have served in Vietnam with Diane, I learned that it was difficult up to that point to find out where the women veterans were, let alone hear their stories. I was interested to find out that this was so, and since then I have had a keener awareness of the issue of women who have served in Vietnam. Secondly, for the last few years I've been part of a survey, which is now completed, to determine how women have adjusted after serving in Vietnam.

Going back to when you were in Vietnam, was there anything that really affected you while you were there?

Let me think. It's all very real, I guess. Probably, the people stories stand out for me. I was stationed for about 15 months at the Naval Hospital, Great Lakes, IL before I left for Vietnam. The patients that I worked with there were casualties from Vietnam who had already been cared for in field hospitals or hospital ships. They came to us for their second, third, possibly fourth, operations for the wounds that they received while in combat. So many of our patients were very involved, meaning that their injuries were very extensive. I believe this time at Great Lakes helped to prepare me for what I found aboard ship. Maybe not for the casualties in triage-that was an eye opener-but for the patients coming from the recovery area. The important thing was to remember the person, not see only the injury. And sometimes that's hard to do.

> *"THE BUDDY OF THE WOUNDED MARINE RETALIATED BY REFLEX AND SHOT MOUI WITH THE M-79 GRENADE LAUNCHER THAT HE WAS HOLDING"*

Do you have any stories that you would like to share?

One fellow that they brought into triage on an evening that I was there was very involved with gunshot wounds over a good deal of his body, and we weren't sure if he would survive. When I was cutting his fatigues so that we could evaluate the extent of his injuries, he asked my name. In the military you are to be proper about names, and to use my last name would have usually been called for. But when someone might be dying, "proper" just didn't seem important, so I told him my first name. Well, he did make it through surgery, and he was admitted to my ward from the intensive care unit. By now this guy was feeling almost cocky from cheating death, and he really had an "attitude." One day, to impress the other guys, he said, "YO, Kath," when he wanted to get my attention. I said, "That's Miss Hickey," to which he replied, "No, you can't do that to me." To which I replied, "This is my ward, and we run it my way." He

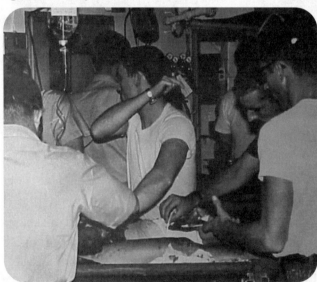

Triage

calmed down and seemed to accept my direction. In the situation of triage, when dealing with life and death, people respond at a gut level, but back in real life (the orthopedic ward) to be able to maintain order with 60 patients, boundaries were needed. Maybe it's not perfect, but that's how it is. As it turned out, he was a sweetie, and as he got better, I think he understood that I wasn't putting him down. So, as time went on, he'd call me by my rank, Lieutenant or Miss Hickey, in front of the other patients but continued to call be by my first name if no one else was around!

I know there is quite a bit of discussion about the misuse of drugs during the Vietnam conflict, but I honestly did not witness this. In fact, often we had to convince patients to take prescribed drugs ordered to alleviate the severe pain that they were experiencing. In fact, if anything, the young men that I met were too dedicated to wanting to do their job over there. Often patients who were being treated for medical conditions were sent back into combat, or "back in country," Usually they wanted to go back to their buddies. In other words, if I'm not sick enough to go home, than send me back "to the bush." It didn't make any sense to me. Gradually, I grew to be impressed by this connection to their buddies, and I really grew to respect it.

One humorous situation that I encountered was that the guys we took care of did not want new fatigue uniforms when they came to the ship or to have us to wash the fatigues they were wearing when they came to us. So, we had to "bag" their fatigues and anything else they were wearing in a plastic bag, and their things were pretty ripe! When they were discharged, we'd give them back their grungy fatigues so that they could return to their unit. One time I offered to wash a guy's socks, and he replied, "No they're my lucky socks." So, he put those crusty things back on his feet, put on his filthy boots, and off he went. I don't know. Maybe the smell from the clothing and boots kept the Vietnamese mosquitoes away! Luck and superstition was part of life for these special guys, and I wasn't going to get in the way.

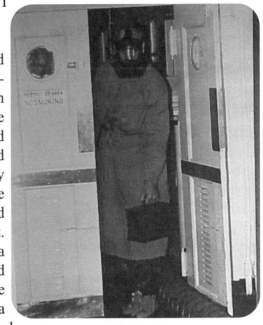

Bomb Squad

I saw another kind of connection displayed while I was aboard the *Repose*. We had a 10-ycar-old North Vietnamese boy recovering in the civilian ward. Moui had no parents and had been brought up in a North Vietnamese camp. In his short life, he had known only war. This little boy looked like an angel and had the temper of a tiger. According to the report, Moui had shot a Marine. The buddy of the wounded Marine retaliated by reflex and shot Moui with the M-79 grenade launcher that he was holding. The grenade lodged in Moui's thigh. The injured Marine and Moui were air lifted to the *Repose* for treatment. The situation that the doctors had to deal with was to remove a grenade from a child's leg without having it blow the poor child to pieces. So they picked a surgical team made up of people who did not have families dependent on them and called in a bomb squad from shore. Excitement mounted as the surgical team prepared Moui, and the bomb squad arrived aboard ship. The squad came off the helicopter looking like people from another planet in their protective garb. They stood ready just outside the operating room, and at the specific time, came in and lifted the grenade out of Moui's thigh and then exited the ship to do whatever bomb squads do to take care of explosives.

The Marine that Moui shot survived and was returned to the States. Moui, on the other hand, stayed aboard ship to recover for the next three months. Moui was placed in a spica cast, which covered one leg totally, and the top half of his other leg as well as his lower body and half way up his chest. What a time Moui put us through. Because of the life that Moui had been brought up in, we were the enemy, and he did not like being held on the ship for this period of recovery. Moui would attempt to flop, spica cast and all, out of his rack in an attempt to get to the railing to get back to his home. One time he got out of his restraints. We had to kind of tie him down so he wouldn't get out, and he actually crawled to the open end of the ward to get out. Apparently he was so adamant about going home that he was willing to attempt swimming in this huge cast. So keeping Moui safe and protected was a full time job for the corpsmen! During this era people would say something was #1 meaning great and #10 meaning really bad. So Moui would always tell us we were #10. He couldn't speak much English, but he certainly conveyed that we were #10! Yet he really did like the corpsmen. I mean, what ten-year-old little kid doesn't like guys, but he'd try not to let it show. Eventually he went back, and I don't know what happened after that. Moui was a real sweetheart; he just acted like he was a forty-year-old soldier.

Did you get to know people very well while you were in Vietnam?
I think I made friendships that come from going through hard times together. These friendships don't usu-

ally last when the crisis is over. The friendships that I made before going to the ship seemed to last longer than those made on the ship. Maybe this is attributed to sharing on more levels than only survival.

You said you were prepared for Vietnam, but when you arrived there and you saw the soldiers after they came off the field, did that change you in any way? Did it make you any more thick- skinned or anything?

"THESE INDIVIDUALS LOOKED ABOUT 180 DEGREES DIFFERENT THAN THE GUYS THAT WE HAD JUST COME WITH FROM THE STATES..."

No. Well, actually I thought I was totally ready to go to a war zone, but my first taste of this new life made me realize that I was in for a reality check! It was in early January that I began my travel to Vietnam. I departed from O'Hare Airport in Chicago wearing my dark blue winter uniform, taupe nylons, heels, and gloves. In California, I had to be in the uniform of the day, which meant my summer uniform. So I went to the restroom and changed into light blue summer uniform, white gloves replaced the black, and buffed my shoes till they shined. I felt very sharp and sophisticated as I waited for the military flight, which would take me on the next leg of my adventure. At this point, I met one other Navy nurse about my age who was also going scheduled on the flight that I was waiting for. So the two of us got on the airplane in our pristine uniforms and found that we were the only military women aboard a whole plane full of military personnel in their fatigues, very much outfitted for war. They looked strained, maybe even scared, and for me the realty of going to war took on a very serious element. I remember finding my seat, taking off the ridiculous prissy white gloves, and shoving them in the bottom of my purse. I did not take them out again till the day I left Vietnam. When we were airborne, it was interesting to see that some of the guys were loud and obnoxious, some introspective. I guess each person was reacting to going to Vietnam in their own way. What they weren't especially interested in was Betty, the other nurse, and me, which suited us just fine.

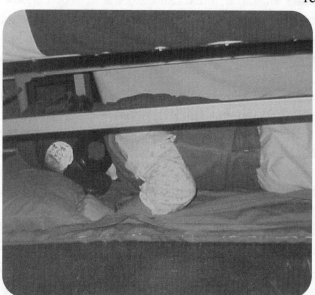

First Night in DaNang

When we got to the airport at DaNang, we were asked to exit the plane first. As we descended to the tarmac, the intense moist heat hit me. I'm from Cleveland, Ohio, and had never experienced such horrible humidity. It was as if a wet blanket was thrown over your face, and you couldn't breathe through it. There was a jeep waiting for us with Marines holding really serious looking guns. They had us climb into the jeep, and the Marines sat around us as if to protect us. I remember thinking, "Oh, this day just keeps getting more serious!" Once in the jeep, I looked over to an area where there were military personnel that were, we were told, waiting to board the plane to go back to the world, the States.

These individuals looked about 180 degrees different than the guys that we had just come with from the States. These troops were clean, but their eyes appeared dead, their faces gaunt, and their bodies were almost listless. This was a small view of what this place did to people.

Betty and I were taken to the Nurses' Quarters in DaNang. That night they had a steak roast inside the nurses' compound, which was supposedly a safe area. At dinner I connected with one of the nurses who was stationed there. Although she did not know me, we had gone to the same college, and I introduced myself to her and shared some messages that I had been given for her. It was a really pleasant night, and we were all talking, and they were filling Betty and me in on all of the info that we needed to know to survive! When we had checked in at the nurses' compound, we had been given a rack to sleep in, a helmet, and flak jacket. I said, "What do I need these for?" And they replied, "Well, in case there's incoming, or bombing, you put it on to protect yourselves." Wanting to look good in the morning when we went to tour the camp, I put rollers in my hair before I climbed into my rack to sleep. Around twelve or so, there was a piercing siren that went on and on. There was incoming, live ammunition noisily swooping right through and over the compound we were in. I thought to myself, "I'm not taking out these rollers," so I got under my rack, and I put the flak jacket on the side of my body and I put the helmet over my face. I decided that if I died, my parents would want to see my face. The things you think of. In looking back now, I have to laugh and say, "Oh my God, that was really bright." The next morning after we discussed the incoming of the night before I really felt pretty stupid.

Betty and I went out to the ship after three days on shore at DaNang. Those couple days were fun and full of great memories. The night before we were to leave for the ship, we were told that our bath that evening would be the last one for a very long time. I didn't really question their comment about the bath until we got to the ship where we found only showers, and then we could only take a GI shower or wet down, soap up, wash off all in the space of about three minutes. Well, since I was really a tub person and liked the relaxing sensation of a tub full of water, I was in for a rude awakening. It was spit baths and GI showers for everyone. Not only was I not going to be able to relax in a tub, I had to learn to bathe and wash and rinse my thick hair in that very short three minutes. Frankly, it was pretty miserable to get used to, you know, never really feeling clean, but we all survived the shower system fairly well.

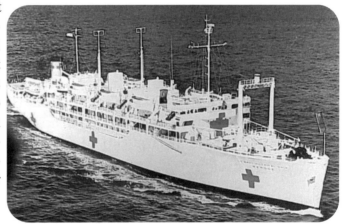

U.S.S. Repose

In the morning we left DaNang to report to the ship. Betty and I boarded a military launch that took us out to where the ship was anchored. When we walked up the ship's ladder, stairway, Betty and I properly saluted, requested permission to board, and gave the officer of the deck our papers…so far, so good. We were taken on a tour of the ship. One of the sailors demonstrated an old Navy custom of sliding down the ladder, or stairs, without touching the rungs. We were shown how to face out from the steps, place your hands behind you and grasp the railings keeping your arms tense and unbending, and you slide down the ladder with your feet out in front of you. I made it down one ladder, then another, but when I attempted to slide down the third ladder my heel caught the step and I was pitched headlong into the boiler room. So I had only been on ship about seventeen minutes, and I had already sprained my ankle. I was taken to triage where initially the corpsmen thought I had been injured on shore. What a klutz. I was so embarrassed. It was really hard that night to begin my big adventure having to meet the people that I would be working with my ankle all wrapped up. So, anyhow, those are some people and things that stick in my mind.

Going back to when you decided to go to Vietnam, did you know what was going on over there?

I had been following the conflict fairly closely in the papers. I was about 12 years old when I first heard about Southeast Asia in a book written by Tom Dooley, a Navy doctor. Dooley would take his corpsmen on their days off to care for families who were hurt by the communists. As a kid I couldn't believe anyone would hurt a child, let alone kill their parents and leave them as orphans. I was really impressed that

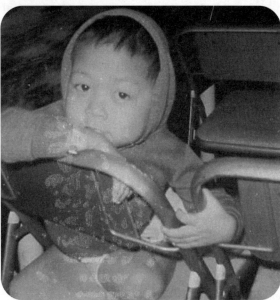

Evening Mass

Dooley and his men were making a difference in the lives of these people. So I had the plight of the people of this war-torn nation in the back of my mind as I read about the conflicts in Vietnam. I imagine that this all played a part in my wanting to be stationed in Vietnam to help those injured by war.

So basically you wanted to help people? It wasn't about war?

Yes.

What coast did you say the ship was patrolling?

Along the coast of Vietnam in the South China Sea.

Do you have any other memories?

We had a Catholic mass every evening in a hospital ward that was converted into a chapel. We would invite the little children from the civilian ward to go with us to mass. For them it was a social thing and a way to get out of their ward. It is a really special memory for me because the children were wonderful and so loving. They truly took everyone's mind off the reality of what was happening around us. The children were really close to our chaplain. Father Joe didn't mind if the children gathered at his feet or leaned against his legs as he said mass. It was really very touching to witness. On my off hours I often went to the civilian ward and helped out with a playgroup outside on the deck. I think being with the children is really a very special memory for me.

One of the doctors from Great Lakes ended up being stationed aboard the ship. I didn't know him at Great Lakes and actually did not really get to know him on the ship because he was in the medical area. After I was on board three months, the ship was decommissioned in DaNang with a formal ceremony. After the ceremony the ship steamed to the Philippines, then to Hong Kong, and finally to Japan. In Japan, the ship's company had a party and a wonderful dinner at a geisha house. Afterward, this doctor came up to me and said that my being on the ship was important to him. I asked him what he meant, and he said that I was kind of a link to his family at home. He explained that when he and his family would go to mass at the Great Lakes Naval Hospital Chapel, they would often see me there too. His comment was surprising to me. I guess I understood what he was saying, but again, when you're twenty-three, those connections don't seem as important to you yet. But to him it was because he really missed his wife and children.

You said that the ship helped North Vietnamese too.

Yes, if someone who was injured were brought to the ship, just like as any other American facility, you'd take care of all patients who were admitted. Actually, there was a German hospital ship there in the area as well, that would also take care of casualties no matter who they were. We didn't have many enemy soldiers, but it did happen.

Why weren't you sent to a hospital on land in Vietnam?

I asked for the ship. If you're in the Navy, it only made sense to ask for a ship. This was just a short time before women were allowed to serve in most capacities aboard ships. At that point in history, the only way to be stationed aboard ship was as a nurse.

After the ship, you went to Guam, so when did you return home?

I was stationed at Guam for eight months. When the ship was decommissioned, I went home for two weeks. The decommissioning of the ship and the steaming from Vietnam to the Philippines to Hong Kong and then Japan actually took almost two weeks. It was a very exciting adventure. When we left DaNang, I was on duty working with patients that had not yet been discharged from the ship. That night I went to bed off the coast of Vietnam and woke up the next day to find out that we were almost in the Philippines.

Let me step back. Aboard ship we had a means of communication termed a patch call. A patch call meant that someone in the States would make a regular phone call to a stateside operator, and the operator would radio the ship. Through this radio connection, you would be able to talk to someone at home. When I had been aboard the *Repose* for a few weeks, Tim, this very special young man that I had been dating, asked me to marry him in a St. Patrick's Day card. I was very excited about the proposal and filled out an application to make a patch call to him to tell him yes. The patch must have been put through very quickly because that same night I was awoke by Benji, the Philippine steward who took care of the nurses' area. He knocked on the outside of my room saying that there was a phone call for me from the States. So I went outside into the passageway or hall and picked up the phone and found, not Tim's voice, but the voice of the Marine sergeant who was in charge of the MARS radio station which made patch calls possible. The sergeant said that he had put through my call to Captain Tim Mero, "But you can't hear him, ma'am, because it's a poor connection, so I'll relay the message." So Tim relayed the message to the lady in Seattle, that he wanted to know what my answer was. The lady in Seattle talked to the sergeant, and the sergeant talked to me, and I said yes, but at no time did I actually speak directly to Tim. During this very unusual conversation, Tim not only asked me to marry him but also asked if I knew any information about the ship being decommissioned and leaving Vietnam. At that point I couldn't tell him much about the ship's status yet, but I definitely said I'd marry him! It was very romantic and a little comic as well. In fact in the morning I wasn't sure if it was a dream or not!

Two days later there was another phone call in the middle of the night, and this time the sergeant had made arrangements on his own to make a patch call to Tim so that we could speak directly to one another! That night when I did get to talk to Tim, I told him yes to marriage, yes to the ship being decommissioned, and that I hoped I'd get leave to come home. I had never met his family, and he'd never met mine. So the next morning when I went to my ward to work, everyone seemed to know about the phone call…so much for privacy. Patients and staff wished us congratulations. It was pretty romantic stuff. The admiral asked me to come and tape the story of our engagement via patch calls. As far as I know, the tape is still in the Navy archives. The day the ship was decommissioned, I went down to my space and found on my bunk an envelope. Inside the envelope was the form that I had filled out for my patch call to Tim, another form that the sergeant in the mars station had filled out for his patch call to play cupid for Tim and me, and a little 'Love Is' cartoon. 'Love Is' cartoons were of cute little sexless naked people doing different activities with the words such as "love is being spending time together." The cartoon that the sergeant had left for me had a little guy and the little wife person holding a suitcase and it said, "Love is when he takes you along." The humor in the line refers to a saying in the Marine Corps, "If the Marine Corps wanted you to have a wife, they'd issue you one." The hard-nosed sergeant must have had some romance in his soul because he shared the cartoon and the sweet message with me. Of course, I still have the cartoon. So that was another really great thing that came out of the whole experience.

What year did you get back to America then?
1971.

Love is...

Did you get any problems from being there from other people?
I was aware of situations of harassment and anti-war sentiment that returning military were encountering in airports and other areas of civilian life, but the group that I returned with did not encounter any of this type of behavior. I don't know how we lucked out. I actually didn't have any problems when I went home either. My family was really supportive. My younger brother was a conscientious objector, and he was even proud of me for working to help those affected by the conflict in Vietnam.

Were you afraid to tell people you were over in Vietnam?
No. I think that's because I was a nurse rather than a soldier. No one really seemed too interested other than my own family and Tim anyway.

Yes, you're not killing people; you're helping them.
Yes. It's different. I think maybe that's it, and I was proud of what the medical personnel were doing in Vietnam. Even though I was going back to the area after my leave, I didn't really talk about the war with many people. Frankly, at that point, I was excited about seeing Tim, seeing my family, and meeting Tim's family. We had only two weeks to do all that, and we accomplished a lot in those two weeks.

When you look back on Vietnam, was worth it to you?
You mean like the war?

Well, helping people, and just being there.
Well, yes, that part of it, sure. Helping people is part of who I am, I guess. But was the war worth it? No. None of it was, I don't think. Just like Desert Storm wasn't; I just hate it all.

Did you have any negative experiences?
I don't know. I'm not a negative person, so I guess I have a tendency to...

Be optimistic?

Yes, I guess so. Yes. I mean, I saw poverty; I saw things that weren't right like evidence of the black market. It was obvious that people had to spend a lot of money for things like soap and other necessary commodities. Civilians were definitely being taken advantage of by individuals trying to make money because of the shortages of goods due to the war. Civilian families were devastated by the war. An example would be the fact that live ordnance, or bombs, often landed in rice paddies. When a family would finally return to their property to try to begin their life again, they might be blown up simply attempting to work their land.

You went to Vietnam when you were only twenty-three; do you think everything that you saw made you grow up a lot faster?
Oh, I'm sure. I thought I was very experienced in life at twenty-three but I know I grew up a lot during this experience. Responsibility is given to you early in the military, and yet on the whole, I felt ready for it because of my educational background and the time that I had spent at Great Lakes.

Were most of the girls there your age?
No, actually aboard ship we went from probably 22 years of age to a nurse who was 40 years old. And our head nurse was probably 49 or *50*. We thought she was pretty ancient. Maybe she wasn't that old. There is a play about women in Vietnam that demonstrates that the ages varied, as did the experiences of the individuals stationed in Vietnam. Are you aware of the play that was here a couple months ago, *A Piece of My Heart*?

Yes, I'm reading the book now.
Tim and I had a chance to go to the play at UW Marathon Center. I thought the play was pretty accurate. As you've probably found out from the book, there are many different women's Vietnam stories. For example, women, say Army nurses or Navy nurses who were in country, would have different experiences than mine. Although a relatively small number of women compared to men died in Vietnam, there were women injured, and you really don't hear about that too much. So I think, probably, my situation is a lot different from the women who were in country. I mean I had one or two nights with the helmet over my face. I didn't have to live with the idea that I need to carry my helmet every day or die. It's not that the ship couldn't get hit or that tracers didn't go over us at night, but I think there was a feeling of safety being aboard ship, warranted or not, that the personnel on shore did not feel. I don't have a personal concept of what their story would be like.

So for the most part, you felt safe while you were in Vietnam?
Yes, when I was aboard ship. If I went in country to help at the Sacred Heart Orphanage, I didn't necessarily feel safe. But on the whole, I would say yes, I felt safe.

Do you think women that were in Vietnam have been overlooked?
Yes. The men returning from Vietnam were certainly overlooked, so it is not a surprise that women were as well. The Vietnam Wall does contain the women who died in Vietnam, and the Women's Memorial is a short distance from the Wall. Although it took quite awhile for either of these memorials to be established, at least they give tribute to the men and women who died in the Vietnam conflict. In the '70s there was interest and growing concern for men who were affected by their experiences of war. The Veterans Administration (VA) hospitals were beginning to see men who couldn't keep a job, were having troubles with their marriages and relationships, and there was a growing rate of suicide in Vietnam veterans. The

Sacred Heart Orphanage

situation of the veterans of Vietnam had been overlooked for far too long. Finally the reality of post-traumatic stress disorder (PTSD) in men was acknowledged as a viable concern. PTSD did not seem to be considered widely in terms of the women's experience though.

While living in Milwaukee in 1980, I interviewed for a volunteer position at the Veteran Administration. The VA was looking for someone with medical background and who had served in Vietnam to facilitate a men's support group. This was my first exposure to the concept of PTSD, and I was very interested in offering my assistance with the group. As it turned out, I did not pursue the VA position because Tim had received orders to Okinawa, Japan, and we went with him on a family tour. But what I had learned from the VA really opened my eyes to the psychological and physical damage to the veterans of the Vietnam War.

In my discovery of information regarding PTSD, I found in particular that the time between the battlefield and returning home and the climate in regard to acceptability of the "war" by the people at home has a tremendous effect on the military person when they return. After WW II and the Korean Conflict, veterans usually returned home by slow means of transportation. The length of time between the battlefield and the States afforded a time of debriefing, or psychologically shedding of the horrors of war. In contrast, the Vietnam veterans flew home to the States from Vietnam sometimes in only 24 hours, to families, friends, and communities who often did not want to acknowledge or know about the war. Without opportunities to unload the horrors that they experienced in battle, combined with never feeling any acceptance as someone who fought for their country, veterans frequently compensated in any way they could. Granted, most veterans were able to balance their lives after the war, but for many veterans, the reality of war has maimed them for life.

I can only speak for myself in regard to my experience of reflecting on my tour overseas. Tim stayed in the Marine Corps on active duty, so we had opportunities to vent about Vietnam with others that had similar experiences. Most veterans were not as fortunate to have found others to help them expel the demons of guilt and sadness that haunted them. Other than talking with Tim about it and discussing with friends, I really didn't dwell on this portion of my life. It wasn't until we lived in Menomonie, Wisconsin, in the late '80s that I began to discuss Vietnam with an acquaintance of ours that was a psychologist. Actually, after hearing that I had been stationed in Vietnam, he related that he saw only men involved with PTSD, but that he was aware of women seeking care for PTSD in some areas. He was trying to figure out why it had taken women longer to come forward to seek help. That day we discussed some of the possibilities for women finally coming for help almost twenty years after their Vietnam tours. We discussed the possibility of the difference of the roles expected of men and women. Often when the guys came home, they might have been harassed by strangers, possibly not given the support from their families. Often they had no job to go to, and in a sense, their identity was vague having no occupation to define them. The women stationed in Vietnam were nurses, women military other than nurses, government officials, USO workers, and Red Cross workers. These roles transcended the return home, and often the women continued in this role on the return to the States. Certainly women might have felt the reality of not having their role in Vietnam appreciated, but possibly their roles as support personnel were more "acceptable" than that of a soldier, who was perceived as a killer. Crude, but I think a reality.

Getting back to the survival of women veterans…I believe that when the women came home, they continued on in their profession, married, and got back to life. Due to their tangible life roles, I believe that women could slip into a pattern of living that allowed them to bury their memories of war as long as they were busy about nurturing a family and maintaining their career. I also think that this suppression of the horrors of war, pushed down for so long in some women, did begin to surface as the life role of the women changed. Possibly as their life roles changed, children began to grow up and no longer need their immediate nurturing, crisis in their career, and marriages in flux, the "stuff" that they had buried for so long began to surface as a result of the personal stress in their life. My friend's concerns were confirmed for me when over the last ten to fifteen years I have read that women are now being treated for PTSD. If approximately 55,000 women served in Vietnam and of that number there have been suicides, and an evident number of women are now being treated for PTSD, I'd say that Vietnam has definitely had a negative impact on the women who served there and possibly this has been overlooked. Naturally these are just my thoughts, but I think we will continue to see the latent effect of Vietnam on female veterans.

It was so traumatic?
Yes. Just as in any trauma. It doesn't matter what it is…a car accident, the Oklahoma bombing, 9/11. It's amazing, your body, your psyche, can only handle so much, and then something has to give, physically, emotionally, or mentally.

Would you say you were close to your friends in Vietnam, even if you don't talk to them now?
Yes, close for that period of time. We had fun, talked about life or our families and dreams for what we'd do back in the world (the States). When we got to Guam, most of the people there had been stationed in Vietnam, so there was a lot of camaraderie. The contingency of nurses lived in a Quonset hut, which is a metal, half-oval building with two floors. There were eighteen of these buildings in our compound and only two occupied when I first arrived. But a battalion of Navy Seabee's returning from Vietnam moved into the other sixteen and offered us nurses another avenue for friendship. We found ourselves being listeners for these men. They needed a big sister, or they needed a mom. The older women kind of became the moms; the younger ones of us became the pals. In effect, the Seabee's offered the nurses a chance to ventilate about the war, and we offered them a chance to ventilate as well.

When you hear the word Vietnam now, what do you think of? What comes to your mind?
I guess glimpses or images. One historical image is of the little Vietnamese girl running down the street after napalm had burned off her clothes. This is an image that will always stay in my mind. I guess glimpses of patients from the ship. They were just great and very brave people, both military and civilian. Memories of trying to convince people it's ok to take a drug for severe pain… in an era when the media was down on young people for drug addiction. The memory of Sacred Heart Orphanage is strong and the little children who lived there. The nuns treated them really well, yet there was never enough food too truly ward off hunger.

When you were working, did you see a lot of the soldiers right after they came off the battlefield?
When I worked in the triage area, yes. I didn't actually pull this duty often. Some nurses were assigned there day in and day out.

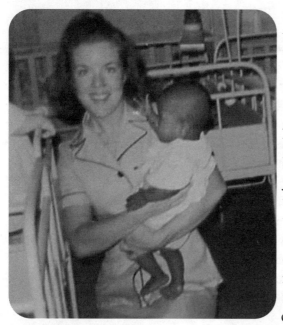

Sacred Heart Orphanage

I read in the book <u>A Piece of My Heart</u> how she had to decide triages and decided those who were expected to die.
Yes, there was a formula to decide who would receive care first and who would be made as comfortable as possible.

Did you ever have to do that?
No. Usually that happened as the injured person was brought down the ramp into triage. One day, a soldier jumped out of the helicopter and began helping to get a litter with an injured person off the helicopter. Because he was walking around on his own, no one had a chance to check his status or ask why he happened to be aboard the chopper. Actually, he had been injured, but his wounds were not obvious, at least compared to his buddies he was helping to get into triage. After a very short time this soldier just collapsed on the deck and died. Apparently he had sustained a bullet or shrapnel to his head. To me this soldier truly displayed selfless courage. He must have been hurting from his head injury and other wounds that we found on his body, yet he was helping get the people who in his mind must have seemed more wounded. Actually, considering his injury, he was possibly the most critically wounded person on the helicopter!

How did you not become emotional when you saw stuff like that?
Oh, I'm not saying I didn't. I did. But you can't shut down. I don't know how to explain it. You have to allow yourself to feel because if you don't, situation by situation, you'd either explode or bury the emotion deeply. I guess you have to be vulnerable. There were times when I would be crying and not even aware of it.

I think that it's amazing how women in Vietnam have been overlooked, and they had such a crucial part in helping these soldiers. Did a lot of them that you treated go back to fight?
The guys who were treated in the medical ward usually went back in country. Those who were in the orthopedic ward most frequently did not return to the bush because in the orthopedic ward patients usually had injuries that were very involved and most often were sent to a military hospital on Guam or Hawaii for more care, and eventually back to a military hospital in the States.

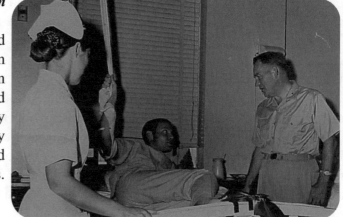

Ward rounds

What were the attitudes of most of the soldiers that came in?

The guys whether aboard ship or at Great Lakes were frequently just 18, 19, 20, 21 years of age. They were friendly, cocky, homesick, sad, defeated, funny, prone to swearing, and great people. There were lots of jokes, pranks, and plenty of buddies helping out buddies, especially keeping their friends' spirits up. When I was in school, the last patient I ever wanted to take care of would be an adolescent guy. Who wants to deal with that? So the first morning in Great Lakes when I went on duty, I wasn't sure I could handle a ward full of adolescent males…but then as the day unfolded and each patient became a separate individual to me, I was fine. Working with the corpsmen was great. I tried very hard to let them know I respected them and also tried to set a good example for hard work. I believe my time at Great Lakes really prepared me for the ship, especially in my work with the military patients and corpsman. My dad had been a Master Sergeant in the Army Supply Corps. When I left to report to Great Lakes, my dad advised me that the person I could probably learn the most from regarding military medicine would be the top enlisted person on my ward. The top person or Senior Corpsman on my ward was Brian Bliss, a wonderful and very gifted person. I came to my first duty station with a fresh degree in nursing and quite a bit of experience in floor nursing but only head knowledge in trauma care. Brian taught me so much in subtle ways, never making me feel stupid or dumb in front of the corpsmen. Often he'd stand in a manner that would allow him to whisper suggestions so that others didn't hear, and I could appear brilliant! I learned a lot in the 15 months that I was stationed at Great Lakes. I will always bless Brian for subtly shaping my skills in trauma care.

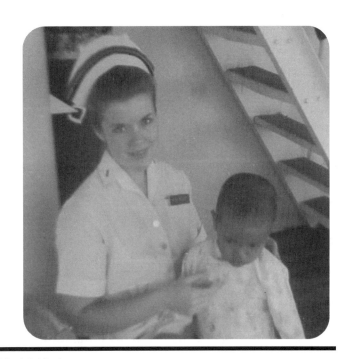

Kathy Mero became engaged to her husband during her tour in Southeast Asia.

Interviewed and transcribed by Katie Anderson

Sandee Reeseman

Reesman provides an insight into the life of a professional soldier's family when they are separated by war. Her husband, Jim, fought in the Vietnam War.

What was it like when Jim, your husband, was in Vietnam? What was it like not hearing from him for long periods of time?

When Jim left it was kind of a tradition from World War II; we decided that we had to have a family get together. We assembled the whole family and went out to a big restaurant before Jim left for Vietnam. We had come back from Germany before he went to Vietnam, so we had to find a place to live. We chose to go back to Milwaukee which is hometown for us because that's where our parents were from. It was nice that we had family support while he was gone. We were the new parents of three children. We had been married for seven years and didn't have any children. When we were in Germany, we'd adopted two boys and had one of our own, so it was an instant family. That made it particularly challenging while Jim was gone. When a soldier is gone to a theater of war, the communication isn't very good. It means that, in effect, I was a single mother. However, I had a lot more support than many single mothers today have. Everything that had to be done other than having to locate a place to live had to be done by me. I had to see to it that the kids got what they needed and the usual things that a woman does in the home. That kind of support is not there when the husband is gone.

"WE HAD A PICTURE THAT I HAD HUNG ON THE WALL AND I TOOK THE BABY TO THE BEDROOM AND SHOWED HIM THE PICTURE AND TOLD HIM THAT THIS IS YOUR DADDY. WHEN JIM CAME BACK FROM VIETNAM, STEVE DIDN'T WANT ANYTHING TO DO WITH HIM."

I think the thing that stands out the most is I tried to keep the children aware of the fact that there was a daddy, too. They were very young. One was an infant, and the others were two and five. We had a picture that I had hung on the wall, and I took the baby to the bedroom and showed him the picture and told him that this is your daddy. When Jim came back from Vietnam, Steve didn't want anything to do with him. The picture was his daddy, not the man. So it took him awhile before he adjusted to the fact that daddy was a man, not a picture.

The other thing that stands out in my mind of my experience in being the wife of a person in a war zone

-- I now sincerely believe in ESP experiences. One night I woke out of a sleep, very startled. I imagined an explosion. I had no idea what it was. A week later I found out a shell had come in and landed close to Jim. We obviously have a way of communicating with one another other than in the spoken or written words. I also think that Jim being in the military made me a much stronger woman. I had to do many things for myself. In fact, when Jim came home at Christmas time, I went out and did all the Christmas shopping. After I got done I thought, "Oh my gosh, Jim's home. I should have had him involved, too, helping me choose toys for the kids." I just went out and did it because it needed to be done. It's interesting the types of things that happen to you. You just do what needs to be done. There's really not much more to tell you. You live your daily life and hope you don't get the knock on the door.

Were there a lot of days when you hadn't heard from him in a while? Would you be really scared that you wouldn't hear from him again?
No, not really. It's something you don't think about. That way it is easier to live from day to day.

Did you just really believe that he was safe?
Like I said, you just hoped you didn't get the knock on the door. Unfortunately, there were some incidents, but I prefer not to think about those. Vietnam soldiers put up with a lot of bad things. Some of it did come down to the wives. I had a couple of nasty comments made and things like that, but I just thought it was a part of the era, and I just tried to forget them.

This picture was taken at the homecoming party.

What was it like when he came home? Did you have a big party?
No, believe it or not we didn't celebrate. When Jim came home we just went back to normal life. He was a career soldier. We just got ready to move to the next post.

Was there was a lot of moving?
Actually, for our family, we didn't move as much as the other soldiers, especially during the Vietnam War. It was done differently than World War II. Men were there literally for the duration of the war. In Vietnam they rotated them in and out every year. They were gone one year at a time.

In other words they would come back, and then they'd leave again?
Yes, soldiers that did jobs like helicopter pilots and the mechanics were there every other year. Jim was really lucky that he had one full and one partial tour. He was one of the last to leave Vietnam.

Did you have any friends that got the knock on the door?
No, because we were living in the civilian community, and there wasn't that kind of contact. The Army gives good support to the wives. If we had not come back from Germany and had been at a military post instead, we could have stayed in quarters. Then you'd have the support of having other Army wives. Instead, I had my family.

Do you think it would have been different for you during the war if you'd have stayed with the other wives to support them and have them support you?

I don't think so; I was fortunate in having a very supportive family. Something I just started to share is the things that were done. For the children and me, we didn't have very much money. Military personnel didn't get paid very much money; they still don't. We lived on three hundred dollars a month. I just recently told Jim about what his mother did; she insisted that we come over to the house once a week to do our laundry. I'd pack up the kids, the laundry, and everything. Then we'd go to their grandma's, and every week she had a twenty-dollar bill sitting on the table. I was supposed to go out and buy groceries with it. It made a difference; not only did we have a good meal that day, but all the leftovers went home with us. It made the food budget stretch. Life was a lot more bearable.

Do you think if you hadn't decided to live in Milwaukee where your family was, it would have been a lot harder to deal with?

It probably would have been more difficult.

So just having your family around made everything a lot easier to cope with?

Oh yes. I never talked much about Vietnam to my family. One other thing that sticks out in my mind was exchanging tapes. I'd make a tape and send it to Jim. That way he got to hear the kids talking. I'd always include them in the tape. A little before Christmas, I got a tape from Jim, and I waited until Christmas Eve to play it. We were playing it, and all of a sudden you hear this "BOOM whoosh," and Jim just continued talking and talking. Every once in a while you'd hear this "BOOM whoosh." Finally, just about at the end of the tape, Jim says, "By the way, that's friendly fire. If you were to hear one coming in, you'd hear the "whoosh" then the "BOOM." He waited until the whole tape was over to tell me that. The other experience…after Jim was back from Vietnam for a while…we had gone to bed when a thunderstorm came. It just so happens it was a very big one. The lightening was the biggest thing. We had our windows open. A lightening bolt came through the window and went out a different window. It woke us up. Before I could reach over, Jim was on the floor and under the bed. That would be the natural reaction if he were under attack. Those are just isolated instances that happened.

Did he talk about the war much when he came home?

No, he didn't want to talk about the war much at all.

Was it hard for him when he came back, to deal with being back to normal life with his family and not having to deal with all the military stuff? Was he different when he came home?

No, it was not really difficult for him. I think that he was glad to be home, of course. Most people would be. No, I don't think he was much different. You hear a lot about post traumatic stress syndrome; I don't think he had any problems with that sort of thing.

Even though you weren't in the war, do you have a message for the young people today about what all happened?

I'm a very patriotic person. I see things in the newspaper that irritate me. There was a story written by a woman that theorized moms and dads ought to be able to go to war instead of their sons. That is utterly ridiculous. I understand her sentiment. I just wish no one ever had to go to war. I do believe so very strongly in this country. I think it's worth defending. Unfortunately, it's the young men and women that have to do it.

Could you define what you think patriotism is?

This is our country. We should care about it. We should be willing to make the sacrifices that are necessary to make the country work for everyone. I feel strongly about my country. Maybe it is my religious upbringing, not only my patriotism. I think that this country has come close to the way all people should live. The people that we are fighting now are oppressive. I don't know if I think the Taliban should be overthrown, but I would like them to understand that they should understand that they need to give others a chance to live as they believe. That's everyone's individual right, or should be. I feel strongly that it would be something nice to have happen.

Reeseman worked for the Red Cross in Health and Safety Education and Disaster Services. She is currently a respiratory therapist.

Interviewed and transcribed by: Connie Fell and Aimee Grosinski

Peggy Reno

Arriving in Vietnam right after the Tet Offensive, Reno served a year in the 8th Field Hospital in Na Trang.

How did you get involved in Vietnam?
I was in the military. When I went in the military, I signed up for Operating Nursing, which was a sure ticket to get into Vietnam.

Were you a nurse before you entered Vietnam?
Yes.

How long were in you Vietnam?
I was in there for about a year, just a few days less than a year.

What years?
I went in '68 through '69. I was there right after Tet, the first Tet offensive.

Can you describe what the facility was like?
I was in the Eighth Field Hospital in NaTrang, and Na Trang is right off the South China Sea. Normally, a field hospital is a mobile hospital. However, there were a lot of permanent buildings, so there was no way we were going anywhere. What we had actually done was we had taken over a lot of buildings that the French had occupied in Vietnam, so the buildings that the nurses actually lived in we called Villas, in a real strange sense, and they were permanent buildings. The operating room itself was a permanent building. A lot of the wards and the post surgery and those areas were Quonset huts.

Did your facility get attacked, or was there combat close by?
We were hit the second day I was there. It was air fire and small arms. Several times a week there was weapon fire near our compound.

Were people injured?
When we were hit the first time, no. One of the guys in the headquarters was hit by weapon fire in a later incident.

Did that make you want to go home right away?

It wasn't a choice.

Did you ever get injured?

No.

What was probably the hardest part of being in Vietnam?

I guess being there during the war. Vietnam is a very beautiful country. It's very war torn. It doesn't matter where you went, you could tell they were in a war. I saw soldiers that had just gotten out of school, and they were going over there, and they were dying. Suddenly it was real; it wasn't TV.

"VIETNAM IS A VERY BEAUTIFUL COUNTRY. IT'S VERY WAR TORN. IT DOESN'T MATTER WHERE YOU WENT. YOU COULD TELL THEY WERE IN A WAR."

Was it like a normal hospital when there were disasters? Did you put them on the floor? Use emergency type conditions all the time?

We triaged before they got to the hospital, kind of like "MASH." A lot of the triage was already done in the field by the time they got there. Probably something that was unusual was we had two operating tables similar to MASH, and of course you don't do that here. As far as stability, it was very similar to state side, except that we didn't have as many supplies.

Did you run out of supplies? And did you have to improvise?

Yes. In the hospitals that I was in before Vietnam, I had friends at those, and I would write and I would say, we need this or we need that, and they would send it to me because the supply system didn't always work.

Surgical nurse at 8th Field Hospital Nha Trang, South Vietnam; July 1968

What were your feelings towards whether or not the US should have been involved in the war?

I think if we win a war quickly, then everybody thinks we should have been there, but if it gets dragged out, then you get that feeling that we shouldn't have been there. I really wanted to go because I didn't know if we should have been there or not, and I still don't know if we should have been. Unfortunately, we weren't allowed to win.

Did you feel that as a nurse you played a significant role in the war?

Yes and no. I wasn't out killing the enemy, but I was saving lives.

What was the most common injury you saw?

There was no common injury. I know there were some Docs who felt like our boys were getting hit more than the Vietnamese were, but the Vietnamese weren't healthy enough to make it as far as us, and they died. Our boys were strong enough and healthy enough to make it to the hospitals and back to the states.

In the movie <u>Pearl Harbor</u>, they showed nurses going out into the field and having to decide which person to treat. Did that happen to you?
This is called triage, and you use the supplies on those people that you can save, not those who are going to die no matter what you do.

Can you describe how the soldiers were brought to you?
They were most always brought in by chopper. They were covered in mud and dirt, soaked from the rice paddies.

Did you ever get close to anyone?
With the injured, but it was a different closeness. It wasn't a personal, even a verbal communication type of thing, but you had those few moments. Sometimes you were very close to that person, without ever really knowing them. Those of us stationed together became like a family.

Did you ever leave your station to go out and help?
No.

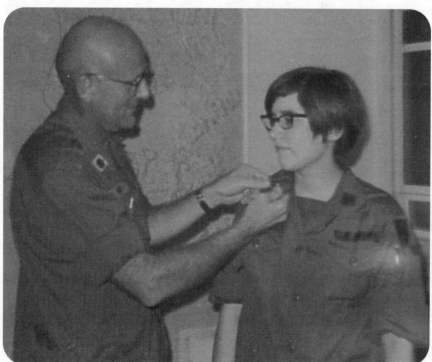
Being promoted upon arriving at 8th Field Hospital; 1968

What was a typical day like?
A typical day was that you worked everyday. We may have worked a 24 or 30 hour day and then maybe you didn't have anything going for a couple of days. There was always normal surgery, the eight-hour day, but there were always casualties coming in. There were mountains around us that they were constantly bombing. At night you could always see the tracers. A tracer is a light that you could see. You could usually hear the bombing on the hills.

What was your most memorable experience?
I think there were a lot of memorable experiences. There were so many kinds of things that happened. The thing that probably impacted my life the most was that I became engaged in Vietnam.

Did you marry him in Vietnam?
No. We were planning to become engaged on Christmas Eve, but we had casualties, so it was Christmas Day. We were married when we returned to the states.

If you had the choice would you go to Vietnam again?

I felt strongly about not saying it's right or wrong because I didn't know enough about it, and I chose an occupation which was sure to get me into the war.

Did you get welcomed when you got home?

I got welcomed in my hometown but not when I got off the plane. They were booing.

It's hard to believe people would do something like that.

I think that people are swept up in the movement. They don't stop and think that the guys that were over there dying didn't really have a choice other than to run away. If everyone would have run away, where would we be?

Were you glad to come home?

I think we looked forward to coming home because we never knew if we were going to make it home. In our last three months we were a short timer, and everyone around us knew how many days we had left.

Do you have any stories?

There aren't really any stories I can share, but it was like living in an unreal place. You reacted differently to things than what you would if you were back home.

How?

One evening, I don't know how long we had been working, but the mice were coming out into our break room. We were feeding them. We were too tired to yell and scream and chase them away, so we fed them. It was just some of the strange things that you did like that. Trying to celebrate the holidays when Christmas came, and everybody had lots of packages coming as delayed as they were. We eventually got them, and you had some of the things you would have had back home. I think one of the hardest things was packing to go and not knowing what to take. I could take a duffle bag. What do you pack first, as a woman? Sanitary supplies because you don't know if they have any over there? If they didn't, then you got them shipped when you needed more. It was hard trying to pick what clothes to bring.

> *"WHEN YOU'RE IN MEDICINE YOU'RE TREATING PEOPLE. YOU'RE NOT TREATING JUST AMERICANS BUT THE ENEMY AS WELL."*

Were there days when you didn't have to do anything?

Yes, there were days when we were on call. We were on call all the time, but there were assigned days you would be called first. Obviously, if the choppers came in full, then everyone went to work. On the off days, we could go swimming in the South China Sea or go into the town.

Did you make close friends?

Yes. I made a lot of friends. There is a retired colonel that I still stay in touch with.

Did you ever have to treat any of the Viet Cong?

Yes. When you're in medicine, you're treating people. You're not treating just Americans but the enemy as well. It was hard to see the kids coming in, the little Vietnamese kids. We knew we had hit them. If you look at the history of Vietnam, all the different countries that conquered and then dumped and then conquered and then dumped. They're so used to being at war, that it was basically their life. When we were in their country, we disrupted their economy. We were paying our mama-san more than the professors and doctors of their country were getting paid. We were paying $60 a month, and we think that is nothing. That was a lot for them.

What message would you send to young people today about the war?

It's important to know and understand that freedom isn't free. People have worked hard

"IT'S IMPORTANT TO KNOW AND UNDERSTAND THAT FREEDOM ISN'T FREE. PEOPLE HAVE WORKED HARD FOR IT..."

for it, and sometimes people think that it's being taken away from them and maybe it isn't. Maybe this is why Vietnam happened. Maybe it didn't mean that we would have lost our freedom, but they would have lost their freedom. I think it's something that needs to be guarded. I think young people today don't have a sense of patriotism, or a sense that the government is working for them in their funny way. Yes, we don't always agree, but in the big picture they are trying to help.

Peggy Reno is currently working as a Parish Nurse at First Presbyterian Church in Wausau. She also does consulting in infection control and performance improvement.

Peggy Reno

Interviewed by Jacalyn Schlutz

THE WAR AT HOME

D.C. EVEREST AREA SCHOOLS

The War at Home

Although subtle acts of protests may have occurred before 1966, the anti-war movement heated up just as American forces in Vietnam escalated to over 300,000 troops. By this time, the New Left had spawned an organization titled Students for a Democratic Society, which was championed by radical thinkers like Tom Hayden and Mark Rudd. In 1967, students at the University of Wisconsin protested DOW chemical recruiters attempts to sign up students for their company. DOW chemical produced Napalm, a chemical firebomb used in Vietnam. At the time Paul Soglin, who would later serve as Madison's mayor during the 70's and 90's, became involved in the DOW chemical riots. His story is featured in this section of the book. Other protests in Madison are also chronicled in Marsh Shapiro's interview, as well as Karl Armstrong's. Armstrong, who led the New Years Gang in its bombing of Sterling Hall tells the story of how student activists worked to remove the Army Math Research Center from the Madison campus. As the war dragged on into 1970 more and more Americans threw their support to the antiwar movement, but few adopted the lifestyle of the anti-war activists. The best organized anti-war groups were those that were connected to religious groups. Michael Cullen of the Milwaukee 14 tells his activist story about breaking into the Milwaukee draft board headquarters and consequently being deported back to his homeland of Ireland. Eventually the Vietnamazation program of the Nixon administration defused the antiwar movement as only 72,000 troops were left in Vietnam by 1972 and all were brought home by 1973.

Karl Armstrong

Armstrong was involved heavily in the antiwar movement in Madison. Before bombing the Army Math Research Center in 1970, Armstrong was employed in a bakery, several machine shops, a steel plant, assembly plants, and restaurants. He also worked on a survey crew, as an encyclopedia salesman, a used car salesman, and was self-employed making bird baths.

When did you start, and what got you started in the anti-war movement?
I got started in the anti-war movement when I observed a demonstration in front of the building where we were being interviewed. People were demonstrating against the war in Vietnam. At that particular point it was just barely moving the meter as far as I was concerned. This was in 1964, 65, and at that time these people were a bunch of commies on campus raising issues that we're aiding and abetting the Soviet Union. I admired their courage for raising the issues, and I wasn't at all convinced in any of their arguments. I think that is when I really started getting interested in what was happening in the war. I finally learned that free elections in Vietnam were cancelled by the US government because Ho Chi Minh, who they considered to be a communist, was going to win the election. To me this went against any principal that our country had, certainly that I had been raised with. People want to freely determine who they want to lead them; they should have that right. When I learned that had happened, I became much more interested in the Vietnam War. That is when I started looking into it more carefully.

Tom Hayden, a founder for Students for a Democratic Society, said that to become a radical is like giving birth to yourself because you had no past, hardly any present, and the future was unknown. Do you agree with this definition of a radical, or what is your definition?
I don't know if I consider myself a radical necessarily, because by his definition it is probably true, and becoming a radical means questioning everything. It means going to the root, and going to the root of your own personal life, and I don't think that I have done that myself because it is a very arduous task. But in many ways I did, and I would definitely have to agree with that definition.

How would you describe Madison during the anti-war movement?
How can I describe it? It depends on what point and time you are talking about. At certain times it was considered a war zone. I remember coming back in the spring of 1970, and people were so paranoid and no one trusted anyone. It was virtually a war zone. I was shocked by the changes that had taken place, of course, the events leading up to that point, clashes with police, clashes with the National Guard, my own personal experience with the DOW riots, and the demonstrations on campus. They were always uniformly violent in one way or another; but then again, during some of the periods when there were riots in the city, I wasn't even here.

In 1966 the Selective Service decided to give deferments to full time college students ranking in the upper half of their class. What is your opinion of schools giving that information to Selective Service Boards?

One of the first big demonstrations in Madison was the issue of Selective Service. That was one of the first demonstrations that I took part in, when we occupied the Administration building because of their collaboration with the Selective Service. Personally, I had gotten my student deferment, II-S, didn't think anything of it; I knew that at some point I was going to be reclassified. I actually had gone to the place where they test you in Milwaukee, and I got a deferment for sleep walking. I passed all their tests with flying colors, but I told them I was a sleep

> *"WHAT TOTALLY SHOCKED ME WAS A PERSON WHO LIVED IN THE SAME BUILDING WITH ME WAS BEING BEAT ON THE HEAD AND HIS GLASSES STOMPED ON."*

walker, and so they gave me a deferment. At that point I was a little bit disappointed because I wanted them to reclassify me so I was eligible for service. Then I could make the decision. My decision at that time was to go to Canada. When that was denied me, I felt that I had an obligation to other students and people serving in Vietnam. I felt that I had some responsibility to end the war, to fight the war.

In October 1967, the students in Madison held protests against the recruiters for the DOW Chemical Company. What part did you play?

I could see every day the developments up to DOW since I was going to school and going to classes and so forth, and I didn't take part in any of the demonstrations until I had a class in the Social Sciences building. I came out from class, and I knew that the building was being occupied, and so forth, and the local police, the sheriff, had gone in to physically remove people from the building. There were four or five thousand students standing there watching what was taking place. The local police, who in local parlance, were kind of "red neck" cops because they were the county cops and they were enjoying going in and beating heads. I saw people being dragged out by their hair, being physically dragged out and beaten in front of the building on the sidewalk. What totally shocked me was a person who lived in the same building with me was being beat on the head and his glasses stomped on. This was a person who I admired very much. I could not conceive of this person taking part in a demonstration in which there were frivolous issues. That had a big effect on me.

For the 1968 presidential election, many students hoped Eugene McCarthy would get elected. Did you take part in his campaign?

I campaigned for McCarthy, going house to house on the east side of Madison. They had a rally for him at the Coliseum. That really geared me up for going to the national Democratic convention later that year.

Could you explain what happened at the convention?

I went to the convention mainly because I wanted to know what a "yippee" (member of the Youth International Party) was. I was curious what a "yippee" could possibly be. I was opposed to the war, and I was willing to take part in the demonstrations, but I was curious about the "yippee" culture. So that was my basic philosophical: quest to find out what that was. I went to Chicago, and my first night there I have my sleeping bag with me and a little bag of clothes, and I am walking through the park, and this Chicago gang comes up and asks me if I was a "yippee". I said that I was a "yippee," and I had my hair cut short, and they promptly picked me up and threw me into the river. That was my first experience with Chicago politics. I spent the better part of that night drying my clothes and sleeping bag. Just before dark on the same night, we went to Grant or Lincoln Park, it was north of there, and the yippees and Blackstone Rangers and a motley crew of people were there protesting the war and occupying the park. I thought this was interesting, and I sat around the campfire with these people including the Blackstone Rangers. Ginsberg was up there reciting his poetry, and they had the "yippee" pig up on the podium. I don't remember what that represented but it was a very good time. Shortly after that, the National Guard under orders decided to remove everyone from the park. They massed on one end with their floodlights on and began shooting tear gas into the park and then just marched through the park with their guns drawn and bayonets, arresting anybody who was foolish enough to stay behind. That was the first night in Chicago.

The second day was when the big demonstrations were taking place. I went to Grant Park and I got my first taste of what police provocateurs were about. I should have seen from the night before that this day was not going to be pleasant. At that point there were National Guard troops in all the buildings with sandbags and sniper nests. All the bridges had machine gun emplacements, and they had tanks out. Probably at any given time there were three or four helicopters flying overhead. We were in Grant Park and the police provocateurs would pick a fight with somebody, and then as soon as they got a fight going, they would call for reinforcements. Now there was an excuse for all the cops to come in and bust heads in Grant Park. I had been told there were police provocateurs, but I could not believe that they actually existed. The crowd swirled around that area, and we got into a demonstration. I don't exactly know how it was organized, but we marched publicly with fifteen thousand people. We marched down Michigan Ave. They let us cross one of the bridges where they had machine guns. I was leery about that. They were channeling us in the direction they wanted us to go. The purpose was to march to the convention center to protest the nomination of Hubert Humphrey for president.

It got darker and darker, and by the time we got to the Blackstone Hotel, we were blocked off and the demonstration stopped there. I could see Hubert Humphrey waving from a window about ten to twelve stories above them. I felt very safe because I was in the middle of the demonstration. I was two rows of people in from the outside. From a side street the cops came to bust heads. I was from Madison, and if you allow yourself to be peacefully arrested it was not going to be too bad. Since I was pretty big, I told the people around me to sit down and allow yourself to be arrested. The people in front of me starting sitting down, and the cops came marching through and started clubbing everyone. I felt rather foolish. They were grabbing people's hair and dragging them over the sidewalks and tossing them into the vans. They also beat them all the way there. The first wave of cops came and waved their clubs which missed me, and I was able to get out of their range. I was able to reach safety on the other side. I had my head down on the asphalt, and I decided never again. I would never put myself in a position like I was in. It crystallized everything for me in that moment.

What was the New Year's Gang?

The New Year's Gang was given to us by the *Kaleidoscope* which was an underground newspaper. The name was given to us because we had dropped an aerial bomb from an ROTC training plane on the Badger Ordnance Plant in Baraboo. That was New Year's Day, and the paper called us that. I called in with a name like "Vanguard of the Revolution" but the newspaper's name was lighter and better. The gang consisted of me and my brother, and we did have help from a woman who will remain nameless. Basically, it was my brother and I at that point.

What do you think of the ROTC burning?

I love the Red Gym, and I loved the building, so it was with a heavy heart that we did the fire bombing of that building. It was a visible symbol housing ROTC offices on campus. The Quonset hut on the far end of campus was also an ROTC training facility.

Why did you decide to place the bomb in the Math Research Center?

It was the ARMY math research center. The Army Math Research Center was placed on the campus during the mid 50s, and it was constructed with heavy metal because it was supposed to stand a bombing from the air. It was a very heavily reinforced building. At the time it housed not only the Army Math Research Center but physics and astronomy, and it was a wing of Sterling Hall. That's why the bombing is always called the Sterling Hall bombing, but that is a misnomer. That's the way the media played it. The reason why it was chosen was twofold. It did research that was vital for the war in Vietnam, and secondly, over a period of time, the students on campus had demanded the removal of the Army Math Research Center, and they had been ignored by the administration. It appeared that no matter how many more demonstrations were to occur, they would be ignored. We had learned that they had developed the math for the infrared devices which was used to track down Che Guerrera in Bolivia. (Ernesto "Che" Guevara was an associate of Fidel Castro who went on an attempt to spread left-wing revolution in Latin America. He was killed in Bolivia in 1967, allegedly by Bolivian troops assisted by the CIA, and in the late 1960s and early 1970s he became a kind of martyr for the Left). They would not have got him without that equipment. They needed the math to develop that piece of equipment. One other thing that they were doing was providing the math to develop bombs that would penetrate deeply before they would explode. They knew that VC and the NVA were in bunkers deep in the ground, and they needed the bombs to penetrate. That was part of the math center to develop those bombs. The same bomb technology is now being used now in Afghanistan. You can look at it as research to destroy the real enemy, but to my way of thinking, this was an evil war fighting a peasant people. We had no business being there. It was totally illegal, and any technology or research being done to aid that war should be destroyed.

Did the Kent State shootings influence your decision?

I was up on campus at the University of Minnesota at the time. I was totally impressed with the peace movement in Minnesota. I thought these people really had it together. I thought that if it could be like that all over the country, we wouldn't have to go to armed struggle against the war. I was thinking that I was willing to "cool my jets" because the peaceful protests really had value in it because everybody from every facet of life was involved, marching in the streets against the war. Then at about the same time, I was in the student union, that Kent State happened. It became clear to me and a lot of other people that the government, rather than ending the war, would

"AT THAT MOMENT I FELT ASHAMED THAT WE HAD TAKEN SOMEONE'S LIFE BECAUSE THAT WAS THE FURTHEST THING WE WANTED TO DO."

kill us instead. They were not going to tolerate these sort of demonstrations. That was the message to me, and I think it was perceived rightly, and it was a calculated response. It was at that point, my brother was in the union with me, that I told him that we are going to have to bomb the Army Math Research Center. The message was clear.

When did you learn about the death in the building, and how did you feel about it?

After the bombing, we had circled around the city in my mother's car. We circled around the city, and the first news reports were over the radio, so there appeared that there were not injuries, and we were so relieved. We were shouting for joy because we had thought that someone might get hurt in the bombing. We stopped at a little truck stop and had a celebratory Coke and tried to be as discreet as possible and then drove on. We got around Waunakee and we heard over the radio that they were pulling a body out of the building, and we were just shocked. We started crying. At that moment I felt ashamed that we had taken someone's life because that was furthest thing we wanted to do. We wanted to level the building as a message to Washington, not to have someone lose their life or even be hurt in the bombing. We knew politically that it would be counterproductive. Secondly, we couldn't fathom that we were responsible for someone's death.

What did you do after the bombing of the building?

What kind of time frame? After we had heard the news on the radio, we decided that we were not going back to Madison. We didn't know what to do. We were shell-shocked by the news. We started driving north, and we went by the Badger Ordnance Plant. We drove by the plant and went on the ridge and on top of the ridge was a county cop. I looked in the rearview mirror and saw that the county cop was starting to follow us. I knew that the car had been IDed after the bombing. In fact, at the time the bomb went off, we were at the same intersection as a cop who was stopped there. The cop was on our right about forty feet away. He had this look of shock on his face from the force of the explosion and drove on. We drove around and finally drove outside the city. The county cop was following us with his partner. I didn't know what to do. The only thing I could think of was going to Devil's Lake, and we took the south shore to Devil's Lake. I told everyone that our story was going to be that we were there to go camping. The rea-

> *"PEOPLE STEPPED WAY BACK AND SAID THEY DIDN'T WANT ANYTHING LIKE THAT AGAIN. THEY FELT THAT IT HAD GOTTEN TOO CRAZY."*

son why we didn't have any camping stuff was that we were going to get the site and someone else would go back and get our gear. That was our story that we concocted in five minutes. The cops pull us over, and they get out with their shotguns, and I was thinking that this didn't look good. I was twenty-two or twenty-three at the time, my brother was eighteen, and David Fine was seventeen, so we were pretty young. The cops tell us to get out and so forth and ask us what we are doing there. They inspected the trunk and see that there is no camping gear. I tell them our story about the camping gear. Radio traffic in the city was so heavy they couldn't reach Madison to find out what to do with us, and we were taken to the ranger station. They held us there until they could find out what to do with us. Finally, they reached Madison after three hours, and when they got back, we were long gone. We made arrangements to leave the city.

Did the bombing of the Army Math Research Center have an effect on the war, the American public, and the anti-war movement?

Not the effect that I wanted because I wanted no one to be killed or injured by the bombing. That was my goal. Without that there wouldn't be the desired effect. In fact, it had a negative effect. The effect I wanted was to destroy the center, and there would be people who would take a step back. By our calculations, it was just property that would be destroyed, and these people would mobilize. Of course, that didn't happen. People stepped way back and said they didn't want anything like that again. They felt that it had gotten too crazy. People prosecuting the war felt that it could get out of hand, and people on both sides took a step back. In that sense that's the effect it had. Certainly not the effect I wanted. If it led to a more non-violent resolution of the war, that was good.

Do you regret the bombing?
I don't regret bombing the research center, but I regret taking someone's life.

Were you against all wars or just the Vietnam War?
When you finally examine all wars, they are all unjust in some way or another. When we step back and see what we are doing in Afghanistan, we are going to find out that we perpetuate a lot of injustices. In retrospect we can see this. The guys that fight the wars don't like talking about it because they hate war. That is how I feel about it.

If the US gets involved in a future war, what would your advice be to students?
Make sure you get a permit first. My advice goes back to Minnesota. If you are really in earnest in bringing a war to an end, people can be organized from all levels of society for support. If you can't do that, then there is a real weakness, and your arguments are wrong. If you can't do that, more violent solutions are just not in the cards. If the government ignores the people, and my perception at the time is that they did, there is a lot of room for organizing in opposition. I knew that thousands of people were being killed weekly, and you have to develop patience.

Was the bombing of Sterling Hall a reaction to the war or a revolution in itself?
We had this notion that we were revolutionaries. It was not true; we were not revolutionaries. A true revolutionary is a person who commits their entire life to the cause, the revolution. Every aspect, every fiber in your being is committed to it, and we weren't in that sense. It was basically an opposition to the war.

Do you have a message for young people about the Vietnam War?
Don't believe your government. They are going to lie, lie, lie because they represent different interests. They represent a tiny minority of people. Those are the interests being represented. This whole thing in Afghanistan is one big lie.

Karl Armstrong is currently a restauranteur; he owns the Radical Rye and several mobile food vending carts on State St. in Madison.

Interviewed by Jessica Dabler and Ryan Prochaska

Michael Cullen

Cullen, resident of Milwaukee during the Vietnam War was a member of the Milwaukee 14. He participated in many acts of civil disobedience in protest of the war throughout the 1960's. Cullen was deported to Ireland for 18 years and did not return to the states until October of 1991.

What were you doing mid to late '60s, while the Vietnam War was going on?
I was married; I still am. We lived in Milwaukee, and we ran a house for the homeless. There were many more then than there are today, the Casa Maria. We ran a house for the homeless in Beverly [WI].

Can you tell me a little bit about the Milwaukee 14? What it was and how were you involved?
The Milwaukee 14 was a group of working people, all males. We had concluded by 1968 that there was a need for a civil disobedience act. The civil disobedience act; we knew from the beginning it was going to enter our personal lives largely because we felt the war was not stopping even though evidence was coming out in 1967 from the government that this was not even a valid war. We were going to get up to our necks into it, no? If you look at the various administrations up at the time, that was true. By 1968, early spring of '69, there were about 27,000 Americans killed by that stage, and that number grew of course, as you know: over 53,000 before the war was over with in 1975. We [the Milwaukee 14] led an action, it was a civil disobedience action, and it was a serious action because we entered the Draft Board and brought out the files illegally and burnt them. These were files of potential members to be drafted into the military, and then many of the draftees went then to war in Vietnam. A huge number of Americans went through that.

Can you tell me a little bit more about the night you broke into the Draft Board?
It was a serious night; it was a serious act. It was September 24th, 1968, about 5:30 in the afternoon; it was just as it was closing, so it was "acceptable" to us. Basically getting the files out and across the street — we had put the files in burlap bags. Someone came on the scene when we were almost through. We were interested in getting the maximum number of files out, but we had agreed to free as many as possible while trying to keep it a non-violent act, no violence involved; but there was a very thin line there. The danger, of course, was real and when we came out, we placed these files (outside of the building) over by a memorial across the street for whatev-

> *"WE WERE INTERESTED IN GETTING THE MAXIMUM NUMBER OF FILES OUT BUT WE HAD AGREED TO FREE AS MANY AS POSSIBLE WHILE TRYING TO KEEP IT A NON-VIOLENT ACT..."*

er war, I think the Second World War. We piled them up, and one of the fourteen had made homemade napalm, a weapon that was being used in Vietnam. The reason was to awaken our consciousness as to the seriousness of the weapon being used. We poured it over the draft files. What it was being used for in the war was to be poured over vegetation and men, some of which were burnt alive. It [the use of napalm] was an attempt to raise awareness, awaken the consciousness on the risks of the war in Vietnam as in any war. Every war has its own risks in terms of weapons and so forth. We surrounded the files, lit a match, and danced around the fire. At the time, people were coming home from work and such, so we quickly drew attention to ourselves. We then stood around the fire and began to pray, more for ourselves I think.

We were frustrated; our hearts were jumping out, at least mine was. Out of breath but full of questions, "Will we survive? Get home?" Of course we were eventually arrested and then put in jail. For a long period of a month, we were all in one jail, and then some were moved to the county jail in Milwaukee. Then we were waiting for an arraignment, bails

> *"THE RESISTANCE WAS TAKING HOLD OF OUR LIVES. EVENTUALLY EVERYONE WAS IMPRISONED..."*

and all that. None of us had ever been involved with breaking the law. It was a first offense, but it was a serious offense. All kinds of personal, emotional life. One seems to be standing at the beginning of it, and the other one, to the side of it, knowing the consequences were going to be quite serious. It was a tremendous outrage against the government because people still believed the war was winnable, and of course, they weren't right. There was a growing movement of young people.

How old were you?
I was in my twenties, early twenties.

Was that pretty typical with the rest of the Milwaukee 14?
Yes, in their twenties. There were a few that were in their thirties, and some of the priests (only one or two) were in their forties. There was a Christian brother who was 50. He taught school for over thirty years and had had too many of his students come back from Vietnam dead. He had to do something. It was quite serious. Looking back after all these years, I can still see that many of the men that came out of that war were either forced to go or went because they felt it was their military duty to replace the several who were wounded or killed. Of course we were finally let out [of prison]; it took a period of about a year before various files came up. Mine didn't come up until the second hearing. The war was still continuing, and we were involved in actual resistance of the war even when we were held on bail—not in any direct action, but reaching out publicly and making people more aware. The resistance was taking hold of our lives.

Eventually, everyone was imprisoned; I was held in a federal penitentiary because I was Irish. I was still an Irish citizen even though I was an emigrant here. Mine [my case] became a little bit more complicated, and I was eventually imprisoned in the federal system in Minnesota for nearly a year before I was set out on probation and I was able to come back here to my family farm, my wife's family farm here in northern Wisconsin. Then we moved back to the city, but the war was still going on, so I got a little bit active again. There were a lot of other movements that were at the beginning of getting rights for the native people, the Indian people. I have been quite involved in the rights movement and had been for quite some time before the act. I think working with the 14 in the city of Milwaukee for many years weakened us, and our priorities were not very balanced. You had people starving in our city, and our cities were rotting. All the money was being spent on the war effort, and many of us didn't know. Many people left the inner city where they couldn't find jobs. The terrible cycle began which many people cant comprehend.

Would you say that as the war progressed, the public climate in regards to the war, became increasingly hostile towards its continuing?

Sure! Oh yes! We had more followers as the body counts soared. If you think about all the times of mass movements, it was all at that stage. It was expressed in all kinds of ways. I guess what you would call the counterculture began among young people; the kind of drop-out mentality was almost like a frustration, not being able to comprehend where their futures were. I think that some of that was part of it. There

"IN MANY WAYS POOR JOHNSON GOT STUCK. HE WAS A DECENT MAN BUT HE GOT STUCK WITH THIS WAR."

were other mass movements going on. A march in Washington; over a million involved in that. Even locally and across the nation, in different states from California to Wisconsin, there were various other efforts. You had a group in Chicago that led demonstrations and democratic conventions which were in 1968 too. Then all the files that followed that, so there were a lot of things going on! It all seemed to raise consciousness, but it's only when you look at it on a whole that you get the full story,

which wouldn't happen until many years later after the war is over with. All these things came up from the national papers, evidence that they *knew* they couldn't get out of it! In many ways poor Johnson got stuck. He was a decent man but he got stuck with this war. I think he began the process of trying to de-escalate, to pull out. Then there were the assassinations that took place of Bobby Kennedy, Martin King, John Kennedy before, but that whole reality for the country as well! How we survived is an unbelievable miracle! I was eventually imprisoned and then deported out of the country during the Nixon era.

What year were you deported?

I was deported in1973, and I wasn't allowed to return for 18 years. I was literally exiled for 18 years! I paid the price right up until 1991 when I was finally given the opportunity to return home to my family. When I had left, we had small children, so now all of them are professionals and working and so on. I think they were grateful that I didn't become bitter as so many had become. Vietnam Veterans as well.

Veterans were just as much victims as we were. We were all victims of this period. You can't say there were good guys and bad guys; this was a horrific period. The miracle is that we survived it, and I trust and hope that we have learned lessons from it, so that now when we march down the road to Iraq, it looks like, from what we're hearing – are we going to be sucked into a war that's just going to bring us more of the same? I'm a citizen of this great nation now, and I say we had better know what we are doing.

Cullen at right during the Milwaukee 14 Trial in Milwaukee Courthouse.

I want to just take a second and say, thank you! That is what we are trying to accomplish with our project here. There are many lessons to be learned. There was a heck of a price that was paid by so many, and we want people to know the stories.

That's right, and it's paid by many. My love for the veterans is the same for those who resisted in a nonviolent way or went out over the border because of their frustrations and such. I think that of all victims, there is a great, special respect for the veterans.

"WE NEED TO HEAR OTHER SIDES! COURAGE TO YOU ALL FOR DOING THIS PROJECT; THIS IS THE BALANCE I'M TALKING ABOUT!"

Did you have any confrontations with veterans?

Many confrontations. I knew many of them, loved many of them, and many were my friends.

Did you feel that when they returned they were mistreated and dishonored?

Sure, every one of them. Many of them were good men that came out of good families. (I think many of them I know here in the North). Then all of a sudden they were put into that situation as any young man or woman today, in today's culture and then having to kill. The implications on their own personal lives must be tremendous. I know training helps them deal with some of that, but there is an underlining. Obviously some of them couldn't handle coming back, and it's also because the war itself wasn't treated with respect. There was great difficulty for them. My own personal experience with most of these men was very good. I felt many of them were against the war when they came back. That was true.

When you came back [from exile] did you find it difficult to acclimate to society, or was it pretty much done and over with?

Yes, it took awhile. It was wonderful to come back to the rural area. Of course I live and work here now in the northern part of the state, but it took awhile I think, locally, because there were a lot of people that thought I was an enemy of theirs. As they came to know me and visa versa, the misunderstandings dissipated, but I had to make the initiative to say that, "Hey, it's okay." This was good. I think what you're doing, too, right now is good. The healing of the nation. But the nation also must make sure that we do not go down these same lines. We are in an extraordinary place in terms of history because of the way the super power reality is and has changed in the past 20 or ten years in fact. What is our situation? How are we going to be in the world, and what kind of people are we going to be?

Do you have an opinion about today's military? You've already mentioned our current situation, but do you have any comment on the military itself?

The military is much more professional as you know. It's a different kind of military from the voluntary military or at least the draftee. People are now pretty much in the military permanently. I really have no big answers, but the danger to being a super power, a militaristic power and the whole culture; there's always that danger. A military can be driven by many things- military industrial complexes at some points- for instance during the Cold War. The military has an extreme amount of power. You can see that since September 11th, the amount of money that has gone towards the military. We need to be watch dogs as people! The military takes a great place in our culture, almost preceding the rights that we have as citizens, and we have to be careful! Balance is very important, and that's not always easy.

Do you think that if we were to come to the same point in the road where we needed to institute the drafting process, would you involve yourself in similar activities to those you had in the 60's?

I wouldn't do the same things; I am fifty years of age now! I think nonviolence and non-cooporation--there's always going to be a place for that—all over the world. I don't believe that violence is the answer, and I'm so convinced of that myself on a personal level and mostly on a faith level. I think that, as Christians we have not sailed the world very well, especially in the last 1,500 years. We have so often been on the side as the believers, the Christian believers, that Christ was so nonviolent and we are the disciples and we are the followers of Christ, and yet nonviolence is almost a bad word. In my mind Christ shows us a way out of the violence that's in the human heart, if you will. And yet for the Muslim world today, Christians are no different than anyone else, and this is a great tragedy in my mind.

> *"THE MILITARY TAKES A GREAT PLACE IN OUR CULTURE, ALMOST PRECEDING THE RIGHTS THAT WE HAVE AS CITIZENS, AND WE HAVE TO BE CAREFUL! BALANCE IS VERY IMPORTANT, AND THAT'S NOT ALWAYS EASY."*

So you wouldn't say that you have regrets? You believe 100% in what you did at the time?

I believe in the resistance. However, I would probably not do the same things again. I have become more clear in my understanding of the non-violent response. Yet we did what we did at the time, and I've had to live with the fullness of the consequences of those actions. It touched my family and me very deeply. We are fortunate to have survived it and been able to return here. There could be other places in the world that we might not have. It could have been a different time, and it could have been different consequences. I'm grateful.

Why did you come from Ireland to begin with? What were your motivations?

I came from Ireland to enter a Catholic Seminary in 1961. I came alone; I was a very young boy and eventually married my wife who is from Rib Mountain, Wisconsin.

It was also brought to my attention that your family helped to hide draft dodgers in the Northwoods. Was this your immediate family?

Yes, young people at that time had been accepted to universities or were attending universities when they got the draft. Usually they were very intellectual young people who couldn't understand why it should cost their lives. They felt it was wrong. They had concluded that the war was wrong. They weren't necessarily passivists, but they were conscientious objectors to that particular war, and that was the difference. There were a lot of people in the

Milwaukee Journal- Thursday October 17, 1991

Vietnam period that became basically upset and conscious to that war [Vietnam], not necessarily against all wars. I have kind of come to that point myself in my own life. War is not going to solve any more. Weapons get worse and worse and the human sacrifices become more and more. We're global people; we're more at risk now when a war breaks out.

I agree with you. For instance, the repercussions following September 11 are much greater.
Yes, the new tactics! To think that we might go to Iraq and drop weapons of our own, not necessarily mass destruction but certainly quite destructive. If we hit some of their attempts at making mass destruction weapons, we set off something that we probably have no idea of the repercussions. They might have some uranium or something, and what if that explodes? We have to start seeing. We have to find a dialogue, you know? I grew up in the highlands during that period, too, and there were so many lessons to be learned from seeing people literally hating each other and spilling blood. I mean they didn't use mass destruction, but they were killing each other. This is not the way, certainly not God's way; not a way for us as human beings to be acting with each other.

Upon returning to the states in the early 90's, Michael continued his calling in the Catholic Seminary and became a Lay Catholic Evangelist. He is currently living in the Northwoods of Wisconsin with his wife and 12 children.

Interviewed and transcribed by Meghan Casta

Harold Dabler

Dabler served with the headquarters company of the 632nd Armor in the Wisconsin National Guard. In 1970 he and other guardsmen were sent to assist police in Madison during the war protests.

Why were you called down to Madison?

We were called to Madison because there were war protests going on. The students and probably some non-students were protesting on campus. They were causing a lot of problems and keeping the students that wanted to go to their classes at the college away. The students were afraid of the other students who were protesting the war over in Vietnam. I guess their intentions were to shut down the campus, but the school administrators and the students that wanted to get an education didn't want that to happen. They brought us to Madison so we could reinforce and help the policemen keep order.

How long were you down in Madison?

We were there for eight days from May 5th, 1970 to May 12th, 1970.

How much of a notice were you given before you had to leave?

As I remember, I was at work in the morning, and they called us and said that we should be down to the armory by noon. Then we left in the afternoon.

Could you explain one day when you were down in Madison?

We would get up in the morning usually by 7:00 and then get dressed to have breakfast. Then we'd wait until the policemen called us. Depending on what was going on, sometimes we'd go down to guard the entrances to the campus and the entrances to the building where the people were congregating. If there wasn't too much going on, we didn't do too much until the evening. Usually the evening is when they would have trouble in the student housing, either by the dorms, or where the students had rented homes in the city. There were some streets, such as Mifflin Street, that had quite a few of these rental units on them, and the kids would congregate there. They would set fires in garbage cans and carry wood and debris out from construction sites to set it on fire. When the police or the firemen came to put it out, the protestors would throw rocks or other things at them just to disrupt the peace of the city.

Do you have any opinions regarding the anti-war movement — the things that the students were doing?

The students really started out to protest the war in Vietnam, but it got out of hand. By creating havoc in the city like they did and on the campus, it probably hurt their cause more than it would have done any good. It kind of got out of hand, and that's why we were called in to help restore order.

What do you think was the hardest thing about being in Madison?
I think the hardest part was just being away from home and not knowing what was going to happen down there. Also, the lost income was a problem because the pay at that time was very little compared to what you could have been making at your job. But it was only for a week, so it wasn't a big hindrance. However, if it had gone on for a long time, it probably would have been.

Was there a lot of emotional or physical stress that you had to endure?
I would say the most stress was just the uncertainty of not knowing what was going to happen, and once in a while when we'd get in with the large crowds of people, there was some apprehension.

Is there one particular experience that stands out in your mind?
One afternoon we were called to the campus in the area of Bascom Hill, and there were probably about 2,000 protestors there. We had driven up in our jeeps to get ready to get out in formation and help the police keep the protestors away from certain areas. Some of the protestors came in real close to our jeeps and were rocking the jeeps, but they didn't hurt the jeeps or us. That was probably the closest call.

Did you ever fear for your life when you were down there?
No, the kids weren't really down there to hurt us, and we weren't there to hurt them. We just went there to restore order, so it was quite peaceful.

Do you think the United States could have won the Vietnam War?
I think they could have won the war if there wouldn't have been so many limits put on the activities. For example, they had the lines that you couldn't cross such as the 17th parallel between the North and South Vietnam, and they weren't supposed to go over into Cambodia. That's where the Vietcong had set up the Ho Chi Minh Trail. By not attacking that supply line, they were able to get supplies into South Vietnam and keep their army supplied, which extended the war.

What weapons or equipment did you carry with you when you went out in the city?
We carried our rifles, and we were in full uniform with our steel helmets. We had facemasks that fit on our helmets to protect our face, and we had our gas masks because the police used tear gas quite often.

What does tear gas do to you?
It makes your eyes tear, nose run, and it makes you cough.

Could you explain what a billy club was?
The policemen carried the billy clubs, and some of us had them in the jeeps with us just for our protection, but we didn't have to use them.

Did you see anybody get arrested when you were down there?
Yes, I saw several students get arrested, or protestors — I'm not sure if they were students. When we formed a line of troops, we were supposed to keep the people in front of us and move them away from any areas we were trying to protect. We were always with the policemen, and if anybody came through

the line, the policemen dealt with them behind the line. I saw one person arrested there. Also, one night when we were by one of the apartments that had a second story porch facing the street, the kids had set some garbage cans on fire. When we went down there, they were throwing rocks at us, and the policemen tear gassed the building and arrested the people that were up there.

Did you ever witness any students, police, or guardsmen get injured?
I only witnessed one protestor who got hit in the head with a billy club by a policeman, but other than that, I didn't see any injuries.

Do you feel that you were trained well enough for doing what you were doing in Madison?
Yes, we had been trained quite extensively for at least a year prior to this happening because as the Vietnam War was getting more intense, there was a lot of protests on other campuses, so we were all put on alert. We were trained especially for riot control and crowd control.

Could you explain what a Molotov cocktail was and how it was used?
It was a glass bottle filled with gasoline, and they would put a piece of cloth material on the top of the bottle, like a soda bottle, or a whiskey bottle. They would light the wick on fire before they threw the bottle, and when it hit the ground or the pavement, it would smash, and the gas would fly all over. Then the wick would ignite the gas.

"WE WERE ALWAYS WITH THE POLICEMEN, AND IF ANYBODY CAME THROUGH THE LINE, THE POLICEMEN DEALT WITH THEM BEHIND THE LINE."

What other kinds of things did you witness?
One other thing I noticed that was done before we got there was that the protestors had gone in the buildings and smashed things in the restrooms. They smashed the fixtures in the bathroom and the dividers between the stalls. A lot of that stuff was marble, which they had just broken into pieces.

Were there any things you were not allowed to do?
We weren't supposed to incite the rioters or antagonize them but just to have an authoritative presence and to assist the police when the crowds got overwhelming for them.

Were you allowed to arrest people, or were the cops just supposed to do that?
We weren't supposed to arrest anybody because we weren't living in Madison, and if their trial dates would have come up later on, we would have had to go back down there. The policemen that we were with were from the Madison City Police Department and from the Dane County Sheriff's Patrol, so they were from that area, and they would go to court when there was a court date. We never arrested anybody. If there were anybody to be arrested, the police would do it.

Where did you stay when you were in Madison?
We stayed in the barracks at Truax Field, which was an Air National Guard base at the Dane County Airport. They had cots and restroom facilities there. Also, that's where we ate our meals. Otherwise they brought us meals out in the city, wherever we happened to be when it was mealtime. They would set-up a place to feed us.

What did the protestors look like? Were most of them friendly or were they unfriendly?

The protestors themselves weren't real friendly, but they were just students that felt that we should get out of Vietnam. There were some people that probably weren't going to school there but lived in Madison. There was also a group of people they called the "hippies," who were usually young, non-working people with long hair and beards.

Is there a message you have today for young people about the war and what you did in Madison?

I guess the only thing I can say is that it was a bad war because we didn't win. The worst part was that the soldiers that were over there weren't treated very well when they came back because of the fact that so many people thought they shouldn't have been there. It wasn't like the previous wars where they were treated like heroes.

What did serving your country or patriotism mean to you when you were down there?

It meant that we were actually trying to help the war effort to support the troops that were over in Vietnam and to also keep the campus open so the students that wanted an education could get it. Some of those students were getting near their graduation time, and if they had closed the campus down, they probably wouldn't have been able to graduate. Instead, they would have kept them back another year from whatever their plans would have been. I believe we did protect the campus, which is owned by the people of Wisconsin, from being destroyed. We also tried to protect business owners in Madison because they did actually destroy some grocery stores that they firebombed and burned. Also, they had broken into the ROTC building, which is the Reserve Officers Training Corp of the military branches. They set fire in the building but didn't do a whole lot of damage because the firemen got there quite quickly. I believe that by being in Madison, we did prevent the protestors from doing more property damage.

> *"THE PROTESTERS THEMSELVES WEREN'T REAL FRIENDLY, BUT THEY WERE JUST STUDENTS THAT FELT THAT WE SHOULD GET OUT OF VIETNAM."*

Is there anything else you would like to add?

One other thing that went on before we got there, when the protests were not as large as they were when we were there, was that they had vandalized some police cars that were parked when the police were out patrolling. They would throw rocks at them or try to burn them. There were 170 guardsmen down there from Wausau, and I guess they had as high as 1,400 guardsmen from Wisconsin there at one time.

Harold Dabler is a coal and yard operator for Wisconsin Public Service at the Weston Power Plant.

Interviewer by Jessica Dabler, Travis Kozlowski
Transcribed by Jessica Dabler

Mark Piette

Piette, an Appleton native, was invlved in the anti-war movement here in the states. In high school he and some friends started an underground anti-war newspaper, and in college he was arrested, beat up, and jailed for anti-war activities. He was later drafted into the Army and served two years as a helicopter crew chief.

How old were you during this time period?

I was born on November 1, 1949, so I was draft age in 1968 when I turned eighteen. That was probably the height of the war or at least the height of the American involvement in the war and also the height of the anti-war movement for the next couple of years.

How were you involved with the anti-war movement?

Do you want to know how I got started in it? I first heard about Vietnam when my older brother, a year older than I, asked me to do some of his homework when I was in grade school in 1961. He said he had to write something about Southeast Asia that was in the news. I didn't even know what countries were in Southeast Asia. So I looked it up on a map, and I found something in Vietnam about American soldiers shooting on each other. And I thought this was a really peculiar thing that they could put American soldiers all over the place. Of course at that age, you really don't know a lot about war.

So I started paying attention to it. And like anyone whose Dad fought in World War II, I thought it would be a romanticised war. I was fourteen when Lyndon Johnson staged the Gulf of Tonkin Incident. I can remember reading PT 109. Oh, this is great. Americans are fighting back seriously against the North Vietnamese, not realising at the time, that that was a brilliant political move on his part to get Barry Goldwater's supporters over to his camp. So LBJ tried to fashion himself as a peace candidate, and at the same time, he wanted the support of the Vietnamese. The Gulf of Tonkin Incident is what he did for them, and it was brilliant. And also around that time, it was when Kennedy was assassinated, it was about a month before that we had President Diem in Vietnam overthrown and subsequently killed. Of course Kennedy might not have been involved in the assassination, but that is pretty much how you're going to eliminate a dictator in that part of the world. So then I remember following it. I was following it pretty closely. At the time, though, I was still pretty much gung ho thinking, yeah, this is what ought to be done. Remember I was born in Appleton. That's the home of Joe McCarthy, the big anti-Communist guy. I was pretty much in favor of it then.

I went off to high school the summer after the Tonkin Gulf Incident, and that's when I began meeting more people whose older brothers had fought in Vietnam. I knew these guys from when I was in grade school because they were brothers of friends. You begin to hear their stories. They were nothing at all like what was in the papers. Nothing at all like the propaganda we were getting from the teachers. I started to look into it a little more, and the more I looked into it, the more horrified I got about it. These guys were coming home with stories of massacres, some of them with cut-off ears, some of them with lost body parts. This was reality. Some of these guys thought it was just hilarious how they would have forklifts put boulders into their helicopters and fly over sandbags and try to drop them on sampans. And of course sink them. This didn't seem at all right to me. This didn't seem like the romantic image of a bunch of wholesome Boy Scouts going off and fighting for freedom. And that's when I really began to change on this, mainly because I began to look more into the history of the war and learned more and more about it. That's when I found out about the election that was suppose to take place before 1956, and it was our side who stopped it. And of course, Ho Chi Minh was no saint, but boy our side certainly wasn't any better. So largely, I first got involved with it because of first the older brothers of kids who were my age before I was draft age and listening to them, and really looking into the history of this whole thing. It didn't seem to have any nobility about it at all. I was just disgusted with it.

Well, come my sophomore and junior years of high school, that's when there were more draftees going over there. Before that, and THIS IS REALLY PITIFUL for the way the war was run, the people, the Americans who were going to Vietnam before then were pretty much people who wanted to go. They were gung ho. There weren't a lot of draftees then. Once draftees were in the war, you had Mr. and Mrs. Middle America's kids going there. It wasn't people who were dead-end, bored, and didn't have any options. And one of the things, by the time you were a junior or senior in high school, you knew that some of these guys were coming back with serious monkeys on their backs. They were hard-core dopers, drunks, smoking dope all the time, trying to find opium.

> *"I FIRST GOT INVOLVED WITH IT BECAUSE OF FIRST THE OLDER BROTHERS OF KIDS WHO WERE MY AGE BEFORE I WAS DRAFT AGE AND LISTENING TO THEM, AND REALLY LOOKING INTO THE HISTORY OF THIS WHOLE THING. IT DIDN'T SEEM TO HAVE ANY NOBILITY ABOUT IT AT ALL."*

What were your views on the war?

Right at the beginning when I was first aware of it, I was aware of it because of them bungling things. There would be articles in the newspapers about American forces firing on other American forces, but none of it was headline stuff. So back then, all I thought was, man this wasn't cool at all, until the Gulf of Tonkin. Now that was cool--American planes going and blasting enemies. Well you know I was fourteen years old when that happened so of course that was pretty exciting. So I guess I was behind it because I believed the propaganda--with no reason not to. As time went on and older brothers of people I knew began going over there and coming back, my opinions changed a lot. Plus as I would read more about it. I like history. Look at the shelf behind you; there's a lot of history there. So here's something that I figured was going to affect my own life. I wanted to know about it.

So I began looking into the history and reading a lot about it. Not just what the government was putting out, not just what the news media were putting out although that was hugely influential. But going back into the deep history, some of the stuff that was a little more difficult to find out. Who was Ho Chi Minh? How did he get that way? Was he really a communist or just some poor third world guy who was just latching on to the most convenient ideology? So as I began to learn more about that, I really began to wonder - what in the world is the U.S. doing over there? Why was it that they were our allies during World War II? And what do we really care if they are communist or not. Man, these poor peasants. Their life wasn't going to be much different by one side or another. So that really began to shift things. And then with the coup that ousted Diem, oh man. That wasn't good. That wasn't good. That got ugly. And the reporting by then was really great. You get guys like David Halverstam (one of the best newspaper reporters in Vietnam and one of the best wrtiers on the subject afterwards) writing from there. It was superb. So that really changed my opinion on the war.

Then I'd get into arguments with my teachers in government classes and history classes in high school. Oh my gosh just to get the ammunition. That made a huge difference in my attitude. And of course when I was in high school again, the older brothers of these guys were coming back, and they were telling stories that, if they were grunts, if they were the guys fighting this war, were absolutely horrifying. And then they ended up a little weird--some of them--when they came back. And the ones who weren't grunts, who were the rear echelon guys, well their stories were a whole different type. And none of them were wholesome; none of them were any good. They all hated the Vietnamese. They were telling you really weird things that they would do. How at first they would get there and they were all idealistic, and they looked at these people almost as little caricatures. Like little Disney creatures. Well they weren't! Then they would find out things were not like they were down in Disney World. So here are these people coming back with terrible attitudes, and a lot of them picked up some really bad habits. It was rare to find these guys who didn't smoke an

> *"None of them ever talked about fighting for freedom. So that's why I became very opposed to the war."*

awful lot. I never smoked, so that I found a little disconcerting, guys who had to smoke all the time. Others were drinking a lot. Then others were smoking a lot of dope. Not all of them, but enough to make me really wonder about this. And the grunts would always say, "If you can get out of it, get out of it." And I would ask these guys (they were only a few years older than I was), "What was it for?" "Would you go back there?" The only answer I would get was, "The only reason I would go back is to kill some more of them. Get revenge for my buddies." Well, there is an idealistic thing. None of them ever talked about fighting for freedom.

So that's why I became very opposed to the war. And it seemed like it wasn't being run very well. There was a lot of bombing up in the North. Man, you bomb the place into oblivion. That makes huge sprawling military complexes that completely demolished the economy of Vietnam. I believe it was between 1966 and 1967 or 1967 and 1968 that Vietnam went from a country that exported rice to one that imported it. Now what good is that? They couldn't even feed themselves anymore because so many of their young men were being drawn off, mainly to work in the huge American complexes, so they couldn't work their fields. The economy got all screwed up; a lot of things got blown up. I didn't like that at all. I didn't like it. It was bad. It was something that the politicians should have avoided. It was totally unnecessary.

Do you think it was right for America to be involved?

I wish there was a real easy answer to that. No, I don't. I don't. We shouldn't have been involved. We shouldn't have been involved the way we were. The U.S. does get involved in things because we had an economic interest there. Tin and rubber came from there. But are you going to ask someone to die because of tin and rubber? This was an old French colony. The U.S. was involved economically. Sure, we had an economic interest. But did that depend on a guy like President Diem? No, it did not. Why couldn't the U.S. have worked with the North Vietnamese? Why didn't they get involved earlier when Ho Chi Minh actually asked for U.S. help in pressuring the French to get out? By the time people over here realised what was happening (when I say people over here, I mean the U.S. government) in North

Vietnam, things had reached such an impasse that there was no more political opposition. If we didn't like Ho Chi Minh, why wasn't there a movement in the North to oppose him? Why did it have to wait for military intervention in the South? That shouldn't have happened. It could have been finessed a lot better, which is really easy to say in hindsight. You got Dien Bien Phu in 1954 when the French got run out of there. I think our State Department was not real interested in what was going on in Vietnam at the time. They were occupied with Korea. They were occupied with the Cold War. Someone should have been paying attention to Southeast Asia, and they weren't. And look what happened. Fifty-eight thousand Americans died over there. We shouldn't have had military involvement over there.

Were any of your friends or relatives in the war?
A lot of them, yeah. Remember, I was born in '49, so in '68, which was the peak of the American involvement, I was eighteen. So those were people I went to grade school with, high school with, the older brothers of people I knew. None of my family was. I can't think of any cousins on either side who were. So I had a lot of people that I knew, a lot of people in my high school and the other high schools over there in Appleton were over there and did fight. In fact just before I went into the Army, when I got drafted, one of the last people I saw in Appleton was a kid I went through high school with, and I had seen him just before he was going to Vietnam. He was an infantryman, and he lived through it. We got to talking, and we stopped in one of the bars there in Appleton. His name was Rick, and he said, "Don't go. Whatever you have to do, get out of it." He used some very crude terms to describe the war, and he said, "It's not worth it." He just hated it. Here I was drafted. It wasn't at this point that I had a whole lot of say-so about it. So I went in anyway. But that was one of the things that I remember was his incredible bitterness about the war.

Then one of my best friends from high school, Jim, went in. He got out when I was in the service, so we didn't see each other until I got back. And he was a real mess. He had been shot and shrapneled and Agent Oranged. He has two kids who have some very, very serious birth defects, and he came back with a pretty serious dope habit, too (marijuana). I don't think he has drawn a straight breath since he got out of Vietnam. He told me everyday, and this was just before we moved up here, it was around thirteen years ago, "You know, Mark, the first thing I do every morning is light up the joint I rolled the night before." Yes, so he has some issues to resolve there too.

What were some of the events that occurred during the anti-war movement?
Oh, you know we lived in Appleton, (Appleton wasn't a hotbed of anti-war activity), but we started an underground newspaper - a bunch of high school kids. In Appleton I think their newspaper is still called the *Appleton Post Crescent*. So we played off that and called it the *Appleton Post-Mortem*, and we wrote articles and printed it out. It was kind of an underground newspaper, and we slipped it to, if I had to look back now, probably a bunch of weirdoes. In that part of the state there, that was kind of active. When I was gone, there was a protest where my younger brother (who was in junior high-was the only junior high kid) he and one of his buddies he talked into walking out of school in protest of the war in Vietnam. So I was really pleased to hear that he did that.

But down in Madison, that's when things got serious. That's when things got serious because Mayor Dyke figured he could really make some political points by opposing the war. Not by opposing the war but by opposing the anti-war movement, which he did. He called out the cops. He called out the riot cops. He called out the National Guard. Man, they'd pop gas at every opportunity. They really encouraged people from the outlying areas to come in and beat people up. Oh yeah. I can remember groups of rednecks coming into town, and the cops would let them ride behind their cop lines. And they'd be yelling, "Yeah, cops. Go out and beat up them damn Jews." You got a lot of that. And then people yelling at long hairs and then of course, "If you don't love America go over to Russia." Heck, these stupid people, they should have gone to Russia. How un-American. Oh that was terrible. And of course the riots, that was pretty bad. People who had no idea of what was going on would get gassed there in Madison. Yeah, people would be studying. One night the police gassed the library, the main library there on campus. But it was ugly.

I got arrested in one of those. I got beat up, got my arm broken, got gassed. They'd cuff you behind your back; twisted my arm till the upper radial bone snapped and cuffed it open. And at first it was kind of-- it hurt. I didn't know it was broken. I thought it was hurt pretty bad, but the tear gas hurt so much worse that it kind of blinded you to the other pain. Oh, yeah. And then of course there was no way you were going to get a fair or a speedy trial. Yeah, it was ugly. And then the hearings they had, what a kangaroo court. They were bringing in only one side. "We want to find out what happened here." Then they wanted to exile people, some of the state representatives. Exile you. And then of course people on the courts occasionally would have a little better sense and say, "No, you can't do that. This is America." Oh I got a real bad attitude back then. Those people in government, you realize just: (a.) they are really self-serving, and (b.) they are really stupid. They have no respect for American traditions at all. They would have loved living in Stalinist Russia. And the more I learned about fascist regimes, the more glad I am that I opposed the war in Vietnam, because the other side, boy, they were very, very strict. They figured that you should be able to control every aspect of a person's life. We cared for that very much. I still have a bad attitude about that.

How did other people react to these movements?
Some loved it. Some were neutral; others figured oh--they were trying to get into the news. Others were dead set against it. They figured if the government said this is what we do, this is what we do. We should go and bomb Vietnam back to the Stone Age, as Curtis LeMay said. That must mean that God wants us to bomb Vietnam into the Stone Age, and who are you as a citizen of America to actually use your right to protest what the government did. They were horrified by that. Mainly people of the greatest generation, as it's now called, they were more than happy to see us get our heads whacked and tossed in jail and get gassed. But then on the other hand, there were people who were totally behind us. Unfortunately they were way far behind us, not giving us a whole heck of a lot of support. That was a real interesting thing. You come in out of those active areas and just back and talking to people who weren't in any danger of going over there, and they couldn't understand it at all. In a lot of cases they couldn't see what the big deal was. So it was interesting. It was really hard to get people to move from one side to the other, I guess.

When or how did you first become aware of how serious the war was becoming?
It was the Tonkin Gulf incident. That's when I knew it was going to grow because there was a lot of publicity about the American mission then, which was suppose to be guarding air bases, and then how it began to get bigger. And right around, I think it was around that time, where they began just putting the casualties on the news at night as light, moderate, and heavy. Well later on because no one really knew what that meant, they began putting the number of dead and then the total number of troops. And this began getting bigger and bigger. It looked like there was no end in sight. The number of enemy dead was staggering. Now it could have been inflated by accounts, which I'm sure in some cases it was. What really bothered me about that wasn't whether or not it was inflated. Even if it was inflated by a factor of ten, there were an awful lot of enemy troops dying. Why? Why was that number going up? And why was it going up so high? It was going up, I figured, because they had that many that they would throw down. When are they going to stop? It was idiotic for them to think that if we are going to get in a war of attrition, that they would win. We had more warm bodies that we could throw. They realized, and this was in all the newspapers, that the U.S. public would get tired of sending young men to war before they would. And they were right. They were right. Who from around here would say, "Yeah, I'm willing to go and die for the government of President Diem in Vietnam." Would you be willing to die for that?

Would you want your brother to die for that? Uh-uh. No, it just seemed a waste of American life and courage, and I hate to see politicians doing stuff like that. But they really have a bad habit in this and other centuries of doing such foolishness. That's when I realized how serious it was. You begin to see these numbers were just staggering. They were going up with no end in sight. And the amount of money they were throwing at it, the number of missions flown; they would put that on there [television].

Man--you kept hearing on the news how Laos has become the most bombed country in history. What? Laos? You think of all the bombing that was done in World War II to Germany which got bombed more than most countries. And Laos got hit harder than that? Why? Then of course it was the Ho Chi Minh Trail. Then you think, they're getting bombed that much. How can they ever make it down? How do these people live? How is this going on? How can they do anything in their fields? Oh, then you realise that this is serious, and it's really serious for them. Our guys would go over for a year, for a year until you were wounded or something. Then you come back. A year - all you had to do was survive. That makes it much more serious for them than for us.

Did you view the war the same then?

That really catalyzed it. Before that, or obviously early on, like any kid who watches a bunch of war movies, I thought this is great. Then later on I begin to think, this isn't very great. Well then I realised how serious it was, and I thought--whoa--this is terrible. This is just awful. A lot of people will say the turning point of the war came with Tet, and I remember Tet. I was a senior in high school when the Tet Offensive happened. In general, the media were surprised. Why they were I don't know. That shouldn't have surprised anyone. But I guess if you are in the media, you believe a lot of politicians. Your really good writers were not surprised by it. But the big turn around came in American attitudes--this when people realised that with half a million guys over there, with bombing this place to the point where they could start mining shrapnel, the Vietnamese were able to mount this offensive. Now most of the Vietnamese who were involved in it died. Militarily it was not a victory for the Vietnamese, North Vietnamese, or Viet Cong at all. But it did make a major shift in American policy, and I agree with that. This is when enough is enough. What kind of pointless nonsense are we dealing with?

> *"TEAR GAS IS EXTREMELY PAINFUL. IT'S HORRIBLE. IT'S EVERY BIT AS BAD AS YOU THINK."*

Describe the demonstration and protest activities in Madison.

Oh yeah. In my freshman year, the males were all required in Madison to take ROTC, whether you wanted to or not. Now there was a way to opt out of it. You could write a letter and say that you don't support this, and you have no desire to get into it. So I thought, "I can do this." But then I got involved because I had already met a bunch of like minded people pretty quickly down there, and said, "No, we shouldn't have to opt out. This is something you should have to opt in." So that was the first demonstration we had. There were probably fifty people out there. Got some speakers - Tom Hayden from California. (I think he was in SDS then - one of those big anti-war guys who later married Jane Fonda.) But he actually got word of this and came out. And those were good, peaceful demonstrations.

That is the way things should be run. They actually did change the policy, and I did not have to go to ROTC. Now some of my friends did, and they took the opposite tactic. They figured you should go and disrupt it. Well, you don't do that. That's rude. There is enough rudeness going on in war and anti-war movements anyway, but that demonstration was peaceful. People from the university showed up. People talked. You got your questions answered. An exchange of ideas, attacked the policy, and boom, things changed.

Now when the demonstrations, the real, big anti-war demonstrations happened, that's where you can bring out thousands of people. The mayor loved that because that gave him a chance to show what a tough guy he was. In the end, it ended up taking him out. But it was an exciting thing to have a bunch of people there, and you're young. This was a very serious thing. You knew what you were on about. It would get ugly when the mayor's people would begin the conflict. The police were nervous; they were outnumbered, and they were fairly young, and I believe they weren't really trained for riots except for riot squads would come in from somewhere else. And they were used mainly just to hammer heads. But the local guys were pretty bad about it. In the one where I got arrested, we were lining University Avenue on either side. The police were in the street blocking traffic. No one, none of the protesters, would get in the street just because we knew that Dyke was looking for an opportunity to really bust some skulls. The news media were out, and they filmed us. Every time the lights would turn green, you had to walk. Thousands of people would walk across. It was hilarious. The cops who were there felt pretty stupid. What are they there for? And then someone about a half a block down, a block, down from me had done something. At any rate the police were giving the order to make everyone disperse--to go home. You can't do that. This was a legal demonstration. Now that's where it got interesting because then they decided to start throwing tear gas. So they popped the gas, and immediately the crowd responds. I had never been gassed before, and I think most of us hadn't. Well I was real curious about it. I wanted to see what that was like. That's why I walked into the gas. You kind of make yourself visible there, so that's when the police decided, we'll get this idiot who is walking in the wrong direction. And two of them came up and the rest was history. But boy one thing, tear gas is extremely painful. It's horrible. It's every bit as bad as you think. If you can imagine taking Tabasco Sauce and putting it in your eyes, every moist part of your body was like that. It was just awful. The other guy who was arrested at that point with me was a black guy by the name of Rob who had taken one of the canisters. This was one of the early ones, before they had it so it shoots the gas out to the sides. He picked it up and had thrown it back at one of the cops and hit him on his mask. They worked him over pretty well. So Rob and I were thrown into a cell with the political prisoners. The other prisoners were there, the normal drunks, thieves, murderers, and rapists. Well, they weren't too happy about it because those of us, the political prisoners who were caught, would be reeking of gas. The stuff is so tenacious. We walked by, and these guys would start burning. Of course, they being a bunch of social misfits instead of a bunch of socially conscious people acting legally like we were, oh they hated it. They started yelling and screaming. They start screaming, "Police abuse." The police were pretty terrible in those places, too. They would go out bop your head even more. Yeah, it was pretty ugly. And that's kind of the pattern those things would follow.

Then there were always the fringe guys. These were people--you could have taken a protest for having underwater sewer mains--and these people would have gone violent. They would just get bags of rocks and bricks and go around campus or downtown or grocery stores and smash stuff. These were not ideologues at all. You could have asked them who Big Mihn was, and who was General Tron, and they wouldn't have had an idea. But they did like the protest. These were the people we always referred to as the crazies, and neither side wanted them because the cops had those guys too. But you really--it's important to purge your ranks of people like this. I don't know what you do with them socially, but they were scary. These were people--you look at them and you realize something isn't quite right here. You wonder what they do if there's not something like this going on. And I think Karl Armstrong was one of those guys--the guy who blew up Sterling Hall. Yeah, what dumbness was this, but Armstrong was like that. I didn't know him, but I knew people who did, and he was just one of those fringe characters. There were a couple of Europeans who went on a rampage associating themselves with this, throwing rocks through all the food stores because they thought American food cost too much, and they thought that is what we were protesting with the Vietnam War. Yeah, oh this makes a lot of sense. Geez guys, welcome to the club here. So for years, all the stores on State Street had very little windows because they all got smashed there in '69. That was ugly.

Were you involved in the protest on the Madison campus when Nixon announced the Cambodian invasion?
No, I wasn't around then, otherwise I would have.

Did you ever confront the National Guard?
Oh, yeah. The guard were not bad guys 'cause these were a bunch of draft dodgers. People did not go into the National Guard to defend their state. They didn't go in there to defend their country. They did it because it was an easy way out of the Vietnam--the possibility of going to the Vietnam War. Well, the last thing they wanted was to get on campus. Well, they had to get their hair cut. You could see that a lot of them had--you know--had fresh white on their skin. It was hilarious. These guys did not want to be there. So they weren't all that scary.

Although the year before with the Dow riots, the year before I got there to Madison, they did actually have the guard out with their unsheathed bayonets. Well what kind of idiocy is this? Man some dumb guard captain must have thought he was in World War I. I mean bayonets, for the love of God. Where did they get these people? There's that great picture, I don't know if you've ever seen it. One of the Madison students took it behind some guardsmen, and you could see the mounted bayonets--mounted and unsheathed. And in front of them, they are marching into the education building. You just see this big sign that says Education, and then the guardsmen. It's a classic poster. I wish I had a copy of it. At the time, I never thought of getting stuff like that. I really wish I had that one now though. What a little gem. So yeah, they weren't scary at all. One of my friends used to like to go, and he'd see the guards and he'd try to surrender to them. He thought that would make a great photo op for people. I don't know if he ever got on TV or not. "What do you mean, you're trying to surrender?" They'd run him off.

What did the <u>Daily Cardinal</u> (one of the UW-Madison student newspapers) have to say about Vietnam and the protests?
They were dead set against the war. They hated the war. The *Cardinal*, man those guys were so radical, and they were really behind the protests and the protesters. It wasn't great writing, but as I recall, they were really behind us. I thought that was good. I liked that.

Did you feel any guilt that you did not serve in Vietnam?
Never, not for a second. Not for a second. If there was any guilt about Vietnam it would be in not protesting enough. Man, those poor guys should never have had to go over there. Like I said, a waste of American courage and manpower. I got drafted, so I was in the military. Maybe I would have felt guilty, and it's hard to say what you would have done if I had gone to Canada, gone to Sweden, or gone into the National Guard and figured that some other guy had to go. But that didn't happen. That didn't happen. I went in.

Did Vietnam vets on campus favor or protest the war?
Just about everyone I knew really protested it. Oh they were dead set against it. That really solidified things for us too. Earlier, when I was a freshman there, these were guys who were there who had a first hand experience, and they were on our side. They were very much against the war. That was good. That was a real good thing, at least for me, that confirmed it. You know, I trust a guy who's been there rather than someone who only knows about it from books or strong feelings. So that helped me a lot. That was a good thing.

Do you have any opinion about Karl Armstrong and the bombing of the Army Math Research Center?
Oh I do. That was terrible. That never should have been done. That was one of the dumbest things of all the protests that I had ever heard. What are we talking about here--Europe in the 1930s? What was

his purpose? People knew about Vietnam. There was nothing he could have hoped to accomplish. He didn't know his target. He didn't know the strength of his bomb. He didn't know whom he was trying to impress. That was a real--just terrible thing to do. Gosh that was stupid.

Was his action justified considering he took a human life?

No, not at all. Even if he wouldn't have killed anybody ,that was a ridiculous thing to do. People who could have been marginally one side or the other, they definitely would have gone the other direction. You know that was a guerrilla tactic in what was not a guerrilla war. If you are trying to destabilize a government, you want to show that you can blow stuff up and inconvenience people. This wasn't a guerrilla war. This is the United States of America. You don't go and blow up a building because you don't agree with a government policy. That was so idiotic. You know what an embarrassment to the anti-war movement he really is. No wonder he is just selling frozen ice cream now. Frozen fruit.

Is there anything else you would like to say about the anti-war movements?

Yeah, you don't hear much about it now. You don't hear much about it except that it was there. Then you hear the really dumb stuff. I know there is a lot of publicity about people going to airports and spitting on returning vets. That might have happened. I don't know. When I came back, I was in uniform. Of course, I landed out in Fort Dix, New Jersey, but then when I got to O'Hare Airport, there was nothing. People were shaking my hand. Yeah, good to see you back. They didn't know if I was in Vietnam or not. As it was, I was not, but I didn't see any of that. And that was a real--if that happened--and like I said, it probably did, that shouldn't have happened. The anti-war movement was not an anti-military movement in a lot of cases, in most cases. For most of us the reason the people were against the war was because of older brothers, people we knew, who were getting involved in it, and we could not see any advantage to sending those guys over to be killed. So to give them grief when they came back, it would have been absolutely pointless. It would have gone totally against what we were trying to do.

And another thing that really changed here was that when I was in high school, the anti-draft movement was pretty strong because that is when more people were being drafted to go to Vietnam. That is one of the things that did help end the war--having so many draftees in there. Before that people were volunteering to go. The general public was not going to be affected. Your ordinary folks who live in an ordinary middle class neighborhood sent their kids off to college before the draft or before the intense draft of '67, '8, and '9. These guys didn't have to worry. They had their II-S deferments, and afterwards they'd go into the military. And if you have a college degree, you weren't going to become a grunt. So Vietnam was affecting people--lower classes, poor people, people who didn't vote a lot, people who didn't read the newspapers, people who didn't make the news. By drafting middle class guys, that got the attention of our parents. Most of our dads thought that was great, and the moms didn't like that very much. It didn't take too long before I realized the draft is a real good thing. I really had become very pro-draft, not because of the character imbued to America's youth, but because that does force a civilian attitude to the military. Any organization left up to its own devices becomes pretty darn insular, and the military can really become that. So by having all these guys coming in, spending their years, and getting out, you're going to limit the military mind set, and that's going to make a huge difference in it. Right now, I don't think there are enough people who are two to four year guys going through the service. There are too many people who are making it a career or hoping to make it a career. I think I would like to see the draft reinstated and have people go back in for two years, particularly young men. As an old guy now, I can say that. But really, that's a time in life when the military will be good for those guys. But more than that, it will be good for the military. So I would very much like to see that. That is one of the changes that I went through, and going from the anti-war movement to being a vet, going through the military, and seeing the benefits of that. Also, I saw a lot of the fallout of the Vietnam War. Most of the people who died in Vietnam, died in 1972 through 1975, but because it wasn't Americans, we didn't pay a whole lot of attention to it. There were more people who died in Vietnam in '72 than in '68, but the American deaths were much higher earlier on. So what do we care about it? That was one of those goofy things, whether or not it was worth the involvement there. I still think it wasn't. The anti-war movement was a good thing. You look who brought down Lyndon Johnson, and he was a really strong president. So it was worth it.

After Piette was discharged in April of 1973, he spent a few years traveling in the Mediterranean and Asia. He then went back to school at the University of Wisconsin, Madison. He now has four children and is employed by a large industrial chemical company.

Interviewed by Meredith Merrill

Marshall Shapiro

Shapiro was a news reporter for Channel 27. He did the Marshall the Marshal Kids Show and later became the owner and operator of Marsh Shapiro's Nitty Gritty restaurant in Madison during the Vietnam Era.

How would you describe Madison during the anti-war movement to the Vietnam War?

Madison was kind of in turmoil all through the 60's. There was a lot of demonstrating going on regarding civil rights and black power. There were all kinds of things happening, and it was just a turbulent time here because of the fact that there were things going on locally in addition to the War in Vietnam and other world events. It was a time when people were more outspoken about what was going on around them. Everybody kind of took for granted what the government had been telling them for years, and all of a sudden, people started questioning the government and some of their credibility. It seemed like they were saying things that weren't true. They said things were going to happen, and they didn't happen. People started to come out of the woodwork a little bit. That was kind of the atmosphere on the campus, not only here, but probably at Berkeley in California and some of the other campuses where there were demonstrations and things happening.

What were you doing at the time of the bombing?

If I'm not mistaken, at the time of the bombing, I was at home out on the west side. I was not affected physically by the bombing, although the Nitty Gritty (a drinking establishment) was shaken. I had a couple of guys working for me living upstairs, and they got knocked out of bed right onto the floor. We didn't have any broken windows this far away, but windows were broken all the way down University Ave. to the corner of University and Park. Everybody in this area obviously heard it, and it scared the hell out of everybody.

Were you involved in the anti-war movement?

I was not; only as a reporter. I actually was still at the television station, at Channel 27, during that time. I was a news reporter in addition to doing my television show, "Marshall the Marshal" kids show in the afternoons at 4:00. I was out reporting the news on radio and TV during the day. In those days, we didn't have a lot of people at the station, which was by design, so everybody had to do everything. It was not unusual for me to be reporting news on the radio in the morning, going and doing television interviews part of the day, coming back here and being "Marshall the Marshal" at night, and doing the sports on TV at 6:00. Everybody out of the station did a lot of things.

I was reporting at the time. I was at a number of the demonstrations. I covered demonstrations, a march they had from Madison all the way to the Badger Ordnance Works in Baraboo. We went out there and covered them as people marched from Madison to the gate demanding that they shut down Badger Ordnance Works because they were making war ammunition and rocket propellant and things like that. I covered a demonstration at Truax Field where everybody marched and wanted them to shut down Truax Field, which was Madison's National Guard base at the time. There were planes and things out there. I covered the riots on the campus. Some of the demonstrations that happened, in fact the Dow Chemical demonstrations that happened in the Commerce Building was the lead story on CBS with Douglas Edwards, 2:00 that afternoon. I was across the street from the Commerce Building, on the telephone to CBS in New York, looking out the window and watching the police taking people away, dragging them in the streets. There was some club swinging, and things were pretty violent at that time. In fact, I had previous to that, tried to get into the building. It was so packed; it was like a sardine can. Students had taken over the building and in essence just sat down and stayed there. This was, of course, when the Dow Chemical recruiters were here trying to recruit people to come to work for their company. They were making napalm, which was looked on as a war tool of the United States, and that we were doing napalm and bombing people in Vietnam was part of that protest.

In 1966, the Selective Service System announced only full time college students ranking in the upper portion of their class would be given deferments. What was your opinion about the college making students take a college qualification test or giving out class rank lists and grade point averages to the Selective Service System?

That was just one of the things that was happening at the time. I don't really have an opinion on that. I had two different lives. My life was as a reporter and working with the establishment during the 60's, working at the TV station being removed pretty much from the demonstrations. I was over here. Now I buy the Nitty Gritty in 1968, and the demonstrations are all around this building. I'm out of television now. I'm down here. My hair is long. I've got a beard. I've got a mustache. I'm kind of "in" with all of these people because that's where my business is. It was just a freaky thing that it happened that way. Now, I'm hearing the other side of the story. I have a unique position of being able to be here during the late 60's and early 70's where a lot of things were still happening on the campus. Yet earlier than that, I was a reporter, and my perspective and views on everything were somewhat different. As a reporter I thought it was kind of disloyal for people not to submit to the draft when they were doing it. Now, after I'm at the Nitty Gritty, I'm hearing all of these things, and I've got people here that are saying, "See ya. I don't know when I'll ever see you again. I'm on the bus to Canada tomorrow." They were getting out of the country so they didn't have to submit to the draft. This was, of course, a couple years later after your question, but that created quite a bit of trouble out on the campus, the whole draft system, the lottery system, and the grade system. As we're finding out now twenty, thirty, forty years later, people with money were buying themselves out of the draft. There were accusations made about a number of high-level politicians

> *"I HAD TWO DIFFERENT LIVES. MY LIFE WAS AS A REPORTER AND WORKING WITH THE ESTABLISHMENT DURING THE 60'S, WORKING AT THE TELEVISION STATION BEING REMOVED PRETTY MUCH FROM THE DEMONSTRATIONS. NOW I BUY THE NITTY GRITTY IN 1968, AND THE DEMONSTRATIONS ARE ALL AROUND THIS BUILDING."*

at the time.

Was it President Clinton that didn't go because he wheedled his way out of it or got some kind of deferment?

There's probably a ton of them. Those people whose number got up, had a hell of a decision to make as to whether they were going to fight in what they considered to be an immoral war or to take off, leave the country, maybe never come back, and be a fugitive. Of course later on, years down the road, there was amnesty for those people. How do you think the people feel whose sons went over there and got killed while other guys went to Canada and said, hell no, I'm not going to go. Now they've got a free ride back here, and they're going on living their life just as if nothing ever happened. There were a lot of inequities, and it was very difficult to be a young person at that time. I'm glad I didn't have to face that decision. I don't know what the hell I would have done. That was something everybody had to deal with.

> "*MY REACTION TO THAT IS, WHAT THE HELL ARE THEY DOING?*"

In October 1967, the students in Madison held sit ins and protests against Dow. How did you react to that?

Again, I'm a newsman there. My reaction to that is, what the hell are they doing? I'm covering this story. I may be sympathetic to them, but I really don't know what my personal feelings were at the time. I'm there to report the story. At the time, I think everybody kind of looked at those people as "off the wall." They were a minority. At the time, at the university, there were probably 20,000 or 30,000 students. You're talking about 200 students, 400 students. A very small minority, but yet total disruption that blocked the streets right out here from where we are. They went into the apartment building next door, took all the furniture out of the downstairs and blocked Johnson St., and threw gasoline on it and lit it up. Traffic was backed up from here to the football stadium. The police would come with barricades on the front ends of their little trucks, and they would break open the barricade, and the traffic would go. By that time, they'd have another one built over on Mifflin St., and by the time the cops got over there, they were going over to Langdon St., and then they were back down here on University Ave. It was fun and games for a long time. It was just disruption. At that time, the police had no idea how to deal with civil disobedience. They had not confronted it before, and they overacted in a lot of instances. That's why they put on the heavy riot gear, and they're beating people on the head, and they're shipping them off to jail.

> "*AT THAT TIME, THE POLICE HAD NO IDEA HOW TO DEAL WITH CIVIL DISOBEDIENCE.*"

People were getting their windows smashed. One of my daily routines during that time was coming down here, even though I was right in the middle of everything, and some of the people that were demonstrating and doing all that stuff were hanging around here. This was a hippie hangout bar at the time. We had live bands seven nights a week. This was kind of the gathering place. I jumped from one extreme to the other. The first thing I would do in the morning is I would go out and walk around the block and look at the telephone poles. That's were the posters were, and they'd say, "Demonstration tonight. Library Mall 7:00." I said ok, I've got to come back here, get the plywood out of the basement, and put it on the windows, because if there's a demonstration there's going to be people out throwing rocks. Even though we were kind of the home base a little bit, we lost our windows a couple of times. If you're familiar with Madison at all, that bank building on the corner of University and Park, that was all glass at one time. Now it's all bricked up. The drug store that's Walgreen's now used to be Renniboms, and that was all glass. All the stores on State St. at that time either had to board up their windows or brick them up because they were getting broken all the time, and they couldn't get any more insurance. They affected life in this area, but yet if you lived on the west side of Madison, or the east side of Madison and unless you drove right through the middle of what was going on here, life was normal. They didn't know what was going on except for what they saw on television or read in the papers. It was a limited guerilla warfare, only in this neighborhood, except for the things that Karl Armstrong and those guys did when they went to other places.

In 1968 at the time of the Democratic National Convention in Chicago, there were mass protests against the war. What was your reaction to that?
At that time again, I'm still in the news media. I'm kind of looking at that and saying, "What are those people doing down there?" It was just a magnified situation compared to what we were seeing here. It was disruption. It was an unhappiness with the direction the government was going. They wanted to disrupt everything, and that's what happened. That was the Chicago Seven and whatever other things were going on down there. The Chicago police at the time with Mayor Daley, the current mayor's father, wasn't going to have any part of it. They're not going to do that in our city, and they had the cops out there with the riot gear, and they beat the hell out of a lot of people and hauled them away. That was national/international news. Television every night. They served their purpose. That's what they wanted to do. They wanted to let people know that there were people against the war in Vietnam. They were against the government's policies. Believe it or not, that was a small minority. People like me or your parents were looking around at that time saying, "What's the matter with those crazies?"

But as it turned out, they probably were right. We were kind of slow getting on the bandwagon. As a result of that, President Lyndon Johnson resigned. He left the presidency.

> *"ALL THE STORES ON STATE ST. AT THAT TIME EITHER HAD TO BOARD UP THEIR WINDOWS OR BRICK THEM UP BECAUSE THEY WERE GETTING BROKEN ALL THE TIME, AND THEY COULDN'T GET ANY MORE INSURANCE."*

It wasn't like it didn't have any effect on anything. That was one of a many series of events. Kent State: people on campus getting killed, all of these demonstrations. Pretty soon the common man in the middle of Middle America started saying, "Maybe these people have a message. Maybe they see something we don't see." Now there are still plenty of people that don't believe that, but at the time, there were a lot of people that did start questioning what we were doing. They and their sons are saying, "Maybe I don't want to go over there and get my ass shot off. Maybe that isn't the right thing to do. I know I'm an American and I got drafted and I should go, but do I want to go get killed for no reason." I don't know. That took a while, but then after all of those demonstrations and all of this disruption all around the country, the message started to get through a little bit to the people in Washington.

You had some candidates that were sympathetic: Eugene McCarthy, who was trying to become a presidential candidate and was running in the primary that year. Then, you've got people like J. Edgar Hoover in the FBI who had planted people in all of these campaigns, and they were doing dirty tricks to all of these people like planting letters like Eugene McCarthy's out messing around with somebody else's wife. Planting stories like that to discredit all of the people that were in that. At one time here at the Nitty Gritty, probably in those days when things were happening here, if there were 200 people in here, probably fifty of them were FBI and undercover agents that were trying to work their way into the underground; trying to work their way into the subculture to find out what was going on. To find out who was doing the next bombing, what were they going to do? Then they were trying to discredit these people and have them arrested. There was a lot of stuff going on on both sides. That was tough times.

When do you think the anti-war demonstrators became violent?
Probably when they got frustrated to the point that nothing was happening from what they were saying. I don't think that the Armstrong brothers and Leo Burt and David Fine [Sterling Hall bombers of 1970] were intending to be violent. I think they just were trying to get their message out. When they bombed Sterling Hall that was just a message. They didn't intend to kill Professor Robert Fassnacht. He just happened to be there at 4 o'clock in the morning doing some work. They had called there to alert the police that there was a bomb. Unfortunately the bomb went off before the message got there to get Professor Fassnacht or anybody out. There were just mistakes that were made. At that point, after all of that happened, people here in Madison started to say, "Wait a minute. We're protesting against all of this killing, and here we just killed a guy. Let's wind it down." I think that was a general consensus, an attitude from the people. From that point on, things started to chill out a little bit. The national picture changed. I'm not saying that this directly affected it, but it was one small part of how it affected everything nationally. That was the mellowing out period. I would say through the 60's it built right to there—Madison bombing—and started to come down. In '72, '73, and '74 things started to chill out. Students got back to drinking beer and partying and dancing and doing normal type things rather than getting stoned out of their minds and coming in and listening to a lot of psychedelic music, doing a lot of drugs, just kind of sitting there with their head on their hands, and trying to solve the world's problems. They called it the military complex. The government and all of those things that in their small way they tried to in effect change, and in the long run, it proved that they did.

Did you ever know Karl Armstrong?
Not previous to the bombing. I probably saw him in here and never gave it a second thought. He was not someone that I sat at the table and had a Pepsi with. Although the bombing was supposedly planned at the Nitty Gritty, I didn't know about that at the time. There were people coming and going. I couldn't tell who were Narcs, and who were customers, and who were students, and who everybody was. Nobody really cared at that time. It was a communal type thing. People were in different circles, and as a business owner here, I was not in the circle with a lot of these people. At that time, it was power to the people and everything was supposed to be free. "How come you're charging fifty cents to see a band? Music is supposed to be free. How come you're charging fifty cents for a hamburger? Hamburgers are supposed to be free. Food should be free. Music should be free. Drinks should be free. Everything should be free. It all belongs to the people." There weren't a lot of businesses that were successful in this campus area. The normal type restaurant businesses in the campus didn't do any business. The barbershops closed up. Nobody was getting any haircuts. The clothing stores closed down. Nobody was buying any clothes. Everybody was wearing torn jeans and work shirts. Nobody was doing a lot of business in this area. The only people doing business were the head shops. They were selling papers for rolling weed and pipes and stuff like that. Like I said, you're talking about a minority pretty much, but still it affected everybody around them and the whole university. You've got John Stielstra going up and taking down the flag off Bascom Hill, and you've got a lot of goofy people that are trying to get attention and saying, "Hey listen to us. We've got a message." Nobody listened. It took it to that point where you got to the bombing, and

then after that they got the message out.

When the bomb was dropped on the Badger Ordnance Works, how did you react to that?
It didn't bother me. That would be like dropping an ant on an elephant's head. That was a comedy of errors. I didn't know about that until after it happened with the New Year's Gang. That's what they got named by the newspapers and television. That again was just a statement, a symbol. Here you've got a guy flying a plane that's never flown a plane before. A snowstorm on New Year's Eve with a bottle of gasoline and a hundreds of thousands of acres ammunitions plant. What were they going to do? I didn't think anything about it anymore than the fact that these guys are really nuts. They are really obviously trying to make a statement of some kind. At that time, it was news but it was at a point where people thought those guys must be crazies. They don't have any credibility. They were trying to say, "Hey! We've got a message." That was that.

What do you remember most about the Sterling Hall bombing, and what was your reaction to it?
I was very upset about it. At that time, I was not in the media. I was here at the Nitty Gritty. I thought it was tragic. I still had a lot of friends in the 'establishment' so to speak, in the police department and the coroner's office, sheriff's department. I talked to these people on a regular basis. Of course, they were very upset, and obviously it was tragic. When it happened, I was there a short time after and saw the building. They did a job. That was real rubble. That changed them around a lot. You wouldn't even know it was there now if you went over there. You'd have to take somebody up there and show different structures, concrete, the driveway going down and everything, and say, "This is where it was, right there." My reaction to that, one of the things that happened along the way, probably my reaction at the time was different. I don't really recall that I specifically made any life changes in my own personal life outside of the fact that I just thought that it was just another thing that was going on. I think at that time my reaction was probably, "This is taking it too far." I don't know if you've seen the movie *The War at Home* which is about that. You'll see me in there if you watch that thing. There was a news reporter a couple of times flashing by with a microphone stuck in somebody's face.

Do you think the individuals responsible for the bombing of Sterling Hall received fair sentencing?
At the time, if they had been captured the next day, they probably would have gotten life. Fortunately for them, the longer things dragged out, the more people were forgiving. Obviously there are people who are not forgiving right now and never will be. There were different groups of people. There was a small group that was the anti-Vietnam, anti-war, the protesters here. In the middle there were a lot of people who didn't know which way to go--maybe they're right, maybe they're wrong. Then over here, is a group of people that no matter what would say if there was the death penalty, they would have killed them. The longer it went, the more sympathetic and the more understanding people got. To their benefit, the longer they evaded arrest, the better off they were. Sure they had to be punished for the crime, but it was not anywhere near what they would have gotten if they would have been captured right away. Did they do enough time? Who's to say? What value do you put on a life? All things considered, I firmly believe that it was not intentional. They didn't intend to kill somebody. It would have to be manslaughter. I wouldn't want to be there at all. I wouldn't want to be in jail at all, but I'm not going to do that kind of stuff. At the time, they were so committed to their beliefs that they didn't care, apparently. Unless they didn't stop to think about the consequences, and I've never had the opportunity to ask them. I could. Karl is around. He's got a restaurant downtown, and I see him frequently. We say, "Hello," and, "Goodbye." We've never ever talked about the bombing. He's just a guy to me right now. I don't condone what he

did. I can understand the message they were trying to deliver, but I don't think violence was the answer. That's where they had to get to. Personally I think it was unintentional. Maybe that doesn't matter to some people. They say, "Well what the hell's the difference if somebody got killed or they blew up a multi-million dollar building? They're still guilty of a crime." Whether or not they got an appropriate sentence, hard to say. I think as they went along, maybe I'm wrong, I think Karl got the worst, Dwight got second or third, David got third; he only got five years or four years. Further along if they found Leo Burt right now, they'd probably pardon him. Who knows where Leo Burt is. He's probably living in Argentina with Elvis.

Do you think the anti-war movement in general had an effect on stopping the Vietnam War?

> *"IT'S A MATTER OF BEATING ON THE DOOR HARD ENOUGH AND LONG ENOUGH UNTIL SOMEBODY PAYS ATTENTION."*

Absolutely. There's no question about it. That affected everything. All of these incidents going on around the country, it's just like anything else. If you're in your class and you say, "Hey teacher, I don't like the way you're doing this." She's going to say, "It's one person." Now everybody in class stands up and says, "I don't like the way you're doing this." You've got her attention. She'll say, "Hey, maybe I'm not doing this right." It's a matter of beating on the door hard enough and long enough until somebody pays attention. That's what that whole thing was all about. I'm not saying that there weren't some people that had other hidden agendas. I have no idea what they were. You had a lot of black militants. You've got the Symbionese Liberation Army with Patty Hearst. You've all kinds of stuff going on at the time. Weird stuff. But for the most part, I think that the anti-war movement was trying to send a message, and every incident that happened, whether it was at Berkeley or at Michigan or Kent State or here or things out east, (You didn't find much in the South. That was a pretty heavy conservative area) I think that eventually and absolutely, I have no doubt, that it affected the national interests.

Do you have a message today for young people about the Vietnam War?

It's hard for me to realize that young people today are only finding out about it by reading it. Those of us that were around then, lived it, and me in this particular environment was able to see it from a number of different perspectives. I don't know what my message would be. Try to understand that you have to speak your mind. The government is supposed to represent you. I think it's absolutely essential that everybody question decisions. They have a right to do that. Just because the government tells you something or does something doesn't necessarily make it right. Up to that time, the government was the law, and it was God. Nobody really questioned the government. Nobody ever thought that anybody could be corrupt. Nobody ever thought that goofy things went on. What about Watergate? How was that possible? Our president being involved in doing stuff like that? There are things going on right now. Do you think that the government and the president may not be involved in the bankruptcy of Enron? That's affected hundreds of thousands of people's retirement funds. Don't you have a little question about that? Maybe something's going on. The attorney for the government shredded all of the records. Everything's gone. Oh, I'm sorry. Everything's gone. Son of a gun, I made a mistake. Doesn't that make you think something's happening there?

I think everybody is a little more reluctant now to take the word of the government as to what they're doing. I'm in favor of what they're doing in Afghanistan. I'm hoping they're going to get Bin Laden and kill him and stuff like that, but I don't know what other hidden agendas there are. Maybe it has something to do with oil. Why haven't they gone into Saudi Arabia? That's where they all came from. Why the hell aren't we in there getting all of the terrorists there? Because that's where the oil is. Why is it there? They won't let us dig in Alaska to get oil, because the environmentalists are hollering over here. There are so many things going on, that you and I as the ordinary citizen have to just kind of sit and watch TV and read the paper and say, "Ya," but what are you going to do? Are there enough people now that want to go out and protest on every issue? In spite of what you may feel or I feel about all of that stuff, it's all done at the ballot box. We still have elections even though you can look back to the last election and wonder what happened in Florida. Some strange things happened in Florida. John F. Kennedy won the election in 1960 because his father bought Chicago. That's common knowledge. They bought all of the votes. It's just like that expression, "Vote early and often." If they went through the cemetery in Chicago, they'd find an awful lot of people that voted in that 1960 election. It's just so big that you can just holler and holler until you're hoarse, and if nobody's listening, then you've got to do other things. That's kind of the story of what was going on.

Do you think the bombing of Sterling Hall was a reaction to the Vietnam War or a revolution of its own?

I think it was probably motivated by the war and everything else that was going on in the country at the time. It obviously was affected by the war because they were looking to bomb the Army Math Research Center, which was in that building. They were supposedly contributing to the war effort. I'm certain there's a direct correlation there.

Shapiro is currently the owner and operator of Marsh Shapiro's Nitty Gritty restaurant in Madison.

Interviewered by Jessica Dabler and Ryan Prochaska
Transcribered by Jessica Dabler

Paul Soglin

Soglin was a University of Wisconsin undergraduate, graduate, and law student during the Vietnam War. He was also a part time bartender, cab driver, and city alderman for the city of Madison.

People were marching in the streets. Certainly, in the spring of 1970 there were a lot of demonstrations around the country protesting the expanding war in Vietnam. This heightened protest against the war led to demonstrations where soldiers shot students at Kent State. That produced more demonstrations. My guess is that by the spring of 1970, 35,000 students were actively participating. I had been involved since 1963. In October 1963, there was a demonstration on the steps of the Memorial Union. We protested the presence of US military advisors and personnel that were involved in advising the South Vietnamese government. We were concerned about the possibility of greater U.S. involvement.

What influenced the bombing of Sterling Hall?

Well, the antiwar movement in Madison and throughout the country quieted down after the bombing of the Army Math Research Center. Some people believed it was a direct result of the bombing. I am not so sure about that. I think what happened is that the antiwar movement grew tremendously during 1967, 1968, and 1969, and with it came a lot of frustration. We were not seeing a response to these feelings, and each time the antiwar movement grew the government expanded the war more. It sort of reminds me of a pot of boiling water. Even though you shut off the source of the energy and reduce the flame, the pot still boils for a while. What happened in 1967-68 was that the antiwar movement grew a lot. It didn't grow in depth. It grew in size, and what we saw happening was that in 1969 and 1970, people became very frustrated and disillusioned, and they didn't know how to make their feelings known. They didn't know the effective way of communicating to the Congress and the President how to stop the war. More and more people were demonstrating in the streets, and we also saw some more violent acts. There was this tremendous sense of frustration that nothing is happening, that nothing is happening. Things were not changing. Now what took place was the movement went in two directions. Some people, even though we had that large number of demonstrators in the spring of 1970, started to drop out. Other people became more militant. It seemed everyone was going in different directions.

What about the bombing itself?

It produced a backlash, produced a reaction against demonstrators. A lot of demonstrators themselves were disillusioned. There was a lot more police presence and undercover activity. It made people rethink of what had happened. I remember talking to a woman named Rena Steinzor. Rena was the editor of the *Cardinal* at the time, and she was trying to assess the morality of the bombing of the Math Research

Center. She said very simply, she looked on herself and she knew that she did not have the capability to do something like that. That simple introspective thought said that this was something very morally wrong.

What was the nation's response to the bombing?
It focused a lot of attention on Madison, that's for sure. The weeks that followed had a lot of national news coverage that came out of Madison. The networks sent their crews here and eventually sent them back here when Karl [Armstrong] was apprehended. But tragically, there were a lot of incidents like this that happened throughout the country. After a while they just moved on to the next big story.

What do you remember most about the bombing?
I suppose I remember the bombing itself. I was in bed when the bomb went off, and I called the fire department to find out what was going on. They told me, and I drove over to the site. I was one of the first people to arrive there, I took a look around because I had this feeling that there was no sense in staying because this awful thing had happened, and it was going to be very hard to change things, so I got back in my car and drove home. I think years later Karl probably had the same thoughts.

Do you have a comment on the 1968 presidential race?
I wasn't that active in the campaign. I actually didn't think McCarthy was that good a candidate. I preferred Bobby Kennedy myself and more or less after the Kennedy assassination gave up looking for a good candidate for the Democratic Party. I didn't feel that the Democrats would nominate Eugene McCarthy. In retrospect, Hubert Humphrey lost a very close election, and I suppose now it would have made a substantial difference if Humphrey were elected. He was Johnson's vice president, so he couldn't, by himself, stand up and repudiate the war; he represented what was wrong with our leasdership. That was the tragedy of Hubert Humphrey and America's tragedy at the time. I guess now in retrospect, Humphrey might have changed the course of the war.

What were the events concerning the ROTC building?
There were a number of campus buildings that were fire bombed during that period and there were a lot of us that set standards for what was acceptable behavior- peaceful marches and stuff like that. Disruption was acceptable. Sitting-in and taking the consequence of being arrested was acceptable, that borrowed from the civil rights movement and the concept of civil disobedience. When it moved up another level to the destruction of property, it was unacceptable. That's probably where the vast majority of anti-war demonstrators stood in drawing a line between what was acceptable and what was not acceptable. There was certainly a group, perhaps no more than one hundred students who condoned violence, who said it was all right to trash the windows of stores on State Street; it was acceptable to destroy property. My greatest anger with them is that they used the cover of a larger crowd to perpetrate their kind of violence. Five thousand people would be peacefully marching down State Street and under the cover of that crowd there would be a handful of people with rocks to trash windows. They couldn't get away with that except in a very cowardly way, using the larger crowd as cover.

Did the bombing of Sterling Hall have an effect on the antiwar movement?
It did, but I am not sure it changed the direction. It did change the movement. It accelerated views that the antiwar movement had to stay within boundaries in how it expressed itself. There was a core of us that spoke out against that kind of violence. It accelerated views of those who wanted to end the war. For

those who supported the war, I am not so sure of the consequence. It probably told them how desperate certain people were. I don't think it accelerated their views.

What is your opinion of the effectiveness of the movement?

I think it sped up the end of the war. It did something else that was more important. It changed the standard by which we would use troops in the future. In other situations that required a military response, it forced presidents to be more selective when they used troops, and it forced them to define how those troops were to be used. I think that was very good. The two most obvious examples are the Gulf War and our intervention in Bosnia. In that regard, the anti-war efforts during the Vietnam era made a major positive contribution because of the larger use of force, and when we do it, there is greater support by the American people.

Do you think the bombing of Sterling Hall was a revolutionary act?

At the time, those who participated in the bombing thought that what they were doing was stopping the war. I don't think they were under the impression that this was a beginning of a revolution. There were others, even more extreme, who thought that this was an act that was leading to revolution. I think in Karl's own words, if I remember them correctly, their main intent was to stop the war of shame, to stop the US from conducting the war. I don't think Karl or Dwight had any notion about the impact of the act, and they were going to start a revolution that would change the government.

Your thoughts on their punishment?

When you balance their actions with the punishment they received, the jail sentence was reasonable. They set off the bomb, they destroyed property and though they didn't intend to kill someone, they did kill someone.

Do you think that if they would have been caught later their sentences would have been less?

That I don't know. The implication of your question is when time went by was there more understanding or sympathy towards their sentencing? Yes, I think that is true, but I couldn't guess about the sentencing happened in 1971. That I couldn't tell you.

Soglin served as mayor of Madison, Wisconsin from 1973 -1979 (three two year terms) and was elected to this office again from 1989-1997. Mr. Soglin works as a financial advisor with Lincoln Financial Advisors Corporation and teaches at Lafollette School of Public Affairs, UW-Madison.

Interviewed by Ryan Prochaska

Courtesy of The War at Home

The Hmong
The Secret War in Laos

D.C. Everest Area Schools

The Secret War In Laos

Excerpted from Hmong Oral Histories

The Geneva Accords of 1954 were signed a few months after the French lost at Dien Bien Phu. The agreement recognized three independent states in what had formerly been French Indochina: Laos, Cambodia, and Vietnam. Vietnam was temporarily divided into northern and southern zones which were supposed to be reunited in two years. The French were required to withdraw their troops from North Vietnam and Laos. Laos was supposed to be a neutral country. However, after the Geneva Accords, internal conflicts continued in Laos between the Royal Lao forces and the Pathet Lao forces (the Laotian communists), with both vying for control of the country. This conflict was intensified when foreign powers offered support. The United States supplied the Royal Lao forces with arms and military advisors, while the Pathet Lao communist forces were aided by the North Vietnamese (NVA), the Soviet Union, and China. The United States feared the domino effect of communism. On his last day in office, President Eisenhower told President-elect Kennedy that if Laos were to fall to communism, the countries of South Vietnam, Cambodia, Thailand, and Burma would soon follow.[2]

The Hmong forces were split along clan lines as the Lo clan supported the communist Pathet Lao and the Ly clan (and other clans) supported the Royal Lao. These Hmong leaders worried about a communist takeover in Laos and felt the Geneva Accords meant nothing to the Vietnamese and would not stop the North Vietnamese Army. One of the Hmong elders warned, "Do not worry about the words in Geneva, they are only words. Worry about the Vietnamese soldiers in Laos, they are real." [3]

The conflict greatly intensified when in 1960, U.S.-supported Kong Le (a Laotian army officer) led a coup d' etat, overthrew the pro-Western government, and demanded a Neutralist government. Kong Le insisted that corruption in the government forced him to take these actions.[4] Within a few months Kong Le was ousted by CIA-backed rightists which threw him into "an uneasy alliance" with the communist Pathet Lao. Kong Le and the Pathet Lao then seized control of most of northern Laos, creating massive turmoil and forever changing the destiny of Laos.

During 1961-62, the Geneva Conference tried to resolve the conflict in Laos. The United States promised not to send "any foreign troops or military personnel" into Laos.[5] Despite this promise, the CIA started recruiting the Hmong to fight against the communists. The United States needed to disrupt the "Ho Chi Minh" Trail, a North Vietnamese military supply line that ran through Laos.[6] This became the job of the Hmong fighters. The Hmong gathered intelligence, fought the ground war, directed air strikes, rescued downed American pilots, and were dropped behind enemy lines to fight. They were paid an average of three dollars a month.[7] While the U.S. military sent half a million troops to fight a conventional war in South Vietnam, only a handful of American personnel were stationed in Laos.[8] This helped keep American activities in Laos secret.

The CIA chose to work closely with a Hmong General named Vang Pao. The CIA supplied General Vang Pao's forces under the cover of a government organization which was supposed to help refugees – the U.S. Agency for Aid an Development since America was not "officially in Laos." [9] Retired CIA director William Colby recalled that "the CIA had identified an officer…originally trained by the French, who had not only the courage but also the political acumen…for leadership in such a conflict." Vang Pao drew " the enthusiastic admiration of the CIA officers." [10] A CIA propaganda film described Vang Pao as a "charismatic, passionate and committed man, a patriot without a country." [11] On two occasions, the CIA flew Vang Pao to the United States, where he was invited to the White House and Disneyland. Vang Pao saw battle for the first time in 1945 at the age of thirteen, while working as an interpreter for French commandos who had parachuted onto the Plain of Jars to organize anti-Japanese resistance. 12 He then moved up the ranks in the Laotian Army to become the first Hmong general in the history of Laos. Many accounts of Vang Pao's heroism and generosity exist. It is said that he always stayed with his men during the battles. Once, Vang Pao ordered a helicopter to take him to Na Khang, where a battle was taking place. "His front line appearances inspired his men, and his unorthodox tactics, often demanding considerable bravery from his soldiers, confounded the enemy and terrified his SKY (U.S.) advisors." 13

Some view General Vang Pao as a much harsher man. One Hmong recalled, "Vang Pao recruited by force. I was very lucky. My father had money and he pay four other men to serve instead of my three brothers and me." General Vang Pao…was said to punish villages that had failed to fill their soldier quotas by cutting off their food supplies. 14

The United States built headquarters and a air base in the city of Long Chieng. "General Vang Pao and the CIA turned corn fields and a cemetery into a city and airport. Long Chieng became the secret city of the secret war in Laos." 15 The CIA had no qualms about delegating high risk military operations to the Hmong, and as a result, Hmong fighters suffered one of the highest casualty rates of any group involved in the Vietnam War – estimtes range from five to ten times higher than that of U.S. soldiers in combat. 16 Between 300,000 and 400,000 Hmong lived in Laos in 1960. There is disagreement over what fraction of the Hmong died with estimates ranging from a tenth (in a 1975 Washington *Post* report) to half (in a 1970 report to the Senate Judiciary Subcommittee on Refugees and Escapees). 17 As early as 1971, many Hmong families had no males left over the age of ten.

The Americans promised the Hmong that the United States would take care of them if the communists took over. 18 The United States became discouraged in Southeast Asia, just as the French had been earlier. In February 1973, the Vientiane Agreement was signed, which called for a ceasefire in Laos and a coalition government. It also called for the end of American air support. The United States also began to cut back on supplies such as the rice, salt, medicine they had been dropping to the Hmong from planes. 19

In 1975, the CIA withdrew completely from Laos. On May 10, 1975 General Vang Pao, surrounded by Pathet Lao and North Vietnamese troops, reluctantly conceded that he could no longer hold Long Chieng. For the next four days, between 1,000 and 3,000 high-ranking Hmong and their families were air lifted to Thailand. 20 As word spread around the countryside that General Vang Pao was leaving, frightened people rushed to Long Chieng with their meager belongings. The crowd at the airstrp grew by the hour. People tried desperately to get on the planes, but were pushed back. Approximately 10,000 (estimates range as high as 40,000) people arrived at Long Chieng hoping to be air lifted. 21

The United States sent a couple of planes to airlift top military staff, but "left the Hmong high and dry." The communists, predictably, viewed the Hmong as a threat. They wanted to drive them out of the country or kill them. 22 The Hmong had been a chief impediment to a communist victory for many years. After the United States pull-out in 1975, most Hmong knew they would not be safe in Laos. On May 9, *the Khao Xane Pathet Lao*, the newspaper of the Lao People's Party, announced that "The Meo [Hmong] must be exterminated down to the root of the tribe." 23 Many Hmong were slaughtered in their villages or at airfields where they waited for evacuation planes that never came. Some died on the long journey out of Laos to freedom in Thailand. 24

Notes

1 Faidman, A. *The Spirit Catches You and You Fall Down: A Hmong Child, Her American Doctors, and the Collision of Two Cultures.* New York, NY: Farrar Stratus, and Giroux, 1997, p.124.

2 Ibid.,p.125.

3 Hamilton-Merritt, J. Tragic Mountains: The Hmong, the Americans, and the Secret Wars for Laos, 1942-1992. Indanapolis, IN: Indiana University Press, 1993, p. 64.

4 Ibid., p. 78.

5 Faidman, A. *The Spirit Catches You and You Fall Down: A Hmong Child, Her American Doctors, and the Collision of Two Cultures.* New York, NY: Farrar Stratus, and Giroux, 1997, p.125.

6 *Farwell to Freedom: The Moore Report.* Videocassette. Bloomington, IN: Indiana University Audio-Visual Center, 1994.

7 Faidman, A. "97/09--Heroes' Welcome." Civilization Magazine *http:/www.civmag.com/articles/C9709F02.htlm.* 1998, p. 2.

8 McCoy, A. *The Politics of Heroin: CIA Compicity in the Global Drug Trade.* Chicago, IL: Lawrence Hill Books, 1991, pg. 308.

9 Faderman, L. and Xiong, G. The Hmong and the American Immigrant Experience: I Begin My Life All Over. Boston, MA: Beacon Press, 1998, p.6

10 McCoy, A. The Politics of Heroin: *CIA Compicity in the Global Drug Trade.* Chicago, IL: Lawrence Hill Books, 1991, pg. 308.

11 *"Journey from Pha Dong: A Decision in the Hills, Secret War in Laos,"* Videocassette, St. Paul, MN: Hmong ABC Publications.

12 McCoy, A. *The Politics of Heroin: CIA Compicity in the Global Drug Trade.* Chicago, IL: Lawrence Hill Books, 1991, pg. 309.

13 Hamilton-Merritt, J. *Tragic Mountains: The Hmong, the Americans, and the Secret Wars for Laos,* 1942-1992. Indianapolis, IN: Indiana University Press, 1993, p. 145.

14 Faidman, A. *The Spirit Catches You and You Fall Down: A Hmong Child, Her American Doctors, and the Collision of Two Cultures.* New York, NY: Farrar, Straus, and Giroux, 1997, p. 129.

15 *"Journey from Pha Dong: A Decison in the Hills, Secret Wars in Laos,"* Videocassette, St. Paul, MN: Hmong ABC Publications.

16 Cao, L. and Novas, H. Everything You Need to Know About Asian-American History. New York, NY: Penguin Books USA Inc., 1996, p. 228. Estimates were also found in Fadiman, A. '97/09 --Heroes' Welcome." Civilization Magazine http:/www.civmag.com/articles/C90709F02.htlm. 1998, p. 2.

17 Faidman, A. *The Spirit Catches You and You Fall Down: A Hmong Child, Her American Doctors, and the Collision of Two Cultures.* New York, NY: Farrar, Straus, and Giroux, 1997, p. 138.

18 Hamilton-Merritt, J. *Tragic Mountains: The Hmong, the Americans, and the Secret Wars for Laos,* 1942-1992. Indianapolis, IN: Indiana University Press, 1993, p. 145.

19 Faidman, A. *The Spirit Catches You and You Fall Down: A Hmong Child, Her American Doctors, and the Collision of Two Cultures.* New York, NY: Farrar, Straus, and Giroux, 1997, p. 138.

20 Ibid.

21 Hamilton-Merritt, J. *Tragic Mountains: The Hmong, the Americans, and the Secret Wars for Laos,* 1942-1992. Indianapolis, IN: Indiana University Press, 1993, pgs. 344-345.

22 *Farwell to Freedom: The Moore Report.* Videocassette. Bloomington, IN: Indiana University Audio-Visual Center, 1994.

23 Faidman, A. *The Spirit Catches You and You Fall Down: A Hmong Child, Her American Doctors, and the Collision of Two Cultures.* New York, NY: Farrar, Straus, and Giroux, 1997, p. 138.

24 "Defending the Hmong: Comments from a Veteran of Vietnam," *http://www.athenet.net/-jlindsay/hmong_tragedy.html.*

Yong Yia Thao

Serving in Laos in the 60s, Thao was a commander of local forces.

In 1960, there was a group led by Kong Le, a Lao descendent, at the state capital Vientiane. We didn't know that there were any North Vietnamese involved at that time. We thought that the conflict was between the Lao people. They fought at the capital city of Vientiane. We lived right on the path where Kong Le withdrew his troops to the Xieng Khoung province. They passed our village, which was on the countryside. When they withdrew to where we lived, we found that Kong Le was siding with the North Vietnamese against the Lao Republic. We tried to cut them off around our village by ambushing the troops. They were well-armed, and we didn't have anything that we could use to retaliate against them. After that, the villagers all dispersed. They burned all our villages. We didn't know that we were even at war with another country. We thought that the conflict was among the Lao people.

When all the villagers dispersed, Americans came to give us support and to gather everyone to fight against the opposition. There were 40 in the first group that went with me to the front line. We went to the border of Xieng Khoung province at the village called Banna. We went to get our military supplies such as guns and other ammunitions. Banna was our new location where we regrouped because we had lost our villages. In this new location, the U.S. airplanes couldn't locate us. They sent two Thai personnel that were equipped with spot guns. They would fire the guns upward to make bright, smoke signals. The planes still couldn't locate us. We didn't get our military supplies. Later, they told me that I needed to gather about 60 more men to my 40 to make 100. Then I would become the commander. I came back to where the women, children, and surveillance were staying. I asked my older brother to replace me in the front line. He became the commander of that group. I remained in the village to oversee the women, children, and those who did not go to the front line.

Now they supplied the troops with ammunition. Once they were armed, those who remained behind still had to be prepared and organized. They had to be ready to move in a moment's notice because we didn't know where the enemy would be coming from. In 1967 or 1968, I became a community leader– Naikong. A Naikong is a surveillance leader that protected the villagers and other surveillancers. When the front troop penetrated and moved the enemy, my group would move to their base. We would stay at that base until the front troop came back to meet us. Then we would come back to the village. Sometimes this would take 2-3 months at a time. This seesawing continued until 1975, when we finally lost the war. We immigrated to Thailand on July 14th, 1975. We left everything behind. We lived in Thailand until March 1978, when my family was interviewed by the U.S. immigration personnel to come to America.

Were there times when you actually fought/confronted the enemy?

We didn't shoot at each other. When they fired at us, we ran and moved to a safer place. But once we were armed, I only served as an army reserve to protect the villagers and surveillance. Only those who served in the army fought in the front line. My brother led his group to fight in a town called NaKhang in the Xieng Khoung province. My brother's troop had 100 soldiers. In that battle, he lost 60 good men; only 40 returned. If he wasn't lucky, he would be dead too. He got wounded in that battle. He got shot in his left elbow. They carried him to safety, and later he recovered.

What year was that?

I don't remember well now, but it might have been in 1968 or 1969. I don't remember which month.

Was there a hospital or medication to treat your brother? Was there any compensation for the wounded?

During the war, the Americans supplied the medication for the wounded. The wounded would be taken to an area where the plane (helicopter) could land and be picked up for treatment. Those who couldn't be saved were left

> *"WE SUFFERED DAY AND NIGHT. WHENEVER THE ENEMY CAME, DAY OR NIGHT, EVERYONE KEPT MOVING TO GET TO A SAFER PLACE. THOSE WHO COULD WALK WALKED, BUT THOSE WHO COULDN'T WALK WERE CARRIED. SOME WERE LEFT BEHIND."*

behind. I only know about those who made it back. For those who didn't return, we assumed them dead. The missing never returned. They took my brother for treatment at the capital city Vientiane. He was in treatment for about 3-4 months before he was well enough to return home to his village. He is still living and can't use his hand. He has some difficulty with blood circulation to his arms and legs. Now, one of his hands and one of his legs is smaller than the other. He still lives in Los Angeles. For those 60 men, they were presumed dead because at that military base they dug a trench around it. Only those who got out of the trench were alive. Those who stayed are all dead. The enemy threw hand grenades into the trenches. No one survived.

Was there anyone who actually saw how many were dead in those trenches?

Once we left, no one ever got back to those places at all. Once the enemy conquered it, we couldn't take it back again.

Who were the people in the plane that came to rescue the wounded soldiers? Were they Hmong or American?

The pilots were American, but I don't know any of their names. They were the helicopter pilots.

Where did you go when you left your village?

When we moved from our village, we moved to Long Cheng, a military base in Xieng Khoung province. Then we moved to Vientiane and crossed the river to Thailand.

When you are constantly moving, how do you get your food?

We suffered a lot during our migration. We couldn't carry any food. We carried only the clothes we had on. The kids were carried on our backs. We grabbed whatever we could find and kept moving. We suffered day and night. Whenever the enemy came, day or night, everyone kept moving to get to a safer place. Those who could walk walked, but those who couldn't walk were carried. Some were left behind. When people still lived in the village and everybody lived together, the Americans supplied the rice. We couldn't plant any rice. Most people remained on the military base. There wasn't any place to farm. The soldiers would survey the outskirts, and the families remained at the base. They lived in trenches so that the artilleries wouldn't hit them. When we lost a base, we moved to another.

How would the Americans drop the rice?
The rice drop would be for the soldiers who had withdrawn from their original position. They would contact the main base, and they would drop the rice for them. For us, if we stayed in one place, then they would drop rice for us. If we kept moving, they wouldn't drop rice for us. Sometimes they wouldn't be able to drop them because we couldn't stay at one place. Soldiers had hand-held phones, and they could communicate and receive food supplies. Those of us with women and children wouldn't be able to receive any food supplies.

How did you protect the women and children?
Those who were still small would ride on the back. The parents would hold hands with those who could walk.

Did you meet with people from other villages, too?
All people in the country (Laos), not only you. Once you got to a larger trail/road, it was filled with people like you who were going to the market. There were no automobiles; everyone marches or walks. Those who had a cart would put their children in it. We only carried food because the trails aren't like the roads you see in this country. The trails go up and down the mountain. It isn't smooth. There are no roads in our country; even a 2-3 day walk was by foot.

"THERE WERE NO ELECTRONIC DEVICES SUCH AS HAND-HELD PHONES. IT WAS BY WORD OF MOUTH FROM ONE TO ANOTHER."

During the war, how did you know that you were fighting the Vietnamese?
We thought that the conflict was among the Lao people, but then Kong Le got support from the Vietnamese. Both Kong Le and the Vietnamese fought against the Republic of Lao. Later, Kong Le had a conflict with the Vietnamese. He moved his forces back into to Laos. That's why we knew that we were fighting the Vietnamese.

Were there Americans who asked you to fight?
They came to our villages and gathered all the men. Later, when they supplied us with ammunition we found that General Vang Pao was the leader.

How do people receive messages? Were there any messengers? Did you have access to any telecommunication device?
There were no electronic devices such as hand-held phones. It was by word of mouth from one to another. For instance, they would say that there will be a drop at the village of Banna, and everyone needs to go there to get weapons to defend themselves.

Were there many young men or boys in the army?
Yes, boys whose ages were around ten years old. Some boys whose height was only about the height of the machine gun, 30/30 caliber, already participated in the army. They were 13-14 years of age when they had to carry guns. Some didn't know how to shoot the gun. It would take 3-4 years before they could carry the guns properly. Anyone who wanted to protect the villages was accepted. When we lost our country, we lost about 35,000 men. That was just the Hmong, not the Lao. The Hmong lost about 35,000 men up until 1975.

How do you know that the Hmong lost 35,000 men?
The leaders accurately kept track of the men. Those who didn't return were considered dead.

When you fought, did you have airplanes or other weapons to assist you? What about the other side?
They had very advanced and powerful guns. They had those long-range guns, such as the DK. They also had the Bazooka. They had more troops and supply lines. We only had small machine guns and what we could carry with us. We depended on the weapons from the airplane drops. At our military base, we couldn't use the small machine guns because the fights usually occur at night. If we used the small machine guns, the enemy would be able to spot the fire/spark when the bullet left the gun barrel. They would use those long-range guns. Most often, hand grenades were the most useful during the dark night. Towards the morning, only then the small machine gun can be used. We were only successful in defending the base when we had enough hand grenades. Using the gun is the last resort. The bases were up in the mountains and heavy or large guns couldn't be hauled up. Small machine guns and hand grenades were the most frequently used artillery. When we used the small machine guns, that meant that we were about to lose the battle because we were out of hand grenades.

How did you know to run towards Thailand?
We didn't know that we would end up in Thailand. We kept leaving our villages behind. Then we heard that America lost the war. We continued to fight, but there was no one to support us. There is a Lao leader – Suvana. The Lao leader, Suvana, told everyone to cease-fire and not to fight anymore. No one kept their guns because everyone knew that if they stayed, they would be killed. Everyone decided to cross the river to Thailand.

What was your trip to Thailand like?
We suffered a lot. We didn't have much to carry, but there was no transportation. We had to hike for 2-3 days before we reached the village of Nasu. Once we reached Nasu, there were vehicles available. From Nasu to the state capital; we traveled by car. Once we reached the state capital Vientiane, we stayed there for a week and crossed to Thailand.

Once you reach Nasu, were there vehicles to pick everyone up?
At that time, the Vietnamese controlled every city and town. We intentionally walked the streets and marched towards Thailand. There was no fear of being killed. If one got killed, so be it. At that early stage, the Vietnamese wouldn't openly kill anyone. Those who wanted to leave left. Those who wanted to stay, stayed. The opposition wanted everyone to leave the country for them. Everyone knew that they wanted things to settle down; then they would ask for people to participate in the education camp. The people who went never returned.

How did you get your vehicle/ride?
They had gates lowered to block the streets. The people who gave us rides told us to walk around the gate so that no one would see. They would wait for us on the other side. Some gates weren't difficult because the driver was able to talk to the gatekeeper into allowing us to pass.

Who were the drivers?
The drivers were all Lao people.

Did you have to pay them?
We had to pay them. We paid one person about 7,000 to 10,000 kip in Lao money. At the state capital Vientiane, we had to pay another person 20,000 kips. You had to multiply 20,000 to the number of people you had. It had to be paid up front before they would take you across to Thailand.

How did you find someone that would take you across?

There were people who came around and asked to see who wanted to go to Thailand. Then the price and boat would be arranged. I believe that the one who agreed to take us bribed the gatekeeper. The driver would give a certain time that he would come to pick us up. If the gatekeeper was someone he didn't trust then he won't come to pick us up. Our driver surveyed the area twice before he came to pick us up. It took our driver three days before he took us to our destination.

At that time, were the borders closed?

Definitely, the border was closed. That was why we had to pay our guide person and the gatekeeper.

"ONE OF MY BROTHER'S SONS STILL LIVES IN LAOS. HE LIVES IN THE JUNGLE AND WON'T SURRENDER TO THE ENEMY."

What do they do when one gets caught?

They would ask, "Where are you from?" If you tell them where you are from, they would send you back to where you came. If anyone refused to go back, they would be killed or jailed. It didn't matter how far away you lived. They would send you back. At that time, they didn't want to expose themselves by killing anyone publicly. They would allow things to cool down. Then they would ask for those who were more intelligent to go to the education camp. Once they got to the Mekong River and while on the boat, some villagers were robbed and dumped into the river. Many villagers died by drowning. Those that I led all crossed safely. Altogether, about 80 people died among my villagers. Some died from hunger and others died from poison by drinking water along the way. One of my brother's sons still lives in Laos. He lives in the jungle and wouldn't surrender to the enemy.

When you came, it was just you and your family and not everyone in your village?

Only my older brother's family and my family; all the others were left behind.

What were the conditions in Thailand when you arrived?

They provided us with food. Later, they built some shelters for all the refugees. The Americans provided the Thai government with some financial assistance so that the Thai official could buy food. They offered food for about two years. Then everyone had to buy their own food. We received one bowl of rice per person every couple of days. All the refugees stayed together. About 8,000 to 10, 000 people lived together in the camp. The Americans provided money to build shelter for all the refugees. In Thailand we didn't suffer much. The only stress was that we lost our homeland. We got enough food and things to meet our immediate needs.

"I WAS ONE OF THE FIRST INDIVIDUALS TO CONTACT GENERAL VANG PAO. WE KNEW THAT HE WENT TO AMERICA ALREADY."

How long did you stay in Thailand before you come to the USA?

We lived in Thailand for about two years. They wouldn't let anyone to go outside to work, only to stay in the camp. I knew that if we didn't find another way out we would suffer greatly. I was one of the first individuals to contact General Vang Pao. We knew that he went to America already. We were interviewed and were the first wave of Hmong refugees. We came to America in March of 1978. We first came to Oklahoma City.

Did you like to live there?
It was okay. When we lived there, they only paid for the rent. They gave us about $200.00 of food stamps. We lived there for three years and then moved to Illinois. We lived in Illinois for a year, then moved to Wisconsin.

How do you get your money?
I tried to work, but I couldn't speak English. Sometimes I only worked for a couple months and was let go because I couldn't speak English. In Wisconsin I was qualified to receive SSI because I came of age. I have lived in Wisconsin ever since.

Following the war, Yong Thao was in the army reserve and a village leader.

Interviewer by Samantha Thao
Interpretered by Lamont Thao

Abraham Yi Vang

Abraham Yi Vang joined the army when he was just a teenager and fought in a combat unit guarding roads in his area of operations.

I was thirteen years old when I joined the CIA. The war was going on, so we had to go to war. I dropped out of school because the Communists came to the village. I had to go out and fight. After the Communists came close to the village, we had to fight them. After that, they went away, and we went back to school. That's how life in Laos was like. After 1968 and 1969, they made everyone fight. I had to go out help the community to fight against the Vietnamese. So our life in Laos became one of fighting. There was no opportunity to go to school and no chance to do business. It was a very difficult life in Laos. After 1975, the Vietnamese took control of the country. They began to look for the people who had served with the American CIA during the Vietnam war. Most of those people, who had a chance, escaped to Thailand. Some of them had been arrested and were sent to refugee camps or prison. The people who could not escape to Thailand gathered their old weapons and went to hide in the forest away from the Vietnamese. Many of them still fight in Laos today.

"OUR LIFE IN LAOS BECAME ONE OF FIGHTING IN LAOS."

The country had become impossible to live in, and we escaped by crossing the Mekong River. I crossed the Mekong about fifteen miles south of Vientiane. I crossed the river to a town called Nong Khai. I stayed there for six months. I was interviewed by the United Nations refugee program that was involved in immigration of the Hmong. One question asked if we knew our leader. They asked questions concerning the medical equipment we used during the war. They also asked questions about the weapons we used. They asked all kinds of questions about the war, to see what you knew. You had to tell them everything to see if you qualify. If you didn't answer truthfully, or if you couldn't answer a question, they would say you were lying, and then you wouldn't qualify for immigration to the United States. If you didn't leave Thailand, you would be forced to stay in a refugee camp.

When we came to the United States, it was very hard for the Hmong people. We knew of life in Southeast Asia. This country was very different. We cannot speak English, and we cannot adjust to the American culture. It was difficult to find a job. It was difficult to become an American citizen and serve a new land and lead a new life. The Hmong families in the community had to come together and talk about how we were going to serve the new land. We called together the family leaders. This happened in 1979 and 1980.

We formed an organization to provide services to help the families who could not speak English. People in our organization provided translation services. Some of our members knew a little English because of our involvement with the Americans during the war. Other than that, we were limited because no one had graduated from high school or college. The Hmong had learned some French and English from working with the soldiers of each country. Our organization also helped the Asian families register for school and would accompany them to the clinics when they needed medical help. Also, our group began to present our history and our traditions to the general public. We wanted the public to understand who we were and why we had come to this country. We tried to do our best. We wanted the public to know our story and see us in the best light. Hmong people work hard and we wanted to be self-supporting. After a number of years, Hmong families are now able to buy homes and our children are graduating from high school and many have gone on to college. Our group will work hard with local governments to help our citizens achieve their goals.

"EVERY COUNTRY HAS TO BUILD A STRONG MILITARY AND SUPPLY IT TO PROTECT THE COUNTRY."

Can you spend some time on your own personal story?

I don't have a whole lot to share about the war because I was thirteen in 1975. I was very young in the early years. The Soviet Union supported China who supplied North Vietnam with weapons and equipment. We stayed in the field every night and day. We often fought at night and hid during the day. We had different weapons that we used that were supplied by the Americans. We had 60mm and 81mm mortars and heavier weapons. We were also supplied with the 40mm grenade launcher that could lob a grenade between 250 and 300 yards. We tried to control the major roads in our area. We would bomb Road Six that led to China and Road Seven that went to North Vietnam during the night. We positioned

our troops so we could control those roads during the night. The North Vietnamese used an 82mm mortar and heavy machine guns. They were also supplied with 130mm howitzers that had a long range. We also could call in aircraft when we needed support.

We knew that North Vietnam could not take over our country and South Vietnam. In our agreements with the United States, we knew that the Americans would help us maintain our sovereignty. We would fight them together. The United States changed direction and an agreement was reached in 1973. Twelve countries agreed on paper to end the conflict. We did not sign that document. The Communist countries wanted control over our country. They got that control after the United States left. The Vietnamese keep our country poor. The government kept all the money. Thailand is a neighbor of Laos, but they would not accept Laotian people. There was no place for those people to go. It was a very difficult life.

Did you get all your fighting supplies from the CIA?

Yes. During the war, in 1966, a friend of mine was named Jerry Donery. He was from Seattle. I was with him until 1972. When I left the country, he was still in Thailand. Later, in 1986, I heard that he passed away in the jungle. I have only a few friends now because most of them have died. The younger generation might know about the war only if we tell the story to them. The army was important. The soldiers protected the people and the territory. Everyone should respect the army and the government that provides the army. Every country has to build a strong military and supply it to protect the country.

Where did all the people go after they fled Laos?

All people that could get away from Laos went to Thailand. A large number of those people made it to the United States. Some went to France, and others went to Canada. Small numbers went to Australia and New Zealand. A few families tried to go to South America. I think China accepted between sixty and eighty families, but China returned those families to Laos about six or seven years ago. China was unable to take care of them. Their life was poorer in China than living in the camps.

Most of the Hmong stayed in the camps?

Yes, they stayed in the camps. Today, there are around thirty thousand that still reside in the north camp in Thailand. Others remain in south Thailand. Those in the south are preparing to return to Laos but the others served with the American CIA. They are writing letters to different authorities to stop the return.

"WE HAD 60MM AND 81MM MORTARS AND HEAVIER WEAPONS. WE WERE ALSO SUPPLIED WITH THE 40MM GRENADE LAUNCHER THAT COULD LOB A GRENADE BETWEEN 250 AND 300 YARDS."

The Thai government has a plan to return these people to Laos. The government of Laos does not want these people back because they fear they will try to take over the government. The Hmong are not allowed to go back, and they must stay in the camps. Guards are located at the gates and by the wire, and people will be injured or killed if they try to escape. Like I said earlier, people will interview you to see what you did during the fighting. If you were part of the CIA, they will find out.

Can you tell us more about the camps?

We appreciated that the Thai government allowed the Hmong to live in the camps in their land. The United Nations and the United States have to pay money to rent the buildings and the land for each camp. Thailand provided the land, but every square foot is paid for with US dollars. The Hmong live in the refugee camps where there is no school. People inside the camp are forced to stay inside the camp. There is no place to go, and there is nothing inside. It is a difficult life.

Did you serve with General Vang Pao?

Yes, I served with General Vang Pao when he made an agreement with the United States government.

Do you have anything to say to the younger generation?

I want to encourage all the younger Hmong to stay in school and become a leader for the future. I would like to see the Hmong children put their best efforts in education and when you finish high school continue on to college. The Americans accepts us in their homeland because we have no place to go. If we want to live here, we have to build everything to make our life like theirs. All the Hmong who live in other parts of the world watch us in the United States. We have come to the right place, and we are headed in the right direction.

Abraham Yi Vang is employed at the Wausau Area Hmong Mutual Association.

Nhia Blia Xiong

Nhia Blia Xiong is from Xeing Khouang Province. He was a student in Laos and then became a paratrooper for the CIA in 1961. In 1962 he got a staff job as a medical and food supply officer. He left Laos in 1978.

The Hmong came to America because in Laos the princes didn't get along with each other. In Laos there were two factions -- the pro-Communist faction and the pro-Western faction. The pro-Communist faction were several princes like Prince Soupanouvong and some of his followers. On the right hand the United States and others sided with the King, General Vang Pao, and some other key leaders. There was some conflict going on in Laos. By 1960 this country was flipped around by Kong Le to form Vientiane. By now South Vietnam started to fight back and to regain the parts of South Vietnam and Cambodia that had been taken. American troops came to help South Vietnam and Cambodia. Because of this, the North Vietnamese started to fight with the South Vietnamese, Cambodians, and Americans to regain the lands that they had taken.

In the early 1960's, the three princes that sided with the communist princes and some others… they took advantage of the conflict in Vietnam. At that time Vietnam was divided into two countries, North Vietnam and South Vietnam. The United States was also involved in South Vietnam. So in Laos, those princes who were on the left-hand sided with the Laotian military leader, Kong Le. He did not favor Laos to choose one side or the other. He seized Laos and neutralized Laos into a neutral country and that neutralization lead to the pro-Communist faction inviting the North Vietnamese to come to Laos and take advantage of going through Laos into South Vietnam.

"BOYS BETWEEN THE AGES OF 13 AND MEN UNDER THE AGE OF 60 HAVE TO JOIN THE MILITARY SERVICES - NO EXCEPTION."

When Americans saw that North Vietnam was using Laos' land to send food, water, and soldiers into South Vietnam and Cambodia to fight they wouldn't have an easy time defending South Vietnam and Cambodia. For this reason, the Americans started to negotiate with the Laotians.

So, the North Vietnamese used Laos territory. They used Laos to transport their military supplies into South Vietnam so they can conduct their war in South Vietnam. Laos was spending time in being neutral. This led the United States to turn to the Hmong and the Laotian government to help with the United States to attack those supply lines and to attack the North Vietnamese troops. Ever since that time, all of us can see if we fight with or help the Americans win South Vietnam. So all of us became soldiers to help the Americans and shoot wherever they started shooting. When they needed help, the Americans wanted us to help.

The Hmong and the Laotians learned that the United States had won World War I and also World War II, so we believed that siding with the United States would lead us to win the Vietnam War. So we sided with the United States. Everyone helped America when the CIA came. They helped the Hmong to become soldiers for the Americans and they named us SGU that stands for Special Guerilla Unit. They named us this to become soldiers to them. Knife, gun, money, food, and clothes were provided and support for us to be their soldiers for that time.

The CIA came to Laos and required the Hmong and Laotians to join the United States to fight the war. The military supplied uniforms, clothes, and food. Boys between the ages of 13 and men under the age of 60 have to join the military services— no exception, but the end turned out that the dream the Hmong had was not achieved and the Hmong or the United States did not win the war. Between 1972-73, America lost the war in Vietnam. Then America began to leave, and all of us lost the war the same as the Americans did too.

In late 1970's...1972-73, the United States withdrew troops out of South Vietnam back to the United States and also their assistants from Laos. The Hmong did not get help from the United States and the result was the Hmong lost the war with the communists.

Then the Hmong who lived in Laos moved out into Thailand. The Hmong continued to fight from 1972-

"...WE HAVE HAPPINESS WHEN WE GOT TO THIS COUNTRY; WE DON'T HAVE ANY MORE WARS, AND WE GOT OUT OF THE FIGHTING AND DEATH."

73, after the United States withdrew from South Vietnam, until 1975 when Laos fell into the hands of the communists and also Cambodia. Then the Hmong escaped from Laos into Thailand, and in Thailand, there was food in the refugee camps set up by the United Nations. Then the United Nations came to buy some land for the Hmong to live. The Hmong won't have any places to go. They are like fishes in a pond, and if the water dries up the fish in the pond die. So that's why they all came to help take the Hmong out during the times of 1976. The United Nations had a commission for refugees to purchase land from the government and built camps, houses for the refugees to live in. Leaders in the United States, France, Canada, Australia— they knew that the Hmong would be without life if they would not allow them to come to other world countries. If they were to be left in the camps it would just be like fish in the pond. When the pond dries up, those fish would be dead. The Hmong were rescued by Western countries so that they would have a better life and have a future. The Americans were the first to come and take all of us out. That's why all the Hmong and Laotians came to the United States. Then France came too, but they didn't get as many people. Australia came too, but they got less people than France did. China came last, and they only got 80 to 200 people to their land. The majority of the Hmong came to the United States. The United States had decided to accept the Hmong to come to this country, and the United States was the first country to come to the camp to interview refugees and to allow refugees to resettle in the United States. The French also did the same thing—interview the Hmong refugees and accept many of them into their country, and then came the Australians...also accepting a lot of refugees into Australia, and then the Chinese came last and they interviewed and accepted about 80 families into China. Canada also accepted many families into Canada.

The ones that came to the United States....all of us are the ones that don't know how to write or speak English, but we just came cause we had no place to live and the Americans accepted us to the United States. When we came here the world was very new and beautiful to us. We have many friends. We live in the United States, and it is a whole new place. We don't know how to speak in their language and don't know how to read, and that makes life hard—not like we lived in our world. Life in the United States is totally opposite of life in Laos. We don't speak the language, we don't have the skills to make a living in this country. Life in Laos is more simple. We have a lot of depression and pressure that just makes life very difficult for middle age and older people, who could not learn, who could not speak the language, who could not find jobs. But aside from that, we have happiness that we got to this country; we don't have any more wars, and we got out of the fighting and death. Everything else we still have problems, and we still have concerns. Only one thing, we're just concerned about is there is no fighting in this country. We are being spared from the war, and we don't have to fight. There is no fighting. Everyone will be safe because there is no fighting like in Laos.

Nhia Blia Xiong and his family migrated to the United States and then moved to Schofield, Wisconsin. Nhia emphasized the importance of getting a good education with his children. Nhia Blia Xiong made many trips back to Laos. He passed away in September of 2002.

Pa Toua Xiong

Trained as a telegrapher, Xiong worked in Thailand. He also received training in weapons and worked with communications with commandos. He served for six years there before returning to Laos in 1975.

Were you drafted?

No, at the time all of Vietnam was at war, since the North was invading the South. There was no war in Laos, but one way of getting to the South was going through Laos, where we lived. So when fighting between the U.S. and North Vietnam started, we were asked to fight alongside the U.S. We then decided to fight because we knew this war wasn't going to be over very fast, and we knew that if it continued, then there would never be peace for us.

What were the base camps like?

Yeah, we had a lot of training. The big camp that us Hmongs were in was located in Long Chiang. Here we were prepared to attack the enemy, and I was at this camp for about a year, from 1969 to 1970. After that I finished my training as a telegrapher for the army and then after this I was transferred to Thailand, but still I'm a telegrapher. This time it was for the commandos. Commandos are special people that are dropped by plane to a certain area and take that area before the army gets there. Anyways, I was trained in Thailand for 3 months, still as a telegrapher, and I was trained to fight some more. Also, I had to learn how to use the machine gun with both sides, the right and the left, because there is a difference between the U.S. and Vietnam's weapons. So it was very beneficial to know that. After I finished training in Thailand, I went back to Laos and stayed there till 1975.

"THERE WAS NO WAR IN LAOS, BUT ONE WAY OF GETTING TO THE SOUTH WAS GOING THROUGH LAOS, WHERE WE LIVED..."

Did you fight against the Viet Cong? Describe them.

Yes, and it was pretty scary because they hated the people who served with the CIA. So if they cannot capture the Americans, then they go for you because you are on the American side, and a lot of people were captured after 1975. This was the reason we had to escape to the jungle. Many leaders, commanders, and soldiers of ours were caught and put in jail. We never knew if they survived or not, but we brought our guns, and while in the jungle, we still fought the communist Vietnamese by ourselves.

Can you describe what an average day was like in the war?

It was a very dangerous situation because the enemy was not only Vietnamese. They were combined with the Laotian people and some of the Hmong. Also, the war was getting bigger and the North had the help of the Soviet Union who were supplying everything. I believe in 1971 to 1973 a lot of Chinese people came and joined with communist to fight against us. We are just a small group of people fighting against a large group, but the Americans have jets and airplanes. The enemy during the day was scared because of the planes and jets we have, but at night they attack. It is very scary at night, especially if you are in the front line; again the most dangerous part is the night. When they come at night they carry bombs, guns, and knives, and they kill anything they see. They also use the knife, which we never use. That was also scary.

> *"I'LL NEVER FORGET IT. IT IS VERY HARD TO FORGET ABOUT THE WAR, AND IT'S OVER THIRTY YEARS NOW."*

Explain an experience that you had?

During my stay in the army, 1969 to 1975, about 6 years, I was involved with a lot of fighting. I was in the front most of the time and saw many people get killed, injured, and dying. But I was lucky that I didn't get injured or died. This was mainly because I stayed in the middle and was well protected because I had to call back to base.

Did you use helicopters to get around? Explain the experience?

We didn't really get to be in the helicopters because at that time it was mainly there to supply us with food and army needs. Also, when we captured an enemy, the helicopters took him away.

Were drugs a big problem in Vietnam?

It wasn't really a bad thing, since there was a rule in the army, and many didn't really break the rules. They didn't do crazy things, but I saw lots of people smoking and gambling. The front line though wasn't able to do this since if you have fun and games then it's easy for the enemy to come and kill you.

How was the relationship between the Hmong and the American soldiers?

It was no problem. The American soldiers and our American commanders treated us in a kind of... it's not friendly, but we know that being a soldier you have to be disciplined. Also, the rules in the army are different from the laws we obey everyday. There we have to do it and we have to respect them, but there really wasn't any problem.

What was the hardest part about being in the war?

The difficult thing was that the Vietnamese army was bigger in size, and we had a small group. Yet we had enough equipment and still fought to protect ourselves, but when the Americans totally withdraw we have nothing to support us, like airplanes and supplies. Also, Laos became communist and then had to isolate. Then finally, we lost.

Will you ever be able to forget the war?

I'll never forget it. It is very hard to forget about the war, and it's over thirty years now.

Do you think that if the U.S. tried they could have won?

No, because the government is smarter but communist at this time was stronger. It was Soviet Union, China, and North Vietnam against the south and the U.S. So I think that it is hard to win this war even if they didn't withdraw. They are smart to withdraw though and at that time we had no idea. So we thought why? Why did they go and run away? So then the communist came for us. Now though I see why the U.S. withdrew, but the good thing is that I'm still alive and made it here.

Did you make lasting friendship? Do you still see them?
Well, I don't really see any of them here, but I still do remember some faces and names. Yet I never saw any of them here. It's a very large country and I have no clue where they could be. But there are many.

Do you have any one moment you'll never forget?
This is one thing that you'll never forget because it is such a big part of your life. Even though you have a new life here, you still once in a while wonder and think about it. The war itself is unforgettable.

"THE WAR ITSELF IS UNFORGETTABLE."

Is there anything you want to say to the younger generation about war?
I want to mention that you don't know how hard our life back in our homeland was, and the one thing is that we were very poor. We had to fight and see many of our loved ones die and get killed. The past was terrible. We hope that the children we have and of others stay in school and get a good education. This is the key to having a bright future. Right now people cannot be without education. We hope that you young guys keep at education and not play a lot. Don't spend your time in gangs and do bad things. This is something we don't want to see. Also you as a Hmong have many loved ones still back in Laos and Thailand and one day we hope that we can go back to help them. We as parents see education as one of the highest goals. In this country we have great technology and it is very modern, yet some kids don't value it and don't care about their future. We want to see our kids have a better life than we did. I remember when I was young, I wanted a sandal, and so I asked my parents. They say they have no money and so I cry because I need them. Also as I grew and went on to higher education, my parents didn't have any money to send me. Here in America there is a lot of help with that, but back then in my homeland it was all parents. Then I wasn't lucky because my father was killed in the war, which complicated things. I cried when I couldn't continue because I love education, but there was no one to help me. I'll never forget it.

Did you have anything else to say?
I had six brothers. One died of sickness and one died returning back to camp. He was killed by the enemy. Another younger brother was captured, but then in 1984 or 1985, he escaped. After that he was captured again and was sent back to Laos. Then after 1987, he escaped again to a camp in Thailand. At this time immigration to the U.S. was limited, and he was sent back to Laos. So I still have a brother in Thailand. I have three brothers here with me and also two sisters.

Pa Toua Xiong was able to emigrate to America and is now involved in the Hmong Association.

Interviewed by Lee Xiong and Vong Lee

Xeng Xiong

Xeng Xiong was recruited to the army at the age of 13 and worked with communications. Later he served as a combat soldier before leaving his country for the United States.

Could you please start by telling us maybe about how you were recruited into the war?
Well, since the war was happening in Laos, I have some Hmong friends who recruited me into the army. During that time I was still going to school. I was around 13 years old when I was recruited for the army.

How old were you then?
I was 13.

What was the hardest part about being in the war and going away?
Well in Laos, the most difficult thing was facing things like monsoons and the rainy season. The jungle had too much mud. A truck or a car could not go into the forest. The United States helped by dropping off supplies and food, but the most difficult thing we faced was the fighting where a lot of people got killed. We did not have transportation at the same time, so we could not move to the headquarters, and many of the soldiers died. They were just buried in the jungle. During the fighting, we had no food and no water and no supplies, so we struggled with so many things.

Did you have contact with many Americans while you were fighting in the war?
I stayed with my brother, and he was the one who operated the radio, talking to the Americans and also the B-52s. We worked closely with the headquarters too.

Can you describe what an average day was like during the war?
I think that the average day was spent sending supplies to the army, and the company stayed close to a position where we could closely watch the communist soldiers of Vietnam. Each day you can hear the bombs explode, and you still hear the explosion of rifle shots everywhere.

Were you worried about the safety of your family while you were in the war?
We do not have safety rules, and we did not have anything to control that much of the family. They can hide by themselves, and they can escape to and from the fighting position or the fighting area. We knew that there was safety for the family from the government of General Vang Pao. He helped talk to the planes so they can get people to different places. When the Communists were getting closer, they have

to move the soldiers and their families before the Communists got too close. Sometimes the Communists just came right away so we never knew about that. It just happened. They used their big guns and rifle as well as explosives that blow things up

Is there one particular experience that stands out in your mind about the war?

I helped the SPN to help my brother to carry the wood burner and the radio equipment to the front line. I carried an M-16 and the explosives, and I was on the front line watching the Vietnamese coming. We would throw the explosives at the enemy. We have to watch the front line during the daytime and nighttime. If the Communists came, we could see them. We can help decide if we have to prepare for precaution. The mission we performed during the Vietnam War was between the south and the north. They were fighting each other, so the United States

"WE RESCUED A LOT OF AIR-PLANE PILOTS FROM 1961 TO 1973."

sent soldiers to South Vietnam. The border of South Vietnam and North Vietnam was very narrow in the north. They are not able to pass over the border. The Communists just passed the border by going through Laos to the south. The Vietnamese were sending their troops and their supplies to South Vietnam, so the CIA involved the Hmong people more than any other Laos minority in Laos because the Hmong opposed the Communists going to South Vietnam. So we are the ones that held the stronghold ,and sometimes the United States fighter pilots got shot down so we can rescue them. The pilots that were shot down and captured would have been shot by the North Vietnamese. We rescued a lot of airplane pilots from 1961 to 1973.

Was there a lot of emotional or physical stress?

I did not have that, but I did see other Hmong men that got wounded from the fighting. They would be depressed. They have many difficulties getting a good life in this country because of their physical problems. They are not able to do some types of jobs in this country. Many medical problems continue to be painful and when they go to see the doctor, the doctor doesn't know how to treat the patient. A whole lot of people got depressed and stressed. I work at the Hmong Association, so I deal with lots of people who have those issues. Sometimes other people keep on crying, and they do not have other members to help them so they suffer. Some still keep talking and asking me when they are sleeping they still have nightmares. They see the killing and fighting back in Laos.

Did you have any family members that were killed?

My two uncles' sons were killed after 1975, so we cannot stay with the Communists. We had to keep fighting until it was over. We lost seven relatives during the war.

What do you know about the United States pulling out of the country?

We did know because it was announced. We knew that before the United States withdrew their troops, so we were ready. We considered that our country would fall to the Communists, so all the civilians and their soldiers discussed what was going on and that the United States had withdrawn their troops.

How did you feel when General Vang Pao was leaving the country?

Lots of people feel very bad that our country would be falling to the Communists. He first announced to the Hmong people and Laotian people, and they cried during that time because he's the main leader that ruled in Laos for fifteen years. A lot of people cried, and they felt sad for him. After he left the country, the Communists took over, and they lied to the people. They took important people into the re-education camps, so that's why the people weren't able to stay in Laos. They felt separated so they just kept on fighting during that time. Lots of people, even their young teenagers, have emotional pain in their minds because of General Vang Pao leaving the country. There was a lot of chaos during that time.

Do you feel that most Americans understand that relationship between the Hmong and the United States CIA?

We are not sure that the United States and the CIA had a good relationship with the Hmong people because they went into the army to support the United States. We fought bravely during that time, so they know we had a good relationship with the United States. Since the country became communist, the United States allowed the Hmong to risk their own people since 1975. Most Hmong people kept fighting quickly to prevent the Communists from getting close to the American headquarters or other American Airlines. We prevented something from happening to the American people and we took care of them. General Vang Pao still sent Hmong troops to South Vietnam to help the United States army there. We helped the United States a lot. The relationship between the United States and Hmong continues.

Do you have a message for young people today about being Hmong?

Well, I do not have a message for the young, but I have a message from the elderly and the other people who still have the idea or considering of how to be Hmong. They should be proud of being able to learn the language and being a part of the Hmong culture. But the young are asking me about how to be a good Hmong.

Do you have anything else you would like to tell us about the war?

I turned 14 or 15 when the United States withdrew their troops from Southeast Asia. During that time we think that the Communists will obey the treaty, and the regulations the United States, the Soviet Union, China, and France signed. They should obey their rules, but since they took over they did not obey the treaty. We obeyed the treaty but the Communists just increased the number of soldiers and they came to control our country. All the major army officers and the professors and students got arrested because the Communists complained that they fought against them because we helped the United States. We helped the United States to defeat them, so they pretty much hate the Hmong people. They say that the Hmong people would be their number one enemy today because we helped the United States. We have about 40 or 45 major leaders that went to the camps, so they didn't come back until recently. In this situation, we can-

not identify how the leaders survived. Sometimes they took them into the camps and they taught them Communist ideas. Then sometimes they just used buried hand grenades in the jungle so people living in the jungle would detonate them, and all the people got killed. They would say that the Americans left those explosives in the ground, and they killed the people. Then they would tell us to support them so they can fight against the United States. They just kept teaching like that.

When the Hmong come to the United States, they weren't able to speak English so they could not find the job. It was difficult because they wanted to help their family. They needed food and they needed money to support their family. Public assistance can only do so much. So that's why a lot of people commit suicide. We want to tell people to understand that the situations are difficult for the refugees who settle in this country. They do not have the experience in life like other people in the world. Most of the people from Laos have a farming background. Most do not have the experience in working in a factory. So when they came here to this country, everything was new in their lives. They do not have an idea of what kind of job they can do. They don't know how to read the directions, but if someone can tell orally they are able to do the job.

> *"I HEARD THAT SOME PEOPLE GOT KILLED AND LEFT THE YOUNG IN THE JUNGLE AND THE YOUNGER CHILDREN STAYED WITH THE DEAD BODY FOR MANY DAYS."*

When did you come to America?
I came here September 11, 1978.

Could you talk about how you got from Southeast Asia to the United States?
I'll tell you how I went from the jungle to a village in Thailand. General Vang Pao put out a directive to leave the country, and many of the civilians in the population suffered and died because they didn't know what to do. We did not trust each other, and when the Communists came and took over, they spread the word to help them fight the United States and kick out the United States CIA. Some people got involved with the Communists. We cannot believe each other because the whole situation was different, so I wanted to escape to Thailand. I cannot tell my brother or my father because they might spread the word to other people that I was leaving to Thailand. Then the Communists will order their soldiers to catch me, so we cannot tell anyone. I had a plan to go to Thailand. We cannot trust anyone during that time, so the situation was very difficult and we just keep fighting, and we helped the family get together.

During 1975 to 1977, I left Laos because we didn't have any support from other countries. We do not have wood to burn, food to eat, education, clothing and other supplies. I escaped to Thailand by myself. I could not tell my family. I came with my friends. During that time we still were sending radio messages. We carried a radio, and we were still talking with the American CIA in Bangkok during that time. We carried those, and we were hiding in the jungle. We stayed hiding in the jungle before we came to Thailand. We came to the Mekong River. We do not have anything to cross the Mekong River, so we just grabbed some bamboo from the jungle, and we floated across the Mekong River. We came to Thailand. At that time they have some people that stayed at the border and robbed the people who were trying to cross. Since I came to Thailand, we did not feel that any other country will help or support the resistance back in Laos. I still have family back in Laos. What can we do? If we came to the United States, I will miss my family. So my brother-in-law cannot do anything. He cannot support or provide anything, so he said if we won, then we can go back to Laos. But my brother-in-law told him that if you send us back into another region, we will not have any support. We do not have any money, so what can we do? It is better to stay here in Thailand or in the U.S. That's why they just take my brother in law and came to this country first. Then I stayed there for over a year before I get an interview. After the interview was done, I got married. Then we came to this country. It was a long way and a long story. I heard that some people got killed and left the young in the jungle and the younger children stayed with the dead body for many days. Some situations like that were very sad.

Why did you leave the children and go?
They were all killed. The fathers died, and there was no one to take care of them. They left their kids in the jungle on the way because the Communist soldiers killed the adults. Some were killed, and some escaped. When they were left behind, they often stayed on the Lao border for six months. They would find food from the village, and they would steal food from the people who do farming and leave their food in their house when they went to farm. They would sneak into the house and grab the food, and they survived for six months. They were able to cross the Mekong River to Thailand.

Xeng Xiong is employed by the Wausau Area Hmong Mutual Association.

PRISONERS OF WAR

D.C. EVEREST AREA SCHOOLS

POW's in Vietnam

The North Vietnamese between 1961 and 1973 imprisoned well over 600 men. These courageous men suffered unfathomably cruel treatment in the protection of their fellow soldiers and most importantly, their country. We were very fortunate to have had the privilege of interviewing Mr. Don Heiliger, a Wisconsin resident who, as a captain, was shot down over Hanoi. Heiliger was imprisoned for six long years in the Hanoi Hilton and graciously shared his story with us. In addition to Mr. Heiliger, we confronted much tribulation with the pursuing of United States Senator John McCain. Due to the senators hectic schedule we were unable to complete an interview, however, he was gracious to allow the use of excerpts from his book: Faith of My Fathers.

Heiliger and McCain are only two of many whom endured mistreatment and exploitation during their incarceration in Vietnam. The expression of their stories and those hereafter are published with intentions of educating the public and to impart proper feelings of gratitude and honor for all prisoners of war and those missing in action.

Don Heiliger

Don Heiliger was an F105 fighter/ bomber pilot who flew missions over North Vietnam in 1966 and 1967. He was shot down and imprisoned by the North Vietnamese. He was a resident of the "Hanoi Hilton." Following the Paris Peace Accords, he and the other POWs were released.

How did you become involved in the Vietnam War?

I was a career military officer in the United States Air Force. I came in the service in 1958 after graduating from the University of Wisconsin. I was a navigator for about four years and went to pilot training in 1964, graduated in 1965, and went to F-105 fighter training. I was assigned to Japan in fighters at Yakota Air Base which is right outside Tokyo. The Vietnam War was just breaking out at that time. As far as Air Force involvement, I was in Japan and did a nuclear alert in Korea every other week. The Vietnam War got more involved, and the USAF was short of fighter pilots. In 1966, I was assigned for sixty days to Takhli Air base in Thailand. All the F-105s flew out of Thailand, and we never flew any missions in South Vietnam—only flew missions over North Vietnam, primarily, and over Laos and the Ho Chi Minh trail. In 1966, I went down in April/May for temporary duty and flew thirty-three missions in the F-105D, a single seat version. I was again assigned back down in 1967, this time to Korat AB, Thailand, and flew special missions that time in the F-105F, the two-seated version. I had a back seater, Ben Pollard, a pilot who was previously an aerodynamics professor at the Air Force Academy. So then, like I did in '66, in '67 we were sent down, to fly for 179 days of temporary duty, half a year. I was on my eleventh mission that time so my total of missions was forty-four. So how did I become involved in the war? I was a professional officer, a professional pilot. Anytime, there is conflict such as Afghanistan or Persian Gulf, or whatever, we become involved because we are professional military people, and when we are called, we serve.

Could you describe a typical day in Vietnam?

Our job was to fly combat missions over mostly North Vietnam, sometimes Laos. In 1966, it was usually a flight of four F-105 aircraft in the flight. We would fly wingtip formation, find the target, and bomb it. In 1967, flying the two-seater F-105F, we would go in at night, just alone, with no other aircraft, to bomb the target. On each mission we would have to refuel inflight, usually once inbound to the target and once returning to our base. A typical day of flying in 1966, was to fly one or two missions a day, normally one, getting up at four in the morning and go plan your mission. By that time it was light out, and you were in your aircraft and take off as single aircraft and then join the other three in a four-ship formation. We flew in a four ship mission to the target. The same thing in '67 but we would always be flying at night, in a single aircraft alone. We would go and brief the day that we were flying, then go and sleep and wake up for the mission. We would fly the mission—about 4 to 5 hours—and then debrief the mission. Nine or ten hours right there, repeated all the time. Then go and have a drink at the officer's club. You would have a stand-down day, probably go out in the sun around the base.

What was it like to be a pilot and a navigator?

I taught navigation first. Fighter pilots are a bit arrogant. It's exhilarating to be a fighter pilot as you are your own boss up there. There is a several million dollar plane under you—such a sense of responsibility sitting in front, seeing nothing around you but air. As to bombing missions you are called upon to do, you are a professional, and you respond. The main thing is to do your job and get your bombs on the target. To be a pilot is the greatest job in the world, fighter pilot being the neatest. My choice when I left pilot training was to be a fighter pilot. I graduated number one in my class and that gave me the opportunity.

Could you describe some of your missions?

On arriving at the target, we would identify it. We would be at about 12,000 feet, and each aircraft would roll in at about a 30 to 45 degree dive angle and release the bombs at about 7,000 feet, pulling out at about 4,000 feet. We would release high enough to avoid some of the flak. We normally carried six 750 lb. bombs, and after release, we would head back to our base in Thailand. We had an internal Gatling gun with about a thousand rounds of 20mm which fired six thousand rounds a minute. On the way back to base, a forward air controller would often call us to use our gun against various targets over North Vietnam or Laos. To summarize, we carried six 750 lb bombs on a single ship, hit our target, head for home, probably refuel on the way home. If you were going to Vietnam, it was a long mission, five or six hours or more, by the time you got back to base.

Heiliger in front of F-105 at Takhi Air Base, Thailand 1966

In 1967, flying the two-seated version, we flew single ship, low-level missions, using radar to go up and down valleys. It was a terrain-avoidance radar on the 105 that showed you what was ahead, including hills and valleys. We would fly at about 750 to 1000 feet during the flight to avoid enemy radar. We would enter the bomb run about six hundred miles per hour, drop the bomb on target, and get out of there as best we could. We would get out over the Gulf of Tonkin, refuel, and go home.

Could you tell us about the mission when you were shot down?

We came in from the Gulf of Tonkin and were targeted against a railroad marshalling yard about thirty miles northeast of Hanoi. We were flying at about 900, feet and we locked on the target. Unfortunately, the enemy radar was locked on us all the way into the target. We were about ten seconds from bombs away, and I felt a little tug on the aircraft. Right away, caution lights went on. We got the bombs off. We knew we were in trouble. We started to climb. There is an old adage among pilots that in bail out, air above you isn't any good; you want air below you. My goal was to climb and get back to the Gulf of Tonkin in case we had to eject, which was about eighty miles away from the Gulf at this point. In the Gulf of Tonkin we had U.S. Navy ships—aircraft carriers, destroyers—and if you could get over the gulf and bail out, you had a good chance of being picked up. Ben and I watched the fire creeping forward. On our aircraft, battery power allowed us to talk by interphone. At 18,000 feet, Ben called that the flames were in his cockpit, and he ejected. I climbed about another five thousand feet and there was a flash fire in the radar console, and I had a choice of either burning up or getting out, so I ejected. You go through this many times in training. Basically you pull the handles on both sides of the seat which arms the system. Then you squeeze the triggers, and the canopy blows. Three hundreths of a second later you go out. One second after you leave the aircraft, there is an explosive charge that goes in your seat-belt buckle, kicking your seat away, leaving you floating in the air. The parachute will open automatically at 14,500 feet. But inasmuch as it was about 9 p.m. on a dark night – no moon – I elected to pull the rip cord immediately. Obviously it was a good chute. It was about a twenty-minute ride down. As I approached the ground, I could see that I was going to be landing in trees. The trees are tall, many 200 feet or higher, and going through the jungle canopy you crossed your legs and you go through trying to minimize your chance of injury. My parachute landed on one tree, and my life support equipment that was dangling about 50 feet below me landed in another. It was like a hammock, and I was in the center. You don't want to fool around in trees at night. I lost a couple of friends trying to free themselves in trees. I carried about 250 feet of let-down rope but decided it was better to wait until morning. I had all kinds of stuff on me in my survival vest. In my pockets were all kinds of equipment. I had a radio and a .38 revolver with ammo, water, candy bars, everything you could load in your pocket. But I was losing feeling in one leg due to the pressure and thought it would be better to hang in the parachute waiting until morning light. I gave my parachute a tug, and I cut myself loose. At that time my parachute gave way, and I came crashing to the ground. Obviously I wasn't that high, maybe eight to ten feet, and I got bruises on my knee and hurt a couple of ribs. Other than that, pretty good. So there I was on the ground about nine thirty, ten o'clock p.m. It was really dark now. There was an absence of light, and I had no idea where I was going, just wanted to get away.

How did the enemy capture you?

Single seat F-105D

I wasn't sure if I was in China or Vietnam. I bailed out right on the border, and it kind of depends on which way the winds were blowing on descent. I was hiding and little by little working my way to the top of a hill. Although I lost my survival equipment when I cut it lose the night before, I had many survival items with me. The map I was carrying showed me that I was about seventy miles from the coast, and my plan was the same as my plan when I was flying. Head for the coast, hill by hill, night by night, if I could. That was my only chance because I was too far north to be rescued—nobody had been rescued that far north. Again, I wasn't sure what side of the border I was on. I tried

©2002 D.C. Everest Area Schools Publications

my radio (I carried a couple of radios) but didn't pick up anything. About three-thirty or four the next afternoon, I heard the villagers coming up the hill. I hid the best I could behind a group of rocks, and one of the villagers saw me. I thought that maybe I could shoot it out. I had fifty rounds of ammo and there were about fifty or so of them. I would have to be a pretty good shot. Some of my friends said they would never be taken alive, but in this case I had no chance unless I could shoot everyone of them. So I gave myself up to them, breaking my gun to make it useless. They took everything off me and left me in my underwear and boots and walked me down the hill to their village. They actually treated me pretty good. They gave me rice and all the cigarettes I wanted. They asked me if I was hurt, and I indicated that I was, my ribs and knee, and they brought in a nurse with bandages. I was looking for sympathy. The villagers were curious, smiling and curious more than anything. Suddenly two Communist cadres showed up, the first uniformed people I had seen. They gathered this group of villagers together and had an electronic powered bullhorn. They put me in the center of the circle. The crowd was yelling and screaming and waving their weapons at me, and I thought they were about ready to lunge at me. Suddenly the entire crowd went silent—you could hear a pin drop. I looked around the circle, and there were 15 or so old ladies, no teeth, and they crossed themselves. I remembered that the French had been there for one hundred years bringing Christianity, and it appeared from their somber attitude that they were giving somebody the last rites. They put me back in the same room where just minutes before everyone was friendly. They threw me up against the wall, and two of the villagers with automatic weapons aimed them at me. I thought this was it. I said my prayers, and one thing I was upset about was that nobody would know where I was. We stayed like this for about 45 minutes and they didn't shoot. The only guy that could speak any English, and that was little, came up to me and said, "no die tonight, tomorrow." I wasn't too much happier about that, and I don't know if it was a joke or a gag, or if he was serious. (U.S. intelligence got word that rewards were being made to villagers for turning in captured pilots.) In the middle of the night, they gave me back my boots and marched me through the jungle. Morning came, at which time we were in a clearing and there was a jeep. We started our trek to Hanoi. I was happy to get out of that village. On the way to Hanoi, about half way the next day, they opened up the back of the jeep and put a life raft in, and on the

Don climbing aboard his F-105 in 1967

life raft was Ben, my backseater. He was pretty delirious as he had hurt his back very badly landing. Upon arriving in Hanoi, they separated us, and I didn't see Ben him for about five years. That's how we got to Hanoi.

What was the POW camp like?
Let me begin by saying everybody was tortured. I won't go into the crude methods used; simple, not electric shock, etc. You are only required by the Geneva Convention and our code of conduct to give only name, rank, serial number, and date of birth. It appeared that the torturing was used to prove to you that they could get something out of you beyond those four items. For a more vivid description, you should

look at a video called "Return With Honor." We were also taught to take a second line of resistance. Before the pain got so severe that you lose your mental faculties, you tell them something, anything, to get rid of the pain. Of course you don't give them anything worthwhile. After some days of the torture, which was done at a special place in the "Hanoi Hilton" (Hoa Loa is the prison name), I was moved to another camp we called "The Zoo" (also in Hanoi). I was put into a cell with two other USAF captains. I must emphasize that during my entire captivity, we were never in a compound situation. That is, the only POWs we could talk with were the ones in our cell. We were never allowed out with men from another cell. It was NOT like *Hogan's Heroes* on TV. That cell was all you get. In the particular building we were in, there were twenty of us: four three man rooms, one four man room, and four single cells. You were not supposed to communicate with any other room. If we were caught communicating, we would be beaten or tortured. But we never stopped communicating. That was one of our main goals all the time we were there. We made sure that nobody was left isolated without communicating. But how do you talk? Talk under the door, but that is dangerous. So we used something that was developed in

Heiliger on a mission over North Vietnam in 1966

order to communicate—the tap code. It is a series of taps that we recognize as letters based on a matrix of five by five. One – One is an "a,", one – two is a "b," two – one is an "f," and so on, until you reach "z" which is five – five. As there are twenty-six letters, "c" and "k" were the same — one - three. We could tap through thick walls. You could tap with your fingers or your knuckles. The tap code was something everybody learned to do, and some of our guys were so good, they could tap as fast as I am talking. We also developed the finger code, similar to the mute code to use when we were in sight of somebody. It is hard to explain over the phone but an "a" is with your index finger straight up, etc.

We were seldom outside the cell. We were twenty-four hours a day in that cell. If we were lucky, we would get a few moments to bathe with water dipped out of a well. Other than that, we spent all of our time in the dark room with one light bulb which was always on. Our cell was about 8 x 10 feet. There were three wooden beds, raised off of the floor. Our normal clothing was shorts due to the heat. We also had a short sleeved shirt and a set of clothing that looked like thin pajamas. Shoes were sandals made from tires, with straps made from inner tubes.

How did we occupy our time? We talked with each other telling stories about ourselves or others. Remember that we averaged 30 years old at the time of shootdown, so we all had a full lifetime to talk about. We told each other about everything, our wives, everything, and so there was very little we didn't know about each other.

After a while, we all lost our "facades" which is how one projects the image of how you want people to think of you. When you are living with the same two people twenty four hours a day, and that's your whole life, and everything happens in that room, a little pot in the corner for your toilet, there is no reason for a façade. You are as natural as you can be and it's a kind of interesting experience. I could never do that again, never would want to; very few people would ever want to tear away the projection that you want to show.

How did they treat you at the camps?

As I said before, we weren't supposed to communicate. The first couple years the guards came on very hard, and somebody got hit at least once a day, whenever the guards felt like it. The first couple of years we got two meals a day consisting of three things, rice most of the time or bread, a soup which was very watery, a vegetable, i.e. cabbage, and also the substance for the soup. My favorite soups were either potato soup or pumpkin soup; I liked pumpkin soup because it was naturally sweet. Two meals a day, late in the morning and one around five o'clock. Later, after Ho Chi Minh, the Vietnamese leader died, meals improved to giving a morning snack in addition to the two meals. It could be a banana, sometimes it was a plate of sugar, now what do you do with a plate a sugar? We also got three cigarettes a day. I didn't smoke for a year and a half. Then in November 1968, after being there over a year, President Johnson announced the bombing halt and the start of peace talks. I thought that it would only be a couple of months before we would be released, so I started smoking. It was something to do. Four and half years later, I was hooked. That's how much longer I was there. We got three cigarettes a day. Later it was upped to six cigarettes a day.   During the first year we had two primary guards. One was a relatively mild guard, and if he hit you, it wasn't very hard, and he didn't discriminate like the other guard who had a chip on his shoulder. The first (or kinder guard) would allow us out and actually give us something to do like fertilizing the vegetable garden—the fertilizer being our own excrement. Sometimes we were outside to sweep, and we used that opportunity to sweep the tap code and put out information to the other POWs. Other than that, it was pretty boring. That is one reason why I started smoking, thirty minutes of your day—ten minutes per cigarette—could be used by smoking.

Two seat F-105F

What were your feelings when you were a POW?

I think that overall we were motivated by one goal, and that is survival. We always felt that if we lived long enough, we would come out. The biggest problem is "time." Time is the one thing they can't teach in survival training, the POW training. When you go into training for a POW situation, you know you are going to be there for only a few days. We were the longest group of POWs that has ever been held captive. World War II was about half the time max, with the exception of the Bataan group and even they were POWs for less time. You have to change your ideas toward time and everything you do. In the cell, there was a radio speaker and they would play the "Voice of Vietnam," and we called the announcer, "Hanoi Hanna." We would listen for the "news" (North Vietnamese style) hoping to pick up something that would encourage us. Somebody would get a letter from home, and we would try to make something out of a simple statement that "the weather was good." You never thought of long term.

You didn't plan long term things. You didn't think about a year from now. You think in days or weeks, maybe months. It was a way to keep your sanity. Even in combat, at least you knew the combat would end at the scheduled tour. In general, we were professional military, fighter pilots. We wanted to be there; that was our job. Being a POW is one of the sad parts of our job. When you are driving down the highway, there is always the sense that an accident is not going to happen to you—and the same thing about being shot down. It's not going to happen to you.

As for our feeling toward the Vietnam War today, I look at it as being only a small part of the cold war which happened after World War II for almost forty-five years. Vietnam was but one battle. Was it a good war or a bad war? In the end we won. The Berlin wall came down; the Communist system basically was destroyed except for a few remnants. Why was that? Because we were able to hold on militarily. Things like Vietnam proved that we were going to be there. That was the feeling we had. We got shot down, but we did what we thought was right. Our feelings about captivity? Of course we wanted to be home. I didn't get a letter for four years, very slow mail. My mother and father sent packages after two and a half years.

I am part of our organization of ex- POWs, chartered in Arizona, called "NAM-POWs, Inc." There are five hundred or so returned POWs. We maintain contact with one another, and I exchange email on a daily basis with many of them. We have an annual (or semi-annual) reunion.

What was it like for you when you knew you were going to be released?

The agreements were signed the 27th of January of 1973 to end the war. By the rules of the agreement, we were supposed to be told within five days. They waited till the very end of the fifth day. We were pretty sure it was the end, as we could hear fireworks and shouting in the streets surrounding the camp. We had been moved from the Hanoi Hilton area up to a camp near China about ten months before. The military started bombing right in the Hanoi area, and I think they wanted to put some of us in a safe zone, so they moved about 208 of us to that camp. We were told on January 20, 1973, that we were moving back to Hanoi, and we knew the end was near. We moved back to Hanoi, and for the first time, we actually got to have a compound situation in the camp. Until this time we never were allowed out of our cell (room) with another room.

That day, the 2nd of February, we were lined up and read the accords. They had cameramen ready to record our "jubilant" reactions, but after the reading of the Paris accords, we just walked back calmly into our room. We were excited inside, and we knew that we would be going home. We were happy.

It has been like having two lives, one before and one after—kind of strange. I was married before, and my wife divorced me while I was a POW. It was kind of strange seeing my three children 15, 13, and 11, after nearly six years. They were living in Ohio, and I had lived apart from them for so long.

Going back, we were in a three man room (cell) for the first year, and in the second and third year, I was in a room with nine men. Those conditions were terrible. We moved outside Hanoi for a short time, but soon they brought us all back into Hanoi into the "Hanoi Hilton." Those couple of years were probably the highlight of the POW experience, and even though we weren't allowed out with other rooms, there were fifty in our room. Remember, we never had any books or reading material. We discovered that the mind is a "hard disc" when you have nothing but your mind to use. It is a fantastic storehouse, and there are things that only in such a situation will you be able to pull out of that mind. In that large room, there was a tremendous education program going on. I learned French, Spanish, and German. We would create dictionaries of the languages out of the memories or those that remembered. We had no paper or pencil, let alone material to draw upon. So we used our minds and made paper out of the toilet paper given to us, ink out of various things like cigarette ashes or medicine, and pens out of any piece of wood we could find. There was always something going on regarding education. We made playing cards. We exercised for two to three hours every morning, and I could go on and on.

How were you treated?

I think the group of POWs is looked at somewhat in awe, and I don't think that is good. We are no different than anybody else. We are not super heroes. I think anybody else can do the same thing. It is just that we in the military are very structured.

When we were released at the airport in Hanoi, we first flew to the Philippines, and there were 3,000 people waiting there at 11:00 o'clock at night. Every time we went anywhere, there were signs welcoming us. A lot of people wore bracelets with our names that had been purchased several years before our release. The treatment was good as opposed to those who came back from Vietnam, the regular soldiers. They were looked down at. People are starting to change now. Soldiers who serviced in Vietnam, Korea, all are starting to get some credit.

What impact did the POW experience have on your life after?

There was a chance there to know yourself better. We had nothing to do, and we all did a lot of soul searching. What kind of person are you? I was in a troubled marriage when I was shot down, and I thought at that time that if I got released, I will make changes.

But as time went on during captivity, I realized that there are certain things about me that are not good, and cer-

Upon his release, Don shakes hands with an American officer

tainly I could be better. But overall the question was, if I basically liked myself. Doesn't mean you can't be better. We can always be better. You don't want to change yourself to only please somebody else. Therefore, the one thing that I came away with was being happy with myself.

You know yourself a lot better when you return from that kind of experience. If you don't, there is something wrong with you. That's what I learned from the experience. Know yourself and satisfy yourself. One of the things that really helped us through was our mental preparation. We had things we could draw upon from our background. We found that it was vital to have something from your past to draw upon—especially something religious in my case.

When I returned from Vietnam, I stayed in the USAF and studied for two years at The George Washington University in Washington, D.C. and got my Masters Degree in International Relations (Latin American Studies). Then I married Cheryl, and from that point on, we have had an exciting time. We have traveled to other countries and have had a great lifestyle. I retired in 1985 after nearly 30 years of service in the U.S.A.F.

Following Vietnam, Heiliger earned a Master's Degree in Latin American Studies from The George Washington University. He is currently a Dane County Supervisor for the 35th District. Heiliger and his wife, Cheryl, have three sons, Don, Jr., Daniel and David.

Interviewed by Jenna Hazaert & Jenni Marcell

Honor, Valor, Courage, Pride
"You are not forgotten"

By Meghan Casta

"Mayday, mayday! We are going down! I repeat we are going down!" The right engine continued to sputter and the thick black smoke swallowed up the craft. The dense jungle floor disappeared into an abyss. Rapid altitude loss made my stomach plummet along with the descent of the helicopter. when suddenly the jungle reappeared. It was all I could see. The waves of branches unforgivingly ripped into the craft as they tossed us back and forth in an angry sea of green. A large piece of debris charged through the shatter resistant windshield; I was knocked unconscious.

Hours passed, maybe days... I had no idea.

I struggled to open my swollen eyes only to see about ten strange eyes staring straight back at me. My first instinct was to try and evade the inevitable capture, but attempts to move were excruciating. I must have broken both legs in the crash and who knows what else. Noticing I was still alive, they began to beat me over the head repeatedly. Coughing blood and fading in and out of consciousness, my angry captors 'paraded me in'...

I was their prize; I was an American.

*   *   *   *   *

(príz'ner) **of war**   *n. a member of the armed forces captured by the enemy during a war (POW)* A standard definition of the term gives little credit to America's POWs, what they've gone through and what many still go through. Those declared missing in action (MIAs) and/or taken prisoner by the enemy (POWs) during the Vietnam War distinguished themselves on their journey back home with their unyielding desire to *return with honor*. In order to understand the respect deservedly bestowed upon POWs/MIAs, one must thoroughly understand their epic tales... horridly gruesome, cultimately heroic, and true.

August 12, 1949, the Geneva Convention relative to the Treatment of Prisoners of War was adopted and entered into force in October of 1950. The Geneva Conventions marked an end to a three and a half month conference in Geneva, Switzerland, in which cruel punishment, torture and violence were outlawed in the capture of military prisoners (Office of the UN -# from bio); "North Vietnam was a signatory (Hubbell, p.58)." However, it was all too soon before the first American prisoner of war, naval aviator Lt. Everett Alvarez, was captured and it became apparent: the Vietnamese seemed to have no intentions in recognizing the previously mentioned Geneva resolutions (Rochester and Kiley, p.98). "Alvarez was downed after taking antiaircraft fire over the base at Hon Gay; after making an attempt to swim to safety he was discovered by a small boat and taken prisoner (Rochester and Kiley, p.88)." Although his initial treatment seemed tentative and new to his captors, they quickly be mastered the profession of torture- inflicting much pain both emotionally and physically upon hundreds of men. The conditions in which the prisoners were held in any of the eight main prisons surrounding Hanoi were horrid.

The Hoa Lo was the main prison, which later staged much propaganda and served as a welcome center for foreign visitors. The façade, including an interior courtyard with flowers, was no indication of atrocities within the prisoner holding areas (Sanders and Mock/ AFF). Upon entering the main gate and administration at Hoa Lo you could go straight through into the "Heartbreak" section of the prison or left into "New Guy Village." To the right was the corner known as "Little Vegas" – home of Calcutta, the Golden Nugget, Stardust, the Mint, Thunderbird, and the Desert Inn. The back one-third of the camp was sectioned off and known as "Camp Unity" which later would become a group holding place before release in '73. Prisons other than the Hilton included: the Zoo, Alcatraz, the Plantation, the Briarpatch etc. Bleak conditions were grotesquely mirrored throughout: "The place was filthy, full of cobwebs, enormous spiders—some measured nine inches across their backs!—cockroaches, rats and an overpowering stench (Hubbell, p.40)." The nature of the food provided by the North Vietnamese was cause for the majority of the prisoners to drop to unhealthy weights, induce vomiting, contract disease, and suffer from a multitude of malnutrition-related complications. One prisoner describes typical rations, "—animal hooves, chicken heads, slimy bits of vegetables, cold and rotten fish, unidentifiable chunks of meat covered with hair (Rochester and Kiley, p.90)."

Hygiene was another health concern due to infrequent bathing and improper medical treatment; the inability to properly clean a small cut or bite often led to serious infection. Medical treatment was inadequate and a farce. Not only were broken bones left unattended but wounds were left to rot:

> A medic showed up to look at Williams' and Cannon's wounds. Williams' fingers were intact, but the top of his right hand had been torn away, leaving a bloody thicket of bone splinters. The VC's field medical technique was typical of what we were to see; he turned his head, held his nose, and poured alcohol on their wounds. It wasn't enough. The wounds of both had begun to turn gangrenous. They insisted on eating separate from Strictland and me so as not to spoil our appetites. Blowflies had laid eggs in Cannon's back wound. Maggots fell out as he walked (PFC David Harker, Hubbell, p.448)."

The following are excerpts taken from United States Senator, John McCain's book- *Faith of My Fathers*. McCain was a naval aviator shot down October 26, 1967, over Hanoi on his 23rd bombing mission and was dragged into Desert Inn (NE corner of Hoa Lo)…

> —Prisoner of War—
> It was hard not to see how pleased the Vietnamese were to have captured an admiral's son, and I knew that my father's identity was directly related to my survival. Often during my hospital stay I received visits from high-ranking officials. Some observed me for a few minutes and then left without asking any questions. Others would converse idly with me, asking only a few innocuous questions. During one visit, I was told to meet with a visiting Cuban delegation. When I refused, they did not force the issue, either out of concern for my condition or because they were worried about what I might say. One evening, General Vo Ngyuen Giap, minister of defense and hero of Dien Bien Phu, paid me a visit. He stared at me wordlessly for a minute, then left.
> Bug arrived one day and had me listen to a tape of a POW denouncing America's involvement in the war. The POW was a Marine, a veteran who had flown in the Korean War. The vigor with which he criticized the United States surprised me. His language did not seem stilted, nor did his tone sound forced.

Bug told me he wanted me to make a similar statement. I told him I did not want to say such things.

He told me I shouldn't be afraid to speak openly about the war, that there was nothing to be ashamed of or to fear.

"I don't feel that way about the war," I replied, and was threatened for what seemed like the hundredth time with a warning that I would be denied an operation because of my "bad attitude."

In early December, they operated on my leg. The Vietnamese filmed the operation. I haven't a clue why. Regrettably, the operation wasn't much of a success. The doctors severed all ligaments on one side of my knee, which has never fully recovered. After the war, thanks to the work of a kind and talented physical therapist, my knee regained much of its mobility—enough, anyway, for me to return to flight status for a time. But today, when I am tired or when the weather is inclement, my knee stiffens in pain, and I pick up a trace of my old limp.

They decided to discharge me later that December. I had been in the hospital about six weeks. I was in bad shape. I had a high fever and suffered from dysentery. I had lost about fifty pounds and weighed barely a hundred. I was still in my chest cast, and my leg hurt like hell.

On the brighter side, at my request, the Vietnamese were taking me to another prison camp. Bug had entered my room one day and abruptly announced, "The doctors say you are not getting better."

The accusatory tone he used to relay this all too obvious diagnosis implies that I was somehow responsible for my condition and had deliberately tried to embarrass the Vietnamese medical establishment by refusing to recover.

"Put me with other Americans," I responded, "and I'll get better."

Bug said nothing in reply. He just looked at me briefly with the expression he used to convey his disdain for an inferior enemy, then withdrew from the room.

That evening I was blindfolded, placed in the back of a truck, and driven to a truck repair facility that had been converted into a prison a few years earlier. It was situated in what had once been the gardens of the mayor of Hanoi's official residence. The Americans held there called it "the Plantation."

To my great relief, I was placed in a cell in a building we called "the Gun Shed" with two other prisoners, both Air Force majors, George "Bud" Day and Norris Overly. I could have asked for no better companions. There has never been a doubt in my mind that Bud Day and Norris Overly saved my life. (p.199-200 Faith of My Fathers)

—Solitary—

It's an awful thing, solitary. It crushes your spirit and weakens your resistance more effectively than any other form of mistreatment. Having no one else to rely on, to share confidences with, to seek counsel from, you begin to doubt your judgment and your courage. But you eventually adjust to solitary, as you can to almost any hardship, by devising various methods to keep your mind off your troubles and greedily grasping any opportunity for human contact.

The first few weeks are the hardest. The onset of despair is immediate, and it is a formidable foe. You have to fight it with any means necessary, all the while trying to bridle the methods you devise to combat loneliness and prevent them from robbing your senses.

I tried to memorize the names of POWs, the names and personal details of guards and interrogators, and the details of my environment. I devised other memory games to keep my faculties sound. For days I tried to remember the names of all the pilots in my squadron and our sister squadron. I also prayed more often and more fervently than I ever had as a free man.

Many prisoners spent their hours exercising their minds by concentrating on an academic discipline or hobby they were proficient in. I knew men who mentally designed buildings and airplanes. I knew others who spent days and weeks working out complicated math formulas. I reconstructed from memory books and movies I had once enjoyed, I tried to compose books of my own, often acting out sequences in the quiet solitude of my cell. Anyone who had observed my amateur theatrics might have challenged the exercise's beneficial effect on my mental stability.

I had to carefully guard against my fantasies becoming so consuming that they took me permanently to a place in my mind from which I might fail to return. On several occasions I became terribly annoyed when a guard entered my cell to take me to the bath or to bring me food and disrupted some flight fantasy where the imagined comforts were so attractive that I could not easily bear to be deprived of them. Sadly, I knew of a few men in prison who had grown so content in their imaginary worlds that they preferred solitary confinement and turned down the offer of a roommate. Eventually, they stopped communication with the rest of us.

For long stretches of every day, I would watch the activities in camp through a crack in my door, grateful to witness any unusual or amusing moment that broke the usual monotony of prison administration. AS I began to settle into my routine, I came to appreciate the POW adage **"The days and hours are very long, but the weeks and months pass quickly."**

Solitary also put me in a pretty surly mood, and I would resist depression by hollering insults at my guars, resorting to the belligerence that I had relied on earlier in my life when obliged to suffer one indignity or another. Resisting, being uncooperative and general pain in the ass, proved, as it had in the past, to be a morale booster for me.

Hypochondria is a malady that commonly afflicts prisoners held in solitary confinement. A man becomes extremely conscious of his physical condition and can worry excessively over ailment that plagues him. After Bud and I were separated, I struggled to resist concern bordering on paranoia that my injuries and poor health would eventually prove mortal. (p. 206-208 Faith of My Fathers)

—Lanterns of Faith (continued)—

He told me the time had come for me to show gratitude to the Vietnamese people and sorrow for my war crimes. Knowing that I was in serious trouble and that nothing I did or said would make matters any worse, I replied:

"Fuck you."

"Why do you treat your guards disrespectfully?"

"Because they treat me like an animal."

Hearing this, Slopehead gave an order, and the guards lit into me. Shouting and laughing, they bashed me around the room, slamming their fists into my face and body, kicking and stomping me when I fell. Lying on the floor, bleeding, I heard Slopehead speak to the interpreter.

"Are you ready to confess your crimes?"

"No."

With that, the guards hauled me up and set me on the stool. They cinched rope around my biceps, anchored it behind my back, and then left the room. The tope hurt and restricted my circulation, but, again, they had not tied it as tightly as they had on others, and I knew I could tolerate it. I remained there for the rest of the night.

In the morning, three guards came in, removed the rope, and took me into an interrogation room, where the deputy camp commander, a dull-witted man we called "Frankenstein" for his bulging forehead and numerous facial warts, waited for me, When I refused his order to confess, I was dragged to the room behind my cell where some time later Ernie Brace would be held.

The room was empty of any furnishings save a waste bucket. I had no bedding or personal belongings. The room didn't have a door, only a louvered window large enough to pass through. I was kept there for four days.

At two-to-three-hour intervals, the guards returned to administer beatings. The intensity of the punishment varied from visit to visit depending on the enthusiasm and energy of the guards. Still, I felt they were being careful not to kill or permanently injure me. One guard would hold me while the others pounded away. Most blows were directed at my shoulders, chest, and stomach. Occasionally, when I had fallen to the floor, they kicked me in the head. They cracked several of my ribs and broke a couple of teeth. My bad right leg was swollen and hurt the most of any of my injuries. Weakened by beatings and dysentery, and with my right leg again nearly useless, I found it almost impossible to stand.

On the third night, I lay in my own blood and waste, so tired and hurt that I could not move. The Prick came in with two other guards, lifted me to my feet, and gave me the worst beating I had yet experienced. At one point he slammed his fist into my face and knocked me across the room toward the waste bucket. I fell on the bucket, hitting it with my left arm, and breaking it again. They left my lying on the floor, moaning from the stabbing pain in my refractured arm.

Despairing of any relief from pain and further torture, and fearing the close approach of my moment of dishonor, I tried to take my life. I doubt I really intended to kill myself. But I couldn't fight anymore, and I remember deciding that the last thing I could do to make them believe I was still resisting, that I wouldn't break, was to attempt suicide. Obviously, it wasn't an ideal plan, but it struck me at the time as reasonable.

Slowly, after several unsuccessful attempts, I managed to stand. I removed my shirt, upended the waste bucket, and stepped onto it, bracing myself against the wall with my good arm. With my right arm, I pushed my shirt through one of the upper shutters and back through a bottom shutter. As I looped it around my neck, the Prick saw the shirt through the window. He pulled me off the bucket and beat me. He called for an officer, who instructed the guards to post a constant watch on me. Later I made a second, even feebler attempt, but a guard saw me fumbling with the shutter, hauled me down, and beat me again. (p.242-243 Faith of My Fathers)

Sustaining multiple injuries during the crash of the A4 Skyhawk in addition to his initial battery and mistreatment, John McCain was, by far, the most critical upon arrival of all POWs. Many other inmates who saw McCain early on were uncertain as to how long he would survive in the 'less than civil' conditions of the prison. However, in a short period of time McCain mentally and physically overcame his injury and pulled forth as a leader amongst his comrades. Navy Lieutenant Commander John Sidney McCain was an American who was determined to resist his imprisonment and to honorably serve his country at all costs.

Throughout the era of conflict with Vietnam, well over 700 Americans were imprisoned, suffering privation and inhumane treatment. The most well known and documented of all prisons in Vietnam was in central Hanoi, the Hoa Lo- meaning *Fiery Furnace* in Vietnamese (Rochester and Kiley, p.88.) Built by the French for Vietnamese incarceration during the Indochina War (Ron Bliss,

Sanders and Mock/ AFF), Americans came to know Hoa Lo as the *Hanoi Hilton*. The Hilton and other surrounding prisons were institutions of brutality obscured by the North Vietnamese persistence to project themselves as humane and civilized captors. Refusing to treat wounds, prolonging dysentery, beatings, lashings, and stringing human bodies from the ceilings are actions which are far from civilized; barbaric would be more accurate a term. Cloaked with foreboding and feelings of malevolence, one would hesitantly enter one of many torture chambers in Hoa Lo. Devices used for inhumane persecution polluted the dim-lit concrete rooms. Meat hooks suspended from the ceilings, ropes, nylon straps, chains, and iron stocks were among many devices which the infamous interrogators and torturers delighted in and prisoners feared. The chief interrogator known as Rabbit, as well as fellow torture specialists including Pigeye (also known as Straps and Bars), Bug, Rat, Slopehead, Hack, Flea, etc. infected the prison system under command of Major Bai, whom POWs referred to as Cat.

> "Stockdale (Navy Commander James Stockdale imprisoned September 9th, 1965) would remember clearly the utter dispassion with which Pigeye approached his work. His eyes were entirely empty of expression. The man was medieval; a professional torturer, one who actually made a life's work of inflicting intolerable pain on other people. There was no humanity to see anywhere in his face, nor in the efficient way he went about his grisly work (Hubbell, p.147)."

Upon capture, a typical prisoner would sustain injury from severe beatings before their initial interrogation. Once the interrogation began, information was demanded as to the prisoner's name, rank, serial number, in addition to other information that seemed vital at the time. What were their orders? Where were they going, and who'd sent them, etc. The majority of the men taken prisoner honorably upheld the code of conduct even though it often cost them much more than broken bones. A method of torture simply referred to as 'the ropes' was an awful contortion of the human anatomy in which wrists and elbows were bound tightly together behind ones backs and then forced up and over to meet their head. Shoulders are popped from sockets, breathing is suffocated, and the pain- indescribable. After being left in the excruciating position for a period of time, usually until submission, the ropes were removed and the pain process worked entirely in reverse (summarized from Rochester and Kiley, p.148). Once the prisoners had submitted or 'broke' due to intolerable pain or the need for medical attention (The witholding of medical care became used as coercion for propaganda statements), they were made to 'confess their war crimes.' Routine 'anti-war' propaganda was forcibly collected from the prisoners and sent back to the states in efforts to con American government officials. False hopes were given to soldiers who "confessed" to committing war crimes by being offered release. Often times, statements of confession that were recorded were altered and falsified before they were sent out.

Despite the North Vietnamese attempts, American intelligence were uninfluenced by these recordings. On one such occasion the Vietnamese staged a propaganda hearing in which several media cameras were present. POW Lieutenant Stratton was photographed bowing almost hypnotically and the Americans began to conspire about Hanoi's brainwashing of its prisoners (Hubbell). This was the reaction Stratton had been striving for despite the Vietnamese's intentions of portraying kind and lenient treatment. Torture continued. On September 3rd the North Vietnamese President, Ho Chi Minh died leaving prison commander Bai (Cat) in charge of the prison system. No longer receiving commands from a higher seat, Commander Bai instituted a slightly more humane atmosphere for

American POWs yet the road to freedom was still off in the distance (Sanders and Mock/ AFF).

> On the very day Ho Chi Minh died Stockdale was again faced with merciless torture; having been caught communicating, Bug promised severe punishment to occur the following morning. Weakened and unsure he would be able to endure torture in order to protect the names of those he was communicating with he decided he'd rather die than suffer and submit. Using shards of glass, Stockdale proceeded to slash his wrists and extract about a quart of blood before his 'high-risk bluff' was discovered. Stockdale had succeeded in proving that he was not afraid to die in order to protect the code and his comrades (Summarized from Hubbell, p.513).

Stockdale, however, was not the first prisoner to resort to thoughts of suicide. Jerry Denton, shot down Sunday July 18, 1965, had thought of and even had a plan for ending his life if need be. "Denton was a devout Catholic and the option of suicide was not open to him. However, his position, which he was prepared to defend before the throne of Heaven, was that he would not have committed suicide, but fallen on the field of battle in defense of his country (Hubbell, p.63)." "The Zoo had become one of the most dismal prisons following a series of U.S. bombing attacks in the spring of 1967 (Rochester & Kiley, p.383)." Persistent mental and physical torture had escalated yet again. Efforts to escape lingered on the minds of many. Some of the more crafty escape attempts lasted for days and sometimes weeks while prisoners evaded recapture by surviving in the ruthless jungles of North Vietnam. Air Force Major George (Bud) Day made a heroic attempt lasting 14 days and nights before he fell less than a mile short of an American base camp (Summarized from Hubbell, p.334). A few years following Bud's escape in 1967 came another such attempt, the Dramesi-Atterbury escape. News of the ill-fated escape echoed through the walls of the prisons and from there on out security tightened and torture grew to excruciating new heights.

> "By nightfall on Sunday, May 11, the day Dramesi and Atterbury were returned to the Zoo, the place had become the closest thing to hell on earth many Americans were ever to know" … "The torture went on for months. Twenty-six men were taken. They were locked in hell cuffs and leg irons. They were beaten with fists and clubs. They were rope-tortured. But the primary instrument of torture now was the "fan belt," the rubber whip that was cut from an automobile tire. Using these, the Vietnamese literally flayed the hides off their American prisoners (Hubbell, p. 494-495)."

Why did so many endure these unimaginable tortures for so long? Why didn't they comply with 'camp regulations' and give the enemy what they demanded? "Honor to the code," was the simple answer, which at times baffled even those who adhered to it every blasphemous day of their incarceration.

Continued from John McCain, "Faith of My Fathers":

—-Lanterns of Faith—

Code of Conduct for American Prisoners of War:

I

      I am an American, fighting in the forces which guard my country and our way of life. I am prepared to give my life in their defense.

II

      I well never surrender of my own free will. If in command, I will never surrender the members of my command while they still have the means to resist.

III

      If I am captured, I will continue to resist by all means available. I will make every effort to escape and aid others to escape. I will accept neither parole nor special favors from the enemy.

IV

      If I become a prisoner of war, I will keep faith with my fellow prisoners. I will give no information or take part in any action which might be harmful to my comrades. If I am senior, I will take command. If not, I will obey the lawful orders of those appointed over me and will back them up in every way.

V

      When questioned, should I become a prisoner of war, I am required to give name, rank, service number, and the date of birth. I will evade answering further questions to the utmost of my ability. I will make no oral or written statements disloyal to my country and its allies or harmful to their cause.

VI

      I will never forget that I am an American, fighting for freedom, responsible for my actions, and dedicated to the principles which made my country free. I will trust in God and in the United States of America

      … Since the Vietnamese invested so much time and energy in coericing our cooperation, our fidelity to the code was almost constantly challenged. Yet its principles remained the most important allegiance of our lives (p.239-241 Faith of My Fathers)

      Honor to the Code was habitually thwarted by extreme torture, but the prisoners persevered. Communication was one stand they could make as a whole group; it qualified as "resistance" under section III of the Conduct Code. Communication among inmates, in every sense was forbidden and if discovered, cause for radical punishment. Again, in the honoring of the code, prisoners would defy authority at every chance. Each letter scribed in code was means for additional torture if discovered. Few letters written to loved ones in the states were eventually released and sent containing coded messages for military intelligence back home. The messages frequently relayed information on the enemy captors, where they were located, and the names, ranks, and conditions of fellow prisoners. Communication was necessary to keep one's sanity under such cruel conditions and means of doing so did not stop at written letters. Contact between the prisoners became an art form as intricate tapping systems were fabricated so that communication could exist without voice. Smitty Harris introduced the "AFLQV Code," originally used by Korean War POWs. "Harris had learned the system of code while attending survival training at Stead Force Air Base, Nevada (Hubbell, p.44)." The code system used a 25-letter alphabet arranged in rows and columns. The letter K was left out and substituted with the letter C. "Code" was tapped through walls, with broom sweeps in the courtyards, etc. The system became widespread and increasingly intricate with abbreviations and diverse methods of code transmission. As prisoners were transferred between buildings they would communicate in a series of coughs, sniffs and scratches which were camp symbols for each of the five rows and columns of code. Navy Cdr. James Mulligan conveys his relentless study of the code in order to enable himself to communicate, a precious commodity which he would later become quite skillful at:

> "I stayed awake most of the night engaged in arduous practice as I firmly implanted the new code in my mind … I was lonesome for human companionship. The eerie silence of complete solitude was an oppressive load that bore down on me mentally like a ton of bricks. I hated every second of it, but now I had a way out. I only needed to master the POW code, and I would have the ability to join the social structure again (Rochester and Kiley, p.104)."

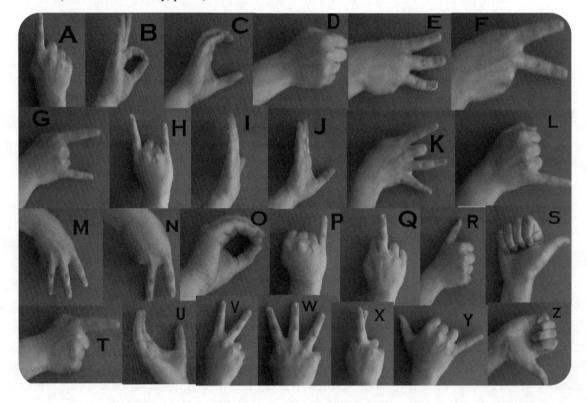

"Even though tap code was the primary means of POW communication (Hubbell, p.46)," tapping rhythms and mute codes were also used. An example of a tapping rhythm would be: "Shave and a haircut" with the response, "Two bits!" which meant the coast was clear— no answer, stop all communication. Occasionally the Vietnamese would intercept this tap and answer back with "Shave and a haircut" [rather than "Two bits"]… this also signified an abrupt halt of communication (Sanders & Mock / AFF). "Mary Had a Little Lamb" and "Pop Goes the Weasel" worked in a similar manor, the latter meaning danger (Rochester and Kiley p.113). Most patriotic tunes: "Anchors Aweigh," "It's a Grand 'Ol Flag," "God Bless America," etc. were signs of the 'all clear.' Mute codes, which slightly mimic American Sign Language, were also used as means of communication.(See above, referenced from Hubbell, p.16) The amount of conversation that was allowed within the newly convoluted tapping systems and mute code was phenomenal and aided the prisoners immensely. Inmates would "tap up" a neighboring cell and converse for hours. Many strong friendships were established this way and it was said that in time, even moods were transferred through the walls in familiarized styles of tapping (Sanders and Mock/AFF).

The passing of time, though camouflaged and accelerated by prisoners' abilities to communicate was still a battle which threatened to conquer many. Morale would rise and fall, unsteady like Wall Street— bleak one moment and hopeful the next.

The death of Ho Chi Minh in the fall of 1969 was the beginning of the end of the POW proverb: …"The days and hours are very long, but the weeks and months pass quickly". On November 21, 1970, an unprecedented event marked the acknowledgement of American prisoners by the United States and came to be known as the Sontay Raid. Although the raid, led by Colonel Arthur "Bull" Simon did not free any prisoners from captivation, it was a colossal success. The prisoners had been acknowledged; they were not forgotten. Anxieties of the North Vietnamese grew in response to the raid; if American troops had gotten in and out of a prison virtually unscathed, it was possible that the prisoners weren't as "secure" as they had previously thought.

The prison authorities now believed that captivity would be more easily controlled if the prisoners were kept in close proximity; a slow migration eventually gathered the majority of prisoners to what was known as Camp Unity in Hoa Lo. A large group of prisoners, now united, was multiplied in strength. Senior Ranking Officers (SRO) promoted comraderie and John Flynn assumed command. The Fourth Allied POW Wing was formally established. The Wing became "Return with Honor." To that end, policy was made and disseminated (Hubbell, p.547).

The new policy, including complete amnesty was abided by the greater part. Much of the strategy further strengthened the Code of Conduct: hand over nothing to the enemy, let them relish in no pleasantries of domination, etc. "Committees were established for such purposes as medical and sanitation procedures, athletics, and communications and escape (Hubbell, p.548)." Many prisoners 'taught classes'- physics, mathematics, architecture, etc. to fellow prisoners. "Camp Unity almost literally hummed with communications (Hubbell, p.550)."

Tribulations had not yet come to and end, however. Cruelties and beatings continued well into 1971some severe (Hubbell, p.574.) The only thing that held the prisoners together in the last years and months was the fact that they were together; they now relied on one another more than ever. "Peace delegations had reached a stalemate and it wasn't until a series of night strikes lit up the skies and shook the prisons' walls that peace negotiations continued between Kissinger and Le Duc Tho (Rochester and Kiley, p.569)." The peace agreements were signed in Paris, January of 1973; however, it wasn't until February or March that the prisoners first gained sight. "It was all so unbelievable—the long nightmare of the war and captivity was ending; people actually were coming back from the grave (Hubbell, p.598)."

Inundated by the initial hysteria, the prisoners rejoiced; some cried, some screamed, and others prayed. The prisoners were to leave in three increments relative to their detainment. They were bussed first to Gia Lam airport in Hanoi where they were met by three silver Air Force C-141 Jetstars. The prisoners filed out as professional and proud as they could, remembering turns and halts as though they had learned them the day before. After boarding the C-141s they were flown to Clark Air Base in the Phillipines where it had been decided that Jerry Denton would be the first to speak on behalf of those who would follow him down the steps out of the Jetstar. He walked assuredly to the microphone; his words were concise, and impacting: *"We are honored to have had the opportunity to serve our country under difficult circumstances. We are profoundly grateful to our Commander-in-Chief and to our Nation for this day..."* He paused. He began again, his voice now quivering as he proudly stated, *"God Bless America..."* The crowd roared.

"Nearly 600 fellow POWs were released and came home, ending the longest incarceration in U.S. history (Straight Talk America)."

The mass return quieted the public in regards to the ongoing POW/MIA situation, but interest was soon fueled once again. Hearings taking place following the return of several hundred prisoners allowed the public's accusation to be expressed: "the government had ill-handled POW cases." Declassification of all documents containing information on prisoners of war and missing in action (MIAs) was a concern, which was addressed early on. However, it wasn't until 1991 that "the McCain Bill was enacted, requiring the Department of Defense to disclose any record, live-sighting report, or other information in its custody that related to the location, treatment, or condition of any Vietnam-era POW/MIA (Ref.InfoPaper 90, Part I-Introduction)." In a conversation Nixon had with Defense Secretary Richardson, he made himself clear in his expectations of the handling of further POW/MIA returns: "I will conclude by saying that we must regain the respect for our military or we will end up with a country and a world which is unsafe. We must also remember and honor our POWs, our MIAs, all of those killed or all of those who served honorably in Vietnam" The President continued to suggest that Congress "give them all the Medal of Honor (1. Mem/Con.)"

The Congressional Medal of Honor is indeed the highest and most prestigious of all congressional and military honors, yet no single inanimate object could ever sum up the honor, valor, courage and pride that were instilled in the fine gentlemen imprisoned for so many years in North Vietnam. Many were eager to leave the country in order serve, defend, and protect freedom in every way possible. When they wereimprisoned, suffering the depths of human pain through years of inhumane treatment by their ruthless captors, they ceased to retract their statements.

> "Before the big iron gates slammed behind me as I entered the Hanoi prison, I found
> it hard to think of freedom as something other than an abstraction that's used in songs,
> Supreme Court debates and political speeches. In this respect I was like many
> Americans today who take freedom for granted. By the time I was released to come

home nearly eight years later, freedom had long since ceased to be an abstraction to me…" Vice Admiral James B. Stockdale*

As Jerry Denton humbly summarized when he stepped off the plane at Clark, imprisonment was another form of dutiful service to their country. America stands for freedom; it fought for its own in days past and continues to fight for others.

Never in the field of human conflict was so much owed by so many to so few.

~ Winston Churchill ~

Let every nation know, whether it wishes us well or ill, that we shall pay any price, bear any burden, meet any hardship, support any friend, oppose any foe to assure the survival and the success of liberty.

—John F. Kennedy Inaugural Address Washington, D.C. January 20, 1961

Bibliography

1. Citation: folder "Feb. 15, 1973 – Nixon, Defense Secretary Elliot Richardson," Box 1, National Security Advisor. Memoranda of Conversations, Gerald R. Ford Libraries
   http://www.ford.utexas.edu/library/exhibits/vietnam/730215b.htm

2. Hubbell, John G, *P.O.W.: a definitive history of the American prisoner-of-war experience in Vietnam, 1964-1973*

3. McCain, John Sidney *Faith of My Fathers* (Excerpts taken courtesy of U.S. Senator John McCain) Need copyright info or publishing co. rights?

4. Office of the United Nations High Commissioner for Human Rights Geneva, Switzerland ©copyright 199 2000 http://www.unchr.ch/html/menu3/b/91.htm

5. Reference Information Paper 90- Records Relating to American Prisoners of War and Missing in Action from the Vietnam War Era, 1960-1994 (Part I – Introduction)
   http://www.merrimack.nara.gov/publications/rip/90/

6. Rochester, Suart I., 1945- *Honor Bound: American Prisoners of War in Southeast Asia* 1961-1973

7. Sanders and Mock/ American Film Foundation Production ©MMI AFF/AOG, USAFA. Tom Hanks Presents—Return With Honor

8. Straight Talk America / United States Senator John McCain's Biography
   http://www.straighttalkamerica.com/About/AboutList.cfm?c=1

Meghan is a senior at D.C. Everest and is planning on attending the University of Wisconsin- Madison in the fall of 2003 where she hopes to major in pre-med. Meghan thoroughly enjoyed being on the Oral Histories Staff and thanks all of the veterans, teachers, and her parents for their continual support and encouragement throughout the production of the book.

STUDENT ESSAYS

Student Writing

D.C. Everest Senior High students researched various topics related to the Vietnam War in their advanced American History Seminar course. They then worked in conjunction with their English class to write poems, essays, and journals. Over 60 students submitted their writings to both history and English teachers. Students edited and revised their writing. Twenty-four students writings were selected for this project by a panel of English and social studies teachers. * The following stories, journals and poems are to be considered historical fiction. (The exception to this is "Letters from Beyond.")

Special Note: Students were instructed on giving credit to their sources.
It is the hope of the Project Coordinator that they have accurately provided credit.

African-American Involvement in Vietnam

By Ben Lindsay

Vietnam is a seemingly insignificant country in Southeast Asia, over 9000 miles away from the U.S. However, in the mid-sixties and early seventies, it was the focal point of the most controversial international combat in which the United States has ever been involved. From the beginning the legitimacy of the war was widely disputed, and there was much prejudice on both sides of the issue. Although the army was the most integrated government institution at that time, many black soldiers found that Uncle Sam was just as prejudiced as the society that created him.

The military did not discriminate against the African-Americans by excluding them, but by placing a disproportionate number of them in high risk positions. From the moment that a black soldier entered basic training, there was a 12 percent greater chance that he would be sent into combat and become a statistical fatality then his white counterpart would. In 1965, African-Americans made up 10 percent of the military, but they made up almost 24 percent of the fatalities of the war. (Starr, p.12) Because of poor education or low test scores, many black men were shuttled right into combat and were passed up for positions that required higher training.

The roots of discrimination were grounded in all aspects of the military and were deeply embedded in the draft board. The Selective Service System was responsible for deciding who was to be called-up for military duty. However, in 1967, blacks made up only 1.3 percent of the draft board members, and many states did not have any black members. (Sellman) Needless to say, the disproportionate number of black men who were drafted was never brought into question.

In 1966 Robert McNamara, the Secretary of Defense under Kennedy and Johnson, proposed Project 100,000 to make it possible for men who had not met the military's physical or mental standards to be recruited for duty. This was promoted as a Great Society program. Politicians claimed that this was a method to "rehabilitate subterranean poor" by teaching them new skills and self-confidence. Despite this project's attempts to "eradicate poverty" and give underprivileged youths a second chance, a few years later it was disclosed that *41 percent* of the men sent to Vietnam were black. (Starr,p.13) The causality rate for Project 100,000 men was more than double the normal rate of casualties. However noble Project 100,000 was in theory, it was in reality merely a means to ship minorities into combat, most without adequate experience.

In training, military leadership supported stereotypes in order to incite the soldiers to fight against the communists. As rifleman Haywood Kirkland states, "Right away they told us not to call them Vietnamese. Call everybody gooks, dinks." (Starr, p. 18) This was an attempt to make them seem less than human and make the bloodshed morally defensible. Also, whenever there were combat simulations in training, it was common knowledge that a minority would play the role of the aggressor. The frustration over this discrimination is vocalized by Reginald Edwards, in the book <u>Bloods</u>.

> "When I first got there (Camp Pendleton), they was doing Cuban stuff. Cuba was the aggressor. It was easy to do Cuba because you had a lot of Mexicans. You could always let them be Castro. We even had Cuban targets. Targets you shoot at. So then they changed the silhouettes to Vietnamese. Everything like Vietnam. Getting people ready for Vietnam. Getting people ready for the little gooks. And, of course, if there were Hawaiians or Asian - Americans in the unit, they played the roles of aggressors in the war games."(p.7)

This was looked at as merely a fact by many black and Hispanic people who had grown used to such stereotypes and prejudice from so many different angles.

On the front lines in Vietnam much racial prejudice was set aside temporarily in order to accom-

plish a mission. Many veterans mentioned that in times of crisis, they had to be able to count on their friends, no matter black or white. However, it was impossible to overlook all of the hatred that some had in their hearts. As one G.I. said, "Our company was one-third Black Panther, one-third KKK, and the rest of us ducked a lot."
(MacPherson,p. 554)

In the rear, however, racial tensions escalated between races, especially after the assassination of Martin Luther King Jr. Confederate flags were flown at base camps and crosses were burned. These things were done as a direct insult to the black soldiers. Because of this, there was a dramatic rise in the black nationalist movement in Vietnam. Both sides were becoming more and more segregated and resentful of each other, and countless times this led to violence.

Also, there was increased encouragement during this time period from black leaders for African-Americans to boycott the war. Muhammad Ali, for example, said, "No Viet Cong ever called me nigger," in response to why he refused to fight. (MacPherson, p.554) This soon became the slogan for the black anti-war movement. The general feeling of this movement was that black people should not be fighting to free another people when in their own country, they were not free. This influence greatly affected the willingness of black soldiers to enter into combat.

Throughout this time, the communists were targeting the black soldiers with heavy propaganda. Hanoi Helen, a communist radio announcer, would constantly assault black soldiers with fabrications like this one that aired the day after the death of Dr. King.

"Soul brothers, go home. Whitey raping your mothers and your daughters, burning down your homes. What are you here for? This is not your war. The war is a trick of the capitalist empire to get rid of blacks." (Terry, p. 43)

After hearing and seeing such propaganda daily, many black people started to believe what they were told. After the death of Martin Luther King, many black soldiers believed that the government was really out to destroy them. All this affected the way that soldiers of different races interacted and encouraged the spread of groups such as the Black Panther Party.

After they returned to the States, many veterans could not cope with the effects of the violence, drug abuse, racism and other horrible things that they saw in Vietnam. In many cases, a few days after men were fighting in combat, they would be back in the U.S., and were expected to act as normal citizen. The anti-war movement also made the veterans feel dishonored, betrayed, and unneeded. This all impacted the black veterans more than their white counterparts. Not only did they have to deal with these factors, but they also had to deal with the original racism and poverty. Many black men resorted to using violence to express their feelings, and there were a huge number of veterans involved in the black nationalist movement. In fact, black veterans were twice as likely to be incarcerated as white veterans. Many times, they were locked away instead of being rehabilitated.

These heroic African-American soldiers of the Vietnam War were the first to be forgotten in the generation that no one wanted to remember. It is appalling that while this country fought for democracy, so many were discriminated against. This prejudice contradicts all the concepts of liberty and equality that the United States was founded upon. All men and women, of any race, who answered the call and served the United States in a time of war deserve the respect of the American people, regardless of opinions about the war. These veterans were not responsible for the war; they were willing to give their lives for their country and an idea that they believed in. That is admirable, in and of itself.

Bibliography

MacPherson, Myra. <u>Long Time Passing</u>. Doubleday & Company, Inc. Garden City, New York, 1984.

Terry, Wallace. <u>Bloods</u>. New York: Random House Inc, 1984.

Sellman, James Clyde. Africana.com. "Politics and the Vietnam War." <http://www.africana.com/utilities/content.html?&../cgi-bin/banner.pl?banner=black world&../articles/tt_933.htm> May, 2000.

Starr, Jerold. <u>Unit Four, Who Fought for the U.S</u>. Center for Social Studies Education, 1988.

Ben Lindsay is currently a Senior at D.C. Everest Senior High School. Where he is president of student council. Ben also participates in choir, drama, clown troupe, cross country, and a lot of church activities.

Agent Orange: The "Cursed Cure"

By Sara Wanless

The Vietnam War was unlike any other war. The United States fought against an unseen enemy, the Vietcong. The Vietcong used guerrilla tactics while fighting. They would appear out of nowhere, ambush U.S. troops, and then quietly disappear into the jungles or through the network of tunnels they had underground. The U.S. faced a problem: "since this war brought on new enemies and new fighting tactics, the United States government needed a new breed of weaponry" (Agent Orange History). The solution to this problem was Agent Orange, a defoliant that would kill the thick jungle-like vegetation and destroy the enemy's cover, thus saving many American lives. Unfortunately, the U.S. did not know that this "solution" would have deadly consequences. The chemical defoliant Agent Orange had a negative impact on U.S. troops, the Vietnamese people, and the Vietnam environment.

Agent Orange was the code name for a defoliant developed for the military. It was named for the orange band that was used to mark the drums it was stored in. Agent Orange was a mixture of two chemicals known as 2, 4, D and 2, 4, 5, T. This product was mixed with kerosene or diesel fuel and dispersed by aircraft, vehicles, boats and hand spraying. The purpose of Agent Orange was to deny the enemy cover and concealment in dense terrain by defoliating trees and shrubbery where the enemy could hide. This protected American and allied troops from ambush or other undetected movement of the enemy.

The effects of Agent Orange can be associated with its prominent use during the Vietnam War. An estimated nineteen million gallons of Agent Orange were used in South Vietnam during the war. "The U.S. has dumped [on South Vietnam] a quantity of toxic chemical amounting to six pounds per person, including women and children" (U.S. Senator Gaylord Nelson). About twelve percent of South Vietnam's land was sprayed with Agent Orange and other chemical defoliants (Bender 107). Agent Orange contained only a small amount of dioxin, an extremely poisonous chemical, but the small amounts accumulated. By the time the spraying had ended an estimated 240 pounds of dioxin had been dumped on Vietnam. One must put these numbers into perspective. It would take only a few ounces of dioxin in the water supply of a major city like New York to destroy its entire population (Paxman 193).

U.S. troops and South Vietnamese people came into contact with Agent Orange daily. On over forty occasions aircraft dumped Agent Orange directly onto American military bases. American troops and South Vietnamese people operating in sprayed areas breathed in the dioxin, drank and bathed in contaminated water, and ate contaminated food. However, American soldiers and South Vietnamese people were not concerned about this because they were told that the chemicals, "are not harmful to people, animals, soil or water" (Paxman 192).

Agent Orange did have many positive effects. The defoliant removed vegetation along roads, canals, railroads, and other transportation arteries to make ambushes more difficult. American officers claim that in some places the ambush rate dropped by ninety percent after the chemical defoliants had been sprayed (Paxman 192). Agent Orange removed the jungle canopy from the network of roads and trails used for moving men and supplies, making it easier to attack from the air. Large forests that hid sanctuaries and bases were cleared, forcing the North Vietnamese and Vietcong to move or risk discovery and attack. "Agent Orange…was every soldier's friend. It cleared the dense jungles exposing the lurking enemy. Thick foliage along the riverbanks was sprayed away in an effort to flush out enemy snipers waiting for their prey" (Living With The Legacy…).

Although Agent Orange had many positive effects during the Vietnam War, these were greatly outweighed by the negative effects it caused to U.S. troops, Vietnamese people, and the Vietnam environment. Agent Orange had a severely negative effect on U.S. troops. There is a "pattern of recurring health problems among veterans who reported having been exposed to a great deal of chemical defoliants" (Bender 159). U.S. troops were exposed daily to Agent Orange and other chemical defoliants. They drank and washed themselves in contaminated water, they ate contaminated foods, and they breathed in contaminated air. One man said, "In the 11 months I was in Vietnam, I had often washed in the waters into which Agent Orange had drained and had eaten local produce which I suspect had been doused with the chemical" (Agent Orange…American Family). Many soldiers in Vietnam who had exposure to Agent Orange began to experience headaches, dizziness, rashes, and stomach cramps. They assumed that these symptoms were caused by the heat.

Only years after Vietnam veterans returned to the states did they hear of reports that Agent Orange had been the cause of their health problems. However, the negative effects of Agent Orange were only beginning to surface; "the soldier's friend had transformed into the veteran's enemy" (Living With…Agent Orange). Thousands of veterans began to come forward with similar ailments they believed had been caused by their exposure to Agent Orange. The veterans suffered from skin rashes, numbness of their limbs, kidney and liver dysfunctions, elevated blood pressure, rapid weight loss, headaches, and various forms of cancer, among other things.

Experiments have been conducted on animals to simulate the negative side effects of Agent Orange on human beings. Dr. Wilbur McNulty fed minute doses of dioxin, a poisonous chemical found in Agent Orange, to rhesus monkeys; he watched as they "grew very quiet, lost their appetite, began losing weight, became thinner and weaker, and finally just laid down and died" (Wilcox 15). Evidence of the unpleasant health effects of dioxin on laboratory animals includes cancer, skin disease, liver disorders, the suppression of the immune system functioning, and birth defects in offspring.

Many Vietnam veterans fathered children with severe birth defects after they returned from Vietnam. Men returning from Vietnam looked forward to starting families, but the children that these veterans fathered had kidney abnormalities, enlarged livers, enlarged heads, club feet, missing or abnormal fingers and toes, and missing, abnormal, or displaced body parts. Jerry Strait served with the 101st Airborne Division in the heavily sprayed A Shau Valley. His daughter was born with one hemisphere of her brain missing (Wilcox 15). Furthermore, Sudden Infant Death Syndrome (SIDS) was four times more likely to kill children of veterans exposed to Agent Orange (Vancil).

In addition to U.S. troops, the Vietnamese people were also negatively affected by the spraying of Agent Orange. Between 800,000 and 1,000,000 Vietnamese suffer health problems linked to Agent Orange, including cancer and birth defects. Agent Orange infiltrated the Vietnamese food supply by contaminating soil, silt, and plants that are ingested by fish and animals. The Vietnamese then consumed those fish and animals as well as contaminated dairy products.

Perhaps the most gruesome legacy of Agent Orange for the Vietnamese was found in their hospitals. In Tay Minh Hospital, in the area most heavily sprayed with Agent Orange, the number of stillborn babies doubled after the spraying of chemical defoliants during the war (Paxman 193). At the Phu Sanh Gynecological Hospital in Saigon, "…some babies have three arms; some have two bodies above the waist; one stillborn has a face on its abdomen; another's umbilical cord protrudes like some Cyclops's eye from the center of its forehead" (Bender 107). Said Vu Trong, director of War Crimes Investigation, "We have over 50,000 children that have been born with horrific deformities…" (The Legacy of Agent Orange). John Pilger stated, "Occasionally I saw these [genetically deformed] children in contaminated villages in the Mekong Delta, and whenever I asked about them, people pointed to the sky; one man scratched in the dust a good likeness of a bulbous C-130 aircraft, spraying" (The Legacy of Agent Orange).

Not only were Vietnamese people negatively affected by Agent Orange, the Vietnam environment was also greatly affected. "Agent Orange had a spectacular effect, sending vegetation on a rapid and self-destructive growing binge. Plants would explode, leaving a surrealistic landscape where weeds had grown into bushes and where trees, bowed down by the weight of their fruit, would lie rotting in the foul-smelling jungle. The Vietnamese peasants called the areas affected by Agent Orange 'the land of the dead'" (Paxman 192). "In some regions it may be several decades before natural vegetation reappears" (Wilcox 12).

The Vietnamese people depend on their crops for income and survival. The use of Agent Orange affected Vietnamese agriculture during the Vietnam War and continues to affect it today. Much of the area sprayed in Vietnam included mountainsides, and the defoliation left these areas exposed. When the monsoon rains hit, no vegetation remained to hold the water, enabling the water to rush down the mountainsides and flood the farmland in the flat coastal areas below (Bender 107). This means that the farmers' crops and incomes are lost. Vietnam has no money to detoxify the land or resettle families; therefore thousands of people are forced to grow crops in contaminated soil and fish in contaminated streams.

For veterans and the Vietnamese people the use of Agent Orange during the Vietnam War not only caused health problems, but also destroyed the Vietnamese environment by contaminating soil, water, and wildlife. Agent Orange was thought to be the perfect solution to the increasing problem of guerrilla warfare. "Defoliation was meant to save lives by denying the enemy cover. But for many the 'cure' was worse than the problem" (Spletstoser).

Bibliography

"Agent Orange And The Anguish Of An American Family." The New York Times Magazine. Sunday, August 24, 1986. The New York Times Company, 1986. October 16, 2001. <http://www.wellesley.edu/Polisci/wj/Vietnam/Readings/zumwalt.htm>

"Agent Orange History." The Agent Orange Files. October 11, 2001. <http://www.aofiles.net/main/aohistory.html>

Agent Orange Website. October 11, 2001. <http://www.lewispublishing.com/orange.htm>

Bender, David and Bruno Leone. The Vietnam War: Opposing Viewpoints. San Diego, CA: Greenhaven Press, 1990.

Buckingham Jr., William A., Ph.D. "Operation Ranch Hand: Herbicides in Southeast Asia." October 16, 2001. <http://cpcug.org/user/billb/ranchhand/ranchhand.html>

Chandrasekaran, Rajiv. "War's Toxic Legacy Lingers in Vietnam." Washington Post. Tuesday, April 18, 2000: AO1.

"Living With The Legacy Of Agent Orange." VFW Magazine. August, 1998. October 21, 2001. <http://www.vfw.org/magazine/aug98/20.shtml>

Mercier, Rick. "Deadly Defoliant Continues To Take A Toll." Special to The Japan Times. Friday, Novemtber 17, 2000.

Paxman, Jeremy and Robert Harris. A Higher Form of Killing. New York, NY: Hill and Wang, 1982.

Spletstoser, Tony. Defoliation. October 16, 2001. <http://www.thehistorynet.com/vietnam/articles/10963_text.htm>

"The Legacy of Agent Orange." October 21, 2001. <http://www.heureka.clara.net/gaia/orange.htm>

Vancil, L. Agent Orange. 1994. October 16, 2001. <http://www.vvvc.org/vvvc/agntor.htm>

"What is Agent Orange?" Homeopathy Online. October 11, 2001.
http://www.lyghtforce.com/HomeopathyOnline/issues/articles/ritchie_orange3.html

Wilcox, Fred and Jerold M. Starr. The Lessons of the Vietnam War: The Wounds of War
and The Process of Healing. 1988. (pages 12-17).

Xuan, Ian Stewart Lam. 1997. October 11, 2001. <http://vvof.org/article.htm>

*Sara Wanless is a junior at D. C. Everest
Senior High School. She participates in march-
ing band, piano lessons at the Wausau
Conservatory of Music, and church youth trips.
She plans on going into medicine somewhere
in Wisconsin.*

Agent Orange/Defoliation in the Vietnam War

By Ashley Zollpriester

Over 20 million gallons of a poison were sprayed over the people and the land of Vietnam. It is no wonder that a large number of people are being affected by it today. A defoliation program called Operation Ranch Hand was conducted by the US between 1962 and 1971. 15 different herbicides were shipped to and used in Vietnam during this time period. Defoliants and herbicides were sprayed in all four military zones of Vietnam, villages, inland forests near the demarcation zone, inland forests at the junction of borders of nearby countries, and mangrove forests. Twin-engine planes, helicopters, trucks, river boats, and backpacks were all used for spraying the defoliants. The object was to clear the areas around the perimeters of American base camps, landing zones, waterways, and communication lines of all the plant life that would have otherwise provided cover and food for the enemy. Very few herbicides were sprayed from 1962 to 1965. However, by 1971, more than 20 million gallons of herbicides were sprayed over six million acres with some areas being sprayed more than once. (There, 2) An area the size of Massachusetts was covered bt these detoliants.

Agent Orange was the most commonly used herbicide. It accounted for 80% of the herbicides used. The name comes from the large orange stripe on the 55 gallon drums in which Agent Orange was stored. Nearly 12 million gallons of Agent Orange was sprayed between January, 1965, and April, 1970. Of the three million people who served in the war, 100,000 were exposed to Agent Orange. However, many veterans believe the number is much larger.

At the time that the defoliants were being used, the people of Vietnam and the fighting, men on both sides had no idea what Agent Orange was and assumed that whatever was being sprayed was used to kill mosquitoes. In the 1970s, veterans began to believe that Agent Orange and other herbicides containing small amounts of the contaminant, dioxin, may have caused delayed health effects. Dioxin, a byproduct of Agent Orange, is one of the most toxic substances known. Any veteran operating in a sprayed area could have been contaminated in many ways: by drinking the water, eating the food, or inhaling the defoliants.

A large number of veterans have developed health problems since serving in Vietnam and believe they are caused by Agent Orange. Research indicates that there are excessive levels of dioxin in the blood of veterans who served in heavily sprayed regions of Vietnam. The spreading awareness of the world's most toxic man-made chemical, dioxin, has caused much frustration, outrage, and fear among the people who were exposed to it.

Studies by the Department of Veterans Affairs acknowledge that there is definite evidence linking type two diabetes and Agent Orange. Because of this, certain veterans are eligible for monthly compensations from the VA. The government expects to pay 63 million dollars in diabetes compensation over five years for 220,000 cases, says Terry Jemison, a VA spokesman in Washington, D.C. The VA also estimates that 9% of the 2.3 million Americans who served offshore or in Vietnam have diabetes. (Umbrigar, 1) Most of these people have no family history of the disease which supports the theory that Agent Orange caused it. Dave Polcyn, who served two years in the war, shares many veterans feelings about their diabetes when he says, "When you get diabetes, that's it. You're gonna die from diabetes. Eventually, I'll have complications." He recalled jumping into rivers there without a thought. "Sometimes I think I did my duty to my country, and now it's going to chop 15 to 20 years off my life. I don't want to feel sorry for myself, but 30 years later it comes back to bite me." (Umbrigar, 2)

Laboratory animals were given amounts of TCDD or dioxin, and it caused a variety of illnesses and death. Most studies suggest that the dioxin in Agent Orange and other herbicides is related to many types of cancer and other disorders. Dr. Wilbur McNulty fed minute doses of dioxin to rhesus monkeys. They grew very quiet, lost their appetite, began losing weight, became thinner and weaker, and eventually laid down and died. (Agent, 15)

Additionally, in a 1987 study, the VA found that former Marine ground troops who served in Vietnam have died of lung cancer and certain lymph cancers at a significantly higher rate than their colleagues who are not Vietnam veterans.

Diseases possibly related to Agent Orange and the other chemicals are a major problem not only in Americans but in the Vietnamese people. There are numerous cases of horribly deformed Vietnamese adults and children with twisted faces and limbs. Dr. Ton That Tung of Hanoi University and his colleagues have found that in 836 Vietnamese soldiers, who fought in the south where there was spraying, there was a miscarriage/premature birth rate of 15.3 percent. Also, 3.6% of all children fathered by the exposed soldiers suffered congenital birth defects. The surveyed children fathered by soldiers who fought in the north had no congenital birth defects. (Agent, 16)

Another study was done by Irva Hertz-Picciotto, a professor of epidemiology at the University of North Carolina at Chapel Hill. It showed a 70% higher risk of AML, a type of leukemia, for children whose parents served in Vietnam. (Possible, 1)

More than 100,000 veterans have filed health claims related to Agent Orange exposure. Hodgkin's disease, non-Hodgkin's lymphoma, and soft tissue sarcoma have all been linked to Agent Orange. Chronic skin rashes and diseases, respiratory problems, nerve disorders, impaired hearing and vision, violent headaches, loss of sex drive, many different types of cancer, and increased rates of stillbirths and birth may all be attributed to Agent Orange. The government, the Center for Disease Control and Prevention, the Air Force, and the National Institute for Occupational Safety and Health, along with many other organizations, state that they will continue to study, the health effects of Agent Orange exposure.

After the chemicals were sprayed, the land remained devastated. Jerry Strait, a Vietnam veteran remembers walking through areas where "The trees are leafless, rotting, and from a distance appear petrified. The ground is littered with decaying jungle birds; on the surface of a slow moving stream, clusters of dead fish shimmer like giant buttons." (Agent, 15) Strait developed cysts that clung to his back, legs, and arms, and experienced headaches, dizziness, rashes, and stomach cramps. The lush forests and jungles are now hundreds of miles of waist-high scrub brush. The soil is dead. A resident of Vietnam returned to his home and with terror said, "not a blade of grass survived... the trunks of toppled coconut trees protruded along the edges of ditches, leafless bamboo stems stood pointing up at the sky... There were no barking dogs, no bird's songs, not even the familiar chirping of insects." It will be many decades before the vegetation will improve and be replenished in many areas in Vietnam. (Agent, 12)

Today, there are many organizations that are designed to help veterans who are concerned about being exposed to defoliants used in Vietnam. The VA set up the Agent Orange Registry health examination program for Vietnam veterans who were concerned about long-term medical effects. The Veterans' Health Care Eligibility Reform Act of 1996, requires the VA to furnish hospital care and medical services and/or nursing home care to veterans exposed to herbicides. Many benefits and services are allowed for these people and their children if they have certain birth defects.

Agent Orange and other herbicides, which were sprayed throughout Vietnam to kill unwanted plants and remove leaves from trees, did much more damage to the people and vegetation involved than anticipated. Many people have illnesses and deformities because of the defoliation program. Much of the land in Vietnam is also destroyed. Even though the VA, the government, and other organizations are working hard to help the exposed veterans, this assistance does not come close to repairing the damages. A large number of veterans who fought for their country never imagined that -- though they lived through the war -- they would eventually die because of it.

Ashley Zollpriester is a junior at D.C. Everest Senior High School where she plays softball. Ashley also enjoys watersking and swimming, and is a member of her church youth group.

Artful Draft Dodgers of Vietnam

By Meredith Merrill

The draft during the Vietnam War changed the lives of many Americans. Fifty-three million Americans reached the age of eighteen, making them eligible for the draft, during the Vietnam War. Throughout the war many people became known as draft dodgers. Sixteen million men avoided this terrifying experience. Some men were lucky enough to have high lottery numbers. Other men, who qualified for the draft, often got out of it in one way or another. Men said they were homosexual, had sight and hearing problems, were physically impaired, had religious conflicts, or were college bound. Sixty percent of twenty-seven million men were able to escape the draft in various ways.

Countless Americans became draft dodgers during the war because they did not want to risk being killed in Vietnam. People made up many excuses to avoid the draft. In the book, *Hell No We Won't Go*, written by Sherry Gottlieb, there is an excerpt written by Chevy Chase. He explained what he did to avoid the draft. " I showed up at my physical examination acting like Soyce. Also, I'd been drinking strong coffee and I hadn't showered in three days, so I was just a teeming nervous wreck, sweaty and stinky. On top of that, I'd put a tube of hair grease in my hair..." He then went on to talk about the written examination he had to take. Men were faced with the decision of marking heterosexual or homosexual on a standard survey before their physical. It was almost sure that homosexual men would not serve in the army. These surveys had other questions such as "Have you ever wet the bed?" By marking "yes" to this type of question, the draft personnel felt the man could be homosexual even though he had marked heterosexual earlier. Those who checked "yes" to these kinds of questions often had to have a session with a shrink. There, they were questioned repeatedly about their sexuality. After their long session in the shrink's office, they often were exempted for being classified as a homosexual.

Other men dodged the draft by saying they were physically unable to go to war. Numerous men said they were visually impaired. In one case, a man borrowed his friend's glasses before his physical. These were the thickest glasses he had ever seen. He then proceeded to stumble around and knock into everything possible. When the doctor told him to read the standard eye chart he replied, "What eye chart?" After a rather long argument with the doctor, he was failed and informed that he couldn't physically fight in Vietnam. (Gottlieb, 147-148)

Other males said they could not pass the hearing tests so they wouldn't be able to hear the crucial sounds while in combat. According to Gottlieb, men had certain ways of preparing to fail these tests. One audiologist actually told a friend how to fail. He said, "What you have to do is: First, you hit the ear with about twice the frequency they test at--a very loud noise for a long time to dull the cells in the ear. Second, take a large dose of aspirin, the absolute minimum lethal dose ever taken divided by two--about twenty-four tablets--which also deadens your high frequencies."

With this, a man by the name of Frederik Hull, prepared to fail the hearing tests. About eight hours before his exam he took the aspirin. He also put his ear up to a stereo with a frequency generator. He had the devices to measure his response, and continued listening to the loud noise until his response was much lower than the flunking level. He went to the doctor and had to do the test twice. When questioned by the doctor, he said that, when he was little he was around some dynamite when it exploded, and his ears rang for a week. He got discharged and was never called back for retesting. His hearing recovered fully after one week. He told this technique to two other guys who also used it to get out of the draft.

In addition to having sight and hearing problems, men would say they had something wrong with their bodies. One man actually planned out a car accident so he could complain of backaches. He knew that the soft tissue injuries would not show up on the x-rays so there was no way they could prove him wrong. Later, he really did suffer from back pains and found out that the wreck had nearly killed him. When the draft board said he was still able to be in combat, he took the case to court. He had the police officers and hospital nurses testify and ended up winning the case. He nearly lost his life but was glad not to have to go to Vietnam.

Furthermore, people dodged the draft by moving to Canada or to other countries. It was illegal for males over the age of eighteen to move out of the country, but if they were still under eighteen, it was within the law. Many males took this to their advantage and moved abroad. They still had to register with a draft board, but this section of the board would be used only as a last resort. Also sons of overseas military personnel were able to avoid the draft by going to a foreign college until they were twenty-six years of age. The males in this draft category rarely were chosen to be drafted; many of them had already turned twenty-six, had a high lottery number, or were able to hold out until they were no longer needed. (Baskir, Strauss, 35)

There were still other ways men avoided the draft. A rather complicated method was claiming conscientious objection. This was a very extensive process because the male often needed numerous religious authorities confirming his claim. One hundred seventy-two thousand males qualified for this option, but in return had to work for at least two years in a low-paying community service job. Those who refused this service were charged with committing a federal crime and sent to prison. (Who Fought For the U.S. Unit 4)

Finally, the easiest way for men to avoid the draft was by going to college. The enrollment of men in colleges increased six to seven percent during the Vietnam War. If it looked as if the male was making steady progress towards his degree, he was "often deferred because of activity in study." (Who Fought For the U.S. Unit 4) For the men who had already gone through college and were still eligible for the draft, graduate schools became very popular. These schools enabled males to further resist the draft. By attending one of these schools, males continued their education until they reached the age of 26 and could no longer be drafted. (Baskir, Strauss, 32) Aside from the standard colleges and universities, divinity schools also became popular. The government thought students there were studying to become rabbis or priests, but the students were often there getting a degree in something as common as accounting.

Throughout the Vietnam era, many men became draft dodgers. They found numerous ways, within and outside of the law, to escape joining the war effort. Some males went to the extreme of staging a car accident or cutting off a limb, while others simply enrolled in college. Whatever their method, thousands of men were successful at it.

Bibliography

Baskir, Lawerence, Strauss, William, Chance and Circumstance. New York:Alfred A.
    Knopf, 1978.

Gottlieb, Sherry Gershon, Hell No We Won't Go. New York: Penguin Books USA Inc., 1991.

Starr, Jerold M. Who Fought For the U.S. Unit Four. Center for Social Studies Education, 1988.

Meredith Merrill will graduate from D.C. Everest High School in 2003. She is involved in clown troupe, chamber choir, Solo and Ensamble, is a captain of the swim team, and enjoys snowboarding. She plans on attending either St.Cloud or Winona University, majoring in social work.

Chaos

By Denise Zilch

A lone girl holds her dying father in her arms.
The horrid stench of blood fills the air.
Bullets whiz past homes
Screams of the dying penetrate the early morning mist.
The living dive under already dead bodies to escape the bloodshed.
A family almost suffocates.
Grenades explode in the ditches of the dying.
Villagers tear through the streets closely followed by soldiers.
A girl cries for her lost father

Bibliography

Hersh, Seymore M. My Lai 4: a report on the massacre and its aftermath. New York: Random House, 1970.

The Lessons of the Vietnam War; when War becomes a crime: the case of My Lai. Center of Social Studies Education, 1988.

Denise Zilch is a junior at D.C. Everest Senior High School. She is active in forensics, orchestra, National History Day, and highway clean-up with her church. Denise would like to become a professor of medieval times.

Diary of a Soldier

By Morgan Klarich

Dear Journal, 1956

I don't know how this can be happening. I'm 19 years old and one minute I'm playing cards and drinking with my friends, the next minute I'm fighting them with machine guns. One minute I'm going to my cousin's wedding and praying at shrines with them, the next minute I'm constructing traps in the jungles we grew up in to kill them. North Vietnam was where I was raised my entire life and now it's turning on me. Many of my friends and cousins have decided to fight with the South. But I represent Vietcong 100%! How could they do this?! They belong *here*. No one wants to fight this stupid war, but since we're being forced to, you might as well fight for the people you grew up with. My cousin Vien yelled at me the night before he left for the south that if I don't see the damage communism will do to Vietnam, and if I'm going to support it, then he will be glad to have me die by his hand. Communism is better than war! And if he's a traitor and turns his back on the rest of his family who are fighting as Vietcong, then *he* deserves to die by *my* hands! We grew up together! We're as close as brothers! Our fathers used to take us fishing together, and he wants to turn his back on me at a time like this?! He is from the North and should fight with the North! I feel my father's spirit with me all the time, but I wish he could give me some advice right now. I don't know what I'm doing. Does he think I'm doing the right thing? I just want him to be proud of me.

Yeu,
Ngoc Trinh

Dear Journal, 1960

This whole thing is totally out of control. Why doesn't the U.S just mind its own business?! As if Ngo Dinh Diem wasn't bad enough on his own, now he's got America's support and help! *He* is the one who is splitting our people, North and South, apart! This is *civil* war, but if those Americans want to make this into a *world* war, then so be it! But no matter how hard they try, the U.S, South Vietnam, and Diem won't be able to defeat *us*! I'm proud to be a guerilla and part of the NLF (National Liberation Front). Ho Chi Minh supporter all the way! I am willing to die for my North Vietnamese people!

Yeu,
Ngoc

Dear Journal, April 30, 1970

With Diem's execution in 1963, you would think the U.S would get its ass out of the war. But it just keeps coming back for more. The U.S is winding down the ground war now, but it has begun air raids and I hear it has about 190,000 troops in South 'Nam (1966). They're probably not even Americans. They've been training South Vietnamese soldiers to replace the U.S soldiers so that the little white boys can go home (1969). Well, I wish *I* could go home. But I don't *have* a home anymore! This once beautiful country has been destroyed. We have to dig tunnels in what were once beautiful gardens and forests. The Vietcong are killing more innocent civilians than we! And when our people aren't being bombed, their crops are poisoned and they die of starvation. My family and friends who haven't already died have gone and sided with the South because they really think they'll have a better chance. The South Vietnamese may think they're so ahead of the game by having their American friends, but we've got plenty of assistance from the Soviet Union and we're supplying our troops in the south through Cambodia. I bet the Tet Offensive (February, 1968) caught 'em off guard, ey? Ha Ha Ha!!! Yet the U.S troop commitment is still growing. Our commander was saying there are already 550,000 of them over here (1969).

Despite massive U.S military aid and heavy bombing, the South Vietnamese Thieu - lovers still can't defeat the Vietcong! We're on the rise! How stupid of our Southern people to trust in those dirty Americans! They can't even make up their minds who to support or whether they want to be in or out of this thing.

Yeu,

Ngoc

Dear Journal,

We have to be so careful now. We have a disadvantage in manpower and firepower so we have to avoid any direct engagements where we don't have numerical superiority. And we're not allowed to visit or have meals in the village homes anymore because those villages friendly to us are being bombed. What I wouldn't give for some steamed banana rice and some durian cakes right about now. When Vien and I were young, we used to sneak them from my mother all the time because we couldn't get enough. My mother was the best cook. I used to watch her when I was little as she would hunch over her big pot, stirring something that always smelled so good. She'd always let me have a taste and then ask me if it needed more spice. But it was always perfect. I haven't heard any word from my family in three months. They were probably all forced out of their homes and made refugees. All those refugees can't be good for the agriculture, and I've heard hundreds of thousands of refugees are dying of starvation. I'd hate to think that my family is part of that statistic.

Yeu,

Ngoc

Dear Journal,

Because of its weak leaders, Cambodia was easy to take over, and we've constructed roadways into South 'Nam. The Cambodians also gave us sanctuaries for retreats and to launch attacks. Impressive intelligence data has been collected in Cambodia, my commander was telling us. The Americans are finally catching on and are bombing the Ho Chi Minh trail in hopes of cutting the flow of men and material. Well, *that* isn't happening, but it is making things difficult for us, forcing us to commit significant amounts of manpower, weapons, and supplies in Laos to keep infiltration routes open. The Americans attacked roads and rail lines from China to North 'Nam to cut supply routes. But just last week the Chinese sent Cambodia's prince, Norodom Sihanouk, a yacht as a gift, down the Ho Chi Minh Trail (1968). Imagine that! A 60-ft yacht amidst bombing missions and everything. Stupid Americans! Ha Ha Ha!!! And then they thought dropping beer along the infiltration areas in southern Laos would slow us down (1969). Ha! Sorry guys, we like Budweiser but not *that* much! They can't kill us as fast as we can recruit replacements and send more troops down the H.M. Trail. They think that once we're cut off from our supplies and reinforcements, our number of men will decrease faster. But North Vietnamese Air Force pilots are gaining more experience by fighting American aircraft and have become quite skillful and aggressive antagonists, if I do say so myself. Sometimes you just gotta look real hard to find the good in things.

Yeu,

Ngoc

Dear Journal,   1970

Parrot's Beak has been the key Vietcong control center in South 'Nam and Kampong Saom has been a very convenient port for getting supplies. But now I'm hearing rumors that we are going to be relocated to Cambodia. Supposedly with the fall of Sihanouk, the U.S might be able to establish military presence in Western Cambodia. And so to prevent this, we have to move away from the border area and move deeper into Cambodia. Our commander said the new command center will be established in the city of Kracheh. Some are staying behind, so tonight we're gonna have a little going - way party. Beer…

girls… music…and… oh, yeah, the smell of dead bodies and smoke and burning trees. Some party, huh? It's times like this when I just can't stop thinking about all those times going to the dance bars with Vien and our boys to pick up girls. It's a good thing I never married one of those girls. I just can't imagine what Vien's wife is going through…fleeing through the woods and streams with their newborn baby girl, not knowing where he is or if he's even alive… crying herself to sleep every night. I would never want my girl going through that. And what about Vien? Never knowing if he will ever see his wife again or get to watch his daughter grow up! But out here you don't think about the future; you just try to make it through the day.

Yeu,
Ngoc

Dear Journal,   1972

No one can trust anyone these days. The Americans betrayed Thieu and now I don't feel so safe trusting the Cambodians. They're having their own problems with Pol Pot and the Khmer Rouge and Lon Nol; *he* was the one who invited the U.S to invade Cambodia! The Khmer Rouge themselves are a reaction against the brutality of U.S-backed Lon Nol. (1970-1975). So I don't see why the U.S and South Vietnam are fighting *against* communism. It seems the *non*-communists are the ones causing all the problems. And then there's the Pathet Lao. When is this going to end?! Just when you think it's going to quiet down, that jackass American president launches secret bombings on Cambodia (April 30, 1970). Some of the guys were saying he wants to keep it secret because not even his own country supports him because Cambodia is a neutral country, and it's just escalating and drawing out the war. Well, it's not like they weren't here *before*. South Vietnamese and U.S troops have been in Cambodia for a while now, spying, conducting sabotage missions and overflights. The Vietcong are not *invading* Cambodia. We thought that moving here would keep us safe because the Americans would never fight here because they know Cambodia's neutral. It has also made it easier to supply our troops in the South from here. And the Ho Chi Minh Trail helps us get supplies from China. If the South Vietnamese can get assistance from the Americans, then we can get assistance from China. If the only way to do that is through Cambodia, then so be it. We aren't doing anything to harm the Cambodians, and we aren't asking them to fight for us. We just needed to move here to get the American troops out of 'Nam. Maybe when they leave, the South Vietnamese will come to their senses, and this will all end. I got to see my sister, Quy, a few days ago. She looks so pale and thin. She said our older sister, Dung, is working as a hooch maid for the Americans somewhere along the border. I swear to God, if they lay a finger on her, I'll rip their hearts out through their throats! The rest of the family was forced into Phnom Penh along with the K.R. Quy's living in the camps along the Ho Chi Minh Trail with some of our other young cousins. They're there to repair roads immediately after being bombed. She's only 13! But the job has to be done. We've built 13,000 kilometers of new roads through Laos, which makes things difficult for U.S targeting analysts. So many trucks coming down different highway systems at one time confuses the enemy, and they have to stop their attacks for at least a week, not knowing which roads to bomb, or how to bomb them. But if one road is bombed, we just open up another one. We have to be cautious with the infiltration networks in Laos, though, because we're in extreme violation of Lao neutrality. I just pray for my little sister's safety.

Yeu,
Ngoc

Dear Journal,

Quy, my little sister, said she talked to ma last night when she snuck away from her bunk. She said they have to dig holes in the sides of mountains and in the forests for protection from the bombings. And to think, Vien is contributing to their torture. His own flesh and blood is forced to live like this, and he goes and fights against them. They can't even see the sun! Not like there's any sun to see anyway. The heat is there for sure, but the skies are black with smoke. The bombing raid that the U.S and South

Vietnamese troops led against Cambodia, suspecting that they were harboring communist base camps, made things worse by forcing the Khmer Rouge deeper into the center of the country with help from democratic Cambodian soldiers. And now civil war has begun between the Khmer Rouge and the democratic government. So now the U.S is focusing troops on 'Nam once again. But you know what they're doing now? They're giving the Cambodian military equipment and economic support! So first they destroy everything; then they try to fix it again?! Screw that! And you know what else? That damn American president then warned the Soviets against supporting the North Vietnamese. The bastard! Why doesn't he just take his damn troops out of here?! He knows they shouldn't be here anyway, and they're just complicating things. If it's the K.R. they're after, they should've just stayed the hell out of 'Nam and focused on Cambodia! Then the K.R. could have been quickly and easily defeated. It's because of their invasion and bombing of Cambodia that so many innocent Cambodian farmers and civilians have been driven deeper into the arms of the K.R. I thought they wanted to keep everyone *away* from communists! Ha! We only want our country back and have no intentions of getting together with the Soviets and going against the U.S. I feel so strange though. I never used to be a hateful person, but the war has made me so angry, and it's boiling up inside me. And I have to admit... it really scares me to think... what I might do.

Yeu,
Ngoc

Dear Journal,   1973

Things are starting to look up for us. A peace treaty was signed between the U.S and North and South Vietnam. The U.S. Congress finally banned the bombing of Cambodia. Military expenditures have been banned anywhere in Indochina, and the War Powers Act was passed, requiring the President to consult Congress before committing troops. We forced the military out of South 'Nam, and the Paris Peace Accords (Jan. 27th, 1973) ended the bombing of 'Nam and Laos. Now the U.S is striking out at the K.R., something they should have done earlier instead of bringing themselves into *our* business and tearing families apart and turning them against each other. Some of the guys were saying that they think things just might start to get back to normal real soon. But in my heart I know that's a false hope. My family is safe back in 'Nam now. But Quy was killed shortly before the signing of the peace treaty, when she was out repairing roads and a plane dove down, exploding bomb fragments everywhere. For the past few days all I do is weep. My eyes bleed because they've run out of tears for my little chi. And they say V.C. are cold-blooded and heartless. We're human! We have families! You wanna know cold-blooded and heartless?! Well, the same evil white demons that killed my sweet young sister, got my older sister, Dung, pregnant. And whatever bastard did this to her is on his way back to the states not knowing how much he has just ruined her life. The family will surely disown her. How could they love that baby with all its dirty American blood? No... no, things will never be normal again. Maybe better than during the *height* of the war... but never *normal.*

Yeu,
Ngoc

Dear Journal,   2002

My wife Kim is waking me up. She said I was screaming and I will wake our grandson. I must have been having the dream again. Kim tries to understand what I've been through and be supportive, but she wasn't there; she didn't see what I saw. She says I should take some herbal tea to help me sleep. But no tea in the world can stop a memory from haunting your mind. It happens every once in a while. It's as if it's being played in slow motion. I'm crouching low in the stream, coming up for a breath every minute or so. My clothes are sticking heavily to my body. Ducks are floating around my head. The stream is surrounded by dense foliage. There is a deafening silence. Then I hear a rustling in the bushes. I see the uniform of a South Vietnamese soldier. I fire two rounds. All the ducks start splashing and quaking and are flying off. I slowly emerge from my hiding spot under the surface of the water. Carefully looking around, I crawl toward the soldier I've just shot down; he's lying face down and blood is gushing from his head and forming a puddle. I nudge him with my gun. Just to make sure. I slowly turn him over and stare into Vien's bloodied face. NOOOOO!!!...

Yeu,

Ngoc

Bibliography

Khmer Rouge Take Over of Cambodia. http://www.wcnet.org/~rstech/khmer.htm.10 Sept., 2001.

Morris, Stephan J. Why Vietnam Invaded Cambodia: Political Culture and The Causes of War. Stanford University Pr. May 1, 1999

Morrocco, John. Rain of Fire. Boston Publishing Co. 1985.

Nixon Anounces Invasion of Cambodia, April 30, 1970. http://chnm.gmu.edu/hardhats/Cambodia.htm1. 10 Sept., 2001.

Nolan, Kieth W. Into Laos. New York Publishing Co. 1982.

Public Papers of the Presidents of the United States: Richard Nixon, 1970. http://vietnam.vassar.edu/docis.html

Rowden, Rick. How U.S Shaped Cambodia.http://www.lightparty.com/misc./Cambodia.html. 10 Sept., 2001.

Vickery, Micheal. Cambodia '75-'82. New York Publishing Co. 1986.

Morgan Klarich is a junior at D.C. Everest Senior High School.

The Elite: Green Berets

By Drew Krueger

"A breed apart; a highly skilled, mature and superbly trained soldier. The Green Berets are unquestionably the world's most unconventional war experts. Teachers first and fighters of uncommon physical and mental caliber, the Green Berets are soldier ready to serve anywhere at any time. Special Forces demands a tremendous amount of invetiveness and salience" (www.specialforces.net/army/special_forces/efault.html pg. 1) The history of the Green Berets, dating back to the years following World War II, began out of a need to shift from a conventional to an unconventional approach to warfare. The intensive training the Green Berets went through left only the best of the best in this elite group. Their role in Vietnam was that of counterinsurgency, combating guerilla warfare, and subversion.

The idea of Special Forces was created after 1945 as the United States and the Soviet Union worked to become superpowers. The United States was faced with the need to create an unconventional warfare unit. General Robert McClore tried to get the Pentagon's support. He faced a great deal of criticism from senior officers who had little time for 'elite' forces and were placing their faith in nuclear weapons. McClore won permission to form the Special Operations Section think tank. In 1952 a base was established at Fort Berg, North Carolina. It was later known as the Special Warfare School. On June 20, 1952, the 10th Special Forces Group was activated, and recruits poured in to begin training. (Brown, Ashley p.6)

In the early 1960s the role of Special Forces underwent a major shift. The groups would now be concerned with counterinsurgency missions. The driving force for this change was President John F. Kennedy. He was concerned about the success the guerrilla soldiers were having in Indochina. This concern was a key force changing the future of the Special Forces. The Green Berets were expected to perform the same sort of hit and run raids that the Rangers carried out in WWII. The focus of the Green Beret efforts throughout the Vietnam War was to create village defense units by training the local natives as Civilian Irregular Defense Groups. The Green Berets were used to infiltrate behind enemy lines in Vietnam. The Special Forces directed Civilian Irregular Defense Groups. Under their direction, strike forces carried out hit and run raids and prolonged reconnaissance missions against the Vietcong. Waging war against an elusive and cunning enemy encouraged the Special Forces to form highly specialized reconnaissance, intelligence gathering. The Green Berets carried the war to the guerillas on their home ground. They patrolled jungles for weeks, captured suspects, gathered intelligence, ambushed Vietcong units, and rescued down pilots from enemy territory.

To accomplish these tasks, the Green Berets had to endure and succeed in one the world's most exhaustive and thorough training programs. "Those who successfully completed the rigorous training, now known as the Green Berets, were the most intellectual, educated, creative and constructive of all United States soldiers." (Halbeistadt, Hans p.4) Green Beret recruits went through a three-stage program in which their mental and physical abilities were evaluated. As many as 75% of the candidates failed this program. (Brown, Ashley p.21) During the first thirty-one days of training, the recruits developed stamina and learned basic combat skills. They would put in seventeen-hour days. These days began with a six-mile march, carrying a forty-five-pound pack and then more exercises. Their instruction emphasized survival, evasion, resistance, and escape techniques. The trainees were put through a seven-day field exercise in the Uwaharrie National Forest. (Brown, Ashley p.22) The last three days were devoted to manhunts. The recruits were armed with only a knife and had to survive by living off the land and evading their enemies.

If they successfully completed the first stage of training, they were permitted to begin the second stage, in which each recruit took a specialist course in one of five skill. These five skills areas were engineering, weapons specialists, communication, medical specialist, and intelligence gathering. The engineers would learn the finer points of construction and destruction. Weapon specialists went through an eight-week intensive instruction. The recruits had to learn how to use eight different types of small arms with an emphasis on marksmanship and proficiency in the building and the use of less conventional weapons such as crossbows. (Brown, Ashley p.23) Communication specialist candidates learned how to work a variety of communication equipment. The largest and most difficult skill group, medical specialist, required a fifty-week course, training the candidates to deal with most types of combat wounds and the treatment of common diseases of the native population. The last of the five skill programs was intelligence gathering. It focused on establishing intelligence networks, organization of guerilla forces, and interrogation of suspects.

Following successful completion of the second stage of basic training, trainees were brought together to learn the operational procedures of Special Forces working in the field. The recruits, in teams, were dropped in the Uwharrie Forest where they had to avoid enemies and form guerilla units. U.S soldiers played the roles of Vietnam natives, and the Green Beret recruits were expected to train them as a guerilla unit within a month. If the trainees were captured or failed to form a guerilla force, they failed the test. (Brown, Ashley p. 25) Successful completion meant the trainees were allowed to wear the honored Green Beret.

The most famous of the Special Forces involved in the Vietnam War were the Green Berets which first appeared in South Vietnam during 1957. Their original mission was to build a conventional army and to repel an invasion from the north. They helped to build an offensive guerilla warfare capability known as the Vietnamese Special Forces. Initial Special Forces efforts in South Vietnam were directed toward training natives who needed expertise in unconventional warfare tactics such as raiding or long-range patrolling. Until then the South Vietnamese had no Special Forces of their own. In the late 1950s the 77th Special Forces group from Fort Bragg trained the beginnings of the Vietnamese Army Rangers. In later years the Vietnamese Ranger Battalions proved to be among the best of the Army of the Vietnamese Republic infantry units.

As time went on, the Special Forces in Vietnam had a number of different roles and missions. Their main and largest mission was organizing the Civilian Irregular Defense Group (CIDG) program. The primary objective of the CIDG program was to block Viet Cong encroachment into Vietnamese rural areas by developing loyalties with the natives and improving their fighting abilities. During the nine years of the existence of this program, the Special Forces became involved in every aspect of counterinsurgency: military, economic, political, and psychological. It involved thousands of U.S. soldiers, hundreds of thousands of Vietnamese civilians, millions of dollars and about one hundred camps spread from the Demilitarized Zone to the Gulf of Siam. The Special Forces taught the Vietnamese how to shoot, build, farm, care for the sick, and run agent operations.

In 1963 the CIA turned over border responsibility to the Special Forces. They recruited and trained border surveillance personnel, established an intelligence system, and gained control of the border through guerilla warfare. The move to establish a chain of fortified camps along the border was not accomplished until the 5th Special Forces Group arrived for permanent duty in Vietnam during October, 1964.

The Green Berets trained CIDG locals to create village defense units. This was the heart of the Special Forces' efforts throughout the Vietnam War. The tribal units and locals in South Vietnam viewed outsiders with distrust. The Green Berets faced an enormous task. To be successful they had to win the hearts and minds of the Vietnamese people. By late 1961, over 200 villagers were protected by 1,200 armed highlanders. Special Forces directed the CIDGs. They were strike forces that performed hit and run raids and prolonged reconnaissance missions against enemies in areas of guerilla activity. These operations were usually carried out under the cover of darkness. Carrying out a prolonged war against an elusive and clever enemy encouraged the Special Forces to form highly specialized reconnaissance units. They carried war to the guerillas on their home ground. The Special Forces patrolled jungles for weeks, snatched suspects, gathered intelligence, ambushed Viet Cong units, and rescued downed pilots from enemy territory. The Special Forces would snatch guerillas and escape quickly with the use of helicopters.

The Green Berets in Vietnam showed much greater concern for the local civilians than conventional soldiers ever had. (Simpson, Charles pg. xii) They helped the villagers find better sources of water by introducing a simple well-digging technique. They helped them build bridges around swamps to their garden plots. They gave locals seeds, which produced better vegetables than they had had before. The Green Berets knew a few words in the villagers' language and talked with them around the evening fire as they shared the villagers' food and drink. (Simpson, Charles p. xii) It was after these friendly relations had been established that the task of training villagers to defend themselves began. Throughout the training and preparations for village security, Green Berets worked with the villagers. When attacks began, the Green Beret fought side by side with the jungle villagers who were now their friends.

In June of 1962, in a graduation address at the United States Military Academy at West Point, President John F. Kennedy advised the newly commissioned, many of whom were soon to serve in Vietnam, " This is another type of war -- a war fought by guerillas, subversives, insurgents, assassins, by ambush instead of by combat; by infiltration instead of aggression, seeking victory by eroding and exhausting the enemy instead of engaging him. It requires in those situations where we must encounter it a whole new kind of strategy, a wholly different kind of military training."(Simpson M, Charles p. X) This was the beginning of the development of the new type of Special Forces later referred to as the Green Berets. In the overall context of the Vietnam War, the Special Forces were a relatively small operation, in size and cost, but they had the beginning elements of counterinsurgency success. The Green Berets became a strategic tool to be used in the new type of unconventional warfare, which had its start in the Vietnam War.

Drew Krueger is currently a junior at D.C. Everest Senior High. He currently participates in football and track. Drew plans on attending the University of Minnesota.

The Failures of the Air War in Vietnam

By Phillip Beck

The United States had become heavily involved in the Vietnam War, a war that appeared insignificant and easily winable in the beginning, but ultimately would not be won. Air attacks had been successful in previous wars for the United States, but the U.S. had carelessly underestimated the determination of the North Vietnamese. Looking back, the air war in Vietnam was undoubtedly a failure in preventing the North Vietnamese Communistic government from overtaking the rest of the country.

Beginning on March 2, 1965, the United States launched an air attack on North Vietnam with the code name Operation Rolling Thunder. The objectives of the operation were to destroy selected targets of importance in North Vietnam, to prevent the flow of personnel and supplies into the South and to break the will of North Vietnamese leaders. By doing so, the United States hoped to place increasing pressure on the North Vietnamese leadership to negotiate a peaceful settlement to the war. The original strategy for Operation Rolling Thunder was to attack targets slightly north of the Demilitarized Zone and then strike progressively more distant targets as the campaign continued. Operation Rolling Thunder involved Air Force and Marine aircraft flying from bases located in South Vietnam and Thailand, in addition to Navy aircraft flying from carriers in the South China Sea. Rolling Thunder was expanded in July, 1966, to include North Vietnamese ammunition dumps and oil storage facilities. By the spring of 1967, the operation increased to bombing power plants, factories and airfields in the Hanoi-Haiphong area. The attacks were later reduced in April, 1968, by a partial bombing halt and were eventually terminated on November 1, 1968. (Summers, 297-198)

When U.S. Air Force planes took off from bases in South Vietnam and Thailand for the first mission of Operation Rolling Thunder, the objective was to launch an assault on an ammunition depot at Xom Bang, thirty-five miles north of the Demilitarized Zone. The force consisted of forty F-100 Supersabres from Da Nang, forty-five F-105 Thunderchiefs based at U.S. airfields in Thailand, and twenty B-57s stationed at Tan Son Nhut, as well as refueling tankers and other support aircraft. Long-range bombers stationed in Guam were included in the original plan, but were canceled at the last minute by President Lyndon B. Johnson. In a chaotic attack, the U.S. successfully destroyed the target, but unexpectedly lost several men in the assault. (Morrocco, 55)

When the aircraft returned from the first attack, General William Westmoreland and Lieutenant Joseph H. Morre asked about the assignment. F-100 pilot Robbie Risner answered, "I guess we destroyed the target, but as best I know we lost about seven airplanes." (Morrocco, 53) As it turned out, six planes were lost, with five of the pilots rescued. North Vietnamese air defenses were considerably better than had been foolishly assumed. "We realized this wasn't going to be a pushover," replied one of the pilots. "We were going to lose some people and some airplanes." (Morrocco, 54)

Following the initial attack, the realization that the United States had badly underestimated the determination of the North Vietnamese would haunt America throughout the rest of the war. Although the U.S. would continue to fight in Vietnam and take action through air attacks and bombings, the North Vietnam air defense and desire to win the war would devastate the United States, South Vietnam and those opposed to the spread of communism.

One of the other primary reasons for the failure of the bombing campaigns was the strict regulations on the bombing campaigns against North Vietnam. Already, several U.S. commanders had openly complained about the strict and inflexible instructions on carrying out the attacks. The United States government prohibited bombing within twenty-five miles of the Chinese border, within ten miles of the Vietnam capital Hanoi, and within four miles of the major port of Haiphong. In fact, the air war in Vietnam soon became regarded as the most limited aspect of the war.

President Johnson envisioned the bombing in North Vietnam as a political tool which could signal U.S. resolve and convince the communist leader Ho Chi Minh to give up without drawing the United States into an even larger war. Fearing that taking excessive actions could escalate into greater warfare, the United States government gave specific instructions on what targets were to be hit, the day and time of attack, the number of planes that would be used, and the types and amount of weapons to be used. Even the direction from which pilots were to approach the target was often determined in Washington, while rescheduling attacks that were canceled due to poor weather also had to be approved back at home. "I won't let those air force generals bomb the smallest outhouse . . . without checking with me," stated President Johnson, using the powers given to him by Congress through the Tonkin Gulf Resolution, which gave the President, as Commander in Chief, "all necessary measure" to protect U.S. interests in Vietnam. (Morrocco, 55) "I spend ten hours a day worrying about all this, picking the targets one by one, making sure we didn't go over the limits." (Morrocco, 57)

Johnson claimed that "a total assault on the North would be rape rather than seduction." (Morrocco, 57) However, while caution was taken with the bombing of Vietnam to prevent further escalation, many others argued that such limited bombing could not win the war for the United States or prevent the spread of communism. By placing such limitations on the bombing efforts in Vietnam, the U.S. Air Force was prevented from attacking nearly every major target. Many U.S. commanders were outraged when they were told that they could not attack surface-to-air missile sites, which were constructed in order to fire AS-2 missiles at U.S. airplanes, until they were entirely operational. Even certain enemy air bases were not allowed to be attacked in fear of taking the lives of technicians from the Soviet Union. Ambassador Maxwell Taylor in Saigon worried, "I fear that Rolling Thunder, in their eyes, has merely been a few isolated thunderclaps." (Morrocco, 57)

The irregular timings of the air attacks against North Vietnam also raised questions of whether the strategic bombing would be successful. Ambassador Taylor continued, "What seems to be lacking is a program covering several weeks which will combine the factors, frequency, weight and location of attack into a rational pattern which will convince the leaders in Hanoi that we are on a dynamic schedule which will not remain static in a narrow zone far removed from them and the sources of their power, but which is a moving, growing threat which cannot be ignored." (Gibson, 325)

Despite controversy over the air war in Vietnam, limited bombing campaigns resumed in hopes of resolving the war. Operation Rolling Thunder continued over the next several years of the war, while other bombing campaigns increased the amount of action taken in Vietnam. Smaller bombing campaigns started before Operation Rolling Thunder was designed, such as Operation Farmgate, Project Mule Train, Operation Able Mable and Operations Flaming Dart I and Flaming Dart II, while additional missions followed, such as Operation Sea Dragon—calling for the sinking of supply craft and identifying targets with spotter aircraft—and Operation Bolo—which turned out to be the largest air battle up to that point in the war. (Air Power over Vietnam)

When twenty-seven B-52F's from Andersen AFB in Guam hit Vietcong strongholds in South Vietnam on June 18, 1965, Operation Arc Light went into effect. By the end of the first year, Arc Light had involved more that 1,500 aircraft that dropped bombs on enemy troop concentrations, bases and supply dumps. Laotian raids followed in December, 1965. While the operation was credited for expanding the bombing campaign, Arc Light was labeled as rather ineffective and criticized for "simply blowing holes in the jungle." (Military Analysis Network)

But none of the missions, including the most important attacks of Operation Rolling Thunder, accomplished the intended goals. There was no clear objective in the air war in Vietnam, and the United States soon realized that these efforts may not have been worthwhile.

Realizing the failures of the bombing efforts, President Johnson announced to the public on March 31, 1968, that he would limit the bombing of North Vietnam by halting Operation Rolling Thunder and negotiate peace. "What has distressed me," wrote President Johnson, "is the notion that air power would provide a strategic route to victory, and the parallel assumption that by bombing the North we could get a cut-rate solution in the South and escape from the problems of building a South Vietnam army." (Lewy, 417)

Johnson decided not to run for re-election in 1968. The next U.S. President, and the last to serve during the Vietnam War, was Republican Richard Nixon. Believing in the idea of détente, the deliberate reduction of Cold War tensions, Nixon assured the American people that the North Vietnamese "have never been bombed like they're going to be bombed." (Werrell, 3)

During the presidency of Richard Nixon, a new mission, known as Operation Linebacker, was created in an attempt to accomplish the goals that failed in Operation Rolling Thunder. Operation Linebacker attempted to force peace negotiations by cutting supply lines in North Vietnam. Unlike former President Johnson's policy of limited bombing, President Nixon gave U.S. military commanders a broad range of power and a long list of targets, allowing them to decide what targets to destroy and when to carry out the attacks.

Operation Linebacker became the most successful bombing effort thus far into the war, but when President Nixon stopped the bombing from October 8 through 23 to discuss peace, negotiations did not go as smoothly as hoped. Wanting to end the conflict, the United States launched another mission known as Operation Linebacker II. Directed by the Joint Chiefs of Staff until further notice, Operation Linebacker II was launched on December 18, 1972, to force the North Vietnamese government to enter into negotiations concerning a cease-fire agreement. A-7s and F-4s carried out the majority of the day-time operations, along with long-range navigation techniques. During the nighttime, B-52s struck Hanoi and Haiphong, while F-111s and Navy tactical aircraft provided diversionary and suppression strikes on airfields and surface-to-air missile sites. (Military Analysis Network).

Finally, perhaps for the first time in the war, there was an apparent objective in the bombing efforts. Experts often consider the Linebacker missions as successful. However, an end to the conflict in Vietnam did not appear to be within reach. The air war in Vietnam had been a failure.

According to one report issued by the Central Intelligence Agency, the cost of the attacks exceeded the dollar value of the targets destroyed by an estimated ratio of 8:1. Figures show that only $600 million of damage was caused by bombing from 1965 to 1968, compared to the six billion dollars cost of lost aircraft shot down on bombing runs. Air Force Major Earl H. Tilford, Jr. stated that the Rolling Thunder campaign itself "cost us $10 for every $1 worth of damage inflicted on Vietnam." (Starr, 16)

The plan was to destroy designated targets in North Vietnam that would weaken the opponents and cause them to surrender, but no such targets existed. The North Vietnamese were able to survive the loss of thermal power plants and overcome the destruction of their only steel mill, an object of extraordinary national pride. Although the loss of such structures was devastating, North Vietnam refused to give up, showing that the U.S. could not beat them by simply destroying carefully selected targets. War planners admitted that "the idea that destroying or threatening to destroy North Vietnam's industry would pressure Hanoi into calling it quits seems, in retrospect, a colossal misjudgement." (Starr, 14)

Rolling Thunder and the other missions also failed to stop the flow of men and supplies to the South. According to the Joint Chiefs of Staff, attacks on facilities would damage the Democratic Republic of Vietnam's "capability to move war-supporting resources within the country and along the infiltration routs to the SVN." (Starr, 14) However, this strategy did not have the effects that were expected. Walt Rostow, an important Presidential advisor, said, "We have never held the view that bombing could stop infiltration." (Starr, 16)

The fact that the United States had badly underestimated North Vietnam once again became evident. By 1972, the number of Americans in Vietnam was reduced from more than 540,000 in 1969 to less than 30,000. When the Paris Accords of January, 1973, were signed, the remaining troops in Vietnam were withdrawn. Throughout the Vietnam War, roughly 58,000 Americans lost their lives. (Newman and Schmalbach, 621)

Defense Secretary McNamara finally admitted to Congress that "the enemy operations in the South cannot, on the basis of any reports I have seen, be stopped by air bombardment—short, that is, of the virtual annihilation of North Vietnam and its people." (Starr, 16)

Bibliography

"Air Power Over Vietnam." <http://www.danshistory.com/vietnam.html>

Bonds, Ray. *The Vietnam War: The Illustrated History of the Conflict in Southeast Asia.* New York: Salamander, 1979.

Gibson, James William. *The Perfect War: Technowar in Vietnam.* Boston, MA: The Atlantic Monthly Press, 1979.

Lewy, Guenter. *America in Vietnam.* New York: Oxford University Press, 1978.

McNarmara, Robert S. *Argument Without End: In Search of Answers to the Vietnam Tragedy.*

Morrocco, John. *Thunder From Above: Air War, 1914-1968.* Boston, MA: Boston Publishing Company, 1984.

Newman, John J. and John M. Schmalbach. *United States History: Preparing for the Advanced Placement Examination.* New York: Amsco School Publications, Inc., 2002.

"Operation Arc Light." Military Analysis Network. <http://www.fas.org/man/dod-101/ops/arc_light.htm>

"Operation Linebacker II." Military Analysis Network. <http://www.fas.org/man/dod-101/ops/linebacker-2.htm>

"Operation Rolling Thunder." Military Analysis Network. <http://www.fas.org/man/dod-101/ops/rolling_thunder.htm>

Starr, Jerold M. *The Lessons of Vietnam.* Center for Social Studies Education, 1988.

Summers, Hary G., Jr. *Vietnam War Almanac.* New York: Facts on File Publications, 1985.

Werrell, Kenneth P. *Linebacker II: The Decisive Use of Airpower?* <http://www.airpower.maxwell.af.mil/airchronicles/aureview/1987/werrell.html> Sep. 1986.

Phillip Beck is currently a senior at D.C. Everest High School where he is a member of the band, peer helpers, Fellowship of Christain Athletes (FCA), and intramural basketball. He is also active in his church youth group. Phillip plans on majoring in education or engineering.

The Fall of the South

By Andy Kryshak

In December of 1974, the North Vietnamese Army (NVA) would begin a massive offensive on South Vietnam. The goal of this offensive: to capture South Vietnam once and for all. The South's forces, the Army of the Republic of Vietnam (ARVN), would try their best to push back the attackers, but the efficient North Vietnamese attack would not relent until Saigon and the whole of South Vietnam were in Communist hands.

The conditions were just right for the North Vietnamese to make their final offensive. In their Tet Offensive of 1968, they had suffered heavy losses, but they had accomplished their goal: to destroy the will of the Americans and the South Vietnamese. The Paris Peace Accords had been officially signed on January 23, 1973. Under this agreement most U.S. forces left Vietnam. Only several thousand Americans remained to aid in Vietnamization, the turning over of the defense to the South Vietnamese. (Griffiths, 22) The bombings of North Vietnam, ordered by Nixon, had stopped after the Watergate scandal had taken the President out of office. The army and political structure in South Vietnam were disorganized and split into factions, but the whole of North Vietnam was united toward a common goal, capturing the South and turning all of Vietnam into one Communist nation.

The commanding Communist general at this time was Van Tien Dung. He and his advisors would organize and lead most of the attacks from the beginning of March to the fall of Saigon. The final goal of the offensive was to capture Saigon, but, however disorganized, the ARVN defended the Saigon area well. The North first needed a way to deliver mass amounts of supplies directly into the South. The Phuoc Long province, on the Vietnam-Laotian border, crisscrossed by networks of trails, would provide the perfect base of operations for the Communists in South Vietnam.

The invasion of Phuoc Long began on December 13. Only a few thousand ARVN rangers and militiamen defended the entire province; no regular army troops were in the area. (Dawson, 25) District after district easily fell to the relentless Communist attack. The attackers cut the province up piece by piece using mass infantry attacks backed by Soviet-made tanks and artillery. By January 2, the only ARVN unconquered city was the capital of the province, Phuoc Binh. After a 4-day resistance, being outnumbered four to one, the South's troops finally retreated from the capital, and the province was left to the NVA. On January 6, the North Vietnamese Army officially "liberated" its first southern province. (Dougan, 20)

General Dung's next move was to take South Vietnam's Central Highlands area, labeled Military Region 2. There were three important cities in the area: Kontum, Pleiku, and Ban Me Thuot. The main target would be the Darlac provincial capital, Ban Me Thuot. It was the largest city in the area, and Dung believed that the whole area would fall easily if he could capture the city. On March 10, the NVA hit Ban Me Thuot with three divisions, against one division of ARVN troops. (Brown, 308) In thirty hours the North had completely captured the city. The ARVN attempted a counterattack to reclaim the city, but it was useless against the superior Communist force. (Griffiths, 7) All ARVN troops in the city had retreated by March 16, or they were captured or killed. (Dawson, 52)

After the fall of Ban Me Thuot, the South's President Thieu decreed that the rest of the highlands were to be abandoned. (Dougan, 54) ARVN troops at Pleiku, Kontum, and other strongholds and outposts in the area withdrew, moving down Route 7B, a road leading to the coastline. The troops were accompanied by thousands of refugees from the abandoned cities. The NVA followed quickly, brutally attacking and killing soldiers and civilians alike in the slow-moving convoy, called the "Convoy of Tears" by many. On March 25, the convoy finally made it to the coastal city of Tuy Hoa, a stronghold reinforced by a large ARVN territorial force. However, only a quarter of the South Vietnamese military troops that started the convoy were alive at the end, and only a third of the civilian refugees made it. (Dougan, 63) It was one of the saddest times in Vietnamese history.

By the time the convoy reached Tuy Hoa, the NVA had already begun its next invasion, on the north part of South Vietnam, Military Region 1. By capturing the Central Highlands, the NVA had effectively split South Vietnam into two. Fresh Communist troops named the B-4 Front forces pushed from North Vietnam into the Quang Tri province (the northern-most province of South Vietnam), where they efficiently destroyed the resistance. (Dougan, 69) Then they pushed towards the ancient capital of Vietnam, the city of Hue. On March 21, the B-4 Front forces reached Hue, and, with the help of numerous other NVA divisions, the Communists sealed off Hue from all major roads. The ARVN held off the Communists for three days, suffering heavy casualties, until they were ordered to retreat and abandon the city on March 24. (Griffiths, 8) With the roads leading out of the city being blockaded by NVA divisions, the ARVN and civilians had to escape by sea. The North shelled the escaping vessels, and only 7,000 ARVN soldiers and 3,000 civilians escaped alive from Hue, south to the coastal city of Da Nang. (Dougan, 74)

The NVA now controlled most of Military Region 1, the north part of South Vietnam. Refugees from all outlying areas of the region had fled to Da Nang, increasing the civilian population to almost 3 million. (Dougan, 75) The city was defended by over 70,000 ARVN troops. The NVA tightened a noose around Da Nang, completely cutting it off from all escape routes as they had done at Hue. The ARVN put up as much resistance as they could, but the NVA war machine kept attacking and destroying the defenders, mostly with artillery. (Griffiths, 9) Da Nang soon turned into a mad rush to escape, by sea or by air. Soldiers would shoot other soldiers or civilians trying to take their place on an already over-laden boat. Of the 70,000 ARVN soldiers only 16,000 made it out alive, and of the 3 million civilians, only 50,000 were evacuated from the city. (Dougan, 83) The remaining soldiers and civilians were left to the Communist troops. Then the massive force turned its attentions southward for the final assault.

The ARVN set up a final line of defense to stop the NVA from reaching Saigon and the deep South. (Dougan, 117) The keystone to this defense was Xuan Loc, a small provincial capital 38 miles northeast of Saigon, and an ARVN stronghold. (Griffiths, 10) If the North captured this, the ARVN would be forced to retreat to Saigon and the whole defense of the South would fall. On April 10, the NVA advanced on the city with three divisions plus artillery support facing one ARVN garrison division. The South put up a tough resistance and the fighting was some of the fiercest in the war. However, the south was outnumbered four to one and attrition became a big factor. On April 16, the North broke into the city, and by April 20, they had captured the city and the nearby airbase of Bien Hoa, the most important South Vietnamese Air Force base in the South. Remnants of the defense were extracted by helicopter on April 21, just as President Thieu officially resigned. Giving a teary eyed speech before the South Vietnamese National Assembly in Saigon, he said that the U.S. "ran away and left us to do the job that you could not do." Thieu then turned over his power to his vice president, who in turn gave it to General Duong Van Minh. (Dougan, 138)

The NVA took advantage of this transition in Saigon politics. The NVA had over 100,000 forces ready for the largest and most important battle of the war. On April 26, the NVA started firing rockets into Saigon as they began encircling the city and capturing its outer defense outposts. The U.S. started large evacuations, using the giant Tan Son Nhut airbase just outside Saigon. First Americans and then important or sponsored Vietnamese were taken aboard planes and helicopters heading out of Saigon. (Church, 5) Vietnamese civilians boarded small boats and attempted to make it to the American evacuation fleet and board the U.S. ships. On April 29, the U.S. conducted Operation Frequent Wind, a major evacuation of remaining Americans and as many Vietnamese as they could take. The operation was successful, and in one day 1,373 Americans and nearly 70,000 Vietnamese were rescued, using helicopters, boats, and planes. (Dougan, 172) While all this evacuation was proceeding, the NVA continued to close in, pushing back Saigon's outer defense borders to the inner city, and shelling the city with artillery. The ARVN defenders fought as fiercely as they could at first, but as the Communist army pushed closer and closer, they became more concerned about their own safety and many deserted.

As April 30 came, the only Americans left in Saigon were the Joint Military Team of U.S. military advisors and a small team of Marines left to guard these men. Four hundred other people were also chosen to be evacuated, including missionaries and foreign dignitaries. At 5:00 a.m. that morning, two CH-46 helicopters swooped down to the embassy rooftop landing pad. Two helicopters were not enough for all of the waiting evacuees, so the civilian Americans were taken out, leaving the Marines and the other 400 behind. The Marines were stuck in the embassy, holding off the Vietnamese civilians attempting to break in. Finally, at 8:00 a.m., helicopters came to the roof of the embassy and flew the Marines out. The four hundred others were left behind, and the evacuations were finished. (Church, 8) Not a single American remained in Saigon.

Exactly an hour after the last helicopter had disappeared, NVA troops moved into the city from five different directions. The South Vietnamese defenders had no chance, and many just surrendered at the sight of the huge Communist force. ARVN soldiers threw away everything identifying them as a soldier and blended in with the civilian population. NVA tanks rolled right through the city without resistance, and up to the capital. At noon on April 30, an NVA tank smashed through the presidential palace gates and claimed the palace. Saigon was officially captured, and the Communist flag flew above the presidential palace. (Dougan, 175)

After the city was taken, President Duong Van Minh signed a surrender. The NVA renamed Saigon Ho Chi Minh City, and went to work at creating the Communist government they had fought for. In the week following Saigon's downfall, celebrations were abundant, and whether they were Communist or not, people celebrated the end of the war. (Church, 10) Yet many people were taken to Communist camps for trials or "reeducation" where they would learn the Communist ways. (Dougan, 184) Life would change for many, but one thing was certain: the fighting and the killing were over. South Vietnam had been defeated, and Vietnam was now a Communist country.

Bibliography

Church, George J. "Saigon: The Final 10 Days." Time. 24 April, 1995.

Brown, Weldon A. *The Last Chopper*. New York: Kennikat Press, 1976.

Dawson, Alan. *55 Days: The Fall of South Vietnam*. New Jersey: Prentice Hall, 1977.

Dougan, Clark and David Fulghum. *The Fall of the South. The Vietnam Experience*. Boston: Boston Publishing Company, 1985.

Griffiths, John. *The Last Day in Saigon*. London: Dryad Press Limited, 1986.

Sorley, Lewis. *A Better War*. New York: Harcourt Brace & Company, 1999.

Andy Kryshak is a junior at D.C. Everest High School. He is involved in track and soccer and likes to golf. After graduation in 2004, he would like to attend UW-Madison or Northwestern University, majoring in business.

From Jeers to Tears: The Kent State Tragedy

By Jessica Dabler

Thursday, April 30, 1970

Today, President Nixon announced that troops are going to be sent into Cambodia to get rid of the communists there.[1] He makes me so angry sometimes. I'm so fed up with this Vietnam War. It keeps going on and on, and now Nixon wants to increase troops when I thought he was pulling them out. Vietnamization is a fraud. He brings troops home, only to add new ones and escalate the bombing and killing. The widening of the war into Cambodia can be seen only as an escalating act in my eyes.

Friday, May 1, 1970

As a journalism student at Kent State, I decided to attend the rally at noon. There were 500 students gathered at the Commons. American citizens were mad at Nixon for not talking with Congress before he ordered the invasion of Cambodia. A few students buried a copy of the U.S. Constitution because they thought no one was following it anymore.[2] The opinion here on campus was to let the administration know that we won't allow another escalation of this war.

At around 10:00 PM my friends and I went to a local bar on Water Street to watch the world championship basketball playoffs. While we watched the game, people outside were yelling and setting off firecrackers.[3] I went outside to see what was going on. People started jumping on a car and smashing its windows. The crowd started yelling, "One-two-three-four, we don't want your f - - - - - - war!"[4]

Since I was taking a journalism class, I decided to see what would happen. At this point, I agreed with the students. I somehow thought that if they rioted enough, Nixon would listen and magically stop the war. I also had some friends who didn't go to college, and they got sent to Vietnam. I really didn't want anything to happen to them. It seems like this war has been going on forever. I wondered how many more dead soldiers it would take to realize that this war wasn't going to be won. However, those feelings weren't strong enough to make me take part in the protests.

People started setting garbage cans on fire in the street. Then the crowd formed a human barricade and stopped a large tractor hauling a semi north down the street, which made everyone cheer. It was complete chaos. I checked in the bar every so often to get the basketball score. A patrol car came down the street, and it was met with a barrage of beer pitchers, bottles, glasses and anything else the students could get their hands on. People started to shout, "Pigs off the street! We won't go to Cambodia."[5]

Then the crowd really got going when the Chosen Few motorcycle gang rode down the street.[6] People left the basketball game to join the crowd that was moving downtown. People started throwing bottles through store windows. At least two stores were looted. A fertilizer spreader was taken from a hardware store and thrown through a bank window. In all, 47 windows were smashed.[7]

Finally, around 12:15 AM, some cops showed up. People started to scatter up alleys and toward the campus. The next move the cops made I don't think was very smart. They closed all the bars, which made most of the people watching the game, including me, angry, so they joined the crowd.[8] The riot squad went up and down Water Street breaking up the crowd and pushing them toward the campus.

At around 1:00 AM, the police had the kids grouped up at the campus line. However, the police weren't allowed on campus, and they had to wait for the campus police to come because they were dealing with other problems on campus.[9] Shortly after that the firemen put out all the fires. The police used tear gas on the crowd that wasn't rounded up. Even though I wasn't actually protesting, I was still affected by that darn tear gas. It made my eyes water and I seriously felt like I was suffocating. Around 2:20 AM, there was a car crash, which diverted the crowd's attention, and slowly the people started to go back to the campus.[10]

Saturday, May 2, 1970

The mayor set an 8:00 PM city curfew today. I heard rumors about burning the ROTC building, so I wasn't surprised when a crowd started gathering by the building at 7:00 PM.[11] At 7:30, a guy by the Victory Bell yelled, "They're trying to keep the kids penned up in the dorms. Let's go." They marched around the dorms trying to get supporters.[12]

The mob which had around 2,000 students now, headed back for the ROTC building, and chanted, "Down with ROTC!"[13] Rocks were thrown, and one group even picked up a gasoline drum and tried to use it as a battering ram to knock down the door, without luck. Groups even threw railroad flares at the building but they all sputtered out. Finally around 8:30 PM, the ROTC was on fire. The crowd yelled, "Burn, baby. Burn!"[14] In celebration, one guy pulled out an American flag and burned it.

At this point I was starting to get angry with my fellow classmates. Sure, I was against the war, but burning down a building? I didn't really see the point of the violence, even though it would catch the attention of more people. But would it be the attention we wanted?

A fire truck came, but the firemen had problems getting to the fire. Protestors cut the hoses with machetes, ice picks, and pocketknives, so the firemen couldn't put out the fire.[15] Three guys dipped rags in the gasoline tanks of motorcycles and threw them in the building. By this time the firemen had given up and left. At 9:20, ten officers arrived and used tear gas to push the crowd away from the ROTC building.[16]

The crowd made its way downtown where it met the National Guard. They were forced back onto campus. Some people vandalized parts of the city again. An air compressor, sawhorses, and other debris were stolen from a construction site and used to make a bonfire in the middle of the street.[17] I didn't really understand the point of destroying businesses. What good was that going to do to stop the war?

The ROTC fire was flaring up again, which excited the crowd. The firemen came back around 10:00 PM, but the ROTC was beyond saving. The Guard forced the students back to campus at 10:30.

Sunday, May 3, 1970.

At 7:10 PM a crowd formed near the Victory Bell. Whether the students knew it or not, they weren't supposed to have any outdoor rallies. Soon, a Guard jeep came driving by telling everyone to disperse.

However, around 9:05 PM, the crowd at the Victory Bell started marching toward University President White's house. Before they could get there, the National Guard tear-gassed them and sent them back in the opposite direction.[18] Again, I felt the disgusting effects of the tear gas.

Around 200 students decided to march into the city even though this was breaking the curfew. An armored personnel carrier with guns stopped them, but then left, making the students think they won.

When the students came back, they joined a group of people sitting, who were protesting the curfew.[19] By 9:45, the National Guard and Kent Police teamed up to surround the students. They left the way back to campus open. The kids started saying to the Guardsmen, "You're just like us. Come over to our side," and, "Are those guns loaded?"[20] I'm sure by now the Guardsmen were irritated with the students.

At around 10:00, more students joined the sitters and the group got wilder. Three students got up and talked with a policeman and asked to talk with President White and Mayor Satrom. They also wanted a warning before arrests were made. The cops gave those same three students a bullhorn, and they told the crowd President White and Mayor Satrom were coming. The students wanted to talk with them about removing the ROTC program from campus, giving amnesty to everyone charged in the ROTC burning, giving total acceptance to the demands of the Black United Students organazation, removing all National Guard troops from the campus by Monday night, lifting the curfew immediately, and lowering tuition.[21]

Shortly after this, news came that the president and the mayor were not coming. The three students with the bullhorn were told this news; however, the students continued to tell the crowd that the president and mayor were still coming.

A few minutes before 11:00, a major told the students with the bullhorn that at 11:00 PM they were going to start clearing out the intersection. When they did, one guy with the bullhorn yelled, "They've lied to us. We've been betrayed." Of course the kids didn't know what really happened, so they got mad and threw rocks. The Guardsmen had their bayonets on and ended up stabbing at least two students in order to get them to go back to campus.[22] It was total chaos.

Those last events really did make me feel betrayed, but not by the police. Those three students with the bullhorn knowingly lied to the group of students who were sitting, just to make them mad at the police and the Guardsmen. I couldn't believe they did that. I was actually starting to feel better that someone was doing something peaceful to protest the war. I also thought it would be good if some of those demands were met. Unfortunately, they never really wanted to be peaceful at all.

Monday, May 4, 1970

People started gathering in the Commons area in anticipation of the noon rally. The school announced, "All outdoor demonstrations and gatherings are banned by order of the government."[23]

Like Sunday, a Guard jeep drove around and told everyone to disperse. At noon, 103 Guardsmen started to use tear gas to move the crowd. [24] The angry students threw tear gas canisters, rocks, wood studded with nails, concrete, and bricks at the Guard. I saw girls bring bags of this rubble to guys who threw it. The Guards were also sworn at and called nasty names.[25] I really thought things were going too far now. The Guardsmen didn't really deserve to get concrete and wood studded with nails thrown at them.

To make things worse, the next class was just getting out, which meant more students were walking in the area. The Guardsmen tried to break up the crowd and walked down the hill onto a practice football field. What they didn't realize was there was a fence around the field, next to which they got trapped. The students seized the moment and began to torment the Guardsmen even more.[26]

In another area of the campus, I saw another group of Guardsmen being harassed by students. I saw the Guardsmen kneel down and aim their guns right at the crowd. Some people still taunted them and one guy waved a black flag right in the Guardsmen's faces. Nothing happened.[27]

The Guardsmen on the football field decided to retreat to the ROTC ruins and were hit with rocks. The crowd yelled, "Kill! Kill! Kill!" Some Guardsmen were knocked to the ground because they were hit so hard. A large group of students started creeping along the right side of the Guardsmen.[28] I was really starting to get alarmed. This was getting out of control. To me it no longer seemed like a war protest.

The next events that happened I will not forget for the rest of my life. Some of the Guardsmen on the right side of the group noticed the students and kneeled down in the ready position. First, I heard one shot, then a pause, then a long spurt of shots, then a pause, and then two more. Four students were killed, and nine students were wounded. The Guardsmen quickly regrouped and retreated to the ROTC.[29]

People were running around screaming. I was in such a state of confusion that I just stood there in the parking lot with my mouth wide open. I couldn't believe my eyes. I just watched the Guardsmen fire at my fellow classmates. I guess I never *really* thought they'd fire and kill someone. I saw one of the dead students lying in a pool of blood. I felt so unbelievably angry with the Guard now that I almost can't describe it. Some of the Guardsmen looked like they had the same reaction of shock as I did. I know the things the students did to the Guardsmen were uncalled for, but did it really justify killing people?

Later today, I found out that the four dead students were William K. Schroeder, Jeffery Glenn Miller, Allison Krause, and Sandra Lee Scheuer. Scheuer was on her way to class and not part of the riot.

October 16, 1970

Today an Ohio grand jury found that the Guardsmen fired in self-defense so they weren't subject to criminal prosecution. They said if the students had dispersed like they were told a number of times to do, the tragedy on Monday, May 4, 1970, would never have happened. The grand jury, however, didn't agree with everything the Guardsmen did.[30]

I think the Kent State tragedy made the American people pay more attention to the war protests. I think it also made people think differently about how they protested, because they thought they could actually get shot. However, this event didn't make President Nixon end the war any sooner because he didn't really pay attention to the protests anyway.

Notes

[1] Gordon, William A. *The Fourth of May: Killings and Coverups at Kent State.* Buffalo, NY: Prometheus Books, 1990. 21.

[2] William Gordon 21.

[3] Michener, James A. *Kent State: What Happened and Why.* New York, NY: Random House, Inc., 1971. 48-49.

[4] "Kent State: Martyrdom that Shook the Country." *Time.* May 18, 1970. 12.

[5] James A. Michener 49-50.

[6] James A. Michener 50-51.

[7] United States. *The Report of the President's Commission on Campus Unrest.* New York, NY: Arno Press, 1970. 241.

[8] "Kent State: Martyrdom that Shook the Country" 12.

[9] *The Report of the President's Commission on Campus Unrest* 242.

[10] James A. Michener 55.

[11] James A. Michener 174.

[12] *The Report of the President's Commission on Campus Unrest* 248.

[13] James A. Michener 176.

[14] James A. Michener 176-177.

[15] *The Report of the President's Commission on Campus Unrest* 249.

[16] William Gordon 23.

[17] *The Report of the President's Commission on Campus Unrest* 251.

[18] William Gordon 23.

[19] James A. Michener 243-244.

[20] James A. Michener 244.

[21] *The Report of the President's Commission on Campus Unrest* 257.

[22] James A. Michener 250.

[23] James A. Michener 294-295.

[24] James A. Michener 299-300; "Kent State: Martyrdom that Shook the Country" 13.

[25] James A. Michener 301-302.

[26] William Gordon 25; James A. Michener 302-303.

[27] William Gordon 29.

[28] "In the Aftermath of Kent State Indictments." *U.S. News and World Report.* Nov. 2, 1970. 34.

[29] James A. Michener 305-307.

[30] "In the Aftermath of Kent State Indictments." 32, 34.

Bibliography

Gordon, William A. *The Fourth of May: Killings and Coverups at Kent State*. Buffalo, NY: Prometheus Books, 1990.

"In the Aftermath of Kent State Indictments." *U.S. News and World Report*. Nov. 2, 1970: 32-35.

"Kent State: Martyrdom that Shook the Country." *Time*. May 18, 1970: 12-14.

Michener, James A. *Kent State: What Happened and Why*. New York, NY: Random House, Inc., 1971.

United States. *The Report of the President's Commission on Campus Unrest*. New York, NY: Arno Press, 1970.

Jessica Dabler is a junior at D.C. Everest Senior High School. She is a violinist for the school orchestra, a member of the Oral Histories Club, and participates in summer softball. Jessica also likes to travel. Future plans include majoring in the science field.

Helicopters
The Role They Played in the Vietnam War

By Dave Zuleger

Although the Vietnam War was not the first conflict in which helicopters were utilized, it certainly saw the most effective use of them up to that time. Vietnam, in fact, provided an extremely successful platform for the Air Force's development of helicopter technology and strategy for its use in wartime. Great advances were made in helicopters' mobility, in their use in reconnaissance, and in the kinds of weaponry with which they were equipped. The helicopter--in a very real sense--accomplished great things in Vietnam.

Its advances in mobility were two-fold: helicopters were ideal for moving troops--in large or small numbers--from place to place, and they contributed immensely to improving medical conditions in the war.

The use of helicopters to move fighting men from base to base, or battle to battle, was not a new tactic, of course, but it was a tactic used repeatedly--and very successfully--in Vietnam. Helicopters--like the Shawnee--were used thousands of times to move troops for quick strikes against remote Vietcong operations or to evacuate them from dangerous areas. Though the element of surprise was often lost because of the noise of the machines, these movements were usually successful. If more soldiers were unexpectedly needed at a certain post, helicopters could get them there within minutes. It was unlikely, consequently, for a small group of American soldiers to be stranded against a large group of Vietcong for an extended period because the Americans could call on more troops to be brought to the battle very quickly. This capability undoubtedly saved thousands of American lives.

Advances in helicopters' speed--more than 100 mph--and maneuverability were even greater assets in the medical arena. Helicopters could fly in and out of battle areas and evacuate wounded soldiers to the safety of hospitals in very short periods of time. Between 1964 and 1973, men were evacuated more than 900,000 times for medical attention. Vietnam also saw the first use of helicopter "hoists." These long ladders--or just ropes--that soldiers could either climb up, or be tied to--to be reeled into the helicopter--saved the lives of countless wounded and immobile soldiers who otherwise would have been stranded or left for dead. In World War II, the average time between a soldier being injured and receiving medical attention or surgery was 10 hours. In the Korean War, this period was nine hours. In Vietnam, however--largely because of improvements in helicopter technology--this critical time span was reduced to just 100 minutes. Experts also agree that the remarkable reduction in the percentage of men hit by gunfire in Vietnam who died (19%) compared with that percentage in other wars (33% in the Civil War, 29.3% in World War II, 26.3% in Korea) was directly attributable to the effectiveness of the medevac, or the evacuation helicopter.

Another key contributor to the saving of American lives was the elaborate radio communications system in the helicopters. This system made possible speedy communication between all elements of the medical operation. When a helicopter pilot called a base radio operator, for example, he could tell the operator the nature of the wounds, give an approximation of the patient's survival time, and convey other vital information regarding the condition of the patient. The radio operator, in turn, could suggest the appropriate hospital for the patient's specific wound, phone ahead to determine if the hospital had a surgeon on staff at the time--or, if not, pick one up along the way--and prepare the hospital for the specific type of surgery that would be necessary. Faster, more efficient trips, equaled much higher survival rates.

The helicopter's exceptional radio system--along with its maneuverability and its capacity to hover near ground level--also made it extremely valuable to American forces as a reconnaissance tool. Vietnam saw extreme advances in the use of the helicopter for reconnaissance. The Helicopters were used frequently for reconnaissance purposes because of their maneuverability, ability to stay near ground level, and exceptional radio systems. Helicopters used in reconnaissance would often fly circle routes, routes in which the helicopter would fly to a certain point, and then circle back to base. The sole purpose of these routes, was to find out if there was any enemy activity in the area. Regardless to the findings of these helicopters on any given day, they would report what they saw to their commanding officer. The job of being a reconnaissance pilot was one which lacked stability. You never knew what you would see, how long you would be patrolling, or if you would come back alive. According to Mark Holbrook, former reconnaissance pilot himself, the pilots would take shifts, and depending on the day, they could be back to base very early in the evening or very late at night. He also stated that sometimes there could be a lot of activity and other days there could be absolutely none. Helicopters were an invaluable resource in gaining information on enemy camps, movements, or equipment. Helicopters would make their route, and then if any action or movement was seen, the pilot could easily radio back to base and immediately alert the base on the situation. Without helicopter reconnaissance many more Americans would have died of surprise attacks, or just plainly walking into an enemy camp that they might not have known was there. Helicopters saved lives by simply gaining information. Also, the information collected by the helicopters helped commanding officers to make decisions in the offensive as well. If a helicopter went by any particular base that looked weak, or was deserted a commanding officer would be notified and usually an American attack would take place on the weak/abandoned base. Without helicopter reconnaissance many more soldiers would have died, and many offensive American missions would have been thwarted. The helicopter was a priceless resource in the Vietnam War.

Another way, in which the success of helicopters was apparent in Vietnam was the significant advance made in the weaponry aboard helicopters. The main helicopter used in attack missions in Vietnam was the Huey helicopter. The need to arm Hueys in Vietnam resulted in field modifications involving the fitting of weapons pylons outboard of the cabin doors and flexibly mounted guns firing through the door aperture. This concept was taken a step farther when new helicopters were built from scratch for the sole purpose of being armed and to negate performance flaws of previous helicopters. This included improving speed, maneuverability and most of all weapons. When looking at weaponry options for helicopters, one realizes that there were over twenty different weapons which a helicopter might have. Here is a list of possible weapons that were used on helicopters in Vietnam:

M2 and M3 .50 caliber machine gun
M24A1 20mm cannon
M37C Flexible .30 caliber machine gun
M39A1/M39A2/M39A3 20 MM automatic gun
M129 40mm grenade launcher
M134 7.62mm machine gun
XM140 30mm automatic gun
XM157 or M158 or XM159B rocket launchers
XM175 40mm grenade launcher
M195 20mm automatic gun
XM196 7.62mm automatic gun
M197 20mm automatic gun

This is just a brief list of the weaponry that could be found in any combination on a combat helicopter in Vietnam. These weapons had more power, rounds, flexibility, mobility, and range than weapons applied on helicopters in any previous war. An average helicopter would have two rocket launchers, and twin machine guns or automatic guns.

These weapons on assault helicopters were used for providing necessary air support for soldiers and by the end of the war the helicopters were the principal air support for ground troops. The helicopter gun ship's rocket launchers could kill vast amounts of enemy men quickly, because of the speed in which they could engage in a battle. They were a pertinent tool, in fighting a war of attrition. Also, they were highly successful in being weapons in the quick strike capacity. Because of the improvements in mobility, maneuverability, and speed, these new technically advanced helicopters could swoop down, attack, and then be gone in the blink of an eye again. This was also an essential role to fight a successful war of attrition. The advances in weapons made helicopters an invaluable assault and battle weapon that was never utilized in previous wars.

In conclusion, the helicopter took revolutionary strides in mobility, reconnaissance and weaponry in the Vietnam War. It vastly improved the survival rate and the kill ratio as compared to previous wars. It was also a key tool in the war of attrition that America was trying to fight. Before this war, helicopters had been used, but not nearly to the success as they were used in Vietnam. They were an invaluable source for mobility, medical services, and as assault weapons. The helicopters may have been the largest part of any success that was had in the Vietnam War. They did all of the dirty work, flying at night or in bad weather to save lives, or to attack the Vietcong. They limited the sucess America achieved in Vietnam.

Dave Zuleger is currently a junior at D.C. Everest Senior High. He participates in basketball, FBLA, Solo Ensemble, and History Day. Dave is planning on majoring in bio-chemistry and education at the UW-Madison.

The Ho Chi Minh Trail

By Michael Wanserski

The Ho Chi Minh Trail, originally called the Truong Son Trail, was an elaborate system of mountain and jungle trails linking North Vietnam, South Vietnam, Cambodia, and Laos during the Vietnam and Indo-China Wars. (Sapeth) It was divided into two main parts. Trails extending from the Ca River Valley in the HaTinh Province and Hai Van Pass in Da Nang, were called the Northern Trails. The trails extending from Hai Van Pass to the Mekong and the Binh Phouc Provinces were called the Southern Trails. (Gami-travel)

During the First Indo-China War, from 1946 to 1954, the trails were very small, and people could only walk along them. These early Ho Chi Minh trails were used to bring supplies from the People's Republic of China to Vietnamese on the battlefields. (Sapeth) During the spring of 1959, the trails began to be used again as communist authorities in North Vietnam tried to take over the Vietcong Army in the south. (MMAS Vietnam Thesis) This is when the trails were changed from the Trung Son Trail to the Ho Chi Minh Trail to honor the Vietnamese Communists' revolutionary leader. (Sapeth) Also during this time, many improvements were made to the trails. Gas, oil, and other fuel lines were put in to transport troops. The trails were expanded across the countryside, and other improvements were made. Many small bases were set up along the trails so that supply trucks and personnel could be hidden during the daytime. (Gami-travel)

Even though the North continuously improved the trail, the roads were still primitive by American standards. The trails consisted of 18-foot-wide tracks carved out of the jungle. Although both gravel and corduroy surfaces were used to strengthen some sections, the roads were mostly dirt and nearly impossible to get through during the wet season. (Gami-travel) The roads were originally built by manual labor, but as time passed, the North Vietnamese made increased use of bulldozers, roadgraders, and other heavy equipment. (Sapeth) The Ho Chi Minh Trail was operated, maintained and defended by an estimated 40,000 to 50,000 personnel organized into geographic units called Binh Trams. Each Binh Tram had the necessary transportation engineers and AAA battalions to ensure movement and security of material and personnel in its sector. (Maclear)

When South Vietnamese officials in Saigon heard of these improvements, they became concerned, and in 1959 the Army of the Republic of Vietnam (ARVN) was sent to negotiate with the Royal Lao Government. Together they established forays west from the Lao Bao along the trails into Laos, to gain better intelligence on infiltration along the trail. At the end of 1959, ARVN and the Saigon government set up an outpost across the border in the Lao village of Ban Houei Sane to patrol the trails.

At the time of the Vietnam War, the Ho Chi Mihn Trail served as the primary roadway for moving North Vietnamese supplies into South Vietnam. The road network extended from Mu Gia Pass in the north, southward along the heavily forested western slopes of the Annam Range, to a series of exit points stretching from just below the demilitarized zone between North and South Vietnam, to the border region of Laos, Cambodia, and South Vietnam. (Maclear) Although the Ho Chi Minh Trail was initially confined to the western slopes of the Annam Mountain Range, North Vietnam continued to build the trails, and the system pushed additional miles further westward in Laos, providing the North an increasingly wide choice of routes along which they could channel supplies. (MMAS Vietnam Theses)

This movement of supplies required a great deal of coordination between various transportation troops and numerous transfers of cargo in and out of vehicles and wayside storage areas. Almost all movement was conducted at night in a series of short shuttles, rather than long-distance hauling. Drivers drove their trucks over the same routes night after night becoming thoroughly familiar with their assigned segments. Periods of high-moon illumination, which allowed travel without headlights, and low cloud cover, were exploited to avoid detection from overhead aircraft. Truck movement began shortly after nightfall and normally trailed off about 3:00 a.m. to allow time for the unloading, dispersal, and concealment of supplies and vehicles before daylight. These strategies were considered highly inefficient by Western standards, but they were the most effective way of moving large quantities of supplies during the Vietnam War. (MMAS Vietnam Theses)

The following statistics show just how effectively the North Vietnamese used the trails. The North Vietnamese truck inventory in Laos alone was 2,500 to 3,000 during the 1970 and 1971 dry seasons with 500 to 1,000 trucks moving per night. Each truck carried about four tons of supplies. (MMAS Vietnam Theses) While the trucks were being shipped down to the South, the North was receiving replacement trucks from large inventories. (Sapeth)

To keep cargo and trucks moving, a group of 440 volunteers was established in 1959 to work on the trail. By 1974, the group included over 300,000 people who helped keep the trail moving. Nearly 20,000 of these young volunteers died. (Sapeth) Besides making things move smoothly, the volunteers played a big role in repairing and defending the trails. The youths used inventive ways to conceal things. For example, when the United States took out a bridge on the trails, they would repair it and then hide it or make it retractable so that it would be harder to destroy the next time.

The United States used tons and tons of bombs and chemicals on the Ho Chi Minh Trail. It used Agent Orange to kill the jungle vegetation so that the pilots could see the trails, but they were never successful in shutting them down. Because the intricate system of trails had so many routes to one place, the destruction at one or two points could not close down the system.

The Ho Chi Minh Trail was the hardest thing to control in the Vietnam War. The intricate system was impossible to stop by anything the United States threw at it. The methods used by the Vietcong to move supplies up and down the trails were very effective for that situation. The will of the people fixing, defending, and helping move supplies along the Ho Chi Minh Trails was very hard to break. In all, the Ho Chi Minh Trail helped the North immensely to win the Vietnam War; if it hadn't existed, the outcome of the war might very well have been different.

Bibliography

Gami-Travel Center the Ho Chi Minh Trail. www.gamitravel.com, 1999-2000

Maclear, Michael. The Ten Thousand Day War, Vietnam: 1945-1975, St. Martin's Press, 1981

Sapeth, Anthony, Ho Chi Minh's Trail. www.cnn.com, CNN, 2001

Unknown Author, MMAS Vietnam Theses.
www.cgsc.army.military/csi/mmas, 1999

Mike Wanserski is a junior at D.C. Everest Senior High School. He plays soccer and hockey, while also partcipating in Key Club. Mike plans on majoring in medicine.

Home Before Morning

By Lynda Van Devanter
Book Review by Alex Hollman

Home Before Morning by Lynda Van Devanter is an autobiography of an Army nurse in Vietnam. This book portrays the hardships that Vietnam veterans had to go through during and after the war.

After attending an intense Catholic school, Lynda and her best friend, Barbara, volunteered their services to the U.S. Army. They were fresh out of basic training when they were sent to different stations in Vietnam.

On June 8, 1969, Lynda Van Devanter's journey began. She was sent to Pleiku and worked at the 71st Evac Hospital. Her first shift was a shock. Lynda saw young boys with their arms and legs blown off, some with their guts hanging out, and others with "ordinary" gunshot wounds. One doctor taught Lynda her first memorable lesson. He told her, "Van, this is an assembly line, *not* a medical center." These words would stick with her for the rest of her life. She and the other nurses learned not to look at these boys as humans, but as packages of meat that were fixed and sent on their way. They couldn't think of them as men or they never would have made it through their course of duty.

As the months progressed, Lynda developed strong relationships with the other doctors and nurses she worked with. They tried to live the most normal life they could under the circumstances. Some held parties where they would get drunk or high, and they would make love whenever the opportunity presented itself. People back in "the world" thought that this behavior was outrageous, but little did they know, this was all they could do to keep their sanity.

One day Lynda was working in surgery and the patient didn't look like he would pull through. As she was moving him to the recovery room, a picture fell out of his pocket. The picture was of his girlfriend and himself. On the back were the words *Gene and Katie, May, 1968*. This was the moment when Lynda saw these patients, these casualties, as men. She saw them as men who had lives back at home; men who had people who loved them, waiting for them to return. These words, too, haunted her for the rest of her life. Lynda began to hate Vietnam and didn't want to have anything to do with it. Sometimes she would break down and cry. Other times she would just sit in a room by herself. The question was: why were all these innocent men dying? What was the cause for it? What exactly were we fighting for?

Vietnam stayed with Lynda for her whole life. After her year was done, she returned to the U.S. and finished her few months in the Army. Adjusting to the return from Vietnam was difficult for all veterans. One minute they were in the middle of a war, and the next they were back in the world. People who knew she was a veteran spit at her and called her names. They treated veterans so horribly. Lynda slowly stopped talking

Author Lynda Van Devanter

about it. She stored it away and tried to forget it. Unfortunately, it was impossible to forget. The nightmares came every night, and every morning she would wake up with the words "Gene and Katie" pictured in her head. She fell into a deep depression. She constantly thought about suicide.

It wasn't until Lynda was able to get into a group with other women veterans that the depression stopped. She was involved in counseling sessions and group therapy. Eventually the therapy worked. Lynda didn't forget Vietnam because she didn't want to. She finally learned that in order to move on with her life, she had to let it go, but she didn't have to forget it. It was a part of her. The war was something that had shaped her personality and helped create the person that she is now.

As time passed, Lynda had a need to go back to the place that held the most painful and important memories of her life. In May of 1982, she was chosen to be part of the delegation of Vietnam Veterans of America to go back to Vietnam. They needed to work with issues such as Agent Orange and the problem of American-Vietnamese children remaining in Vietnam after the war.

They went to Vietnam for a second time, but this time they went in peace. Lynda learned that the Vietnamese were good, friendly people. She realized that it wasn't Vietnam that had sucked; it was the war. Lynda had wanted to go back to find something she had left-- her youth and her innocence. She now knows that she will never be able to get those back, but it's okay. She knows where they went, and she knows what they are. Her second trip to Vietnam washed away the war. She proceeded to move on and live a good life.

Lynda wasn't the only nurse from Vietnam who had a difficult time coping with the war. Lynn Kohl, who was also stationed in Pleiku, hated what was happening in Vietnam. When asked why she volunteered, Lynn replied that she was tricked into volunteering. Lynn was a senior in nursing school when she talked with the recruiters. They told her that there were so many wonderful opportunities and she would even go into the Army as an officer. The recruits assured Lynn and her friends that there was no way they would go to Vietnam. They would be stationed in California and work there. Lynn got orders to go to Vietnam after a month of serving in the Army.

When she arrived in the Central Highlands of Pleiku, she was ordered to work in surgery. During normal times Lynn worked a minimum of six-day weeks and twelve-hour shifts. Since they were constantly under rocket and mortar attacks, they dealt with a high number of casualties a day, and she also had to witness the horrors of war.

Lynda Van Devanter and Lynn Kohl were both treated with high amounts of respect when they were in Vietnam. They both learned to use the minimum number of instruments when performing a surgery of any type. It was a big change when they returned to America. They were treated with little or no respect, and the doctors needed all their sophisticated instruments and made a fuss when they didn't get what they wanted.

Just like Lynda, Lynn had to go through multiple counseling and therapy sessions to get rid of her depression and constant nightmares. It seemed that the only jobs she could get were in surgery. It followed her for most of her life. It was a long time before she could get into OB. Lynn worked in the nursery and absolutely loved it. She was finally able to work with life instead of death.

If Lynn could give a message to the people of America she would say how very proud she is to have served her country. Everybody who went to Vietnam gave 110% at all times. They were very brave and courageous, and it's a shame that America confused the warrior with the war.

Lynn saw a poster once that really said it all. It read, "For those who fought for it, freedom has a taste those protected will never know." (WWII Vet)

Lynda Van Devanter and Lynn Kohl are friends from Vietnam. They can talk about the war, but they don't let it eat them away. They can concentrate on the lives that they did save, and they both now live happy lives.

Home Before Morning gives a clear understanding of all the difficulties those nurses in Vietnam went through. Women veterans weren't even recognized until many years after the war. Many experienced depression or PTSD, but many were able to overcome it. People should be proud of these women for saving the lives of so many young men. It's a shame that these women weren't recognized earlier for their accomplishments.

Alex Hollman is a junior at D.C. Everest Senior High School where she plays volleyball and softball. She is also a member of the student council and does community service at nursing homes.

The Kent State Tragedy

By Kyle Goertz

It is a warm, sunny day in Ohio. You and your fellow students are protesting the presence of the National Guard on your Kent State University campus. You have marched onto the practice football field and the parking lot of Prentice Hall. Rocks are thrown at the Guardsmen as the protestors scream angrily at them. The Guardsmen are armed with tear gas and possibly live ammunition. You know what you are doing is illegal on campus, but it gives you a sense of danger that you love. Imagine the panic; imagine the confusion. Imagine how fast your heart would be beating in a situation like this.

Then imagine yourself being on the other side, as one of the Guardsmen. How would it feel to have rocks thrown at you while college students shout angrily at you? One can easily see how the shootings broke out on May 4, 1970, on the campus of Kent State University in Ohio. There were several events that occurred in the days prior to the horrible shootings. The actions that happened during the shootings left several students dead, and even more students wounded. After the event, there were several trials to attempt to figure out who was responsible for the tragic events that happened on May 4, 1970.

With many of the college-aged students around the nation being called off to war in Vietnam, there were sure to be many protests on college campuses. There had been a few small protests on the campus of Kent State in previous years, but none had drawn much attention from the outside community or the student body. The first protest took place in 1967, but drew very little interest (Calkins pg. 2). In the fall of 1968, the Students for a Democratic Society, the SDS, became a major force on campus. It organized with the already existing Black United Students (Calkins pg. 2). The two groups worked together to take over the Student Activities Center where the Oaklawn Police were recruiting (Calkins pg.2). The Oaklawn Police Department was notorious for racism at the time(Calkins pg.2). The students were stopped by police when they became trapped in the Music and Speech Building. There were 58 students arrested (Calkins pg.3). Overall, this led to a feeling of distrust and anger among students on the campus (Calkins pg.3).

The past events on the Kent State campus built up and seemed to be coming to a climax in early May of 1970. The National Guard was called into Kent State by Mayor Satrom at 5 p.m. on May 2, 1970, because there were rumors that radical students were planning to destroy the city and the University (Hensley pg.2). When the National Guard arrived, it found the ROTC Building ablaze with 1000 demonstrators surrounding it (Hensley pg.2). The protestors interfered with fire fighting efforts, and the Guardsmen were forced to send tear gas into the crowds (Hensley pg.2). The ROTC Building eventually burned to the ground (The pg.2).

The following day, May 3, there were 1000 Guardsmen on the campus of Kent State University (Hensley pg.4). The governor of Ohio, James Rhodes, held a press conference and called the protestors the worst type of people in America and said that every force of law should be used against them (Hensley pg.4). He also stated that they were worse than brownshirts and that he'd keep the Guardsmen on the campus "until we get rid of them all." (The pg.3). This, of course, angered many of the students who were protesting the war in Vietnam. That night, the protestors set to the streets and threw rocks in the town. The Guardsmen fired tear gas into the crowds as many of the protestors were arrested (Hensley pg.5). All of this added to the tension created on the following day, May 4, 1970.

The protest on May 4, 1970, had been planned on Friday, May 1 (Hensley pg.5). The protestors began to gather around 11 a.m. and by noon, there were 3000 protestors (Hensley pg.5). The crowd con sisted of 500 core demonstrators, 1000 "cheerleaders," and about 1500 spectators (Hensley pg.5). This protest was not a protest against the war in Vietnam, but more a protest against the presence of the National Guard on the campus of Kent State, but there was still a strong anti-war sentiment among the demonstrators (Hensley pg.6). Prior to the protest, school officials had handed out 12,000 leaflets on how demonstrations of any kind were illegal on campus, but that did not stop the demonstrators, who had planned nothing but a peaceful rally (The pg.3).

The police and the Guardsmen were sent in to disperse the gathered protestors. Several policemen and Guardsmen drove through the commons area telling the students to leave, or legal action would insue (Hensley pg.6). They were met by angry shouts and rocks being hurled toward them. The National Guard fired tear gas into the crowd in hopes of causing the protestors to disperse (Calkins pg.3). They then began to march toward the group, but the protestors began to move up a steep hill, known as Blanket Hill, and then down into the Prentice Hall parking lot and an adjacent practice football field (Hensley pg.5). The Guardsmen followed the protestors, but soon found themselves somewhat trapped because of the fence on the football field (Hensley pg.6). The Guardsmen stayed there for about ten minutes as the rock throwing intensified to its highest point (Hensley pg.7). The men then turned and backtracked up the hill toward Prentice Hall. Upon reaching the top of the hill, 28 of the 70 Guardsmen turned and fired live ammunition toward the crowd of demonstrators. Most of the men fired either into the ground or into the air, but a few shot directly into the crowd (Kent pg.3). In a matter of 13 seconds, there were 61-67 shots fired by the Guardsmen.(In pg.4) Chaos broke out after the shots were fired; students ran all over the place, not knowing and not believing what had just occurred. Students looked around to see many of their fellow students wounded, and several dead.

There were several students wounded by the Guardsmen's shots, nine to be exact. In an essay written by Jerry M. Lewis and Thomas R. Hensley, it appears that the victims were very spread out in relation to each other. One of victims was Joseph Lewis. Lewis was standing 60 feet away from the Guardsmen holding his middle finger up when he was hit in the right abdomen and lower left leg. Another victim was Thomas Grace. Thomas was also about 60 ft. away and was hit in the left ankle. John Cleary, who was around 100 ft. away from the Guardsmen, was hit in the upper left part of his chest. Also, Alan Canfora, who was standing 225 ft. away, was struck in his right wrist. The most seriously wounded student was about 300 ft. away from the Guardsmen. The man was Dean Kahler, who was struck by a bullet leaving him paralyzed from the waist down. Another victim, Douglas Wrentmore, who was standing about 330 ft. away, was struck in his right knee. James Russell was struck in the right thigh and the right side of his forehead. He was standing 375 ft. away. Robert Stamps, who was positioned about 500 ft. away, was shot in the right buttock. The victim who was the furthest away from the Guardsmen, Donald Mackenzie, was shot in the neck. He was about 750 ft. away (At pg.5-9).

Along with the nine students who were wounded, four of the protestors were killed by the volley of shots. None of them, however, was a protest leader or even a radical (At pg.7). William K. Schroeder, a 19 year old psychology major was one of the four (At pg.7). He was from Lorain, Ohio, and was the second-ranking student in the Kent State's Army ROTC unit.(At pg.7) He was only a spectator at the rally. He was a high school basketball and track stand-out, and was the perfect image of a clean-cut Middle American Boy (At pg.7). Even with this, his mother said,"My so was very opposed to the Vietnam war, and his feelings against the war were growing."(At pg.7)

Another student who was killed by the Guardsmen shots was Sandra Lee Scheuer. She was a 20 year old junior from Youngstown, Ohio (At pg.8). She wasn't the type of person to be caught up in the whole protesting and rioting scene. She was described as a bubbly honor student type of girl (At pg.8). Her best friend, Eileen Feldman, said, "Sandy lived for what everyone else lived for--to find someone to love and someone who loved her" (At pg.8).

Jeffrey Glenn Miller was also shot and killed on May 4, 1970. He was a 20-year-old transfer student from Michigan State (At pg.8). He wasn't a militant activist type, but told his mother that he felt as though he needed to join the demonstrations occurring on campus. He was a psychology major at Kent State who wore his hair long, liked bell-bottoms and rock music. His mother said, "I know it sounds like a mother, but Jeff didn't want to go to war, not because he'd be hurt, but because he might have to hurt someone else" (At pg.8).

The fourth student who was shot and killed was Allison Krause. She was a 19-year-old honor student in art (At pg.9). She was said to be more of a listener than a talker and never preached of her deeply held views. She opposed the war and was among the spectators at the protest on May 4, 1970, alongside her boyfriend Barry Levine (At pg.9). Earlier, she had placed a flower in a Guardsman's rifle and said softly, "Flowers are better than bullets" (At pg.9). Allison's father said, "Is dissent a crime? Is this a reason for killing her? Have we come to such a state in this country that a young girl has to be shot because she disagrees deeply with the actions of her Government?" (At pg.9)

Sadly, none of the students killed by the volley of shots from the guns of the Guardsmen were even involved in the protest. They were simply onlookers, passersby. Innocent lives were lost in the shootings.

In the years following that day in early spring of 1970, several trials were held to bring justice and rest to what happened on the campus of Kent State on May 4, even though no official investigation had ever been carried out (Kent pg.2). In each of the trials, the Guardsmen said they fired because they felt that their lives were in danger (At pg.9). In 1974, District Judge Frank Battisti dismissed the case against eight of the Guardsmen at mid-trial because he felt the government had such a weak case that the defense didn't need to state its case (At pg.10).

In a longer and more complex trial in 1975, a jury voted nine to three that none of the Guardsmen could be held responsible, and that their lives were, in fact, in danger. This ruling was appealed, and the Sixth Circuit Court of Appeals ruled that they had to have a new trial because of the mistreatment of a jury member (At pg.11).

The trials finally came to an end in January, 1980. An out-of-trial settlement was signed by 28 defendants. The wounded students and parents of the students killed were awarded $675,000. This amount was paid by the state, not by the Guardsmen. It equalled the amount of money the government estimated it would cost to take the matter back to court. The Guardsmen looked at the agreement not as an apology or admission of wrong doing, but as a declaration of regret (At pg.12). The statement read as follows:

In retrospect, the tragedy of May 4, 1970, should not have occurred. The students may have believed that they were right in continuing their mass protest in response to the Cambodian Invasion, even though this protest followed the posting and reading by the University of an order to ban rallies and an order to disperse. These orders have since been determined by the Sixth Circuit Court of Appeals to have been lawful.

Some of the Guardsmen on Blanket Hill, fearful and anxious from prior events, may have believed in their own minds that their lives were in danger. Hindsight suggests that another method would have resolved the confrontation. Better ways must be found to deal with such a confrontation. We devoutly wish that a means had been found to avoid the May 4th events culminating in the Guard shootings and the irreversible deaths and injuries. We deeply regret those events and are profoundly saddened by the deaths of four students and the wounding of nine others which resulted. We hope that the agreement to end the litigation will help to assuage the tragic memories regarding that sad day.

In conclusion, what happened on May 4, 1970, was tragic and surrounded in sorrow. Were the

Guardsmen correct in shooting at the crowd of protestors because their lives were in danger? To them it probably seemed that way. Were the students right in protesting when they had been told to disperse and they knew the protest was declared illegal by the University? No, they weren't. There were many events that led up to what happened on May 4, 1970, which caused the growing tension between the students and Guardsmen. The protest on May 4 could have easily gone on peacefully or could have become even more violent than it turned out. The events that followed the tragic event left no real closure for the victims and their families because not one Guardsmen was found to be solely responsible. Could the events of May 4, 1970, have been avoided by different methods of handling the situation?

Kyle Goertz is a junior at D.C. Everest Senior High School. He participates in football, basketball, and baseball, and enjoys playing other sports for fun. While his college plans are undecided, he is interested in physical therapy.

Left Behind,
the Story of a Prisoner of War

By Amanda Zimmerman

Every day I would sit and pray
to try and ease my worried mind,
"Oh Lord, let this not last another day,
and let us not be left behind."

It began one day when it had started to rain,
and I was crawling through a thick haze,
wondering how I'd get off enemy terrain,
and trying to make my way through a maze. (1)

And as soon as I stepped on that little stick,
a noise I thought no one would ever hear,
a thousand rifles I heard click,
and there I stood frozen in fear.

With guns pointed and cocked,
the Vietcong soldiers took me away,
the intensity and depth of my shock,
mere words could never display.

To which camp would they take me?
I desperately wanted to know,
Hanoi Hilton, Mountain Retreat, or Camp B,
Citadel, Plantation, or perhaps Skidrow? (3)

When we got to the camp sometime the next day,
they asked me about things I should know,
but information I would not say,
and my hate for them started to grow.

When answers I would not give,
their reaction to that was torture,
the beatings would last until I thought I would not live,
until they thought I would talk for sure.

The solitude was hardest to bear,
and I had to keep a sharp mind,
I had to remember that I had people who care,
and my country would come get me out of this bind.

For days I waited but no one came,
and the months began to pass.
Do they realize this war was not game?
And I wondered if I still had a chance.

The years have gone by,
and I am still here,
forgotten by my country-left to die,
and rescue attempts to this prison didn't near.

So here I sit forgotten by all,
abandoned by my country too.
For the enemy, I have no use at all,
and I wonder what I should do.

So every day I would sit and pray,
To try and ease my worried mind,
"Oh Lord, let this not last another day,
and let us not be left behind.

Bibliography

Notre Dame Magazine. "Pure Torture." Thomas N. Winter '95-'96.

"The Vietnam Conflict." http://www.deanza.fhda.edu

Three's In ***-the Vietnam POW home page." Paul Ganti.

http://www.eos.net/rrva/nampows.html

Amanda Zimmerman is a Junior at D.C. Everest Senior High.

Letters From Beyond
A Soldier's Point-of View from the Vietnam War

By Jenna Tomcek

These letters were written by Bill Tomcek, a soldier in the Vietnam War. He was assigned to Company E, 3/39th Infantry, 9th Infantry Division. He served from January 15, 1968, through November 18, 1968. These letters were written to his Mom, Dad and his brother Leonard. To Bill's surprise, his mother saved all the letters. When Bill left for Vietnam, his mother told him to write home every week so that she would know that he was still alive.

The tone of these letters change throughout his tour of duty. In the beginning the letters relate first impressions and a sense of unfamiliarity to his surroundings. As time goes on, the letters begin to express doubt and frustration as to what he is trying to accomplish and as to what everything means. Ultimately, he begins to express some anti-war feelings as members of his unit are killed and supplies are not readily available. He expresses happiness and relief, as he is able to leave Vietnam for R & R and eventually the end of his tour of duty and his return to the "world."

19 Jan 68

Dear Mom and Dad,

After leaving Fort Lewis at 3 a.m. on Thursday, we arrived at Honolulu by 8 a.m. From there we flew to the Philippines. This was a 10-hour flight. From the Philippines we flew to Cam Ranh Bay where I am now. Altogether, it was an 18-hour flight. I was supposed to go to Pleiku, but presently I'm being shipped to Saigon. Right now I'm in the 504th company of the 22nd battalion. I will be going to the USARV Trans Det in Saigon. There I will be assigned to something else.

God Bless,

Bill

21 Jan 68

Dear Mom, Dad and Len,

Here I am in Saigon. I am waiting to be shipped from here, the 90th replacement battalion, to the 9th division. This is a change in my orders; I was supposed to go to the 4th division. I've heard that the 4th is really bad so the change is for the better. I really don't prefer to climb the mountains in the Central Highlands. The mountains are quite steep at times, and with 16-inch-thick undergrowth the going would be rough. The 9th operates in the Delta so I'll be wading through the paddies -- but there won't be any steep mountains. I had quite a ride from Cam Ranh Bay to Tan Son Nhut, which is on the outskirts of Saigon. We rode in a transport, camouflaged, four-prop carrier. There weren't any seats, so we sat on our duffle bags. The ride wasn't anything to talk about. It was a good thing I didn't eat dinner. Since I'm going down into the Delta, I plan on volunteering for either the River Rat patrol or door gunman on a helicopter. Both ways I'll be riding instead of hoofing it. One thing that seems funny around here is that it's hard to believe that I'm in a country that's at war. It seemed like the war was more real back in the states. So many people are in transit that you wonder who is in the field.

God Bless,
Bill

21 Jan 68

Dear Mom and Dad,

Now I am at the Bear Cat Camp, 9th division HQ. This camp is in the Bien Hoa Province, III CORP, 20 miles east of Saigon. We're staying in squad tents. They're comfortable, and there's not much problem in keeping them clean. I should say that everything is so dusty that it doesn't pay to clean anything. We have all our gear now including our personal M16 rifles. Our field gear is the same as always issued. I was expecting to be issued a couple of sheets, but I was just clued in that we're in a combat zone. From now on it's just one big bivouac. This place is in the boonies. The chow is pretty good -- had turkey for dinner. Today is Sunday. I was surprised to hear that. The days of the week don't have any meaning. The numbers are what count. Each month has so many, and they go by one at a time.

God Bless,
Bill

24 Jan 68

Dear Mom, Dad and Len,

Today we zeroed in our weapons, and now we're ready for a firefight. The artillery keeps popping off the rounds into the jungle. This is mainly done to keep Charlie awake and moving. This war seems funny. It's not a conventional war, so nothing is clear-cut. Here we are with VC on the other side of our perimeters. Even here it doesn't seem like we're really at war. Things just seem endless.

God Bless,
Bill

31 Jan 68

Dear Mom and Dad,

Right now I'm at Tan An. Yesterday, I flew from Bear Cat to Dong Tam and then took a helicopter to Tan An. Last night we had a red alert. I guess they hit Saigon last night. Anyway, a lot of activity was taking place. We stayed in the med ward along with the wounded. There're not too many here. This is one of the three places in Vietnam that treat VC wounded.

God Bless, Bill

A bunker in the perimeter defense at Rach Kien. Before night-fall Bill noticed a gap in the roof over the firing porthole. He piled bags of mud in the hole.

That night a mortar round hit this bunker and exploded in the bags of mud which were piled on top of the firing porthole. Bill and Flegal were inside the bunker when the round hit..

4 Feb 68

Dear Mom and Dad,

I am now in Rach Kien. The last two nights have been pretty peaceful. Before that we were hit by mortar three nights in a row. We took some casualties, but nobody was seriously hurt. Boy, I was scared when those mortars were coming in. One day we got hit in the evening around 8 p.m., then 12 a.m. and then 6 a.m. If that doesn't keep a person jumpy, nothing will. A lot of guys sleep out right by the bunkers. Hence, when the mortars come, they don't have to run for cover. Last night there were twelve of us in one bunker. This all coincides with the big push all over the country.

God Bless,
Bill

21 Feb 68

Dear Mom, Dad and Len,

Today is the third day since we sustained a mortar attack. To illustrate how jumpy we are right now, I'll relate a funny event that happened last night. The VC have hit our mess hall in every mortar attack, and one time they dropped a few rounds in while a movie was playing. Well, with all this in one's mind, you're pretty jumpy when sitting in the mess hall. Last night, we were watching a movie in the mess hall. Just then the artillery fired their full charges. This sudden explosion sent everyone to their feet, and guys began to dart out of every possible exit. We ran into the street and were met by the bewildered looks of other guys who were walking by. Others came out of hootches, and everyone was asking, "What's going on?" After finding out that it was our own artillery, we filed back into the mess hall and proceeded with our movie. It was amazing how fast that mess hall was cleared. I wonder if a civilian theater could be cleared out that fast.

God Bless,
Bill

24 Feb 68

Dear Mom and Dad,

Everything is going OK. Today we suffered two more casualties. The recon platoon got themselves into a situation where they were almost wiped out, but ended up with one wounded. They were on a night patrol when they came under heavy enemy fire: mortars, and small arms. The whole platoon dove for the moats, and immediately sunk into mud up to their chests. A dike was between them and Charlie so they were able to watch the tracers fly right over their heads. One guy, the man who was wounded, went a little bisserk (sic). He thought that our own artillery was firing at them since once before it did happen. Hence, he ran on top of the dike waving his rifle and shouting, "Stop, Stop, what kind of war is this that you shoot your own men?" No one could stop him since everyone else, scared for their lives, had jumped in the moat. He was finally hit in the mouth by some shrapnel. It tore his teeth up a bit but didn't kill him. This morning one guy was shot while inside his hootch. Someone accidentally discharged a grease gun (an automatic, 30 round clip 45 caliber). He was just shot through the arm and side so he's not in too bad of shape. We have to make up all the casualty reports and accident statements. As I mentioned before, whenever something happens around here, we are able to get gunships in 15 minutes. That is the reason why we only have to hold off a ground attack for 15 minutes. Once the ships get here, they strafe a 60 degree area with their mini-guns. These guns fire 6,000 rounds a minute and literally tear the place up. You can see why Charlie would commit suicide if he ever attempted to over-run us. He will try though and as before, he will suffer a severe defeat.

God Bless,
Bill

26 Feb 68

Dear Mom, Dad and Len,

Everything is OK. The weeks go by fast. Around here we don't go by the days of the week; we go by the numbers, and then the numbers don't actually mean too much because all we do is live from daylight to dark, and dark to daylight. Hence, a week could fly by and you wouldn't even realize it. The mosquitoes and bugs are flying around me like I'm a ferris wheel. This place is sure buggy, and needless to say this place does bug a person. Please send me my pipe. I get the urge to act like a General once in a while. War is really mixed up, funny, crazy, and so forth. If you don't get hurt, which is a miracle around here, you must have done something right.

God Bless,   Bill

9th Infantry
Base Camp
entertainment.

1 Mar 68

Dear Mom, Dad and Len,

Well, Mom, I hope you have a happy birthday. I've celebrated it here, halfway around the world. Just think, I've celebrated your birthday a day before you did. Everything is fine with me. I get a little teed off once in a while at this place but not bad enough to shoot anybody.

Bill

17 Mar 68

Dear Mom and Dad,

For some reason my spirit is dragging. I guess I have a feeling of uselessness. A good firefight would probably boost my morale. Recon went out a few nights ago and killed five VC where the Falcons had been ambushed. They caught the VC building a roadblock.

God Bless,
Bill

5 Apr 68

Dear Mom and Dad,

The monsoons are really getting close. The air is getting damper, the mornings are getting foggy, and the sky cloudy. I haven't seen a drop of water fall from the sky for three months. I guess it's time for some rain. Soon everything will be mud. At least Charlie won't be able to mortar us. It's still hot here, 120 to 130 degrees in the sun, 95 or 100 degrees in the shade. Our room fluctuates between 80 degrees at night and 90 degrees during the day. 80 degrees is pretty cool; it gives you the chills. Well, they're talking about peace again. Charlie will just build up his supplies, and when the time is right Hanoi will walk out and blame the U.S. for aggression, and all this mess will break open again. Oh well, everyone not over here seems to have all the answers. Everything is OK with me. Is Mary still planning on getting married in August?

Good Night,
Bill

30 Apr 68

Dear Mom and Dad,

I have just returned from my three-day in-country R & R. I had a good time and got a wicked sunburn from the South China Sea. Vung Tau is an R & R (Rest and Relaxation) center, but it's just like the rest of Vietnam. The people are dirty. The streets are dirty, and filth just lies wherever it pleases. The people try to get everything they can out of you. While walking down a street, it's not uncommon to be mobbed by a bunch of Vietnamese kids who will even try to slit your pockets to get the contents. The merchants charge wild prices, but you can usually talk them down. I bought a chess set for 120 piasters, after the man initially wanted 450 piasters for it. I do enjoy haggling with these people.

God Bless,
Bill

©2002 D.C. Everest Area Schools Publications

8 May 68

Dear Mom, Dad and Len,

First of all I must wish mom a Happy Mother's Day. I hope you enjoyed yourself. You can bet that I'm proud to have you for my mother. If you haven't sent the rat traps yet, you don't have to(sic). We got a hold of one trap and some other guys got a few, and all together we have caught over 40 rats. Now we don't have any running over us at night. The rains have started and at times it really pours. For a while things cool off. The humidity is getting pretty high, and after a rain the heat is almost unbearable. Just sitting in one spot is enough for sweat beads to run down your face, back, stomach, and arms. Along with the rain and heat come the bugs. They're everywhere -- it's unbelievable.

God Bless you all,

Bill

While building a bunker for defense, he is pausing to admire his growing mustache.

13 May 68

Dear Mom and Dad,

Last night was really something else. Between the hour of 1 a.m. and 4 a.m., we were mortared ten different times. The VC exhibited the same type of accuracy they had once before. They must have infiltrated another FO (Forward Observer) into the village. For what they did they must have had inside help. The mess hall took four or five hits. The club took three hits. Many rounds exploded on the street, and several hit around our hootches. The building we live under took a direct hit. The tile roof was blown apart at the spot where the round hit. It made about a 6 ft hole. We stayed in our own hootch. I really don't know how safe and sound we are, but no one was hurt. Today I received orders promoting me to Sergeant E-5. I will now be wearing three stripes. Heavy casualties and constant rotation of soldiers back home make for fast promotions. Now I'll be paid $292.50 a month. Wow!

God Bless,
Bill

9 June 68

Dear Mom, Dad and Len,

Well, five months have passed. What a way to go. Rumors have it that we will be moving to Dong Tam to replace the Riverine Force. Last week some tactical genius dropped the 2/39th Infantry into a VC Battalion-sized ambush. Needless to say, the 2/39th needed quite a few replacements. As the rains keep increasing, so does the heat. Right now it is 92 degrees in our hootch and it is nearly 10 p.m. Well, I heard Kennedy was shot. Counting King, that makes two. In a way, I feel safer over here. I have a bunker and if someone would attempt to shoot me, I wouldn't hesitate to empty a clip. At least we can shoot back over here. The only man who has said anything realistic about this war is Reagan -- who proposes to attack North Vietnam. We could airlift troops into North Vietnam and raise some holy hell. Then North Vietnam would have to use their resupplies in their own country, and while we are tearing up North Vietnam, the VC in the South could be wiped out. Well, I guess we will have to leave it up to the politicians. I'm pretty tired so I'm going to get some sleep. Maybe tomorrow will be a better day. This letter doesn't portray very much happiness, does it?

God Bless,
Bill

13 June 68

Dear Mom, Dad and Len,

Well, we're at it again. Our whole battalion is picking up and moving. E company is being split up. We will be going south, to the mud holes deep in the Delta. I am going to Dong Tam first. Well, whatever happens, we'll have to live with it. Boy, I sure get irritated at some of these stupid lifers who have been in the Army for 20 years, more or less. They're supposed to lead us "inexperienced ones." They are the ones who get people killed. Over here you just can't make enemies and live to tell about it. After these guys spend six months or more on line (and being slightly off anyway) they won't hesitate to shoot someone they don't like. The best time to shoot a person is during an assault. Since bullets are flying all over, no one can tell who shot whom. Well, such are the hazards of war. It's getting late and I have to get up at 5:30 A.M tomorrow. We plan on hitting the road early in the morning. Keep praying and let's hope for the best.

Bill

While traveling through the Mekong Delta, he is alert, watching the countryside for enemy activity.

14 June 68

Dear Mom, Dad and Len,

We are now at Dong Tam. There are 15 of us from Echo Company, and we're setting up a base of operations. The rest of our company is at Fire Base Moore, about 10 miles from here. That firebase has all sorts of big guns and firepower. We are west of My Tho. We definitely are deep in the Delta. In a few weeks we will be mounting the boats and begin the amphibious assaults. It promises to be quite a change and definitely exciting. I'm getting to see quite a bit of the Delta, and my tour will at last be interesting. Dong Tam is the most forward base of operations in the Delta for the 9th Infantry.

God Bless,
Bill

20 June 68

Dear Mom, Dad and Len,

You know, this war just seems unreal. We're not losing, and there's no way of knowing if we're winning. One's whole life over here is lived in a background of artillery blasts and uneducated people who don't even understand what's going on. I just can't learn to trust these people. You even check the little kids to see if they're carrying grenades before you talk or play with them. Also, I don't believe that anyone fully realizes the extent of the corruption that goes on. I'm referring specifically to our own supplies. Through our own selfish desire for wealth and through extreme laziness and negligence, from the trooper who will discard 500 rounds of M60 machine gun ammo because it's too heavy -- not caring that Charlie will find it and use it to kill GI's -- to the dock manager who can reap a kickback by not noticing that an unmarked barge is loaded with American supplies and lets it casually disappear down one of the many waterways; to the black markets which sell items marked "A gift from the American people: Not to be sold"; to company supply rooms being out of boots or poncho liners (but ask some shop owner, he'll get you one for a price) and it goes on and on. All I want to do is get out of this country and out of the army.

Bill

Infantry men of Company E hold a memorial service for SGT. Carl Johnson who was killed when satchel charges blew him out of the lookout tower at Firebase Moore. The boots, weapon with bayonet, and the hat of SGT. Carl Johnson are displayed during a three gun salute.

29 June 68

Dear Mom, Dad and Len,

My latest possession is a National Radio-Tape, $45.50. It is really cool. You can play the radio and tape at the same time. I'll send a few tapes home, and you can send me some. Next month, I will be going to Sidney, Australia, for R & R. It promises to be a big change. Just think, I will be among English speaking people. Wow! Take care of yourselves so that when I come home, everyone will be lean and mean.

Bill

He is resting under a tent shelter and listening to ARVN out of Saigon on his National Radio-Tape.

13 July 68

Dear Mom, Dad and Len,

In 8 days I'll be leaving for Bear Cat and eventually Australia. I'm sure looking forward to leaving Vietnam. On the picture you see one of the scout dogs we have around here. They are beautiful and vicious, weigh about 80 lbs, and really have a nose for VC. Next to my left arm you can see a gravestone. As I said before, we are set up in a grave-yard, and these graves are all over. Someday someone will accidentally dig up old Papasan (Father, househead). We make firing positions out of the grave-stones.

Bill

15 July 68

Dear Mom, Dad and Len,

Another Monday morning is here. It looks like another sunshiny day. It's raining quite regularly now at noon, around 5 p.m. and later at night. The rain is really refreshing. The clouds are taking over the sky, so it's hard for pilots to run air strikes and it's especially difficult to see at night. Our main night device is a starlight scope. This scope works off of starlight, and when the clouds fill the sky there's no starlight. It's as simple as that. Did you get my tape yet? I'm wondering how it worked out. I have also sent more slides home.

Take care,
Bill

Hall, Tomcek, and Harings are unofficially using the 9th Infantry Base Camp swimming pool at Bear Cat.

23 July 68

Happy Birthday Dad,

Just don't worry -- I'm just about a quarter of a century old myself. I hope you had a good day and will have many more to come. My location is now Saigon. I'm at the 90th Replacement Battalion awaiting a flight to Australia. I will be leaving tomorrow at 1345. It definitely promises to be a grand time. Oh, yes -- I won't do anything that you wouldn't do. I plan on going to the countryside and living on a ranch. Yup, I'll be riding some of those Australian horses. Maybe I'll go skiing in the mountains. Anyway no matter what I'll end up doing, I will enjoy it. Getting out of this place will seem like heaven.

God Bless,
Bill

3 Aug 68

Dear Mom and Dad,

I have returned! Australia was great! When I got back to the unit, I found out that our battalion had moved back to Dong Tam. Now our whole battalion is together – who knows for how long. I no longer have the job of liaison between the field and rear attachment. I am now a member of the Radar Section. Our job is to detect enemy movement and prevent surprise attacks. I enjoy this work much more. It's much more physical than mental, but I'm sick of the mental run-around that goes on with the First Sergeant. The whole section consists of 11 men. The way I look at it, I only have five months left, so I'll be able to stick anything out. I have received the birthday box. Thanks very much. The cookies were fresh and tasted very good. Just think, I'm a quarter of a century old (25). Wow! I really don't know what to say about my stay in Sidney. I had a lot of things to say before, but once I got back to the unit, I found I didn't have much to talk about. I guess coming back had a depressing effect. It seems senseless to write about it.

God Bless, Bill

2 Sept 68

Dear Mom, Dad and Len,

Just think, I'm getting short over here. The end is definitely in sight. I get happier every day. I received the cookies a few days ago. They came at the right time and were delicious. We were deep in the boonies. Yes, they are already gone.

God Bless,
Bill

He is sitting on the edge of a French gravestone in a grave-yard among the rice paddies in the Mekong Delta. Since the rice paddies were filled with water, this was the only place that was dry.

15 Sept 68

Dear Mom, Dad and Len,

Today is the first day of my ninth month. When I first arrived at Beat Cat and the 9th Infantry and then the 3/39th Infantry at Rach Kien, I was one of several replacements. After last night's little action, I am now the only man left. Everyone else who came to the 3/39th Inf. with me is either dead or seriously wounded and evacuated to the states. Martinez and I had 120 days left last night. We were beginning to kid each other whenever we would meet that we were the only two left and that we were getting short. I guess we were getting sort of cocky about it. By this time we figured that we'd make it unscratched. Last night while on a security patrol, he was hit with fragments from a B40 rocket and an AK-47 round pierced his head and shoulder and came out of his back. Things seemed to get a little more personal during these last two nights. I and my other radar partner barely sleep at night. On Friday the 13th, we were walking on the road at 12:30 a.m., going to brush our teeth at the water wagon. We saw flashes to our right and soon afterwards heard the very distinct whistling sound of airborne rockets. We went flying for cover, which amounted to a grain of sand. When I was lying as flat as possible on the road, I thought that the end was here. I attempted to push my body through the hard ground. After the explosion and a realization that I was still alive, I took a tremendous leap into a rice paddy. Here, when I look back at it, the funny part starts. I had leaped right through a barbed wire fence. I tore my clothes up but received no serious scratches. I then completely submerged myself in the paddy. I was hanging on to rice stalks. Then I heard and saw two more rockets, which seemed to be bearing down on my soggy position. Again, I thought, this is it. These two rounds hit dead center in the middle of the road, but 100 meters west of me. I then crawled like a beaver through that rice paddy. I think that I was still shaking two hours later. In the morning, you could see the path I created in the paddy. We've decided not to brush our teeth after dark anymore. We're both to short too mess around with rockets. Well, nothing else is going on. It's the same old bullet and bean story.

God Bless, Bill

20 Sept 68

Dear Mom, Dad and Len,

    We're still at Can Giuoc. I'm making a tape, which represents the sounds of Vietnam: gun shots, grenades, footsteps in the paddies, helicopters, and anything else that's heard over here. I'll probably hand carry this one home.

                    Will write again,
                    Bill

2 Oct 68

Greetings,

    No need to worry about me. I'm taking good care. If anything would happen, you'd know about it within 24 hours or so. We're at Dong Tam right now. We may move out any day. I'm going to start sending some of my stuff home. In twenty days or so I should be in Hong Kong. As it looks now, I almost, for sure, will be home for Christmas -- maybe Thanksgiving. Wouldn't that be wild? Well, it's about noon now; I didn't feel like sleeping.

    God Bless, Bill

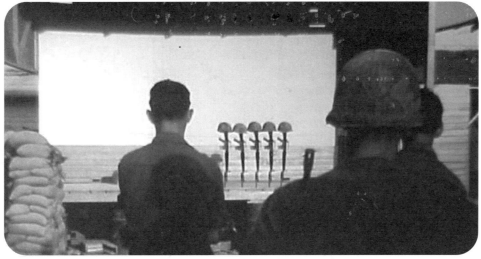

Following the ambush of Falcon platoon, Company E, 3rd Battalion, 39th Infantry, 9th Infantry Division, a memorial service is being held at their camp for the five men who were killed.

4 Oct 68

Dear Mom, Dad and Len,

    Everything is going fine. I am now in charge of a PPS-5 Radar Team. I have eight men besides myself. We are on 24-hour alert to deploy anywhere into the Delta from Dong Tam. I was to go out today with 4 people from the 2nd Brigade. It's going to be interesting. It will be the first time I'm taking out a team by myself. Everything is going great. I'm really looking forward to coming home. I left the 3/39th just in time. Four of my friends were killed yesterday and five others were dusted off. They were blown away by a command-detonated mine. Well, I must get some sleep.

                    God Bless,
                    Bill

16 Oct 68

Dear Mom and Dad,

   I have just experienced the most rewarding week and mission since I have arrived in this country. I took a five-man team to AP Cho, Vietnam, 10 miles from nowhere. We lived with the village chief and got to know quite a few Vietnamese. It would actually be hard to describe. I was extracted last Tuesday night before I was scheduled to go into a classroom full of Vietnamese kids. I was planning on going over the numbers and a few English phrases. I was disappointed when I had to leave. I was supposed to go to Hong Kong. I will probably leave in a few days. I plan on buying a couple of good suits and a very good camera.

   God Bless, Bill

In the village of AP Cho, Bill had the tailor make him a set of black pajamas which he wore for several days before he decided that it was unhealthy!

24 Oct 68

Dear Mom and Dad and Len,

   Well Len is now another year older. I hope he had a happy birthday last week. Not too much is going on as far as I'm involved anyway. I'm not going to the field anymore. As far as I know, I'm going to be home for Thanksgiving. Don't prepare any extra food. I won't eat too much. I haven't decided on my route of travel yet. I am getting an early out so I can attend the Winter Quarter at Ball State University, Muncie, Indiana. School starts December 5. Things will be in a rush but I'll make it. I'm leaving tomorrow for Hong Kong. There is no need for me to go into all the detail, but I do have everything coordinated. After November 7, don't send any more mail this way. I won't get it anyway. Well, I'm not really in the mood for writing letters. It gets harder and harder.

      See you all soon,
      Bill

5 Nov 68

Dear Mom and Dad,

I'm back in Vietnam–Hong Kong was just too much. I saved so much that I just about went broke. I really had a wild time in Hong Kong. I never had such a time in my life. Well, everything is great and ok.

God Bless
Bill

Footnote: The 5 November 1968, letter was the last letter saved by Bill Tomcek's mother, Theresa, my grandmother. Bill Tomcek was sent home on November 18th, 1968 and discharged from the Army on November 25th, 1968 – in time for Thanksgiving Day. On December 5th, 1968, he was attending classes at Ball State University, Muncie, Indiana.

In the fall of 2001, I reviewed and edited my father's letters. These letters had not been read for over 30 years. From a soldier's point-of-view, these letters gave me insight into how my Dad felt about the war, and what he went through. In the beginning he was willing to do what his country asked him to do. As time went on, he became disgusted and frustrated with how the war was being conducted. He did what he had to do in order to survive, and then he went back to the "world." As a result, I am able to share these letters with you.

Jenna K. Tomcek
A proud daughter

Jenna Tomcek is a junior at D.C. Everest Senior High. She is involved in the school choir and has participated in History Day twice. Jenna's college decision is undecided, but future plans include working in the psychology field or social work.

Media in the Vietnam War: Who Really Made Us Lose?

By Ben Simmerman

Is it possible for a battle to take place in your living room? Many battles did during the Vietnam War. Television showed many battles of the war to the average American household. Bloody battles were common dinnertime occurrences. This was the first war with such extensive media coverage.

The media in the Vietnam War greatly affected the outcome. According to Peter Braestrup, a Vietnam veteran and writer, the pictures from Vietnam were unprecedented in war coverage. The media and the press showed raw violent footage, sometimes reported incorrect information, and, in general, gave the war a bad name.

First of all, the media showed raw footage of the war, which the government did not censor. Many of these photos were graphic and violent, and should have never made it onto television programs. The reason for this was the disorganized manner in which stories were sent out of Vietnam. Films and photos were often taken out by unexpected routes--returning soldiers even carried them with them--so the U. S. government could not always control what information reached the American people. For example, after the Tet Offensive in 1968--because of the surprise of the attacks--many raw photographs appeared on television news programs and in newspapers. Many reporters' movements were not controlled during this time, and in the confusion, the government could not determine what made it back to the United States. The graphic images of wounded and dying young American men had the power to leave lasting impressions on the nation. Moreover, the government also gave news crews relatively easy access to the battlefields. Reporters and cameramen were flown by plane or helicopter to the battlefields (which also led to the--often widely publicized--deaths of many reporters and press staff). It was estimated that in any one battle there was an average of forty press members in the field at one time. This allowed lots of raw battle footage, most of which was not censored, to reach the American people.

Secondly, the information the press reported was often incorrect. After the Tonkin Gulf incident, for example, in which the U. S. was reportedly attacked at sea by North Vietnamese forces, the alternative press printed a story that contradicted the U.S. government's account of the incident, saying that the event may have never even occurred Though it was never proven, at the time, that the government was not truthful, the contradiction in the press left the suspicion with some segments of the population that the government may have lied. A good deal of incorrect information also reached the American public after the Tet Offensive. Because the government did not comment officially for two months after the events, reporters speculated widely, and false accusations and stories were rumored. It was reported, for example, that during the offensive, 26 communists had infiltrated the U.S. embassy. Though they had, in fact, gotten into the compound, three U.S. marines had stopped them from actually entering the embassy building. The Tet Offensive was ultimately one of the most successful aspects of the Vietnam War for U.S. forces, but the films and photographs taken during the event left the opposite impression by emphasizing American losses and weaknesses in our security and forces. Vietnam was also one of the few conflicts in American history in which newspaper reporters and writers at home were allowed to join anti-war rallies. Their personal opinions often leaked into their articles, causing a biased view for their readers.

Consequently, the press often gave the Vietnam War a bad name. Though President Johnson was extremely sensitive to this "negative" coverage and occasionally considered World War II-like censorship, this was never accomplished, due to a lack of support in Congress. Instead the media was accused by many of showing too much violence by both Vietnamese and American troops. The coverage in the U.S. of the Tet Offensive actually boosted communist morale, instead of simply showing America what was happening. In World War II, veterans were treated with respect and sympathy, and their stories made to be heroic. This was not the case in Vietnam. The focus shifted off of heroic efforts of fighting men and women onto the battle aspects of the war. In many ways, the media was responsible for the lack of support for the war by giving the impression that the U. S. was losing, even when that was not the case. The press continued to report on the war with increasing skepticism. In the 1960s, many people were looking for peace in the world, and this war didn't fit with what they wanted. The media showed them images of the exact opposite of their ideals. It was clear that the television reporting of the war focused primarily on American troops, and often when they were in trouble. Issues like drugs and desertion contributed to the negative atmosphere beginning to spread around the U.S.

The outcome of the war, then, was almost certainly affected by the media and press coverage in Vietnam. The raw footage of the war, the incorrect information that was reported, and the negative image conveyed by many of the reporters were all factors in the outcome. Robert Elegant, a former *LA Times* reporter explained, "The outcome of the war was determined not on the battlefield but…on the television screen." This was true because of the huge role the media played in the lives of normal Americans. Had the media not been so intense in its coverage of the war, it is possible that the result may have been different.

Bibliography

Biesel, Frank R. Interview. Nov. 2, 2001. D. C. Everest High School.

Braestrup, Peter. *The News and Media in the Vietnam War--Myths and Realities*.

Elterman, Howard; Jarold M. Starr. *How the War was Reported*. Center for Social Studies Education. 1988.

Heanue, Megan. May 10, 2000. "Vietnam War: Media". <caribou.cc.trincoll.edu/~mheanue/final.htm>. (Nov. 1st, 2001)

Ben Simmerman is a junior at D.C. Everest Senior High. He participates in choir, Solo Ensemble, drama, and soccer. Ben is also a memeber of his church youth board.

My Lai Masacre

By Erin Lukensmeyer

On March 16, 1968, Charlie Company, a unit of the U.S. Eleventh Infantry Brigade, stormed into the hamlet of My Lai in the Son My village of Quang Ngai Province. Four hours later, an estimated 200-500 unarmed civilians, including women, children, and the elderly, were brutally murdered. It was a massacre that seems to have been forgotten, but will always haunt the conscience of the U.S. Army and the American people. (Wallechinsky, 1)

Charlie Company conisited of 150 soldiers, led by Lieutenant William Calley, was considered one of the best units in the army. The company had been in Vietnam for three months and had not engaged in any major battles, but had still suffered a lot of casualties from snipers, mines, and booby traps. (Wallechinsky,1) The soldiers were agitated because of all the casualties of their company in the weeks preceding the massacre. (My Lai Massacre,1) The soldiers were ready to prove themselves and seek revenge on the enemy. When the soldiers entered My Lai they expected to be locked into fierce combat with the Vietcong believed to be stationed at My Lai. (Wallechinsky,1)

When the company arrived at My Lai they discovered that there were no Vietcong in sight, so Lt. Calley ordered the troops to slaughter the civilians. People were rounded up into ditches and machine-gunned; some were even mutilated by having "C Company" carved into their chests. (Wallechinsky,1) According to an eyewitness report, several old men were bayoneted, praying women and children were shot in the back of the head, and at least one girl was raped and then killed. (My Lai Massacre,1) Any survivors trying to escape were immediately shot. It is also said that when Calley spotted a baby crawling away from the ditch, he grabbed her, threw her back into the ditch, and opened fire. One GI later said, " You didn't have to look for people to kill, they were just there, I cut their throats, cut off their hands, cut out their tongues, scalped them. I did it. A lot of people were doing it and I just followed. I just lost all sense of direction."(Wallechinsky, 1) The objective of the American military mission was certainly clear: search and destroy My Lai, but what wasn't clear was what to do with any civilians who were encountered in My Lai. (Wallechinsky,1)

There were actually some heroes in My Lai although you rarely hear of them. Helicopter pilot Hugh Thompson was flying above My Lai at the time, and sickened by what he saw. He landed his aircraft and started rescuing the Vietnamese civilians. He also gave orders for his machine gunner to open fire on any American soldiers who continued to fire on the villagers. He radioed for help from other helicopters and in complete graphic detail reported to his section leader what he had seen. Soon afterward, the company was ordered to quit killing the civilians. (Wallechinsky,2)

Coverup of the massacre occurred immediately. Many stated it was a stunning combat victory against a Vietcong stronghold. Even *Stars and Stripes,* an army newspaper, ran a feature story applauding the courage of the American soldiers who risked their lives. People even sent personal congratulatory notes to Charlie Company. (Wallechinsky,2)

There were two separate investigations that uncovered the truth of My Lai. The initial investigation just concluded that My Lai was a combat operation in which twenty civilians were accidentally killed. In the second investigation eighty soldiers were extensively interviewed. An army photographer even produced photos of the carnage of My Lai. Twenty-five officers and enlisted men were eventually charged with crimes, but only six cases were even tried. In a lot of cases the evidence was overwhelming and a lot of soldiers admitted to killing civilians. The only soldier found guilty of murder was Lt. William Calley. (Wallechinsky,2)

The court martial for Lt. Calley began on November 17, 1970. For over four months witness after witness came forward to tell their stories in front of a six-officer jury. (Wallechinsky,2)

Calley testified, "I was ordered to go in there and destroy the enemy. That was my job that day. That was the mission I was given. I did not sit down and think in terms of men, women, and children. They were all classified the same." Some soldiers said Captain Ernest Medina made it clear that the civilians should be killed, but others disagreed. Some also said he did not put it in those exact words, but he did imply it. (Wallechinsky,2) Calley also testified that Captain Ernest Medina ordered him to kill everyone in My Lai, but the evidence was only enough to convict Lt. Calley alone of murder. (My Lai Massacre,1)

The jury found Lt. Calley guilty of killing only 22 civilians at My Lai, and he was sentenced to life imprisonment. The final army estimate for the number killed total was 347. (My Lai Incident,1) Calley had only served three days in prison, and President Nixon ordered him to be taken to Fort Benning, Georgia, to be held under house arrest. His life sentence was reduced to twenty years, and then again reduced to 10 years, but in 1974 he was paroled after only serving three years under house arrest. (Wallechinsky,3)

Many Americans did not see Lt. Calley as a murderer, and they thought his verdict was unjust. Many thought he was either a hero fighting against communism or a scapegoat used to mask enormous blunders made by the US Army. (Wallechinsky,3) Others questioned the conduct of the US soldiers in Vietnam as the gruesome details of the massacre reached the public. A Military Commission investigating the My Lai Massacre found widespread failure in leadership, discipline, and morale among the Army's leaders and fighting units. (My Lai Massacre,1)

In normal times, a poorly-educated man like Lt. Calley would not have even been allowed to become an officer. However, because the army did lower its standards, it should share in the guilt of the massacre. (Maclear,272) Many said that if the educated middle class (the "Harvards" they were called) had joined in the fight, a man of Lt. Calley's emotional and intellectual stature would never have been issuing orders. (My Lai Massacre,1) Calley was considered a below-average, dull, and inconspicuous boy. It is said that Calley did not even know how to read a map. Seymour Hirsh wrote in a report of the massacre, "If there was any concurrence among former members of Calley's platoon in Vietnam, it is the amazement that the army considered Calley officer material." (Maclear, 272-273)

My Lai is a very good example of when war becomes a crime. No one really knows whose fault it was. Either Captain Medina or Lt. Calley? Or was it the American Army's fault for letting someone with emotional problems be a leader issuing orders and putting others' lives at risk? The only thing we really do know is that there was no reason for the killings of hundreds of civilians in My Lai. They were all unarmed and posed no threat whatsoever to Charlie Company. Abraham Lincoln once said to the troops during the American Civil War, " Men who take up arms against one another in public do not cease on this account to be moral human beings, responsible to one another and to God." (Wallechinsky,3)

Bibliography

Maclear, Michael. *The Ten Thousand Day War*. New York: St. Martin's Press, 1981.

"My Lai Incident." http://www.encyclopedia.com/articles/08921.html> (22 Oct. 2001)

"My Lai Massacre." http://www.pbs.org/wgbh/amex/vietnam/trenches/mylai.html> (22 Oct. 2001)

Wallechinsky, David. "The 20th Century: The My Lai Massacre." http://www.dreamscape.com/morgana/mylai.htm> (22 Oct. 2001)

Erin Lukensmeyer is a junior at D.C. Everest Senior High School.

My New Life

By Jenna Hazaert

The following are sample journal entries of a Vietnam veteran, who is suffering from post traumatic stress disorder. The Vietnam experiences that follow are based on actual letters from Vietnam veterans.

July 4, 1969

Dear Journal,

Today has been a bad day because I have been thinking about all my buddies who went to college, and are now enjoying fireworks and celebrating the birth of our country. I would do anything to be with them right now. I can't believe it is a day of celebration at home, and thousands of us are here grieving for the men we saw die today.

I am mostly thinking about my buddy, Keith. He was killed a few days ago. Keith, Robert, a few other men, and I were searching a deserted Viet Cong base camp. Robert and I were looking at a radio system when we heard an explosion. We looked up to see Keith's body in three pieces flying through the air. He had stepped on a booby trap and killed himself. I had to pick up pieces of his body and wrap them in a poncho to be carried back to camp. The smell of the body is something I will never forget.

I got a letter from Frank the other day. He left months ago to go to nursing school. He is talking about his apartment and how he is refurnishing it. He is also saving money to buy a color television. I wish those were the kinds of things I was worried about here. Everyday all I can think about is how to stay alive. Frank asked about Keith and Robert. I regret having to tell him Keith was killed in action. I guess it is just another day here in Vietnam.

October 30, 1969

Dear Journal,

Today is the two-month anniversary of the day Robert climbed into a spider hole and was killed. I'll never forget that horrible day. We were best friends and the two smallest men in our company. We usually took turns going into spider holes and had been very lucky not to be killed yet. However, August 30, his luck changed. Robert agreed to go in the spider hole because I wasn't feeling well that day. It was my turn, though; I would just go the next two times. So, Robert went in the hole, and the rest of us stepped back. Seconds later there was a huge explosion which knocked over some men. The spider hole had been booby-trapped, and he was killed, right in front of me. It was supposed to be me in that hole not him. I will never get over the guilt I feel over Robert's death.

I am at Namo Bridge right now, and I have too much time to think. I have all this time because we are just sitting around cleaning out our weapons and resting. It is hard to sleep at night with all the nerves. I am on alert all the time. Thinking is not healthy for me; it is better for me to live without thinking about what is going on around me. I just go through the motions, not thinking about the impact of our actions. I am simply making sure I survive.

December 25, 1969

Dear Journal,

Merry Christmas to me! I am alone in a foreign country and have been watching my friends being killed for the last year. I'm done and out of here on January 1, 1970. I can't believe I only have seven days left in this hellhole. The G. I. Bill is going to pay for my college education. I plan on using every cent. I figure anything is better than this place.

October 14, 1984

Dear Journal,

My wife, Jane, made me go to see a psychologist today. She said if I didn't do something about my drinking, she was going to take the kids and leave me. The psychologist thinks that I have post traumatic stress disorder (PTSD) from the Vietnam War. He wants me to see a specialist. I've been out of the war for fifteen years and they are just telling me this now!

I have a lot of the symptoms of PTSD. My frequent flashbacks of the war, nightmares, emotional numbness, sleep disturbances, depression, anger, anxiety, and the feeling of guilt of surviving. My drinking may also be a side effect of the disorder. The psychologist said that at least 30% of men and women who served in war zones suffer from PTSD. Over one million Vietnam veterans have the disorder. (1)

Jane and the kids think I should make an appointment with the specialists. Jane made me realize how I was not a part of my children's lives when she pointed out that I do not communicate with them, or her, for that matter. I do not attend my son's baseball and football games. I forget to pick my daughter up from dance and school. I spend most nights in my room watching television and sitting on my bed. I usually drink so much at night that all I can do is lie in bed. The worst part is that I did not even realize I was doing all this. I can't explain my own actions, and now that it has been brought to my attention, it aggravates me. After letting this all sink in, I made an appointment for November 27.

November 29, 1984

Dear Journal,

I went to the specialist two days ago, and he officially diagnosed me with post traumatic stress disorder. I scored a 65 on the Global Assessment of Functioning Scale. This scale is based on 100 points, and the lower the number, the more disabled the person is (American Psychiatric Association). So, I guess things could be much worse. The specialist talked about how he believed Vietnam veterans suffered from PTSD for two main reasons. The first reason is the average age of the veterans when they were in the war. The average age was 19-years-old compared to 26, which was the average age of a World War II soldier. At age 19, the soldiers were unsure of their future and were not mature enough to handle what was happening to them. The second reason is the fact that the soldiers were sent over to the war as individuals rather than a team. When the men got to the war, they felt alone and had no friends. Many of the men were scared to make friends because the friend would be there one day and gone the next. As a result, when they got home, they felt like they had no one to talk to about their experiences. There was no "welcome home" feeling. To make matters worse, at home the men were treated poorly and not respected. They got home too quickly, often within forty-eight hours of their discharge (Wilson). They were sent home alone and often went through a culture shock. When the specialist was saying this, I was thinking, wow, this is exactly how I feel.

The specialist made me talk about what I think my biggest problems are. I said they were fear of crowds and emotional numbness. I am unable to do something as simple as take my children to a movie. The lines of people there and darkness make me anxious. I hardly ever speak to my children or my wife because I feel like they don't understand me.

We then talked about reliving my experiences to help me recover and become a part of my children's lives. He told me about an organization called the Vietnam Veterans of America (VVA). The VVA is an organization that helps families get all the benefits and services they deserve (VVA's Guide on PTSD). I also found a twelve-step program online. Dr. Joel Brende originated the program. His twelve steps are:

1. Power-- accepting the fact that I am powerless to live a meaningful life.
2. Seek Meaning-- finding that there is meaning in the fact that I survived.
3. Trust-- finding trust in God and my family and friends.
4. Self-Inventory-- looking for the good in me.

5. Rage-- admitting that I have a lot of angry feelings.

6. Fear-- tell God and my family the traumatic experiences I had in the war.

7. Guilt-- ask God to forgive me for my lack of living.

8. Grief-- ask God and family for help in grieving for those I left behind.

9. Forgiveness vs. Self-Condemnation-- telling myself and God that I have self-destructive wishes and commit to wanting to live from now on.

10. Forgiveness vs. Revenge-- admit that I want revenge and ask for the strength to give it up.

11. Finding Purpose-- look for God's knowledge to find a new purpose in life.

12. Loving & Helping Others-- love others and help those who suffer from the same thing I do (Brende).

     I can now realize that PTSD will never go away and that I must learn to live with it. In the near future with the help of my family, psychiatrist, and the above twelve steps, I would like to make a life for my family and myself.

December 23, 2001

Dear Journal,

It has been almost a year since my diagnosis, and I feel like a better man. I have learned how to manage my PTSD. My disorder has less of an affect on my day-to-day function. In the last year I tried my best to follow the twelve-step program and visited my psychiatrist on a regular basis. I am no longer drinking and am able to take my children to the movies. We have made it a weekend tradition. I also talk to my wife and children freely after telling them my stories of the Vietnam War. I no longer feel guilty about living through the war. But, not a day goes by that I do not think about Keith and Robert. I contacted Frank, and he is arriving tomorrow to spend Christmas with my family. My entire family is coming to our house for the holidays to celebrate my newfound life. My life has purpose and direction now. And I cannot wait for the first Christmas in 32 years, in which I will feel the true Christmas spirit.

Bibliography

American Psychiatric Association. *Diagnostic and Statistical Manual of Mental*

    Disorders: Fourth Edition (DSM-IV). 1994.

Anxiety Disorders: Post Traumatic Stress Disorder.

    <http://www.nmha.org/infoctr/factsheets/34.cfm> Oct. 21, 2001.

Brende, Joel, MD. PTSD. From the VietNow National Magazine.

    <http://www.vietnow.com/artptsd.htm> Oct. 28, 2001.

Fassio, Ray. To Daniel Hazaert. June 3, 1969.

Fassio, Ray. To Daniel Hazaert. June 30, 1969.

Fassio, Ray. To Daniel Hazaert. August 22, 1969.

Fassio, Ray. To Daniel Hazaert. August 24, 1969.

Fassio, Ray. To Daniel Hazaert. September 21, 1969.

Fassio, Ray. To Daniel Hazaert. October 24, 1969.

Fassio, Ray. To Daniel Hazaert. December 23, 1969.

Russ. Post Traumatic Stress Disorder Personal Stories.

<http://www.mhsancturay.com/ptsd/story.htm> Oct. 19, 2001.

Stover, Phillip. To Daniel Hazaert. June 29, 1969.

VVA's Guide on PTSD. <http://www.vva.org/Benifts/ptsd.htm> Oct. 21, 2001.

Wilson, R. Reid. Post Traumatic Stress Disorder Summery. 2000.

<http://www.cyberpsych.org/anxieties/6Trauma/PTSD_intro.htm> Oct. 19, 2001.

Jenna Hazaert is a junior at D.C. Everest High School. She is involved in Chamber Choir, the Oral Histories Club, Solo Ensemble, and National History Day. After she graduates in 2004, she is planning on going into the field of sociology.

The Tonkin Gulf Incident

By Matthew Nohelty

The country of Vietnam has been a trouble spot marked with conflict and controversy throughout the twentieth century. Troubles began when numerous European countries, mainly France, attempted to colonize Vietnam and convert its people to Christianity. Soon opposition to the French arose, and after many years of bloody conflict, Vietnam won its independence. The Geneva Accords, signed on July 21, 1954, forced the French to withdraw their troops and divided Vietnam into a communist north under Ho Chi Minh and a democratic south under Ngo Dihn Diem. Elections were scheduled in 1956 to once again reunite Vietnam under a common leader elected by the public. As the election approached, the CIA collected information which indicated that Ho Chi Minh had gained much support and was likely to win. In fear of losing Vietnam to communism, the United States encouraged Diem to cancel the elections, which he did.

Because of these actions, many South Vietnamese were outraged with Diem, and support for communism grew. In 1958, civil war broke out between the communist supporters and Diem. As the war continued, Diem began disobeying the United States' orders, which eventually led to the U.S.-backed coup led by the South Vietnamese military in 1963. The United States then helped establish a new government, the Military Revolutionary Council, and the focus was once again placed on the communist north. The events that soon followed would be flawed with deception and half-truths leading to the escalation of the most controversial war in the history of the United States.

During July, 1964, the United States was gaining valuable information from its aircraft reconnaissance missions. The information pertained to the size and location of the North Vietnamese troops. Despite this success, many U.S. government officials felt the time had come for stronger measures.

General William C. Westmoreland, leader of the U.S. Military Assistance Command, asked officials in Washington to support a South Vietnamese attack on the coastal defenses of North Vietnam in the Tonkin Bay. His request was approved, and the attack was planned in coordination with the South Vietnamese leaders. ("Tonkin Gulf Yacht Club" 2) The operation began at 2:00 a.m. EDT on July 30 when Nasty boats were released from Da Nang. The Nasty boats under OPLAN 34A, Operation Plan 34 Alpha, attacked the islands of Hon Me and Hon Ngu. These attacks lasted approximately 39 minutes. During these strikes, North Vietnamese radar sites and defense facilities were destroyed. (Goulden 253)

Because of these attacks, the United States anticipated the North Vietnamese troops would become active, especially around the coast where the attacks had occurred. Because of this activity, the United States felt it could learn a great deal about the North Vietnamese forces. On July 31, the United States dispatched the *USS Maddox* to conduct a DeSoto Patrol in the international waters off the coast of North Vietnam in the Tonkin Bay. The purpose of this mission was to gather information about the coastal defenses of the North Vietnamese and to discover the amount of damage caused by the attacks of the previous morning. The *Maddox* used electronic espionage, which gave it the ability to intercept both radar and radio waves from North Vietnam.

In the early hours of August 2, the *Maddox* intercepted a radio message that indicated the North Vietnamese might undertake hostile actions. As the *Maddox* continued its patrol, it intercepted more information that confirmed there would be an attack somewhere in the Gulf of Tonkin. The *Maddox* reported these messages and also stated that the continuation of its patrol would be an unnecessary risk. However, the commander of the Seventh Fleet, Admiral Roy L. Johnson, ordered the *Maddox* to continue its patrol despite the feelings of the crew. (Goulden 254)

As it passed by the island of Hon Me, the *Maddox* began to pick up radar signals indicating that three, small, fast moving objects were headed its way. As the vessels approached, they were identified as North Vietnamese PT boats traveling at speeds between 45 and 50 knots. As the boats came within 9,800 yards, the *Maddox* fired three warning shots in the direction of the boats. The shots had no affect on the PT boats, and they continued to approach rapidly. The crew of the *Maddox* knew they would soon be under attack and sent a message to the aircraft carrier, *USS Ticonderoga*. When the *Ticonderoga* received the call from the *Maddox*, it was in the process of performing test flights. The *Ticonderoga* immediately dispatched the four F-8 Crusaders that were already in the air to assist the *Maddox*. By this time, the PT boats were nearing the *Maddox* and two had already launched one torpedo apiece. Both of the torpedoes missed to the starboard side of the *Maddox* by 100 to 200 yards. (Goulden 27) The other PT boat continued to approach and was hit directly with a 5-inch round fired from the *Maddox*. Slightly before it was destroyed, the PT boat launched a torpedo, which also missed the *Maddox*. The two remaining PT boats fired numerous rounds of 37-mm gunfire toward the *Maddox*. The *Maddox* continued to return fire on the two remaining PT boats with its 5-inch gunfire. Eventually, the F-8 Crusaders, led by Lieutenant Dick Hastings, arrived and attacked the PT boats with 20-mm gunfire and Zuni rockets. The remaining two boats were forced to retreat back to the coast. As they retreated, they were pursued by the F-8 Crusaders, whose gunfire heavily damaged both boats. The fuel supplies in the aircraft began to deplete so they were forced to return to the *USS Ticonderoga*. ("Tonkin Gulf Yacht Club" 3) The two PT boats managed to return to the coast but suffered heavy damage. The only damage taken by U.S. forces was a single bullet hole in the side of the *Maddox*, which was inflicted by a machine gun aboard one of the PT boats. ("The Tonkin Gulf Incidents of 1964" 2)

On the nights of August 3 and 4, the Nasty boats from Da Nang were once again authorized to attack North Vietnamese coastal defenses. Just like the attack on July 30, the mission was under the authority of OPLAN 34A. This time the targets were on the mainland of North Vietnam rather than on nearby islands. The attacks damaged numerous facilities on the coast of North Vietnam, and the mission was considered a success just as the previous mission had been.

The United States refused to let the attack on the *Maddox* disrupt its plans of electronic espionage but didn't want to leave the *Maddox* alone and unprotected. Admiral Thomas H. Moorer decided to place another United States destroyer, the *C. Turner Joy*, in the Gulf of Tonkin along with the *USS Maddox*. Before the attack, the *Maddox* stayed near the coast at all times. Now the United States decided it would be safer for the two destroyers to patrol near the coast during the day and then move out into the middle of the Tonkin Gulf at night. (Goulden 255)

On August 4, the United States gained information that North Vietnam believed the patrol of the destroyers was linked with the attacks by OPLAN 34A. This information brought the fear of another attack on the *Maddox* and the *C. Turner Joy*. Shortly after this information reached the destroyers, they asked for constant air protection. The request was denied, but aircraft would be available on nearby aircraft carriers should trouble arise. (Goulden 256)

As the night of August 4 was approaching, the *Maddox* and the *C. Turner Joy* were completing their patrol and were heading out into the gulf. On their way out to the middle of the gulf, they began picking up strange signals on their radar indicating that numerous small, high-speed vessels would soon attack the destroyers. The signals appeared nearly identical to those seen by the crew of the *Maddox* on August 2. The captains of both destroyers called for air support from the nearby aircraft carriers. The *Ticonderoga* dispatched six A-1H Sky Raiders, one F-8 Crusader, and two A-4D Sky-Hawks within minutes. A short time later, the *USS Constellation* sent out seven more aircraft to support the *Maddox* and the *C. Turner Joy*. ("Tonkin Gulf Yacht Club" 3) The night was very foggy and pitch black, making visibility very poor. The ships began to fire in the direction the radar indicated the crafts were coming from. As the planes arrived, they too began to fire into the water under the direction of crewmembers of the two destroyers. The *C. Turner Joy* reported sinking three of the attacking vessels. The destroyers reported that their sonar detected a total of 22 torpedoes had been fired at them as well as heavy machinegun fire. (Goulden 259) In total, the *Maddox* and the *C. Turner Joy* fired 249 shells from their three-and five-inch guns. ("Tonkin Gulf Yacht Club" 3)

The strange thing about the attack was that the images and sonar readings were different on both ships, especially the number of boats that were attacking them. This caused many to believe that the images were "ghost images" and the attack had not actually taken place. After the incident, the majority of the pilots said they saw no enemy movement in the water. James B. Stockdale, the pilot of the F-8 Crusader said, "Not a one. No boats, no wakes, no ricochets off boats, no boat impacts, no torpedo wakes-

-nothing but the black sea and American firepower." ("Gulf of Tonkin Incident 1964" 1) Stockdale and other pilots may have been unable to see the attacking boats because of poor visibility. Other pilots, along with some crewmembers of the destroyers, claimed they did see the attacking boats, which adds to the overall controversy surrounding the attack. John J. Herrick, captain of the *Maddox*, was unsure about these attacks and said, "freak weather conditions and an overeager sonar-man" may be the reason for the reported torpedo attacks. (Goulden 259) After researching the attack, Secretary of Defense, Robert S. McNamera, and Pacific Commander, Admiral Ulysses Grant Sharp Jr., concluded that the attacks actually had occurred. They reported their findings to President Lyndon B. Johnson.

On August 5, the following day, the United States retaliated with attacks of its own, which were authorized by President Johnson upon hearing the reports of McNamera and Sharp. The *Constellation* and the *Ticonderoga* were ordered to send aircraft to bomb numerous targets near the coast of North Vietnam. The majority of these targets were part of the North Vietnamese Navy including patrol boats and other vessels located at Ben Thuy, Quang Khe, Hon Gay, and in the Lach Chao River. The planes also hit a large petroleum storage facility in the city of Vinh, which was considered the most valuable target the aircraft destroyed during these attacks. ("Tonkin Gulf Yacht Club" 3)

On the seventh of August, President Johnson proposed the Tonkin Gulf Resolution which would allow him to use any means necessary including military force to stop the military action in Vietnam. President Johnson manipulated the truth about the attacks and explained to the public and to Congress that the North Vietnamese had used military force against United States troops in two unprovoked attacks. He also said that the *Maddox* was in the Tonkin Gulf only to keep peace in the Vietnam area. He also conveniently failed to mention the possibility that the second attack had never even occurred. His proposal passed by a vote of 416 to 0 in the House of Representatives and 88 to 2 in the Senate. ("The Gulf of Tonkin Incident 1964" 1) Because of the resolution, President Johnson was able to send hundreds of thousands of troops to Vietnam without first getting the approval of Congress.

Because of the events that occurred in these nine days, United States involvement in the Vietnam area grew rapidly, eventually escalating to the Vietnam War. The truth about the American involvement in the events leading up to the retaliation by the North was not discovered until 1968. However, by this time, it was too late to reconsider U.S. policy in Vietnam and to prevent the 58,000 American soldiers from giving their lives. A person truly has to wonder what would have happened if the truth had been revealed earlier, but because it was repeatedly covered up and continuously hidden from the public, the United States became heavily involved in a war that has shaped a generation.

Bibliography

Goulden, Joseph C. *The Truth is the First Casualty - The Gulf of Tonkin Affair - Illusion and Reality.*

Chicago, New York, San Francisco: Rand McNally & Company, 1969.

The Gulf of Tonkin Incident 1964. [Online] Available, http://campus.northpark.edu/history/WebChron-/USA/GulfTonkin.html, October 7, 2001

The Tonkin Gulf Incidents of 1964. [Online] Available, http://www.cs.ruu.nl/wais/html/nadir/vietnam-/tonkin-gulf.html, October 7, 2001

Tonkin Gulf Yacht Club. [Online] Available, http://home.pacbell.net/lchevato/tonkin.htm, October 7, 2001

Weitzman, Kim. The Relevance of the Tonkin Gulf Incidents: U.S. Military Action in Vietnam, August 1964. [Online] Available, http://www.ttu.edu/~vietnam/96papers/maddox4.htm, October 17, 2001

Matt Nohelty is a junior at D.C. Everest Senior High School. He participates in football and baseball, and enjoys golf. He is currently undecided about his college plans.

Torn by Society

By Greg Peterson

O say can you see?
18 and I can do what I want,
fighting soldiers from the sky
eight miles high, then you touch down
wordlessly watching
there's a man with a gun
over there telling me I've got to beware,
this summer I hear the drummin'
four dead in Ohio,
freedom, freedom, freedom,
yeah, yeah, yeah yeah yeah yeah,
one, two three what are we fighting for?
volunteers for America, volunteers for America,
war, huh, yeah, what is it good for?
absolutely nothing, good God y'all,
shapes of things before my eyes will they
teach me to despise or will I make man more wise?
R-E-S-P-E-C-T!
the times they are a changing,
it ain't me it ain't me I
ain't no fortunate one,
ball of confusion that's what
the world is today,
be sure to where some flowers in your hair,
my country 'tis of thee
sweet land of liberty;
all we are saying is
give peace a chance,
America, love it or leave it
hell no, we won't go,
California dreamin'
in restless dreams I walk alone,
purple haze is in my mind
excuse me while I kiss the sky,
where have all the flowers gone?
Sunday will never be the same,
do you believe in magic?
God bless America, land that I love,
to everything there is a season

turn, turn, turn,
hey what's that sound everybody
look what's going on,
I heard it through the grapevine,
21 and as strong as I can be,
heat wave, dancing in the streets,
I was so much older then
I'm younger than that now,
all you need is love, everybody,
we've got to get out of this place
boom, boom, boom, boom;
I've got to run to keep from hiding,
O beautiful for spacious skies,
God shed his grace on thee,
take another little piece of my heart now baby,
doctor my eyes have seen the tears
it's too late; it's too late,
no where to run too baby, no where to hide,
incense and peppermints,
come hear Uncle John's Band,
break on through to the other side,
it's all over now baby blue…

gk peterson
10/31/01

Bibliography

This bibliography is in the order of the song as it appears in the poem.

Smith, John Stafford (Music) 1750 and Key Francis Scott (Words) 1814, *The Star Spangled Banner*, Traditional. Performed by any high school band.

Cooper, Alice, Buxton, Glen, Dunaway, Dennis, Smith, Neal and Bruce Michael, *Eighteen*, Bizarre Music Company, Alive Enterprises 1970. Performed by Alice Cooper.

Sadler, Barry and Moore, Robin, *The Ballad of the Green Berets*, Music, Music, Music Inc., 1966. Performed by Staff Sergeant Barry Sadler.

Clark, Gene, Crosby, David and McGuinn, Jim, *Eight Miles High*, Tickson Music, 1965. Performed by The Byrds.

Stills, Stephen, *Helplessly Hoping*, Gold Hill Music, 1969. Performed by Crosby, Stills and Nash.

Stills, Stephen, *For What Its Worth*, Ten-East Music/Cotillion Music Inc and Springalo Toones, 1966. Performed by Buffalo Springfield.

Young, Neil, *Ohio*, Cotillion Music Inc. and Silver Fiddle Music, 1970. Performed by Crosby, Stills, Nash and Young.

Havens, Richie, *Freedom*, Traditional arrangement adapted from Motherless Child, 1969. Performed by Richie Havens.

McDonald, Joe, *I-Feel-Like-I'm- Fixin-To-Die-Rag*, Alkatraz Korner Music Company, 1965. Performed by Country Joe and the Fish.

Balin, Marty and Kanter, Paul, *Volunteers*, Ice Bag Corp., 1969. Performed by Jefferson Airplane.

Whitfield, Norman and Richards, Brinley, *War*, Stone Agate Music Corp., 1970. Performed by Edwin Starr.

Samwell-Smith, Paul, Relf, Keith and McCarty, James, *Shapes of Things*, B. Feldman and Company/Unart Music Corp., 1966. Performed by The Yardbirds.

Redding, Otis, *Respect*, Irving Music Inc.-East Memphis Music, 1965. Performed by Aretha Franklin.

Dylan, Bob, *The Times They Are A Changing*, M. Whitmark and Sons, 1963. Performed by Bob Dylan.

Fogerty, John, *Fortunate Son*, Jondora Music, 1969. Performed by Creedance Clearwater Revival.

Whitfield, Norman and Strong, Barrett, *Ball of Confusion (That's What The World Is Today)*, Stone Agate Music Corp, 1970. Performed by The Temptations.

Phillips, John, *Are You Going To San Francisco (Be Sure Tom Wear Some Flowers In Your) Hair*, Honest John Music 1967/ MCA Music, 1967. Performed by Scott McKenzie.

Harris, H. (Music) 1744 and Smith, Samuel Francis (Words) 1832, *My Country 'Tis Of Thee*, Traditional Song. Performed by Marion Anderson.

Lennon, John and McCartney, Paul, *Give Peace A Chance*, Northern Songs LTD, England, 1969/ Maclen Music Inc, 1969. Performed by John Lennon and the Plastic Ono Band.

Slogan of the Time Period.

Slogan of the Time Period.

Phillips, John and Phillips, Michelle, *California Dreamin*, MCA Inc, 1965. Performed by The Mamas and the Papas.

Simon, Paul, *Sounds of Silence*, Paul Simon Music, 1964. Performed by Simon and Garfunkel.

Hendrix, Jimi, *Purple Haze,* Canadiana-Six Continents, 1967/Yameta Co. Ltd, 1967/Unichappell Music-Six Continents, 1967. Performed by The Jimi Hendrix Experience.

Seger, Pete, *Where Have All The Flowers Gone?*, Fall River Music Inc, 1961. Performed by The Kingston Trio and Peter Paul and Mary.

Pistilli, Gene and Cashman, Terry, *Sunday Will Never Be The Same*, Pamco Music Inc, 1966. Performed by Spanky and Our Gang.

Sebastian, John B.*, Do You Believe In Magic?,* The Hudson Bay Music Co., 1965. Performed by The Lovin Spoonful.

Berlin, Irving, *God Bless America*, Irving Berlin Music Co., 1939. Performed by Kate Smith.

Seger, Pete (Music) and The Book of Ecclesiastes (Words), *Turn, Turn, Turn, (To Everything There Is A Season)*, Melody Train, 1962. Performed by The Byrds.

Stills, Stephen, *For What Its Worth*, Ten-East Music/Cotillion Music Inc/Springalo Toones, 1966. Performed by Buffalo Springfield.

Whitfield, Norman and Strong, Barrett, *I Heard It Through The Grapevine*, Stone Agate Music Corp., 1966. Performed by Marvin Gaye.

Leadon, Bernie, *Twenty-One*, Kicking Bear/Benchmark Music ASCAP, 1973. Performed by The Eagles.

Holland, Eddie, Dozier, Lamont and Holland, Brian, *(Love Is Like A) Heat Wave*, Jobete Music Corp., 1963. Performed by Martha and The Vandellas.

Stevenson, William, Gaye, Marvin and Hunter, Ivory Joe, *Dancing In The Streets*, Jobete Music Co. Inc./Stone Agate Music Corp., 1964. Performed by Martha and The Vandellas.

Dylan, Bob, My *Back Pages (I'm Younger Than That Now)*, M. Whitmark and Sons, 1964. Performed by The Byrds.

Lennon, John and McCartney, Paul, *All You Need Is Love,* Northern Songs Ltd. England/Maclen Music Inc., 1967. Performed by The Beatles.

Weil, Cynthia and Mann, Barry, *We've Got To Get Out Of This Place*, Abkco Music Inc., 1965. Performed by The Animals.

Hooker, John Lee, *Boom, Boom, (I'm Gonna Shoot You Right Down), Conrad* Music A_Division of Arc Music Corp. BMI, 1962. Performed by John Lee Hooker and The Animals.

Allman, Greg and Payne, Kim, Midnight Rider, Unichappell Music Inc., 1970/Elijah Blue Music, 1970. Performed by The Allman Brothers Band.

Bates, Katherine Lee (Words) 1893 and Ward, Samuel Augustus (Music) 1895, *America The Beautiful*, Traditional Song. Performed by The Mormon Tabernacle Choir.

Bernes, Bert and Ragovoy, Jerry, *Piece Of My Heart,* Web 4 Music Inc., 1967/ Unichappell Music Inc., 1967/ Canadiana-Unichappell Music, 1967. Performed by Big Brother and The Holding Company with Janis Joplin.

Browne, Jackson, *Doctor My Eyes*, Atlantic Music Corp./Open Window Music Co., 1970. Performed by Jackson Browne.

King, Carol (Music) and Stern, Toni (Words), *Its Too Late*, Colgems-EMI Music Inc., 1971. Performed by Carol King.

Carter, John and Gilbert, Tim, *Incense and Peppermints*, MPL Communications Ltd., 1967. Performed by The Strawberry Alarm Clock.

Hunter, Robert and Garcia, Jerry, *Uncle John's Band,* Ice Nine Publishing Inc., 1970. Performed by The Grateful Dead.

Morrison, Jim, Manzarek, Ray, Krieger, Robby and Densmore, John, *Break On Through To The Other Side,* Doors Music Inc./ ASCAP, 1967. Performed by The Doors.

Dylan, Bob, *Its All Over Now Baby Blue*, M. Whitmark and Sons, 1965. Performed by Bob Dylan.

Growing up in the 1960's and 1970's was not easy. There were so many decisions to be made at such a young age. Up bring and being patriotic would come into conflict with the thoughts and views of society. Music also would contribute to the decision making process. The words and melodies that paid respect to our flag and forefathers that had sacrificed for our rights and freedoms came into conflict with the words and music of the younger generation, who were exercising their rights and freedoms. It was hard to make a choice. Listening to the music brings back the memories and time for reflection occurs.

We are still a great country that learned to survive through difficult times intertwining the music of many different sources to evolve as a better society.

Greg Peterson teaches U.S. History and Government courses at D.C. Everest Senior High. Mr. Peterson's American History Seminar students played an instrumental part in the production of this oral history book.

Tunnel Rats

By Liz Novak

Imagine yourself being put in a pitch black tunnel underground, with little air, and crawling around, never knowing when something or someone could attack. The Tunnel Rats in Vietnam faced situations that were similar to these. The Viet Cong built extensive tunnel systems in and around the city of Saigon. The tunnels used in the Vietnam War had hospitals, sleeping chambers, fighting positions, and often times mothers and children lived in the tunnels for security[1] .The tunnels allowed the VC to slip away after a battle into these underground tunnels, where they would be secure. The entrances to the tunnels were often hard to detect. The tunnel systems were a big advantage that the VC had in the war. These were just one of the things the VC knew inside and out, but the U.S. hard time understanding them. They could easily move wounded men into the tunnels, reload ammunition, and seek protection. U.S. troops eventually found out about the tunnels, and started sending men down to look through them. The people, who went into the tunnels and looked at them, were the Tunnel Rats and they helped the U.S, understand what these tunnels were and the secrets of the VC. The following is my story of an American Tunnel Rat.

I never thought when I first went to Vietnam, that I would be a Tunnel Rat. I got into Vietnam and I heard about these Tunnel Teams. It was strictly people who volunteered to go and search through tunnels [2]. I do not know what attracted me to it, but I knew that I had the physical and mental capability to do it. I remember getting ready to join the other guys, and get ready for our tunnel rat training. A man who had obviously been in Vietnam for awhile, looked at me and simply said, you don't know what you are getting yourself into. Those simple words are the exact truth, what was I getting myself into? That's something I learned when I got into training.

The training to become a Tunnel Rat was intense. I guess I never expected it to be the way it was. You go in Vietnam thinking you will be a big hero, and then come out as a scared little boy. To be a Tunnel Rat you had to be a person with little fear of enclosed spaces, and could stay relaxed easily. I recall being taught how to try to crawl through the tunnels[3], and we were always warned when in small spaces try to breathe as little as possible, and never panic. I have heard that there have been guys who go into the tunnels and can't stop crying and yelling, they get pulled up, and are never let down again[4]. We are all here for the same reason to go home alive and well. Yet we are all on the same boat, we are scared. We were called Tunnel Teams, and the majority of us on the team were volunteers. A lot of us were the small guys, but I do remember there were a few big guys too. I heard all the horror stories. Fact or Fiction? I believe a lot of them are fact. I know first hand that suffocation is a killer. I watched one of my tunnel teammates get pulled up out of the tunnel, he suffocated to death. Meeting up with a VC in the tunnel is not that uncommon either. My good tunnel friend fought a VC. HE said they fought with knives, and the light he saw was the VC's candle [5]. He said he never felt so terrified before, you see the whites of their eyes, and then you know you have to kill him, before he gets you. He's the man we wish we were, the ones that fight and get out safely, because as I knew it, it is life or death down there.

The VC also put booby traps into the tunnels. They were the worst. You could not fight back. The VC often planted snakes, ants and scorpions in the tunnels. Poisonous snakes that with one bite you die almost instantly. There were red ants and scorpions that bite, and mice that just chew on everything [6] I have only heard about one of our guys encountering these animals. He saw a rat and killed it, and then brought it back up as a momento. I remember the tunnels being destroyed by using explosives. Also CS gas was let throughout the tunnels, in order to kill any VC that would go through them. The CS crystals get embedded in the walls when it is pumped in the tunnels, it gets breathed in by the VC as they are crawling through. It irritates the skin and lungs and caused a lot of pain or even death. We also pumped acetylene into the tunnels, which would burn up the oxygen in the tunnel. That was another way to kill anything inside of the tunnels; it was an instant death [7]. The hardest thing was knowing that you were killing men that you did not know. That is the most haunting memory. We are killing men just like, who really do not want to kill, but don't want to die either.

We were always ordered to explore the tunnels before putting in any gases or explosives. Sometimes important documents were found, and they helped other tunnels. Also, bodies of U.S. soldiers were found in them. The VC would take dead U.S. soldiers and put them down in the tunnel, they did it so our body counts were not right later[8]. The stench in the rooms where the bodies were was the most intolerable smell. I had to go in one of those rooms, and count the number of men down there; it was so unbearable to smell.

I can remember like it was yesterday, when I found that tunnel entrance, and I had to go down. It was early in the morning and I was with another teammate. We were walking in this graveyard that we were supposed to check. There was some ground that when my friend stepped on it, it was soft. He thought we should really check it out, so we did the test. You stick a long pointy stick into the ground. If you hit a coffin, then there was no entrance. If you do not hit a coffin, a possible entrance. We probed the ground in a few spots, and found no coffin[9]. We made our reports to the Captain, and he came and took a look. He ordered us to dig, and that's when we saw it, the entrance to the tunnel. However this entrance looked to be an old one, as if it had not been used in awhile. He told us all that we were going to check the tunnel today; tomorrow's weather would not be good.

I was supposed to go down this tunnel with one of my friends. He would lead and I would follow. The Captain thought it would be a good idea to send me into an older looking tunnel. I remember him reminding me of everything I learned, but it was so hard to concentrate. I remember thinking about all the things the Captain had said before. This sticks out in my mind when a guy stayed in the tunnel to long; the captain screamed "get the hell out of there." The Captain was a smart guy, he could feel when we were panicking, and always knew what to do. The most memorable and meaningful statement the Captain made that stuck in my head was, " I never thought when I went to Vietnam as a chemical officer, that I'd be crawling around on my hands and knees underground."[10] I remember thinking that's how it was for all of us, we never thought we'd be crawling through these spaces and tunnels.

I recall being armed with some kind of knife, a pocketknife of some sort, and a gun. The captain told us to look around and not to stay down too long. I trusted everyone helping out up top. We were told that if a communication line ever broke someone would come down and get us out. I knew that if we were injured, we would be rescued immediately, and if you died in there you were brought up too[11]. It kind of comforts you to know you'll be brought out safe if you are injured.

When it was time to send us down, I felt a fear I have never experienced before. I had the fear of everything and anything. I remember watching him go first; it was like a never-ending pit. I went down next We went further and further down, and it grew darker and darker. Finally we reached the bottom. There was another entrance, and I remember it to my right. It is cool and moist in the tunnels; it reminded me of an old basement or cellar. That's when we started crawling. Minutes seem like hours in the tunnels; it felt like we were crawling forever. It is impossible to tell how long I was down there. I tried not concentrating on my breathing, because I knew I would panic. I also tried not to follow too close, in case of booby traps. My body was going crazy. My heart was in my throat, my muscles tense, and the adrenaline rushing. We continued through the tunnel, and my family kept passing through my mind. Finally we reached this room. It was nice to be able to stand and breathe. We thought the room to be about 10x10, it was small. We turned on the flashlights and looked around the room. There were two cots, and we both assumed this was once a hospital. On one of the cots there was a blanket with holes in it, probably chewed out by mice. There were needles on the ground, there was a canteen, and a bag. At first I thought the bag might be a booby trap. That thought obviously had not crossed my partner's mind, because he picked it right up. Luckily the bag was safe, and there was just medication and gauze in it. We thought we should bring the bag back. I couldn't believe how the VC had had these tunnels with these hospitals. I could just see that at one time injured VC used to lie in beds. There was a woman helping them, and trying to get them to drink water from their canteen. I can envision the room and how we saw it, so well. We found it fairly obvious that the hospital had not been used in awhile. We had to head back, so I carried the bag, and back we went. You wasted no time in the tunnels, you look and leave.

On the way back it seemed harder to crawl. I think the tunnel had an incline, so we were trying to go up hill. I remember panicking once on the way back up. My partner's foot slipped. It made my heart literally jump. I was breathing so heavy after that. I just wanted to get out as fast I could. I was still excited though that we found the room. I remember wanting to go back, oddly enough. I felt I needed to look around more and continue through the light pouring through the entrance from the hole. We got up and out of the tunnel, and were so excited to tell what we saw.

We gave the bag to the Captain, and he took it back to camp to look at it. When we got up out of the tunnel, I couldn't stop gleaming. I was so proud of what we did and what we found. My first time going into the tunnels was an experience that has changed me forever. I learned the meaning of fear, and to cherish life.

I look back on going through that tunnel for the first time and realize how lucky I am. There are so many things you can encounter in these tunnels, and I was truly lucky. A lot of Tunnel Rats panic, but I felt I did well and stayed calm. It takes certain people to do this job. I now know that we are special people who do this, and for some reason we are not like any other unit in the Vietnam War[12]. We are considered men of great aggression, and I know first hand that you look at life so differently after experiencing something so unique. I know a lot of men did not consider themselves humans after going through the tunnels. They often explained it that we were animals; because humans do not crawl around in little tunnels looking for things[13]. Men also said this was fear they had never encountered before. I can agree with that, because this was fear I had never felt before.

The men who were Tunnel Rats bring a new meaning to the word courage. All these men were able to face hardship in a time of need, but these men had more than courage. It takes more than that to go into a pitch black tunnel, navigate yourself around, breathe lightly, and know at any minute something or someone could surprise you, and you could die. The people who were Tunnel Rats risked their lives for the South Vietnamese people so they could have the freedoms like we do in the United States of America.

End Notes

1 Tunnel Rats. October 10, 2001. http://ww w.diddybop.demon.co. uk/tunnel.html

2 Mangold, Tom, John Penycate. The Tunnel Rats of Cu Chi. Random House Incorperated 201 East 50th street, New York, New York 10022

3 Mangold, Tom.

4 Mydans, Seth. Visit the Vietcong's World: Americans Welcome. The New York Times. July 7, 1999. http://www.mishalov.com/Vietnam Cu-Chi.html

5 Browne, Malcolm. The New Face of War. Bantam Books Incorperated,   666 Fifth Avenue, New York, New York 10103, 1986.

6 Mydans, Tom.

7 Tunnel Rats.

8 Tunnel Rats.

9 Mangold, Tom.

10 Browne, Malcolm.

11 Browne, Malcolm.

12 Mangold, Tom.

Bibliography

Browne, Malcolm. The New Face of War. Bantam Books Incorporated, 666 Fifth Avenue, New York, New York 10103, 1986.

Mangold, Tom, John Penycate. The Tunnels of Cu Chi. Random House Incorporated 201 East 50th street, New York, New York 10022,1986.

Mydans, Seth. Visit the Vietcong's World: Americans Welcome. The New York Times. July 7, 1999. http://www.mishalov.com/Vietnam_Cu-Chi.html

Tunnel Rats. October 10, 2001. http://www.diddybop.demon.co.uk/tunnell.html

Liz Novak is a junior at DC Everest High School. She enjoys running in track and field and playing many other sports for fun. She likes to watch football and basketball. In the future she hopes to attend the University of Wisconsin, Madison, and compete in track and field. Her favorite subjects are anything related to politics, and science classes.

Tunnel Rats: Creepy, Crawly, Heroes:

5 fictional journal entries from Private José Rodriguez during his tour as a tunnel rat

By Jessica Gelhar

María Rodriquez- Dallas, TX
Private José Rodriguez
August 7, 1966
1st US Infantry: Dong Zu, South Vietnam
Querido María,

How I've missed you so! This is the first I've been able to write since the last letter from Saigon, South Vietnam. Since then so much has happened, not much of it being good. As you know, I belong to the 1st US Infantry, and as a member and a Mexican, I face racism each and every day. To gain respect, I thought about volunteering as a tunnel rat. From what I've heard, a tunnel rat is a man of small but strong stature who has nerves of steel. It sounded as though I could handle it. Plus, these men are highly thought of and even receive extra pay. I've seen how they can become heroes overnight, so without fully understanding the job, I signed up! I was transferred to Dong Zu, a base camp maybe veinte (20) miles from Saigon and merely cinco (5) miles from the Vietnamese town of Cu Chi. (Mangold, 103) While there, I passed the preliminary tunnel rat test, where decisions are based on such things as the ability to withstand claustrophobia and to stay calm in extremely tense situations. I barely passed the test, but I did, and now I am a registered tunnel rat, whatever that may be. I'm now settling into the tents with the others, after being briefed on what I will be doing here for the next cuatro (4) months. I'm to go out with a few other "rats" and find the hidden tunnel entrances, then blindly explore them, looking for the enemy. To put it simply, I have to crawl on all fours into a pitch black Viet Cong tunnel, where Gooks are stationed and waiting for us. It seems dangerous, but it's worth the respect and extra "hazardous pay." I've heard the other men talking and now at least somewhat understand the importance of these tunnels to the Gooks. They are the basis for all of their guerilla operations and even contain kitchens and hospitals, along with barracks and even small theaters. I learned that these tunnels have been in existence since 1948, when the Vietnamese used them against the French. Tunnels have been discovered in many different areas -- ranging from Cambodia to Saigon. It has also been noted, by retired tunnel rats, that all through the tunnels there are varying turns and dips. This makes it very difficult to shoot or use explosives inside them. (Martin, 3) Maria! One soldier even discovered a second level to the tunnels! What if there's more no one has discovered yet? Oh, I'm sorry for being silly! The Gooks could never secretly construct all of that. It's just all so new to me!

I've also been warned of the many booby traps in and around the tunnels. Tomorrow should be very interesting. I'll write about it soon! Con amor,

José

María Rodriguez- Dallas, TX
Private José Rodriguez
August 9, 1966
1st US Infantry: Dong Zu, South Vietnam

Querido María,
I'm writing again to you very soon because I've heard so much that I need to write it all

down just to remember it. I am going to tell you about my newest comrade. On the morning of the 8th, he was one of the older "rats" to introduce himself to me. His name is Donald Smith, from Pennsylvania. He also has a wife waiting for him at home, and her name is Joy. Well, to the point, he is the single reason I am still alive and writing to you today! Don explained every single one of the Gook's booby traps to me, along with ways to protect myself against them. Early in the morning, before roll call, he took time to introduce me to my new way of life. It helped me greatly, and now I feel the need to explain them to you, too. One trap I was warned about is a simple artillery shell that is dug into the ground. It would blow a man to bits if he stepped on it. There is also a crossbow and arrow, adapted by the VCs, so a trip-wire releases the arrow, allowing it to fly straight towards you. Another is a trip-wire-detonated mud ball, with spiked bamboo stakes coming out of the middle. Mines are other types of boobies. There is the coconut mine, which is a hollow nut, packed with explosive powder, and another is the bamboo mine, which is a hollow bamboo pole filled with nuts, bolts, broken glass, scrap metal, and some sort of explosives. Both are trip-wire-detonated. There are more yet, María! Some are used with camouflage to hide the entrances. These include the ever-famous pungi stakes, which are extremely sharp bamboo stalks, dipped in dung to insure infection. You also have to be careful of these inside the tunnels. (Mangold, 120) I owe everything to Don for explaining the dangers to me. He insisted booby traps were a huge part of the VC's protection of their tunnels and land. He suggested rolling up my pant legs when walking through fields or forests, because trip-wires are set high enough so you can not step over them. Once you feel it on your leg, you can stop and save yourself. He also advised me to stop and look for wires inside tunnels before entering them. You have to get down on your stomach and carefully, *CAREFULLY* look. Your life depends on it. Now you can see why I think so highly of Don, because I know where I would be without him. Con amor,

      José

María Rodriguez- Dallas, TX
Private José Rodriguez
August 13, 1966
1st US Infantry: Dong Zu, South Vietnam

Querido María,

    This is all still so new for me, María! I'm still learning more of the dangers every single day. It seems new dangers keep popping up! I've been told that the Gooks wait in the tunnels for unsuspecting GIs to come through. Also, there are many natural dangers in their underground world. The Gooks bury all of their dead men in the walls of the tunnels. They do this solely to aggravate us, knowing how important the body count is to us. Besides being deprived of the body count -- the only thing to keep up our morale -- whenever we go into a tunnel in search of the enemy we have to put up with raunchy, rotting bodies. It makes a lot of men lose their lunch right then and there. It's unbelievably horrible; no words come close to describing it.

    In addition to all of that, we have to constantly beware of tomb bats, fire ants, rats, snakes, spiders, giant centipedes, and scorpions. There are also highly poisonous bamboo vipers and kraits.

    After all of the warnings, I went out with older GIs to be introduced to the tunnels. I quickly learned that the entrances are so incredibly well hidden that hardly any one is able is see them. Mostly they are covered with small brush and thousands of leaves. We were instructed to always be on the lookout. Only trained eyes can sense the entrance hints: broken tree branches, crushed grass on both sides of the trail, and rotting, dark leaves. Also, spongy dirt and unexplained high knolls indicate a tunnel entrance. (Mangold, 112)

    Everything that has happened is so hard to believe. You never could have imagined anything like this before. It's amazing, in a bad way. I must go, but I will write again soon. Con amor, José

María Rodriquez- Dallas, TX
Private José Rodriguez
August 15, 1966
1st US Infantry: Dong Zu, South Vietnam

Querido María,

I know my last few letters weren't very exciting; this one, however, you should find a bit more adventurous. Yesterday was my first day in actual combat, and I will never, ever, forget it. I went in search of tunnels yesterday morning with a boy by the name of John Edmond. Luck was with us when we found an entrance within an hour of separating from the others at the base camp. We slowly, but, oh, so, carefully, pulled the dark leaves away from the opening. We had our pistols in hand, in case an armed VC was waiting for us. There was nothing but pungi sticks, and we were able to slip in without disturbing them. We immediately got down on all fours to look for trip-wires and, when we knew we were safe, proceeded into the tunnel. With our headlamps on and grenades in our hands, we began our first journey. Johnny and I split up to take different turns into the tunnel, and...he never came out again. Early this morning, Donald saw his body inside of one of the tunnel walls. I don't think I'll ever be able to forgive myself for letting the boy go off on his own. More than that I feel the need to get that Gook that did it to him. I need to find some way to deal with these feelings. I can assure you that I am definitely going to Heaven, María, because I have already been to hell: Vietnam. (Martin, 4) Con amor,

José

María Rodriguez- Dallas, TX
Private José Rodriguez
August 30, 1966
1st US Infantry: Dong Zu, South Vietnam

Querido María,

I know I haven't written in a long while, but the truth is that nothing significantly new has happened since my last letter. Every day is the same! We wake up, go into the tunnels and kill. I must say I did feel some satisfaction from the first Gook I blew up. That must sound extremely graphic to you, María, but it's the truth. It was young Johnny's revenge. You will never be able to understand; you're not here, and I cannot explain it to you. Not because I don't want to, but because the right words don't exist. There is nothing I can say that would make you understand. I don't even feel anything. I feel nothing when someone is dead on my account. It's just life to me. War is just life. I killed either my 9th or 10th Gook today. I've stopped counting. Body count stopped mattering a long time ago. Everything stopped mattering a long time ago. Yesterday, however, I did find something kind of exciting. While exploring a tunnel, I discovered a vacated VC hospital. It had, of course, been deserted a while ago, but bunks and their used bandages remained inside! It was something new and exciting, but not exciting enough to raise my morale. It doesn't even surprise me, though it would have when I first arrived here. I've learned not to underestimate the VC. María, war changes people. It has changed me. I'm stationed here another tres (3) months as a rat, but after that I will finish my dos (2) years in Vietnam and then be home with you. You're what keeps me going, María! Con amor,

José

Bibliography

Mangold, Tom and John Penycate. *The Tunnels of Cu Chi.* New York: Berkley Books, 1985.

Martin. Robert W. "The Tunnel Rats: Subterranean Battles and Modern Warfare." <http:militaryhistory.about.com/library/weekly/aa0927la.htm>. April 2002.

"Tunnel Rats." <http://dspace.dial.pipex.com/luhusen/nam/proprats.htm>. April 2002.

Jessica Gehlar is currently a junior at D.C. Everest Senior High School. She has been involved with History Day twice and is on the dance team. She plans on attending college after graduation, but is undecided on where.

A Wall of Remembrance

By Melissa Beck

The Vietnam Wall --
A testimonial to remembrance.
Gazing into the stone-cold wall,
Our generation
Remembers sadness, sorrowful years,
Hatred, hardships, hostility, fears,
Those who fought for us.

    The fifty-eight thousand names reflect
    Loyalty to our country,
    Selflessness, respect.
    Reflecting those men and boys
    Who fought with all their hearts, their strength,
    Who would not stop at any length.

        The fifty-eight thousand names reflect
        Loyalty to our country,
        Selflessness, respect.
        Reflecting those women and girls
        Who mended hearts, bodies, minds, souls,
        Who tried their best to fix the holes.

            The fifty-eight thousand names reflect
            Loyalty to our country,
            Preserving respect.
            Reflecting the countless viewers
            Paying tribute each day,
            Showing gratitude in their own way.
            They lay flowers, shed tears,
            Bring notes to say "thank you" or "I'm sorry."
            They think back years,

Determined to conquer their fears.
They wonder and ponder
What it must have been like
To be a soldier, his children, his wife.
They search the wall;
They look for a name.
And once they find it, they are never the same.

The Vietnam Wall--
A testimonial to remembrance.
Gazing past the stone-cold wall,
We
Remember the years,
Courage that overcame the fears,
Those who helped the wounded,
Who fought and survived,
Who died in the call of duty,
Died for us,
Died for us all.

Melissa Beck is a junior at D.C. Everest Senior High. She is a member of the dance team, and the school band. Melissa is also involved in her church. After graduation in 2004, she would like to start college at the UW-Marathon County and then transfer to the UW-Eau Claire or UW-Stevens Point, earning a degree in elementary school education.

Women in the War: A Journal

By Kim Anderson

August 17, 1968

Dear Journal,

Today was my first day as a nurse in Vietnam. The hours drag by here; it seems like everything moves at a much slower rate and things blur together. Everybody looks the same. Every man looks like the rest, and every Vietnamese person looks like the next. I can already tell this is going to be a very long year. The plane ride over here was endless. It was a really pretty sight, though, from the window. Vietnam is really beautiful. I met a guy named Frank; he's from Wisconsin just like me. It was calming talking to him. Neither of us wants to be here. His dad made him, just like I feel obligated to be here because of Lyn, my perfect sister. When I got off the plane, I couldn't believe the heat! And the humidity! It's nothing like the US here, and I can't decide if that is good or bad. We drove to the compound in a big truck; there were about eight men, and I was the only woman. The compound I'm stationed at is in Cu Chi, which is near Saigon.(2) I'm hoping to be able to get to Saigon before I leave because I've heard it's really something. The hospital here looks fairly modern, and there are almost ten other women here with me; about half are new like me. The head nurse is Sue Ellen. She seems really nice; she has that voice that just calms you down. I don't know if she's always had such a great voice or if it's something that she has developed over here to calm down the men. I got to talking with another nurse, Mary. She's almost 23 and from Iowa. She has been here for about eight months already and told me a lot of helpful tips for my months to come. I'm tired, I'm going to bed.

August 18, 1968

Dear Journal,

Looking back over what I wrote yesterday just now. What a joke! That last line, how I was tired, I take it back. Today was hell. It's almost midnight now, and I'm nowhere near ready to sleep. I can't sit still. Today was a shock. I can't even put into words what it was like. I'm not ready for this; I don't have the experience as a nurse. I'm only twenty for God's sake! I woke up early today, around dawn. I quickly got ready and walked to breakfast with some of the other girls. It was barely 9:00 a.m. when some seriously injured men came in. One guy barely had a face left, and the other was missing a leg. I got to talk to the one with a missing leg. He's only 19, his name is Bill, and he's a real nice guy. Later in the afternoon, what seemed like a whole platoon of men came in. It was total chaos here. Blood was on everyone; everything got all hazy for me, and I couldn't think straight. Thank God for Mary, another nurse; she really helped me out. I kept dropping needles and bandages. I feel like an idiot looking back at it. Seriously though, I need to get everything together because it's life or death for many of these men, and I play a very large role in that. I still can't shake the images of those men, the looks on their faces, so young and so very afraid. The once beautiful, youthful, and excited eyes and faces now look run-down and depressed. I wanted to break down and cry, but I knew I couldn't. I've heard about how strong army nurses must be (www.womenin-vietnam.com). I held it in, but then when I got back to my bunk at lunch, I cried my heart out for those men until I had no more tears that could fall from my tired eyes. It made me feel better, though, to cry. Tomorrow night I'm supposed to go to a club with the other women and some men. I don't really want to, but I feel obligated to go, so of course I will.(4) These men deserve to talk to some women; many of them haven't in so long…I just hope I don't start to cry in front of them. I still can't put my head around what happened today. Nothing could prepare me for this, nothing. I know it doesn't sound the same, writing it down. What I'm really worried about is that if this is just day two, what are the next eleven months going to be like? I can't do this! I have to stop worrying so much. I'm going to bed.

August 19, 1968

Dear Journal,

Today the compound was attacked. I have never been so scared in my life. There aren't words to describe what I felt. I wasn't really sure what had happened until I asked a guy named Charlie. He told me that the Vietcong were in tunnels underneath the entire city and were ready to attack us, but we caught on and attacked them before they did any real damage (Walker). I ended up sitting in the kitchen with about twenty other people for around four hours. At the end of the four hours, I, along with the rest of the women, went to the hospital, which was crammed full with injured men. It was insane, dying men were lying on the floor because there was no room for them on beds that had already been occupied. I worked a 12-hour shift, and because of the attack, I missed the first four. The eight hours I did work flew by! I know I've only been here for a little less than 72 hours, but already everything feels routine. No, routine isn't a good word. I can't explain it. It's like I'm a robot and don't have feelings. I just care for the patient's wound, and that's the last I see of him, unless he comes back in worse condition. I don't know how I'm feeling right now. I ended up going to that club. Charlie went too; that's where he filled me in about the attack. I don't really like to drink, but tonight I did, and it made me feel better, which makes me feel pathetic that I need a drink to cheer myself up. The men here are all really sweet. None of them tried anything, which was a surprise because I've heard what dogs the army men can be (Litt). It's just a real nice group of men, really, and all they want from me is to talk, which I don't mind doing at all. Charlie was telling me about his family back home, and it made me feel better about the whole situation here. I'm beat, need sleep.

August 20, 1968

Dear Journal,

Today was just like yesterday; I'm too tired to talk. I've been working non-stop since 6:00 a.m. this morning. The men just keep pouring in. I don't understand what is going on out there. Honestly, I know it's war, but I could never see myself injuring another human being like this. I would be so petrified and paranoid. I give so much credit to these brave men. It's late and I'm tired.

August 22, 1968

Dear Journal,

Today was the worst day of my life. I hate war. I hate everything about it. I can't stand this stupid place. I want out of here right now. I still can't believe it. I keep hoping that I'll fall asleep and today will have never happened. I worked the first 12-hour shift. Right before I was supposed to get off, a mob of men came in. It seemed like about 30 or 40 of them, all seriously injured. I was walking around, trying to find someone I could save, because over half of the men couldn't be saved. I came across a man who I knew would be dying within the hour; he was so badly burned and his skin was so crisp. I was about to walk by him, when he held up his hand. I stopped, and he tried to speak to me. He said, "Grace, Grace, it's me, Charlie." It was Charlie! My wonderful and caring friend Charlie! He was always there for me, always listened to my fears and never asked for anything in return; I loved that guy. I could barely make out what he was saying because his vocal cords had been burned and he was so hoarse. I just held his hand and tried to keep him out of pain by giving him as much morphine as I could get my hands on. We were looking at each other, and I knew he was about to go, and I just started weeping. I couldn't help it; I tried so hard to fight it, but I just couldn't. I looked into his eyes and he looked into mine, and he was gone the next second. I so badly wanted to go back to my bunk and be alone; I had no choice but to gather myself together and get back to work. He was my best friend here, and now he is gone. I can't do this anymore. I want to go home.

November 27, 1968

Dear Journal,

I gave up on writing in here a long time ago, but decided to today because it's my birthday. Today I am 21 years old, and it feels like any other day. I was reading what I had written in my first couple of days here. How stupid I was to think that I had already experienced war in my first 72 hours. I understand things better now. I haven't even been here four months, and I know that this isn't even the tip of the iceberg. In the beginning I acted so foolish, to think that someone actually cared how I was feeling. I've put up a big wall since then. I can barely get through it myself sometimes, but I have no choice because I have to make it through this. I have met a lot of Charlies since then as well. You'd think I would have learned not to get close to any men, but I haven't, and I regret caring for them as soon as I see their bodies lying on my table. I was promoted to head nurse because Sue Ellen left for Saigon. It's not that much different; I just have to keep track of all of the other nurses (Walker). We haven't been attacked lately. Everyone feels something coming, though; we're all really paranoid. I have changed so much since I've been here. I wrote a letter to my folks a few weeks ago. I didn't tell them how many dead bodies I've seen since I got here; my mother would faint. I also didn't tell them how I feel. I just said that I'm kept busy and that things aren't so bad. Things are actually worse; this place is hell on earth. Nobody back home knows what it's like here; they don't understand and probably never will. I still cry every night by myself. It's the only way to relieve myself of all the pain. The other nurses cry too, but no one ever talks about it. We're supposed to be strong and always stay calm (www.spencergroup.com). I have changed so much since I've arrived here. To think I felt obligated to come here. I had to compete against Lyn; I definitely won. I just feel proud in a sense now. I made the right decision to come here. I regret it at times, but I know I'm helping out my country. I should just stop writing because I know in a few months when I pick this old thing back up I will make fun of myself for thinking that I knew so much after a little over three months. I know my feelings will change by then. I'm just hoping to still be alive to write about them.

Bibliography

Litt, Marilyn Knapp. To Vietnam and Back Again: A Nurse's Tale. www.illyria.com

Walker, Keith. A Piece of my Heart. Presidio Press. 1985

www.spencergroup.com

www.womeninvietnam.com

Kim Anderson is a Junior at D.C. Everest High School. Anderson is involved in soccer, student council, and enjoys running. She hopes to attend UW Madison or The University of Minnesota after graduation.

Women in the War: Unsung Heros

By Katie Anderson

The roles women filled during the Vietnam War have been greatly overlooked for numerous years. While the U.S. Department of Veterans Affairs knows the exact number of men who served, men who were killed, and many other interesting statistics, it does not know the official number of women sent to Vietnam. An article on a website points out that "accurate records on how many women were there, what decorations they earned, where they served, and effects they suffered are close to nonexistent." It is estimated that 15,000 women had been in Vietnam, but that number could actually range from ten to twenty thousand.

While approximately 90% of the women who served were nurses in the Navy, Army, or Air Force, it's essential to know that they had other occupations as well. They also served at support staff assignments, hospitals, crewed on medical evacuation flights, MASH units, hospital ships, operation groups, information offices, service clubs, headquarter offices, and held numerous other clerical, medical, intelligence, and personnel positions. (VMA.org) There were over 500 WACs in Vietnam, women marines, women in the Air Force, civilians, USO Club women, and news correspondents. Only recently have we learned the crucial part they played during the "war that wasn't a war."

Women went to Vietnam to help and assist the Americans fighting there. Some were for the war, others against it. By 1967, most military nurses went right after graduation from a nursing school. It was the youngest group of medical personnel ever to serve in wartime. (VWM.org) Veteran Saralee McGoran explained she went because "I was single, there was a war and American boys were in it, and they needed American nurses." Many weren't prepared for the extent of the injuries they would see. In order to do their job properly, women had to quickly adjust to the condition of the soldiers brought in. For some of them, Vietnam was their first nursing experience. It forced them to grow up quickly; and to do that, some became callous and bitter. Women grew up knowing it was okay to show emotions, yet during the Vietnam War, they were forced to build a wall and be tough. As war veteran Kathy Mero says, they learned to treat the injury, not the patient.

When nurses arrived in Vietnam, they were sent mainly to Saigon, the Mekong Delta, or Long Bihn. (Salon.com) Nurses worked twelve to fourteen hours a day, six to seven days a week. Sometimes, after a heavy attack, they had to work days without rest. Linda J. McClenahan explained that they quickly filled in as mother, sister, sweetheart, and confidante to the men. (Walker 27) At the same time, they were working to save the soldiers' lives. Some of the different tasks they had to do were change bandages, clean wounds, make the beds, clean the rooms, operate, give medicine, and do triages. Triages determined the severity of the wounds, and in most Vietnam hospitals, there were three options, as Rose Sandecki explains. "You had to make the decision about those people who were wounded so bad that no matter how much time you spend on them, they would die." (Walker 16)

Vietnam was a booby-trap war, creating the biggest percentage of leg amputees in any war. Soldiers could be brought in with only half a body, or limbs missing. Peggy DuVall stated, "When you finally saved a life, you wondered what kind of life you saved. We put their bodies together *as best we could.*"

(MacPherson 447) What many people didn't realize was that nurses were always there for their patients. Lynda Van Devanter sums it up perfectly when she said, "Somebody would always go and take their hand and speak to them quietly, just in case they could hear. The people of this country have no concept of that. Their sons might have died in vain for a cause that was horrendous-- but they didn't die alone." (MacPherson 446)

When the women returned to the states, some of them faced the same hostility that returning soldiers faced. Others, like Kathy Mero, did not confront any harassment from people opposed to the war. She believed that since she was a woman, and was not there fighting against people, they did not target her. Still, many women, such as Saralee McGoran, hid the fact that they were in Vietnam. "I was the *enemy*. All the riots were going on. I didn't tell *anyone* I was a Vietnam Veteran." (MacPherson 441)

Many women veterans also felt the same alienation the men did. Some explained that they simply felt safer in Vietnam. Also, in Vietnam, nurses were respected for their work and in crisis situations performed as associate doctors. In the States they returned to rank-and-file pettiness. (MacPherson 449)

In recent years we have learned that almost half of the women who served in Vietnam suffered some form of Post Traumatic Stress. They faced nightmares, drinking problems, social problems, job instability, and countless other problems, all due to Vietnam. A survey conducted in 1982 concluded approximately one third of post traumatic stress symptoms were identified by 25 percent or more of the returned surveys as presently occurring between ten and thirty times a month. Some 27.6 percent reported having suicidal thoughts between one and nine times a month, 19.2 percent reported feeling depressed between fifteen and thirty times a month, and 16.1 percent reported feeling an inability to be close to someone they cared about between fifteen and thirty times a month. Seventy percent of those who reported having stress symptoms stated that those symptoms are still present today. (MacPherson 450)

Each veteran, male or female, has different stories, different memories, and different feelings as to what happened in Vietnam. Yet each one has endured the same pain, viewed the same horrors of war, and received some form of hostile treatment coming back to a country unappreciative of his or her efforts. The difference is women were given almost no recognition. For years, people overlooked the fact that women had been there, and suffered the same hardships men did. Both genders equally faced the same terrors, yet our country failed to remember the women. It is time to give credit where credit is due, and realize the outcome of the Vietnam War would have been even worse had women not been there.

Bibliography

"During the Vietnam Era..." On-line. Internet. http://www.vietnamwomensmemorial.org/pages/frame-sets/setvwmp.html, 22 April 2001.

MacPherson, Myra. *Long Time Passing: Vietnam and the Haunted Generation.* Doubleday & Company, Inc: Garden City, New York, 1984.

"Unarmed and Under Fire: An Oral History of Female Vietnam Vets." On-line. Internet. Nov. 11 1999. http://archive.salon.com/mwt/feature/1999/11/11/women/, 18 April 01.

"Vietnam Southeast Asia." On-line. Internet. 1996, http://userpages.aug.com/captbarb/femvetsnam.html. 18 April 2001.

Walker, Keith. *A Piece of My Heart: The Stories of Twenty-Six American Women Who Served in Vietnam.* Presidio Press, 1997.

Katie Anderson is currently a senior at D.C Everest Senior High. She is involved in basketball, Student Council, and Key Club. Future plans include attending either the University of Madison or Minnesota, working towards a degree in medicine.

Women in Vietnam: The Legacy of Operation Babylift

By Shannon Whitman

Operation Babylift was a humanitarian project in Vietnam. The US sent voluntary women over to help bring Amerasian orphans to America. These children were neglected in Vietnam because of their mixed racial background. As a result of these women's efforts, thousands of children were saved.

Women's help in Vietnam,
Saved thousands and thousands of lives.
These women were not trained for battle;
Instead they were mothers and wives.

Operation Babylift
Was a humanitarian project in Vietnam.
Even though they only handled children,
There was always fear of the Vietcong.

Compassion and love for the children
Were the motives that made these women stay,
For those Amerasian orphans brought to America,
Are American citizens today.

The floors were covered with sheets;
A sea of babies crying.
The 100 degree heat was hard to handle,
So there were children dying.

The air reeked of vomit,
And orphanage workers were weeping.
They had to feed and change them,
And hurry to give them safekeeping.

Hundreds were driven to airports
In their brand new clothes of lace.
They had to look nice for their parents
In a far-away brand new place.

Frightened toddlers boarded the plane,
Unaware of the long flight ahead.
But 40,000 were left behind,
And many would end up dead.

The plane was lined with metal benches,
And boxes were put on the floor.
The workers tried to keep them calm,
Even though they were tired and sore.

Once the plane arrived in America,
The children were safe at last.
Their new parents gave them a future,
Unlike anything in the past.

Women contributed greatly in Vietnam,
Saving thousands and thousands of lives.
The kids they saved are now grown up;
They now are mothers and wives.

Shannon Whitman is a junior at D. C. Everest Senior High School. She is involved in Peer Helpers, work, and tennis. She would like to be a pyschologist or social worker and attend the University of Wisconsin, Madison.

Student Interviewers and Transcribers

Anderson, Katie
Anderson, Kim
Barr, Megan
Beck, Melissa
Beck, Philip
Bernard, Stephanie
Berry, Nicole
Bolan, Matt
Boyton, Colin
Brown, Mike
Burrows, Kristina
Casta, Meghan
Chadi, Ahmed
Dabler, Jessica
Derby, Tyler
Doescher, Eric
Erdman, Carmen
Esch, Amber
Fasula, Ryan
Fell, Connie
Geisnedorfer, Ashley
Gelhar, Jessica
Gierczak, Jackie
Gliniecki, Amanda
Goertz, Kyle
Grahm, Jennifer
Grosinske, Aimee
Hansen, Shanna
Harder, Ashley
Hazaert, Jenna
Ho, Karen
Hollman, Alex
Isberner, Kristy
Jackson, Eli
Jenks, Kesa
Jenks, Kortney
Karcher, Vicki
Klarich, Morgan

Klein, Katie
Kozlowski, Travis
Kreger, Drew
Kryshak, Andy
Lindsay, Ben
Line, Joel
Luekensmeyer, Erin
Marcell, Jenni
Marquardt, Kim
Martindale, Melissa
McBain, Lesley
McCulloch, Shannon
Meinel, Chad
Merkx, Sally
Merrill, Meredith
Michalik, Adam
Miller, Andy
Moore, Matt
Moua, Pader
Ng, Jenessa
Nohelty, Matthew
Novak, Elizebeth
Orzel , Steph
Peter, Melissa
Plisch, Ryan
Powers, David
Priebe, Jenny
Prochaska, Ryan
Radant, Chelse
Reger, Callie
Reuter, Jenny
Rupel, Chris
Schippers, Scott
Schultz, Jacalyn
Simmerman, Ben
Stewart, Katie
Strong Gehl, Tabitha
Thao, Lamont

Thao, Samantha
Theisen, Jaime
Thersen, Jamie
Tomcek, Jenna
Vang, Kazoua
Vang, Mary
Walstrom, Lindsey
Wanless, Sara
Wanzerski, Mike
Whitman, Shannon
Wodalski, Michael
Wolf, Jessica
Xiong, Lee
Xiong, Liz
Zeihen, Zack
Zilch, Denise
Zimmerman, Amanda
Zollpriester, Ashley
Zuidema, Natasha
Zuleger, Dave

Connecting With the "Person"

By Jenni Marcell

When interviewing a veteran you need to connect with them so they feel they can talk to you about their experience. This will help the quality of your interview a lot. It helps to pretend like you were there with them. You don't want to be too blunt about things or too shy. Be comfortable with them. Let then know that you are interested, and they will open up to you. Don't be a stranger; be one of their friends. Show compassion towards them. Remember that they went through a really hard time. You need to connect with them. Asking straight out," Can you tell us about the bloody details?" doesn't work well. You need to care about their feelings. Ask," Was there any certain times you remember that you would like to share?"

Interviewing relatives is harder than a stranger. My first interview was with my uncle. He was open, but I went into the interview expecting something different. Also, with relatives you tend to feel more uncomfortable around them than a stranger. Not only do you want to get the person open up, but also, you need to be open and ready for anything. When I interviewed Lynn Kohl (a nurse in the Vietnam War) she was open and willing to tell all, so it was a plus. But I also went into the interview ready for anything. You never know how the vet will react to what is going on. If the vet were to start to get emotional, let them know that it is ok, and it is very important that you stay calm. Sometimes if you give them comfort, they will feel that they can trust you more with their feelings.

Another thing to remember is try not to jump around too much and keep it flowing. Even if you have all your questions all planned out, ask more. If you get on a topic you're interested in a lot or have a question about something-ask it. Most veterans will open up. It is a lot easier for a veteran to open up if you do. Don't make them feel like they are on the spot. Think about the questions in your head, and ask yourself them. If you think it would be a question that would make you feel uncomfortable then that probably means that it would make the vet uncomfortable. Sometimes while you are giving the interview you can tell that it wouldn't bother the vet, Then give it a try. Your interview will be 100% better if you show interest and compassion. Try to relate your personal life to theirs. The veterans are usually nervous just like you, so chat a little before to get to know them a little. For me I found that I could connect ten times better with the women in Vietnam then the men, so it was easier for both the vet and me. Pick someone you feel like you connect with.

I can't stress enough that if you show interest and compassion the veterans WILL open up to you because they feel that you actually care and it is not just some assignment. It's not enough just to show it. You actually do need to be interested and compassionate about it. Also, care about their feelings. If it is a hard topic for them don't make them talk about it. Find something they will want to talk about, and maybe when they feel more comfortable, they will then talk about it.

Glossary of Terms -
Used During the Vietnam War

Advisors, U.S.

First American military advisers sent to Vietnam arrived in Saigon in 1950 as the U.S. Military Assistance Advisory Group Indochina. These early U.S. advisors worked with all the branches of the Republic of Vietnam military.

Agent Orange

A chemical herbicide used against the NVA and VC to defoliate jungles and has been identified as a cause of cancer, birth defects, and other medical problems among servicemen and their children

Armored Personnel Carrier (APC)

A replacement for the M-113, the APC could carry more than 11 infantrymen plus a driver, and was constructed from aluminum armor welded over a watertight hull. It was designed to carry troops to combat, and it provided protection from small arms fire up to .50 caliber.

ARVN

Founded by President Diem, the Army of the Republic of Vietnam was America's ally in South Vietnam.

Babylift, Operation

Program begun by President Gerald R. Ford to evacuate South Vietnamese and Cambodian orphans to the United States before the communist takeovers of those countries in April and May 1975

Base Camp

Semi-permanent field headquarters and center for a given unit, usually within the unit's tactical area of responsibility

Boat People

Millions of Southeast Asians, including tens of thousands of ethnic Chinese-Vietnamese, took to the ocean in anything that could float in order to escape the new, 1970s communist regimes. Nicknamed the "boat people," 250,000 of their ranks died at sea.

Body Count

Unlike previous wars, the Vietnam War was a war of attrition rather than a war for territory along a specific front. Troops did not hold ground, the traditional measure of military success. Because of this, the body count became the measure of military success for the U.S. The body count was casualty statistics to indicate the damage U.S. and ARVN forces inflicted on VC and NVA troops.

Booby Traps

Concealed explosives or deadly devices activated by human contact. VC extensively used booby traps such as hidden pits with stakes (punji stakes) or hand grenades and other explosives attached to trip wires.

Boot Camp

Military training and orientation process where civilians are transformed into soldiers

Charlie

GI slang for the Viet Cong, a short version of Victor Charlie, from the U.S. military phonetic alphabet for VC

Claymore Mines

Antipersonnel mine designed to emit a fan-shaped spray of fragments about three feet above the ground when detonated. U.S. commonly used these and VC forces who captured the mines used them in booby traps

Click/Klick

One kilometer

Cold War

Period from 1945 through 1991 when the world democracies, led by America, waged an economic, ideological and military struggle against communist expansion, largely led by the Soviet Union

Communism

The political philosophy based on common poverty or equal distribution of wealth.

Conscientious Objector

A person who refused to serve in the military on religious or ethical grounds; they often performed alternative services, such as working in hospitals in the U.S.

Containment

The political theory that Communism was like a disease and it must be "contained" or quarantined within the countries where it existed or it would spread

Credibility Gap

The wide difference between official White House and Saigon regime statements about the progress of the war versus the facts reported by the news media and others in Vietnam.

De-escalation

During its Tet Offensive debates, the Johnson administration disagreed on a working definition of de-escalation. Some said it meant pulling out U.S. troops. Others said it meant maintaining current troop strength levels.

Dominoes

In 1946, President Truman dispatched a State Department expert on Asia, Abbot Low Moffat, to evaluate the Vietminh and its leader Ho Chi Minh. Moffat reported that Ho was "probably" a passionate communist, and that Vietnam, Laos, Cambodia, and Thailand would soon fall like "dominoes" to communism.

Domino Theory

The idea that individual Communist countries within a region destabilize the region as a unit, so that neighboring countries are then more likely to "go Communist" versus remaining democratic, free market nations

Enclave Strategy

By mid-1965 , the Johnson administration favored an enclave strategy for the thousands of fresh U.S. troops arriving in Vietnam. That meant protecting key coastal towns and existing U.S. military bases only.

Fire Base

A temporary artillery firing position, often secured by infantry

Firefight

Exchange of small arms fire between opposing units

Fragging

Assault or murder of military superior by U.S. troops, usually using fragmentation grenades

Free Fire Zone

An area where permission was not needed before firing on targets

Friendly Fire

Term for combat deaths or wounds accidentally caused by friendly forces

Gook

A derogatory slang term for Asians usually Vietnamese

Green Berets

U.S. Special Forces troops

Grunts

U.S. military slang for infantry troops

Guerrilla Warfare

Nontraditional warfare strategy where the main tactics are infiltration, ambush, pretending to be part of the civilian population, and political terror

Gulf of Tonkin Resolution

Congressional resolution submitted by the Johnson administration of 5 August 1964 in reaction to the 2 and 4 August Tonkin Gulf incidents where two U.S. destroyers reported that North Vietnamese PT boats fired upon them in the Gulf of Tonkin. The resolution gave the president a broad authority to conduct an undeclared war in Vietnam.

Hanoi

Capital of North Vietnam

Hamburger Hill

The battle of Ap Bia. It was a play on General Abrams's "meat-grinder" approach against the North Vietnamese, and a recognition of their own high casualties in the effort.

Hawk and Dove

The term hawk dates back to the congressional "War Hawks" of 1810-1812 who favored a war with Britain in the name of honor, pride, and a deep hatred for anything English. The dove is a product of 1967-1968 Vietnam War debates, and refers to the desire for a peaceful, nonviolent foreign policy.

Ho Chi Minh Trail

The North Vietnamese infiltration supply route into the South Vietnamese Central Highlands through Laos and Cambodia.

Hooch

Wooden structure with a thatched roof

Hot Pursuit

Policy allowing U.S. troops to chase VC and NVA soldiers across the border into Cambodia

Incursion

Learning a lesson in semantics from Eugene McCarthy's 1968 presidential campaign, Nixon did not announce that the U. S. was invading Cambodia in 1970. Instead he said that the U.S. was involved in an incursion, thereby downplaying his widening of the war.

Khmer Rouge

This homegrown nationalist and radical communist movement was responsible for the Cambodian Holocaust of the 1970s.

MACV

America's Military Assistance Command in Vietnam (MACV) became a household term to most Americans by the November 1964 election.

Main Forces

Regular army forces of the North Vietnamese and Viet Cong

Napalm

A sticky, gel-like, gasoline-based, incendiary that burns at about 2,000 degrees Fahrenheit, used as a defoliant and antipersonnel weapon by U.S. It could be dropped from aircraft in canisters or fired from flamethrowers.

New Left

The New Left welcomed the humanist and liberal side of socialist and communist philosophies. Borrowing from leftist thinkers ranging from Karl Marx to Mao Tse-tung, New Left adherents despised imperialism, capitalist excess and corruption, and preferred an isolationist U.S. foreign policy. The support for isolationism was reminiscent of conservative Republican views of the 1920s and 1930s. Hence, the New Left complicated the political scene, preferring political debate to political action. The New Left was more a state of mind than political group.

NVA and PAVN

Both NVA (North Vietnamese Army) and PAVN (People's Army of Vietnam) refer to North Vietnamese troops.

Pacification

U.S. program in South Vietnam aimed at engaging civilian population in a common effort to defend and develop their communities; initiated under President Johnson (1967-68) also called CORDS. It involved the effort to secure U.S and ARVN control over south Vietnamese villages, win the locals' allegiance to the Saigon regime, and deprive the enemy of all strongholds in the countryside.

Pathet Lao

This Laotian guerrilla force was also one of the first communist movements in Southeast Asia.

Punji Stake

During 1947, terrorist tactics represented the heart and soul of the Vietminh war against the French. A sharpened bamboo pole tipped with poisons and even "night soil" (human fecal matter), the punji stake was concealed near jungle trials, rice paddies, or wherever French troopers walked on patrol.

Refugees

Individuals who left the country of Vietnam during or after the war, because of fear for their safety or because of opposition to a Communist form of government

Saigon

> Capital of South Vietnam

Scorched Earth

> This term has been used to describe one opponent's effort to lay waste to the territory of another. Meant to break an enemy's will to fight as well as deprive him of anything and everything in a given area, scorched earth can be employed by both an attacking and a retreating army.

Search and Destroy

> Offensive operations designed to find and destroy enemy forces rather than establish permanent government control

Secret War

> War fought secretly in Laos. U.S. CIA recruited Hmong to fight against communist Pathet Lao and disrupt the Ho Chi Minh Trail supply route of the NVA.

Selective Service

> A federal agency that drafted male citizens and residents aged 18 to 26 into the armed forces. If they met certain criteria, draft-age men could avoid induction by qualifying for a deferment.

Seventeenth Parallel

> Temporary division line between North and South Vietnam

Student Deferment

> Any male student in an institution of higher learning could apply for student deferment status in the 1960s. By maintaining a B to B-plus average or above in his studies, he was spared from a military draft system that most likely would quickly send him to Vietnam.

Viet Cong

> Tracing its roots back to the Vietminh of the 1940s and early 1950s, the Vietcong were the Hanoi-backed armed opposition to the South Vietnamese government. American GI slang, such as Victor Charlie, VC, or simply Charlie and Chuck, comes from this title. The term Viet Cong is slang even in Vietnamese. The official title for the anti-Saigon regime forces is National Liberation Front, or NLF.

Vietnamization

> President Nixon's program to gradually turn the war over to the South Vietnamese while pulling U.S. troops out

Weathermen

> One of the smallest and most extreme anti-war protest groups was the Weathermen. They got their name from a line from Bob Dylan's "Subterranian Homesick Blues": "You don't need a weatherman to know which way the wind blows."

Chronology of the Vietnam War 1942-1975

1942

U.S. pilots attached to the Flying tigers fly combat missions in Vietnam against Japanese military installations.

1943-1945

The Office of Strategic Services a forerunner to the CIA (OSS) funds Vietminh actions against the Japanese in Vietnam. OSS operatives work with the Vietnamese to rescue downed U.S. flyers and go on espionage and sabotage missions with them.

1945

August   Japan surrenders. Ho Chi Minh establishes the Viet Minh, a guerilla army. Bao Dai abdicates after a general uprising led by the Viet Minh.

Sept.   U.S. supports the French efforts to re-impose colonialism in Vietnam.
Seven OSS officers, led by Lieutenant Colonel A. Peter Dewey, land in Saigon to liberate Allied war prisoners, search for missing Americans, and gather intelligence.

Sept. 2   Ho Chi Minh reads Vietnam's Declaration of Independence and establishes the Democratic Republic of Vietnam in Hanoi. Vietnam is divided.

Sept. 26   OSS Lieutenant Dewey killed in Saigon, the first American to be killed in Vietnam. French and Vietminh spokesmen blame each other for his death.

1946

Ho Chi Minh attempts to negotiate the end of colonial rule with the French without success.

Nov.   The French army shells Haiphong harbor, killing over 6,000 Vietnamese civilians.

Dec. 19   The Vietminh attack French forces in Tonkin, formally beginning the first Indochina War.

1948

June 5   The French name Bao Dai head of state of Vietnam.

1950

The U.S., recognizing Boa Dai's regime as legitimate, begins to subsidize the French in Vietnam; the Chinese Communists, having won their civil war in 1949, begin to supply weapons to the Viet Minh.

May 8	U.S. signs an agreement with France to provide the French Associated States of Vietnam with military assistance.
June 27	President Harry S. Truman announces increased U.S. military assistance to Vietnam.
Aug. 3	A U.S. Military Assistance Advisory Group (MAAG) of 35 men arrives in Vietnam to teach troops receiving U.S. weapons how to use them. By the end of the year, the U.S. is bearing half of the cost of France's war effort in Vietnam.
Dec. 30	U.S. signs a Mutual Defense Assistance Agreement with France, Vietnam, Cambodia, and Laos.

1951

Sept. 7	The Truman administration signs an agreement with Saigon to provide direct military aid to South Vietnam.

1952

Nov. 4	Dwight D. Eisenhower is elected president.

1953

July 27	Korean War armistice is signed.
Sept. 30	President Eisenhower approves $785 million for military aid for South Vietnam.

1954

April 7	At a news conference, President Eisenhower, stressing the importance of defending Dien Bien Phu, uses the domino theory to explain the political significance of Indo-china.
May 7	The French are defeated at Dien Bien Phu. General Vo Nguyen Giap commands the Vietnamese forces.
May 8	The Geneva Conference opens.
July 20	France signs a cease-fire ending hostilities in Indochina. The Geneva Conference on Indochina declares a demilitarized zone at the 17th parallel.
Sept. 8	U.S. signs the Manila Treaty forming the Southeast Asia Treaty Organization (SEATO).
Oct. 24	President Eisenhower sends a letter to the new leader in southern Vietnam, Ngo Dinh Diem, pledging U.S. support and agreeing to send $100 million to build up Diem's military forces. Eisenhower begins the U.S. commitment to maintaining a non-Communist government in South Vietnam.

1955

July 6	Ngo Dinh Diem repudiates the Geneva Agreements and refuses to plan for open elections throughout the country.
Oct. 26	Diem, after defeating Bao Dai in a rigged election, declares himself to be president of the Republic of Vietnam (South). The U.S instantly recognizes his government.

1956

July 20 The deadline for holding reunification elections in accordance with the Geneva Accords passes. U.S. supports Diem's refusal to hold elections.

1957

May 5-19 Diem makes a triumphant visit to the U.S. Eisenhower praises him lavishly and reaffirms U.S. support for his government.

Oct. Small-scale civil war begins in South Vietnam between Diem's forces and Vietminh who have remained in South Vietnam after the partition at Geneva.

1959

April 4 Eisenhower delivers a speech in which he makes his first commitment to maintain South Vietnam as a separate state.

July 8 First American servicemen (Major Dale Bius and Master Sergeant Chester Ovnard) killed by Viet Cong attack at Bien Hoa.

Dec. 31 Approximately 760 U.S. military personnel in Vietnam.

1960

Dec. 20 The National Liberation Front (NLF) is formed. It is the Vietminh reborn. The Communist-controlled NLF takes charge of the growing insurgency against the Diem regime. Diem calls the NLF the 'Viet Cong' meaning Vietnamese who are Communists.

Dec. 31 Approximately 900 U.S. military personnel in Vietnam.

1961

Jan. 21 John F. Kennedy becomes president.

Jan. 28 Kennedy approves a Vietnam counterinsurgency plan.

May 9-15 Vice President Lyndon B. Johnson visits South Vietnam and recommends a strong U.S. commitment there.

May Kennedy approves sending Special Forces to South Vietnam.

June 9 President Diem asks for U.S. military advisers to train the South Vietnamese Army.

Dec. 31 Approximately 3,200 U.S. military personnel in Vietnam.

1962

Feb. 6 MACV (U.S. Military Assistance Command, Vietnam) is established in Saigon, General Paul Harkins commanding. Major buildup of U.S. forces begins.

Feb. 14 Kennedy authorizes U.S. military advisers in Vietnam to return fire if fired upon.

March 22 U.S. begins the Strategic Hamlet (rural pacification) Program.

Dec. 31 Approximately 11,300 U.S. military personnel in Vietnam. 109 Americans were killed or wounded in 1962.

1963

May 8	In Hue, 20,000 Buddhists celebrating the birthday of Gautama Siddhartha Buddha are fired on by government forces.
June 11	Thich Quang Duc, an elderly Buddhist monk, immolates himself by fire at a busy Saigon intersection to protest Diem's suppression of the Buddhists.
Aug. 21	Military forces loyal to Diem and to his brother Nhu attack Buddhist temples. Kennedy denounces these actions.
Nov. 1	A coup, led by General Tran Van Don and General Duong Van Minh, with the foreknowledge and encouragement of U.S. officials, overthrows the Diem regime. A military directorate, led by General Minh, succeeds Diem.
Nov. 2	Diem and his brother Ngo Dinh Nhu are assassinated.
Nov. 22	President John F. Kennedy is assassinated in Dallas, TX.
Dec. 31	Approximately 16,300 U.S. military personnel are in Vietnam. About 489 U.S. troops have been killed or wounded during 1963.

1964

	President Johnson approves covert military operation against North Vietnam to be carried out by South Vietnamese and Asian mercenaries. Called OPLAN 34A, in includes espionage, sabotage, psychological warfare, and intelligence gathering.
July	Both sides engaged in covert warfare in violation of the 1954 Geneva Accords. North Vietnam is using the Ho Chi Minh trail to infiltrate NVA troops south to supply the Viet Cong. U.S. implements the OPLAN 34A operation. OPLAN 34A uses U.S. destroyers to conduct surveillance missions off the North Vietnamese coast. These are called DESOTO Missions.
Aug. 2	Vietnamese patrol boats in the Gulf of Tonkin allegedly attack U.S. destroyer *Maddox*, which was on a DESOTO Mission.
Aug. 4	U.S destroyer *C. Turner Joy* claims attack by North Vietnamese patrol boats in the Gulf of Tonkin.
Aug. 5	President Lyndon Johnson asks Congress for a resolution against North Vietnam following the Gulf of Tonkin incidents. Congress debates.
Aug. 7	Congress enacts the Gulf of Tonkin resolution allowing President Johnson to "take all necessary measures to repel any armed attack against the forces of the United States and to prevent further aggression…including the use of armed force…." Johnson uses this power to conduct an undeclared war.
Dec. 31	Approximately 23,000 U.S. Army personnel are now serving in Vietnam. A full-scale undeclared war rages on in South Vietnam, and there is also fighting in Laos and Cambodia. 1,278 U.S. casualties have occurred in 1964.

1965

Feb. 13	Johnson orders a sustained bombing campaign against North Vietnam called Operation Rolling Thunder.
March 2	Operation Rolling Thunder begins.

March 8	First U.s. combat troops arrive in Vietnam.
April 6-8	President Johnson authorizes the use of U.S. ground combat troops for offensive operations. The next day he offers North Vietnam aid in exchange for peace. North Vietnam rejects the offer.
April 17	Students for a Democratic Society sponsor the first major anti-war rally in Washington, D.C.
July 21-28	President Johnson makes a series of decisions that amount to committing the U.S. to a major war in Vietnam. Draft calls will be raised to 35,000 per month, 50,000 additional troops will be sent to Vietnam with additional increases as the situation demands, and the air war against North Vietnam is expanded.
Oct. 15-16	Anti-war protests are held in about 40 American cities.
Dec. 31	Approximately 184,300 U.S. troops in Vietnam. 1,369 Americans are killed in action and 5,300 are wounded in action during the year. There are also 22,420 Allied troops in Vietnam.

1966

June 29	U.S. bombs oil facilities in Haiphong and Hanoi.
Oct. 26	Johnson visits U.S. troops in Vietnam.
Dec. 31	The Vietnam War has become the dominant event in world affairs. Approximately 385,300 U.S. troops are in Vietnam. 5,008 Americans were killed and 30,093 were wounded during 1966. Also about 22,420 Allied troops are present in Vietnam.

1967

Jan. 8	Operation Cedar Falls begins.
Jan. 26	Operation Cedar Falls ends.
Feb. 22	Operation Junction City begins.
April 15	100,000 anti-war protesters rally in New York.
May 14	Operation Junction City ends.
Sept. 29	Johnson offers to stop bombing of North Vietnam if they will immediately come to the negotiating table.
Oct. 21	50,000 anti-war protesters rally at the Pentagon.
Dec. 31	Approximately 500,000 U.S. troops are in Vietnam. The war cost taxpayers about $21 billion for the year. Casualties: 9,353 KIA and 99,742 WIA.

1968

Jan. 3	Senator Eugene McCarthy announces his decision to seek the Democratic presidential nomination with an anti-war platform.
Jan. 30	The Tet Offensive begins. On the first day of the Tet truce, Vietcong forces, supported by NVA trooper, launch the largest offensive of the war. Simultaneous attacks are mounted in South Vietnam's largest cities and many provincial capitals. The offensive is crushed by American and GVN forces. Tet is a decisive military victory for the Allies, but turns out to be a psychological and political disaster.

Feb. 1	Richard M. Nixon announces his candidacy for the presidency.
March 12	Senator Robert Kennedy announces that he will seek the Democratic nomination and run on an anti-war platform.
March 16	In what will become the most notorious atrocity committed by American soldiers during the war, a platoon of troopers killed hundreds of unarmed villagers in the hamlet of My Lai.
March 31	Johnson stuns America with his announcement to not seek reelection.
May 3	America and North Vietnam agree to begin formal negotiations in Paris on May 10.
June 6	Robert Kennedy is assassinated.
Aug 5-8	The Republican National Convention, meeting in Miami, nominates Richard M. Nixon for president. The Republican platform calls for an honorable negotiated peace in Vietnam and for the progressive "de-Americanization" of the war.
Aug 26-29	The Democratic National Convention meets in Chicago. Democrats adopt a platform endorsing the administration's war policy and nominate Vice President Hubert H. Humphrey for president. On the evening of August 28, there is a full-scale riot in the streets between Chicago police and anti-war protesters.
Oct. 31	Johnson announces end of bombing of North Vietnam. Operation Rolling Thunder ends.
Nov. 5	Richard Nixon defeats Hubert Humphrey in the 1968 presidential election.
Dec. 31	Approximately 536,000 U.S. troops are in Vietnam. 14,314 KIA, 150,000 WIA. Cost, about $30 billion. 65,600 Allied troops in Vietnam.

1969

Jan. 25	The first plenary session of the four-way Paris peace talks among the Americans, the North Vietnamese, the South Vietnamese, and the National Liberation Front occurs.
June 8	Nixon announces that 25,000 U.S. troops will be withdrawn by the end of August and that they will be replaced by South Vietnamese forces. The gradual phase-out of the American war in Vietnam has begun.
Sept. 3	Ho Chi Minh dies.
Oct. 15	National Moratorium anti-war demonstrations staged throughout the U.S.
Nov 15.	More than 250,000 come to Washington, D.C. to protest the Vietnam War.
Nov. 16	My Lai massacre described in the press.
Dec. 31	U.S. troops decline to approximately 479,000. GVN forces have increased and now number over 900,000. American KIA: 9,414. 70,300 Allied forces in Vietnam. The U.S. forces show signs of declining morale, discipline, and fighting spirit.

1970

April 30	U.S. invades Cambodia.
May 4	National Guard troops kill four students at Kent State University during demonstration against the Cambodian invasion.
May 6	More than one hundred colleges and universities across the nation shut down because of student protests and rioting in response to the Cambodian invasion and the killings at Kent State.

June 24	The Senate repeals the Gulf of Tonkin resolution.
June 30	Operations in Cambodia end.
Dec. 31	The U.S. war in Vietnam is winding down. At year's end there are about 335,000 U.S. troops in South Vietnam. U.S. KIA's number 4,221 for the year. Allied forces total 70,300. However, the war has spread to Cambodia, and no progress is reported at the Paris peace talks.

1971

March 6-24	ARVN forces invade Laos to interdict enemy supply routes down the Ho Chi Minh trail. Communist counterattacks drive the invaders out of Laos and inflict heavy casualties. It is a major defeat for the GVN.
Dec. 31	The U.S. war in Vietnam is ending. 156,800 U.S. remain in Vietnam. There were 1,380 KIA in 1971. As the Americans withdraw, the Communists intensify their attacks in Laos, Cambodia, and parts of South Vietnam. U.S. morale continues to deteriorate. Vietnamization is not working, and the Paris talks remained stalled.

1972

March 23	U.S. suspends Paris peace talks until North Vietnam and the NLF enter into "serious discussions."
April 15	U.S. bombing of Hanoi begins again.
April 27	Paris peace talks resume.
May 4	U.S. suspend peace talks.
June 22	Watergate break-in and arrests.
July 1	Paris peace talks resume.
Nov. 7	Nixon is reelected president.
Dec. 14	U.S. breaks off peace talks.
Dec. 18-31	Nixon announces the resumption of bombing and mining of North Vietnam. The most concentrated air offensive of the war begins, mostly aimed at targets in the vicinity of Hanoi and Haiphong.
Dec. 28	Hanoi announces that it is willing to resume negotiations if the U.S. will stop bombing above the 20th Parallel. The bombing ends on December 31.
Dec. 31	At the year's end approximately 24,000 troops remain in Vietnam. 312 Americans were KIA. Allied troops totals drop to 35,500.

1973

Jan. 8-18	Henry Kissinger and Le Duc Tho resume negotiations in Paris, and they reach an agreement.
Jan. 23	Nixon announces that the Paris Accords will go into effect at 7:00 PM EST, Jan. 27, 1973. He says that "peace with honor" has been achieved.
Jan. 27	The draft ends.

Feb. 12-27	U.S. POWs begin to come home.
March 29	The last U.S. troops leave South Vietnam. Only a DAO contingent and Marine embassy guards remain. About 8,500 U.S. civilian officials stay on.
June 4-	The Congress blocks all funds for any U.S. military activities in
Aug. 15	Indochina.
Nov. 7	Congress enacts the War Powers Act over Nixon's veto. It requires the president to report to Congress within 48 hours after committing American forces to combat on foreign soil. It also limits to 60 days the time that the President can commit soldiers to foreign combat without congressional approval.
Dec. 31	The Vietnam War continues without U.S. involvement. Most of the provision of the Paris agreements are not observed by either side. During the year there were 13,788 RVNAF KIAs and 45,057 Communist KIAs.

1974

Aug. 5	Congress makes sharp cuts in the amount of military aid going to the South Vietnamese government.
Aug. 9	Nixon resigns the presidency. Gerald Ford is inaugurated as the president of the U.S.
Sept. 16	Ford offers clemency to draft evaders and military deserters.
Dec. 31	U.S. military personnel in Vietnam remains at 50.

1975

Jan. 6	NVA troops take control of Phuc Long Province.
March 10	NVA captures Ban Me Thuot.
March 19	NVA captures Quang Tri Province.
March 26	Hue falls to the NVA.
March 30	Danang falls to the NVA.
April 29-30	Operation Frequent Wind evacuates all American personnel and some South Vietnamese from Vietnam.
April 30	NVA captures Saigon. Vietnam War ends in victory of the VC/NVA forces. The long American effort to create a non-Communist state in southern Vietnam fails.

Guide to Abbreviations and Acronyms of the Vietnam War

1A	Draft Eligible
2S	Student Deferment
11B	A Military Occupational Specialty code
11b 10	A Military Occupational Specialty code
11F	A Military Occupational Specialty code
24b 10	A Military Occupational Specialty code
96B	Combat intelligence
A,B,C,D,E,F,G,H,I	Alpha, Bravo, Charlie, Delta, Echo, Foxtrot, Golf, Hotel, and Indian Company
A-1H Sky Raiders	Aircraft used by U.S. and South Vietnamese with the ability to carry large bomb loads, absorb heavy ground fire, and fly at low altitudes
A-4D Sky Hawks	U.S. light attack-bomber aircraft with ability to carry a variety of aerial weapons
A-7	Carrier-based, single-engine, light-attack all-weather U.S. bomber aircraft
AAA	Antiaircraft artillery
AFB	Air Force Base
AFVN	Radio Station
AIT	Advanced Infantry Training; Advanced Individual Training
AK-47	Assault Rifle used mainly by the Viet Cong
AML	Type of leukemia
AO	Area of Operations; Aerial Observers
APC	Armored Personnel Carrier
ARA	Aerial Rocket Artillery
ARVN	Army of the Republic of Vietnam
ASA	Army Security Agency
ASROC	Anti Submarine Rocket
AWOL	Absent Without Leave; Desertion
B-4 Front	Communist forces
BAR	Browning Automatic Rifle
BIC	Battlefield Information Center
BICC	Battlefield Information Control Center
B-40	Rockets used by Viet Cong
B-52	Large U.S. jet bomber
B-52F	Modified version of B-52 bomber
B-57	"Canberra" Modified version of the English Electric Canberra; light bomber and recon aircraft
C-4	Plastic Explosives
C-130	"Hercules" U.S. Air Force transport aircraft

C-Rations	Canned and packaged food that came in boxes
C&C	Command and Control
CAG	Combined Action Group
Cav	Cavalry
CH-46	"Sea Knight" Twin-turbine, tandem-rotor, medium assault helicopter designed to transport troops and cargo
CH-47	"Chinook" Twin-engine, tandem rotor helicopter designed to transport cargo, troops, or weapons
CH-53	"Sea Stallion" Marine Corp's heavy lift helicopter designed to transport heavy equipment and supplies during ship-to-shore movement
CIA	Central Intelligence Agency
CIDG	Civilian Irregular Defense Group
CO	Commanding Officer
CP	Command Post
DFC	Distinguished Flying Cross (medal)
DMZ	Demilitarized Zone
E-1	Private (rank/ 1st pay grade)
E-4	Corporal (rank/ 4th pay grade)
E-5	Sergeant (rank/ 5th pay grade)
E-6	Staff Sergeant (rank/6th pay grade)
EDT	Eastern Daylight Time
ER	Emergency Room
ETS	Enlisted Time Served
F-4	"Phantom" U.S. twin engine, all-weather tactical jet fighter-bomber
F-8	"Crusader" Supersonic carrier-based fighter, attack, and recon aircraft
F-100	"Super Sabre" Aerial combat aircraft also used as a fighter-bomber
F-105	"Thunderchief" U.S. Single engine fighter-bomber
F-111	"Aardvark" U.S. low-altitude, all weather strike fighter aircraft
FAC	Forward Air Controller
FBI	Federal Bureau of Investigation
FNG	F——— New Guy
FO	Forward Observer
G4	Army or Marine Corps component logistics staff officer
GI	General Issue; General name for U.S. troops
GP	Group
HQ	Head Quarters
I Corps	Northernmost military region in South Vietnam
II Corps	Central Highlands military region in South Vietnam
III Corps	Military region between Saigon and the Central Highlands
IV Corps	Southernmost military region in South Vietnam
JP-4	Jet Fuel
KIA	Killed in Action
KKK	Ku Klux Klan

KP	Kitchen Police
L-19	"Bird Dog" Aircraft used as a forward air controller for U.S. supersonic jet fighters
LBJ	Lyndon B. Johnson (President during Vietnam War)
LCM-8	Landing Craft, mechanized
LOH	Light Observation Helicopter
LP	Listening Post
LRRP	Long Range Reconnaissance Patrols
LSD	Illegal drug used by some GIs
LST	Landing Ship, Tank
LZ	Landing Zone
M-1	Training rifle; also used when there was a shortage of M-14 and M-16 rifles
M-10	Semi-automatic pistol
M-14	Semi-automatic rifle, was the standard service rifle until replaced by the M-16 rifle
M-16	Automatic Rifle, standard service rifle replacing the M-14 rifle
M-48A3	Diesel-powered tank; the main tank used by U.S. and ARVN
M-50	"Ontos" Self-propelled, recoilless anti-tank vehicle
M-51	Heavy Recovery Vehicle, equipped with a 30-ton capacity crane to retrieve damaged tanks and other equipment
M-60	Machine Gun
M-67	Flamethrower variant of the M-48A3 tank
M-79	Grenade Launcher
MAB	Marine Amphibious Brigade
MACV	Military Assistance Command, Vietnam
MARS	Military amateur radio services; Military Affiliate Radio System
MASH	Mobile Army Surgical Hospital
Medevac	Aeromedical Evacuation; Medical evacuations of critically injured soldiers made by helicopters and taken directly to a military hospital
MI	Military intelligence
MIA	Missing in Action
MiG	Main fighter aircraft used by North Vietnamese
MOS	Military Occupational Specialty
MP	Military Police
MPC	Military Payment Certificates
NATO	North Atlantic Treaty Organization
NCO	Non-commissioned officer
NLF	National Liberation Front, the political organization of the VC until 1969
NSA	National Security Agency
NVA	North Vietnamese Army
OCS	Officers' Candidate School
OD	Olive Drab (color)
OH-6A	"Cayuse" Light Observation Helicopter used for command and control, observation, target acquisition, and recon

OH-13	"Sioux" Light Observation Helicopter used before OH-6A
OJT	On the job training
OP	Observation Post
OPLAN 34A	Operation Plan 34 Alpha, July 1964 U.S. aided South Vietnamese attack against North Vietnamese Coastal Defenses in Tonkin Bay
OR	Operating Room
P-38	Small can opener for C-Rations
PBR	Patrol boat, river
PFC	Private First Class (rank)
POL	Petroleum, oils, and lubricants
POW	Prisoner of War
PPS-5	Short range ground surveillance radar
PT-109	Patrol boat commanded by JFK during WWII and sunk by a Japanese destroyer in 1943
PT Boat	Patrol Torpedo Boat
PTSD	Post Traumatic Stress Disorder, a condition that can appear many years after combat service; symptoms may include uncontrolled panic, rage, or depression; it may also be accompanied by incidences of divorce, drug addiction, suicide, alcoholism, and crime
PX	Post Exchange, a store for troops to buy various items such as food, books, and small electronics
PZ	Pickup zone
R&R	Rest and Recuperation, time period lasting a few days or weeks where troops were allowed to leave the combat zone or even the country to stay somewhere in the Pacific basin
Recon	Reconnaissance
REM	Rapid Eye Movement, type of therapy to help minimize flashbacks
RN	Registered Nurse
ROK	Troops from the Republic of Korea
ROTC	Reserve Officer Training Corps
RPG	Rocket Propelled Grenade
RTO	Radio Teletype Operator
RVN	Republic of Vietnam
S-1	Battalion or brigade adjutant
S-2	Battalion or brigade intelligence staff officer
S-3	Battalion or brigade operations staff officer
S-4	Battalion or brigade logistics staff officer
S-5	A civic military opperation
SA-2	Medium-range Communist surface to air missile
SDS	Students for a Democratic Society, a radical youth movement involved in anti-war protests
SEALs	U.S. Navy Sea, Air, Land commandos
SP Pack	Special Purpose Pack, box containing playing cards, cigarettes, books, and candy

SSI	Supplemental Security Income, program for Hmong and Lao legal refugees
SVN	South Vietnam
TCDD	Dioxin, a byproduct of Agent Orange
Tet	The Asian Lunar New Year celebration, a major religious holiday in Vietnam; Also referring to the Tet Offensive of 1968 which was on that holiday
TH-55A	U.S. Army's main helicopter trainer
TOC	Tactical Operations Center
UH-1	"Iroquois" Nicknamed "Huey" most widely used helicopter for Medevac, ommand and control, air assaults, personnel and material transportation and as a gunship
UH-1B	Variant of the UH-1 helicopter
USARV	U.S. Army Vietnam
USO	United Service Organization, a place for troops to go to shows with various entertainers
VA	Department of Veterans Affairs
VC	Viet Cong, communist forces fighting in South Vietnam
VFW	Veterans of Foreign Wars
VN	Vietnam
VVA	Vietnam Veterans of America Americaans of America

Bibiliography for
Glossary, Chronology, and Abbreviations

Air War Over Vietnam. 22 July 2002 <http://www.danshistory.com/airwar.html>.

American Postwar Aircraft: Vought F-8 Crusader. Ed. Milan Bo?ok, et al. 19 July 2002. Military.cz.
22 July 2002 <http://www.military.cz/usa/air/post_war/f8/f8_en.htm>.

Cessna O-1A (L-19) Bird Dog. 27 Sept. 2001. Smithsonian National Air and Space Museum. 23 July
2002 <http://www.nasm.si.edu/nasm/aero/aircraft/cessna_o1.htm>.

CH-46 Sea Knight . 2002. The Boeing Company. 20 July 2002 <http://www.boeing.com/companyof-
fices/history/boeing/seaknight.html>.

Douglas A-4D-2N/A-4C Skyhawk. 4 Sept. 2001. Smithsonian National Air and Space Museum. 21 July
2002 <http://www.nasm.si.edu/nasm/aero/aircraft/douglas_a4.htm>.

Douglas Skyraider - The Able Dog. 2001. JS Firm, LLC. 22 July 2002
<http://www.jsfirm.com/onefact.asp?ID=39>.

F-100C Super Saber. 17 June 2002. Grisson Air Museum. 22 July 2002 <http://www.grissomairmu-
seum.com/f-100.htm>.

Foreign Relations of The United States 1964-1968 Volume IV Vietnam. U.S. Department of State. 22
July 2002 <http://www.state.gov/www/about_state/history/vol_iv/abbreviations.html>.

Ground Surveillance Radar. 1 Apr. 2002. Grunt!. 22 July 2002
<http://www.soft.net.uk/entrinet/radar1.htm>.

Historic U.S. Army Helicopters. 8 July 2002. 22 July 2002 <http://www-
acala1.ria.army.mil/lc/cs/csa/aahist.htm>.

Joint Acronyms and Abbreviations. 23 July 2002. U.S. Department of Defense. 23 July 2002
<http://www.dtic.mil/doctrine/jel/doddict/acronym_index.html>.

Kendall, Mike. *US M50 Multiple 106mm Self-Propelled Rifle 'Ontos', Part 1* . 2001. AFV Interiors
Web Magazine. 21 July 2002 <http://www.kithobbyist.com/AFVInteriors/ontos/ontos1.html>.

KSC M11A1. 23 May 2002. RedWolf Airsoft. 22 July 2002

<http://www.redwolfairsoft.com/ksc_m11a1.htm>.

M1 Garand Rifle. 21 July 2002 <http://www.fastpapers911.com/aessays/a98.html>.

Maga, Timothy P. *The Complete Idiot's Guide to the Vietnam War*. Indianapolis, IN: Macmillan USA,
    Inc., 2000.

Moss, George D. *Vietnam: An American Ordeal*. Englewood Cliffs, NJ: Prentice Hall, 1990.

Olson, James S., and Randy Roberts. *Where the Domino Fell: America and Vietnam 1945-1990*. New
    York, NY: St. Martin's P, 1991.

Pike, John. *B-57 Canberra*. 10 Mar. 1999. Federation of American Scientists. 22 July 2002
    <http://www.fas.org/nuke/guide/usa/bomber/b-57.htm>.

Pike, John. *M14 7.62mm Rifle, M21 7.62mm Sniper Rifle, M24 7.62mm Sniper Rifle* . 22 Feb. 2000.
    Federation of American Scientists. 22 July 2002 <http://www.fas.org/man/dod-
    101/sys/land/m14.htm>.

Pike, John. *UH-1 Huey Helicopter*. 12 Mar. 1999. Federation of American Scientists. 22 July 2002
    <http://www.fas.org/man/dod-101/sys/ac/uh-1.htm>.

*Restoration of SSI Benefits to Hmong and Lao Legal Refugees and other Legal Immigrants in the
    United States*. 17 Nov. 1997. Lao Human Rights Council, Inc. 22 July 2002
    <http://home.earthlink.net/~laohumrights/laoact03.html>.

Ross, Brian. *Articles Relating to the Indochina Wars: The US and Allied Forces AFV's of the Vietnam
    War* . 2 Feb. 1999. 22 July 2002 <http://www.vwip.org/articles/usarm.htm>.

The Moving Wall. 2001. The Baxter Bulletin. 23 July 2002
    <http://www.baxterbulletin.com/ads/movingwall/page16.html>.

United States Armour: Tanks and Recovery Vehicles. 1 Apr. 2002. Grunt!. 22 July 2002
    <http://www.soft.net.uk/entrinet/armour9.htm>.

U.S. Helicopters: CH-47 Chinook Cargo Helicopter. 1 Apr. 2002. Grunt!. 22 July 2002
    <http://www.soft.net.uk/entrinet/us_helos7.htm>.

U.S. Helicopters: OH-13 Sioux Light Observation Helicopter. 1 Apr. 2002. Grunt!. 22 July 2002

<http://www.soft.net.uk/entrinet/us_helos1.htm>.

U.S. Helicopters: OH-6A Cayuse Light Observation Helicopter. 1 Apr. 2002. Grunt!. 22 July 2002

<http://www.soft.net.uk/entrinet/us_helos12.htm>.

USMC/Sikorsky CH-53 (S-65) Sea Stallion and Super Stallion Helicopter. 22 July 2002

<http://www.polyweb.com/danno/ch53/ch53e.html>.

Vietnam: Echoes from the Wall. Washington, D.C.: Vietnam Veterans Memorial Fund, 2000.

Warriner, Russ. *Blue Max Aerial Rocket Artillery Association*. 21 May 2002. 22 July 2002

<http://www.bluemax-ara-assoc.com/>.

Webster's New World Dictionary of the Vietnam War. 1999.

Where are they Now? 22 July 2002 <http://www.cris.com/~ogre1538/bogue.htm>.

Oral History Procedures Used

The D.C. Everest Oral Vietnam History Project took place during 2001-2002 time period. Vietnam veterans and anti-war protesters have shared their experiences. Most participants were from the Central Wisconsin area. These oral history interviews have captured only a small portion of their experiences during the war. Still, one gets a sense of the daily life of a soldier during the war.

The following steps were taken to ensure the accuracy of the oral histories as they went from interview to a written transcript.

Step One: Preparing

Procedures for conducting oral histories were reviewed using a variety of sources. Materials from the Oral History Association (OHA) were obtained and examined. In addition, specific guidelines for the transcription of oral interviews were reviewed. Oral history interview techniques were discussed with James Lorence and Kris Paap at U.W.M.C. during three earlier oral history projects.

Step Two: Identifying the Participants

Participants in the project included: Vietnam veterans from the Central Wisconsin area, anti-war protestors and other home front persons (the interview subjects), D.C. Everest junior high and senior high students, largely those in the American History Advanced Placement and Seminar class (who conducted the interviews), and staff from the D.C. Everest Social Studies Department (who trained students, set up the interviews, and compiled the interviews). Additional staff from the school district was also involved (i.e. English, Math, and Special Education teachers were also involved in the process). William Skelton (Professor of History at UWSP), Paul Mertz (Professor of History at UWSP), and Michael Stevens (Wisconsin Historical Society), author of *Voices from Vietnam* helped critique student essays and were project consultants. Additionally, Dennis Uhlig, an English teacher (Milwaukee Hamilton) critiqued student essays. Vietnam veteran interviewees were identified primarily via "word of mouth." In a few cases, oral histories were obtained from relatives of the student interviewees.

Step Three: Training the Interviewers

A formal training session prepared the students to conduct oral interviews. A training manual, entitled *Conducting Oral History Interviews: Guideline for Students*, was developed for the use of the interviewers. Questions for the interviews were adapted from the manual. The junior high students used these questions, while the senior high students developed their own questions for the interviews. In a few cases, D.C. Everest staff developed questions. Prior to the interviews, students studied the Vietnam War in their classes. Each student then wrote an essay on a specific Vietnam related topic (e.g., Tunnel Rats, Agent Orange, Kent State) Students worked with English teachers to edit/revise the essays. The essays were then submitted for possible inclusion in the book. Thus, students developed a solid foundation of content knowledge regarding the Vietnam War prior to conducting the interviews.

Step Four: Interviewing

Many interviews took place in the classroom setting with approximately four-five students listening to and interviewing a veteran. Sometimes pairs of students went to a veteran's home to conduct the interview. The purpose for collecting the oral histories was explained to the intervicwees by the student interviewers. Interviewers reviewed the Interview Consent Form with the interviewees and obtained the appropriate signatures.

The length of the interview varied; however, most interviews lasted approximately one hour. The quality of the interviews varies. Some of the interviewers were proficient at drawing out information from the interviewees by asking open-ended questions or trying to clarify details. Conversely, some of the interviewees shared information more freely than did others. Most interviewees were asked to "tell their story" and interviewers asked questions toward the end of the interview. This strategy encouraged interviewees to freely tell of their experiences and not be inhibited by the question/response approach. Questions were usually asked to clarify information.

A brief biographical sketch providing basic information was compiled for each interviewee. In addition, pictures of the interviewees were obtained whenever possible. (The biographical information and photograph appears at the beginning of each person's interview transcript.)

Step Five: Transcribing

After completion of the interviews, students transcribed the tapes. Typically the same student/s who conducted the interview transcribed the audio recording. These transcribers used a similar form for all the transcriptions. Once students had completed the transcription of their tape, they took the actual transcript back to the interviewee so that the interviewee could check for accuracy. Changes were then made to the transcript.

Step Six: Proofreading

After the transcribing was completed, the transcript was given to a social studies staff person to be proofed for spelling/punctuation errors. Copies of the interviews were then mailed to each veteran and they were again asked to critique the interviews.

Step Seven: Editing

The oral history interviews were then edited. The edited version was prepared so that the reader can focus on the meaning of the responses and not be distracted by grammatical errors or "clutch words" such as "ah," or "hmmm." The syntactical errors of the responses have been "cleaned up" so that the meaning is more easily discerned (e.g., present tense was changed to past tense). However, the grammatical structure has not been corrected to perfection. The "flavor" of the language used still remains. Names of villages/people were spelled to the best of our ability. The interviews were edited several times by students and school staff. Some veterans came to school and worked with the students to edit their interviews. Some interviews include pictures the veterans took while in Vietnam.

Step Eight: Compiling the Book

The edited interviews were then organized by the role the interviewee played during the Vietnam War (e.g., Infantry, Women and War, Navy). A team of social studies and English teachers selected student essays for inclusion in the book. Rotographics, a local printing company, had their staff train students to use a desktop publishing program entitled QuarkXPress. Students then compiled edited interviews using Quarkexpress.

Step Nine: Storing the Tapes

The tapes will be stored at the Marathon County Historical Society.